Publishing and Bookselling

PUBLISHING AND BOOKSELLING

Part One: From the Earliest Times to 1870
FRANK ARTHUR MUMBY

Part Two: 1870–1970
IAN NORRIE

ERRATA

Pages 78 and 79

The last four lines on page 79 should be read as
the first four lines on page 78

Pages 129 and 130

The references to Chartwell are incorrect. Though
Mr. Christopher Mann has a house on the Chart-
well estate, Chartwell itself is, of course, a
National Trust property.

JONATHAN CAPE
THIRTY BEDFORD SQUARE LONDON

FIRST PUBLISHED 1930
SECOND EDITION 1949
THIRD EDITION 1954
FOURTH EDITION 1956
FIFTH EDITION REVISED AND RESET 1974

PART ONE © 1974 BY JONATHAN CAPE LTD
PART TWO © 1974 BY IAN NORRIE

JONATHAN CAPE LTD, 30 BEDFORD SQUARE, LONDON WCI

ISBN 0 224 00827 7

PRINTED IN GREAT BRITAIN
BY BUTLER & TANNER LTD, FROME AND LONDON

The original edition was dedicated by Frank Mumby

TO MY GRANDSON
ROBERT MUMBY ALLAN

Contents

7

Acknowledgments

From the long list of all those who helped me in revising this work it may seem invidious to select eleven names for special mention. However, more demands were made on some than on others, and I am especially grateful to the following for the time they spent in researching on my behalf and/or in reading my typescript: Norman Askew, Ronald E. Barker, G. R. Davies, Peter du Sautoy, John Elsley, Ian Parsons, the late F. D. Sanders, A. E. Skinner, Alan Steele, David Whitaker and J. Alan White.

I am much indebted also to the undermentioned who provided me with the information I sought from them and would, I am certain, have readily given more assistance had they been asked. Only those who are not mentioned in the text are described by more than their name: K. W. H. Adlam, R. Olaf Anderson, John Attenborough, David Austick.

Irene Babbidge, A. R. Bacon, H. E. Bailey, J. R. Bailey, Jocelyn Baines, the late John Baker, J. A. Bardsley (Oldham Bookshop), Eric Baker, Arthur E. Barker (S.P.C.K.), Christopher Barclay, P. H. Bartholomew, J. C. Bartle, Gerald Bartlett, Brian Batsford, M.P., W. F. Bauermeister, John Beech (Deighton, Bell), F. T. Bell, Sir Basil Blackwell, Richard Blackwell, Ronald Blass, G. W. M. Blewett, Anthony Blond, John Boon, G. N. Boddy, Peggy Bowyer (Thames & Hudson), K. J. Bredon, E. M. Broadhurst (Southport), A. J. Bryant (Mowbray), Handasyde Buchanan, John Bush, Paul Burns (Burns, Oates), W. E. Butcher.

Carmen Callil (Granada), John Calder, Mrs U. A. Card (Combridge, Hove), Sam Carr, Harry Carter, H. G. Castle (McGraw-Hill), A. S. Chambers (W. & R. Chambers), I. P. M. Chambers, Joe Cheetham Jnr, Charles Clark, J. S. Clegg (Wills & Hepworth), Robert Clow, J. A. Cochrane, R. B. Cochrane (Promenade Bookshop, Cheltenham), T. C. Collocott (W. & R. Chambers), W. G. Corp, G. F. Cousins, Trevor Craker, Marcus Crouch, Mary Curtis.

W. T. Dally, M. W. Dashwood, C. P. Davies (Reference Librarian, Folkestone), R. G. Davis-Poynter, F. J. Martin Dent, S. L. Dennis, John Denton, André Deutsch, Cedric Dickens, I. C. Dickson (Butterworth), A. Donati, Basil Donne-Smith, Kathleen Downham (S.C.M. Press), T. Robson Dring, Dorothea Duncan (Penguin).

Colin Eccleshare, Charles Ede, Cyril Edgeley, Andrew George Elliot, David Elliot (The World's Work), Desmond Elliott, A. G. S. Enser (Borough Librarian, Eastbourne), A. Dwye Evans, Martin Eve.

J. H. Fall, G. A. Ferguson, D. G. Filleul (St Helier, Jersey), Elwyn Fisher, John A. Ford, Norman Franklin, Noel Frieslich, Monique Fuchs.

David Gabbutt (Seed & Gabbutt), the late Francis B. Gabbutt, J. F. Gabbutt (Seed & Gabbutt), J. G. Galloway, John Gibbins, I. A. Gibson (J. & A. Churchill), B. L. Gilbert, W. R. Gisborne, Benjamin Glazebrook, P. N. Godfrey (George Philip), Anthony Godwin, Martyn Goff, R. H. L. Goffin, Pauline Goldsmith, Mark Goulden, W. Gordon Graham, Ian R. Grant (John Grant), the late Arthur Gray, Don Gresswell.

John Hale (Robert Hale), Anthony Hamilton, Hamish Hamilton, C. G. Harris (George Over), Philip Harris, F. N. Harrison (E. J. Arnold), D. M. Hay (of Exeter), Raymond Haynes, Ernest Hecht, Reuben Heffer, W. G. Henderson (E. & S. Livingstone), Richard Henwood (Scholastic Productions), Ross Higgins, Alan Hill, Ken Hills, Jack Hobbs, Ernest Hochland, F. S. Hodges, Michael Holman (Anglebooks), Rathbone Holme (The Studio), Lord Horder, Simon Hornby, W. Houben, Michael S. Howard, Pat Hudson, J. Hume, J. F. Hyams, Robin Hyman.

B. H. Jackson, J. S. Janiurek, H. F. Johns, T. L. Jones, Thomas Joy.

Antony Kamm, Harry Karnac, W. Kay, Edward King (King's, Lymington), A. L. Kingsford (B.B.C.), R. J. L. Kingsford, Elizabeth Knight (O.U.P.), John M. Knox.

The late Charles Lahr, Dr E. M. Lancet, the late Sir Allen Lane, T. Langdon, Lt.-Col. J. M. Langley (Ancient House, Ipswich), Gordon Larkins, T. J. Law, D. A. Leck, C. R. Leegood (B.B.C.), J. Lehmann, Brian Levy (Pan), David Liell, George Linfoot, the late Mark Longman, Norman E. Lucas, Sir Robert Lusty.

James MacGibbon, Douglas Miller, William Miller, C. R. Milne, John Milne (James Bisset), Sir Thomas Moore, D. J. Morrell (Woodfield & Stanley), F. J. Morrish, John Grey Murray.

J. D. Newth, George Henry Nicholls, Gordon Nicholas, Harold Nockolds (Temple Press), Allen Nolan (Browne & Nolan), Eric Norris.

E. O'Keeffe (James Duffy), Malcolm Oram (J. Whitaker), Peter Owen.

H. Paroissien, Max Parrish, Catherine Paton, the late R. Charlton Paton, Judith Patten (Hamlyn), Hilary Pattison, John G. Pattison, Ben Perrick, John Philip (Philip, Son & Nephew), Stanley Pickard (Laye-Ward), Sir James Pitman, Charles Pizzey, C. R. Place (S.P.C.K.), T. G. Preston (Hills, Sunderland), John Prime.

Norman A. Rae, George Rainbird, George Rapp, Piers Raymond, M. A. C. Reavell, Max Reinhardt, L. A. Rich (Wheaton), T. Robinson, J. G. Ruddock (of Lincoln), Thomas Russell, John Ryder (The Bodley Head).

A. A. Sales (Albert Gait), John Sandoe, Elise Santoro, H. L. Schollick, Graham Scott (Bookseller, Friern Barnet), the late E. W. Sheppard, J. H. Simpson (Jas. Golder), T. E. Smith (W. & R. Holmes), F. T. Spencer (Students' Bookshop), Maisie L. Stevens, Paul Stobart (Technical Press), Peter Stockham, Harold Sweeten.

John Tannahill (Blackie), John Taylor (Lund, Humphries), James Thin, David St John Thomas, Philothea Thompson, Nicolas Thompson, N. G. Thompson, Alec Tiranti, G. A. Turll.

Philip Unwin, Rayner Unwin, the late Sir Stanley Unwin, M. H. Varvill (George Bell), Ralph Vernon-Hunt.

Peter Wait (Methuen), P. C. B. Wallis, G. B. Walmsley (Eason & Son, Belfast), F. J. Warburg, Alan Ward, E. P. Warner, G. R. Wasley, Graham Watson, W. M. Watson (Municipal College of Commerce, Newcastle-upon-Tyne), Captain O. M. Watts, Michael Wayte, Frank Weatherhead, Maurice Webb (B.B.C.), Elizabeth Weiler, John F. Welch, Kenneth Welham (Pitman), R. F. West (Baillière, Tindall & Cassell), H. Ewart Wharmby, Leslie A. Wheeler, F. M. Whitehead, Peter Whiteley, J. M. Whiting, Ronald Whiting, Alan Wilson, Arnold Wilson (Henry Young), Charles Wilson, Hubert Wilson, Humphrey Wilson, Ben Winter-Goodwin, Peter Wolfe, Noel Woolf, T. C. Woolston.

Edward Young, K. H. Young, Desmond Zwemmer,

And to the City Librarian of Hull, and several members of the staffs of the Guildhall and the London Borough of Camden Libraries.

From many of those mentioned I received kind hospitality as well as information, especially when my wife and I were out doing 'field work'.

I should also thank my publisher, Graham C. Greene, who was always encouraging and never mentioned the fact that my revision had failed to meet delivery date by several years; his personal assistant, Frances Bundock, whom I pestered during six long years and who was unfailingly helpful and patient; and his secretary, Elizabeth Robinson, who coped admirably whenever Graham and Frances were unavailable.

Also my daughter, Amanda, who chored through the hundreds of letters to make an index of those whose help demanded acknowledgment, and Mavis, my wife, who accompanied me on many of my journeys and always gave sympathetic ear to my constant spoken ruminations, as did so many friends inside and outside the trade.

Finally, I must thank my colleague, Monica Carolan, for bringing the bibliography up to date, and my friend, Bruce Stevenson, for compiling the index.

IAN NORRIE

Preface to the Second Edition

So much has happened since the last edition of this work appeared that it not only needs drastic revision but also supplementary chapters to bring it up to date. A whole volume could be devoted to the war years of 1939–45 alone: and the story of the British book trade's part throughout that long ordeal is one of which it has reason to be proud. Here, however, it has been possible only to gather up the main threads while the happenings are still fresh in one's memory, and string them together as part of the larger history of the world of books through the ages. Gaps there must inevitably be in a narrative covering so vast a field, but it is hoped that the result will still be acceptable as a brief survey of a vital trade which has existed from time immemorial. Though much of the present book is new, the original preface may perhaps be allowed to stand, almost as it was written, many years ago:

My reason for offering this work is that no one else has attempted to write an adequate history of English bookselling and publishing. Wherever I looked for information on the subject I was faced with regrets that so little had been done to explore this evaded field of research. 'No great trade has an obscurer history', wrote Augustine Birrell in one of his essays. 'It seems to lie choked in mountains of dust which it would be suicidal to disturb. Men have lived from time to time of literary skill—Dr Johnson was one of them—who had knowledge, extensive and peculiar, of the traditions and practices of "the trade", as it is proudly styled by its votaries; but nobody has ever thought it worth his while to make record of his knowledge, which perished with him, and is now irrecoverably lost.' And I met the familiar saying of Carlyle—that 'ten ordinary histories of kings and courtiers were well exchanged against the tenth part of one good History of Booksellers'—so many times that I was ashamed at last to face it again until I had done something to remove the reproach which seemed to lie hidden in his words.

Curwen's *History of Booksellers*, issued in 1873, and long since out of print, is not, strictly speaking, a history at all, consisting mainly of a collection of articles on the leading publishers and booksellers of his day. Much material lies scattered through Nichols's *Literary Anecdotes of the Eighteenth Century*, and Charles Knight has made abundant use of this in his *Shadows of the Old Booksellers*, a work which, though pleasantly written, is not always

12

trustworthy. W. Roberts's *Earlier History of English Bookselling* is most valuable for its records of the seventeenth and eighteenth centuries, to which it is chiefly devoted; but the source-book of supreme importance for the early history of the trade after the invention of printing is Professor Arber's great *Transcript of the Registers of the Stationers' Company*, privately printed in five volumes, and carrying the record down to the year 1640.

In my own book an attempt has been made to tell in outline the whole story of English bookselling—tracing its origin as far as possible in the days of ancient Rome; its struggle for existence through the Dark Ages; and its subsequent organisation and development through the centuries down to the present day.

Those who wish to probe deeper into this subject are referred to the comprehensive bibliography by the late W. H. Peet. This originally appeared in *Notes and Queries*, and was reprinted in the first edition of the present work by permission of the proprietors of that publication. It has since been amplified and brought up to date, my chief regret in doing so being that Mr Peet did not live to do this himself.

If I may be permitted a personal note, I would wish this edition to be accepted as my farewell salute to all those with whom it has been my present lot to be associated throughout my journalistic and literary career.

FRANK A. MUMBY, 1949

Preface to the Fourth Edition

With the words printed above, Frank A. Mumby took leave of his unique *History of the Book Trade in Great Britain*. Starting with classical times in his first chapter, he thereafter rooted himself in London, in which city, indeed, he was born in 1872. He had had experience of literary editorship when in 1923 he joined the staff of *The Times Literary Supplement* and became a regular contributor of articles on bibliography and history.

He was for a long time the writer of one of the most important features of the *Literary Supplement*, namely the weekly notes on forth-coming books. He had an intimate as well as an extensive knowledge of the publishing and bookselling worlds, and, in spite of a lameness which afflicted him for a prolonged period, there was no more frequent (and more welcome) visitor to publishers' offices.

In spite of his work for the *Literary Supplement*, he was an active author and editor on his own account, as will have been perceived from the bibliography on p. ii. Besides *The Romance of Bookselling* he compiled five volumes of *History in Contemporary Letters* and edited *Letters of Literary Men* and an account of the Kaiser's war in several volumes. He retired from Printing House Square in 1940, though he was active as a contributor and as editor of the 1949 edition of his *Publishing and Bookselling* almost to the last. He died in August 1954, at the age of eighty-two.

This new edition brings the story to Easter 1956, while keeping to the words and to the structure of *Mumby* (as this standard work deserves to be called) as far as possible.

MAX KENYON, 1956

Preface to the Fifth Edition

This drastically revised version of Frank Mumby's history was born in June 1967, when Graham C. Greene suggested to me that I should 'bring it up to date'. Neither of us on that summer evening in Bedford Square knew what we were letting ourselves, and others, in for. Or if Graham did, I did not.

I re-read the work that I had long admired, and noted, as will some future reviser in his turn, that there were many omissions. After long heart-searchings I concluded that only major surgery would meet the case, because Mumby had recorded little of the history of bookselling, as distinct from publishing, in the twentieth century, and had also overlooked many specialist imprints. So that if I were to attempt a coherent narrative of the trade as a whole it would be necessary to start at a date earlier than that of the fourth edition of 1956. At first I thought it would be satisfactory to go back only as far as 1945; then 1919 seemed a more convenient date. Finally I opted for 1870 as my starting point.

This has necessitated cutting off Mumby's history at around p. 260 of the fourth edition but, for practical purposes, it has involved excisions in his text earlier than that and much mutilation of it for several pages after. From p. 269 of that edition I have incorporated the facts he used in my words, or discarded them, and I have added very considerably from my own research. Chapters 1–13 remain almost exactly as Mumby wrote them and I have not done any original research on them. These, plus a bridge chapter, remain Mumby's part of the history; for the rest, I must take responsibility.

In the first four editions the university presses were dealt with in a separate chapter at the end of the book. I have incorporated their history in my half of the book, which has meant recording their stories long before 1870. There is also overlap, both ways, concerning many other imprints and businesses, and therefore neither section can be regarded as completely self-contained. Some of Mumby's text relies on my further exposition; more of mine demands study of what his first half relates. I feel some guilt at truncating his text as I have done, because he is dead and cannot express either approval or condemnation, and because no author takes kindly to unbidden subbing, but in the circumstances there seemed no alternative apart from writing a completely new history 'from the earliest times' of the title. This would have taken even longer than the six years I have spent, and I believe that Mumby's history up to 1870 is worth preserving anyway. What he wrote of the period after that was not bad history but needed to be reviewed in the light of later events, just as, in due course, my half will be.

My research for this edition has involved me in many journeys to visit bookshops in Scotland, the north of England, the Midlands, East Anglia, Wales, the West Country and the Home Counties; to see publishers at work in the new towns and in their more traditional quarters in London; and to Booksellers' Association conferences and the Frankfurt Book Fair. I had hoped it would be possible to visit all the major towns of the United Kingdom, but although I have covered thousands of miles this has not been achieved.

There has also been vast correspondence. Most of those publishers and booksellers to whom I applied for information gave it unstintingly and quickly; some ignored my requests, usually because they were too busy to comply, but, in most cases I was finally able to gain satisfaction, although I formed the impression that a great many publicity departments have very few facts to hand out about their own companies. A few never answered at all and, in these instances, I have had to find out what I can from other sources or omit reference to them altogether.

The bibliography has been brought up to date by my colleague, Monica Carolan, but many of my sources lie in private letters and the spoken word, and in what I have seen for myself. I have followed that great historian J. E. Neale (published by Jonathan Cape) in keeping footnotes to a minimum, but in writing so close to one's own time some are inevitable. Each week's issue of *The Bookseller* records some new major change or the death of an important figure, and although this work officially ends at 1970, certain events thereafter cannot be ignored whilst there is still an opportunity of including them; but a final cut-off point was made at March 1973.

I have not attempted to survey the activities of secondhand booksellers during my period. The antiquarian trade, different in structure and outlook from the new book trade (although many businesses have a foot in each), is essentially parasitical and often incestuous. Dealers spend much time selling to one another, and their prosperity depends on the scarcity value of particular works. In the antiquarian world it is not what is printed in the book which matters so much as the rareness of the edition. In theory the secondhand trade is useful for those wanting out-of-print books (although the organization existing to locate them is lamentable) and for those students who actually buy the books on their set lists without parental aid, but its organization in the twentieth century requires a separate study.

In mentioning individuals I have tried to follow a policy of naming principals only, except when reference is made to a person to illustrate a specific point; the result may seem to some to make for an invidious selection, but no offence is intended to those who are not featured in these pages although they may have contributed a lifetime of constructive work in publishing and bookselling.

Hadley Wood, 1973   IAN NORRIE

Part One

FROM THE EARLIEST TIMES TO 1870
Frank Arthur Mumby

I

The Beginnings of the Book Trade

The secret of the philosopher's stone is not more difficult to discover than the name of the Father of the Book Trade. We should look for it in vain among the records of the baked clay tablets of Babylonia and Assyria, and other ancient writings. Though a well-worn phrase in Ecclesiastes tells of the endless making of many books in biblical days there is no mention in the Scriptures of any bookseller or publisher by name. The legend that Barabbas was a publisher, erroneously attributed for many years to Lord Byron, has no more foundation in fact than 'Peter Pindar's' malignant epigram on the publishers' habit of drinking out of authors' skulls.

In groping among the annals of antiquity it is disconcerting to find that the first bookseller about whom there appears to be any definite information was an undertaker as well. The undertaker's claim, however, need not be taken too seriously. He was an Egyptian, and his bookselling was only carried on in connection with his funerals, at which he had the disposal of copies of the *Book of the Dead*—a work which was not only bought by the mourners and preserved by them as a memorial, but placed with the body in the tomb, to serve as the soul's passport and guide in the after-life. Leaving this lugubrious quasi-bookseller and flitting through the ages which saw the rise and fall of other ancient civilisations, we find an extensive literature of every description, including novels, but no actual records of organized bookselling until we come to the classic days of the Greeks and Romans. Bookselling does not seem to have had any tangible existence as a trade in Greece until the fifth century B.C., and it did not grow to considerable dimensions until the reign of Alexander the Great, a century or so later. Authors sought no share in whatever profits it may have made. They would not insult their Muse by any sordid dealings with booksellers. Contemporary fame and perhaps the hope of posthumous glory were the only things that mattered to the authors of ancient Greece. Lucian, 'the last great master of Attic eloquence and Attic wit', as Macaulay calls him, does not give a flattering picture, in his satire on *The Illiterate Bibliomaniac*, either of the Athenian booksellers of his day or of some of their wealthy patrons:

You think, [he writes] that by purchasing a great number of

21

fine books you may be taken for a good scholar. But, on the contrary, you will only make your ignorance the more conspicuous.
Not only do you buy the books which are not the best, but you are
easily persuaded by the first man who praises the book; so that the
booksellers who know you sacrifice to Mercury are as lucky as if
they had found a treasure, for they could never hope for a better
opportunity of converting their vilest trash into solid cash ... Even
supposing that you were just discerning enough to buy the manuscripts of such a dealer as Callinus, so much admired for their
elegance, or the publications of an Atticus, so celebrated on account
of their accuracy, of what good, my dear sir, is such a possession to
you? You can no more appreciate their excellence than a blind
lover the fine eyes and rosy cheeks of a charming mistress. You may
have collected the works of Demosthenes, including one of the eight
copies of Thucydides which he wrote with his own hand, or all
the books which Sulla, when he made himself master of Athens,
seized and sent to Italy; yet how could that avail you? If you made
your bed on the best copies of the great authors, or were decked in
manuscripts from head to foot, would you be less ignorant than you
are? There is a proverb that says, 'An ape is still an ape though
adorned with jewels and gold' ... You men of wealth would have
too many advantages over us poor scoundrels if you could buy in an
instant, for a mere sum of money, all the store of learning which has
taken us so long to collect. If that were so, no scholar would venture
to contend in erudition with the booksellers, with the vast stores of
learning in their possession; but, on closer inspection, you will find
that these worthy persons are no less lacking in taste and discernment than yourself, though their days and nights as well are spent
among books.

This, it must be remembered, was written in the declining days of
the book trade in Athens, long after the conquest of Greece by the
Romans had shifted the home of culture and the centre of literary
life to Alexandria. Here, undoubtedly, was developed an extensive
system of book-production, by means of which the best editions were
published of the collected literature of Greece, Rome, Egypt and India,
based on the texts contained in the famous Alexandrian Library.
Details of the trade itself, however, are sadly lacking, and of the men
directly connected with it not a name is now known. We are forced,
therefore, to turn to Rome, which subsequently became the chief seat
of the book trade, though the intellectual supremacy of the city of the
Ptolemies was long maintained under the Romans. It was not until the
second half of the first century A.D. that the centre of the publishing
world passed to Rome itself, taking with it, according to Strabo, the

groundwork of the system upon which the Alexandrian book trade had been built.

Once in the book market of ancient Rome we are on firmer ground; and there is much to remind us of the book world of today. We stand in the Argiletum, and the atmosphere of books is as strong as in Charing Cross Road today. The pillars outside the shops are covered with the titles of the works to be obtained within, and the whole place is evidently a favourite haunt of literary men. The authors and scholars are plainly distinguishable from the slaves who go about their masters' business. If we look inside the larger publishers' offices we shall find other slaves hard at work on a new edition of the latest book that has been lucky enough to hit the popular taste. The thing that surprises us most is the marvellous cheapness of the books—often no more than a few pence. The main reason for this—to drop the pleasant fiction of the present tense—was not so much that the Roman author did not receive his share of the profits as that the publisher was able to employ his own slaves on an economical system which is as obsolete today as the gladiatorial combats in the amphitheatre. Slave labour, with all its drawbacks, made it possible for ancient Rome to manage remarkably well without the printing press. With his trained staff of readers and transcribers a publisher could turn out an edition of any work at very cheap rates and almost at a moment's notice. There was no initial expense of typesetting before a single copy could be produced; no ruinous extras in the shape of printer's corrections. The manuscript came from the author; the publisher handed it over to his slaves; and, if a book of modest dimensions, the complete edition could be ready, if necessary, within twenty-four hours. There was a beautiful simplicity about this system, which, in spite of its technical deficiencies—chiefly in the form of corrupt and badly written texts—must fill the breasts of some of our modern publishers with envy, when they think of their own complicated methods of production.

The slaves, it need scarcely be added, were specially trained and educated for their work. Martial, our most entertaining if not our most trustworthy guide through the book mart of ancient Rome, tells us at the beginning of his second book of *Epigrams* that the transcriber could copy the manuscript of that book in an hour, 'and his services not be confined to my trifles alone'; but as there are between five and six hundred lines in the book in question Martial's estimate need not be taken as strictly accurate. Even this system of editions 'while you wait', so to speak, with its obvious advantage of making it possible to cope at once with any demand, did not always save publishers from the evils of over-production. From Cicero's letters to Atticus, and other references, we gather that the Romans were not without some sort of 'Remainder Market'—the grave then, as now, of so many blighted hopes. The

remainders of today suffer a less ignominious fate than that of a large
proportion of the unsold copies in ancient Rome. There seems to have
been no secondhand bookseller then to act the part of foster-father to
them; or kindlier pulping machine to put an end to their misery at
once. The more fortunate, apparently, were shipped to the provinces,
but their common fate would seem to have been found in the fish-
dealers' and other shops of the Roman tradespeople, there to be used
for wrapping-up purposes. 'If Apollinaris condemn thee', writes
Martial, in one of his addresses to his book,* 'thou mayest run forthwith to the fish-sellers, to have thy back scribbled upon by the boys' —
evidently with the customer's address, and possibly the price.

How many classics were destroyed in this way, or perished in the
household fires of Roman citizens, it is useless to speculate, but in all
the rubbish that was sold as wastepaper there must have been lost many
precious fragments. The shape of the book in those days lent itself
admirably to these base uses. The volume as we understand it did not
come into vogue until about the fifth century A.D. In ancient Greece and
Rome, as in Egypt, it took very much the form of the mounted maps
of modern days. The rolls were made of papyrus or parchment, and
were written on one side only. The size of the roll naturally depended
on the length of the work. The editions varied, according to the estimate of Theodor Birt, from five hundred to one thousand copies. In one
of his letters Pliny writes slightingly of a book which Regulus had
written on the loss of his son — 'a whole book upon the life of a boy!' —
and for causing as many as a thousand copies to be distributed throughout the Empire.†

This publishing trade, like Rome itself, was far from being built in a
day. It was only when the Romans became their own manufacturers,
instead of sending to Alexandria for the books which were turned out
wholesale there by trained staffs of copyists, that the publishing trade of
Rome began to reign supreme. With the Augustan age, in the latter
half of the first century B.C., we arrive at last at something like a clear
conception of what that trade amounted to. It is here that we reach the
days of Titus Pomponius Atticus, the prince of friends and booksellers.
Atticus stands apart from and above all other publishers of ancient
Rome. He was the first man to lift the craft above the ordinary ranks
of commercialism, to lay the foundations of its most honourable traditions; and though by no means the first publisher on record, there is
none more worthy of the foremost place in the Booksellers' Roll of
Honour. A scholar and author himself, he was Cicero's literary adviser,
as well as publisher; and being possessed of great private wealth, was
able to conduct his publishing business with something of that liberality

* Book IV, 86.
† *Epistles*, Book IV, 7.

and public-spiritedness which prompted George Smith in the nineteenth century to spend a fortune on the *Dictionary of National Biography*.

Atticus, like George Smith, seems to have been a man of enterprise and marked business ability. 'You have sold my discourse on Ligarius so well', writes Cicero,* 'that I shall entrust you with this duty for all my future works.' Atticus evidently developed his publishing business on a large scale. He was not content to rely upon Alexandria for editions of the Greek classics; he had his own trained staff of slaves for copying, and *Attikians*, as his editions came to be known, were the hallmark of excellence. According to Theodor Birt, Atticus in course of time opened retail branches not only in Rome, but in the provinces as well.

Some of the Roman emperors exercised a strict censorship over literary property. Augustus on assuming the office of high priest had the bookshops, as well as private houses, searched for books of spurious Sibylline prophecies, both Latin and Greek, and committed the whole collection, amounting to upwards of two thousand copies, to the flames. Much more brutal outrages both on authors and publishers were perpetrated by Domitian. On one occasion, according to Suetonius, Domitian not only put to death Hermogenes of Tarsus because of certain passages in his history to which the tyrant objected, but crucified also the copiers who had issued the work.

What money was to be made out of Horace's books evidently fell to his publishers, for in the *Ars Poetica* he suggests that while his works, which pass even across the sea, bring gold to the Sosii, he himself reaps only widespread fame. Horace makes several references to the bookseller brothers who issued his works from their shop in the neighbourhood of the Temples of Janus and Vertumnus. One of these (Epistle XX) is best translated in verse by Sir Theodore Martin, from which we may be permitted to quote the following lines:

> I read the meaning of that wistful look
> Towards Janus and Vertumnus, O my book!
> Upon the Sosii's shelves you long to stand,
> Rubbed smooth with pumice by their skilful hand.
> You chafe at lock and modest seal; you groan
> That you should only to a few be shown,
> And sigh by all the public to be read,
> You in far other notions trained and bred.
> Well, go your way, whereso you please and when,
> But, once set forth, you come not back again.
> 'Fool that I was! Why did I change my lot?'
> You'll cry when wounded in some tender spot,

* *Ad Att.*, xiii, 12.

And out of fashion and of favour grown,
You're crumpled up, and into corners thrown.

*   *   *   *   *

You will be liked by Rome while in your bloom,
But soon as e'er the thumbing and the soil
Of vulgar hands shall your first freshness spoil,
You will be left to nibbling worms a prey,
Or sent as wrappers to lands far away.

We come down to Martial's day—sixty years or so after Horace's
death—for another literary complaint, as well as a further illustration of the extensive circulations commanded by the popular
Roman authors. 'It is not the idle people of the city only', writes
Martial, 'who delight in my muse; nor is it to listless ears alone that
these verses are addressed; for my book is thumbed amid Getic frosts,
near martial standards, by the stern centurion; and even Britain is said
to sing my verses. Yet what do I gain by it? My purse knows nought of
my fame.'* But his chief cause of complaint, he proceeds, is that when
the gods gave to the earth a second Augustus (by which he means
Domitian) 'they did not give thee, O Rome, a second Maecenas.'
Martial, like all the needy poets of his day, never ceased to think of the
prizes that had fallen to the poets of a happier reign—the Sabian
estate which Horace had received from Maecenas, the 10,000,000
sesterces (about £50,000) which had fallen into Vergil's lap. But times
had changed; the court and aristocracy had now little but praise to
bestow on the poets dependent upon them; and Martial begged
Domitian's assistance in vain. Authors, no longer rich enough, like
Catullus and Lucretius, to employ their own slaves in copying their
books for private circulation, were forced into the hands of the booksellers. They had to make their reputation before they could hope for
imperial favours or wealthy patronage. Martial evidently thought that
one of his booksellers at least made a a handsome profit by his works,
for he informs his reader† that 'this thin little book' (the *Xenia*) will
cost him four sesterces (about 4p), but if four be too much 'perhaps you
may get it for two, and Trypho, the bookseller, will even then make a
profit'.

Trypho is more favourably remembered as the bookseller to whom
Quintilian dedicated the *Institutio Oratoria*, acknowledging that it was
owing to his friendly importunity that his books were published, and
begging him to see that they were issued as correctly as possible. Though
Martial grumbled at the bookseller's profit, it was to his own interest
to obtain for his writings as wide a circulation as possible. He did not

* Book XI, 3.   † Book XIII, 3.

hesitate even to write his own advertisements, for no one was less ashamed than Martial of the gentle art of puffing. 'That you may not be ignorant where I am to be bought', he writes,* 'and wander in uncertainty over the town, let me guide you to where you may be sure of obtaining me. Seek Secundus, the freedman of the learned Lucensis, behind the Temple of Peace and the Forum of Pallas.' There was no imprint, it should be added, on Roman books, and such directions were by no means superfluous. Martial, like some of our modern authors, perhaps thought it worth while to set up a sort of rivalry among the publishers of his books, for he mentions yet another of them by name†—one Quintus Pollius Valerianus, who had preserved the immature verses of the poet's youth, and also sold other trifles which he had himself forgotten. Possibly it was in order to prevent competition of this sort that the first Publishers' Association was formed; for Dr Putnam records, on the authority of Theodor Birt, that such a society was founded at the beginning of the second century.‡ Little is known about it except that it was organized by the leading publishers of Rome 'for the better protection of their interests in literary property, and that each member bound himself not to interfere with the undertakings of his fellow members'.

Roman authors had other grievances besides those against their publishers and friends. It was not only from motives of vanity that they indulged in the public and private recitations which became one of the features of their social life. The recitations, in addition to affording them their best form of advertisement, lessened, though it by no means removed, the risk, which every Roman author ran, of some unscrupulous plagiarist taking a new book and in the most barefaced manner reissuing it, or large portions of it, as his own original work.

Even the public recitations were not without some dangers of the sort, for, like the public libraries of Rome—of which we are told there were between twenty and thirty—they were free to all citizens. It was by no means an unknown thing for some one among these audiences to commit a new piece to memory and, hurriedly issuing it through the bookseller, put his own name to it as author. This is not so improbable as it may seem when we remember what remarkable memories were possessed by the citizens of ancient Rome and Greece. Memory was then cultivated as a gift of the highest order, and some of the achievements in this direction would be incredible were they not corroborated by so many writers. Pliny tells us, in one of his letters, of a Greek philosopher who was able, at the close of a long extempore oration, to repeat it word for word from beginning to end. Cyrus is said to have remembered the name of every soldier in his army.

* Book II, 24.   † Book I, 113.
‡ *Authors and Their Public in Ancient Times*, 1894.

But we have strayed into the tempting byways of purely literary history, and must return to the booksellers, remembering that even in those remote days literature was distributed as far afield as the conquered land of Britain, with which our history henceforth is chiefly concerned. Roman literature, and with it the Roman book trade, rapidly declined after the Silver Age of Latinity, and when Constantine I, early in the fourth century, transferred the capital of the Roman Empire to Byzantium the age of classical Latin was practically over.

2

Through the Dark Ages

It is no easy task to write an account of the restricted book trade in this country through the 'long night of the Dark Ages'. We find only faint traces here and there as we stumble through the centuries until we come to the system of distribution as it gradually developed in the days of the monks. The Anglo-Saxon invasion in the fifth century destroyed whatever remnants of intellectual life remained in the island, save for a handful of refugee scholars in the west, and the monastic schools of Wales — whence proceeded the men who founded the seats of learning which now sprang up in Ireland. Safe from the devastation of Europe by the barbarians, Ireland became the sanctuary of thousands of fugitives, and its monasteries the training-ground for missionaries, who in turn carried back their scholarship to the English and other nations. To England came not only this monastic learning, but, in the seventh century, the educational stimulus of the Roman missionaries under the influence of which three great schools were to rise into prominence — Canterbury, Jarrow and York — until England in turn led the van of intellectual progress.

There must have been some sort of recognized system of book distribution at the back of this intellectual revival. The epics of the Anglo-Saxons were spread by recitation and preserved by memory, but among the scholars themselves a considerable traffic in books was inevitable. This traffic probably was based on the long traditions of Rome brought by the Roman missionaries, but of this we can judge only by inference. There are occasional scraps of evidence to show that in the downfall of the Empire the book trade had not been completely extinguished in Italy — and perhaps in Gaul as well — but the attempt to bridge the gulf between the classic trade and the English reading world of the early manuscript days is at the best unsatisfactory. We read of Benedict Biscop's several journeys to and from Rome, and elsewhere, laden with precious volumes for the great twin abbeys of Wearmouth and Jarrow, the first of which he founded in 674 and the second in 682; of the literary additions made by his successor Ceolfrid; of book-lovers like Aldhelm, Bede and Acca; of Aldfrith of Northumberland ordering copies of Adamnan's book *De Locis Sacris* for the use of 'lesser persons'; of Ælbert's noble library at York; and of other evidences of England's scholarly activity in these early Middle Ages. But the system of book

distribution which lay behind this development was not such an
organized trade as in the days of Imperial Rome. Books were now
written and published by the authors themselves, as in the more distant
ages of antiquity.

Bede kept in touch with the monasteries not only of England, but of
the Continent, and had copiers at work as far away as Rome. He may
be said to have published his *History* from the monastic cell at Jarrow
in which he spent most of his life, for when it was finished—in or about
the year 731, at which it is brought to an end—he sent the book thence
to his friend Albinus, an ecclesiastic who had urged him to undertake
the work and helped him with information. 'Wherefore', he writes, 'I
have with great propriety sent it to you to be copied. But I intend to
repay you by forwarding to you another volume for the same purpose
... namely, that which I have lately published on the building of
Solomon's Temple, and its allegorical signification. And I humbly
beseech you, most loving father, and Christ's servants who are with
you, to intercede fervently with the righteous in behalf of my frailty;
and to admonish those to whom you shall show my work to do the same.'

That was the pious way they had of publishing books in those days,
just as, later in the Middle Ages, we can see, in several illuminated
manuscripts, John Lydgate on his knees before Henry VI, or some other
generous patron, presenting him with a copy of his new book of poems.
Such a presentation, as in the case of Bede's offering to Albinus,
practically constituted the first publication of a new work. When Bede
died—to return to our restricted book world of the eighth century—the
seat of learning passed from Jarrow to York, which then became the
centre of education in Western Europe. It was Ælbert's famous library,
already referred to, which furnished us, thanks to Alcuin's metrical
account of its treasures, with the earliest book list of which we have any
knowledge. The catalogue shows us that in addition to the books of
such native scholars as Bede and Aldhelm, York possessed the works of
Augustine, Jerome, Hilary, Ambrose, Gregory, Athanasius, Pope Leo,
Basil, Chrysostom and other Fathers of the Church. Virgil, Statius and
Lucanus were among the classics, together with Propertius, Aratus,
Juvencus, one of the earliest of the Christian poets, and Lactantius, the
'Christian Cicero', who enjoyed a great vogue in the Middle Ages.
Among historians and philosophers were Pliny, Boëthius, Orosius,
Aristotle and Cicero; and the formidable list of grammarians includes
Phocas, Donatus, Probus, Priscianus, Servius, Eutchius and Commianus.

The fame of this library spread throughout Europe. It was a literary
treasure-house to which most scholars turned until Alcuin left England
for Charlemagne's Court towards the end of the eighth century, when
the centre of education was transferred to the schools of Charles the
Great. The decay of learning in England had already set in before

Alcuin left the country, and in the ninth century the Danes completed its destruction. We are again forced to wander abroad for our next traces of the book world, and these are to be found only in the monasteries.

The production and preservation of books, as well as their serious study, had been one of the leading principles of monastic life since the early part of the sixth century, when St Benedict, striking at the roots of the evil which threatened the very existence of monachism, branded idleness as 'the enemy of the soul', and added the vow of labour to the other rules of poverty, chastity and obedience. The later orders followed St Benedict's sagacious example, and the monasteries became the one recognized home and refuge of Letters — the Vestal Virgins, as a French writer has said, who, through all the vicissitudes of the Dark Ages, prevented the sacred lamp of learning from burning out. The phrase is specially appropriate when applied to the nuns, who played a noble part in the preservation and distribution of sacred literature. Some of the most beautiful manuscripts that have come down to us were produced by medieval nuns.

How religiously the scribes approached their work may be gathered from an eighth-century manuscript, in which we find one of the *scriptoria* receiving the following form of benediction: 'Vouchsafe, O Lord, to bless this *scriptorium* of thy servants, and all that dwell therein; that whatsoever sacred writings shall be here read or written by them, they may receive with understanding and bring the same to good effect, through the Lord, ...'* The monks have often been accused of scraping ancient parchments in order to substitute their own writings for the texts of Greek and Latin classics, but as most of these palimpsests were made after the Norman Conquest, when parchment became increasingly valuable, it is more probable that the manuscripts of the earlier Middle Ages were thus treated rather than the older parchment of the classics.

Our losses in this respect, however, have been greatly exaggerated. And our gains have been by no means inconsiderable — legends of the saints, treatises of the Fathers of the Church and possibly some of the early chronicles with which English history especially is so richly endowed. For almost every monastery of importance had its own historiographer, whose duty it was to carry on the annals left by his predecessor.

Some at least of the monastic book-makers of the Dark Ages proved themselves worthy successors of Atticus in the pains which they took to secure the accuracy of their texts.

In England monachism, after falling into complete decay, was only just beginning to revive. Alfred worked wonders in his efforts to kindle a new enthusiasm for education and literature towards the end of the

* Maitland's *Dark Ages*.

ninth century, and in the following century his efforts bore fruit in the re-creation of the monasteries under St Dunstan and King Edgar. But the people themselves were too busy fighting for their lives and homes against the Danes to profit greatly by the revival. It is not until the Norman-French cultivation made its way into England in the eleventh century that we can follow the book trade in this country with any degree of continuity. With the Norman Conquest England was brought definitely into the full current of European culture, and received an impetus which she sorely needed to her whole national life.

But in the ecclesiastical settlement under William the Conqueror and Lanfranc both the Anglo-Saxon books and the monks who had so patiently compiled them were often shamefully treated, however much the intellectual standard of the Church may have been raised in the process. The Norman bishops and abbots by whom the native ecclesiastics were displaced despised the Anglo-Saxon writings which they found in their new monasteries. Many Anglo-Saxon books were cut up for binding, or erased to make room for some transcript in Latin, Latin gradually superseding the Anglo-Saxon which had been employed in all the national literature since Alfred's day. Norman monks were doubtless introduced for their skill as transcribers and decorative artists, though the art of illuminating manuscripts, which is as old almost as humanity itself, had already been brought to a high state of perfection in England, having been introduced from Ireland centuries before. The finest of the existing specimens bear witness both to the skill and infinite patience of these unknown craftsmen. It is not surprising that books in those days could be so costly, or that the *scriptorium* of the monastery in which such work was done was sometimes so jealously guarded that no visitors were allowed there except the abbot, the prior, the sub-prior and the precentor. That, at least, was one of the rules of St Victor, and similar restrictions were probably in force at most monasteries where gold and jewels were freely used in the binding and illuminating of books. The art of decoration and illumination became everywhere so splendidly ornate that Odofredi, the Bolognese jurist, had some cause for complaining, in the thirteenth century, that writers were no longer writers, but painters. For law books were frequently as resplendent as missals, psalters and prayer-books. It is not fair, however, to regard the cost of such sumptuous works as these as a true index to the prices of books in the Middle Ages. Doubtless it was more for its binding and decoration than its intrinsic worth that the Countess of Anjou paid in the year 1056 for a copy of the homilies of Haimon, Bishop of Halberstadt, two hundred sheep, a hogshead of wheat, another of rye, a third of millet and a certain number of marten skins. The simple truth, as Maitland says, is that there has always been such a thing as bibliomania since there have been books in the world.

As the manuscript period reached its more elaborate stage the makers of books in the monasteries specialized in their different departments of work. One monk would prepare the parchment by rubbing it with powdered pumice-stone, or obtain suitable 'pounce', such as the powdered bone of the cuttle-fish. Then he would cut it into sheets of the required size, and, having ruled the pages, hand it to the monk whose particular forte was writing. The scribe himself would leave the initials and borders for the illuminators, whose work seems frequently to have been neglected—or, maybe, stayed by the hand of Death, if we are to judge by the number of unfinished manuscripts which have come down to us. It is not difficult to imagine ourselves back in one of these secluded bookshops as we turn over the pages of an early fourteenth-century missal, for example, with its glowing splashes of burnished gold, and decorative effects as vivid in colouring today, almost, as when the monks themselves were putting the finishing touches to the work. The small 'leading letter' for one of its elaborate initials, left by the transcriber for the guidance of the illuminator, has been left as it stood; and on the last page the outline sketches have never been filled up. It recalls the story of that monk of Wedinghausen, in Westphalia, who died at his desk, his pen still in his hand. Years afterwards, we are told, his grave was opened, whereupon it was found that his good right hand was as fresh and firm of flesh as on the day of his death. And, lest anyone should doubt this story, the hand and pen may be seen to this day among the holy relics preserved in the monastery chapel.

There was a strict, if variable, system of lending and borrowing books, even in the monasteries themselves. In certain cases books could not be lent except to neighbouring churches, or to persons of distinction and substantial means; and then only on the deposit of books or other articles of at least equal value. King John, when he borrowed 'the book called *Pliny*' which had been in the custody of the Abbot and Convent of Reading, had to give a pledge for it. Some monasteries went so far as to refuse to make any loan of the kind, under no less a penalty than that of excommunication. This appears to have been the case at the Abbey of Croyland, where, according to the so-called *History of Ingulph*, 'the lending of their books, as well the smaller without pictures as the larger with pictures', was thus strictly forbidden. For greater safety the books in the libraries were often chained to the desks. 'Cursed be he who shall steal or tear out the leaves, or in any way injure this book', is the anathema which will be found inscribed in some of these old volumes; as, indeed, was advised by that prince of fourteenth-century book-lovers, Richard de Bury, Bishop of Durham, in *Philobiblon*: 'There are also certain thieves who enormously dismember books by cutting off the side margins for letter paper, leaving only the letters or text, or the fly-leaves put in for the preservation of the book, which they take away

for various uses and abuses, which sort of sacrilege ought to be prohibited under a threat of anathema.' A choice collection of these
monkish warnings will be found in J. W. Clark's learned work on *The
Care of Books*.

If all that the worthy bishop says in *Philobiblon* be true the monks of
his day had sadly degenerated. They had little of his own reverential
devotion to study, being more intent on the 'emptyings of bowls' and
'such things as we are accustomed to forbid to secular men' than on the
wisdom and companionship of books. They were, indeed, reverting to
the old order of things which, centuries before, had induced St Benedict
to institute the vow of labour, and a century or so later was to lead to the
downfall of monachism in England. Though books in manuscript were
never so brutally treated as during the suppression of the monasteries by
Henry VIII, they now suffered many cruel indignities through the
laxity of discipline and morals among those whose predecessors had
proved so worthy of the trust imposed upon them. Every student of the
subject knows the story of how Boccaccio paid a visit to the famous
monastery of Monte Cassino, the foundation of which was laid by
St Benedict himself, and was horrified at the deplorable condition in
which he found the library there. Dust and dirt lay an inch thick
everywhere, covering and corroding manuscripts which would now be
of priceless value. The weeds on the window-sills had grown so thick
and tall that the whole room was darkened; but Boccaccio saw clearly
enough to notice that many of the books had been brutally mutilated,
some having half their contents forcibly removed, and others — as in the
cases complained of by his English contemporary, Richard de Bury —
having their margins cut away. More in sorrow than in anger, Boccaccio
went to one of the monks in the cloisters and asked how it was that the
books had been so treated. The monk admitted quite frankly and un-
concernedly that when they wanted a few pence they cut off the blank
margins of the old manuscripts or erased some of the pages and turned
them into small devotional books, for which there seems to have been a
ready sale. Not a word about the shameful state of neglect into which
everything had been allowed to fall.

Records of this description are mostly from the Continent, but
Richard de Bury's bitter complaint, and other references, leave us
little room for supposing that our own monks at this period were much
better. In a passage in Richard de Bury's *Philobiblon* which we are
tempted to quote at length the books themselves are allowed to air
their grievances:

In the first place, we are expelled with heart and hand from the
domiciles of the clergy, apportioned to us by hereditary right,
in some interior chamber of which we had our peaceful cells:

but, to their shame, in these nefarious times we are altogether banished to suffer opprobrium out of doors. Our places, moreover, are occupied by hounds and hawks, and sometimes by a biped beast; woman to wit — whose cohabitation was formerly shunned by the clergy, from whom we have ever taught our pupils to fly, more than from the asp and the basilisk; wherefore this beast, ever jealous of our studies, and at all times implacable, spying us at last in a corner, protected only by the web of some long deceased spider, drawing her forehead into wrinkles, laughs us to scorn, abuses us in virulent speeches, points us out as the only superfluous furniture lodged in the whole house; complains that we are useless for any purpose of domestic economy whatever, and recommends our being bartered away forthwith for costly head-dresses, cambric, silk, twice-dipped purple garments, woollen, linen and furs: and indeed with reason, if she could see the interior of our hearts, or be present at our secret councils, or could read the volumes of Theophrastus and Valerius, or at least hear the 25th Chapter of Ecclesiasticus with the ears of understanding.

We complain, therefore, because our domiciles are unjustly taken from us — not that garments are not given to us, but that those which were formerly given are torn off by violent hands, insomuch that our souls adhere to the pavement, our belly is agglutinated to the earth, and our glory is reduced to dust. (Ps. xliv. and cxix.) We labour under various diseases; our back and sides ache, we lie down disabled and paralysed in every limb, nobody thinks of us, nor is there anyone who will benignly apply an emollient to our sores. Our native whiteness, perspicuous with light, is now turned tawny and yellow; so that no medical man who may find us out, can doubt that we are infected with jaundice. Some of us are gouty, as our distorted extremities evidently indicate. The damp, smoke and dust with which we are constantly infested, dim the field of our visual rays, and super-induce ophthalmia upon our already bleared eyes. Our stomachs are destroyed by the severe griping of our bowels, which greedy worms never cease to gnaw. We suffer corruption inside and out, and nobody is found to anoint us with turpentine; or who, calling to us on the fourth day of putrefaction, will say, 'Lazarus, come forth' ...

Again: we complain of another kind of calamity, that is very often unjustly imposed upon our persons; for we are sold like slaves and female captives, or left as pledges in taverns without redemption.

Richard de Bury himself kept his own staff of transcribers, and took advantage of all the facilities then available for adding to his beloved library. Churchmen eager for his favours searched for him in all parts of the Continent, and he never missed an opportunity, when calling at a monastery, of visiting the library chests and other repositories of books; 'for there, amidst the deepest poverty, we found heaped up the most exalted treasures'. In addition to these exceptional facilities, he adds that: 'We easily acquire the notice of the stationers and librarians, not only within the provinces of our native soil, but of those dispersed over the kingdoms of France, Germany and Italy, by the prevailing power of money. No distance whatever impeded, no fury of the sea deterred them; nor was cash wanting for their expenses when they sent or brought us the wished-for books.' Unfortunately neither the bishop's library which he collected with so much care and devotion, nor the 'special catalogue' which he drew up for the use of his scholars, is any longer in existence. The books were destroyed or dispersed in Henry VIII's reign, during the suppression of Durham College, which the bishop founded at Oxford on the site now occupied by Trinity College.

The ready means of private book distribution in England in the fourteenth and early fifteenth centuries are indicated in the wide circulation of the completed translation of the Bible by John Wyclife, who died in 1384. This version, revised by John Purvey, was severely proscribed by the Convocation of Canterbury in January 1409, yet copies of it were spread all over the country by various unauthorized means until superseded by Tyndale's translation and other printed versions in the first half of the sixteenth century. There is additional evidence of some early system of book distribution in the signs which exist of the extensive circulation of William Langland's *The Vision of Piers Plowman*. Langland, who died somewhere about the year 1400, issued his poem in three distinct forms, or editions, and some fifty manuscript copies are known to be still in existence. He sought no pecuniary reward, preferring, apparently, to live the life of poverty and unselfishness which he preached so earnestly in the old alliterative measure of his Middle-English poem. Doubtless he was his own publisher — if we may use such a term in this connection — issuing copies of his work in his own hand from his house in Cornhill, where he lived with his wife Kitte for many years.

The growth of the medieval university marks the beginning of a new chapter in the history of bookselling. The coming of paper and the increasing demand for books among the people had already given birth to another class of book-makers, the scriveners and *stationarii* — so called, according to Kirchoff, to distinguish the stationary, or resident, booksellers from the wandering pedlars. Thomas Fuller offers a similar derivation, but it is much more quaintly put in his seventeenth-century English: '*Stationarii* — publicly avouching the sale of staple-books in standing shops (whence they have their names) as opposite to such circumforanean pedlars (ancestors to our modern Mercuries and hawkers) which secretly vend prohibited books.' Henry Hallam, in his *Literature of Europe*, says that 'these medieval booksellers were denominated *stationarii* perhaps from the open stalls at which they carried on their business, though *statio* is a general word for shop, in Low Latin. They appear by the old statutes of Paris, and by those of Bologna, to have sold books on commission; and are sometimes, though not uniformly, distinguished from the *librarii*; a word which, having originally been confined to the copyists of books, was afterwards applied to those who traded in them. They sold parchment and other materials for writing, which, with us, though, as far as I know, nowhere else, have retained the name of stationery, and naturally exercised the kindred occupations of binding and decorating. They probably employed transcribers.'

In Paris, which in the fourteenth century was the great bookmarket of the world, the stationers were controlled by the universities, and appear to have acted at first mainly as book-lenders. Their shops were in reality circulating libraries for the scholars. They sold books only as agents for the owners of manuscripts committed to their care, receiving a commission in this case of a bare 2 or 3 per cent. When they came to issue books of their own copying, every work of the kind had to be submitted to the university for approval, and sold only at the price at which it was then assessed. There was reason in all this, for the Paris book trade appears to have owed its organization and development largely, if not entirely, to the university, and the university saw to it that it fulfilled the purpose for which it was originally intended, namely, that of supplying the educational needs of the scholars, without at the same time contaminating their minds with doubtful or heretical books. Much the same system of control prevailed at the older University of Bologna, and other Italian universities, as well as at Oxford and Cambridge.

Some curious facts regarding the status of the university booksellers in England may be gleaned from George Gray's work on *The Earlier Stationers and Bookbinders, and the First Cambridge Printer*, issued for the Bibliographical Society in 1904. The first reference to the Cambridge booksellers is in a decision of 1276, in which it is declared that the 'writers, illuminators and stationers, who serve the scholars only', were subject, like the members of the university, to the jurisdiction of the chancellor, and could not be interfered with by the Archdeacon of Ely, who had claimed jurisdiction over the university, as well as over the town. The wives of the said writers, illuminators and stationers were rather heartlessly abandoned to the tender mercies of the archdeacon. For these, it is added, 'being under the charge of adultery or any other crime, the cognizance and correction of which pertains to the

archdeacon in similar cases concerning other persons under his jurisdiction, and the rest of their family, not especially deputed to the service
of the scholars, shall be under the archdeacon's jurisdiction in all and
everything, like other lay persons in the town of Cambridge and our
diocese of Ely'.

The stationers could only sell books which had been approved by the
chancellor as being free from heretical opinions. The power of the
Oxford and Cambridge Universities as censors of the book trade in
those days is seen in the series of resolutions for the suppression of
Lollardism passed at the Convocation of Canterbury early in 1409.

Among other things it was ordained that no book or tract compiled
by John Wyclife, or by anyone else in his time or since, or to be compiled hereafter, should be read or taught in the schools, hostels, or other
places within the province, unless it should first be examined by the
Universities of Oxford or Cambridge, or at least by twelve persons to
be elected by each of these bodies, and afterwards expressly approved
of by the archbishop or his successors; that, when approved, the book
should be delivered, in the name and by the authority of the university,
to the stationers to be copied; and a faithful collation being made, the
original should be deposited in the chest of the university, there to
remain for ever.

The first 'stationarius of the University' of Cambridge of whom we
have any record is one John Hardy, referred to in one of the records as
early as 1350, but for a hundred years after Hardy's death there is no
mention of anyone holding such a post. From 1449 onwards, however,
there is a constant succession of them. Their peculiar position and
duties are thus defined by Sir Stanley Leathes in his edition of the
Cambridge *Grace Book A*.*

> *Stationaries*: These persons occupied an anomalous position. They
> were not students, nor were they exactly servants or tradesmen.
> They were the official agents of the University for the sale of
> pledges,† and official valuers of manuscripts and other valuables
> offered as security [by needy students]. They seem to have received
> an occasional fee from the chest. The analogy of other Universities
> suggests that they were bound to supply books to the students at a
> fixed tariff, and that they also acted as intermediaries between
> buyer and seller when a student had a book to sell. Like the servants
> and tradesmen dependent on the University, they were under the
> University jurisdiction.

As at Oxford, there appears in the fifteenth century to have been

---

* *Grace Book A, 1454–88*, edited by Sir S. M. Leathes, 1897.
† Pledges, or 'cautions', were deposited by every student as a guarantee that he would
perform the requisite acts on admission to a degree. The 'cautions' were forfeited if he failed
in the performance.

only one stationarius appointed—though the number increased after the introduction of printing—and various entries suggest that he was paid a yearly sum by the university. Other entries point to the interesting fact that the stationarius was also supplied with a gown as a distinctive mark of his office. He was responsible for the binding and repairing of books, as well as the chaining of them. The chains cost from 2d. to 4d. each. 'That the University did not monopolize the whole of the time of their stationarius', says George Gray, 'is shown by John Hardy (1351–4) being also an official in the Corpus Christi Gild, and by Walter Hartley, the last of the fifteenth-century stationers, who added to his work the post of parish clerk to the university church of St Mary the Great, and saw to the cleansing of the pavements leading to the university buildings.'

The first stationer to figure in the Oxford records is one Robert, who was a 'notary and stationer in cattestrete' in the year 1308, but there are references to scribes and illuminators as far back at least as 1180. At the beginning of 1374 the number of booksellers in Oxford appears to have been so excessive that the university decreed that none except the sworn stationers, or their deputies, should sell any book exceeding half a mark in value. According to the terms of that statute, there were a great many booksellers in Oxford at that time who were not sworn to the university, with the result that 'books of great value are sold and carried away from Oxford, the owners of them are cheated, and the sworn stationers are deprived of their lawful business'.*

The Oxford booksellers evidently continued in rather a bad way, for we learn from the same authority that in 1411 the university enacted that, 'as the duties of the university stationers are laborious and anxious, every one on graduation shall give clothes to one of the stationers'. But the Oxford stationer was not the only book-maker of his century to find himself short of clothes. In the *Paston Letters* there is a pitiful appeal from Sir John Paston's scrivener, who, writing from Sanctuary for a settlement of his account for books copied, adds that he will be grateful for the gift of an old gown.

In London the scriveners, or Writers of the Court Hand and Text Letters—the forerunners of the Stationers' Company—have been traced back in the civic records to the year 1357, while Chaucer was still a royal page and his Canterbury Pilgrimage probably as yet undreamt of; but they must have been in existence as recognized copiers and sellers of books long before then. Later—on July 12th, 1403—we find all the various members of the original fraternity grouped together in a memorial to the Mayor and Aldermen of London, dated July 12th, 1403,† as 'the reputable men of the Craft of Writers of Text-letters,

---

* *Early Oxford Press*, by Falconer Madan, 1895.
† Arber's *Registers of the Stationers' Company*, vol. i, 1875.

those commonly called Limners [Illuminators] and other good folk; citizens of London, who were wont to bind and to sell books'. In their memorial these reputable men prayed for authority to elect wardens 'diligently to oversee that good rule and governance is had and exercised by all folks of the same trades in all works with the said trades pertaining, to the praise and good fame of the loyal good men of the same trades, and to the shame and blame of the bad and disloyal men of the same'. The petition was granted by the mayor and aldermen, 'for the reason especially that it concerned the common weal and profit'. The five-hundredth anniversary of the guild thus founded was commemorated by the Stationers' Company in 1904.

In Chaucer's day—and, indeed, throughout the Middle Ages—the copiers of books attached little importance to authors' names, unless posterity had already made them famous. New books had nothing in the shape of a title-page. There is reason for supposing that Chaucer read Boccaccio's tales without knowing the name of the author to whom he was so deeply indebted. The modern title-pages came in with the printing press, though Caxton, who, like most early printers, transferred many features of the manuscript book into the printed copy, never seems to have adopted this new idea. Conservative in his tastes, it is not unlikely that he had many an argument on the subject with his friend, assistant and successor, Wynkyn de Worde, who introduced the title-page almost immediately after his master's death.

3

The Dawn of Printing

With the introduction of printing it is less difficult to gather up our scattered threads, though by no means easy to weave them into a satisfactory web. Our own early printers, heavily handicapped by their lateness in practising the new art, were faced by foreign competition, keen and well organized, and they were wise to feel their way cautiously. Caxton, who set up his press at Westminster in 1476, appears to have begun modestly enough, and to have made sure of a certain subscription before embarking on some of his larger ventures. In his *Legend of Saints* he tells us: 'I have submysed [submitted] myself to translate into English the *Legend of Saints*, called *Legenda aurea* in Latin; and William, Earl of Arundel, desired me — and promised to take a reasonable quantity of them — and sent me a worshipful gentleman, promising that my said lord should during my life give and grant me a yearly fee, that is to note, a buck in summer and a doe in winter.' The nobility were then the chief patrons of printed literature in England, for the simple reason that there were not enough readers among the common people to justify the printing of a large edition of any book; and naturally the more limited the number of copies the higher would be the price charged for each.

Unfortunately Caxton's account-book has not been preserved, so that it is impossible to say how much he charged for the works which are now worth more than their weight in gold. The only clue that we have lies in the fact that the fifteen copies of *Legends* which he left to St Margaret's, Westminster, realized prices ranging from 5s. 4d. to 6s. 8d. Even this fact is not so illuminating as it seemed down even to William Blades's day, for Caxton's biographer, like every other authority until the present century, assumed that the books bequeathed by the printer were copies of his *Golden Legend*, the largest book produced by his press, containing 499 folio leaves, with illustrations. Fragments have, however, been discovered of a *Sarum Legenda*, printed for Caxton in Paris by Guillaume Maynyal, who in 1487 produced for Caxton an edition of the *Sarum Missal*; and it was probably this service-book, rather than the *Golden Legend* itself, that was left to St Margaret's Church.

That there was some system of 'sale or return' among the booksellers in Caxton's time is evident from the list of Thomas Hunte, stationer of the University of Oxford, which Falconer Madan prints at the end of his edition of *The Day-Book of John Dorne*. This list is an inventory, written on the fly-leaf of a French translation of Livy (printed at Paris in 1486, and now in the Bodleian Library), recording the books received by Hunte in the year 1483 from Peter Actors* and Joannes de Aquisgrano. These were two foreign stationers settled in London who appear to have travelled about the country in partnership as wholesale booksellers. Hunte gives a written promise faithfully to restore the books or pay the price affixed in the list. Most of the leading stationers of London had their travelling booksellers, if they did not always do the travelling themselves. Their chief markets were the great fairs, such as that of Stourbridge, which had been as early as the thirteenth century the chief fair in the kingdom. The importance of Stourbridge to booksellers lasted for several centuries after the invention of printing, for it is known to have had its Booksellers' Row as late as 1725. The leading stationers of London in the early days of printing also made a point, whenever possible, of attending the great book-market which was held twice a year at the Frankfurt fair. It was here that accounts could be settled and the new books of the world seen. Frankfurt, it may be added, remained the centre of the Continental book trade until after the Thirty Years War in the seventeenth century. It was then gradually superseded by the fair at Leipzig.

The dawn of printing brought with it, among other changes, a new form of binding in the shape of pasteboards—layers of waste sheets pasted together—instead of the old solid boards. Fearful as well as wonderful were some of the great tomes of the older style. The covers between which the leaves were fastened were literally wooden boards, as thick as the panel of a door. The wood used was commonly beech: it is from the German word *buche* (beech) that we get our 'book'. The boards were covered with leather and often beautifully embossed, with elaborate corners, clasps and brass nails on the outside; but they made the book so heavy that, as Erasmus said of Thomas Aquinas's *Secunda Secundae*, 'No man could carry it about, much less get it into his head.'

Pasteboards came into vogue towards the end of the fifteenth century, and were often composed of printed sheets that had been discarded as of no use. Many rare typographical fragments have been brought to light in modern days from the search among the linings of these old bindings. A remarkable find of the kind was made by Blades in the library of the St Albans Grammar School. Blades was examining a number of volumes in connection with his life of Caxton, and pulled out one book which was lying flat upon the top of others. 'It was in a most deplorable state, covered thickly with a damp, sticky dust, and with a considerable portion of the back rotted away. The white decay fell in

* Afterwards appointed Stationer to Henry VII. See p. 47.

lumps on the floor as the unappreciated volume was opened. It proved to be Geoffrey Chaucer's English translation of *Boecius de consolacione philosophie*, printed by Caxton, in the original binding as issued from Caxton's workshop, and uncut! ... On dissecting the covers they were found to be composed entirely of waste sheets from Caxton's press, two or three being printed on one side only. The two covers yielded no less than fifty-six half-sheets of printed paper, proving the existence of three works from Caxton's press quite unknown before.'

Some slight evidence of book prices in England at the beginning of the sixteenth century is afforded in the 'Privy Purse Accounts of Elizabeth of York', one entry showing that in 1505 twenty pence were paid for a Primer and a Psalter. Now in 1505, as Charles Knight observes in his life of Caxton, twenty pence would have bought half a load of barley and were equal to six days' work of a labourer. In 1516 *Fitzherbert's Abridgement*, a large folio law book, then first published, was sold for forty shillings—equal at that time to the cost of three fat oxen. Small wonder, if books fetched such prices as these, that Caxton declared that his works were not for the 'rude uplandish man'.

The printer little dreamt that the 'rude uplandish man' was in course of time to become a ruling patron of the press. Already he was making his influence felt on the Continent, thanks very largely to the papal encouragement of cheapness, but even there he was not yet in sufficient force to warrant the large editions which some printers were induced to place on the market. The result of this is seen in the petition presented to the Pope in 1472 by the two German printers Sweynheim and Pannartz, who had settled in Rome. 'We were the first of the Germans', they wrote—though Ulrich Hahn claims the same distinction—'who, with vast labour and cost, introduced this art into your Holiness's territories; and by our example encouraged other printers to do the same. If you read the catalogue of the works printed by us, you will wonder how and where we could procure a sufficient quantity of paper, or even rags, for such a number of volumes. The total of these books amounts to 12,475—a prodigious heap—and unbearable to us, your Holiness's printers, by reason of those unsold. We are no longer able to bear the great expense of house-keeping, for want of buyers, of which there cannot be a more flagrant proof than that our house, though otherwise spacious enough, is full of quire-books, but void of every necessary of life.' The immediate result of this appeal is unknown to us, but the fact that Pannartz abandoned printing for the art of engraving in the following year suggests that the Pope's assistance, if forthcoming at all, was not sufficient for the purpose. Sweynheim, who died some three years later, seems to have continued to print to the end, but not, apparently, with any enthusiasm.

The Church is known to have helped its early printers with funds, and long continued to support cheap books for the encouragement of learning among the people, as well as the propagation of works of approved theological teaching. When Leo X, in 1533, granted a privilege to the second Aldus for printing *Varro* he required that the book should be issued in a cheap edition. Gradually, however, as Dr Putnam points out in his history of *The Censorship of Rome*, it dawned upon the ecclesiastical authorities that there was another side to the shield. The leaders of the Reformation as well as the rulers of the Church had given a warm welcome to the printing press, and were making full use of their new opportunities to spread their doctrines far and wide. Before a hundred years had passed the danger to the Church was met by the promulgation of a special edict prescribing penalties for the reading of heretical or doubtful works. The first Italian list of prohibited books and authors appeared in 1542, and seventeen years later was inaugurated the series of Papal Indexes which continued until the 1960s.

In England — to return to the dawn of printing in this country — the first printers and publishers were not so subject to the approving or disapproving nod of the Pope. Caxton, indeed, for his earlier services as 'Governor to the English Nation at Bruges' and as secretary or steward to the sister of Edward IV — Margaret, Duchess of Burgundy — could count on court influence to support him in his new enterprise. Though never officially appointed Printer to the King, he was patronized both by Edward IV and Richard III, and printed several works under their 'protection'. Of the hundred books which were issued from his press before his death in 1491 he was personally responsible for the translation of about twenty-five, besides editing almost every one of them.

Caxton has been taken to task by Gibbon for neglecting the classics, but our first printer-publisher knew what he was about. The favourite literature of the age among his chief patrons, the princes and nobility, was the 'joyous and pleysaunt romaunce', just as printed service-books were then the need of the clergy. Caxton, who, as he tells us in *Charles the Great*, had now to earn his living by his press, showed his common sense in issuing books for which he knew there was a demand. He realized that the classics could be obtained from abroad in editions which made competition on his part both unnecessary and futile. What he did for us — and for which we cannot be sufficiently grateful — was to produce works of Chaucer, Gower, Lydgate, Thomas Malory and other gems of pure literature at one of the momentous stages in the development of the English language.

To Caxton we owe the first printed book-advertisement in this country of which we have any knowledge — a little poster not unlike the leaflets of some of our present-day publishers, except that, instead of stating that the work in question — the *Sarum Ordinale*, or *Pica*, containing the Salisbury order of Church services—could be obtained 'of all booksellers', it invited the reader to come to his office for it:

> If it plese ony man spiritual or temporal to bye ony pyes of two or three comemoracions of Salisburi use, enpryntid after the forme of this preset [present] lettre whiche ben wel and truly correct, late hym come to Westmonester in to the almonesrye at the reed pale, and he shal have them good chepe.

Below this is a line by itself, appealing to the public not to tear down the bill, and printed in Latin: 'Supplico stet cedula'. Pye, it should be explained, was the English form of the Latin *pica*, or service-book, and the explanation of the term 'pyes of two or three comemoracions' accepted by Blades is that a pye of two commemorations contained the rules for Easter and Whitsuntide, and a pye of three commemorations those for Easter Whitsuntide, and Trinity.

Wynkyn de Worde, the German assistant who inherited Caxton's business, and remained in the same house until 1500, was a craftsman of a very different stamp—'a man', in the words of E. Gordon Duff,* 'who was merely a mechanic, and who was quite unable to fill the place of Caxton either as an editor or a translator, one who preferred to issue small popular books of a kind to attract the general public rather than the class of book which had hitherto been published from Caxton's house'. He described himself, in common with most other makers and sellers of books in London, as a 'citizen Stationer'. In 1500 he moved to the sign of the Sun, in Fleet Street, renting two houses close to St Bride's Church and immediately facing the entrance to Shoe Lane. Evidently affairs were prospering with the printer and publisher of popular books. Some years later he had another shop in St Paul's Churchyard. Probably he had a bookstall in front of his Fleet Street house as well, for this appears to have been a custom of the craft which even the King's Printer in those days was not ashamed to follow.

St Paul's Churchyard, however, was already the chief centre of the book trade, not only for London, but for the whole of the country. Many of the more important printers and stationers lived and carried on their business in the main row of houses which surrounded the church. Their smaller brethren, who were forced to have their printing offices elsewhere, and the foreign stationers, who now crowded to England as agents for the Continental printers, seized every available nook and corner for booths and stalls and unpretentious little shops of one story that served as 'lock-ups'. The competition of the foreigner with the native printer and stationer led to a Book War more bitter than anything of the sort that we have experienced in modern times. There was much to be said for both sides. The printing press and the

* *The Printers, Stationers, and Bookbinders of Westminster and London from 1476 to 1535.*

book trade developments which sprang immediately from it had made vast strides on the Continent long before they were established in this country. In 1484, when Richard III passed the Act which contained a direct encouragement to foreigners to bring their printing and their books to England, there were fifty printers at work in Venice alone, and in Germany, France and Spain they could be counted by the score.

Yet England at this date could boast of only three other presses at work besides Caxton's—that of the Oxford printer whose imprint of 1468 for 1478 threatened at one time to deprive Caxton of his glory as England's first printer; that of the mysterious schoolmaster of St Albans who printed a few books between 1479 and 1486; and that of John Lettou, the accomplished foreigner who set up the first press in the City of London (1480), four years after Caxton had started at Westminster, and continued for a time in partnership with an inferior Belgian printer named Wilhelmus de Machlinia. Such a limited number of presses could not supply anything like the growing demands of the reading public in England.

There was no English paper-mill, it may be added, until the end of the fifteenth century, the first English printers being dependent for their supplies upon various Continental countries where the making of paper —introduced originally from the East—had been understood for several centuries. John Tate, afterwards Lord Mayor of London, was the first paper-maker in England. The first book to be printed on his paper was Bartholomaeus' *De Proprietatibus Rerum*, published in 1495–6, in which the historic fact is thus quaintly announced:

> And John Tate the younger,
> Joy mote he broke,
> Which late hath in England
> Doo make this paper thynne,
> That now in owre Englisshe
> This boke is prynted Inne.

In order to develop the new art of printing and all its accessories, the Act passed in 1484 for regulating the trade of foreigners in England carefully exempted every stationer, scrivener, illuminator, or printer of books, no matter 'of what nation or country he be', and gave him full licence to sell any books, and to settle within the said realm for the exercise of the said occupation.

This open invitation was readily accepted by Continental craftsmen. England, too, became a sort of dumping-ground not only for classics and educational works printed abroad, but for liturgical books, in which French printers especially excelled. So lucrative did the English trade become that type of English character was employed by many of the printers in the Low Countries, who sent across countless books printed in the vernacular. For half a century there was practically free trade in the English book-market, much to the disgust of the brethren of the Stationers' Company, who, though they did not obtain their charter until 1557,* dated their corporate existence, as explained on p. 39, from 1403. Unfortunately their guild records up to 1554 are lost, but it is evident that they protected their interests before that time as well as they could. The government's special encouragement of foreign printers and booksellers was a prolonged and bitter grievance, resulting at times in ugly encounters between the aliens and the hot-blooded English apprentices. The feeling against foreign craftsmen in general culminated in the memorable Evil May Day of 1517, when 2,000 apprentices and the rougher element of the populace attacked the French and Flemish quarters and sacked the houses. Nearly a score of the ringleaders were afterwards hanged. When the aldermen sought the king's presence to ask pardon for the riot, says Holinshed, his Majesty sternly refused, saying that although the substantial citizens did not actually take part in the riot, it was evident, from their supineness in putting it down, that they 'winked at the matter'.

By restricting their trade to St Paul's Churchyard or within the liberties of St Martin's or Blackfriars, the foreign printers and booksellers who had neither become naturalized nor had taken out letters of denization were outside the jurisdiction of the Stationers' Company. Duff estimates that of all persons living in England connected with the book trade, printers, binders and stationers, from 1476 to 1535, something like two-thirds were aliens. It was a foreigner, Peter Actors, a native of Savoy but resident in London, who in 1485 was appointed Stationer to Henry VII. Actors was succeeded by William Faques, a native of Normandy, who had established himself as a printer in London, and so had the official title altered to that of Printer to the King—the first man to hold that position in England. Faques was followed, on his death, by another Norman, Richard Pynson, knowledge of Norman French probably proving a special recommendation for the post.

Richard Pynson, one of the best of the early London printers, suffered, like many other foreigners, from the national prejudice against alien workmen. On one occasion—in 1500—he brought an action in the Star Chamber against Harry Squier and others for leading a murderous attack against himself and his servants, 'having made great oaths and promise that there shall neither Frenchman nor Flemming dwell nor abide within the said parish of Seynt Clementes'.† At other times Pynson deposed that his workmen had been waylaid in

* Not 1556, as stated by most writers on the subject. This point was first cleared up by E. Gordon Duff in 1905, in *A Century of the English Book Trade.*

† *Select Cases in the Star Chamber,* edited for the Selden Society by I. S. Leadam, 1903.

Fleet Street, and there 'cruellye assaulted, sore bete, and wounded, and put in such fear and peril of their lives that they durst neither go to church nor out of doors to do their master's business. For which assaults and menaces the said servants have departed from the said Richarde Pynson and have left righte greate besynez, which he hath in hande, to be undone, to his greate hurte and utter distrucion.' After that it is not surprising to learn that Pynson removed for better protection from the parish of St Clement's, which was outside the City, to a house within Temple Bar, 'in fletestrete at the sygne of Ye George'. Here, doubtless, he became naturalized before receiving his appointment as Printer to the King. Pynson retained this title on the accession in 1509 of Henry VIII, in whose reign, however, the barriers of protection against foreigners were erected and increased until at length the great bulk of the alien printers, stationers and binders dwindled away to nothing.

Not only were they forced to pay double subsidies, but by an Act of 1523 they were allowed to employ none but English-born apprentices and not more than two foreign workmen, and were placed under the strict rule of the wardens of the Stationers' Company. Six years later they were further handicapped by a law which enacted 'that no stranger artificer not a denizen, who was not a householder the 15 of February last past, shall set up nor kepe any house, shop, or chambre wherein they shall occupy any handycraft within this realm'. The climax arrived with the Act which came into operation on Christmas Day 1534, and formally annulled the free trade in books which had existed since the passing of the Act of 1484.

The chief object of the Act of 1534 — especially the clause prohibiting any but wholesale purchases of foreign books — was as much to prevent the surreptitious importation of heretical writings as to protect the native craftsman. Its chief result, however, was the suppression of the more skilful alien, who, whatever harm he may have done to the pockets of his English brethren, had at least provided them with a healthy stimulus in the new art of printing.

Another royal proclamation was issued in 1530 against 'blasphemous and pestiferous Englishe bokes, printed in other regions and sent into this realme', as well as 'the admission and divulgence of the Olde and Newe Testament translated into English'. This proclamation, like many others on the same subject, was printed by Thomas Berthelet, who, besides being printer to Henry VIII — having succeeded to that position on the death of Pynson — was also bookseller and bookbinder to the king. Berthelet's address was in Fleet Street, 'nere to ye conduit at ye signe of Lucrece'. The bookstall which he kept outside his shop figured in a lawsuit brought in 1536 for assault on some Frenchmen, one of whom, it was stated, had endeavoured to hide himself under the King's Printer's stall.

The selling of prohibited books was too hazardous to tempt the regular bookselling trade—save in a certain number of isolated cases —but there were many illegitimate ways and means of smuggling them over, and no lack of enthusiastic reformers willing to run the risk of martyrdom in disseminating them among the people. 'Luther's inexhaustible fecundity flowed with a steady stream', writes Froude, 'and the printing presses in Germany and in the Free Towns of the Netherlands multiplied Testaments and tracts in hundreds of thousands.' It is more than probable, however, that the number of heretical books of foreign origin is much smaller than is commonly supposed, and that many of these so-called foreign books were actually printed in England.

The first edition of Tyndale's New Testament, with which the history of our present English Bible begins, was circulated in 1526 by the irregular booksellers—more especially by the 'Christian Brothers', who formed, in Froude's words, the first 'Religious Tract Society' in England. Hitherto the Reformers had been dependent on the manuscript translations of the scriptures, and how eagerly even portions of these were bought up by the people is shown in Foxe's striking passage to the effect that in 1520 'great multitudes ... tasted and followed the sweetness of God's holy Word almost in as ample manner, for the number of well-disposed hearts, as now ... Certes, the fervent zeal of those Christian days seemed much superior to these our days and times, as manifestly may appear by their sitting up all night in reading and hearing; also by their expenses and charges in buying of books in English, of whom some gave five marks [equal to about £100 in our money], some more, some less, for a book. Some gave a load of hay for a few chapters of St James or of St Paul in English ... To see their travails, their earnest seekings, their burning zeal, their readings, their watchings, their sweet assemblies ... may make us now, in these days of free profession, to blush for shame'. That was written in 1563, and more than three centuries later, as Bishop Westcott says in reprinting this extract in his *History of the English Bible*, the 'contrast is still to our sorrow'. But it was ever the way of the world to value most that which was hardest to come by.

The secret demand for Tyndale's New Testament was so great that in spite of all the Council's threats and the bishops' anathemas six editions were exhausted before 1530. Yet so fierce and systematic was the persecution both then and afterwards that Bishop Westcott estimates that of these six editions, numbering perhaps fifteen thousand copies, there remain, of the first one fragment only, which was found in 1834 and is now preserved in the British Museum; of the second edition but two imperfect copies; and of the others two or three specimens which are not satisfactorily identified. The story of the memorable burnings of these works at St Paul's and at Oxford, at which the prisoners were compelled to do penance by casting their faggots and books into the flames, and of Tyndale's betrayal and martyrdom, is beyond the scope of our narrative, though we shall have more to say presently on the progress of the Battle of the Bible itself.

Some of our brightest sidelights on the regular book trade in England in those early years of the sixteenth century are provided by *The Day-Book of John Dorne*, edited for the Oxford Historical Society by F. Madan in 1885. John Dorne appears to have been a Dutchman who settled in Oxford as a bookseller, and probably acted, apart from his English trade, as agent for a number of enterprising printers on the Continent. In the account-book edited by Madan we find a methodical record of practically all the books sold by him in the course of the year 1520 — an early edition, as it were, of *Book Prices Current*. There is a great preponderance of Latin books, especially in theology and the classics. *A.B.C.*s are met with repeatedly, but as they rarely fetched more than a halfpenny each — and even at that price thirteen on one occasion were sold 'as twelve' — they probably, as the editor suggests, took the form of a single leaf of parchment or paper. Erasmus appears to have had the largest sale of any author, but Luther was also in considerable demand, the prices realized for his works ranging from threepence to three shillings. One shilling in those days, it may be pointed out, would be worth well over £4 of our money.

The list of English books, though fewer in number, is even more illuminating. There are penny almanacks, and 'prognosticons in Englis' for the same price — the larger ones two for threepence — these answering the same superstitious purposes as the prophecies of Mother Shipton and the more modern 'Old Moore'. John Dorne had plenty of customers in his shop for his 'balets', or ballads, which could be had from a halfpenny upwards. Towards the end of the year there is a small run on 'kesmes corals', or Christmas carols, sold as single leaves for a penny, or in two leaves for twopence. *Robert the Devill* could be bought for threepence, *Roben Hod* for twopence, and *The Notbrone Mayde* for a penny. Housewives will be interested to learn that *The Bocke of Kokery* (Cookery) was to be had for fourpence.

Information as to the customs of the trade in London at this period is aggravatingly meagre. The nearest approach to a contemporary account that we possess is the following brief description (reprinted from Professor Arber's *Transcript*) written by Christopher Barker, the Queen's Printer, in 1582, the year in which he became warden of the incorporated Stationers' Company: 'In the tyme of King Henry the eighte, there were but fewe Printers, and those of good credit and component wealth, at whiche tyme and before, there was another sort of men, that were writers, Lymners of bookes and dyverse thinges for the Churche and other uses called Stacioners; which have, and partly to this daye do use to buy their bookes in grosse [wholesale] of the saide printers, to bynde them up, and sell them in their shops, whereby they well mayntayned their families.' The addition of the 'saide printers' had greatly strengthened the forces and power of the first fellowship of London stationers, for the whole system of book production and distribution was now in their hands. The ups and downs of religious opinions in the later years of Henry VIII made it extremely difficult for some of them to steer a safe course, but on the whole they seem to have been singularly astute.

In 1535 came the first complete edition of the English Bible—the work of Miles Coverdale, though the New Testament was based on Tyndale's version. The names of the original publisher and place of printing of Coverdale's Bible remain somewhat of a mystery. But whoever was the printer—and most authorities agree that he was Christopher Froschauer, of Zurich—there is no doubt that the edition for sale in England was bought by James Nycolson, or Nicolai, and issued by him at Southwark. Coverdale's Bible, though first published in 1535, was not definitely 'set forth with the Kinge's moost gracious licence' until the corrected edition appeared two years later. Then, in 1537, came the English Bible which John Rogers brought out under the name of Thomas Matthew—and has been known as 'Matthew's Bible' ever since—combining the labours of Tyndale and Coverdale. This was printed by Jacob von Meteren at Antwerp, where the sheets were bought by Richard Grafton—a member of the Grocers' Company, with strong leanings towards the reformed religion—in association with Edward Whitchurch, a fellow merchant. In 1538 Grafton and Whitchurch were also entrusted with the preparation of the Great Bible, and compensated for their outlay on the translation which that edition superseded.

Another new translation which suffered through the publication of the Great Bible was that of Richard Taverner, 'printed at London by John Byddell for Thomas Barthlet' (sic), and issued, like the larger work, in 1539. Taverner's Bible was only once reprinted. In November, 1539, while Grafton was preparing the Great Bible, letters patent were received from the King wherein, 'for the diversity of translations', Henry appointed Thomas Cromwell 'to take special care that no manner of person should attempt to print any Bible in the English tongue of any volume during the space of five years, but only such as should be deputed by the said Lord Cromwell'.*

* *Ecclesiastical Memorials*, Strype, 1824.

The Great Bible itself was printed (under Coverdale's direct super-vision) in Paris—for the reason, according to Strype and Henry's letters on the subject to the French king, that 'better paper and cheaper' was to be had there than in London, 'and cheaper and more dexterous workmen'. Grafton and Whitchurch were largely financed in this undertaking by Anthony Marler, a wealthy member of the Haber-dashers' Company; and Grafton, at least, was in Paris with Coverdale while the printing was being done at the press of Francis Regnault. All went well until the text was on the point of completion, when the Inquisitor-General for France stepped in and not only stopped all further progress, but forbade the removal of the sheets already printed. Luckily both Coverdale and Grafton succeeded in escaping, and, steal-ing back to Paris shortly afterwards, managed to buy up the whole plant and remove it to London—presses, type and workmen as well. They even rescued 'four dry-vats full' of the prohibited sheets, which the authorities had sold as wastepaper to a local tradesman, the re-mainder having been burnt in Maubert Place as heretical books. The interference of the Inquisition, therefore, was really a blessing in disguise, for with all the necessary material safely established in London there was nothing now to prevent the printing of as many copies as were wanted.

The Reformation must have seriously disturbed the regular book trade. Hardly anyone ventured to publish story-books, and even educational works were at a discount. The 'Summary Declaration of the Faith, Uses and Observances in England', dated 1539,* tells us that 'Englishmen have now in hand in every Church and place, almost every man, the Holy Bible and New Testament in their mother tongue, instead of the old fabulous and fantastical books of the *Table Round, Launcelot du Lac, Huon de Bourdeaux, Bevy of Hampton, Guy of Warwick*, etc., and such other, whose impure filth and vain fabulosity the light of God has abolished utterly'.

The freedom of the Scriptures, however, was soon restricted. With the Catholic reaction and the execution of Cromwell in 1540, the publishers of the Bible found themselves in anything but an enviable position. The bishops complained to the King of the notes which had been added to certain of the Bibles in English, and, repenting also of ever having sanctioned the Great Bible, proceeded to undo and pro-scribe much of the work in this direction which had been done under Cromwell's auspices. The free use of the Scriptures, they urged, had been responsible for all the heresies which had taken such deep root in Germany, and spread thence so dangerously into England. Grafton especially seems now to have fallen into disfavour, for he was rash

* Collier's *Ecclesiastical History of England*, 1708–14, vol. ii; *Collection of Records*, No. 47.

enough, soon after Cromwell's death, to publish a 'ballade' in his patron's praise.

Conflicting accounts are given of the origin and upshot of this incident, but Burnet's version, which we are inclined to accept, is to the effect that 'Audley, the Chancellor, was Grafton's friend, and brought him off'. According to Strype and Foxe, however, he fell into more serious trouble not long afterwards for his share in the production of the now prohibited Matthew's Bible, 'which he, being timorous', says Strype, 'made excuses for'. Then he was examined about the Great Bible, and the notes that he was charged with intending to add thereto. 'He replied that he added none to his Bible, when he perceived the King and clergy not willing to have any. Yet Grafton was sent to the Fleet, and there remanded six weeks, and before he came out was bound in three hundred pounds that he should neither sell nor imprint any more Bibles till the King and the clergy should agree upon a translation.'

The situation was deplorable for those who were pecuniarily interested in the Bible trade. Early in 1541 Anthony Marler, the haberdasher, who had largely financed the Great Bible, presented a petition to the Privy Council pointing out that he would be ruined unless his Bibles were sold, and praying for a proclamation that every church still unprovided with it should purchase one, according to the King's former injunction. It was thereupon agreed 'that there should be such a proclamation, and that the day limited for having the said book should be Hallow Mass'.* The Privy Council had already fixed the price at 10s. for unbound copies and 12s. for copies stitched and bound. The proclamation, which was issued on May 6th, 1541, confirmed the injunctions heretofore set forth by which the King 'intended his subjects to read the Bible for their instruction humbly and reverently; not reading aloud in time of Holy Mass, or other divine service, nor, being laymen, arguing thereupon. Many towns and parishes having failed to accomplish this, they are straightly commanded, before All Saints' Day next, to provide and set up Bibles of the largest volume, upon penalty of 40s. for every month's delay after All Saints' Day, half to go to the informer. The sellers of such Bibles are taxed to charge for them not above 10s. for Bibles unbound, or 12s. for Bibles well bound and clasped.'† On March 11th of the following year, as may also be seen in the *Letters and Papers of Henry VIII*, Marler further succeeded in obtaining a patent appointing him 'sole authority to print the Bible in English during the space of four years next ensuing'.

The authorities further tightened their hold over the press in this year of 1542 by issuing a proclamation which, in addition to forbidding anyone, after the ensuing August 31st, to 'receive or keep the text of

* *Letters and Papers of the Reign of Henry VIII*, vol. 16, May 1st, 1541.
† *Ibid.*, vol. 16, May 6th, 1541.

Tyndale's or Coverdale's translation of the New Testament, nor any other than is permitted by the Act of Parliament made', declared that henceforth no printer was to issue 'any English book, ballad or play, without putting his name and the name of the author and day of the print; and the printer shall present the first copy to the mayor of the town where he dwells two days before allowing any other copy to leave his hands. From the day of this proclamation no person shall bring into the realm any English book printed beyond sea concerning Christian religion, nor shall sell any English book printed beyond sea without the King's special licence.'*

On turning up this proclamation we discovered an interesting fact in connection with the history of the Stationers' Company itself. The dearth of records before the royal incorporation under Mary I has been frequently remarked upon, but no writer on the subject, so far as we know, has ever mentioned that the Company applied for a charter in the reign of Henry VIII. The fact is revealed in the seventeenth volume of the *Letters and Papers of the Reign of Henry VIII*, edited by Dr Gairdner (1900). In an account of the proceedings of the Convocation of Canterbury, dated March 17th, 1542, there appears the bald statement to the effect that 'the Prolocutor exhibited a book in parliament for the incorporation of the Stationers, to be referred to the King'. That is all. And it is impossible now, unfortunately, to say what happened. Perhaps the king, who had beheaded his fifth queen only a month previously, was too busy seeking a sixth wife to be bothered about such a trifle as a charter for London's stationers; but, whatever happened to the application, we know that the stationers had to wait another fifteen years for their incorporation. It is significant that on both occasions when they applied for this the Catholics were doing their utmost to stem the rising tide of the Reformation. Either the leanings of the stationers were on the side of the Catholics, or they stifled whatever religious convictions they may have possessed in order to seize the best opportunity for increasing the power and importance of their craft. For, as a long-established civic guild, they were strong enough already to be invaluable to the authorities in their crusade against prohibited books; and it was as much to their advantage as to the ecclesiastical authorities' to suppress the lawless bookseller.

For all this zeal in the closing years of Henry VIII, the number of prohibited books still circulated in England caused increasing alarm. In April 1543 proceedings were taken against eight printers, including Grafton and Whitchurch, and twenty-five booksellers, for issuing unlawful books. Each of the prisoners was compelled to send in a true list of all the books and ballads he had bought and sold during the three preceding years—lists which, unfortunately, cannot now be traced.

* *Letters and Papers of the Reign of Henry VIII*, vol. 17, March 1542.

This fresh disgrace was the more unfortunate for Grafton and Whit-church since, only three months previously—on January 23rd—having regained the fickle favour of the authorities, they had received the exclusive privilege of printing all the Church service-books, 'for Sarum use', within the King's dominions for seven years. Most of the prisoners on the present occasion were released in a fortnight, but Whitchurch and Grafton were detained for nearly a month. Further restrictions against the English Bible were imposed in 1543. For, declared Parliament in that year:

The King's Majesty perceiveth that a great multitude of his said subjects, most specially of the lower sort, have so abused the same that they have thereby grown and increased in divers naughty and erroneous opinions, and by occasion thereof fallen into great division and dissension among themselves, to the great unquietness of the Realm and other his Majesty's Dominions. For remedy thereof be it enacted by the authority aforesaid that from and after the first day of July next coming, no women nor artificers apprentices, journeymen, serving men of the degrees of yeomen and under, husbandmen nor labourers, shall read within this Realm, or in any other the King's Dominions, the Bible or New Testament in English, to himself or any other, privately or openly, upon pain of one month's imprisonment for every time [of so] offending contrary to this Act, and being thereof convict in such manner and form as is aforesaid.

The Reformation remained in this state of reaction when Henry VIII died (1547). The English Bible at once leaped into power again. In the few short years of Edward VI's reign there were published no fewer than thirteen or fourteen editions of the complete Book, as well as thirty-five Testaments. 'In King Edward the sixt his Dayes'—to come back to Christopher Barker's account—'Printers and printing began greatly to increase: but the provision of letter [type], and many other thinges belonging to printing, was so exceeding chargeable that most of those printers were dryven throughe necessitie to compound before [hand] with the booksellers at so lowe value, as the printers themselves were most tymes small gayners, and often loosers.' The trade at this time was busy not only with the English Bible, but with the new Prayer-book. The printer and publisher of this was Richard Grafton, who, rewarded at length for his leanings towards the Reformation, was appointed King's Printer on the accession of Edward, and held that post throughout the reign. When the first English Prayer-book of Edward VI was published in 1549 all the old service-books had to be destroyed; and on August 13th of the same year proclamations were issued by the Privy Council ordering that from henceforth no printer should print or 'putt to vente' any English book 'but such as should first be examined by Mr Secretary Peter, Mr Secretary Smith, and Mr Cecil, or the one of them, and allowed by the same'. This Mr Cecil was the future Lord Burghley, now the Protector Somerset's secretary and right hand, and already in the Princess Elizabeth's confidence. Not many weeks after this proclamation the Protector was arrested by Warwick, and Cecil discreetly withdrew from public life—to reappear in the following year as Secretary of State under Somerset's rival.

With the swing of the pendulum which brought in the reign of Mary I on the death of Edward VI in 1553 came yet another reaction, the full force of which must have been felt by the booksellers at once, well stocked as they were with English Bibles and other literary products of the Reformation. For though the royal proclamation issued on July 19th—after Mary had defeated the machinations of Northumberland and the reign of his unhappy 'nine days queen' had come to a close—assured her 'loving subjects' that in taking Mary for 'their liege sovereign Lady and Queen they should find her as benign and gracious a lady as others her most noble progenitors had been', there were ominous signs that must have made some of the booksellers at least change the complexion of their stock-in-trade as quickly as they could. Grafton, who printed this proclamation of the Queen's accession, had also issued the similar announcement of poor Jane Grey, and for this, as well as for having printed the Bible in English and other Protestant books, he was at once deprived of his office as Royal Printer, John Cawood being appointed in his stead. 'Nor was this all her measure he found,' remarks Strype, 'for in the next month he was clapped up in prison.' Whitchurch also was imprisoned for his share in the production of the English Bible, and they were both exempted from the pardon proclaimed by Mary at her coronation.* Prebendary Rogers, whose edition of the Scriptures they had published in 1537 under the name of 'Matthew's Bible', was summoned on August 16th before the Council as 'John Rogers, alias Matthew', and eighteen months later suffered at the stake at Smithfield as the first victim of the Marian persecutions. Coverdale, more fortunate, succeeded in escaping to the Continent. On August 18th, 1553, a proclamation was issued which showed the book trade clearly what it had to expect from the new rule:

* Grafton and Whitchurch practically retired from business on their release later in the year. Whitchurch married the widow of Archbishop Cranmer, and died in 1562. Grafton, who, among his general works, had issued this year Wilson's *Arte of Rhetorique*, lived eleven years later, becoming twice M.P. for London and subsequently (1562–3) Member for Coventry. Much of his later life he spent as a rival of John Stow in the compilation of English *Chronicles*, and, like Stow, is said to have died in very needy circumstances.

Forasmuch as it is well known that seditious and false rumours have been nourished and maintained in this realm by the subtilty and malice of some evil disposed persons ... and printing of false found Books and Ballads, Rimes, and other Treatises in the English tongue, containing doctrine in matters now in question, and controversies touching the high points and mysteries in Christian religion; which Books, Ballads, Rimes, and Treatises are chiefly by the Printers and Stationers set out to sell to her Grace's subjects of an evil zeal for lucre and covetousness of vile gain; her Highness therefore straightly chargeth and commandeth all and every of her said subjects ... that none of them from henceforth print any Book, Matter, Ballad, Rime, Interlude, Process, or Treatise ... except they have her grace's special license in writing for the same, upon pain of incurring her Highness' indignation and displeasure.*

The English Bible, strangely enough, does not seem to have figured in any special measure for its destruction in Mary's reign. No new edition was permitted, and public copies found in churches were burnt, but no injunctions appear to have been issued against its private use. And in spite of the strict regulations of the Crown, the scattered army of Reformers on the Continent still saw to it that England was well supplied with 'seditious and heretical' literature. In June 1555 it was found necessary to issue a further proclamation authorizing the warden of every company in London to search for such books as had either been smuggled over from the Continent or secretly printed in England. Another proclamation was issued at the same time against the service-books of Edward VI. The campaign of seditious literature went steadily on, increasing in activity as the time drew near for the Spanish marriage. Parliament now issued an order against the circulation of any book to the slander of the king or queen under penalty of the loss of the right hand. And after the marriage there still seemed urgent need for further powers of repression. It was a ripe moment for the London stationers again to demand the royal charter, to which they had long considered themselves entitled. Philip and Mary, as they listened to the prayer for incorporation, saw in it a means of obtaining further control over the all-powerful and obnoxious printing press, and it was for this reason, more than anything else, that the charter of May 4th, 1557, was granted.

That Mary and Philip hoped to make effective use of the newly incorporated Company in suppressing seditious and heretical books is clear from the preamble of the charter. The government of the 'community of the said mistery or art' was vested in one master and

* Collier's *Ecclesiastical History*, 1708–14; *Records*, No. 58.

two keepers, or wardens; and no person within the realm was permitted to print anything for sale within the kingdom unless he belonged to the Company or held some licence by letters patent from the
Crown. Furthermore, the master and wardens were empowered 'to
make search whenever it shall please them in any place, shop, house,
chamber, or building of any printer or bookseller whatever within our
kingdom of England or the dominions of the same, for any books or
things printed, or to be printed, and to seize, take, hold, burn, or turn
to the proper use of the foresaid community, all and several those books
and things which are or shall be printed contrary to the form of any
statute, act, or proclamation, made or to be made'. The pains and
penalties for breaking these regulations, or hindering the officers in the
course of their duties, were three months' imprisonment for each
offence, and a fine of 'a hundred shillings of lawful money of England,
one half thereof to us, the heirs and successors of the foresaid Queen,
and the other half thereof to the foresaid Master, Keepers or Wardens
and community'.

Flushed with its new importance, there can be little doubt that the
Company used its powers with no half-hearted zeal, especially as the
first master, Thomas Dockwray, was himself an ardent Catholic.
Dockwray did not long survive his new honour, for he died in the first
year of Elizabeth's reign. Meantime the war against heresy and heretical
books was pursued with grim but unavailing energy. The Company
might keep the regular trade under its drastic rule, but nothing could
stop the ceaseless flow of surreptitious literature during the two and a
half years of bitter disillusionment which the unhappy Mary had still
to live. To what extreme lengths the forsaken queen was prepared to go
in the last six months of her life is seen in the following proclamation,
dated June 5th, 1558, while Philip, who had dragged this country into
his conflict with France, and had already lost Calais for England, was
absent on the Continent:

> Whereas divers books filled with both heresy, sedition and treason
> have of late and be daily brought into this realme out of foreign
> countries and places beyond the seas, and some also covertly
> printed within this Realme, and cast abroad in sundry parts thereof,
> whereby not only God is dishonoured, but also an encouragement
> given to disobey lawful princes and governors. The King and
> Queen's Majesties for redresse hereof, by this their present pro-
> clamation, declare and publish to all their subjects that whosoever
> shall after the proclaiming hereof be found to have any of the said
> wicked and seditious books, or, finding them, do not forthwith
> burn the same, without showing or reading the same to any other
> person, shall in that case be reputed and taken for a rebell, and shall

without delay be executed for that offence according to the order of Marshall lawe.*

It is curious that Robert Caley, the most prominent printer on the Catholic side, was not at this time a member of the Stationers' Company; nor did his religious fervour save him, in the year of incorporation, from being fined for printing without a licence. Mary's death put an end to Caley's press, yet this was the very time that he chose to take the freedom of the Company. Perhaps he cherished the hope that Elizabeth meant to make no drastic change, and that in course of time it might be safe for him to start afresh. If so, the gradual triumph of the Reformation must have shattered his hopes, for we hear of no more books issuing from Caley's press.

---

* Arber's *Registers of the Stationers' Company.*

4

The Book Trade Under Queen Elizabeth

The momentous event which stopped the Catholic printer from issuing any more books also brought back John Day, the distinguished printer and bookseller, who was as ardent a disciple of the Reformation as was Caley of the older faith. John Day was destined to play a leading part in the book world of Elizabeth's reign. Born in 1522, he started printing in 1546, moving, after a few years of partnership with William Seres,* to the old city gate called Alders Gate. 'John Day, Stationer, a late famous printer of many good books,' says Stow in his *Survey*, 'in our time dwelled in this Gate, and builded much upon the wall of the citie, towards the parish church of St Anne.' Apparently he joined the Stationers' Company from the Stringers' in the following year, but ceased printing when Mary, in the summer of 1553, became the first queen regnant of England. Day seems to have withdrawn to Norfolk at this time, for a note in *Machyn's Diary* proves that he was brought thence with his servant, together with a priest and another printer, and sent to the Tower for printing 'noythy bokes'. Whether these were books issued in Edward's time or surreptitious productions of the new reign it is impossible to say, and we have no means now of learning how long he remained a prisoner. According to the *Dictionary of National Biography* and other authorities, he fled abroad after his release, but if this were so he would not have been absent long, as he was included among the original members of the incorporated Company, in the Charter granted by Philip and Mary in 1557. After Elizabeth's accession he was rewarded for his services and sufferings in the Reformers' cause by a large share of patronage from the leaders of that party, becoming, as will presently be seen, the printer and publisher of the works of Bishop Latimer, Archbishop Parker and Foxe, the martyrologist.

Twelve months after her accession Elizabeth—to return for the moment to the story of the Stationers' Company—confirmed the charter granted by 'Lord Philip King and Lady Mary, late Queen of

---

* William Seres afterwards joined partnership for a time with the printer and translator Anthony Scoloker, and in 1554 received letters patent for the printing of psalters, primers and prayer-books. This privilege he lost on the accession of Mary, when he seems to have sought safety on the Continent, but it was renewed by Elizabeth. In his old age he assigned his business for a yearly rental to Henry Denham, another worthy of the Elizabethan book trade, who became a member of the Stationers' Company in 1560. Seres lived to be master of the same company for several years in succession, and died about 1579.

England, our dearest sister'. This was succeeded by the formal creation of the stationers as a livery company on February 1st, 1560, by the Lord Mayor of London. The origin of the ecclesiastical licensing of books which now followed, and hampered the trade for many years, is seen in the *Injunctions given by her Majestie* — issued in the first year of Elizabeth's reign — which Professor Arber, in quoting the more important of the items in his *Transcript of the Stationers' Registers*, regards as the earliest printed notice of the Company in existence. One of these 'Injunctions' ordered the clergy, as in Cromwell's time, to provide each parish within three months with a copy of the English Bible of the largest volume. Later they were also enjoined to set up in some convenient place within the said church the "Paraphrases of Erasmus" ', also in English, ' "upon the Gospelles" '.

Several editions of these and other injunctions were issued before the confirmation of the Company's charter by Elizabeth in November 1559. The order was never observed with any strictness, the licensing being left more often to the Stationers' Company, the officers of which, however, were always made to keep in their hearts the fear of the higher powers. The earliest injunctions of the Ecclesiastical Commissioners preserved by the Company were dated the following year, when the master and wardens were directed to prevent certain persons from printing the primers and psalters in English which had been licensed to privileged printers. Shortly after this we find the first record of an order relating to the entering of copies on the Company's registers — a rule which played an increasingly important part in the securing of copyright, for all members were now required to enter the title of any book which they regarded as their particular property, a fee being charged for each entry. Books printed under special privilege or State monopoly were exempt from registration, but otherwise every book published had to be entered in the Company's records — with the result that the Stationers' Registers now form a record of contemporary literature which, though not complete, is of supreme bibliographical value.

We have not long to wait in the new queen's reign before meeting with the real Elizabeth in her dealings with the stationers. It was a time of much royal wooing, for the number of Elizabeth's suitors, both among foreign princes and her own subjects, was legion. When, in 1560, she went so far as to accept the preliminary gifts of the handsome King Eric of Sweden, the matter was regarded by many people as a settled thing. The result was that the more enterprising stationers — eager as any pictorial publisher of the present day — promptly issued portraits of the happy couple united. Whereupon they were gravely admonished by the Queen's Secretary of State, Sir William Cecil, afterwards Lord Burghley, in the following letter which he wrote to the Lord Mayor:

It may please your lordship, the Queen's majesty understands
that certain bookbinders and stationers do utter certain papers,
wherein be printed the face of her Majesty and the King of
Sweden; and although her highness is not miscontented that
either her own face or the said King's should be printed or por-
traited, yet to be joined in the same paper with the said King, or
with any other prince that is known to have made any request for
marriage to her Majesty, is not to be allowed. And therefore her
Majesty's pleasure is that your lordship should send for the wardens
of the stationers; or for the wardens of any other men that have
such papers to sell, and to take order with them, that all such
papers be taken and packed up together in such sort that none be
permitted to be seen in any part. For otherwise her Majesty might
seem touched in honour by her own subjects, that would in such
papers declare an allowance to have herself joined, as it were, in
marriage with the said King, where, indeed, her Majesty hitherto
cannot be induced (whereof we have cause to sorrow) to allow of
marriage with any manner of person.*

A few years later the Queen's self-esteem was tried so sorely by the
wide circulation of ill-favoured likenesses of her majesty that Cecil was
forced to draw up another energetic proclamation on the subject. The
document is worth giving in full:

Forasmuch as through the natural desire that all sorts of subjects
had to procure the portrait and likeness of the queen's majesty,
great numbers of painters, and some printers and gravers, had and
did daily attempt in divers manners to make portraitures of her,
wherein none hitherto had sufficiently expressed the natural representation of her majesty's person, favour, or grace; but had
for the most part erred therein, whereof daily complaints were made
amongst her loving subjects, — that for the redress hereof her
majesty had been so importunately sued unto by the lords of her
council and other of her nobility, not only to be content that some
special cunning painter might be permitted by access to her majesty
to take the natural representation of her, whereof she had been
always of her own right disposition very unwilling, but also to
prohibit all manner of other persons to draw, paint, grave, or
portrait her personage or visage for a time, until there were some
perfect pattern or example to be followed:

Therefore her majesty, being herein as it were overcome with the
continual requests of so many of her nobility and lords, whom she
could not well deny, was pleased that some cunning person should
shortly make a portrait of her person or visage to be participated

* Haynes's *State Papers*, 1740.

to others for the comfort of her loving subjects; and furthermore commanded, that till this should be finished, all other persons should abstain from making any representations of her; that afterwards her majesty would be content that all other painters, printers, or gravers, that should be known men of understanding, and so therein licensed by the head officers of the places where they should dwell (as reason it was that every person should not without consideration attempt the same), might at their pleasure follow the said pattern or first portraiture. And for that her majesty perceived a great number of her loving subjects to be much grieved with the errors and deformities herein committed, she straightly charged her officers and ministers to see to the observation of this proclamation, and in the meantime to forbid the showing or publication of such as were apparently deformed, until they should be reformed which were reformable.*

Elizabeth did not deprive John Cawood of his official post as royal printer to which he had been appointed by Mary, in succession to Richard Grafton, in 1553, at a salary of £6 13s. 4d., but she made him share the office with Richard Jugge. It was Jugge who published the first edition of the Bishops' Bible in 1568, between which date and 1574 he was four times appointed master of the Stationers' Company. John Cawood was, in his turn, three times master of the Company, and took a deep interest in its affairs to the end of his life.

But let us return to Master John Day, whose story helps us better than any other to realize the new era which was beginning for the book trade with the coming of 'Great Eliza'. Day himself strikes the keynote of that epoch in his trade device, the design of which represents the rising sun, and a boy awakening his sleeping companion with the words 'Arise, for it is Day' — a double allusion to the printer's name and to the dawn of the Reformation. John Foxe, who published the first (Latin) part of his *History of the Acts and Monuments of the Church* — popularly known as Foxe's *Book of Martyrs* — at Strasbourg in 1554, while seeking safety on the Continent during the Marian persecutions, issued the first English edition through John Day in 1563. Anthony à Wood tells us that on his return to England he was handsomely entertained at the Duke of Norfolk's 'Manor place called Christ Church' — the Duke having been one of Foxe's pupils — and 'from that house he traversed weekly every Monday to the house of John Day the printer, to consummate his Acts and Monuments of the Church, and other works in English and Latin'.

Day issued four folio editions of the *Acts and Monuments* in his lifetime, and was also associated with Foxe in other undertakings, the

* *Archaeologia*, Society of Antiquaries, vol. ii.

martyrologist probably acting for him as one of the learned correctors of the press who were then employed by the leading publishers of the time. Foxe had been so employed during his exile on the Continent, when he served as reader of the press to Oporinus (Herbst), who published his *Christus Triumphans* in 1556. Thanks to the patronage of that scholarly churchman and true booklover, Archbishop Parker, Day was the first printer to issue a book in Saxon characters — Ælfric's Saxon homily, edited by the Archbishop himself under the title *A Testimonie of Antiquitie* in 1567; and five years later, at the archbishop's private press at Lambeth, he printed Parker's own work, *De Antiquitate Ecclesiae Britannicae*, which not only appeared in a new italic letter, but is believed to have been the first privately printed book ever issued in this country.

At this time, and for long afterwards, English books were almost entirely printed in the type known as black-letter, Roman type being but sparingly used, and that only for quotations and the like, while the new italic letter, for which the archbishop had a strong partiality, was rarer still — as may be seen in the following extract from a letter which he addressed to Lord Burghley in 1572. The letter relates to the work which he had arranged to be written by Dr Clarke in reply to the great book of the Catholic controversialist Nicholas Sandars, entitled *De Visibili Monarchia Ecclesiae*, which had appeared the year previously, and incidentally tells of Day's troubles with rival booksellers, who were evidently envious of his success:

> ... As for some particular matters which be not known to me I trust to have your counsell furthermore to the better accomplishment of this work, and others that shall follow. I have spoken to Day the printer, to cast a new Italian letter, which he is doing, and it will coste him forty marks, and loathe he and other printers be to printe any Latin booke, because they will not here be uttered, and for that bookes printed in England be in suspicion abroad. Now, sir, Day hath complained to me that, dwelling in a corner, and his brotherne envying him, he cannot utter his bookes which lie in his hande, two or three thousand pounds' worthe. His friends have procured of Pawles a lease of a little shop to be sette up in the church-yarde, and it is confirmed. And what by the instant request of some envious booksellers, the Mayor and Aldermen will not suffer him to sett it up in the church-yarde, wherein they have nothing to do but by power. This shop is but little and lowe, and leaded flatt, and is made at his great cost to the sum of forty or fifty pounds, and is made like the terrace, fair railed and posted, fitt for men to stand uppon in any triumph or show, and can in no wise either hurte or deface the same. And for that you of the Councell have written to me and others of the Commission to help Day, etc., I praie your lordship to

move the Queen's Majestie to subscribe her hand to these or such letters, that all this entendment may the better go forward, wherein your Lordship shall deserve well both of Christ's Church and of the prince and state.*

With such powerful patrons to help him, Day eventually succeeded in getting the little shop which had been the cause of so much agitation and pother. He used it like most other stationers in the churchyard, merely for the purpose of selling his books, his printing still being carried on at his dwelling over Alders Gate. In addition to his Saxon and Italian types, Day is said to have vastly improved the Greek. 'Day seems, indeed,' according to Dibdin, 'to have been (if we except Grafton) the Plantin of old English typographers; while his character and reputation scarcely suffer diminution from a comparison with those of the illustrious contemporary just mentioned.' To which it may be added that he was one of the earliest music-printers in this country. He was also the publisher, among other notable books, of the first authorized editions of *Gorboduc* and Ascham's *Scholemaster*. Day lived until the summer of 1584—four years after attaining to the highest office of his craft, that of master of the Stationers' Company—and was buried at Little Bradley, in Suffolk. His epitaph is worth recording:

> Here lies the Day that darkness could not blynde;
> When Popish foggs had overcast the sunne
> This Day the cruel night did leave behynd.
> To view and shew what bloodi Actes were donne
> He set a Fox to wright how Martyrs runne
> By death to lyfe. Fox ventured paynes and health
> To give them light; Day spent in print his wealth.
> But God with gayne returned his wealth agayne
> And gave to him as he gave to the poore.
> Two wyves he had partakers of his payne,
> Each wyfe twelve babes and each of them one more.
> Als [Alice] was the last increaser of his stoore,
> Who mourning long for being left alone,
> Set up this toombe, herself turned to a Stone.

The meaning of the last line, it is necessary to add, lies in the fact that the widow of John Day sought consolation in a second marriage. Day left the book trade at a time when it was full of troubles both from within and without. It had long been a grievance among the unprivileged men that all the plums of the trade had been picked by such monopolists as Day and Richard Tottel, the last of whom was also among the best known of the sixteenth-century publishers. He issued

---

* Wright's *Elizabeth and her Times*, vol. i, 1838.

from the Hand and Star in Fleet Street not only law books, which he had
the sole right to print, but the collection of poetry known as Tottel's
Miscellany, as well as Lydgate's *Fall of Princes* (1554), the Earl of
Surrey's *Aeneid* (1557), and various editions of Grafton's *Chronicles*,
Tottel having married a sister of that worthy chronicler and printer.
Monopolies similar to those just mentioned — and there were many others
of the kind — pressed heavily and unfairly on the smaller and unprivileged men. They led to murmurings and a growing discontent
which extended over many years of Queen Elizabeth's reign. In a
document which Arber dates 'about August 1577', containing 'The
Griefes of the Printers, glass sellers and Cutlers sustained by reason of
privileges granted to private persons', the victims of these monopolies
— printers and stationers to the number of 175, together with such
others 'as do lyve by bookselling', who, though not members of the
Stationers' Company itself, were free of other civic guilds, and thus
qualified to practise any other trade — complained that the privileges
lately granted by her Majesty 'hath and will be' their overthrow:
'Besides their wyves, children, apprentizes and families, and thereby
the excessive prices of bookes, prejudiciall to the state of the whole
Realme, besides the false printinge of the same.'

Among their grievances was that 'John Jugge, besides being her
Majestie's printer, hath gotten the privilege for the printing of Bibles
and Testaments, the which was common to all ye printers; Richard
Tottel the printing of all kinds of lawe books, which was common to all
Printers, who selleth the same at excessive prices, to the hindrance of a
greate number of pore students; John Daye the printinge of *A.B.C.*:
and Catechisms, with the sole selling of them by the collour of a Commission. There books were the onelie releif of the most porest of ye
printers.'* It is curious to find among the signatories to the petition the
name of Christopher Barker, who, in this same year of 1577, on the
death of John Jugge, bought his patent for the printing of the Old and
New Testament in English, succeeded him as her Majesty's printer, and
became as stout a defender of privileges as any of the monopolists against
whom he had just been pleading. It was one of the evils of this system
of patents that they were generally granted for life, with the right of
reversion to the owner's successor, so that as the popular books were
seized upon one by one in this way it became more and more difficult
for the poorer stationers honestly to secure even a hazardous living.

Small wonder that the more ardent spirits among the unprivileged
members of the craft rebelled when they found that their petitions led
to no redress. Since the authorities made it impossible for them to
compete on fair terms, they declared war, and adopted methods which
warfare alone could seek to justify. They began by surreptitiously

* Arber's *Registers of the Stationers' Company*, vol. i.

pirating their licensed rivals' copyrights, printing whole editions of their smaller and more popular properties under forged imprints, and selling them mainly in the provincial towns and among the country fairs, where there was less risk of detection. Two years before his death John Day took action against Roger Ward for printing, and William Holmes for selling, great numbers of the *A.B.C.* with his forged imprint, this leading to a memorable Star Chamber case extending from February to July 1582. Holmes pleaded ignorance, 'beinge a yonge man lately come owt of his yeares and but lately set upp for hym selfe'; but Ward, who was one of the most determined opponents of the monopolists, confessed to the printing of no fewer than 10,000 copies of the *A.B.C.*, prevaricated as to his responsibility, and pleaded in his defence that 'a verye small number in respecte of the rest of the Companye of Stacioners Prynters have gotten all the best bookes and coppyes [copyrights] to be printed by themselfes by Privyledge, whereby they make bookes more dearer than otherwise they wolde be, and have lefte verye littell or nothinge at all for the resydue of the Company of Printers to lyve upon, unless they sholde worke under them for suche small wages as they of them selfes please to geve them, which is not sufficiente to fynde suche workemen and their famylies to lyve upon, whereby they through their Priviledges inriche themselfes greatly and become (some of them) greate purchasers of Landes and owners of large possessyons. And the owners of the reste of the sayd Prynters beinge manye in number and moste of them howshoulders so extremely poore, that by reason of pretend Priviledges and restrayntes that happenethe thereby can scarce earne breade and Drinke by their trade towards their lyvinge ...'*

Roger Ward seems to have suffered several terms of imprisonment for thus defying the authorities, but he stood to his guns; and not only Ward himself, but his stalwart wife, who on one occasion later in the same year held the 'fort'—in his feigned absence, so it was said— against the officials of the Stationers' Company, who had been sent to search his house, but had perforce to retire discomfited. It was but a few months later (December 1582) that Christopher Barker drew up his report on the printing patents granted since the Queen's accession. Here he complains, among other things, that the Psalms in metre, which had been granted to Day by the Earl of Leicester, as well as the Small Catechism which Day printed with his *A.B.C.*, now properly belonged to him. These books, 'being occupied of all sorts of men, women and children, and requiring no great stock for the furnyshing thereof', were profitable 'copies'. This was not his only grievance, for William Seres, he writes, also 'encrocheth farther' upon his preserves with the privilege for the printing of psalters, primers and prayer-books, which rightly belonged to Barker. Yet Master Barker really had small cause

* Arber's *Registers of the Stationers' Company*, vol. ii.

for complaint, and he frankly admitted that 'as it is I have the printing of the Olde and Newe Testament, the statutes of the Realme, Proclamations, and the Book of Common Prayer by name, and, in general works, all matters for the Church', which, shorn though these patents were of much of their profit, were nevertheless privileges to be thankful for.

From the same report of 1582 we can detect the gradual but continuous parting of the ways between the printer and the bookseller. We have already quoted the reference to this cleavage as noticed by Barker in dealing with the condition of the trade in the days of Edward VI, when the provision of letters (type) and other material for the press was so costly a matter that most of the printers were driven through necessity to compound beforehand with the booksellers at costs which were so low that the printers themselves 'were most tymes small gayners and often loosers'. And in coming down to the days of 'our soveraigne Lady the Queen's Majesty that nowe is', he shows how the booksellers had pursued their advantage, and incidentally how necessary it was for some few printers at least to be protected by the Crown:

The booksellers [he explains] being growen the greater and wealthier nomber have nowe many of the best Copies and keepe no printing howse, neither beare any charge of letter, or other furniture but onlie paye for the workmanship, and have the benefit, both of the imprinting, and the sale of all 'Commentaries of the Scriptures', and (till of late yeres of all Schoole bookes, Dictionaries, Cronicles, Histories) bookes of Phisick, and infinite others; most whereof are free to all: so that the artificer printer, growing every daye more and more unable to provide letter and other furniture, requisite for any good worke; or to gyve mayntenaunce to any such learned Correctours as are behovefull, will in time be an occasion of great discredit to the professours of the arte, and in myne opinion prejudiciall to the common wealth ... I speake not this (though it be very true) as wishing any restraynt to Bookesellers, or Bookebinders, but that they may print, and have printed for them such good bookes as they can orderly procure: for even some of them, though their skill be little or nothing in the execution of the art, have more judgement to governe, and order matters of printing, than some Printers themselves: But unless some few printers be well mayntayned it will bring both the one and the other to confusion and extreme povertye.*

Let us give Master Barker his due for writing thus honestly and manfully; for, when all is said and done, he cannot be blamed for looking after his own interests, and his treatment of the pirates, as he now regarded his old associates, is not ungenerous. A whole volume could

* Arber's *Registers of the Stationers' Company*, vol. i.

be filled with the tangled story of this Elizabethan book war, but we are compelled merely to glance at it in passing. The prime mover in the revolt was John Wolfe, a printer from the Fishmongers' Company, who openly defied the authorities, and twice went to prison for his pains. He still declared that he could and would print any lawful book, in spite of any commandment of the Queen to the contrary. ' "Tush", said he,' to quote from the reports of the Stationers' Company on the subject,* ' "Luther was but one man, and reformed all the world for religion, and I am that one man, yet must and will reform the government in this trade." ' Wolfe, it is also stated, 'hath oftentimes delivered most disloyal and unreverent speeches of her majesty's government, not once giving her highness any honourable name or title, as "She is deceived", "she shall know she is deceived", also "she is blindly led, she is deceived" '. The end of it all was a special commission and a compromise in which the monopolists, at the beginning of 1584, yielded a number of their copyrights for the benefit of their poorer brethren—John Day, most liberal of them all, surrendering as many as thirty-six, including Ascham's *Scholemaster*—and John Wolfe, having 'acknowledged his error, was relieved with work'.† But this was not quite the end, for while the printers and booksellers were thus quarrelling among themselves, the Crown seized the opportunity still further to tighten its hold on the trade.

Two days after the monopolists made their concession to the insurgents the authorities, as if to illustrate their proclamations against prohibited books with an object-lesson which would not be forgotten, condemned the Catholic printer William Carter for treason, and on the following day had him hanged, disembowelled and quartered at Tyburn. This was the time, it must be remembered, when Mary Stuart's supporters were plotting against Elizabeth's life. The authorities had reason to be on their guard against such men as Carter, who had already been in prison 'for printinge of lewde pamphlets', and only three years previously had been traced by Bishop Aylmer as the publisher, 'amongst other nawghtye papystycall books', of one written in French on *The Innocency of the Scottish Queen, who was then a prisoner for laying claim to the crown of England and endeavouring to raise a rebellion*—'a very dangerous book', adds Aylmer, in his letter to Burghley on the subject. Carter for some reason was not prosecuted on that occasion, which

* *ibid.*, vol. ii.

† Prosperity, as in so many cases of the kind, seems to have altered the point of view of this once doughty champion of liberty, for John Wolfe, who had already been admitted to the Stationers' Company, was afterwards as zealous as anyone in protecting the privileges which now came his way, as well as in routing out secret presses as an official of the company at the time of the Marprelate troubles. He lived to become printer to the City of London, and, after publishing works by Gabriel Harvey, Robert Greene, Thomas Churchyard and others, died a pattern of respectability.

perhaps explains his rashness in issuing the book which cost him his life — Gregory Martin's *Treatise of Schism*, alleged to contain a veiled incitement to Catholic gentlemen at Elizabeth's Court to assassinate the Queen. Carter denied that the offending passage had any such meaning, but his denial proved of no avail.

Earlier in Elizabeth's reign, as may be seen in Arber's *Transcript*, the Queen had occasion to issue numerous proclamations against seditious books other than those to which we have referred. All serve to prove how difficult the authorities found it to prevent the determined activity of the Romanist press, especially at the time of the rebellion in the North and the other ill-starred endeavours on behalf of Mary Stuart. Later there is similar evidence of trouble with the Puritans, for proclamations were printed showing the stern attempts that were being made to repress certain of their printed books, as well as 'the insolent and inordinate contemptes of such as refuse to come to common prayer and divine service, according to the order established by Parliament'. The most vindictive instance of the queen's vengeance in this connection occurred in 1581, in the case of the hot-headed Puritan John Stubbs, bencher of Lincoln's Inn, and William Page, his bookseller, the one for having written and the other for having published the book entitled *The Discovery of a Gapyng Gulf, whereunto England is like to be swallowed by another French marriage, if the Lord forbid not the banes by letting her Majestie see the sin and punishment thereof.* Among other indiscretions, the hapless Stubbs had protested against this 'imp of the crown of France' venturing to pay Elizabeth a personal visit incognito — which he stoutly denounced as 'An unmanlike, unprince-like, French kind of wooing'.

The punishments threatened under her own proclamations were not sufficient to appease Elizabeth's wrath in this case, so she fell back on one of the more violent acts of Philip and Mary, and both author and publisher were condemned to suffer the loss of their right hands, which were accordingly chopped off with a butcher's knife and mallet in the market-place at Westminster. Stubbs redeemed this brutal business by a remarkable display of fortitude and loyalty. 'I remember', says Camden, 'standing by Stubbs, who, as soon as his right hand was off, took off his hat with his left, and cried aloud, "God save the Queen!" ' The next moment he fainted. Yet even this display of dauntless courage and devotion did not save him from the additional miseries of a long and rigorous imprisonment in the Tower.

Five years later — in June 1586 — the Star Chamber strengthened its control of the press by a decree which consolidated and extended its powers defined in the earlier proclamations, and remained in force until the Star Chamber of Charles I superseded it in 1637 by an injunction which, while it lasted, was even more peremptory and strict. For all their threatening enactments the authorities found it as impossible as ever to stop the flow of prohibited books, their chief trouble now being the growth of the Puritan movement against Elizabeth's official episcopacy. Whitgift's high-handed policy was not calculated to extinguish the smouldering fire of dissent. Persecution has ever been but the means of adding fuel to the flames of religious controversy in this country. One result of Whitgift's hard, uncompromising rule was the fierce war of words known as the Martin Marprelate controversy, which raged at its hottest about 1589. Unable openly to publish their opinions, the Elizabethan Puritans had recourse to the customary means of secret presses and the mysterious machinery which always seemed ready at hand to scatter forbidden literature all over the land, no matter to which side it belonged, the Church of Rome, the Church of England, or the Nonconformists.

It is no part of our purpose to relate in detail how these Puritan zealots, led by the young Cambridge graduate John Penry (afterwards hanged), spread broadcast the violently worded and often scurrilous pamphlets which appeared under the one pseudonym of 'Martin Marprelate'. We need only refer to the controversy as showing the difficulty experienced by Elizabeth's Government in repressing the illegitimate publishing which went on throughout her reign. Whitgift, who was attacked with a fury of invective which exceeded the bounds even of Tudor decency in matters of this kind, did his best to stop the slanders, personally organizing the search for the hidden presses which were distributed over various parts of the country, but without meeting with much success. There were always sympathizers ready to cover up the tracks of the offenders. The 'Anti-Martinists', as they were called, who included among their champions John Lyly and Thomas Nash, were more successful in carrying the campaign into the enemy's camp by means of counter-attacks. It was only when both sides were worn out with their exertions that the end came in sight — to quote the wise words of Bacon in his *Advertisement touching the controversies of the Church of England* (1590) — 'of this immodest and deformed manner of writing lately entertained, whereby matters of religion are handled in the manner of the stage'.

It is a relief to turn from all this turmoil of religion to the birth of the Golden Age of English literature — to watch it as far as possible from the bookshops of the men who were destined to play the midwife's part in ushering it into the world. Much of their work was unauthorized or unworthily done. But this was not altogether the booksellers' fault, as we hope presently to show; and some of the men who mounted to fame on the shoulders of the great Elizabethans were honourable enough according to their lights. The fine record of William Ponsonby is a case in point. Ponsonby, who was admitted to the Stationers' Company in 1571, started in business for himself in St Paul's Churchyard, at the sign of the Bishop's Head—close by the shop of Gabriel Cawood (son and successor of John Cawood, the royal printer), who there published, in 1578, the first English novel of contemporary life, Lyly's *Euphues*.

Perhaps Ponsonby had the success of *Euphues* in his mind when, eight years later, he sought permission from Sidney's old Oxford friend, Sir Fulke Greville, to publish Sir Philip's *Arcadia*, already well known by its wide circulation in manuscript copies. *Euphues*, with its marked originality of style and purpose, had received an enthusiastic welcome from the cultured classes of England, each part running into four or five editions in the first three years, and maintaining a steady sale for many years afterwards. 'Sir,' wrote Fulke Greville to Sidney's father-in-law, Sir Francis Walsingham, in a letter endorsed November 1586—only a month after Sir Philip's death at Zutphen—'this day one Ponsonby, bookebynder in pole's churchyard came to me and told me that there was one in hand to print Sir Philip Sidney's old Arcadia, asking me if it were done with your honour's consent, or any other of his frendes. I told him, to my knowledge, no; then he advysed me to give warninge of it, either to the Archbishope or Doctor Cosen, who have, as he says, a copy to peruse to that end.'* The letter proceeds to suggest that 'some deliberation' would be advisable before publishing Sidney's book, but adds: 'Gayn ther wilbe, no doubt, to be disposed by you: let it be to the poorest of his servants: I desyre only care to be had of his honour, who, I fear, hath carried the honour of these latter ages with him.'

Sidney's relations appear to have shown some reluctance in thus giving the *Arcadia* to the world, but Ponsonby eventually received their permission, and entered the work in the Stationers' Register on August 23rd, 1588, his 'copy' being 'authorized under the Archbishop of Canterbury's hand'. The first edition did not appear until 1590, and was not even then an accurate text. In 1593 another edition appeared, 'augmented and ended', and five years later, by arrangement with the same publisher, the whole was revised by Sidney's sister, the Countess of Pembroke, who also added Sir Philip's *Apologie for Poetrie*, the Sonnets, and *Astrophel and Stella*. Ponsonby has a higher claim to fame as the publisher of *The Faerie Queene*. Probably the close and tender friendship which had existed between Sidney and Spenser had something to do with the more illustrious connection, but, however that may be, Spenser published all his works, with the exception of *The Shepherd's Calendar*, through the same bookseller. *The Shepherd's Calendar* had been issued years before (in 1579) by Hugh Singleton, 'dwelling in Creede Lane, near unto Ludgate, at the signe of the Gylden Tunne', and after being assigned by him in the following year to John Harrison the younger, of Paternoster Row, passed through five editions in the poet's lifetime. Ponsonby entered *The Faerie Queene* (Books I-III) in the Stationers'

* Printed by Dr Grosart in the introductory essay to his edition of the poet's works, 1877.

Register on December 1st, 1589, Spenser having entrusted him with
the manuscript on his arrival in London from Ireland in the previous
month. Sidney's *Arcadia* was then passing through the press, and both
works appeared in the following year.

Disappointed in the hope of preferment which had brought him
back to Court—though Elizabeth, to whom the work had been dedicated, loosened her purse-strings to the extent of a pension in his
favour of £50 a year—Spenser returned reluctantly not long afterwards
to his lonely home at Kilcolman Castle. The poet's reputation now
encouraged his publisher to collect his minor verse, which he issued
under the title of *Complaints, containinge sundrie small poems of the world's
vanity,* prefaced with Ponsonby's own address to the reader, to the
following effect: 'Since my late setting foorth of the Faerie Queene,
finding that it hath found a favourable passage amongst you; I have
sithence endeavoured by all good means (for the better encrease and
accomplishment of your delights) to get into my handes such small Poems
of the same author's as I heard were disperst abroad in sundrie hands;
and not easie to bee come by, by himselfe, some of them havinge bene
diverslie imbeziled, and purloyned from him, since his departure over
sea.' The publisher proceeds to hold out a promise of a further collection
of lost or scattered pieces, 'when I can either by himselfe or otherwise
attaine to ... in the meane time praying you gentlie to accept of these,
and graciouslie to entertaine the *new Poet*'.* The pieces promised in
this letter, however, were never recovered; but in 1594 Spenser sent
Ponsonby for publication his sonnets *Amoretti* and *Epithalamion,* which
Ponsonby entered in the Stationers' Register on November 19th that
year, and issued in 1595 with a dedication to Sir Robert Needham. 'To
gratulate', to quote the publisher's words, 'your safe return from Ireland I had nothing so ready, nor thought anything so meet, as these
sweete and conceited sonnets, the deede of that wel-deserving gentleman, maister Edmonde Spenser; whose name sufficiently warranting
the worthinesse of the work, I do more confidently presume to publish
in his absence.'

Spenser's later works were all issued by the same publisher, who also
had the distinction of bringing into the world, among other notable
books, Greene's *Mamillia,* and Bedingfield's translation of Machiavelli's
Florentine History. Ponsonby was warden of his company in 1597–8. He
figures for the last time in the Stationers' Register on July 5th, 1604, as
one of the publishers of a new edition of Sir Thomas North's translation
of Plutarch's *Lives*—the chief source of Shakespeare's classical learning.
This was first published in 1579 by Thomas Vautrollier and John
Wright, and was one of the best-read books of the age.

* The name which had been applied to Spenser on the publication of *The Shepherd's
Calendar.*

Several of the privileged men were enterprising and public-spirited enough not only to invest some of their profits in learned and costly works which must have involved no inconsiderable risk, but to suggest books themselves and engage authors to write them. 'It was at the expense of Christopher Barker', writes H. G. Aldis in the *Cambridge History of English Literature*,* 'that George Turberville undertook the compilation of *The Noble Arte of Venerie or Hunting* (1575), the publisher himself seeking out and procuring works of foreign writers for the use of the compiler. When William Fulke was at work upon his *Confutation of the Rhenish Testament*, he and two of his men, with their horses, were maintained in London for three-quarters of a year by the publisher of the book, George Bishop, who also supplied Fulke with such books as he required, and at the finish paid him forty pounds for his work.'

Fulke was luckier than most writers of his day. For the booksellers, having now got the upper hand of the printers, gradually drew the professional authors into their power. The day was rapidly passing when authors wrote only for the love of the thing, or because they could not help it—when they could say with Alvan of *The Tragic Comedians*, 'My pen is my fountain—the key of me; and I give myself, I do not sell; I write when I have matter in me and in the direction it presses for, otherwise, not one word!' Men of letters, who were also men of fashion, long continued to hold themselves aloof from any commercial dealings with their publishers, but writing was gradually becoming a none too creditable trade. Men could now be lured for a miserable pittance to turn out anything, from one of those noble translations which formed such a feature of the Elizabethan book trade, to controversial pamphlets, or street ballads, the last of which came from the press in quantities so vast that one publisher who specialized in these sheets—Richard Jones—entered in the Stationers' Register in 1586 no fewer than 123 at one time. John Stow, the most accurate historian of his age, told Manningham the diarist that he 'made no gains by his travails'. It is true that he received £3 and forty copies for his great *Survey of London*, published by John Wolfe in 1598, and that 'for his pains in the *Brief Chronicle*' he was paid twenty shillings and fifty copies, but these were humiliating returns for labours in which he had spent not only the best part of his life, but all his little fortune.† Let us not forget, however,

---

* Vol. iv, H. G. Aldis's chapter on 'The Book Trade, 1557–1625', an illuminating account of a very obscure period.

† Stow's *Annals* first appeared in 1588, 'published by R. Newberie at the assignment of H. Bynneman'—who were both well known in the Elizabethan book trade. Ralph Newberie, or Newbery, as it is generally spelt, issued many important works between 1560 and his retirement in 1605, including Barnabe Googe's *Eclogues* and Hakluyt's *Voyages*. Henry Bynneman printed mainly for other stationers, and his name is frequently met with in the considerable undertakings of his day, sometimes in association with other printers.

that James I rewarded him in 1604 with a beggar's licence—in other words, with royal letters patent authorizing him to appeal for 'kind gratuities'! He seems to have set up basins for alms in the streets, but, fortunately, did not long survive his Majesty's magnanimity.

5

Shakespeare's Publishers

Meanwhile the first fruits were being gathered of the Golden Age of our dramatic literature, mainly by men who, according to modern ideas, had little right to the harvest. The privileged booksellers, if not content merely with fat monopolies, were too busy with weightier undertakings to bother their heads about the chance plays of contemporary dramatists. It was left to their less fortunate brethren to search the byways as well as the highways for new manuscripts that seemed likely to make 'vendible copies', and thus bring a little grist to their mill. So that these served their purpose it mattered little to the printer or bookseller how the 'copies' found their way into his hands. If he thought of author's rights at all it was but to remember that the author himself was only too well aware of their non-existence – indeed, the very idea of author's copyright was regarded in some high quarters as prejudicial to the public interest – and with a shrug of the shoulders he could well afford to dismiss such a trivial matter from his mind. A pirate, if you like, but it was an age of buccaneering; and let us, in denouncing him as a mere unprincipled money-seeking bookseller, remember not only that he was so hedged about with monopolies and privileges that it was extremely difficult for him to make a living in a more legitimate way, but also that, for the very same reason, he all unwittingly performed services to literature the value of which it is now impossible to over-estimate. For it is to the unprivileged and often piratical bookseller that we owe the preservation in print of the greater part of the dramatic work of the reigns of Elizabeth and James I, and much of the poetical and popular literature as well.

It was a pirate who, in the year 1594, first paid Shakespeare the compliment of publishing one of his plays. The pirate was John Danter, the play *Titus Andronicus* – much of which is attributed to Kyd as well as to Shakespeare – and it was published jointly by Edward White and Thomas Millington. Three years later Danter followed this up with his surreptitious first edition of *Romeo and Juliet*, printed in quarto from an imperfect copy, and published anonymously. A more ignoble beginning to a series destined to immortality could scarcely be imagined. 'Danter the Printer' was notorious as a dealer in disreputable literature, being introduced as such in the satirical play *The Return from Parnassus*, publicly acted about 1601 at St John's, Cambridge – 'that most famous and fortunate Nurse of all learning', as Nash wrote of it in 1589. Danter was thus probably the first printer or bookseller to be impersonated under his own name in English drama, though Ben Jonson has a reference to 'Master John Trundle', the publisher of ballads, in his *Every Man in his Humour*, which was first produced, with Shakespeare among the players, in 1598. It was this same Trundle who, in 1603, published, with Nicholas Ling, the first quarto of *Hamlet* (see p. 83).

Danter was also the publisher of Nash's attacks on Gabriel Harvey, the most scurrilous of whose tracts, *Have with you to Saffron Walden,** appeared in the year before his surreptitious editions of *Romeo and Juliet*. Hence Harvey's contemptuous reference to Nash as 'Danter's man'. It was in *Have with you to Saffron Walden* that Nash himself admitted, in defence of some of his more shameless productions, that he had been forced by poverty and 'in hope of gain' to write *Amorous Villanellos and Quipassas* for 'new-fangled Galiardos and senior Fantasticos'.

To the reading public Shakespeare was known as a poet before his plays began to issue from the press, though he made his name first of all in his double role of actor-dramatist. He was more fortunate in the printer of his two narrative poems, *Venus and Adonis* and *Lucrece*, the first of which appeared in 1593 and the second in 1594. This printer was his fellow townsman—and, it is assumed, his personal friend—Richard Field, who left Stratford in 1579 and served his apprenticeship in London with Thomas Vautrollier,† in due course marrying his master's widow and succeeding to the business in 1590. Blades once suggested that when Shakespeare drifted to London in 1586 Field found temporary work for him in Vautrollier's office, but this theory is discredited. Shakespeare's poems attracted far greater attention than his plays. *Venus and Adonis*, which appears, from its unusual accuracy, to have been printed from the author's own manuscript, ran into seven editions in the first eight years, while *Lucrece* reached a fourth edition in the poet's lifetime. A fifth edition of *Lucrece* was published in 1616—the year of Shakespeare's death—by Roger Jackson, who issued it, with the poet's name, as 'newly revised'. This, however, was only one of the tricks of the trade, the text being inferior to the earlier editions.

It was not long after the first appearance of *Venus and Adonis*—the Christmas of 1594—that Shakespeare received his summons to act at Court with other leading players—Elizabeth, like James I, becoming an open admirer of his genius. Sir Sidney Lee suggests that Shakespeare's friendly relations with Field may have secured him some part of the profits in the large sale of the poems; but if that were so, it is strange

* Where Gabriel Harvey was then living.
† Thomas Vautrollier was a Huguenot refugee and an excellent printer. He made two attempts to establish a bookselling business in Edinburgh, but does not seem to have met with much success. He finally returned in 1586 with John Knox's *History of the Reformation* in manuscript, but his impression of that work was suppressed.

that Shakespeare should apparently have been content with literary earnings from these narrative poems alone. Is it possible that he came to regard all such dealings with booksellers as beneath his dignity? It is worth remembering that it was just after his first return to Stratford-on-Avon in 1597 — to raise the prestige of his family and to buy New Place, the largest house thereabouts — that his father, it is presumed at the poet's instigation, made his original application for a coat of arms, and that henceforth William Shakespeare was formally described as 'of Stratford on Avon, gentleman'.

Shakespeare knew well enough that no one in those days could hope to take rank as a man of fashion if he condescended to strike a bargain with any publisher or bookseller. Sir Philip Sidney would not allow any of his books to be printed during his lifetime; and, as Professor Pollard remarks in his bibliographical study of the 'Shakespeare Folios and Quartos', to have offered Sidney money for his *Defence of Poesie* or his *Astrophel and Stella*, 'would have been to run a serious risk of being thrown downstairs'. Our suggestion that Shakespeare may have adopted similar views is only worth considering on the assumption that Shakespeare was something of a snob, or rather, a natural aristocrat, with — as we can see from his plays — a great contempt for the proletariat. In any case it is a remarkable fact that not only were all his plays published without the slighest sign of interest on his part, but his *Sonnets* as well, which had been circulated in manuscript for at least eleven years before their unauthorized publication in 1609. The plays might be accounted for by the fact that it was then customary for dramatists to sell their works outright to one or other company of players, and to realize that they had no further right in them; but this does not hold good in the case of the *Sonnets*. Nor is there any record of a single word of protest when the worst freebooters of the press went so far as to publish seven worthless dramas with Shakespeare's name or initials fraudulently attached as author.

Obviously he had now become a valuable asset in any of these six-penny ventures — for that was the usual price at which a new quarto of this character was published: a price equal to something like forty shillings in 1970. Yet, apart from one protest to which reference will presently be made, he seems to have treated everything respecting the publication of his works with an indifference which almost amounted to contempt. Some of the quartos were shamefully produced, not only in their general makeup, but in the all-important matter of textual accuracy. It seems incredible that Shakespeare did not see the printed editions of his sixteen plays published during his lifetime, or that, having seen them, he did not take some steps to ensure that they were at least accurately printed.

He was fond of litigation, and even in the absence of any legal right as author of the plays, it would not have been impossible, with the powerful influence which he could bring to bear upon the Stationers' Company, to call the pirate publishers to book. Was not the patron of his company the Lord Chamberlain himself? It might have been a troublesome business, but, as Professor Pollard points out, injured authors were not without means of obtaining redress in the shape of a fine or imprisonment through the Stationers' Company. And that the Company itself was not always ready to license a play merely on the production of the sixpenny fee is clearly shown by such entries as those in which James Roberts, for example, in 1598, was credited with the 'copy' of *The Merchant of Venice* only on condition that the book was not to be printed by the said 'James Roberts, or anye other whatsoever, without lycence first obtained from the Right Honorable the Lord Chamberlain'; and again in 1603, when he received permission to print *Troilus and Cressida* only 'when he hath gotten sufficient authoritye for yt' (see p. 83).

The out-and-out pirates rarely ran this risk of refusal, preferring to take their chance of a fine or imprisonment to seeking anyone's authority. This was not invariably the rule, however, in Shakespeare's case; but that the pirates regarded him as fair game, and unlikely to retaliate, is suggested by the cool manner in which Thomas Thorpe, the publisher of the *Sonnets*, both in the Stationers' Register and on the title-page of the book itself, brusquely designated the work *Shakespeare's Sonnets*, instead of following, as Sidney Lee observes, 'the more urbane collocation of words invariably adopted by living authors, viz. *Sonnets of William Shakespeare*'. The one protest of which we have any record survives in Thomas Heywood's *Apology for Actors* — issued in 1612 — wherein he tells us that Shakespeare resented the unwarranted use of his name by William Jaggard in 1599, when that worthy issued, under the title of *The Passionate Pilgrim, by W. Shakespeare*, an unauthorized collection of scattered verse, the bulk of which was not by Shakespeare at all. Among the contents, however, were two of the *Sonnets* which subsequently appeared in the complete, but still surreptitious, edition of the poems. Heywood was treated in similar fashion by the same publisher in a later edition of *The Passionate Pilgrim*, and airs his grievance in his dedicatory epistle. He knew, he added, in referring to Shakespeare, that he was 'much offended with Mr Jaggard that (altogether unknown to him) presumed to make so bold with his name'. It was perhaps as a result of this objection that Shakespeare's name was removed from the title-page of some of the copies.

Sir Sidney Lee, according to Professor Pollard, had pirates on the brain, regarding practically all the printers and publishers of Shakespeare's day as tarred with the same brush, and equally dishonest. Pollard is so eager to whitewash their characters that he goes to the other extreme, holding that the amount of wrong done to professional authors was much less than might have been expected, and that piracy was the exception rather than the rule. Nevertheless he makes out a strong case for the legality of most of the Shakespearean quartos, his evidence seeming to prove that 'good' copies are found in the plays duly entered in the Stationers' Register, and that these were obtained by the publishers from their lawful owners, the playhouse authorities to whom the manuscripts had been sold by Shakespeare himself. The pirated editions—those not entered in the Register—he writes, 'were few and clearly distinguishable from the honest ones, and they have left no trace whatever on our present texts'.* The whole question is of great importance in any critical consideration of Shakespeare's plays, but too controversial and involved to be discussed at length in the space at our disposal.

Thomas Thorpe, who first issued the complete collection of the *Sonnets* in 1609, belonged to a bookselling class plentifully represented among Shakespeare's publishers—a class which picked up its living largely by the procuring of manuscripts for the press. Its members were not over-scrupulous as to the means employed to achieve their purpose. If the playhouse managers objected to the publishing of their plays, or demanded too high a fee, needy actors could be bribed to lend or sell their written copies; or, failing that, shorthand writers could be sent to take the piece down as well as they could. That *Romeo and Juliet* was first printed from a copy obtained, wholly or in part, by this last-named means can hardly be doubted, according to Pollard, who also ascribes to a similar origin the first and imperfect editions of *The Merry Wives of Windsor* (published in 1602 by Arthur Johnson 'at the sign of the Fleur de Luce' in St Paul's Churchyard) and *Pericles* (published by Henry Gosson 'at the sign of the Sunne in Pater-noster Row' in 1609). Heywood complains in the prologue to his play of *Queen Elizabeth*, which had been published surreptitiously for the first time in 1605:

> That some by stenography drew
> The plot: put it in print: (scarce one word trew:)

and so compelled him to prepare a corrected text for the revival of 1637. Heywood is also our authority for knowing that some dramatists at least sold their plays to publishers as well as to the playhouse managers, though the practice was evidently regarded as double-dealing of a somewhat shady character. The reference is in the preface to Heywood's *Rape of Lucrece* (published by Nathaniel Butter in 1630), when he speaks of playwrights who incur great 'suspition of honestie' by arranging 'a double sale of their labours, first to the stage, and after to the Presse'—a thing which he prides himself on never having done. Some

---

* *Shakespeare Folios and Quartos*, 1909.

of his plays, unknown to him, had found their way into the printer's hands, and were so corrupt and mangled that he had been 'as unable to know them as ashamed to chalenge them'. In the case of *The Rape of Lucrece*, therefore, he had obtained the consent of the stage authorities to furnish it out in its native habit, 'because the rest have been so wronged in being publisht in such savadge and rugged ornaments'.

Thorpe was probably not worse than many others of his kind. He was less fortunate than most, for whereas the majority of these men only employed such means as stepping-stones to more dignified positions in the trade, Thorpe, apparently, began and ended his career as a sort of homeless publisher, though for one brief period, in 1608, he blossomed forth with a shop of his own, at the sign of the Tiger's Head, in St Paul's Churchyard. Apart from the three books which he is known to have issued from this address—one of them being George Chapmans' *Conspiracie and Tragedie of Charles Duke of Byron* and another Ben Jonson's *Masques of Blackness and Beauty**—the whole of the books with which he was associated were printed and sold for him by other stationers. His first literary prize was Marlowe's *Lucan*, a manuscript copy of which fell into his predatory hands in 1600. He dedicated the first edition to his friend Edward Blount, who, two years previously, had himself come into possession of Marlowe's *Hero and Leander*, and, being but a stationer's assistant at the time, had issued it through other members of the trade. Blount, whose later career is dealt with on pp. 83–4, declared in his preface to *Hero and Leander* that he published it out of respect for Marlowe, whose intimate friendship he claimed, and whose memory he defended against the attacks of his detractors.

When Thorpe published the first edition of Shakespeare's *Sonnets*, he had given up his shop at the sign of the Tiger's Head, and, after getting the printing done by George Eld, arranged for the sale of the copies with two other stationers—William Aspley and John Wright. Having entered the copy in the Stationers' Register, and thus proclaimed himself proprietor of the work, he asserted his right by inditing the dedication which has led to so much discussion:

> To the onlie begetter of these insuing sonnets, Mr W. H., all happinesse and that eternitie promised by our ever living poet, wisheth the well-wishing adventurer in setting forth. T. T.

Sir Sidney Lee settles this perplexing phrase almost conclusively in his life of Shakespeare. The mysterious 'Mr W. H.,' did not, as so many students had previously assumed, indicate the initials of the sonnet's youthful hero, but were merely those of Thorpe's partner in the speculation. 'He is best identified', says Sir Sidney, 'with a stationer's

---

* Thorpe succeeded in publishing four of Ben Jonson's works altogether and three of Chapman's.

assistant, William Hall, who was professionally engaged, like Thorpe, in procuring "copy". In 1606 "W.H." won a conspicuous success in that direction, and conducted his operations under cover of the now familiar initials. In that year "W.H." announced that he had procured a neglected manuscript poem—*A Foure-fould Meditation*—by the Jesuit Robert Southwell, who had been executed in 1595, and he published it with a dedication (signed "W. H.") vaunting his good fortune in meeting with such treasure-trove. When Thorpe dubbed "Mr W. H." with characteristic magniloquence "the onlie begetter [i.e. obtainer or procurer] of these insuing sonnets", he merely indicated that that personage was the first of the pirate-publisher fraternity to procure a manuscript of Shakespeare's sonnets and recommend its surreptitious use.' Thorpe's venture was the only edition of the *Sonnets* published in the poet's lifetime. We have already seen that his two narrative poems had been frequently reissued during the same period; and most of his published plays were reprinted before his death, six of them running into three and four editions, and two of them (*Richard III* and the first part of *Henry IV*) into as many as five.

The circumstances surrounding the origin of each of these quartos are of the deepest interest, but any serious attempt to discuss them here would not carry us outside the scope of our inquiry, but bring us at once to debatable matters upon which the most distinguished critics have agreed emphatically to differ.

One of the more substantial of Shakespeare's early booksellers was James Roberts, who, unlike most of the play publishers, was something of a monopolist, holding the patent with R. Watkins to print almanacks and prognostications,* which, in the complaint of the unprivileged, 'were the onelie relief of the most porest of ye printers', besides taking over in 1594 a number of theological and other copyrights which had belonged to John Charlewood, whose widow he seems to have married not long afterwards. For nearly twenty years Roberts also held the privilege of printing and publishing the 'players' bills', or programmes, and in this way must have enjoyed exceptional opportunities of picking up manuscript copies of Shakespeare's plays from the managers and actors. In 1600—if we are to believe the title-pages—he printed the quarto editions of *The Merchant of Venice* and *Midsummer Night's Dream*, as well as the second edition of *Titus Andronicus*; and, four years later, the complete quarto of *Hamlet*. At one time he was held responsible for the printing of the mutilated first quarto of *Hamlet*, but later researches have led to its being assigned to the press of Valentine Simmes, who

---

* The patent lasted until the end of Elizabeth's reign, James I handing over the privilege to the Stationers' Company and the Universities of Oxford and Cambridge. After lasting for nearly two centuries the monopoly was broken down by Thomas Carnan, a London bookseller (see p. 171).

also printed the first quartos of *Richard II*, *Richard III*, *Much Ado about Nothing* and the second part of *Henry IV*. Only the publishers' names — Nicholas Ling and John Trundle — appear on the title page of the first edition of *Hamlet*.

Roberts figures as publisher, as well as printer, of the first edition of *The Merchant of Venice*, but in the other quartos with which he is associated he appears for the most part as printer only. He was associated with other notable works besides Shakespearean quartos, including Marston's *Metamorphosis of Pigmalion's Image* (published by Edmund Matts in 1598), and *The Scourge of Villanie*, by the same dramatist, in the following year; Jervis Markham's *Tragedie of Sir Richard Grinvile* (1595); Tuberville's *Songs and Sonnets*, and a new edition of *Euphues*. In 1603 he nearly added *Troilus and Cressida* to his list, for the licence, as stated on p. 79, was made out in his name in that year, but the players in this case seem to have exercised their right to intervene, for nothing came of it. In or about 1608 Roberts's printing business was transferred to William Jaggard, who had a bookselling shop in the churchyard of St Dunstan's-in-the-West, where he now developed the other branch of his craft, and in 1611 became Printer to the City of London. Roberts's publishing stock, Pollard tells us, was not taken over by him until 1615. The business included the right to print the players' bills — a privilege which Jaggard must have found of the greatest value when the time came to collect the plays of Shakespeare for the famous folio of 1623.

Much of the credit for the First Folio belongs, however, to Edward Blount, who learnt his craft under William Ponsonby, helping him in the great days of his association with Spenser, Robert Greene and Sidney's *Arcadia*. Though admitted to the Stationers' Company in 1588 — at the end of his ten years' apprenticeship — he did not start publishing on his own account until 1594, but, once established, he soon launched out in a series of enterprises which ensured him, quite apart from the First Folio, an honourable place in the bookselling annals of his day. He not only published John Florio's Italian–English Dictionary (issued in 1598 under the title *A World of Words*), but also commissioned him to undertake the English version of one of the noblest of Elizabethan translations, Montaigne's *Essays*. This was published by Blount in 1603, while still content with the modest shop — 'little more than an open stall'* — which he had taken against the great north door of St Paul's Cathedral in 1594.

With the development of his business Blount was compelled to move, in 1603, to a more substantial house at the sign of the Black Bear, in St Paul's Churchyard. 'The conditions of the trade', says Sir Sidney Lee, 'did not permit him to contribute substantially — if at all — to the

* Sir Sidney Lee, in the study of Edward Blount which he contributed under the title 'An Elizabethan bookseller', to *Bibliographica*, vol. i, 1905.

support of authors. But in private life he was honestly interested in literature and was ambitious of social intercourse with its creators.' Blount
published works for Ben Jonson and Daniel, and his connection with
Marlowe we have already touched upon in our references to Thomas
Thorpe. His other great ventures before sharing in the production of
the First Folio included Thomas Shelton's translation of *Don Quixote*,
the first part of which appeared about 1612 — while the publisher was in
temporary partnership with William Barret — and the second part in
1620. His association with Shakespeare's name began before this with
the collection of verse entitled *Love's Martyr; or, Rosalin's Complaint*, which
included *A Poetical Essaie on the Turtle and Phœnix*, signed with the poet's
name in full. 'Happily', as Sir Sidney Lee remarks in his life of the
poet, 'Shakespeare wrote nothing else of like character.'

The First Folio was beyond the individual resources of either Blount
or Jaggard, so a small syndicate was formed such as became the custom
of the trade in later years in most undertakings involving considerable
expense. William Jaggard had just retired from active business, but he
played a prominent if not the leading part in the preparation of the
folio, his connection with the playhouses doubtless helping considerably.
He is probably entitled to divide the chief honours of the enterprise with
Blount, who not only took a large share in the financial risk, but is
credited with much of the literary and editorial work involved in its
production. The three other stationers concerned were Isaac Jaggard,
William's son, who had just succeeded him in the printing business,
John Smethwicke, and William Aspley, the last being one of the two
booksellers entrusted by Thomas Thorpe with the sale of Shakespeare's
Sonnets, and joint publisher with Andrew Wise of the first quarto of
Much Ado about Nothing, and the second part of *Henry IV*. Aspley had
also been associated with Blount in several of his earlier undertakings.
Smethwicke, who was a neighbour of the Jaggards in St Dunstan's
Churchyard, knew something of Shakespeare's value from two late
editions which he had published of *Romeo and Juliet*, as well as one
edition of *Hamlet*.

The First Folio came from the press of Isaac Jaggard, and included
not only the plays published in Shakespeare's lifetime, as well as the
posthumously printed *Othello* (1622), but seventeen other works which
had never hitherto been printed. The names of Blount and Isaac
Jaggard alone appear as publishers of the book, the colophon stating
that it was printed at the expense of William Jaggard, Smethwicke,
Aspley and Blount. The publishers claim on the title-page that the
whole thirty-six plays are printed 'according to the true originall copies'.
Unimpeachable evidence of former piracy is given in the dedication
addressed to the two Herberts — 'the incomparable pair of brethren' —
the Earls of Pembroke and Montgomery, the first of whom was Lord

Chamberlain and patron of the playwright: 'As where you were abus'd
with diverse stolne and surreptitious copies, maimed and deformed by
the frauds and stealthes of injurious imposters that expos'd them: even
those are now offer'd to your view cur'd and perfect in their limbes,
and all the rest absolute in their members as he conceived them.' The
dedication was written by the two editors, Shakespeare's old friends
and brother-players, John Heming and Henry Condell, who protested,
probably with truth, that they were actuated in their share of the work
'without ambition either of selfe-profit or fame', and solely with a
desire to 'keepe the memory of so worthy a friend and fellow worker
alive as was our Shakespeare'. This First Folio, our supreme glory in
literature, if not our proudest achievement in the matter of typography,
has ensured for its promoters an enduring place in the annals of English
publishing. Whatever were their faults as revisers of the press, as Pollard
says, they preserved nearly twenty of Shakespeare's plays from total
destruction besides printing greatly improved texts of several others,
'and for these inestimable benefits, had each of the venturers received
the whole proceeds of the edition as his share of the profits, who shall
say that they would have been overpaid?' Running into nearly one
thousand pages, the First Folio was sold for what was then the high
price of twenty shillings. In 1970 a copy fetched £3,000.

6

Through the Reign of James I

The seventeenth century brings us to a new phase in the history of bookselling. In 1601 Queen Elizabeth, realizing that the system of monopolies, which formed so large a part of her whole fiscal policy, was at length rousing her subjects to serious discontent, issued proclamations suspending all privileges of the kind until their legality had been examined and approved by the law officers of the Crown. But however much this may have benefited the book trade for the two remaining years of her life, it was soon nullified by the action of her successor, who expressly excluded books from the provisions of the statute by which monopolies were practically done away with. James not only confirmed individual privileges among the stationers, but permitted the Company itself, while still under strict State control, to become a sort of book trust for its own benefit. C. R. Rivington, who throws some light on this development in his sketch of *The Records of the Worshipful Company of Stationers*, says that there were originally five different trading stocks, called respectively the Ballad Stock, the Bible Stock, the Irish Stock, the Latin Stock and the English Stock, the Company also holding for some years a patent for printing in Scotland, granted by the Scottish Parliament.

On October 29th, 1603 the partners in the English Stock obtained the first of these grants from the new King, which secured to the Company the exclusive right to print all primers and psalters (the King's Printer excepted), as well as all almanacks and prognostications. Other valuable grants followed, and gradually a formidable trade monopoly was set up, the one good thing that could be said for it being that the poorer members of the Company, and the widows of earlier partners, participated in the profits. 'The monopoly long claimed by the Company under these charters', wrote C. R. Rivington in 1883, 'has been swept away now nearly a century, but the English Stock still flourishes, and a considerable annual profit continues to accrue from the publication of almanacks and the *"Gradus ad Parnassum"*, the sole survivor of a long list of school-books which formerly issued from Stationers' Hall.' The monopoly began by the founders of the English Stock buying out the stationers who had held their privileges in Elizabeth's time, 'the which composition, together with a stocke raised by them, coste them great sommes of money'. It then pleased his Majesty (to quote an

86

extract from the State Papers printed by Professor Arber in his introduction to the third volume of his *Transcript*) 'to grante the same unto them for the generale good of the whole Companie ... The peticioners have ever since the granting of the said Letters patents yearelie distributed, and by an Ordinance in that behalfe made, are to distribute £200 per Annum for ever, among the poore of the said grante.' The profits from each Stock, apart from these charitable contributions, were divided among the partners according to their individual stake in the concern.

This grant led to long and bitter murmuring among the 'poor Freemen and journeymen printers', who, in a petition to the Lords (printed by Professor Arber), complained that the benefits of the charter, intended for the general good of the whole Company, had, under colour of relieving the poor, been converted to the monopolists in particular, 'and the petitioners utterly ruined thereby'. They prayed that the charter of privilege might be dissolved; but nothing, apparently came of it.

The partners in the Bible Stock, however, who divided the right of issuing the Scriptures with the King's Printer, played a creditable part in the so-called 'Authorized Version' of the Bible (1611), which originated out of the Hampton Court Conference of 1604. This familiar edition was printed at the expense of Robert Barker, son and successor to Christopher Barker as King's Printer, whose privileges included the right to print not only Bibles and New Testaments, but all Statute Books, as well as Acts of Parliament and proclamations. The king himself, to whom the translators dedicated the work as its 'principal mover and author', paid nothing towards its expenses, the sole remuneration received by the learned divines, apart, of course, from its honour and glory, being 30s. weekly, a sum which each of the seven revisers received from the partners of the Bible Stock in the Stationers' Company during the last nine months of their labours. The Company also provided them with a room at Stationers' Hall, where the work was completed. The owners of the Bible Stock had no reason to complain of their own reward, for Rivington tells us that no fewer than eight auditors were at one time required to examine the accounts, and that the profits were sufficient to enable the partners to lend money to the Company at 6 per cent. Today the copyright of the Authorized Version, as well as the Book of Common Prayer and *The New English Bible*, is vested in the Crown, the right to print them being granted by charter to Oxford and Cambridge Universities, and by licence to the King's Printer. The Revised Version is the joint property of the two Universities, which paid £20,000 towards the expenses of publication.

We are still sadly lacking in information concerning the actual profits and losses of individual members of the trade in the early years of the seventeenth century, though the printer continued to complain that the bookseller—or publisher as we should call him—had matters too much his own way, and secured too many of the prizes. It was certainly easier and less expensive to start simply as a bookseller or publisher, without waiting for permission to set up a printing establishment. The young stationer could begin with a bookstall; and he had only to pick up a manuscript—it did not much matter how—have it entered as his 'copy' in the Stationers' Register, get someone to print it for him if he had no press of his own, and start publishing at once. A half-forgotten book that seemed worth reprinting, or even a ballad, would answer the purpose. The system of interchange which became a recognized practice at once provided him with an opportunity of stocking his booth or shop with other books at comparatively little expense.

That was how John Dunton started his business later in the century, when, as he explains in his *Life and Errors*, by exchanging through the whole trade the first book which he issued, 'it furnished my shop with all sorts of books saleable at that time'. There are references in the Stationers' Registers to show that this was a common practice at the time. Many an apprentice who started in this humble way knew nothing of the printer's craft, having served his time with a bookseller or bookbinder; and having completed his apprenticeship, he was made free of the Stationers' Company whether he could print or not. Books in those early days were usually sold unbound, so that no great outlay was involved on that account, the binding belonging, for the most part, to a distinct branch of the stationer's craft. As the young bookseller prospered so he could extend his business, stocking bound as well as unbound copies, and presently adding to his staff as many hackwriters as he condescended to patronize.

With the printers it was different. In the early seventeenth century, and onwards to the time of the Long Parliament, when for a time there was greater freedom, they were handicapped by the Star Chamber Decree of 1586, which limited the number of master printers to twenty-five. That was a liberal allowance in the eyes of the ecclesiastical authorities, fearful as ever of the growing power of the press. Had not Christopher Barker, the Queen's Printer, in his official report of 1582, declared that eight or ten presses at the most 'would suffice for all England, yea, and Scotland too'? Even the twenty-five printing houses, with their fifty odd presses which they boasted between them, were hopelessly insufficient to find promotion or even work for all the increasing number of journeymen and apprentices. Vacancies occurred among the master printers only at rare intervals—to be filled up in each case with the sanction of the archbishop. Steps were taken to relieve the distress which inevitably ensued by restricting the number of apprentices, and limiting the number of copies of any one edition—

except in special cases—to 1,250 or 1,500 copies, the whole work having to be reset in the event of a reprint being called for.

There was one way, however, as Professor Arber points out, in which the would-be master printer could come to a printing business of his own, independently of the court of assistants and the archbishop, and that was to marry a master printer's widow. The good apprentice of tradition was wont to marry his master's daughter. In point of fact, in the stationer's case at all events, it was more often his master's widow. 'It must have been a lively time among eligible young printers', remarks Arber, in the introduction to the fifth volume of his *Transcript*, 'when it was known that a master printer was dying.' We meet with more than one widow, in the course of this *Transcript*, who married three printers in succession, carrying her business with her in each case.

The trade still had its headquarters in St Paul's Churchyard. Paternoster Row did not take its leading place until the days of Queen Anne, after Little Britain had had its reign and, in its turn, been superseded. Meantime the 'Row' was more noted for its mercers, lace-men, haberdashers and sempstresses than for its publishers, though these began to put in their claims towards the end of the sixteenth century, when we find one or two noted stationers located there. The westward movement started in the reign of James I, when booksellers' shops sprang up here and there along Holborn, and down the Strand towards Charing Cross. Little Britain came to the front towards the middle of the seventeenth century, when London Bridge also had its spell of bookselling popularity, though one stationer, William Pickering, chiefly remembered as a ballad-monger, had a shop there as early as 1557. 'In the next year', writes H. G. Aldis, in his chapter on 'The Book Trade, 1557–1625', in *The Cambridge History of English Literature*, 'he was "dwellying at Saynt Magnus Corner", which, if not actually on the bridge, was at least hard by, and at this address the business continued for upwards of a century. As might be expected from its situation at the port of London, many nautical books were published here, and the seaman making his preparations for a voyage would step into the well-known shop and purchase *The Art of Navigation*, or perhaps, if he were thither bound, a *Card or rutter of the sea lyenge betwene Holland and Ffryse-land*, and, were he so minded, he might fortify himself with *The Sea-mans sacred Safetye or a praier booke for seamen*.'

From the same authority we learn that the Frankfurt fair still held so important a place in the English trade that John Bill, one of the leading London stationers, who was patronized by King James, Sir Thomas Bodley, and other distinguished men, thought it worth while in 1617 to begin the issue of a London edition of the half-yearly Frankfurt *Mess-Katalog*. This he continued for about eleven years, adding, from 1622 to 1626, a supplement of 'Books printed in English'. This supplement, as H. G. Aldis points out, was not the first attempt at a catalogue of English books. 'The credit for that enterprise is due to Andrew Maunsell, who, induced, one may believe, by a love of books, deserted the calling of a draper to become a bookseller and the earliest English bibliographer.' Maunsell's *First Part of the Catalogue of English printed Bookes* had been issued from his shop in Lothbury in 1595, and was devoted to works of divinity. The second part, which he published in the same year ,'concerneth the science Mathematicall, as Arithmetick, Geometrie, Astronomie, Astrologie, Musick, the Arts of Warre and Navigation; and also of Physicks and Surgery', and was to have been followed by a third part dealing with rhetoric, history, poetry and art, but this, unfortunately, never appeared. Maunsell printed but few books himself, but he was well known as a publisher.

Apart from the evil of monopolies, which remained a very real grievance among the unprivileged stationers, the trade enjoyed a period of comparative peace during the reign of James I. Whatever his faults and failings as a monarch, James was a genuine scholar, as well as something of an author, and could take a personal interest in the affairs of the Stationers' Company. His *Basilicon Doron* was written in 1599, but the first edition was not published until shortly before his accession to the English throne, when it was issued in Edinburgh by the King's Scottish printer, Richard Waldegrave. Copies evidently soon found their way to the English capital, for within a week of Elizabeth's death we find it entered in the Stationers' Register—'A booke called *Basilicon*, or his Majestie's instructions to his Dearest sonne Henrie the prince'—as the 'copie' of six London stationers. One of these enterprising booksellers was Master Simon Waterson, who published the last of Camden's great works, the *Annals of the Reign of Elizabeth*, which is entered in the Stationers' Register on March 21st, 1615, as '*The History of England in Latin from the yeare* 1558 *to the yeare* 1588, licensed to be printed by the Kinge's Maiesties Letter under the Signett directed to Sir Robert Cotton, knight, and Master William Cambden, Clarenceaux'.* In November of the following year Waterson entered the *Annals* in an English translation, 'to be printed when it is further authorized', but no English version appeared until 1627, several years after Camden's death.

Francis Bacon, who had just received his knighthood from James, published his *Advancement of Learning* in 1605 through Richard Ockhould, the first part being entered to him on August 19th of that year, and the second part exactly one month later. Ockhould published nothing else worth remembering in the course of his career, and even the *Advancement of Learning* he assigned to one William Washington on

* Camden's *Britannica* was published by Ralph Newbery in 1586, and ran through five editions before the end of the century.

January 15th, 1629, some two or three years after Bacon's death. There is more interest attaching to the first edition of the famous *Essays*, which Bacon authorized Humphrey Cooper to publish in 1597. Only ten essays went to make up this slim octavo volume, and in his dedication 'to Mr Anthony Bacon, his deare brother', the author explains his reasons for thus issuing 'these fragments of his conceites'. He publishes them now, he says, 'like some that have an Orcharde ill neighbored, that gather their fruit before it is ripe, to prevent stealing', meaning that he is doing so to forestall an unauthorized edition that he knows to be in preparation; 'only I dislike now to put them out because they will bee like the late new halfe-pence, which though the silver were good, yet the peeces were small'. Not to do so 'had been to adventure the wrong they mought receive by untrue coppies, or by some garnishment'.

Sure enough the essays were entered by one of the pirates, Richard Serger, on January 24th, 1597, but against the entry is written in the margin of the Register—*cancellatur ista intratio per curiam tentam 7 februarij* (Arber). Twelve days later came the authorized entry in favour of Bacon's publisher, Humphrey Cooper—'A book intituled *Essaies, Religious Meditations, Places of Perswasion and Disswation*'—and the volume itself appeared on February 7th. The *Essays* were immediately successful, Cooper, whose shop was at the sign of the Black Bear, in Chancery Lane, issuing a new edition in 1598. Numerous other reprints, authorized and unauthorized, appeared during the author's lifetime.

Bacon, like Ben Jonson, Beaumont and Fletcher, Thomas Heywood, and other dramatists who linked the great Elizabethan era with Jacobean days, had almost as many different publishers on his title-pages as Shakespeare himself. And, in the same way, many of the works of the playwrights have been preserved to us in print by wholly unauthorized means. Beaumont and Fletcher's *Knight of the Burning Pestle*, for example, was published anonymously in 1613 by Walter Burre, who writes in his dedicatory letter to Robert Keysar that he 'had fostered it privately in his besom these two years', adding incidentally that the play was a failure when first produced on the stage. It was a great success upon its revival in 1635. Walter Burre was the bookseller who, in 1614, published the first edition of Sir Walter Ralegh's unfinished *History of the World*, written, as we all know, while the author was in the Tower.

A circumstantial story, but now rejected as apocryphal, of a dramatic interview four years later between Sir Walter Ralegh and his bookseller, is told by Winstanley in his *English Worthies* (1660) and repeated by Aubrey and other antiquarians. 'Some few days before he suffered', so the story runs, 'Sir Walter sent for Mr Walter Burre, who formerly printed his first volume of the *History of the World*, whom, taking by the hand, after some other discourse, he asked him how it had sold. Mr Burre returned this answer: "It sold slowly; it had undone him." At which words of his, Sir Walter, stepping to his desk, reaches his other imprinted part of his history which he had brought down to the times he lived in, and, clapping his hand upon his breast, said with a sigh, "Ah! my friend, hath my first part undone thee? The second part shall undo no more; this ungrateful country is unworthy of it": and immediately going to the fireside, threw it in, and set his foot on it until it was consumed. As great a loss to learning as Christendom could have sustained; the greater because it could be repaired by no other hand but his.' The real fact was that the volume published by Burre was a conspicuous success from the first, two editions being called for in the same year. It is true that James, who had expounded his views in his *Basilicon Doron* as to the divine right of kings, condemned the work — 'for divers exceptions', says John Chamberlain, the letter-writer, 'and specially for being too saucy in censuring princes' — but although the Archbishop of Canterbury, at his majesty's command, ordered the Stationers' Company to suppress all the copies, the publisher appears to have surmounted the difficulty by cancelling the title-page, for the circulation of the book was allowed to continue. It reached another edition before Sir Walter's death, and remained one of the best selling books throughout the seventeenth century.

Two years before Ralegh died Bishop Montague published through the King's printers, Robert Barker and John Bill, the collected works of James himself, though his majesty was no more popular as an author than as a King. This was in 1616, the year of Shakespeare's death, as well as the less-remembered death of Francis Beaumont. The band of immortals associated with the old convivial gatherings at the *Mermaid*, of which Beaumont wrote so feelingly to Ben Jonson, was fast breaking up. Ralegh, who followed Shakespeare and Beaumont two years later, had himself originated these 'merry meetings' in the more heroic days of Elizabeth. Less than a fortnight after Beaumont's death we find an entry in the Stationers' Register of one of the fifty-odd plays that he wrote conjointly with John Fletcher. This was *The Scornful Lady*, entered as the 'copie' of Miles Patriche, by whom it was assigned in the following year to Thomas Jones. It was in 1616, also, that Ben Jonson collected his plays and verses in his First Folio, to which he ventured to give the title of his *Works*, thus bringing down upon his head the scorn of contemporary wits for prostituting that term by such ephemeral things as plays.

The 1616 Folio was prepared for the press by Jonson himself, and issued by William Stansby, one of the most considerable stationers, and certainly one of the best printers, of his day. Stansby fell into serious trouble on one occasion for printing a seditious book, the Stationers'

Company punishing him by nailing up his shop, though he was eventually allowed to resume his business. There was not the same demand for Ben Jonson as for Shakespeare, whose First Folio, published seven years later, went to its second edition in 1632,* while Ben Jonson's Second Folio, sold in a succession of fragments by Robert Allot, Andrew Crooke, Richard Meighen and H. Herringman, was not completed until 1641.

To Ben Jonson, as to most professional authors of his day, the choice of a patron who would pay for the dedication of his book was even more important than that of a publisher. He succeeded in securing the patronage of James I, who conferred a pension of a hundred marks† a year upon him, and subsequent but more uncertain bounties from Charles I. Jonson sent a characteristic petition to Charles begging that his pension of a hundred marks might be turned into pounds:

> Please your majesty to make
> Of your grace, for goodness sake,
> Those your father's marks, your pounds.

The poet also drew a pension of a hundred nobles as the city of London's chronologer. William Herbert, Earl of Pembroke, patron of so many needy writers, used to send Jonson a regular New Year gift of £20 wherewith to purchase books. Another of his more generous supporters was the Duke of Newcastle, to whom Jonson, in his letters, could humble himself in a manner which, though characteristic of the age, is nevertheless distressing to read. 'Your lordship's timely gratuity', he tells the duke on one occasion, 'fell like the dew of heaven upon my necessities'; and some of his begging letters form pitiful commentaries on the state of authorship in those unprotected days.

But authors were already beginning to rebel against their inadequate rewards from the book trade itself. John Minsheu, the lexicographer, like John Ruskin and other independent authors in more recent times, became his own publisher, printing his *Guide into Tongues* in 1617 at his own charge, and, since the booksellers refused to have anything to do with the work, sold it himself to the subscribers. This was the first book published by subscription in England, but apparently the venture was not very successful.

The case of George Wither, the poet and pamphleteer, is better known. His *Schollers Purgatory* gives the most graphic, if somewhat

---

* The Second Folio Shakespeare was printed by Thomas Cotes for John Smethwick, William Aspley, Richard Hawkins, Richard Meighen and Robert Allot, each of whose names figures as publisher on different copies. To Allot, whose name is most often met with on the title-page, Blount had transferred, on November 16th, 1630, his rights in the sixteen plays which were first licensed for publication in 1623.—LEE.

† The mark was formerly a current coin in England and Scotland, and is equal to about £10 in modern money.

prejudiced, portraits of contemporary booksellers that we possess. Wither had obtained from James I in 1623 letters patent granting him for a period of fifty-one years not only the monopoly or copyright of his own *Hymns and Songs of the Church*, but an order for their compulsory insertion in every copy of the authorized *Psalm-book in meter*, the privilege of issuing which had been granted to the Stationers' Company by the King at the beginning of his reign. The Stationers' Company at once came to loggerheads with him, and the bitter controversy ensued which the author perpetuated in his *Schollers Purgatory*, published at the time of James's last Parliament. If the Star Chamber, as it did on occasion, chastised the stationers with whips, Wither chastised them with scorpions:

> Nevertheless [he writes], conceive me not, I pray you, that I goe about to lay a general ymputation upon all Stationers. For, to disparage the whole profession, were an act neither becomming an honest man to doe, nor a prudent Auditory to suffer. Their mystery (as they not untruly tearme it) consists of divers Trades incorporated together: as Printers, Booke-binders, Claspemakers, Booksellers, etc. And of all these be some honest men, who to my knowledge are so greeved being over-born by the notorious oppressions and proceedings of the rest, that they have wished themselves of some other calling. The Printers mystery, is ingenious, paynefull, and profitable; the Booke-binders necessary; the Claspmakers useful. And indeed, the retailer of bookes, commonly called a Booke-seller, is a Trade, which being wel governed, and lymited within certaine bounds, might become somewhat serviceable to the rest. But as it is now (for the most part abused) the Bookseller hath not onely made the Printer, the Binder, and the Claspmaker a slave to him: but hath brought Authors, yea the whole Commonwealth, and all the liberall Sciences into bondage. For he make all professors of Art labour for his profit, at his owne price, and utters it to the Commonwealth in such fashion, and at those rates, which please himselfe.

Wither complains, among other things, of the excessive number of books. It is a complaint which we are familiar with in our own day; and will be heard, probably, to the end of the chapter; for is it not the oldest cry in literature. 'Good God!' writes Wither in 1632, 'how many dungboats full of fruitless works do they yearly foist on his Majesty's subjects; how many hundred reams of foolish, profane, and senseless ballads do they quarterly disperse abroad!' Yet the total number of entries in the Stationers' Register for 1632 does not amount to more than 109 — an average of but two a week. This is not a strictly accurate list of the actual number of books published, for many works were issued without being entered, but it is sufficiently striking when we compare it with the totals in recent years, printed on pp. 570 and 571.

Wither made good his claim to his monopoly for the time being, but ten years later the council disallowed the offending patent. The Stationers' Company clung to its privileges in no spirit of compromise, whether dealing with refractory authors or provincial printers. The long-standing rivalry between the Londoners and the University stationers, which began in Elizabeth's day, continued intermittently through the reign of James I. Timperley quotes an anecdote about the learned Ussher which is said to mark the beginning of the contest between the Stationers' Company and Cambridge University about the right to print Bibles. Ussher 'one day hastening to preach at Paul's Cross, entered the shop of one of the stationers, and inquiring for a Bible of the London edition, when he came to look for his text, to his astonishment and his horror, he discovered that the verse was omitted! This gave the first occasion of complaint to the King of the insufferable negligence and incapacity of the London press'. The best known of many corrupt editions of the Scriptures published in the seventeenth century was that which has so well earned the name of the 'Wicked' Bible, making the seventh commandment read: 'Thou shalt commit adultery'. The omission of the one small but all-important word cost Robert Barker and Martin Lucas, the King's printers who issued this edition in 1631, a heavy fine, yielding a sum out of which a fount of Greek type and matrices was, at the suggestion of Charles I, bought by Archbishop Laud, and a press for the publishing of special editions in Greek established at Blackfriars. Not many books were issued as a result of this admirable plan, and the press itself does not seem to have survived the shock of the Civil Wars.

7

Charles I and the Commonwealth

The story of the book trade through the reign of Charles I is largely a record of restriction and persecution. The plague, which played havoc with the trade at the time of his accession — leaving, as in earlier outbreaks, significant gaps in the Stationers' Register — was a small matter compared with the ecclesiastical tyranny now exercised over the press. Authors and publishers, comparatively speaking, had not had much to complain about in the matter of state control during the preceding reign, but with the predominance of Laud and his party under Charles I they were harassed unmercifully. Most branches of literature were hard put to it to keep their heads above water in the new flood of theological writings, and few stationers, whether they were printers or publishers — or both — escaped a fine or imprisonment. They were not so cruelly used, however, as such authors as Alexander Leighton, the Scottish divine, who, besides being twice whipped and branded, had his ears cut off and his nose slit, and was kept in prison until the Long Parliament released him; or the more celebrated Puritan, William Prynne, whose *Histrio-Mastix*, with its attack on stage plays and acting which was supposed to cast reflections on the morals of the Court — because the Queen herself had recently taken part in a masque! — was published by Michael Sparke in 1632.

Prynne and his publisher were both thrown into prison, together with the two printers of the book, 'W.J.' (William Jones) and 'E.A.', though these last escaped further punishment. Brought up before the Star Chamber in February 1634, Prynne was sentenced to a fine of £5,000, to be degraded from the Bar, to stand in the pillory at Westminster and Cheapside, where he was to have one of his ears cropped at each place, and to be imprisoned for life. An eyewitness of his punishment in the pillory at Cheapside says that while he stood there 'they burnt his huge volumes under his nose, which had almost suffocated him'. Sparke had to pay a fine of £500 and to stand in the pillory as well, but this was the extent of his punishment, though he had incensed the authorities and suffered imprisonment for similar offences on more than one previous occasion. Three years later the irrepressible Prynne found means to publish under a pseudonym the tract, *Newes from Ipswich*, which cost him his second fine of £5,000, together with the renewed degradation of the pillory, the loss of what remained of the stumps of his ears, and, most infamous of all, the mutilation of both cheeks with the letters 'S. L.' — 'Stigmata Laudis', according to the grim humour of Prynne's own interpretation, though 'seditious' or 'scurrilous libeller' was the official meaning.

Though ostensibly printed at Ipswich, the work was produced in London, John Lilburne being found guilty in February 1637 of printing and publishing this among several seditious books. Lilburne was condemned, says Timperley, to be whipped at the cart's tail to Old Palace Yard, Westminster; then set in the pillory there for two hours; afterwards to be carried back to the Fleet there to remain until he conformed to the rules of the Court; also to pay a fine of £500 to the king; and, lastly, to give security for his good behaviour. He underwent the sentence with undismayed fortitude, uttering many bold speeches against the bishops, and dispersing pamphlets from the pillory. The Star Chamber thereupon ordered him to be gagged; but, not to be suppressed, he proceeded to stamp with his feet. His rebellious spirit earned for him the name of Freeborn John.

It was in this year of 1637 — on July 11th — that the Star Chamber, bent on repressing such obnoxious literature at all hazards, published the drastic decree concerning printing which preceded the darkest age in the history of the English book trade since Caxton set up his press at Westminster. This Act, while confirming existing ordinances, consisted of no fewer than thirty-three additional clauses, the former decrees, it states in its preamble, having 'been found by experience to be defective in some particulars: And divers abuses have sithence arisen, and beene practised by the craft and malice of wicked and evill disposed persons, to the prejudice of the publicke; and divers libellous, seditious, and mutinous bookes have beene unduly printed, and other bookes and papers without licence, to the disturbance of the peace of the Church and State'. The number of printers was reduced to twenty-three, including the King's printers and the printers allowed for the universities; all books had to be licensed according to classification — law books, by the Lord Chief Justice and the Lord Chief Baron; all books of English history or other books of State affairs, by the principal Secretaries of State; works dealing with heraldry, by the Earl Marshal; and all other books, 'whether of divinitie, phisicke, philosophie, poetrie, or whatsoever, by the Archbishop of Canterbury, the Bishop of London, or the Chancellors or Vice-Chancellors of Oxford or Cambridge University'.

Every book had still to be entered in the Stationers' Register, and to bear the name of the printer, the author and the publisher. Native printers, however, were protected by a clause which prohibited the importation of English books printed abroad, and the interests of legitimate booksellers were also studied, in Clause X, with a consideration which would be gratefully received by some members of the book trade today: 'That no haberdasher of small wares, ironmonger, chandler, shop-keeper, or any other person or persons whatsoever, not having beene seven yeares apprentice to the trade of a booksellor, printer, or book-binder, shall within the citie or suburbs of London, or in any other corporation, market-towne, or elsewhere, receive, take or buy, to barter, sell againe, change or do away, any Bibles, Testaments, Psalm-books, Primers, Abcees, Almanackes, or other booke or books whatsoever upon pain of forfeiture of all such books so received, bought or taken as aforesaid, and such other punishment of the parties so offending, as by this Court, or the said high Commission Court respectively, as the severall causes shall require, shall be thought meet' (Arber). To ensure good behaviour each of the master printers was bound in sureties of £300, and the penalties for all stationers and others who offended against this or any other decree of the kind included heavy fines, imprisonment, confiscation of stock, and such corporal punishment as a whipping at the cart's tail. One clause which caused a good deal of dissatisfaction was that which required not only first editions, but all reprints to be licensed, though in the case of reprints no fee was charged for registration, and printed copies only had to be submitted for inspection, instead of the two written copies demanded in the case of original works.

The final clause marks an early stage in the evolution of the custom, prevailing at the present day, of sending copies of all new works to the British Museum, and four or five of the leading university libraries in the United Kingdom and Ireland: 'That whereas there is an agreement betwixt Sir Thomas Bodley, Knight, Founder of the University Library at Oxford, and the Master, Wardens, and Assistants of the Company of Stationers, viz. That one Booke of every sort that is new printed, or reprinted with additions, be sent to the University of Oxford, for the use of the publicke Librarie there; the Court doth hereby Order, and declare, that every printer shall reserve one Book new printed, or reprinted by him, with additions, and shall before any publique venting of the said book, bring it to the Common Hall of the Companie of Stationers, and deliver it to the officer thereof to be sent to the Librarie at Oxford accordingly, upon paine of imprisonment, and such further Order and Direction therein, as to this Court, or the high Commission Court respectively, as the severall causes shall require, shall be thought fit' (Arber).

The formidable Decree of 1637 soon lost its effect under the gathering clouds of the Civil Wars, and when the Long Parliament abolished the Star Chamber in 1641 the Act became to all intents and purposes a dead letter. This was not at all to the liking of the Stationers' Company, which was virtually left for the time being not only powerless to act, but in serious danger of losing its privileges. The most law-abiding stationers under the old regime began to print and sell both books and pamphlets without troubling either to obtain a licence or to enter them in the Company's Register, which now shows an average of scarcely more than one entry a week. The more lawless members seized the opportunity to trade in books belonging to the monopolists. 'Within these last four years' — to quote from 'The humble Remonstrance of the Company of Stationers' to Parliament in April 1643, eight months after Charles had raised his standard at Nottingham — 'the affairs of the Presse have grown very scandalous and enormious, and all redresse is almost impossible, if power be not given by some binding order to reduce Presses and Apprentices to the proportion of those times which did precede these last four years. This is so farre from an Innovation that tis the removall of a dangerous Innovation, and without this removall, the Company of Stationers being like a feeld overpestred with too much stock, must needs grow indigent, and indigence must needs make it run into trespasses, and break out into divers unlawfull shifts; as Cattle use to do, when their pasture begins wholly to fail. Besides the same disorder which undoes Stationers by too great multitude of Presses and Apprentices among themselves, causes also Strangers, as Drapers, Carmen, and others to break in upon them, and set up Presses in divers obscure corners of the City and suburbs; so that not only the ruine of the Company is the more hastened by it, but also the mischief — which the State suffers by the irregularity of all, is the lesse remediable.'

Among other 'considerations' offered in the same document, which fills nearly five pages in Arber's great *Transcript*, is one modest paragraph of four lines pointing out the present discouragement to authors. 'Many men's Studies', it observes, 'carry no other profit or recompence with them but the benefit of their copies [copyrights]; and if this be taken away, many Pieces of great worth and excellence will be strangled in the womb, or never conceived at all for the future.'

Parliament, as well as the Stationers' Company, had already taken alarm at the manner in which authors, printers and publishers made use of their new-found freedom, and, two months after receiving this Remonstrance, a new Ordinance was passed, 'to prevent and suppress the license of printing'.

This reactionary Ordinance, inspired by the very Presbyterians who, in other days, had been loudest in protesting against the wickedness of such restraints, had scarcely been issued when Milton's offending treatise on the *Doctrine and Discipline of Divorce* was ready for publication. Milton had already treated the earlier Decree with contempt by issuing his Anti-Episcopal pamphlets without leave or licence from anyone. The new Ordinance suffered a similar fate. The idea of any censorship over books, which left the decision as to what should be published, and what suppressed, in the hands of a few men, and these—as he wrote years afterwards—mostly unlearned and of common capacity, filled him with indignation. Disregarding the new Act—knowing indeed that there was little likelihood of persuading any of the new authorities to license the work—he sent forth his divorce treatise without either official sanction or entry in the Stationers' Register. The Company at once took action against both this and another unlicensed work, but, though the matter was taken to Parliament, and referred to a Commons Committee on Printing, nothing came of it.

Milton, however, did not intend to let the matter rest there. He took his revenge in the finest piece of prose that he ever wrote, the *Areopagitica*, now one of the leading documents in the history of the liberty of the press. Seizing the bull by the horns he addressed the *Areopagitica* to Parliament itself, calling it 'A Speech for the Liberty of Unlicensed Printing'. It was published in 1644 in his own name, but unlicensed, and without the name of either printer or bookseller—a small quarto breathing throughout its forty pages the author's ennobling love of liberty—'which is the nurse of all great wits'—and letters. 'As good almost kill a man as kill a good book', he writes in a celebrated passage, which reminds us of no one so much as that earlier book-lover, good Master Richard de Bury—'Who kills a man kills a reasonable creature, God's image; but he who destroys a good book, kills reason itself, kills the image of God, as it were, in the eye. Many a man lives a burden to the earth; but a good book is the precious life-blood of a master-spirit, embalmed and treasured up on purpose to a life beyond life.' Milton proceeds to pour out his eloquence on the lessons of the past, carrying them back to ancient Rome and Athens, and reminding them that 'this authentic Spanish policy of licensing books ... was the immediate image of a Star Chamber Decree to that purpose made in those times when that Court did the rest of those her pious works, for which she is now fallen from the Stars with Lucifer ... It may be doubted', he concludes, shrewdly enough, 'there was in it the fraud of some old patentees and monopolizers in the trade of book-selling; who under pretence of the poor in their Company not to be defrauded, and the just retaining of each man his several copy (which God forbid should be gainsaid) brought divers glossing colours to the house, which were indeed but colours, and serving to no end except it be to increase a superiority over their neighbours.'

Anxious that he should not make his reputation solely as a pamphleteer, Milton, shortly after this, consented to the publication of the first collection of his poems by Humphry Moseley, who issued the edition, revised for the press by Milton himself, on January 2nd, 1646.

Moseley had his shop at the sign of the Prince's Arms, in St Paul's Churchyard, and was the one stationer above all others who stood out conspicuously at that time as a publisher of poetry and the miscellaneous class of literature, leisurely and elegant, politely known as 'belles-lettres'. When we remember how little was issued in pure literature in the troubled days of the mid-seventeenth century, his record in this respect is remarkable. 'By 1646', writes Dr Masson, 'Moseley had distinguished himself as the publisher of original editions of books, not only by Howell and Waller, but also by Milton, Davenant, Crashaw and Shirley, and moreover as the ready purchaser of whatever copyrights were in the market of poems and plays by Beaumont and Fletcher, Webster, Ludwick Carlell, Shirley, Davenant, Killigrew and other celebrities dead or living. To this group of Moseley's authors Cowley and Cartwright were soon added; and it was not long before he snapped out of the hands of duller men Denham's Poems, Carew's Poems,* various things of Sir Kenelm Digby, and every available copyright in any of the plays of Shakespeare, Massinger, Ford, Rowley, Middleton, Tourneur, or any other of the Elizabethan and Jacobean dramatists. For at least the ten years from 1644 onwards there was, I should say, no publisher in London comparable to Moseley for tact and enterprise.'

To Dr Masson's list should be added the works of Sir John Suckling, 'the darling of the Court' of Charles I, the majority of which appeared in print for the first time in the *Fragmenta Aurea*—'published by a friend to perpetuate his memory' in 1646, four years after their author's death. This volume comprised Suckling's poems, his *Letters to Divers Eminent Personages*, and three of his plays, *Brennoralt*, *The Goblins*, and *Auglaura*—the tragi-comedy which the poet had produced in folio form in 1638 with margins so wide, and text so slim, that it provoked the ridicule of the wits, who declared that the type resembled a baby lying in the great bed at Ware. His fourth and unfinished play, *The Sad One*, was published by Moseley in 1659 with a publisher's note to the reader, stating that he thought it better 'to send it into the world in the same state I found it, without the least addition, than procure it supplied by any other pen ... I could not have answer'd myself, to the world', he concludes, 'if I had suppressed this tragedy, and therefore may hope for some favour by its publication.'

English literature would have been the poorer for a good many other pieces had it not been for worthy Humphry Moseley. In the same year as that of this first edition of *The Sad One*, he published Suckling's *Last Remains*, having obtained permission to transcribe them for that purpose from the poet's sister, Lady Southcot, in whose safe

* The first edition of Carew's poems was published by Thomas Walkley, 'at the signe of the Flying Horse, between Brittains Burse, and York House', in 1640. The second edition came from the same publisher in 1642, with eight additional poems, including one by Waller. Moseley published the third edition, which appeared in 1651.

keeping they had been left. 'I could tell you', writes our publisher in his characteristic address from *The Stationer to the Reader*, 'what a thirst and general inquiry hath been after what I here present you, by all that have either seen or heard of them. And by that time you have read them, you will believe me, who have, now for many years, annually published the productions of the best wits of our own and foreign nations.'

Milton, to step back a few years, had meantime been swept into the whirlpool of politics as Latin Secretary to the newly appointed Council of State (1649), writing in the same year the best known of his official papers, *Eikonoklastes*, in reply to the famous *Eikon Basilike* of Charles I (or John Gauden, Bishop of Worcester, as seems more likely), which, appearing at the time of the King's execution, had a sale so remarkable that some fifty editions of it are said to have been exhausted in the same year. The manuscript copy of this mysterious book was not received by Richard Royston, the royal bookseller, at the Angel, in Ivy Lane, until December 23rd, 1648, and great efforts were made to issue it before the King's execution at the end of the following month. It was printed by William Dugard, headmaster of Merchant Taylors School, where he had set up a private printing press; and the work was ready, if not immediately before the day of execution (January 30th, 1649), at least immediately after, for we have it on Toland's authority that a copy was bought on January 31st. It has been suggested that had this book appeared a week sooner it might have saved the King's life. Dugard shortly afterwards printed Salmasius's *Defensio Regia*, whereupon the Council of State committed him to Newgate, turned his wife and family out of doors, seized all his printing plant, and ordered the Governors of the School to elect a new master. Subsequently Dugard made his peace with Parliament, and being reinstated at his school, and having his printing effects returned to him, he served the ruling powers with the loyalty which he had hitherto displayed for the Royalists. Among other things he printed Milton's official reply to Salmasius.

The book trade, as sensitive then as now to outside disturbance, was naturally affected during these years of strife. Most of the reading matter of the day took the form of controversial pamphlets or news-sheets, each side having its own organs, published two or three times a week in the more stirring stages of the wars.* But all pure literature, as we have shown, did not cease to issue from the press. Sir Thomas Browne,

---

* It was due to the indefatigable pains of a bookseller that we possess at this day—in the British Museum—the remarkable series formerly described as the 'King's Pamphlets', but now better known as the 'Thomason Collection'. George Thomason, who had these ephemeral publications bound into nearly 2,000 volumes, and preserved them through many vicissitudes, kept his shop at the sign of the Rose and Crown in St Paul's Churchyard. He does not seem to have prospered as a bookseller, for when he died in 1666 he is said to have been buried 'out of Stationers' Hall (a poore man)'.

forced by the pirated editions of his *Religio Medici*, which appeared in
London in 1642, from an imperfect manuscript text—for though not
intended for publication he had allowed it to be copied by one friend
after another—issued the first authorized edition in 1643. Nothing shows
the effrontery of these crafty publishers of the seventeenth century
better than the circumstances surrounding the publication of the
Religio Medici. The publisher in question was Andrew Crooke, who was
no mere pirate in a small way of business, but one of the principal
members of the Stationers' Company. Coming into possession of a manuscript copy of the *Religio Medici*, he published two unauthorized and
anonymous editions in 1642, and only communicated with the author
to inform him that Sir Kenelm Digby was writing animadversions on
the work. Thereupon Sir Thomas Browne wrote to Digby the letter
which is now printed with the *Religio Medici*, and, notwithstanding
Crooke's behaviour in the earlier editions, supplied him with the
revised text for the authorized version. This appeared in the spring
of 1643, Crooke being quite ready to announce it as 'a true and full
copy of that which was most imperfectly and surreptitiously printed
before'.

'This piece', writes Sir Thomas, in his prefatory letter to Digby,
'contrived in my private study, and as an exercise unto myself, rather
than excitation for any other, having past from my hand under a broken
and imperfect copy, by frequent transcription it still runs forward into
corruption, and after the addition of some things, omission of others,
and transposition of many, without my assent or privacy the liberty of
these times committed it unto the press; whence it issued so disguised,
the author without distinction could not acknowledge it.' Common
justice compels us to perpetuate the name of the pirate who had thus
forced Sir Thomas's hand; and let us not be unthankful that the *Religio
Medici* has come down to us even by such dubious means as those employed by the barefaced Crooke.

Other famous works continued to make their appearance in spite of
the storm and stress of national affairs. We have already referred to
several of the authors who issued their best, if not their all, during the
period covered by the Civil War, the Commonwealth and the Pro-
tectorate. To these may be added Thomas Hobbes, who published his
Leviathan in the summer of 1651; Jeremy Taylor, who wrote and issued
his best work before the Restoration; Sir William Dugdale, the first
handsome folio of whose *Monasticon Anglicanum* came from the press of
Richard Hodgkinson in 1655; Brian Walton, whose great Polyglot
Bible (1657) is the finest monument we possess of seventeenth-century
printing, and the second English book to be published by subscription;
and Izaak Walton, whose *Compleat Angler* made its first appearance in
1653, the year in which Oliver Cromwell was first installed Protector

of the Commonwealth. The following advertisement has been preserved of the first edition of *The Compleat Angler*:

> There is published a Booke of Eighteen-pence, called the Compleat Angler, or the Contemplative man's Recreation; being a Discourse on Fish and Fishing. Not unworthy the perusal of most anglers. Sold by Richard Marriot in St Dunstan's Churchyard, Flete-street.

Gentle Izaak Walton, a quiet man and a follower of peace, 'as most anglers are', was sixty when this advertisement appeared. He had long since retired from Fleet Street, and the noisy neighbourhood of St Dunstan's, where once he had carried on his business as a linen-draper, in the close friendship of Dr Donne, vicar of the parish, as well as Dean of St Paul's, whose life he had written thirteen years before. He lived long enough to see his *Compleat Angler*, 'this Booke of Eighteen-pence'— a single copy of which now realizes over £1,000—run into four editions.

It was Richard Marriot of St Dunstan's Churchyard, appropriately enough, who published the first separate edition of Walton's life of Donne—originally written as a preface to the first folio of the poet-dean's *Sermons* (1640)—and who subsequently reissued it in the first collection of Walton's *Lives* (1670), which ran into its fourth edition in the next five years. The earliest surviving edition of Donne's poems* was issued from the same shop in St Dunstan's Churchyard in 1633, by John Marriot, presumably Richard's father, who published there until 1640. Strong efforts were made by Donne's son to suppress this edition, as well as a similar volume of Donne's *Juvenilia*—both posthumous productions—on account of the looser pieces of the poet's youth, which scandalized not a few of the great dean's ardent admirers. In a letter to the Archbishop of Canterbury dated December 16th, 1637, John Donne the younger begs him to take the matter in hand, and punish the publishers for daring to issue poems which he protests were none of his father's. 'Of which abuses', he writes, 'they have been often warned by your petitioner, and tolde that if they desisted not they should be proceeded against before your Grace, which they seem so much to slight, that they professe soddainly to publish new impressions, verie much to the greife of your petitioner,—and the discredite of ye memorie of his Father.'†

Had John Donne the younger not been the hateful man that he was— and his clerical cloth made him the more despicable—it is obvious that

---

* In a letter to his friend Sir Henry Goodere, written towards the close of 1614, Donne mentioned that he was about to issue a small private edition of poems—'not for much public view', as he expresses it, 'but at mine own cost'. Unfortunately no copy of this edition can now be traced.

† Published by Dr Grosart for the first time in his edition of Donne's poems in the Fuller Worthies' Library, 1873.

a good deal might be said from his point of view regarding this disreputable business. Donne's son, though admitted to holy orders about this time, was already notorious for his profligate habits, and his character never seems to have possessed a single redeeming feature. The hypocrisy of his 'greife' is apparent when we find him issuing through Henry Herringman in 1669 not only all the pieces complained of in Marriot's edition of his father's poems, but 'divers copies under his own hand never before printed', including a number of contributions which the dean must have repented of in his virtuous old age as sincerely as of anything else that he wrote in his unregenerate youth. John Donne the younger probably came to some mercenary arrangement with the original publishers of the poems, for, within a year or two of his letter to the Archbishop, Marriot came out with an edition practically identical with that which he had published before. Donne's son showed himself in his true colours in 1653, when he reprinted a translation of his father's *Conclave Ignatii* as a newly discovered work of the dean's, and recently translated by Jasper Maine, though he himself had suppressed an edition of exactly the same English version which had been published nineteen years before. He left manuscripts of his own which, from all accounts, are unspeakably obscene, and succeeded in publishing one volume of his indecencies only six months before his death in 1662.

8

The Restoration and the Revolution

The Restoration not only brought a renewal of the censorship, but introduced to the book trade the indefatigable Roger L'Estrange, who, not content with disturbing every individual connected with the press, had designs on the Stationers' Company itself. The Licensing Act of 1662, in which the Royal prerogative was strongly reasserted, was a crushing blow to the administrative powers of the Company, whose interests were practically ignored by it, a new office being created in the following year under the title of 'Surveyor of the Imprimery and Printing Presses'. The number of printers at work in London, which had then grown to sixty, was again reduced to twenty, and most of the clauses of the Star Chamber decree of 1627 were reinforced. The new Act and its administration were hotly debated, and led, among other things, to a petition from the Stationers' Company to the effect that their ancient privilege of controlling unruly members and searching for unlicensed books might be restored to them.

Roger L'Estrange was appointed to inquire into the whole matter. On June 3rd, 1663, he published his *Considerations and Proposals in order to the Regulation of the Press*, addressed to Charles II — a long-winded document full of immoderate denunciations of the Stationers, 'for they are the principal authors of those mischiefs which they pretend now to redress, and the very persons against whom the penalties of this intended regulation are chiefly levelled'. The same arguments, he maintained, held good against the printers, between whom and the stationers a distinct line was now drawn. 'To conclude,' he added, 'both printers and stationers, under colour of offering a service to the publique, do effectually but design one upon another. The printers would beat down the bookselling trade by managing the press as themselves please, and by working upon their own copies. The stationers, on the other side, they would subject the printers to be absolutely their slaves; which they have effected in a large measure already, by so encreasing the number, that the one half must either play the knave or starve.' This tribute to the triumph of the stationer, or bookseller, over the printer, who, in the earliest days of the press, had matters much his own way, corroborates the older statements of Christopher Barker and George Wither and explains the abortive attempt made by eleven of the leading London printers either in 1660 or 1661 to found a new company, independent of the Stationers, to look after their own special interests. Evelyn will be found to bear later and similar testimony on p. 109. L'Estrange was not content with the ordinary penalties which he found available for inflicting upon his offenders, such as death, mutilation, the pillory, stocks, whipping, carting, stigmatizing, 'standing under the gallows with a rope about the neck at a publique execution', and a sufficient variety of other punishments, one would have thought, even for a man of his catholic taste. He had, however, a great idea of making the punishment fit the crime; or making the penalty, as he expresses it, 'bear proportion to the malice'. So, with a sort of Gilbertian ingenuity, he proceeded to draw up a list of suggestions:

> In some cases, they may be condemn'd to wear some visible badge, or mark of ignominy, as a halter instead of a hatband, one stocking blew and another red; a blew bonnet with a red T or S upon it, to denote the crime to be either treason or sedition: and if at any time the person so condemned shall be found without the said badge or marque during the time of his obligation to wear it, let him incurre some further penalty, provided only that if within the said time he shall discover and seize, or cause to be seized, any author, printer, or stationer, liable at the time of that discovery and seizure, to be proceeded against for the matter of treasonous or seditious pamphlets, the offender aforesaid shall, from the time of that discovery, be discharged from wearing it any longer.

L'Estrange agreed that these proposals might seem 'phantastique', but there are many men, he shrewdly added, 'who had rather suffer any other punishment than be made publiquely ridiculous'. L'Estrange was obviously too good a man to be wasted; besides, his unflinching loyalty to the King in the darkest days of his exile had long cried out for adequate recompense; so on August 15th, 1663, he was appointed to succeed Sir John Birkenhead as 'Surveyor of the Imprimery', with similar police powers to those previously held by the Stationers' Company. In addition he was one of the licensers of the press, and had the sole privilege of printing and publishing anything in the shape of a newspaper or public advertisement. Until the outbreak of the Plague, when it was mercifully allowed to lapse, the new Act, under L'Estrange, was more rigorously enforced than the short-lived Star Chamber decree of 1637.

The energetic Surveyor took to making midnight raids on printing houses, and had not been many months in office before he caused the arrest and execution of John Twyn—he was hanged, drawn and quartered—for printing a pamphlet entitled *A Treatise on the Execution of Justice*, described as 'a seditious, scandalous, and poisonous book', and alleged to form part of a plot against the king's life and government.

This was not, however, as some one has stated, 'the first time in English history' that 'a printer suffered the penalty of death for the liberty of the press', for William Carter, as we have shown, was done to death in the same horrible way eighty years before, in Elizabeth's reign.

Worse disasters fell upon the book trade than the appointment of Roger L'Estrange. The Plague of 1665 ruthlessly thinned the ranks of all classes of stationers, and with the withdrawal of the Court to Oxford,* and the wholesale flight of the citizens, the trade was brought practically to a standstill. Then, in the following year, came the more sweeping disaster of the Great Fire, which, in addition to other bookselling quarters, wiped out the very centre of the trade in St Paul's Church-yard. Here the booksellers lost an immense stock of books, which they had stored for safety in the vaults of the church. 'I hear', says Pepys, on September 26th of this year, 'the great loss of books in St Paul's Church-yarde, and at their Hall also, which they value at about £150,000; some booksellers being wholly undone, and among others, they say, my poor Kirton' — Joseph Kirton being the bookseller in St Paul's Churchyard of whom we hear a good deal in the course of Pepys's Diary.† Later he learnt that poor Kirton was 'utterly undone, and made £2,000 or £3,000 worse than nothing, from being worth £7,000 or £8,000'. All the great booksellers, he was told, had been similarly ruined; 'not only these, but their warehouses at their Hall, and under Christ Church, and elsewhere, being all burned. A great want there will be of books', he adds, 'specially Latin books and foreign books; and, among others, the Polyglottes‡ and new Bible, which he believes will be presently worth £40 a-piece.' Evelyn expresses the same fear in a letter to the Earl of Clarendon, not long before the Lord Chancellor's downfall.

> Since the late deplorable conflagration [he writes], in which the stationers have been exceedingly ruined, there is like to be an extraordinary penury and scarcity of classic authors, etc., used in our grammar schools; so that of necessity they must suddenly be reprinted. My Lord may please to understand that our booksellers follow their own judgment in printing the antient authors accord-ing to such text as they found extant when first they entered their

* It was during this stay at Oxford that Arlington, the Lord Chamberlain, licensed the publication of the *Oxford Gazette*, notwithstanding the exclusive privilege held by L'Estrange, who now had two similar sheets running in London—the *Intelligencer*, published on Mondays, and the *News*, which appeared on Thursdays. The Oxford rival was produced bi-weekly and reprinted in London, where, upon the King's return to his capital, it became the *London Gazette*, effectually silencing L'Estrange's publication, and continuing its useful existence down to the present day.

† The Diaries of both Pepys and Evelyn remained in manuscript until the nineteenth century, when they made their first appearance in print within seven years of each other —Evelyn's in 1818, and Pepys's in 1825. Henry Colburn was the publisher in each case.

‡ Walton's Polyglot Bible, referred to on p. 103.

copy, whereas out of MSS collated by the industry of later critics, those authors are exceedingly improved ... The cause of this is principally the stationer driving as hard and cruel a bargain with the printer as he can; and the printer, taking up any smatterer in the tongues, to be the lesse losser; an exactness in this in no wayes importing the stipulation; by which meanes errors repeate and multiply in every edition, and that most notoriously in some most necessary schole-bookes of value, which they obtrude upon the buyer, unless men will be at unreasonable rates for forraine editions. Your Lordship does by this perceive the mischievous effects of this avarice and negligence in them.

Evelyn then considers what might be done to remedy this condition of things. First, he suggests an inspection as to what texts of the Greek and Latin authors should be followed in future editions. Secondly, that a censor be established to see that all printers are adequately provided with able correctors of the press. Thirdly, that the whole cost be borne by the Stationers' Company. He considers the time ripe for such a move, for 'this sad calamity has mortified a Company which was exceedingly haughty and difficult to manage to any usefull reformation'.

If the stationers needed any chastening—and no doubt many of them did—they had surely had their full share of it during the last two years. Apart from their private sufferings they had experienced a grievous loss in the destruction of their Hall, with their original Charter and other irrecoverable treasures. Most fortunately the registers escaped. This was the third hall owned by London stationers, for they appear to have possessed a home of their own, as an ordinary Brotherhood, somewhere in or near Milk Street before their incorporation in Mary's reign. 'The supposed site of the first hall', writes C. R. Rivington, in his brief but useful *Records*, 'is still in the possession of the Company.' The second hall, to which a move was made some time before 1570, was probably on the south side of St Paul's Churchyard, but this was leased in 1606 to a vintner who turned it into a tavern. Five years later the partners in the English Stock bought Abergavenny House, lying back between Amen Corner and Ave Maria Lane, and converted it into a hall for the Company's use. When it had to be rebuilt in 1654, being then hopelessly out of repair, the Company settled the cost by the sale of Foxe's *Book of Martyrs*, the copyright of which had come into its possession many years before, and was still of very great value. It was not, however, until 1670 that the Stationers appointed a Committee to rebuild the hall, and four years later we hear of Stephen College—the 'Protestant Joiner' afterwards executed at Oxford—being commissioned to wainscot the new building for the sum of £300.

It was in March of the year following the Great Fire—which burnt his own birthplace—that Milton, who had long since resigned his political hopes, and settled down to his life-work as a poet, signed the celebrated agreement with Samuel Simmons for the publication of *Paradise Lost*. His old publisher, Humphry Moseley, had died six years before, and the struggle for supremacy in the trade thereafter rested with Richard Marriot (or Marriott), whom we have already seen in St Dunstan's Churchyard, and Henry Herringman, who had a share in the Third Folio Shakespeare, and issued the first authorized edition of Waller's poems, one or two of Milton's early pamphlets, the three obituary panegyrics on Oliver Cromwell by Marvell, Dryden and Sprat, first editions of Cowley and Denham, and many other works of the kind. Dr Masson, who made a special study of the book trade in Milton's day, writes:

On the whole, at the time of Moseley's death, while the advantage was with Herringman, Marriot's chances were considerable; and the publication from his shop of the first part of *Hudibras* in 1662 was another incident in his favour. Somehow he could not follow up that success. The second part of *Hudibras*, a year after the first, was not published by him, but by Martin and Allestree; and though he published the poems of Katherine Philips instead, that was a poor substitute. Meanwhile, Herringman had been gaining ground remarkably. Already in possession of Davenant, Lord Orrey, Sir Robert Howard, and Dryden, he had brought round him also Cowley and Boyle, having published the essays of both in 1661, and a volume of Cowley's poems in 1663. In April 1664 he acquired the copyright of all Waller's poetry; and from that time his super-iority to Marriot, and his title to be regarded as Moseley's successor in the primacy of the book trade, admitted of no dispute. He was to publish more and more for Waller, Howard, Dryden, and other poets and dramatists; the scientific connection he had won through Boyle drew round him the chiefs of the Royal Society as well as the wits of the Court; *Hudibras* and the poems of Katherine Philips were to be his when he chose; and, whenever any stock of old plays and poems was in the market, and especially when Anne Moseley, withdrawing from business, wished to dispose of any of her late husband's copyrights in such things, who so ready to pur-chase as Herringman? In fact Herringman and his shop are one of the most vivid traditions of the Restoration. The shop was 'at the sign of the Blue Anchor in the Lower Walk of the New Ex-change', this New Exchange, so called to distinguish it from the Old Exchange in the city, being on the south side of the Strand, on the site of the present Adelphi [which was demolished in the

1930s]. Any time before the Great Plague and the Great Fire, but perhaps more distinctly after those events than before, this shop of Herringman's was the chief literary lounging-place in London.

Samuel Simmons, whose address was 'next door to the Golden Lion in Aldersgate Street', was practically a beginner, without any record or distinction behind him, but it is probable that he was a son of the late Matthew Simmons, of the same address, who had published Milton's *Eikonoklastes*, as well as several of his earlier tracts, and had become official printer to the Commonwealth during the first year of Milton's secretaryship. *Paradise Lost* may have gone to Samuel Simmons, therefore, for old associations' sake. The agreement itself is printed by Masson, as follows. There were, of course, as he points out, two copies, and it is the copy signed for Milton by proxy, and kept by Simmons, that has been preserved:

These Presents, made the 27th day of Aprill 1667, Betweene John Milton, gent., of thone ptie, and Samuel Symons, Printer, of thother ptie, Wittness:—That the said John Milton, in consideration of five pounds to him now paid by the said Samm$^{ll.}$ Symons and other the considerations herein mentioned, hath given, granted, and assigned, and by these pnts doth give, grant, and assigne, unto the said Samm$^{ll.}$ Symons, his executors and assignes, All that Booke, Copy, or Manuscript of a Poem intituled Paradise Lost, or by whatsoever other title or name the same is or shalbe called or distinguished, now lately Licensed to be printed, Together with the full benefitt, profitt, and advantage thereof, or w$^{h.}$ shall or may arise thereby. And the said John Milton, for him, his ex$^{rs.}$ and ad$^{s.}$, doth covenant with the said Sam$^{ll.}$ Symons, his ex$^{rs.}$ and ass$^{ns.}$, That hee and they shall at all tymes hereafter have, hold, and enjoy the same, and all Impressions thereof accordingly, without the lett or hinderance of him, the said John Milton, his ex$^{rs.}$ or ass$^{ns.}$, or any pson or psons by his or their consent or privitie, And that the said Jo. Milton, his ex$^{rs.}$ or ad$^{s.}$ or any other by his or their meanes or consent, shall not print or cause to be printed, or sell, dispose, or publish, the said Booke or Manuscript, or any other Booke or Manuscript of the same tenor or subject, without the consent of the said Sam$^{ll.}$ Symons, his ex$^{rs.}$ and ass$^{ns.}$. In consideracion whereof, the said Sam$^{ll.}$ Symons, for him, his ex$^{rs.}$ and ad$^{s.}$, doth covenant with the said John Milton, his ex$^{rs.}$ and ad$^{s.}$, the sum of five pounds of lawfull english money at the end of the first Impression which the said Sam$^{ll.}$ Symons, his ex$^{rs.}$ or ass$^{ns.}$, shall make and publish of the said Copy or Manuscript; Which impression shalbe accounted to be ended when thirteene hundred

Books of the said whole Copy or Manuscript imprinted shalbe sold and retaild off to pticular reading Customers; And shall also pay other five pounds unto the said Mr. Milton, or his ass[ns]., at the end of the second Impression, to be accounted as aforesaid; And five pounds more at the end of the third Impression, to be in like manner accounted; And that the said three first Impressions shall not exceed fifteene hundred Books or volumes of the said whole Copy or Manuscript a peice: And further, That he the said Samuel Symons, and his ex[rs]., ad[s]., and ass[ns]., shalbe ready to make oath before a Master in Chancery concerning his or their knowledge and beleife of or concerning the truth of the disposing and selling the said Books by Retail, as aforesaid, whereby the said Mr. Milton is to be intitled to his said money from time to time, upon every reasonable request in that behalfe, or in default thereof shall pay the said five pounds agreed to be paid upon each Impression, as aforesaid, as if the same were due, and for and in lieu thereof. — In witness whereof the said pties have to this writing indented interchangeably sett their hands and seales, the day and year first abovewritten.

JOHN MILTON

Sealed and delivered in the
    presence of us,
       JOHN FISHER,
       BENIAMIN GREENE, ser[t.] to Mr Milton.*

On the face of it, it seems an iniquitous bargain that Milton should receive for such a stupendous achievement as *Paradise Lost* the miserable sum of £5 down, with the promise of a further £5 when the first edition was exhausted, and two similar sums at the end of the second and third editions, if called for. But a number of not unimportant points must be remembered before passing judgment on the publisher. In 1667 £5 would be equal to about £110 in our present money, and as Milton

---

* 'The original [writes Masson] is in the British Museum, having been presented to that collection in 1852 by Samuel Rogers, the poet, who had purchased it in 1831, for a hundred guineas, from Mr. Pickering, the publisher. It had come down in the possession of the famous publishing family of the Tonsons, who had acquired part copyright of *Paradise Lost* in 1683 and the whole before 1691, and had thus got into their hands this evidence of the original sale. Notwithstanding the vague history of the document between 1767 and 1824, there is not the least doubt as to its genuineness. It is the actual copy of the agreement as kept by Simmons. But there has been a general mistake as to the signature. The poet Rogers, who was proud of the relic, never doubted, when he showed it to his friends, that the signature was Milton's own; most of those who now look at the relic in the British Museum never doubt it. Most certainly, however, the signature is not Milton's own, but a signature written for him by someone else, and certified by the touch of Milton's finger and by the annexed Milton family seal of the Spread Eagle. This might have occurred to anyone on reflecting that Milton in 1667 had been fifteen years totally blind.'

himself received one further sum of £5, for a second edition was already
demanded by the spring of 1669, his returns, in present-day reckoning,
would amount to about £220. In 1680, six years after the poet's death,
his widow resigned the full copyright to Simmons for a third and
final payment of £8—equal now to some £176, so that the publisher
paid for *Paradise Lost* sums which, all told, would amount at the present
time approximately to £396; still wretchedly inadequate, but hardly
warranting all the abuse that has been heaped on the publisher's head
by succeeding generations of authors. It must not be forgotten, too, that
when Milton ventured from his retirement with *Paradise Lost*, he was
not exactly every publisher's choice. His name still stank in the nostrils
of the Royalists as that of a hated Republican, and author of *Eikonoklastes*. If he had been mentioned at all since the Restoration it was but
as 'that serpent Milton', or in an expression of regret that he had not
been either hanged with the regicides or at least sent with some of them
to lifelong imprisonment.

It is not impossible that he took *Paradise Lost* to Herringman, who,
like Simmons, had escaped the fire, or some other leading publisher,
and could only find Simmons willing to take the risk. Simmons, as it
happened, made by *Paradise Lost*, according to Dr Masson's calculation,
about five or six times as much as he paid its author—a vastly disproportionate return, it is true, but he seems to have worked uncommonly hard, and with striking success, to get the book firmly established.
At least nine successive bindings, and a curious variety of title-pages,
were issued before the first edition was exhausted, the publisher's plan,
to judge from the number of booksellers who figure as his agents in the
various imprints, being to scatter the edition as widely over the town
as possible.

Simmons does not seem to have been at all anxious to keep the
copyright of *Paradise Lost*, for at the end of 1680, or early in 1681, he
sold it for £25 to Brabazon Aylmer, 'at the sign of the Three Pigeons
in Cornhill'. How it would have fared had the copyright remained in
Aylmer's possession it is idle now to speculate, but, as it happened,
before the work was reprinted, it fell into the hands of Jacob Tonson,
who had just started in business, and was soon to become, in Masson's
phrase, 'the third man after Humphry Moseley and Henry Herringman
in the true apostolic succession of London publishers'.

The great Tonson deserves a whole chapter to himself, but to follow
him alone through his long career would spoil the structure of our
narrative. He must take his place therefore with the rest of his craft: a
young man as we see him at first, following the example of his brother
Richard, who, like Jacob, had been left £100 by his father. Richard
had opened a bookshop in 1676 within Gray's Inn Gate, where, among
other things, he had already published Otway's *Don Carlos*. Jacob

started business in 1678 at the Judge's Head, in Chancery Lane, where he too became one of Otway's booksellers, as well as one of Nahum Tate's. More ambitious than his brother, Jacob began to cast his net for Dryden, now Poet Laureate. Dryden was one of Herringman's authors, but Tonson had not been in business two years before he succeeded in tempting him with £20 for his play, *Troilus and Cressida; or, Truth Found Too Late*, which he published in 1679, sharing the venture with another bookseller of the name of Abel Swalle. A few years later came the half-share in *Paradise Lost*, which he bought from Brabazon Aylmer on August 17th, 1683, paying more for it than Aylmer had given to Simmons for the whole copyright some three years previously. It was not, however, until 1688 that Tonson first turned this investment to profitable account by issuing his handsome folio edition of the work with Dryden's well-known lines engraved beneath the portrait of Milton. This edition was published by subscription, and proved so successful that Tonson did not hesitate, in 1690–91, to buy 'at an advanced price' the second half of the copyright, subsequently acquiring the rest of Milton's poetry—or at least the leading share in it—from other publishers. According to Spence, Jacob admitted on one occasion that *Paradise Lost* brought him in more money than any other poem that he published.

Meanwhile Dryden and Tonson had been associated in other great works—not always, unhappily, in the friendliest spirit. 'He was the bookseller to the famous Dryden', says John Dunton in 1705, 'and is himself a very good judge of persons and authors; and as there is nobody more competently qualified to give their opinion upon one another, so there is none who does it with a more severe exactness, or with less partiality; for, to do Mr Tonson justice, he speaks his mind upon all occasions, and will flatter nobody.' We need not take this estimate of Tonsonian candour too literally. His letters to Dryden at the time of their disputes are more often in the nature of soft answers endeavouring to turn away wrath. The truth is that great changes were taking place in the book trade, and no one was quicker than Tonson to recognize, among other signs, that professional writers with a popular following were becoming a power to be reckoned with. This had been due largely to that omnipotent person the general reader, who, slowly but surely, had been altering the literary outlook. Books which hitherto had been regarded as appealing only to the leisured and cultured classes had a wider audience. Authors, as well as publishers, now looked for a proportionate addition to their profits. How rapidly things were changing in this respect may be seen in the difference between Milton's original £5 for *Paradise Lost*, and the £1,200 which Dryden, in the next generation, is said by Pope to have received, all told, for his *Virgil*, or the two hundred and fifty guineas which Tonson paid the same poet for the first edition of his *Fables*, with an engagement to bring that sum up to £300 on sending the book to a second edition.*

Dryden realized as soon as anyone the altered state of the literary market, and needed no Society of Authors to look after his interests. He had some of the contempt for the booksellers which characterized the old Court poets, but none of their delicate scruples about accepting money from the trade. 'Some kind of intercourse must be carried on betwixt us', he wrote tartly during one of his little differences with Tonson, 'while I am translating Virgil. Therefore I give you notice that I have done the seventh Aeneid in the country; and intend, some few days hence, to go upon the eighth; when that is finished, I expect fifty pounds in good silver; not such as I have had formerly. I am not obliged to take gold, neither will I; nor stay for it beyond four-and-twenty hours after it is due ... I told Mr Congreve that I knew you too well to believe you meant me any kindness.'

Debased coinage was the cause of much of the trouble between Tonson and his angry poet, who either could not or would not realize that Tonson, like everybody else, was suffering from the same cause. 'These complaints and demands', as Macaulay justly says, 'which have been preserved from destruction only by the eminence of the writer,

* The memorials of this transaction, given by Dr Johnson in his life of the poet, are to the following effect:

'I do hereby promise to pay John Dryden, Esq., or order, on the 25th of March 1699, the sum of two hundred and fifty guineas, in consideration of ten thousand verses, which the said John Dryden, Esq., is to deliver to me, Jacob Tonson, when finished, whereof seven thousand five hundred verses, more or less, are already in the said Jacob Tonson's possession. And I do hereby farther promise and engage myself, to make up the said sum of two hundred and fifty guineas three hundred pounds sterling to the said John Dryden, Esq., his executors, administrators, or assigns, at the beginning of the second impression of the said ten thousand verses.

'In witness whereof I have hereunto set my hand and seal, this 20th day of March, 169$\frac{8}{9}$.

'JACOB TONSON

'Sealed and delivered, being
first duly stampt, pursuant
to the acts of parliament for
that purpose, in the presence
of
          'BEN PORTLOCK'
          'WILL CONGREVE'

'*March* 24, 1698.

'Received then of Mr Jacob Tonson the sum of two hundred sixty-eight pounds fifteen shillings, in pursuance of an agreement for ten thousand verses, to be delivered by me to the said Jacob Tonson, whereof I have already delivered to him about seven thousand five hundred, more or less; he the said Jacob Tonson being obliged to make up the foresaid sum of two hundred and sixty-eight pounds fifteen shillings three hundred pounds, at the beginning of the second impression of the foresaid ten thousand verses;

'I say, received by me,
          'JOHN DRYDEN

'Witness, CHARLES DRYDEN'

Dryden's death in May 1700, only six months after the first publication of the *Fables*, robbed him of the supplementary sum. The second edition was not published until 1713.

are doubtless merely a fair example of the correspondence which filled all the mail-bags of England for several months.' In justice to Dryden it is only fair to add that when he wrote in this strain to his publisher he had been deprived by the Revolution of his post as laureate and historiographer, and was now mainly dependent for his income upon what he could earn by his works. 'The inevitable consequence of poverty', says Dr Johnson in his life of Dryden, 'is dependence. Dryden had probably no recourse in his exigences but to his bookseller. The particular character of Tonson I do not know; but the general conduct of traders was much less liberal in those times than in our own; their views were narrower, and their manners grosser. To the mercantile ruggedness of that race, the delicacy of the poet was sometimes exposed. Lord Bolingbroke, who in his youth had cultivated poetry, related to Dr King of Oxford that one day, when he visited Dryden, they heard, as they were conversing, another person entering the house, "This", said Dryden, "is Tonson. You will take care not to depart before he goes away; for I have not completed the sheet which I promised him; and, if you leave me unprotected, I must suffer all the rudeness to which his resentment can prompt his tongue."'

There is no trace of this alleged rudeness in any of the surviving correspondence between Dryden and his publisher; the boot is rather on the other foot. The letters begin hopefully enough in 1684 with the poet's acknowledgment of two melons which had been sent as a present from the publisher, and end with the final reconciliation in 1697, when he thanks him 'heartily for the sherry', and, in another note, hopes that his *Ode for St Cecilia's Day* has done him service, 'and will do more'.

Dryden apparently decided to make the best of what he regarded as inevitably a bad job. 'Upon trial', he told him a few months later, 'I find all of your trade are sharpers, and you not more than others; therefore I have not wholly left you.' In his life of the poet, Sir Walter Scott has some pertinent remarks to make not only on the subject of these disputes with Tonson, but also on the whole eternal question of the pecuniary rewards of authorship:

Whatever occasional subjects of dissension arose between Dryden and his bookseller, mutual interest, the strongest of ties, appears always to have brought them together, after the first ebullition of displeasure had subsided. There might, on such occasions, be room for acknowledging faults on both sides; for, if we admit that the bookseller was penurious and churlish, we cannot deny that Dryden seems often to have been abundantly captious and irascible. Indeed, as the poet placed, and justly, more than a mercantile value upon what he sold, the trader, on his part, was necessarily cautious not to afford a price which his returns could not pay; so that while, in one point of view, the author sold at an inadequate price, the purchaser, in another, really got no more than value for his money. That literature is ill recompensed, is generally rather the fault of the public than the bookseller, whose trade can only exist by buying that which can be sold to advantage. The bookseller, who purchased the *Paradise Lost* for ten pounds, had probably no very good bargain.

Tonson, like all of us, had his failings, but he did yeoman service in helping to develop a popular literary taste. His liberality to his leading authors, notwithstanding Dryden's grievances, fairly entitles him to be regarded as our first Prince of Publishers. Apart from his own authors, he not only introduced Milton to a far larger public than he had ever known before, but, with Rowe's octavo edition in seven volumes (1709), was practically the first to open Shakespeare to the general reader, the four folio editions, apart from their expense, having already become scarce. Jacob had moved to the sign of the Shakespeare's Head in Gray's Inn Gate—probably his late brother's shop—when he published Rowe's edition, but before following him there, and entering upon the Golden Age of Bookselling, as some one has called the eighteenth century, it is necessary to gather up a few of the remaining threads of seventeenth-century history.

John Bunyan and his publishers take us back to the early days of Roger L'Estrange's surveyorship. More than one of Bunyan's booksellers, as well as the author himself, was unpleasantly familiar with the prison-house. Francis Smith, who published his earlier works at the sign of the Elephant and Castle, near Temple Bar, fell into official disfavour from the very beginning of the Restoration. He was known as Anabaptist, *alias* 'Elephant Smith', and became quite accustomed to having his house searched, and his windows smashed. Dr John Brown, in his exhaustive life of Bunyan, tells us that in 1660—the very year of Charles II's proclamation—'Elephant Smith' was three times a prisoner for publishing a little book entitled *The Lord's Loud Call to England*, and similar productions, being kept, apparently, in the hands of the King's Messengers at a noble a day, the total cost amounting to £50. In August of the following year Smith and piles of his books were seized. Smith was taken to the Gate-house Prison for 'having a hand in printing and compiling dangerous Books'—which surely were not so very dangerous, remarks Dr Brown, seeing that those who carried them off straightway sold the sheets to the trade again, and put the money into their own pockets.

During the imprisonment, he recorded, 'I was locked up in a room where I had neither chair nor stool to rest upon, and yet ten shillings per week must be the price, and before I had been there three nights

£7 15s. was demanded for present fees. That is to say, £5 to excuse me for wearing irons, ten shillings for my entrance-week lodging, five shillings for sheets, five shillings for garnish money, and the rest for Turnkey's fees.' Elsewhere he describes how he fell into the toils of L'Estrange and his men, evidently being a marked man. Brown suggests that it was because this shop was no longer safe that Bunyan changed his publisher, for until *Grace Abounding* was issued by George Larkin in 1666 all his prison books were published by 'Elephant Smith'. The *Pilgrim's Progress* came from yet another publisher—Nathaniel Ponder, whose shop was then in the Poultry, at the sign of the Peacock. Ponder published for John Owen, the great Nonconformist theologian, who had helped to secure Bunyan's final release from prison. It was probably on this account that *Pilgrim's Progress* obtained its introduction to its publisher, who, after its successful production, became known among his brother craftsmen as 'Bunyan Ponder'. He was an agreeable man to have dealings with. 'He has', says Dunton, 'sweetness and enterprise in his air which plead and anticipate in his favour.' Notwithstanding his pleasant manner, however, 'Bunyan Ponder', like 'Elephant Smith', had in the previous year found his way to the Gate-house Prison, as may be seen from the Privy Council Minutes, where there is the following record: '1676. At the Court at Whitehall, May 10th (the King present), a warrant was issued to commit Nathaniel Ponder to the Gate-house, for carrying to the presse to be printed an unlicensed Pamphlet tending to Sedition and Defamation of the Christian Religion.'

Ponder, however, had in his composition little of the stuff of which martyrs are made, for we find another entry on the 26th of the same month to the effect that: 'Nathaniel Ponder, Stationer, was discharged upon his humble petition, setting forth his hearty sorrow for his offence, and promising never to offend in like manner.' He also had to pay his prison fees and enter into a bond of £500 as surety for his good behaviour. Ponder entered *Pilgrim's Progress* in the Stationers' Register as his copy on December 22nd, 1677, and published it early in the following year, 'price bound 1s. 6d.' The book met with a success which surprised no one more than Bunyan himself, three editions being called for within the first twelve months. Bunyan took the opportunity with each of these reprints to make several notable additions, and was encouraged by their continued popularity to venture upon the second part, which came from the same publisher early in 1685, bearing on the reverse of the title-page the significant warning: 'I appoint Mr Nathaniel Ponder, but no other, to Print this Book. John Bunyan.' It was necessary to print this, for spurious books were already in circulation purporting to be *The Second Part of the Pilgrim's Progress*, one by a writer who signed himself T. S., and closely resembling the original book in shape and type, coming from a John Malthus, whose shop, at the sign of the Sun, was actually in the same thoroughfare as Ponder's—the Poultry. Eleven editions of the *Pilgrim's Progress* were published altogether during the author's lifetime, all by Nathaniel Ponder, though after Bunyan's death in 1688 his name disappears from the imprint until the fifteenth edition of 1695, when he makes his final appearance as the *Pilgrim's* publisher.

Before Bunyan first walked into his shop with the manuscript of the *Pilgrim's Progress*, Ponder had numbered Andrew Marvell among his authors. That was in the earlier 'seventies, when he displayed his sign of the Peacock in Chancery Lane. Whether he published any of Marvell's political poems cannot now be said, for most of these, appearing probably as broadsides or pamphlets immediately they were written, have long since disappeared in their original form.

A more distinguished worthy to whose memory justice has never yet been done in our scanty bookselling annals is Thomas Guy, better known as the founder of the great hospital which still bears his name. Charles Knight, who has given currency to most of the legends surrounding this shadowy figure, embroiders his facts with so much idle, if amiable, imagining, and makes assumptions so wide of the mark, that it is by no means easy to disentangle fact from fiction. It was not until Dr Samuel Wilks and G. T. Bettany published their *Biographical History of Guy's Hospital* in 1892 that anything approaching an adequate account of Guy's bookselling career, as well as of his public life and benefactions, found its way into print. From all accounts it is clear that Guy, like various other publishers who have since left fortunes which are frequently, but unfairly, compared with the miserable rewards of authorship, made the bulk of his wealth by financial speculations quite outside the bounds of bookselling business. He was fortunately situated for combining stocks and shares with bookselling.

The little shop which he opened for the first time in 1667, with a stock worth, it is said, some £200, stood at the angle formed by Cornhill and Lombard Street, in view of the new Exchange which was springing up from the ruins of Sir Thomas Gresham's original building, swept away, like everything else in the neighbourhood, by the Great Fire of the preceding year. Guy evidently caught the speculative spirit from his surroundings. His early Bible trade was itself not a little risky. The printing of Bibles was still largely in the hands of the London monopolists, who, secure in their privileges, produced copies of the Scriptures which were a disgrace both to their craft and their religion. Cambridge occasionally exercised its right to print Bibles, but Oxford had bartered away its similar privilege to the Stationers' Company in 1637 for an annual payment of £200. The London printers in Guy's early days therefore had matters much their own way, with the result that Bibles were not only expensive to buy, but so shamefully printed that one edition is said to have contained no fewer than six thousand errors.

Perhaps it was in the pious hope of remedying this evil, as Charles Knight would have us believe, that Guy joined with others in encouraging the printing of the English Bible in Holland, importing whole editions for circulation in this country, and doubtless making a handsome profit thereby. This trade, writes William Maitland in the account of Guy and his hospital included in his history of London in 1739, 'proving not only very detrimental to the public revenue, but likewise to the King's printer, all ways and means were devised to quash the same; which, being vigorously put in execution, the booksellers, by frequent seizures and prosecutions, became so great sufferers that they judged a further pursuit thereof inconsistent with their own interest'. Thomas Guy and Peter Parker—one of the booksellers who had shared in the sale of the first edition of *Paradise Lost*—were presently able to turn this defeat into a greater victory by becoming associated with Oxford University, which, under the generous influence of Dr Fell, had begun to awake—in the words of Mr Falconer Madan in his *Brief Account* of the Oxford University Press (1908)—'not merely to the fact of its privileges, but also to the duties belonging to them'.

In 1675 the agreement with the Stationers' Company lapsed, and Oxford began again to print Bibles and Prayer Books, to the considerable annoyance of the London monopolists, who at once did their best to stifle the competition by imitating and underselling all these new editions. 'So persistently was this done', says Mr Madan, 'that it was found advisable to bring in some London booksellers into the Oxford business. Moses Pitt and William Leake were first chosen, but they were soon followed by Guy and Parker, and Oxford Bibles between 1679 and 1691 bear the imprint of these four Stationers, sometimes alone, sometimes two or three together.'

Now began a battle royal between the London Stationers and Oxford, in which first honours fell to the university, which sturdily maintained its right to its privileges before the Council, Parker and Guy bearing a large share of the legal expense, amounting in all to many hundreds of pounds. The two printers thereupon made an agreement with the Delegates of the Oxford Press by which, upon payment of £240, being the arrears of the annual sum hitherto received from the Stationers' Company, they should be appointed University Printers with the sole right of printing there. This was carried into effect in March 1684, and the agreement lasted until 1691, when the Stationers' Company, enraged at what they doubtless considered the usurpation of Parker and Guy, determined to get them removed, alleging, among other things, that they had made a profit of £10,000, or even £15,000, by their connection with Oxford, and had thus advanced 'from a low and mean condition to considerable fortune'. The whole story of this unworthy campaign, too long for our pages, is told by Wilks and Bettany, but it seems that the Stationers' Company at last succeeded in prejudicing the university authorities against Guy and Parker to such an extent as to get them removed — January 1692.

During all these years Guy, though doubtless paying occasional visits to Oxford, had been steadily developing his business at his corner shop in the heart of London, apart from the considerable sales of his Oxford Bibles. For a time at least he appears to have taken his younger brother into partnership. He published a large number of school books and books of Divinity, while among his other ventures were the fourth edition of Howell's *Familiar Letters* and the third edition (with Parker) of Ogilvy's translation of Virgil. He was steadily building up his capital, too, in other ways. The story is told by Maitland to the effect that he acquired some of his fortune by the purchase of seamen's tickets at an inordinate profit. 'England being engaged in an expensive war against France, the poor seamen on board the Royal Navy, for many years instead of money received tickets for their pay, which these necessitous but very useful men were obliged to dispose of at thirty, forty, and sometimes fifty in the hundred discount. Mr Guy discovering the sweets of this traffic, became an early dealer therein.'

There is probably more in this story than Charles Knight is willing to admit in his *Shadows of the Old Booksellers*, though his profits both from the Bible trade, and in his investments in government securities before the foundation of the South Sea Company, would alone account for his consistent and increasing prosperity. He invested largely in South Sea stock, long before the Bubble burst, being one of the shrewd shareholders who sold out in time at an immense profit. Within three months he is said to have made from that source alone upwards of a quarter of a million sterling. Perhaps Thomas Guy had some qualms of conscience when he thought of the wretched investors who had lost their all; but, however that may be, it was largely out of his own huge profits in this connection that Guy's Hospital was built and endowed, so that some good at least rose, phœnix-like, from the ruins of what has been described as 'the most enormous fabric of delusion that was ever raised among an industrious, thrifty, and prudent people'.

Success did not tempt Thomas Guy into extravagance. He was as close-fisted in his home as open-handed outside. He denied himself a wife — which was, perhaps, just as well, if there be any truth in the story that he broke off his one matrimonial engagement because his prospective bride had dared to give an order without his permission. Yet he spent his money outside with rare unselfishness. He seems to have been a sort of fairy godfather to whole crowds of poor relations. Long before he built Guy's Hospital he made large benefactions to the Stationers'

Company for the less fortunate members of his craft; built three new wards and made other additions to St Thomas's Hospital, besides being one of its principal governors and a regular subscriber of £100 a year; and not only supplied almshouses to Tamworth, where he was educated, but furnished the place with its new town hall.

Tamworth at first showed its gratitude to Guy by returning him to Parliament in the Whig interest in 1695, and he continued to represent the same town until 1707, when that fickle constituency rejected him. He was mortally offended, and though begged to stand again by the repentant burgesses — who now remembered his oft-repeated promise, that if they supported him faithfully he would leave the whole of his fortune to the town — he declined peremptorily ever to run the risk of a second refusal. He was seventy-five when he made his South Sea fortune in 1720, and had the satisfaction of seeing his hospital roofed in before he died in 1724. At his death he endowed that institution with the residue of his estate, which was worth more than £200,000, after leaving at least half as much again in other bequests and charities.

Meanwhile new laws and customs had been coming into force affecting not only authors and publishers, but the whole book trade. The stringent Licensing Act of 1662, which had been allowed to lapse at the time of the Great Fire, never recovered its original strength, and was not, indeed, renewed by Charles II, though L'Estrange did his best as Surveyor of the Press to make things as lively as possible both for printers and booksellers. He found a monarch more in sympathy with him when James II came to the throne in February 1685, the Act of 1662 being renewed for the first time for twenty years on the new King's opening Parliament. On April 30th L'Estrange himself received his knighthood, and, three weeks later, his warrant to enforce the regulations with all necessary severity. Dunton, who reveals a good deal of the human interest of the book trade in those far-off days, tells us that there was a yielding side even to L'Estrange's stubborn heart. The Surveyor, he says, was always susceptible to the influence of the better-looking sex, and 'would wink at unlicensed books if the printer's wife would but smile on him'. And Dunton, whose fondness for flirting was only equalled by his boundless egotism, knew what he was writing about.

The time came when King James was 'frighted' away, and Nemesis, in the shape of William of Orange, not only deprived L'Estrange of his licence, but sent him to prison for his avowed hostility. In the end the man who had made so many booksellers' lives a burden was forced to eke out his existence mainly on the wretched payments which they made him for his hack work as a translator. Though the Licensing Act, which had been renewed in 1685 for a period of seven years, was renewed in 1692 for one more year, it does not appear to have been in the least effective. It lapsed altogether at the end of the twelve months' renewal, leaving literary property without any statutory protection until the passing of the Copyright Act of Queen Anne in 1709. The disappearance of the Licensing Laws, and the end of the active history of the Stationers' Company—their police powers having become obsolete, and their political uses long since superseded—thus brought the book trade at the end of the seventeenth century to another new chapter in its history.

Bookselling by auction had also found its way into England by this time, with far-reaching results. William Cooper seems to have been the first bookseller to try the 'Auctionary Way' in this country, though the method seems to have been practised on the Continent, by the Elzevirs and others, between seventy and eighty years before. The earliest book auction of which we have any record took place in Holland on July 6th, 1599, when the library of the scholar and patriot, Philip van Marnix, Lord of St Aldegondi, was dispersed in this way. 'Reader', says William Cooper in the preface to the catalogue of the first English sale—which began on October 31st, 1676, at his bookshop at the sign of the Pelican in Little Britain—'It hath not been usual here in England to make sales of Books by way of Auction, or who will give most for them; But it having been practised in other countreys to the Advantage both of Buyers and Sellers; It was therefore conceived (for the encouragement of Learning) to publish the Sale of these Books this manner of way; and it is hoped that it will not be unacceptable to Schollers.' The catalogue deals with between five and six thousand lots—forming the library of Dr Lazarus Seaman, one of the Assembly of Divines—and Cooper realized about £3,000 from them. The second sale, which was also held by Cooper in Little Britain, was that of the library of the Rector of Hitchin. These first attempts, according to the catalogue of the third sale—which took place at the Turk's Head Coffee House in Bread Street—gave 'great content and satisfaction to the gentlemen who were the buyers, and no discouragement to the sellers.'

Other booksellers followed suit, and the sales soon became common in London; but it was apparently ten years before the method found its way to the provinces—introduced by Edward Millington—and twelve years before it reached Scotland. John Dunton, 'who', to quote the elder d'Israeli, 'boasted that he had a thousand projects, fancied he had methodized six hundred, and was ruined by the fifty he executed', took a shipload of books in 1698 to sell by auction in Dublin. He quarrelled with the Irish booksellers, but returned to London boasting that he had done greater service to literature by his auctions 'than any single man who had come into Ireland these hundred years'. His financial troubles increasing, Dunton took to scribbling, although he declares that he 'could not stoop so low as to turn author'—which he nevertheless thinks was what he was born to. His *Life and Errors of John Dunton, late Citizen of*

London, written in Solitude, has been described as the 'maddest of all mad books', but it is extremely useful in the annals of bookselling.

He tells us that when he started bookselling on his own account (about 1681) the first book he published was a work by Thomas Doolittle, the Nonconformist tutor whose academy was ruined by constant removal. 'The book fully answered my end', says Dunton, 'for, exchanging it through the whole trade, it furnished my shop with all sorts of books saleable at that time', showing that the custom already alluded to in the earlier history of the Stationers was still in vogue. 'Hackney authors', adds Dunton, 'began to ply me with specimens as earnestly, and with as much passion and concern, as the watermen do passengers with oars and scullers.' Later he complains bitterly of these scribblers, 'that keep their grinders moving by the travail of their pens. These gormandizers will eat you the very life out of a copy so soon as ever it appears; for, as the times go, *original* and *abridgment* are almost reckoned as necessary as man and wife; so that I am really afraid a bookseller and a good conscience will shortly grow some strange thing in the land.' The mischief to which Dunton refers, remarks Mr Birrell, in his all too brief essay on *Old Booksellers*, in *In the Name of the Bodleian*, 'was permitted by the stupidity of the judges, who refused to consider an abridgment of a book any interference with its copyright. Some learned judges have, indeed, held that an abridger is a benefactor, but as his benefactions are not his own, but another's, a shorter name might be found for him. The law on the subject is still uncertain.'*

Fortunately for Dunton he married, in 1682, a daughter of Samuel Annesley, another of whose daughters became the mother of John Wesley. Dunton's wife not only kept him in the paths of honesty, but 'managed all my affairs for me, and left me entirely to my own rambling and scribbling humours'. He took full advantage of this freedom three years later to adventure upon a voyage to the American Colonies with a cargo of books for which apparently there was then little demand at his shop, the Black Raven, in Gracechurch Street. 'There came an universal damp upon trade by the defeat of Monmouth in the west; and at this time, having £500 owing to me in New England, I began to think it worth my while to make a voyage of it thither.' The trade had not as yet made much progress in that part of the world.

The first book printed in New England came from the press established at Harvard College in 1639, with Stephen Day as printer, but his successor, Samuel Green, remained the only printer in the colony until 1660, when Marmaduke Johnson was sent over to join him with a fresh plant for the printing of Bibles for the Indians. Printing was started at Boston in 1675 by John Foster, a Harvard graduate, who was succeeded

---

* Authors' rights in this respect have since, however, been safeguarded under the Copyright Act of 1911.

on his death in 1681 by Samuel Green, junior; and Green was at work there when John Dunton arrived after a four months' voyage from home, during which half of his cargo of books, to the value of £500, had been cast away in the Downs. He consoled himself in New England mainly in aimless flirtations with maids and widows, for his dealings appear to have been anything but satisfactory with the four booksellers of Boston, to whom he was 'as welcome as sour ale in summer'. 'He that trades with the inhabitants of Boston', writes John, in much bitterness of spirit, 'may get plenty of promises, but their payments come late'.

At the end of a year's wanderings, during which he opened warehouses in Salem and other places, visited Harvard, and learned something of Indian life and habits, he returned to his 'lovely Iris', only to find it necessary first to hide from his creditors at home and then to seek shelter from their insistent demands by an involuntary visit to the Continent. He made a fresh start upon the accession of William and Mary, having been able to settle with his creditors. For a time fortune smiled on him. Among other things he issued the *Athenian Gazette*, which Charles Knight describes as the precursor of a 'revolution in the entire system of our lighter literature, which turned pamphlets and broadsides into magazines and miscellanies'. Then came renewed financial straits, and, to add to his troubles, his Iris died. Her successor proved but a bitter disillusionment. It was about this time that he turned from publishing to book-auctioneering and, as already stated, set sail for Ireland with his shipload of books. Disappointment dodged poor Dunton's footsteps for the rest of his life. He made a pitiful appeal to George I in 1723, entitled *Dying Groans from the Fleet Prison, or last Shift for Life*, claiming to have played a distinguished part in bringing about 'the general deliverance' accomplished by the Hanoverian succession; but, meeting with no reward, he lived on in misery for another ten years.

Dunton has something to say in his *Life and Errors* of that other book-auctioneer, Edward Millington. Millington is said to have sheltered Milton during his temporary absence from home in or about the year 1670, when, after his third marriage, he parted with his three daughters. 'About 1670', says Jonathan Richardson, the authority for this story, who gives it in the life of Milton which he prefixed to *Notes on 'Paradise Lost'* in 1734, 'I have been told by one who then knew him that he lodged some time at the house of Millington, the famous auctioneer some years ago, who then sold old books in Little Britain and who used to lead him by the hand when he went abroad.' Millington, it seems, had a rare way with him with his role as auctioneer-bookseller. 'He had a quick wit and a wonderful fluency of speech,' writes Dunton. 'There was usually as much wit in his "One, two, three!" as can be met with in a modern play. "Where", said Millington, "is your generous flame for learning? Who but a sot or a blockhead would have money in his pocket, and starve his brains?'''

There is no doubt that the new system of auctioneering greatly encouraged the love of reading throughout the country. One catalogue mentioned in John Lawler's little book on the subject (*Book-Auctions in England in the Seventeenth Century*) specially invites the country clergy to buy at low prices for distribution among their parishioners. A penny bid was often accepted. The book auction was soon a regular feature at the country fairs, and gradually became a distinct branch of the bookselling trade. There were book lotteries as well, and sales by inch of candle, announcements to that effect being found in the newspapers of the period. The first English auctioneer to compile good, classified catalogues was Samuel Paterson, of King Street, Covent Garden, who died in 1802 – 'a man', wrote Johnson, who was godfather to his son Samuel, 'for whom I have long had a kindness'. Samuel Paterson was a first-rate bibliographer, but he loved his books too well to make a good business man. We are told that when he came across a book that was new to him he would sit reading it for hours, and the time appointed for the sale could go by for all he cared. No wonder he frequently failed in business. Samuel Baker, in 1744, founded (in York Street, Covent Garden) the first auction room instituted in this country exclusively for the sale of books, MSS, and prints. It was here that Baker's nephew, John Sotheby, entered the business – the first of a long and distinguished line which has been associated with book-auctioneering ever since.

9

The Early Eighteenth Century

The dawn of the eighteenth century found the book trade in a sorry state of indiscipline. The lapse of the old Licensing Laws in 1694 had left both authors and publishers without the uncertain protection which even those arbitrary measures afforded. The value attaching to the entry of books in the Stationers' Register is seen in the ridiculous totals for the following years:

1701	3	books
1702	2	,,
1703	4	,,
1704	5	,,
1705	5	,,
1706	2	,,
1707	3	,,
1708	2	,,

In 1709, however, came the much-abused Copyright Act of Queen Anne—the first copyright Statute ever passed in any country. It was high time that something was done to put an end to the lawless state of things prevailing since the expiration of the old Licensing Acts. The Stationers' Company did its best to maintain its ancient usage in the matter of duly registered 'copies', passing bye-laws forbidding any member to print, bind, or sell any book belonging to another member; but their printed regulations were as so much wastepaper. The free-booters of the press were never so openly defiant as now. They were the 'set of wretches we authors call pirates', says Addison in the *Tatler*, 'who print any book, poem, or sermon as soon as it appears in the world, in a smaller volume, and sell it, as all other thieves do stolen goods, at a cheaper rate'. Even John Dunton declines to praise when he includes 'felonious Lee'—perhaps merely for the sake of the pun—in the character sketches of his *Life and Errors*. 'Such a pirate, such a cormorant', he writes of this 'Mr Lee of Lombard Street', 'was never before. Copies, books, men, ships, all were one; he held no propriety, right or wrong, good or bad, till at last he became to be known; and the booksellers, not enduring so ill a man to disgrace them, spewed him out, and off he marched for Ireland, when he acted as felonious Lee, as he did in London.' Ireland remained more or less free to pirates until the Union of 1801, when the Copyright Act was extended to that country, thus putting an end to the unauthorized editions, cheaply printed in Dublin, and surreptitiously imported into Great Britain, which had been a grievous source of trouble since the early days of printing.

The London booksellers, finding their bye-laws wholly inadequate as a means of protecting themselves against one another, applied to Parliament for a new Licensing Act in 1703, again in 1706, and for a third time in 1709, when they were at length rewarded with the Statute of Queen Anne. Tradition has it that the original Bill was drafted by Swift, whose draft was cut up in Committee. However that may be, it did something which no other Act had ever done—it made some attempt to provide for the due recognition of the rights of authorship. Authors, as well as publishers—provided they had not parted with their property—were given the copyright of books already printed for a period of twenty-one years, dating from April 10th, 1710, and no longer. New books were placed on a different footing, copyright in this case lasting only fourteen years, with the proviso that in the event of the authors surviving the said term they were to be granted another period of fourteen years. Among other things, piracy was to be punished by forfeiture and the fine of a penny per sheet—half to go to the Crown and half to the informer; and registration at Stationers' Hall was again demanded as a necessary condition of protection.

This well-meaning but, as Augustine Birrell calls it, 'perfidious' measure, though it did (and for the first time) confer upon authors statutory rights in their literary property, spoilt the whole case for perpetual copyright. Hitherto the belief in this perpetuity had been general, the booksellers believing that any literary property which they purchased became theirs and their successors' for all time. Authors held the same view, and sold or retained their copyrights accordingly. Amid all the judicial differences on the subject during the eighteenth century, said Birrell in his lectures as Quain Professor of Law at University College London,* 'there was a steady majority of judges in favour of the view that but for the Statute of Anne an author was entitled to perpetual copyright in his published work. This right (if it ever existed) the Act destroyed. Whether this judicial opinion as to the existence at Common Law of perpetual copyright in an author and his assigns was sound may well be doubted, and possibly if the House of Lords had held in *Donaldson* v. *Becket*† that perpetual copyright had survived Queen Anne, an Act of Parliament would, sooner or later, have been passed curtailing the rights of authors. But how annoying, how distressing, to have evolution artificially arrested and so interesting

* *Seven Lectures on the Law and History of Copyright in Books*, 1899.
† See pp. 190–91.

a question stifled by an ignorant Legislature, set in motion not by an irate populace clamouring for books ... but by the authors and their proprietors, the booksellers'.

It is pleasant to find that while the booksellers were in the thick of their troubles in the early years of the eighteenth century they still had time and inclination to make a practice of the trade sale dinners. The sale dinner, like piracy itself, was something of an institution among the London booksellers long before the eighteenth century, but the earliest direct evidence of its existence is the catalogue* of the stock-in-trade of Mrs Elizabeth Harris, deceased, to be sold at 'The Bear in Avey-Mary-Lane, on Monday the Eleventh of this Instant Decemb. 1704, Beginning at Nine in the Morning: Where the Company shall be entertained with a Breakfast; and at Noon with a good Dinner, and a Glass of Wine: and then proceed with the Sale in order to finish that Evening.' They knew the way to a man's pocket in those days. But it was a genial custom, and the friendly gossip over the nuts and wine must have done much to soften the asperities of trade competition. Nothing is more surprising than to turn from some of the stories of petty bookselling wars and personal spite to the social amenities and cooperative spirit associated with the historic Chapter Coffee House, which, in eighteenth-century publishing, filled the place occupied by the Mermaid Tavern in Elizabethan literature. The Chapter Coffee House had many literary as well as bookselling associations. Goldsmith dined there, and poor Chatterton may or may not have tasted its hospitalities. 'I am quite familiar at the Chapter Coffee House,' he writes in one of his proud, boastful letters, 'and know all the geniuses there.' In its later history Charlotte and Anne Brontë stayed there during their first visit to London after the triumphant appearance of *Jane Eyre*. The Chapter House was converted into a tavern in 1854.

Before the early Chapter Coffee House days—in the year 1719—a regular association was formed by a number of booksellers for trade purposes under the strange name of the 'Conger'—a term which, according to Nichols, 'was supposed to have been at first applied to them individually, alluding to the Conger Eel, which is said to swallow the smaller fry; or it may possibly have been taken from *Congeries*'. Whatever the origin of its name, the society itself flourished for many years. In 1736 a similar partnership was formed, under the title of the New Conger, by Charles Rivington and Arthur Bettesworth, two of the Paternoster Row booksellers. Both associations were succeeded by the Chapter Coffee House in Paternoster Row, where the old custom of cooperative publishing—on the lines of the combined enterprise of the

---

* This is one of a series of sale catalogues, 1704–68, in the possession of Longmans, Green and Company. An account of them, by the late W. H. Peet, will be found in *Notes and Queries*, 7 S. ix, 301, also see *Library*, 5th Series, vol. v.

Stationers' Company under the Charter of James I—gradually developed into the systematic division of individual books, or series of books, into shares, each shareholder being responsible for his portion of the expenses, and receiving his proportionate number of the books at cost price, or, in certain cases, his proportionate amount of the profits. Many works, such as Johnson's *Lives of the Poets*, were brought into the world under this cooperative system. 'Chapter Books' they were at first called; a name which subsequently gave place to 'Trade Books'.

Bookselling localities were more specialized in the early eighteenth century than at the present day. 'The booksellers of ancient books in all languages', writes Macky in his *Journey through England* (1724), 'are in Little Britain and Paternoster Row; those for divinity and the classics on the north side of St Paul's Cathedral; law, history, and plays about Temple Bar; and the French booksellers in the Strand. It seems, then, that the bookselling business has been gradually resuming its original situation near this Cathedral ever since the beginning of George I, while the neighbourhood of Duck Lane* and Little Britain has been proportionately falling into disuse.' In its palmy days Little Britain was a favourite resort of Swift and other great bookmen and booklovers of his time. Scholars went there for their Greek and Latin texts, or their favourite French and Italian authors, afterwards forgathering in the old 'Mourning Bush' in Aldersgate to discuss both their spoils and the current gossip of the town. Swift mentions several visits to Christopher Bateman, one of the best known of these Little Britain booksellers, in his *Journal to Stella*. On January 6th, 1711, he tells her that he 'went to Bateman's, the bookseller's, and laid out eight and forty shillings for books', for which he seems to have bought 'three little volumes of *Lucian* in French, for our Stella'. A few months later he was at the same bookseller's, 'to see a fine old library he has bought, and my fingers itched as yours would do at a china shop'.

Bateman was a competent man. 'There are few booksellers in England (if any)', says Dunton, 'that understand books better than Mr Bateman, nor does his diligence and industry come short of his honesty.' There appears to have been a custom among some of his brethren to permit customers to have the run of their shops and read the books without taking them away, for which privilege they had to pay a small subscription. Reading chairs or stools were kept in the shops for this purpose. If the books were not finished at a single sitting they were kept until the readers returned to finish them. Bateman, however, abandoned this custom. 'I suppose', he said, 'you may be a physician or an author, and want some recipe or quotation; and if you buy it I will engage it to be perfect before you leave me, but not after, as I have

* Duck Lane was one of the arteries of Little Britain, which, like those in the neighbourhood of Paternoster Row, were given up largely to the booksellers.

suffered by leaves being torn out, and the books returned to my very great loss and prejudice' (Nichols' *Literary Anecdotes*). Book lotteries, as mentioned on p. 126, were also in vogue. Swift, on April 27th, 1711, tells Stella that he spent £4 7s. in thus gambling with a bookseller, winning six books in return. That Little Britain itself had long passed its prime before the middle of the eighteenth century is confirmed by Roger North, who, in 1744, regrets its vanished glories in a passage which has scarcely a good word for the booksellers of his own day.* In John North's time (he died in 1683), writes his biographer:

Little Britain was a plentiful and perpetual emporium of learned authors; and men went thither as to a market. This drew to the place a mighty trade; the rather because the shops were spacious, and the learned gladly resorted to them where they seldom failed to meet with agreeable conversation. And the booksellers themselves were knowing and conversible men, with whom, for the sake of bookish knowledge, the greatest wits were pleased to converse. And we may judge the time as well spent there, as (in latter days) either in tavern or coffee-house; though the latter hath carried off the spare hours of most people. But now this emporium is vanished, and the trade contracted into the hands of two or three persons, who, to make good their monopoly, ransack, not only their neighbours of the trade that are scattered about town, but all over England, aye, and beyond sea too, and send abroad their circulators, and in that manner get into their hands all that is valuable. The rest of the trade are content to take their refuse, with which, and the fresh scum of the press, they furnish one side of a shop, which serves for the sign of a bookseller, rather than a real one; but, instead of selling, deal as factors and procure what the country divines and gentry send for; of whom each hath his book-factor, and, when wanting anything, writes to his bookseller, and pays his bill. And it is wretched to consider what pickpocket work, with help of the press, these demi-booksellers make. They crack their brains to find out selling subjects, and keep hirelings in garrets, at hard meat, to write and correct by the great; and so puff up an octavo to a sufficient thickness, and there is six shillings current for an hour and a half's reading, and perhaps never to be read or looked upon after. One that would go higher must take his fortune at blank walls, and corners of streets, or repair to the sign of Bateman, Innys, and one or two more, where are best choice, and better pennyworths. I might touch other abuses, as bad paper, incorrect printing, and false advertising; all which and worse is to be expected, if a careful author is not at the heels of them.

* Roger North's *Life of Dr John North*.

This was the tribe which Pope lashed so unmercifully in the *Dunciad*, but it is only fair to add that the satirists have had matters too much their own way in this connection. Jacob Tonson and Bernard Lintot, the two great publishers of the early eighteenth century, whatever their faults may have been, certainly helped to give a better tone to the trade. Against Lintot's benevolence and general moral character, says Dr Young, 'there is not an insinuation'. And Jacob Tonson, as we have seen, was a very worthy fellow, in spite of his latter-day snobbery. For Tonson, after Dryden's death in 1700—where we left him in the last chapter—had entered upon a new, and, from the social point of view, more dazzling phase in his career. He became secretary, and probably had some share in the founding, of the famous Kit Cat Club, hobnobbing with dukes and the leading men of wit and fashion among the Whigs, having his portrait painted, like every member of the Club, by Sir Godfrey Kneller, and flattering his vanity to his heart's content in the celebrated room which he built for their meetings at his own villa at Barn Elms.* Tonson was liked none the better by some of his friends for this illustrious association, if we are to credit the friendly criticism of Rowe, who writes, in his *Dialogue between Tonson and Congreve, in imitation of Horace*, which appeared in 1714:

> While in your early days of reputation,
> You for blue garters had not such a passion,
> While yet you did not live, as now your trade is,
> To drink with noble lords, and toast their ladies,
> Thou, Jacob Tonson, were, to my conceiving,
> The cheerfullest, best, honestest fellow living.

The Club was not allowed to interfere with the course of Tonson's regular business, which he was doubtless shrewd enough to see would benefit by such friendly intimacy with writers of the stamp of Addison and Steele. He had published Addison's *Poems to his Majesty* in 1695. In 1705 he issued his *Remarks on several Parts of Italy*; in 1713 his tragedy, *Cato*; and two years later his comedy, *The Drummer*, for which he paid fifty guineas. In addition, and above all these, he became, in October 1712, joint publisher of the *Spectator* with Samuel Buckley, of the Dolphin in Little Britain,† who advertised the first number in his *Daily*

* Kneller painted his well-known series of portraits for this room—forty-eight in all—on canvas of uniform size (30 in. × 28 in.), a size which has ever since been known as 'Kit Cat'. The Kit Cat Club held its summer meetings at the Upper Flask Tavern in Hampstead, on the edge of the Heath.

† Buckley, who owned the *Daily Courant*—the first daily newspaper to appear in England—which he had taken over from a bookseller named Mallet, was one of the best known of the early newspaper proprietors. 'He was originally a bookseller,' says Dunton, 'but follows printing. He is an excellent linguist, understands Latin, French, Dutch and Italian tongues, and is master of a great deal of wit. I hear he translates out of the foreign papers himself.' In 1714 he disposed of the *Daily Courant* to take over the publication of the *London Gazette*.

Courant of that date as follows: 'This day will be published a paper entitled *The Spectator*; which will be continued every day. Printed for Samuel Buckley at the Dolphin in Little Britain, and sold by A. Baldwin in Warwick Lane.' From the sixteenth number the imprint stated that it was also sold by 'Charles Lillie, Perfumer, at the corner of Beauford Buildings in the Strand'.* Tonson's name as joint publisher was added from No. 499. The first two volumes of the revised edition in volume form, 'well bound and gilt, two guineas', were issued to subscribers by Buckley and Tonson in January 1712, the third and fourth following in April of the same year. In November 1712 Addison and Steele sold a half share in these four volumes, and in three others not yet published, to Jacob Tonson, junior—old Jacob's nephew and now his partner—for £575, Buckley taking the other half share for a similar sum. Two years later Tonson junior bought Buckley's half for £500. The collected edition of the *Tatler* was also published by the Tonsons, being issued at a guinea a volume on royal paper, and ten shillings on medium paper. The *Guardian* came from the same busy press. According to Pope, Steele threw down that journal on October 1st, 1713, because of a quarrel with Tonson; but later authorities regard it as more likely that he gave it up in order to start a paper which would give him a wider political scope. It is significant, however, that the *Englishman, Being the Sequel of the Guardian*, the first number of which appeared on October 6th, 1713, was published by Samuel Buckley.

One or two references in Steele's correspondence suggest some jovial evenings at the bookseller's shop at Gray's Inn, before the Tonsons moved in 1712 to the Shakespeare Head, in the Strand, opposite Catherine Street. Nor is it very difficult to imagine how 'genial Jacob' and 'poor Dick Steele'—as Thackeray has called him in one of the most lovable of all his portraits—became closely associated both in business and social relations. Tonson published at the end of 1701 the first of Steele's plays to be produced on the stage, *The Funeral, or Grief-à-la-Mode*, and a few years later the author is seen writing to 'dear Prue' regretting that he is 'obliged to dine at Tonson's, where after dinner some papers are to be read, whereof, among others, I am to be a judge'. In 1714 we find our 'reprehended spouse' writing to have three bottles of his wine removed from the same hospitable house. Alas! he returned this hospitality—according to Aitken in the scholarly biography of Steele already alluded to—with a base ingratitude which no one would regret—when too late—more than Dick himself. 'His frank, hearty nature and his love of companionship led him into temptation; like those around him he sometimes indulged in excesses at the table, and

---

* G. A. Aitken's *Life of Richard Steele*, 1889. It is added that 'there was often a note stating where sets of the back numbers could be obtained, and the increase in the names of shops mentioned shows the continued growth in the sale'.

he had a natural daughter by a daughter of Tonson the publisher.' This could not have been a daughter of Tonson I, for the elder Jacob was childless; but a daughter of the nephew and namesake whom the founder of the House took into partnership after moving to Gray's Inn from Chancery Lane.

It is not always easy to distinguish between Jacob Tonson I and Jacob Tonson II in their business dealings after the removal to the Shakespeare Head, but as the founder appears to have retired from active business in 1720 later references may be assumed to relate to his successor. That being the case it must have fallen to Jacob Tonson II to publish the most successful of Steele's plays, *The Conscious Lovers*, produced at Drury Lane Theatre in November 1722, and printed in December of the following year. In February 1718 Bernard Lintot had entered into an agreement with his old rivals the Tonsons—probably through Tonson junior—to become joint partners in all plays which they should buy after eighteen months following the date of that agreement, and Lintot, accordingly, bought half the copyright of *The Conscious Lovers*.

Some years before this agreement was signed, Lintot himself had negotiated with Steele for *The Lying Lover*, the copyright of which cost him £21 10s. In November 1722 both publishers issued the first collected edition of Steele's *Dramatic Works*, part of the edition appearing with title-pages bearing the joint names of Tonson and Lintot, and part with separate title-pages. In 1722 old Jacob Tonson assigned over to his nephew the privileges of his office as stationer, bookbinder, bookseller, and printer to a number of the great public offices—privileges which he had secured in 1719–20 as some reward for his devotion to the Whigs. The younger Jacob secured a renewal of the original grant for a further term of forty years, a nice little monopoly which the Tonson family contrived to hold until the end of the century. At one time Jacob Tonson and his nephew held the privilege of printing the *Gazette*, but this was taken away from them not long after Steele lost his gazetteership. 'Mr Addison and I have at last met', writes Swift to Stella in telling her, on July 26th, 1711, of a memorable meeting at the publishers' house; 'I dined with him and Steele to-day at young Jacob Tonson's. The two Jacobs think it is I who have made the secretary take from them the privilege of the *Gazette*, which they are going to lose, and Ben Tooke and another are to have it. Jacob came to me t'other day to make his court; but I told him it was too late; and that it was not my doing.'

Swift's influence with the Tory ministers at this time was also sought by his old acquaintance Alderman Barber (afterwards Lord Mayor), for whom he had already obtained several lucrative posts. 'My printer and bookseller', he writes on January 16th, 1712, 'want me to hook in another employment for them at the Tower, because it was enjoyed before by a stationer, although it be to serve the Ordnance with oil, tallow, etc., and is worth four hundred pounds per annum more. I will try what I can do. They are resolved to ask several other employments of the same nature ... Why am I not a stationer?'

Gulliver's Travels was the only book for which Swift ever received any payment. Hitherto his writings had been scattered, without reward, over a great number of booksellers, both in Dublin and London. *Gulliver's* birth, partly due to fear lest its political satire might have disagreeable consequences for its author, was surrounded with a vast amount of mystery. It was offered to its publisher, Benjamin Motte, by Swift himself, in a letter written in a feigned hand and signed 'Richard Sympson', ostensibly on behalf of 'my cousin, Mr Lemuel Gulliver'. The sum of £200, he declared, was the least sum that he could receive on his cousin's account, 'because I know the author intends the profit for the use of poor seamen'. Pope had a hand in the business, but the final negotiations were conducted through Erasmus Lewis, at whose house in Cork Street, behind Burlington House, a meeting took place between 'Richard Sympson' and the publisher. *Gulliver* appeared in November 1726 and at once became the talk of the town. 'The whole impression sold in a week', wrote Gay and Pope to the author on the 17th of that month. 'It is generally said that you are the author, but I am told the bookseller declares he knows not from whose hand it came.' Motte was not able to pay the money on the date fixed, but must have satisfied the author in due course, for we find Swift writing to him in 1732 to the effect that he was 'assured of your honest and fair dealing', and declaring that he would never publish with anyone else.

Jacob Tonson shared his printing in partnership with John Watts, with whom young Benjamin Franklin worked after his year's service at Palmer's, in Bartholomew Close. 'Here', writes Franklin in his *Autobiography*,

I continued all the rest of my stay in London. At my first admission into a printing-house I took to working at press, imagining I felt a want of the bodily exercise I had been used to in America, where press-work is mixed with the composing. I drank only water; the other workmen, near fifty in number, were great drinkers of beer. On occasion, I carried up and down stairs a large form of types in each hand, when others carried but one in both hands. They wondered to see, from this and similar instances, that the *Water American*, as they called me, was *stronger* than themselves who drank *strong* beer! We had an alehouse boy, who attended always in the house to supply the workmen. My companion at the press drank every day a pint before breakfast, a pint at breakfast with his bread and cheese, a pint between breakfast and dinner, a pint at dinner, a pint in the afternoon about six o'clock, and another when he had done his day's work. I thought it a detestable custom ... Watts, after some weeks, desiring to have me in the composing-room, I left the press-men ... From my example, a great many of them left their muddling breakfast of beer, bread, and cheese, finding they could be supplied from a neighbouring house with a large porringer of hot water-gruel, sprinkled with pepper, crumbled with bread, and a bit of butter in it, for the price of a pint of beer, viz., three halfpence ... My constant attendance (I never making a St Monday) recommended me to the master; and my uncommon quickness at composing occasioned my being put upon work of despatch, which was generally better paid. So I went on now very agreeably.

It is quite possible that Jacob Tonson, walking round the printing office with his partner, had this energetic young colonial pointed out to him—little dreaming of the part which he was destined to play in the separation of the American Colonies from the Mother Country.

One government appointment—that of printing the Votes—was shared from 1715 until 1727 between Jacob Tonson, Bernard Lintot and William Taylor, the last of whom takes us back to Paternoster Row, and links us with one of the great publishing houses of the present day. For it was William Taylor who built up the business in Paternoster Row bought by young Thomas Longman in 1724, thus founding the firm which still bears as its emblem the Ship though not now the Black Swan. These were the signs of the two houses which Taylor had amalgamated out of the profits of *Robinson Crusoe*. The first part of that immortal tale was published on April 25th, 1719, when Defoe was nearly sixty years old, and a thoroughly discredited man. Taylor's enterprise was at once rewarded, for so great was the run on the book that he had to employ several printers to cope with the demand. Three editions were exhausted within four months, bringing the publisher the handsome profit of over a thousand pounds. The second part appeared in August of the same year, and a third part, containing the *Serious Reflections of Robinson Crusoe*—now rarely printed with the narrative proper—in the following year. Taylor, publishing books in all departments of literature, continued in business until 1724, when, as already stated, he was succeeded by Thomas Longman, then in his twenty-fifth year.

Born when Dryden was still alive, and Dr Johnson as yet unborn, Thomas Longman I was the son of a prosperous citizen of Bristol—a not insignificant fact when we remember the close connection in later generations between the Longmans and Bristol's more famous son, Robert Southey, as well as his local bookseller friend, Joseph Cottle.

Young Longman came to London in 1716 as an apprentice to John Osborn, stationer and bookseller in Lombard Street, and in due season, like the good apprentice that he was, married into his master's family. His 'prentice days over he bought William Taylor's business for a sum which, to be exact, amounted to £2,282 9s. 6d., and was not long in making his influence and energy felt in the book trade of London in the days of George I. Thirteen years before Longman stepped into Taylor's shoes was founded another historic publishing firm — the House of Rivington — Charles Rivington taking over in 1711 the business of Richard Chiswell the Elder, of the Rose and Crown, in St Paul's Churchyard, and hoisting his own sign of the Bible and Crown in Paternoster Row, where he soon became the leading theological publisher in London.

Tonson's chief rival, however, was the Bernard Lintot already alluded to — Barnaby Bernard Lintot, to give him his name in full. He was nearly twenty years younger than Tonson senior, and was not made free of the Stationers' Company until shortly before Dryden's death. He opened his shop not long afterwards at the sign of the Cross Keys, between the Temple Gates, in Fleet Street. Among his early investments, as shown in his account-book, were a third share of Cibber's *Love's Last Shift* (1701), which cost him £3 4s. 6d.; a half share of Dennis's *Liberty Asserted* (1704) for £7 3s.; the whole of the same author's *Appius and Virginia* (1705) for £21 10s.; and a seventh share of Captain Cook's *Voyages* (1711), which he bought of a Mr Gosling for £7 3s. Gay's first entry in the account-book is for his *Wife of Bath*, which cost the publisher on May 12th, 1713, £25, and a later entry shows that for the revival of the *Wife of Bath* he paid another £75. The same author's *Trivia* cost him £43 in December 1715, and his *Three Hours after Marriage*, on January 8th, 1717, £43 2s. 6d.

Long before this date Lintot had begun the association with Pope which, more than anything else, was to make him famous. Pope was one of old Jacob Tonson's disappointments. As early as 1706, while Pope was still in his teens, Tonson had spread his net for him in a letter of diplomatic politeness. After mentioning that he had been shown the manuscript of one of his *Pastorals*, which he thought 'extremely fine', he added: 'I remember I have formerly seen you in my shop, and am sorry I did not improve my acquaintance with you. If you design your poems for the press, no one shall be more careful in printing it, nor no one can give greater encouragement to it than, Sir,' etc. The letter succeeded, the *Pastorals* finding their way into Tonson's *Miscellany* in 1709, and Pope himself into Tonson's mixed band of 'eminent hands'. 'I shall be satisfied', he writes on May 20th, 1709, to Wycherley, who had introduced him to town life, 'if I can lose my time agreeably this way, without losing my reputation. I can be content with a bare saving game, without being thought an *eminent hand* (with which little Jacob has graciously dignified his adventurers and volunteers in poetry). Jacob creates poets, as kings do knights, not for their honour, but for their money.'

'You will make *Jacob's Ladder* raise you to immortality,' was Wycherley's reply. But the young and inconstant Pope not only took his anonymous *Essay on Criticism* to an obscure bookseller named Lewis,* who published it in 1711, but allowed the first edition of the *Rape of the Lock*, besides other pieces, to appear in Bernard Lintot's rival *Miscellanies* in 1712. This was the beginning of a regular connection which may be clearly traced in Lintot's account-book. Here are some of the items and the amounts paid for them by the publisher:

	£	s.	d.
Windsor Forest (Feb. 1713)	32	5	0
Ode on St. Cecilia's Day (July 1713) . . .	15	0	0
Additions to the *Rape* (Feb. 1714) . . .	15	0	0
Temple of Fame (Feb. 1715)	32	5	0
Key to the Lock (April 1715)	10	15	0

More important than all these was Pope's acceptance of Lintot's offer in 1714 to publish his translation of Homer's *Iliad*, on terms which were far in advance of anything that Tonson had ever paid Dryden. Pope and his friends had already ensured its financial success by securing a list of subscribers of unprecedented strength. The poet had issued his proposals for the translation in October 1713, and Swift worked as hard as anyone to secure the support of his political friends; but the leaders of both parties were included in the list, together with a host of patrons among the nobility. Lintot paid Pope £200 for each of the six volumes, and supplied him free of cost with all the copies for his subscribers, as well as presentation copies.

Bookselling by subscription on these lines continued right through the eighteenth century, authors issuing their 'Proposals' themselves, and getting as many influential friends as possible to tout for subscribers. It was the next thing, indeed, to becoming their own publishers, but though it occasionally accounted for such sums as were received in this way by Pope, it did not tend to increase the dignity of the profession. 'He that asks subscriptions', said Johnson, who made a bed of

* Lewis was a Catholic bookseller in Covent Garden. Isaac d'Israeli, in his *Quarrels of Authors*, tells the following story in this connection. 'From a descendant of this Lewis', he writes, 'I heard that Pope, after publication, came every day, persecuting with anxious inquiries the cold impenetrable bookseller, who, as the poem lay uncalled for, saw nothing but vexatious importunities in a troublesome youth. One day Pope, after nearly a month's publication, entered, and in despair tied up a number of the poems, which he addressed to several who had a reputation in town as judges of poetry. The scheme succeeded, and the poem, having reached its proper circle, soon got into request.' In 1716 a new edition was published conjointly by Lewis and Lintot, the last of whom paid £25 for the privilege.

thorns for himself when he undertook the subscription edition of *Shakespeare* in the middle of the century, 'soon finds that he has enemies. All who do not encourage him defame him.' And gradually the system fell into disuse, subscribing, with occasional exceptions, being now left to the publisher.

According to Johnson, Pope received altogether for the *Iliad* sums amounting to £5,320, though the publisher's own memorandum-book, quoted by Nichols, makes the total not much more than £4,000. Lintot apparently was not so happy in his bargain. 'It is unpleasant to relate', says Nichols in his *Literary Anecdotes*, 'that the bookseller, after all his hopes, and all his liberality, was, by a very unjust and illegal action, defrauded of his profit. An edition of the *Iliad* was printed in Holland in duodecimo and imported clandestinely for the gratification of those who were impatient to read what they could not afford to buy.'* This action compelled Lintot to bring out a still cheaper edition, which seems to have had a very large sale, but at a price so low as not to be profitable. It was the *Iliad* which led to Pope's so-called quarrel with Addison, whom he unjustly suspected of being the real author of Tickell's version of the same work, the first volume of which was published by Tonson three days after the announcement that Pope had finished the first volume of his translation.

For the copyright of the *Odyssey* for which Pope issued his proposals in January 1725, Lintot paid only half the sum he had been ready to give for the *Iliad*, and trouble ensued in connection with the poet's collaborators, William Browne and Elijah Fenton. Pope's profits amounted to £4,500, out of which he had to pay Browne and Fenton something like £700. Pope and Browne called Lintot a scoundrel, and other harsh names, because he declined to provide free copies for Browne's subscribers as well as Pope's; Lintot threatened a suit in Chancery; and the end of it all was their separation, and the poet's ignoble taunt in the *Dunciad*. Accounts differ, however, as to the real origin of Pope's spite against Lintot. 'Undoubtedly', says Nichols, 'at this time Pope had conceived a very ill impression of his *quondam* bookseller. His principal delinquency seems to have been that he was a stout man, clumsily made, not a very considerable scholar, and that he filled his shop with rubric posts.' Pope refers more than once to these bookseller's posts, adorned with red advertisements of the latest publications:

> What though my name stood rubric on the walls,
> Or plaistered posts, with clasps, in capitals.

Which takes us back to Ben Jonson's good-humoured protest against the pushful practices of the trade in one of his *Epigrams*, and farther

---

* Lintot's original edition was published at a guinea for each of the six volumes. The first volume appeared in June 1715; the last in May 1720.

back still to the advertisement posts of the bookshops of ancient Rome.

Among other works published by Lintot were poems and plays by Farquhar, Fenton and Rowe—to whom he paid £50 15s. for *Jane Shore*, and £75 5s. for *Lady Jane Grey*. When he retired, evidently in comfortable circumstances, he settled down in some considerable style in Sussex. Here, in November 1735, he was nominated High Sheriff for the county, but, dying in the following February, was succeeded in that office by his son Henry, who carried on his father's business until his own death in 1758.

Pope, to hark back to earlier days, returned for a time to his old publishers, the Tonsons, to edit their edition of Shakespeare in 1725, for which he was paid, roughly, £217. The edition was not particularly successful. Only about 600 copies were sold at the original price, out of a total edition of 750, the balance having to be 'remaindered'. 'Old Jacob Tonson', wrote Pope to a correspondent in 1731, 'is the perfect image and likeness of Bayle's Dictionary, so full of matter, secret history, and wit and spirit, at almost fourscore.' Tonson had retired ten or eleven years before this, leaving the business to be carried on by his nephew and name-sake. Like Thomas Guy, the elder Tonson had amassed, apart from any profits that he may have made as a publisher, a large fortune by South Sea stock and other investments, notably in Law's Mississippi Scheme. He died within two months of his old rival Bernard Lintot—on April 2nd, 1736.

Outwardly they were a curious, misshapen breed of men, these early publishers of the eighteenth century, if we are to accept the lines which have handed them down to posterity. Dryden, in one of his financial squabbles with Tonson, who would not satisfy all his demands for money, is said to have sent him the following lines, with the threatening message: 'Tell the dog that he who wrote these lines can write more':

> With leering looks, bull-faced, and freckled fair;
> With two left legs and Judas-coloured hair,
> And frowzy pores, that taint the ambient air.

The lines are from a satirical fragment attributed to Dryden and preserved in a Tory poem published as a joint attack on the Kit Cat Club and its bookseller-secretary. Jacob's unfortunate legs proved an irresistible mark for the satirist, for we find them again in Pope's *Dunciad*, following his portrait of 'great Lintot':

> As when a dab-chick waddles through the copse
> On feet and wings, and flies, and wades, and hops;
> So lab'ring on, with shoulders, hands, and head,
> Wide as a windmill, all his figure spread,

With arms expanded, Bernard rows his state,
And left-legg'd Jacob seems to emulate.

Himself misshapen—'a crooked mind in a crooked body'—Pope, as he dipped his pen in gall, seemed to gloat over any physical peculiarity in his victims. But Pope could not be more virulent in this respect than Thomas Amory, when damning Curll to unenviable immortality. 'Curll', writes Amory, in his curious autobiographical romance of *John Buncle*, 'was in person very tall and thin—an ungainly, awkward, white-faced man. His eyes were a light grey—large, projecting, goggle, and purblind. He was splay-footed and baker-kneed'—whatever baker-kneed may be. 'He was a debauchee to the last degree,' adds the same authority, 'and so injurious to society, that by filling his translations with wretched notes, forged letters, and bad pictures, he raised the price of a four shilling book to ten. Thus, in particular, he managed Burnet's *Archaeology*. And when I told him he was very culpable in this and other articles he sold, his answer was, "what would I have him to do?" He was a bookseller; his translators in pay lay three in a bed at the Pewter Platter Inn, in Holborn, and he and they were for ever at work to deceive the public. He likewise printed the lewdest things ... As to drink, he was too fond of money to spend any in making himself happy that way; but at another's expense he would drink every day till he was quite blind and as incapable as a block. This was Edmund Curll. But he died at last as great a penitent (I think in the year 1748) as ever expired. I mention this to his glory.'

'Left-legged Jacob'—or 'Genial Jacob', as Pope calls him in another passage—suffered from the *Dunciad* less than most of the unfortunate booksellers with whom 'Pope Alexander' had any dealings. Edmund Curll, his particular *bête noire* in the bookselling world, was better able to retaliate than Tonson or Lintot. Pope 'has a knack at versifying', admitted Curll, with consummate coolness, when called to appear at the Bar of the House for publishing his enemy's correspondence, 'but in prose I think myself a match for him'; and indeed he did his best, all through his long squabble with the irascible poet, to give as good as he received. His unabashed retaliations probably amused his contemporaries as much as Pope's venomous abuse, but posterity only remembers the *Dunciad*'s unsavoury description:

Obscure with filth the miscreant lies bewrayed,
Fall'n in the plash his wickedness had laid.

Curll had been trained in the unprotected days when a bookseller, were he so minded, could break all bounds of decency and honour with little risk of the law's interference. Curll and Pope had been deadly enemies years before the affair of the letters. The feud began with the

Court Poems, published in the spring of 1716 by James Roberts, of Warwick Lane, though the profits, apparently, were to be divided between Curll and two other booksellers, John Oldmixon and John Pemberton. This was the privately printed edition of the pieces by Lady Mary Wortley Montagu, afterwards published as *Town Eclogues*. We need not give the whole of its complicated history, with the side issue of its effect on the relations between Lady Mary Wortley Montagu and Pope. Curll and Pope have both given their own versions of the so-called 'poisoning', which the poet inflicted on the publisher when he heard that Curll had had a hand in the publication of the book. Pope's *Full and True Account of a Horrid and Barbarous Revenge by Poison on the Body of Mr Edmund Curll, Bookseller, with a faithful Copy of his last Will and Testament*, was published in Pope and Swift's *Miscellanies*, and much of it will hardly bear reprinting, but the following passages may be quoted:

> History furnishes us with Examples of many Satyrical Authors who have fallen Sacrifices to Revenge, but not of any Booksellers that I know of, except the unfortunate Subject of the following Paper; I mean Mr Edmund Curll, at the Bible and Dial in Fleetstreet, who was yesterday poison'd by Mr Pope, after having liv'd many Years an Instance of the mild Temper of the British Nation. Every Body knows that the said Mr Edmund Curll, on Monday the 26th Instant, publish'd a Satyrical Piece, entituled Court Poems, in the preface whereof they were attributed to a Lady of Quality, Mr Pope, or Mr Gay; by which indiscreet Method, though he had escap'd one Revenge, there were still two behind in reserve. Now on the Wednesday ensuing, between the Hours of Ten and Eleven, Mr Lintott, a neighb'ring Bookseller, desir'd a Conference with Mr Curll about settling a Title-Page, inviting him at the same Time to take a Whet together. Mr Pope, (who is not the only Instance how Persons of bright Parts may be carry'd away by the Instigation of the Devil) found means to convey himself into the same Room, under the pretence of Business with Mr Lintott, who it seems is the Printer of his Homer. This Gentleman, with seeming Coolness, reprimanded Mr Curll for wrongfully ascribing to him the aforesaid Poems: He excused himself by declaring that one of his Authors (Mr Oldmixon by Name) gave the Copies to the Press, and wrote the Preface. Upon this Mr Pope (being to all appearance reconcil'd) very civilly drank a Glass of Sack to Mr Curll, which he as civilly pledged; and tho' the liquor in Colour and Taste differ'd not from common Sack, yet was it plain by the Pangs this unhappy Stationer felt soon after, that some poisonous Drug had been secretly infused therein.

In a note in the *Dunciad* the same poet alleged that, 'being first threaten'd and afterwards punish'd for intending to publish the *Court Poems* as by "A Lady of Quality", Curll transferred it from her to him, and has now printed it twelve years in his name'. Curll retorted in the *Curliad* by declaring that the whole of this charge was false.

The matter of fact [he writes] stands thus: About the year 1715, Mr Joseph Jacobs (late of Hoxton, the Founder of a Remarkable Sect called the Whiskers) gave to Mr John Oldmixon three Poems at that time handed about, entitled The Bassett Table, The Toilet, and The Drawing Room. These Pieces were printed in Octavo, and published by Mr James Roberts, near the Oxford Arms in Warwick Lane, under the Title of Court Poems. The Profit arising from the Sale was equally to be divided between Mr John Oldmixon, Mr John Pemberton (a Bookseller of Parliamentary Note in Fleet Street, tho' he has not had the good fortune to be immortalized in the Dunciad), and myself. And I am sure my Brother Lintot will, if asked, declare this to be the same state of the Case I laid before Mr Pope, when he sent for me to the Swan Tavern in Fleet Street to enquire after this Publication. My brother Lintot drank his half Pint of Old Hock, Mr Pope his half Pint of Sack, and I the same quantity of an Emetic Potion (which was the punishment referred to by our Commentator), but no threatenings past. Mr Pope, indeed, said, that Satires should not be printed (tho' he has now changed his mind). I answered, they should not be wrote, for if they were, they would be printed. He replied, Mr Gay's Interest at Court would be greatly hurt by publishing these Pieces. This was all that passed in our Triumvirate. We then parted, Pope and my brother Lintot went together, to his Shop, and I went home and vomited heartily. I then despised the Action and have since in another manner sufficiently Purged the Author of it. In the Advertisement prefixt to the Court Poems, the Hearsay of the Town is only recited, some attributing them to a Lady of Quality, others to Mr Gay, but the Country-confirmation was (Chelsea being named) that the Lines could come from no other hand than the laudable Translator of Homer. This is a Demonstration of the Falsehood of our Commentator's Assertion, that any transfer was made, from a Lady to Mr Pope, they being originally charged upon him as his lawful issue; and so I shall continue his Fame, having lately printed a new edition of them and added them to his Letters, which come next under consideration.

Before dealing with Pope's *Letters*, however, it may be as well to say something more about Curll's earlier record. The year in which the memorable meeting took place in the Swan Tavern, in Fleet Street, saw the bookseller tossed in a blanket by the Westminster scholars for printing, without permission, a funeral oration delivered by the captain of the school. The story of his humiliation at their hands is best told in the following letter, which is printed by W. J. Thoms from the *St James's Post* of that year:

King's College, Westminster
August 3, 1716

Sir,—You are desired to acquaint the public that a certain book-seller near Temple Bar, not taking warning by the frequent drubs that he has undergone for his often pirating other men's copies, did lately, without the consent of Mr John Barber, present Captain of Westminster School, publish the scraps of a Funeral Oration, spoken by him over the corpse of the Rev. Dr South. And being on Thursday last fortunately nabbed within the limits of Dean's Yard, by the King's Scholars there, he met with a college salutation, for he was first presented with the ceremony of the blanket, in which, when the skeleton had been well shook, he was carried in triumph to the School; and after receiving a grammatical construction for his false concords, he was reconducted to Dean's Yard, and on his knees asking pardon of the aforesaid Mr Barber for his offence, he was kicked out of the Yard, and left to the huzzas of the rabble.

I am, Sir, yours, etc.

T.A.

In the same unlucky year Curll also made his first appearance at the Bar of the House of Lords. This was for printing an account of the trial for high treason of the Earl of Wintoun, the privilege of which had been granted to Jacob Tonson, who had issued it at a price which only a monopolist could afford to charge. Curll's attempt at underselling brought him on his knees before the Lord Chancellor, but the reprimand which he then received does not appear to have had any permanent effect, for he was at once busy again in other disreputable practices.

Both Nichols and Thoms, without seriously attempting to whitewash the character of 'the infamous, the dauntless, the shameless Edmund Curll'—as Lord Campbell called him in his speech of July 28th, 1845, when the order against publishing the works, life, or last will of any member of the House of Lords was rescinded*—have made some attempt to show that he was not quite so black as he was painted, but when all is said and done in his favour he remains an ugly blot on the history of eighteenth-century bookselling. On November 30th, 1725, he was convicted of 'printing and publishing several obscene and im-

* Curll paid his second visit to the House of Lords in 1722 for announcing that he intended to publish the late Duke of Buckingham's works; which led to the passing of the Standing Order forbidding any publication of the kind without the authority of a peer's executors, or other legal representative.

modest books, greatly tending to the corruption and degradation of manners', including *The Nun in her Smock*, but was not, as commonly stated, 'set in the pillory as he well deserved' for this offence, but, after five months' imprisonment, fined fifty marks and kept in surety of £100 for his good behaviour for one year. It was for the political offence of publishing the *Memoirs of John Ker of Kersland*, as W. J. Thoms clearly proves, that he was ordered, at the same time, 'to pay a fine of twenty marks, to stand in the pillory for the space of one hour, and his own recognizance to be taken for his good behaviour for another year'.

The *Dunciad*, in which Curll was pilloried after another fashion, made its appearance with all the air of mystery with which both Pope and Swift delighted to surround the origin of their satires. It was published anonymously on May 28th, 1728, professing to be the work of a friend of Pope, and a reprint of a Dublin edition. How great a stir it made in London on its publication is seen in a contemporary account attributed to Pope himself, though said to have been written by Richard Savage:

> On the day the book was first vended a crowd of authors besieged the shop; entreaties, advices, threats of law and battery, nay, cries of treason, were all employed to hinder the coming out of *The Dunciad*. On the other side, the booksellers and hawkers made as great an effort to procure it. What could a few poor authors do against so great a majority as the public! There was no stopping a torrent with a finger, so out it came. Many ludicrous circumstances attended it. The Dunces (for by this name they were called) held weekly clubs to consult of hostilities against the author. One wrote a letter to a great Minister, that Mr Pope was the greatest enemy the Government had; and another bought his image in clay, to execute him in effigy; with which sad sort of satisfaction the gentlemen were a little comforted. Some false editions of the book having an owl in their frontispiece; the true one, to distinguish it, fixed in its stead an ass laden with authors. Then another surreptitious one being printed with the same ass, the new edition in octavo returned for distinction to the owl again. Hence arose a great contest of booksellers against booksellers, and advertisements against advertisements; some recommending the edition of the owl, and others the edition of the ass, by which names they came to be distinguished, to the great honour also of the gentlemen of *The Dunciad*.

Pope published the enlarged edition of the *Dunciad* in March 1729, assigning the property to Lord Bathurst, Lord Burlington and Lord Oxford, and copies could only be obtained through them. Later in the same year, when there seemed to be no longer any risk of publication, they reassigned the property to Lawton Gilliver, who, having now become Pope's publisher, issued a new edition in November, though Pope himself did not openly acknowledge the poem until it appeared in his Collected Works in 1735. The complete history of the publication of Pope's correspondence, in which the poet, by tortuous intrigues which were quite beyond the ingenuity of the bookseller, surreptitiously made Curll his publisher, and then had him summoned before the House of Lords, would fill a whole chapter by itself. The true facts have only come to light within comparatively recent years, but there is no doubt that Pope merely used Curll in this matter in order that he might gratify his insatiable vanity by publishing an authorized edition of his letters. Curll had published in 1726 the *Familiar Letters* addressed by Pope in his youth to his friend Henry Cromwell, the originals of which had been bought by the bookseller for ten guineas from a Mrs Thomas, who had been Cromwell's mistress. Whether Pope seriously objected to the publication of these letters or not does not matter. They undoubtedly suggested Curll as the agent who should publish his *Literary Correspondence for Thirty Years*. This appeared in 1735, and Pope secretly arranged that the collection should be announced as including a number of letters of Peers, which he knew to be an offence against the law. Though careful enough to arrange that no such letters were actually sent to Curll for the purpose, Pope nevertheless saw to it that the books were seized on publication by a warrant from the House of Lords, and the publisher himself summoned to explain what he meant by his advertisement. Curll in defence pleaded ignorance. He explained that the advertisement was sent to him with instructions to copy it and have it inserted in the papers. All he knew about the person who sent it was that he signed himself 'P. T.'. He told the Lords that he wrote to Pope to acquaint him that a Gentleman, who signed himself 'P. T.', had offered him a large collection of his (Pope's) letters to print. 'That Mr Pope did not send him any answer to his letter, but put an Advertisement in *The Daily Post Boy*, that he had received such a letter from E. C. That he knew no such person as P. T. That he believ'd nobody had such a collection of letters, but that it was a Forgery, and that he should not trouble himself about it; And then read an Advertisement which he put into *The Post Boy* in answer to the said Advertisement of Mr Pope.'*

In the end, the Lords, finding that the book did not, as announced, contain any letters of Peers, and thus was not contrary to the Standing Order of the House referred to in a footnote to p. 144, dismissed the publisher and ordered the copies to be returned to him. The Lords and the bookseller, however, had served Pope's purpose, and he at once proceeded to prepare his 'authorized' edition. Curll, nothing abashed, and determined also to profit by the publicity given to the affair, boldly announced his intention to publish a third volume:

* From the Proceedings in the *Lords' Journals*.

The Third Volume of Mr Pope's Literary Correspondence, I shall publish next Month, ORIGINALS being every day sent to me, some of them, to a certain DUCHESS, which I am ready to produce under his own Hand. I know not what Honours Mr Pope would have conferr'd on him: — 1st I have hung up his Head for my Sign; and, 2ndly, I have engraved a fine view of his House, Gardens, etc., from Mr Rijsbrack's Painting, which will shortly be publish'd. But if he aims at any further Artifices, he never found himself more mistaken than he will in trifling with Me.

And Curll was as good as his word. He added volume after volume — with much extraneous matter — until he had a whole series of six in stock; and in the fifth of these he had the effrontery to criticize the textual accuracy — not without a certain amount of truth — of Pope's authorized edition. 'Many considerable passages are omitted,' he declares, among other things; 'others are interpolated; and upon the whole the *Genuine Edition* is so far from an *authentic one* that it is only a *Select Collection* of Mr Pope's Letters, more old letters being omitted than new ones added.' Pope's own edition appeared in May 1737 and the copyright was bought by Robert Dodsley, the publisher who may be said to have followed old Jacob Tonson in the 'apostolic succession'. Jacob, now spending his last days in retirement, lived until the following April, surviving his nephew and successor rather more than four months, the business being carried on by the son of Jacob Tonson Junior — Jacob Tonson III. Bernard Lintot had also been succeeded by his son Henry, but the great traditions of both houses were passing away.

IO

In Dr Johnson's Day

It was a ripe moment for the right man, and Robert Dodsley, who holds a place apart in the bookselling annals of the eighteenth century, made the most of his opportunity. The generality of his craft in that Golden Age may be roughly divided into two distinct classes. To one of these belonged such notorious members as Edmund Curll, and his lineal descendant, Ralph Griffiths, who tortured poor Goldsmith's soul in his poverty-stricken Grub Street days. The other class included such publishers as Bernard Lintot and Jacob Tonson, men who were practically the fathers of the modern book trade, possessing the first real sense of the rights of authorship and a respect for the dignity of letters. None of these, however, had anything of the true literary instinct, and it was this possession which gave Robert Dodsley his unique position.

He strayed into poetry while still in his footman's livery. It was probably because he did not disguise this fact that his earliest appearances in print, beginning with *Servitude* in 1729, and including *A Muse in Livery; or, The Footman's Miscellany* (1732), won for him many influential friends, not only among people of quality, to whom anything in the shape of a novelty was welcome, but among such authors as Defoe and Pope. Defoe, who was then sixty-eight, took an interest in the footman-poet from the first, young Dodsley having found some means of obtaining access to him. According to Lee's *Life of Daniel Defoe* (1869), he 'not only revised the poem [*Servitude*], but also—seeing it would not fill a sheet, wrote a preface and introduction of some ten pages, and then kindly added, as a postscript, six pages of quiet banter on his own popular tract [his recently published *Every Body's Business*], in order to give his humble protégé the reflex benefit of such popularity'. It is probable that he also assisted in the publication of the pamphlet which was issued by the bookseller Thomas Worrall. Success turned Dodsley's ambitious thoughts to playwriting. He wrote *The Toy-Shop*, and after issuing his *Muse in Livery* in 1732, ventured to send the play to Pope for his opinion as to its merits. Pope did more than Dodsley asked him; he recommended it to John Rich, who was then preparing to move to his new theatre in Covent Garden. It is not difficult to imagine Dodsley's delight when he read Pope's letter.

If fame and fortune were not already within his grasp, they were near enough to justify the doffing of his lackey's livery. Exactly when he left service, however, or what he did personally before embarking, in 1735, upon his career as a bookseller, is not known. As for the *Toy-Shop*, which he described as a 'dramatic satire', it was not produced on the stage until February 3rd of that year; but it scored an immediate success, and did even better when published, for the first time, three days later, by Lawton Gilliver, Pope's latest publisher, who had already issued several small volumes of Dodsley's verse. The book went through four editions within its first two months, and was only taken over by Dodsley himself when it reached its eighth edition. More important than the number of its editions, it secured for Dodsley, according to his biographer, Ralph Straus,* the money he needed, 'and with that, his own small savings, and a present from Mr Pope he was enabled to start upon the career which must of all others have appealed to him'.

The new publisher made an appropriate start on May 17th 1735, at Tully's Head, in Pall Mall — soon to become famous as a favourite haunt of distinguished booklovers and literary men — with a share in the second volume of Pope's *Works*, the other partners being Gilliver, whose address was at Homer's Head, in Fleet Street, and J. Brindley, of 29 New Bond Street. Pope had at last found a publisher after his own heart. 'I beg you,' he writes to the elder Duncombe on May 8th of that year, 'to accept of the new volume of my things, just printed, which will be delivered you by Mr Dodsley, the author of the *Toy-Shop*, who has just set up as a bookseller; and I doubt not, as he has more sense, so will have more honesty, than most of [that] profession'. The bookseller was not ungrateful for Pope's patronage, and sincerely mourned the poet's death in 1744.

Dodsley had his occasional disputes with authors, but they were few and far between. His own literary gifts helped him no doubt, but the reason for his success in this field is not easy to appreciate to-day. His poems are as dead as his ill-starred literary journal, the *Public Register*; and his contemporary vogue as a playwright is difficult to understand. The real reason for his popularity in the literary world was that he had a 'way' with him which almost everybody liked. Perhaps it was because he was never ashamed to admit that he began life as a footman. 'You know how decent, humble, inoffensive a creature Dodsley is; how little apt to forget or disguise his having been a footman,' writes his friend Horace Walpole to George Montagu on one occasion, when telling him how Dr John Brown had been ill-mannered enough to reply to one of Dodsley's letters with a card saying, 'Footman's language I never return.'

Brown's mind was none too well balanced, or probably he would never have done such a thing; for the publisher-poet, as Sir Edmund

* *Robert Dodsley, Poet, Publisher, and Playwright*, 1910.

Gosse says in a letter quoted by Straus, 'was just "Doddy"—everybody's friend, in love with books and bookish people, a delightful, serviceable, bourgeoise personality'. Lord Chesterfield and Lord Lyttelton, as well as Sir Robert Walpole, were among the bookseller's earliest patrons. Rivals watched the rapid progress of the rising star with envy and uncharitableness. Curll could not forbear to show his malice in the lines which he addressed to Pope in 1737, when that poet made over to Dodsley the sole right in the publication of his letters:

> 'Tis kind indeed a Livery Muse to aid,
> Who scribbles farces to augment his trade.

To Dodsley belongs the place of honour in the great group of booksellers attracted by that magnetic personality, Samuel Johnson—just as their less scrupulous predecessors revolved round Shakespeare and Ben Jonson a century before. Dodsley's shop was already fashionable when Johnson, then practically unknown, went to him on the matter of the anonymous *London*. Later, like many other distinguished men of letters, he was to share in the social gatherings of wit and fashion which Dodsley delighted to encourage at his hospitable Tully's Head. 'The true Noctes Atticae are revived at honest Dodsley's house', he afterwards said. But for the moment he was only an outsider, ostensibly acting for an unknown author friend. Himself the son of a bookseller he knew something of the hardships and uncertainties of the trade, and always had a good word to say for it. His early experience was mainly confined to his father's shop at Lichfield, and Warren's at Birmingham, where, after leaving Oxford, and his dreary days as usher at Market Bosworth Grammar School ended, he lodged when staying with his friend Hector. Warren was the first established bookseller in Birmingham. When Michael Johnson started in business at Lichfield, as Boswell tells us, 'booksellers' shops in the provincial towns of England were very rare, so that there was not one even in Birmingham, in which town old Mr Johnson used to open a shop every market-day'. Michael Johnson carried his books in the same way to Uttoxeter, and it was here that Dr Johnson, in his old age, performed his penance for his youthful pride in refusing to accompany his father to market. The story as told by Boswell bears repeating:

> To Henry White, a young clergyman, with whom he now formed an intimacy, so as to talk with him with great freedom, he mentioned that he could not in general accuse himself of having been an undutiful son. 'Once, indeed', said he, 'I was disobedient; I refused to attend my father to Uttoxeter market. Pride was the source of that refusal, and the remembrance of it was painful. A few years ago I desired to atone for this fault; I went to Uttoxeter in very

bad weather, and stood for a considerable time bare-headed in the rain, on the spot where my father's stall used to stand. In contrition I stood, and I hope the penance was expiatory.'

It was for Warren, the Birmingham bookseller, that Johnson's first prose work was written — his translation of Lobo's *Voyage to Abyssinia*, for which the bookseller paid him five guineas. The work was published in 1735, with 'London' printed on the title-page, though in reality it came from a local press in Birmingham; but this, says Boswell, was 'a device too common with provincial publishers'. When Johnson moved to London in 1738 he obtained his first regular employment from the publisher Edward Cave, who had founded the *Gentleman's Magazine* seven years previously, and carried it on under the name of *Sylvanus Urban*,* but it was Dodsley who gave him his real introduction to the great reading public in town. Johnson submitted his *London* to Cave, who forwarded the poem to Dodsley, and Johnson, still preserving the pretence of being merely a friend of the author, called anxiously at Tully's Head to know the result. As he told Cave in one of his letters on the subject, the mysterious author was then 'under very disadvantageous circumstances of fortune'. Then came the letter to the printer with the joyful news that Dodsley was willing to publish the poem:

I was to-day with Mr Dodsley, who declares very warmly in favour of the paper you sent him, which he desires to have a share in, it being, as he says, a creditable thing to be concerned in. I knew not what answer to make till I had consulted you, nor what to demand on the author's part, but am very willing that, if you please, he should have a part in it, as he will undoubtedly be more diligent to disperse and promote it. If you can send me word to-morrow what I shall say to him, I will settle matters, and bring the poem with me for the press, which, as the town empties, we cannot be too quick with.

The result was a further meeting between Dodsley and Johnson, at which he gave Johnson ten much-needed guineas. 'I might perhaps have accepted less', said the author to Boswell, years afterwards, in relating this incident, 'but that Paul Whitehead had a little before got ten guineas for a poem; and I would not take less than Paul Whitehead.' Whitehead's poem — his satire, *Manners* — cost its publisher a good deal more than ten guineas before he had done with it, for early in the following year the Lords voted the piece 'scandalous', and a libel on several members of the House. In the absence of the author Dodsley was kept in prison for a week, at a cost of £70 in fees, but was then

* Cave was subsequently the printer of Johnson's *Rambler*.

released through the intercession of influential friends, after being brought to the Bar of the House, where, upon his knees, he received a final reprimand for his offence from the Lord Chancellor.

An interesting experiment was started about this time, which, though outside the regular course of bookselling, deserves some mention. In 1736, the year after Dodsley opened his shop at Tully's Head under such influential patronage, the trade was threatened with another form of competition. This was an association nominally called 'The Society for the Encouragement of Learning', and aiming, among other things, 'to assist authors in the publication, and to secure them the entire profits of their own works'. The scheme had for its president the Duke of Richmond, and its Committee of Management included other noblemen and scholars of the highest rank, as well as Paul Whitehead and James Thomson as representatives of professional authorship.

It began with a flourish of trumpets, a membership of over a hundred, and a secretary, one Alexander Gordon, who is said to have 'made a trial of all the ways by which a man could get an honest livelihood'; but whose correspondence, so far as we have seen it, does little credit to his tact. 'You have no doubt heard', he writes to Dr Richardson, Master of Emmanuel College, Cambridge—whose assistance he sought in order to secure the offer of Dr Middleton's *Life of Cicero*—'in what a discouraging way Dr Bentley has used our Society: for, though his work of *Manilius* was ready to be printed, and he desired by several persons to have it published by the Society, he not only raised such ill-grounded objections against the institution itself, but chose to throw it into the hands of a common bookseller, than in those of the Society, which has not only made several gentlemen of letters and high life exclaim against the discouraging and ungenerous act, but will be recorded to the learned world when he is dead and rotten.'

It is hardly surprising that the Society did not meet with much encouragement from the 'common booksellers', though a few chosen members of the regular trade were at various times appointed to act for it, and issue such works as fell into his hands. Not meeting with much success by these means the Society appointed its own retail booksellers in different parts of London, allowing them 15 per cent on all the Society's publications that they sold; but its affairs were never flourishing. Even Thomson, though a member of the committee, would not leave his old friend Andrew Millar, who had published his *Seasons* in 1730, not long after opening his shop near St Clement's Church in the Strand. Millar remained Thomson's publisher until the poet's death in 1748. The Society for the Encouragement of Learning, in spite of all the drawbacks, made a brave and generous struggle against odds for thirteen years, publishing, among other things, Carte's *Original Letters*, Roe's *State Papers*, and Bishop Tanner's *Notitia Monastica* and *Bibliotheca*

Britannica. According to Knight, who dwells on the incident with a professional satisfaction which would not be unpardonable were he strictly accurate in his facts, the Society 'made an end without publishing any work that had a chance of being profitable either to author or bookseller, and it left to some of its patrons, irresponsible or not, a legacy of two thousand pounds debt'.

A very different version of the Society's end is given by William Jerdan in a pamphlet published in 1838, and based on the manuscript volumes of the Society's Proceedings, now in the British Museum. From this it appears that the distinguished promoters of the scheme 'closed their humane and honoured exertions by balancing the accounts of the association and bestowing the residue of their funds upon that noble charity, the Foundling Hospital. At this time the Duke of Leeds was President, and the sum so congenially appropriated was £24 12s. — the last legacy from the Foundlings of Literature to the hardly more forlorn Foundlings of Benevolence.'

Though Johnson's *London* — to return to our story — proved a great success, it was nine years before Dodsley published anything else of his; but then it was to be associated with him in the great *Dictionary*, which Dodsley appears, indeed, to have been the first to suggest. He was not only one of the 'gentlemen partners' in this arduous enterprise, but also the one with whom alone the lexicographer did not pick a quarrel. 'He invariably', writes Ralph Straus, 'caused Dodsley to act as intermediary during the many little quarrels and disagreements which arose during the seven years of toil.' We all know the story of the mutual satisfaction expressed by Johnson and one of the other partners, Andrew Millar, when the last sheet was at length received from the unpunctual author. 'Thank God, I have done with him!' exclaimed Millar, upon whom had fallen the chief responsibility of seeing the work through the press. 'I am glad', said Johnson, when this remark was repeated to him, 'that he thanks God for anything.'

This, however, was not Johnson's final opinion of Millar, who, 'though himself no great judge of literature', says Boswell, 'had good sense enough to have for his friends very able men to give him their opinions and advice in the purchase of copyright; the consequence of which was his acquiring a very large fortune, with great liberality'. Johnson said of him, 'I respect Millar, sir; he has raised the price of literature.' Next to Dodsley, Millar was the best-known publisher of his day. He was Fielding's publisher as well as Thomson's, and, with the histories of Robertson and Hume, played no inconsiderable part in developing the popular taste for historical works in the mid-eighteenth century. How disappointed was Hume with the reception of the first volume of his *History*, which was issued at Edinburgh, he has told us in his own words:

I thought that I was the only historian that had at once neglected present power, interest, and authority, and the cry of popular prejudices; and as the subject was suited to every capacity, expected proportional applause. But miserable was my disappointment. I was assailed by one cry of reproach, disapprobation, and even destestation; English, Scotch, and Irish, Whig and Tory, Churchman and Sectary, Freethinker and Religionist, Patriot and Courtier, united in their rage against the man who had presumed to shed a generous tear for the fate of Charles I and the Earl of Strafford; and after the first ebullitions of their fury were over, what was still more mortifying, the book seemed to sink into oblivion. Mr Millar told me that in a twelvemonth he sold only forty-five copies of it. I scarcely, indeed, heard of one man in three kingdoms, considerable for rank or letters, that could endure the book. I must only except the primate of England, Dr Herring, and the primate of Ireland, Dr Stone, which seem two odd exceptions. These dignified prelates separately sent me messages 'not to be discouraged'.

Burton attributes much of the subsequent success of the *History* to the exertions of Millar. 'An arrangement was made, by which he should take the history under his protection—publish the subsequent volumes, and push the sale of the first.' The arrangement is said to have been recommended by Hume's Edinburgh publishers; and it shows how much, in that age, as probably also in this, even a sound work may depend on the publisher's exertions, for securing a hold on the public mind. The *History* was concluded in 1761, and Hume now wrote in a very different strain: 'Notwithstanding the variety of events and seasons to which my writings had been exposed, they had still been making such advances that the copy money given me by the booksellers much exceeded anything formerly known in England. I was become not only independent but opulent.'

Boswell places Dodsley at the head of the list of booksellers who, for the sum of £1,575,* contracted with Johnson for the execution of the *Dictionary*. The others are given as 'Mr Charles Hitch [son-in-law and successor of Arthur Bettesworth of Paternoster Row], Mr Andrew Millar, the two Messieurs Longman, and the two Messieurs Knapton'. Unfortunately the fame which the *Dictionary* brought him did not improve Johnson's financial position. The whole of the £1,575 was spent before the last page was written, the cost of amanuenses and paper, and other expenses of the kind, running away with no small portion of the sum. Boswell once said to him: 'I am sorry, Sir, you did not get

* This, by a coincidence, was exactly the amount received by the widow of Philip Stanhope for Lord Chesterfield's *Letters to his Son*.

more for your *Dictionary*.' His answer was, 'I am sorry too. But it was very well. The booksellers are generous, liberal-minded men.' Upon all occasions, adds Boswell, 'he did ample justice to their character in this respect. He considered them as the patrons of literature; and indeed, although they have eventually been considerable gainers by his *Dictionary*, it is to them that we owe its having been undertaken and carried through at the risk of great expense, for they were not absolutely sure of being indemnified'. Though Millar took the principal charge of conducting the publication of the work, Dodsley seems to have been responsible for most of the preliminary arrangements.

The Doctor himself, in a letter to Dr Burney, asks him to direct his friends to send their orders to Dodsley 'because it was by his recommendation that I was employed in the work'. It was at Dodsley's desire, too, that the 'Plan' was addressed to Lord Chesterfield—with what result we all know. The publisher was afraid that Johnson's caustic letter to the Earl, after his belated praise of the *Dictionary* in Dodsley's own journal, the *World*, would cost him that nobleman's patronage; but his fears were groundless. Dodsley told Dr Adams that Chesterfield himself had shown him the letter. 'I should have imagined', replied Dr Adams, 'that Lord Chesterfield would have concealed it.' 'Pooh!' said Dodsley, 'do you think a letter from Johnson could hurt Lord Chesterfield? Not at all, sir. It lay upon his table, where anybody might see it. He read it to me; said, "This man has great powers," pointed out the severest passages, and observed how well they were expressed.'

It would be interesting to trace the growth of literary patronage up to this period from the time of Caxton, who, as mentioned on p. 41, was encouraged to continue his task of translating and printing the *Legend of Saints* by Lord Arundel's promise 'to take a reasonable quantity of them', and grant him, in addition, a yearly fee—'that is to note, a buck in summer and a doe in winter'. There are already, however, too many allied topics to admit of this; but it seems clear that the individual patron gradually gave place to the collective patronage of subscribers referred to on p. 138. A striking instance of this was the four thousand guineas received by Prior for the folio edition of his poems issued by his admirers on his release from prison in 1717. By the middle of the eighteenth century, with the steady growth of the reading public, the patron, both collective and individual, was no longer a necessity. 'At present', wrote Oliver Goldsmith, 'the few poets of England no longer depend on the great for subsistence; they have now no other patrons than the public.' And the publisher, at the same time, had superseded the patron as the author's paymaster.

'My good friend Mr Dodsley', as Lord Chesterfield calls him in one of his papers, continued to receive both his Lordship's patronage and his contributions to his periodical, the total number of his papers in the *World* eventually amounting to twenty-four. In the meantime Dodsley had been strengthening his connection with Johnson by publishing his imitation of the tenth satire of Juvenal, *The Vanity of Human Wishes*, and his tragedy *Irene*, both in 1749. The poem was none too handsomely paid for, as is proved by the copy of the agreement printed by Boswell:

> Nov. 25, 1748. I received of Mr Dodsley fifteen guineas, for which I assign to him the right of copy of an imitation of the *Tenth Satire of Juvenal*, written by me; reserving to myself the right of printing one edition.
>
> SAM. JOHNSON

Johnson made a practice in his agreements with publishers of reserving to himself this right of printing one edition, 'it being his fixed intention', says Boswell, 'to publish at some period, for his own profit, a complete collection of his works'. Dodsley was more liberal in regard to *Irene*, paying Johnson £100 for it, notwithstanding its failure on the stage at Drury Lane, and its refusal at the hands of other booksellers. Space prevents us from doing justice either to Dodsley's own highly successful tragedy, *Cleone*, or such literary work as the authorship of *The Oeconomy of Human Life*; and we can only glance at his subsequent career in the bookselling trade—a career bound up with some of the best chapters in our literary history. How he came to publish Gray's *Elegy* is best told in Gray's own letter to Horace Walpole, to whom he had sent a copy of the poem in the summer of 1750, when Walpole incautiously circulated it among his friends:

> *Cambridge, February* 11, 1751
>
> As you have brought me into a little sort of distress, you must assist me, I believe, to get out of it as well as I can. Yesterday I had the misfortune of receiving a letter from certain gentlemen (as their bookseller expresses it), who have taken the *Magazine of Magazines** into their hands. They tell me that an *ingenious* poem, called *Reflections in a Country Churchyard*, has been communicated to them, which they are printing forthwith: that they are informed that the *excellent* author of it is I by name, and that they beg not only his *indulgence*, but the *honour* of his correspondence, etc. As I am not at all disposed to be either so indulgent, or so correspondent, as they desire, I have but one bad way left to escape the honour they would inflict upon me; and, therefore, am obliged to desire you would make Dodsley print it immediately (which may be done in less than a week's time) from your copy; but

---

* A literary journal recently started by a bookseller of small renown, named Owen.

without my name, in what form is most convenient for him; but on his best paper and character; he must correct the press himself and print it without any interval between the stanzas, because the sense is in some places continued beyond them; and the title must be — *Elegy, written in a Country Churchyard.* If he would add a line or two to say it came into his hands by accident, I should like it better.

Dodsley, also through the agency of Walpole, who made him his regular bookseller, had already issued Gray's first published work, *An Ode on a Distant Prospect of Eton College.* This appeared anonymously in the spring of 1747, but attracted no attention. Walpole must have rushed to Tully's Head with a copy of the *Elegy* as soon as he received Gray's reproachful letter, for although this did not leave Cambridge until February 11th, the poem itself was published anonymously as a quarto pamphlet on the 15th. Even so, they only beat the rival bookseller by twenty-four hours, the poem appearing in the *Magazine of Magazines* on the 16th. The *Elegy* leaped into immediate fame, running through four authorized editions in two months, apart from numerous pirated editions. 'The success of the poem, however,' as Edmund Gosse says in his life of Gray, 'brought him little direct satisfaction, and no money. He gave the right of publication to Dodsley, as he did in all other instances. He held a Quixotic notion that it was beneath a gentleman to take money for his inventions from a bookseller, a view in which Dodsley naturally coincided.' After Gray's death it was stated by another bookseller that Dodsley had made nearly a thousand pounds by his poetry.

Gray lowered his exalted ideals when he walked into Dodsley's shop in June 1757 with his two later poems, *The Bard* and *The Progress of Poetry,* and parted with the copyright of both for forty guineas. These were the two poems with which Walpole started his private press at Strawberry Hill. 'On Monday next', writes the enthusiastic Walpole to Chute in July of this year, 'the Officina Arbuteana opens in form. The Stationers' Company, that is, Mr Dodsley, Mr Tonson, etc., are summoned to meet here on Sunday night. And with what do you think we open? *Cedite, Romani Impressores* — with nothing under *Graii Carmina.* I found him in town last week: he had brought his two *Odes* to be printed. I snatched them out of Dodsley's hands, and they are to be the first-fruits of my press.'

The first-fruits were a long time in the making. Gray began to lose patience with Walpole's new plaything, but copies were at length safely delivered in quarto pamphlet size, and issued on August 8th at a shilling each. In the following year Walpole printed at the same press his *Catalogue of Royal and Noble Authors,* though it was Dodsley who brought out the second edition in 1759. Earlier in the same year, while making his preparations to retire from the business, in which he was to be succeeded by his brother James, Robert Dodsley entered into negotiations with Laurence Sterne for the publication of *Tristram Shandy*. Probably through an old apprentice, John Hinxman, who had taken over the bookselling business of H. Hildyard, of Stonegate, York, Sterne wrote to Robert Dodsley offering *Tristram* for fifty pounds. The substance of Robert's reply may be gathered from Sterne's second letter, which is worth giving in full. Our text is from Straus's *Life of Dodsley*:

Sir,

What you wrote to me in June last, in answer to my demand of £50 for the Life and Opinions of Tristram Shandy—that it was too much to risk on a single volume, which, if it happened not to sell, would be hard upon your brother—I think a most reasonable objection in him, against giving me the price I thought my work deserved. You need not to be told by me, how much authors are inclined to overrate their own productions—for my own part, I hope I am an exception, for, if I could find out, by any arcanum, the precise value of mine, I declare Mr James Dodsley should have it 20 per cent below its value. I propose, therefore, to print a lean edition, in two small volumes of the size of Rasselas, and on the same type and paper, at my own expense, merely to feel the pulse of the world, and that I may know what price to set on the remaining volumes from the reception of these. If my book sells, and has the run our critics expect, I propose to free myself of all future troubles of the kind, and bargain with you, if possible for the rest as they come out, which will be every six months. If my book fails of success, the loss falls where it ought to do. The same motives which inclined me first to offer you this trifle, incline me to give you the whole profits of the sale (except what Mr Hinxman sells here, which will be a great many) and to have them sold only at your shop upon the usual terms in these cases. The book shall be printed here, and the impression sent up to you; for as I live at York, and shall correct every proof myself, it shall go perfect into the world, and be printed in so creditable a way, as to paper, type, etc., as to do no dishonour to you, who, I know, never choose to print a book meanly. Will you patronize my book upon these terms, and be as kind a friend to it as if you had bought the copyright? Be so good as to favour me with a line by the return; and believe me,

Sir, Your most obliged and most humble servant,

L. STERNE

What followed, as Straus says, is obscure, but it is probable that Dodsley advised his brother to come to terms with Sterne. What these terms were—if, indeed, any terms were made—it is impossible to say, but the work appeared on the first day of the new year, and took both London and York by storm. What that success meant to its author is shown in the fact that for the new editions of the book, and his two volumes of sermons, James Dodsley was ready to pay him £480. Robert himself retired in 1759 with a fine record. Apart from the books already named and others too numerous to mention, he published the works of Shenstone, whose close friend and biographer he became; *The Pleasures of Imagination* and other poems of Mark Akenside, who also edited the *Museum*; Swift's *Directions to Servants*, as well as a number of the Dean's minor writings; the first three works of Edmund Burke, besides starting with him the historic *Annual Register*; the first six parts of Young's *Night Thoughts*, for the copyright of which he paid 220 guineas; and Goldsmith's *Inquiry into the State of Polite Learning*, which rescued the author from the clutches of the bookseller Griffiths.

As a fitting close to his reign at Tully's Head, he issued the first edition of *Rasselas*, written, according to the story told to Boswell by Strahan the printer, in order that Johnson, with the profits, 'might defray the expense of his mother's funeral, and pay some little debts which she had left. He told Sir Joshua Reynolds that he composed it in the evenings of one week, sent it to the press in portions as it was written, and had never since read it over. Mr Strahan, Mr Johnston, and Mr Dodsley purchased it for a hundred pounds, but afterwards paid him twenty-five pounds more, when it came to a second edition.' The work was published on April 19th, 1759, and went to a second edition in the following June. Dodsley has other claims to remembrance apart from his own writings and his record as a publisher. His twelve volumes of *Old Plays* and three volumes of *Poems by Several Hands*—all compiled and edited by himself—remain an enduring memorial of his services to letters.

It is time to glance at some of the provincial booksellers as they might have been found in the early sixties of the eighteenth century, about the time of Robert Dodsley's death. There were more booksellers in Birmingham than in Dr Johnson's early days, among them William Hutton, who had established a circulating library there in 1751, but was now more intent on his paper warehouse, from which, as he tells us, he acquired an ample fortune. He is remembered as the author of a number of useful topographical works, and as a friend of Priestley who suffered heavily in the Church and King riots of 1791. His circulating library was not, it has been discovered, the first of its kind in Birmingham. This distinction apparently belongs to Thomas Warren, whose library is referred to in an advertisement which appears in a book printed by him in 1729.

To whom belongs the honour of founding our first circulating library in Britain is a vexed question. According to Benjamin Franklin there was no such thing in London in 1725. It was in that year, if we are to believe Robert Chambers's *Traditions of Edinburgh*, that Allan Ramsay started his in the Scottish capital. The *Dictionary of National Biography* gives the year as 1726, 'but the first known reference to it is in 1728'. Other early circulating libraries were established at Bristol, by Thomas Sendall (1728); Bath, by James Leake (by 1735); Cambridge, by Robert Watts (about 1745); and at Norwich, where the City Library, to quote from the Report of the Select Committee on Public Libraries issued in 1849, 'appears to partake of this double character, of a town and subscription library'. This library was founded in 1608, but the earliest reference to it as a subscription library appears in the preface to its catalogue of 1732. Hull still boasts a Subscription Library, now housed within a large shop in George Street, which traces its history back to 1775. Liverpool long had one of the best institutions of this kind in the Lyceum, founded in 1758 and surviving until 1944. Newcastle, always a book-loving centre, with its own Stationers' Hall on Tyne 'Brigg' in the eighteenth century, possessed two such libraries in 1755, according to Curwen—one founded by William Charnley, who lived until 1803, when he was succeeded by his son Emerson, described by Dibdin as 'the veteran Emperor of Northumbrian booksellers'.

William Charnley, before succeeding him in business, had been apprenticed to another local worthy, Martin Bryson, a friend of the bookseller-poet Allan Ramsay, who, as just mentioned, had already launched a circulating library in Edinburgh. Ramsay once sent him a letter addressed in verse:

> To Martin Bryson, on Tyne Brigg,
> An upright, downright, honest Whig.

York, which had been one of the earliest cities to encourage the printing-press in England, was not specially encouraging to booksellers in the eighteenth century. John Hinxman, as we have seen, had succeeded Hildyard there in 1757, and published the first edition of *Tristram Shandy* in 1760, but he soon returned to London, taking over the very considerable publishing business of Mrs Mary Cooper, relict of Thomas Cooper, at the Globe, in Paternoster Row. York's best-known printer was Thomas Gent, who, like William Hutton, was a topographer as well, with a similar fondness for relieving his pent-up feelings in occasional verse. His autobiography, which was not discovered until long after his death, is useful for its information regarding the state of the press in his lifetime, though, like the record of Samuel Richardson's business, in which Gent was at one time employed, it belongs more to the story of printing than to that of bookselling proper.

Dublin had no lack of printers and booksellers in the last half of the eighteenth century, but they were a notorious lot, taking full advantage of the fact that Ireland remained out of the jurisdiction of the Act of 1709. Richardson's grievance, which he printed in 1753, under the title 'The Case of Samuel Richardson, of London, Printer, on the Invasion of his Property in the *History of Sir Charles Grandison*, before publication, by certain Booksellers of Dublin', was that of many another author of his age. He explains that he had planned to send to Dublin the volumes of *Grandison*, as in the case of *Clarissa Harlowe*, to have them printed there before they were issued in London. But the pirates surreptitiously anticipated him. 'The sheets were stolen from his warehouse, and three Irish booksellers each published cheap editions of nearly half the book before a volume appeared in England. Richardson had heard an Irish bookseller boast that he could procure, from any printing-office in London, sheets of any book while it was being printed there. "At present", he writes in conclusion, "the English writers may be said, from the attempts and practices of the Irish booksellers and printers, to live in an age of *liberty*, but not of *property*." The *Gray's Inn Journal*, in referring to his case, observed that "a greater degree of probity might be expected from booksellers on account of their occupation in life, and connections with the learned. What, then, should be said of Messrs. Exshaw, Wilson, and Saunders, booksellers in Dublin, and perpetrators of this vile act of piracy?" '

Glasgow was perhaps the most striking exception to the general rule that the best work at this period was being done in London. The Foulis Press at Glasgow—founded in 1741 by Robert Foulis, with whom was associated his brother Andrew as partner—issued some of the finest books ever printed. 'The works produced by it', says Professor Ferguson,* 'are quite entitled to rank with the Aldines, Elzevirs, the Bodonis, Baskervilles, which are all justly renowned for the varied excellences they possess, but no provincial, and certainly no metropolitan, press in the country has ever surpassed that of the two brothers.' They became printers to the University of Glasgow, and confined their publications mainly to editions of the classics—notably the celebrated 'immaculate' Horace—and reprints of standard works in English. But they devoted too much of their attention and capital to their luckless scheme for a sort of Scottish Academy of Arts, and when, after their death, their affairs were finally wound up in 1781, their debts were found to amount to over £6,500.

Edinburgh, at the same period, had not specially distinguished herself in bookselling annals. Her great days under Constable were still to come, her most interesting bookseller up to this time, Allan Ramsay, the poet, having retired from business in 1755, and died three years later. Alexander Donaldson, who began in Edinburgh, had

* In the *Library* for March 1889.

opened his shop in London, where, as will presently be seen, he conducted a campaign against the Londoners which had far-reaching
consequences. Other booksellers, like Thomas Miller, of Bungay, who,
in 1755, as recorded by Dibdin, 'set himself up in the character of
grocer and bookseller', were springing up all over England, keeping
pace with the gradual increase in the reading public, and being supplied
by the wholesale dealers who had now become a recognized branch of
the business; but few other provincial worthies have left their names in
the records of the trade.

We must return to London for our contemporary glimpse of what
Lackington called 'the grand emporium of Great Britain for books'.
The Strand was a great highway of letters right through the eighteenth
century. Did not Pope place the race-course for the stationers in the
centre of that thoroughfare? Here, too, Andrew Millar installed himself
in old Jacob Tonson's house at the Shakespeare Head, opposite
Catherine Street, honouring a brother Scot by changing the name to
Buchanan's Head. Jacob Tonson III, who deserves to be remembered
for never having learned 'to consider the author as the under-agent to
the bookseller'—to quote Steevens's eulogy in the advertisement
prefixed to his edition of *Shakespeare*—had left the old address for another
house on the opposite side of the Strand, where he died in 1767, leaving
no one of his name to succeed him. It was Jacob Tonson III who, in
1765, with a number of other booksellers, published Johnson's long-
delayed edition of *Shakespeare*, and after his death was referred to by the
Doctor as 'the late amiable Mr Tonson.' And not without reason, for
the publisher who had all the troublesome dealings with Johnson in
connection with the new *Shakespeare* seems also to have proved a real
friend in need when, in February 1758, nearly two years after signing
the agreement for the book, his editor was arrested for a debt of £40.
The facts were given by H. B. Wheatley in the *Athenaeum* of September 11th 1909, in which he printed for the first time a number of
documents relating to this edition. From these it appears that, all told,
Johnson must have received upwards of £1,300 for his *Shakespeare*,
which is nearly three times as much as it was hitherto supposed to have
brought him. The work was published by subscription, Johnson issuing
his proposals in 1756, and promising the work before Christmas of the
following year. Yet nine years elapsed before it was ready, and Johnson
admitted that he 'lost all the names and spent all the money' before it
was finished.

Like the third Jacob Tonson, Henry Lintot, old Bernard Lintot's
only son, died (in 1758) without leaving a successor, and also without
adding much to his father's laurels as a publisher. James Dodsley
continued the business left by his greater brother Robert, but appears
to have closed the ordinary bookselling department, developing more

on the lines of a publishing house of the present day; keeping a carriage, too, but dreadfully afraid all the time that any of his friends should hear of it. It was James Dodsley who was first approached by Chatterton, before the 'marvellous boy' made his unsuccessful bid for the patronage of Walpole. 'I take this opportunity to acquaint you that I can procure copys of several Ancient Poems', he writes from Bristol to Tully's Head on December 21st, 1768. Among them, he says, is 'an interlude, perhaps the oldest dramatic piece extant; wrote by one Rowley, a Priest in Bristol, who lived in the reign of Henry VI and Edward IV'. If these pieces were likely to be of service to the publishers, copies would be sent at his command by his 'most obedient servant De Be'. The answer was to be directed 'for D. B. to be left with Mr Tho. Chatterton, Redclift Hill, Bristol'.

It has been assumed that no reply was sent, from the fact that nothing of the sort has been traced, but J. H. Ingram,* in his study of the poet from original documents, makes it fairly obvious that some correspondence did take place. The later letter to Dodsley, in which Chatterton described the finding of his masterpiece, the tragedy of *Aella*, and regretted that he had not the guinea which the owner demanded for a copy of the manuscript, seems clearly to prove that some intervening communications must have passed between the two. 'If it should not suit you', adds Chatterton, in his grand manner, 'I should be obliged to you if you would calculate the expenses of printing it, as I will endeavour to publish it by subscription on my own account.' Chatterton, remember, was then little more than sixteen; the tragedy itself, as now printed, contains over twelve hundred lines. What happened is not clear, though the result of the subsequent appeal to Walpole is well known. Chatterton called on Dodsley soon after his arrival in London, and it must have been there that he first realized how hard was the struggle which he had set himself to face. The rest of the unhappy story is known to every reader. It was a tragedy for Chatterton that the publisher to whom he applied was not Robert Dodsley—though some of his biographers evidently assume that it was —instead of his brother James, for Robert himself had the literary instinct, and might have sent Chatterton away as joyfully as Johnson, after that more fortunate interview in the matter of the poem *London*.

Gray's Inn at this time still had its bookseller in Thomas Osborne, an ignorant but enterprising man, who was not only pilloried by Pope in the later edition of the *Dunciad*,† but personally chastised by Johnson.

* *The True Chatterton*, 1910.

† Osborne earned this distinction, according to William Roscoe, in a footnote to his edition of the *Dunciad*, for publishing advertisements pretending to sell Mr Pope's subscription edition of Homer's *Iliad* at half the price; 'of which books he had none, but cut to the size of them (which was quarto) the common books in folio, without copper-plates, on a worse paper, and never above half the value'.

There were at least five Osbornes or Osborns in the London book trade at that period. One was John Osborn, of the sign of the Golden Ball in Paternoster Row, who is more honourably remembered for his share in 1740 in persuading his brother stationer, Samuel Richardson, to undertake something more ambitious in literature than the indexes and dedications which had hitherto contented him. Richardson himself relates how this came about in a letter to Aaron Hill:

> Two booksellers, my particular friends [John Osborn and Charles Rivington], entreated me to write for them a little volume of Letters, in a common style, on such subjects as might be of use to those country readers who were unable to indite for themselves. 'Will it be any harm', said I 'in a piece you want to be written so low, if we should instruct them how they should think and act in common cases, as well as indite?' They were the more urgent with me to begin the little volume for this hint. I set about it; and, in the progress of it, wrote two or three letters to instruct handsome girls who were obliged to go out to service, as we phrase it, how to avoid the snares that might be laid against their virtue. And hence sprung *Pamela*.

So successful was the novel that it ran through five editions within the first twelve months. It was in the following year that Johnson undertook to catalogue the Harleian Library, which Thomas Osborne had bought for £13,000 — not more, according to Oldys, than the mere cost of the binding of the books. 'It has been confidently related, with many embellishments', says Boswell, 'that Johnson one day knocked Osborne down in his shop, with a folio, and put his foot upon his neck. The simple truth I had from Johnson himself. "Sir, he was impertinent to me, and I beat him. But it was not in his shop: it was in my own chamber."' The story reminds us of the scuffle between Oliver Goldsmith and Thomas Evans* the bookseller who, in 1773, published a letter in his *London Packet* reflecting on Goldsmith and Miss Horneck; and of the earlier scene between David Hume and the Fleet Street bookseller who published the review called the *History of the Works of the Learned*, which had ventured to criticize his anonymous *Treatise of Human Nature*. This was a circumstance, according to Burton's *Life of Hume*, 'which so highly provoked our young philosopher, that he flew in a violent rage to demand satisfaction of Jacob Robinson, the publisher, whom he kept at bay, during the paroxysm of his anger, at his sword's point, trembling behind the counter, lest a period should be put to the life of a sober critic by a raving philosopher'. Obviously, as

---

* Not to be confused with another Thomas Evans, the scholarly bookseller of Pall Mall, who first collected Goldsmith's writings, and himself edited Shakespeare's Poems, Prior's Works, and a volume of Old Ballads on the lines of Percy's *Reliques*.

his biographer suggests, the author had not yet acquired the command over his passions of which he afterwards made a boast.

Johnson's treatment of Osborne did not in the least affect his high regard for booksellers in general. He is nowhere seen to better advantage than in his dealings with 'our poor friend Mr Thomas Davies', as Boswell calls him—the actor turned bookseller,* who in the back parlour of his little shop in Russell Street, Covent Garden, on that memorable Monday, May 16th, 1763, first introduced Boswell to the 'extraordinary man' of whom he had heard so much:

At last, on Monday the 16th of May, when I was sitting in Mr Davies's back-parlour, after having drunk tea with him and Mrs Davies, Johnson unexpectedly came into the shop, and Mr Davies having perceived him through the glass-door in the room in which we were sitting, advancing towards us,—he announced his awful approach to me, somewhat in the manner of an actor in the part of Horatio, when he addresses Hamlet on the appearance of his father's ghost, 'Look, my lord, it comes.' I found that I had a very perfect idea of Johnson's figure, from the portrait of him painted by Sir Joshua Reynolds soon after he had published his Dictionary, in the attitude of sitting in his easy chair in deep meditation; which was the first picture his friend did for him, which Sir Joshua very kindly presented to me. Mr Davies mentioned my name, and respectfully introduced me to him. I was much agitated; and recollecting his prejudice against the Scotch, of which I had heard much, I said to Davies, 'Don't tell where I come from.' 'From Scotland,' cried Davies, roguishly. 'Mr Johnson', said I, 'I do indeed come from Scotland, but I cannot help it.' I am willing to flatter myself that I meant this as light pleasantry to soothe and conciliate him, and not as a humiliating abasement at the expense of my country. But however that might be, this speech was somewhat unlucky; for with that quickness of wit for which he was so remarkable, he seized the expression 'come from Scotland', which I used in the sense of being of that country; and, as if I had said that I had come away from it, or left it, retorted, 'That, Sir, I find, is what a very great many of your countrymen cannot help.' This stroke stunned me a good deal; and when we had sat down, I felt myself not a little embarrassed and apprehensive of what might come next.

Poor Bozzy was snubbed worse than that before the interview was over, but he counted himself well rewarded by the conversation which the great man condescended to utter in his presence. Later we find

* It is said that Tom Davies was driven from the stage by Churchill's sneer in the *Rosciad*—'He mouths a sentence as curs mouth a bone.'

them dining together at Tom Davies's house, and it was the same publisher who, with Strahan and Cadell, waited upon Johnson on behalf of the Chapter House in 1777 to solicit the *Lives of the Poets*. Four years before this Davies had risked his friendship by publishing a pirated edition of Johnson's *Miscellaneous and Fugitive Pieces* in two volumes, but the Doctor took pity on his needy circumstances, and forgave him. 'Sir', he said to Boswell on one occasion, 'Davies has learning enough to give credit to a clergyman'; but his learning did not prevent him in 1778 from becoming bankrupt. It was Johnson who used his influence then to help him out of his difficulties, and touching memorials of his sincere regard for his old bookselling friend are preserved by his biographer in two letters written by the Doctor when stricken with illness in the last years of his life.

Nor must we forget those dinner parties at 'my worthy booksellers and friends, Messieurs Dilly, in the Poultry, at whose hospitable and well-covered table', remarks Boswell, 'I have seen a greater number of literary men than at any other, except that of Sir Joshua Reynolds.' It was here that Bozzy so artfully negotiated the meeting between Johnson and Wilkes in 1776; and it was Charles Dilly—at one time in partnership with his brother Edward—who not only published Boswell's *Tour to the Hebrides* (1780) but the *Life of Johnson* (1791).

We are wandering, however, from our general view of the book trade as it existed in London within a few years of Robert Dodsley's death. Among the men who helped to make the neighbourhood of the Strand a favourite haunt of booklovers was Tom Payne, whose annual catalogue of literature, old and new, English and foreign, brought him customers from all parts of the kingdom. His shop was at the Mews-Gate, so named from the Royal Mews, which stood on the site of the present National Gallery. Here, in 1777, he published the first edition of the *Rowley Poems*—seven years after Chatterton's tragic death.* 'His little shop', says Knight, 'acquired the name of a Literary Coffee House; for there, rummaging over his shelves, or glancing at the books upon his counters, were to be found a succession of scholars always eager to purchase at the very moderate prices at which "Honest Tom Payne" marked his books.' Thomas Mathias, in his *Pursuits of Literature*, describes him as 'that *Trypho emeritus*, Mr Thomas Payne, one of the honestest men living, to whom, as a bookseller, learning is under considerable obligations'.† Pall Mall already had other book-sellers, besides the Dodsleys. Thomas Becket settled there after leaving Andrew Millar's shop to become a partner in the firm of Becket & De

---

* All Chatterton's literary work printed during his lifetime appeared in the periodicals. The first of his pieces to be published separately was *The Execution of Sir Charles Bawdin*, issued by W. Goldsmith, of 20 Paternoster Row, in 1772, two years after the poet's death.

† Thomas Payne the younger succeeded to his father's business in 1709, transferring it to more pretentious quarters in Pall Mall in 1806, and retiring in 1825.

Hondt, who, succeeding James Dodsley as Sterne's publishers, issued the fifth and sixth volumes of *Tristram Shandy* at the end of 1761, and not only completed the work, but published the same author's further volumes of *Sermons* in 1767—with a subscription list which included the names of Voltaire, Diderot and Hume, and brought him £300 in addition to copyright money—and the *Sentimental Journey*, which appeared in February 1768, less than three weeks before poor Yorick's melancholy end.

While the Strand and farther west were thus widening the book circle of London, Fleet Street and the neighbourhood of St Paul's still held their own, though the Churchyard itself had long since lost its old importance. Paternoster Row, standing in the shadow of St Paul's and the new Stationers' Hall, made amends for the Church-yards' loss by steadily increasing its influence with the growth of such firms as the Rivingtons and Longmans. A stone's-throw away at the sign of the Bible and Sun dwelt 'the philanthropic publisher of St Paul's Churchyard', as Goldsmith in *The Vicar of Wakefield* calls John Newbery, the good-natured, pimple-faced bookseller, who combined the sale of literature with that of Dr James's celebrated Fever Powder, and other patent medicines. Newbery was the first publisher to prove that the time had come to furnish children with a special library and a light literature of their own. It was not until the eighteenth century that Englishmen began to study the needs of children in this respect. The horn-books, with their prayers and their alphabets, and the chap books which the pedlars carried about from village to village as far back as the sixteenth century, were out of date.

Newbery understood children better. *Little Goody Two Shoes*, *Giles Gingerbread*, *Tommy Trip and his Dog Jowler*, and other of his 'Nursery Classics', as Charles Lamb calls them, all owed their origin to him, if he did not write them himself. In this connection America honours his memory today with the Newbery Medal, awarded for the best children's book of the year. His inexhaustible energy—playfully caricatured by Johnson under the character of 'Jack Whirler' in the *Idler*—led him into many undertakings in practically every branch of literary and newspaper enterprise, but his fame rests chiefly on his books for children and his connection with Oliver Goldsmith. This connection began after Dodsley had published the *Inquiry into the Present State of Polite Learning* in 1759, which, as already stated, marked the end of Goldsmith's miseries at the hands of the grinding bookseller, Ralph Griffiths, who had given him hack work on the *Monthly Review*, providing him with board and lodging in return over his shop in Paternoster Row. Escaping thence, Goldsmith found other rooms elsewhere, though still in the pay of Griffiths, who lent him, or became security for, a small sum of money in order that Goldsmith could buy a suit of clothes for his examination at Surgeon's Hall. He promised to return the money in the shape of book reviews. As luck would have it, his landlord was just then thrown into prison, and the good-natured Goldsmith must needs pawn the suit in order to secure his release, at the same time leaving the books which he had reviewed for Griffiths as security for a trifling loan advanced by a neighbour to relieve his own immediate wants. Unfortunately the parsimonious publisher happened to see the suit of clothes at the pawnbroker's, and denouncing Goldsmith as a knave and sharper, threatened to send him to prison. Here is Goldsmith's reply:

January 1759

Sir,—

I know of no misery but a jail to which my own imprudences and your letter seem to point. I have seen it inevitable these three or four weeks, and, by heavens! request it as a favour—as a favour that may prevent something more fatal. I have been some years struggling with a wretched being—with all that contempt and indigence bring with it—with all those passions which make contempt insupportable. What, then, has a jail that is formidable? I shall at least have the society of wretches, and such is to me true society. I tell you, again and again, that I am neither able nor willing to pay you a farthing, but I will be punctual to any appointment you or the tailor shall make; thus far, at least, I do not act the sharper, since, unable to pay my own debts one way, I would generally give some security another. No, Sir; had I been a sharper—had I been possessed of less good nature and native generosity, I might surely now have been in better circumstances.

I am guilty, I own, of meannesses which poverty unavoidably brings with it: my reflections are filled with repentance for my imprudence, but not with any remorse for being a villain; that may be a character you unjustly charge me with. Your books, I can assure you, are neither pawned nor sold, but in the custody of a friend, from whom my necessities obliged me to borrow some money; whatever becomes of my person, you shall have them in a month. It is very possible both the reports you have heard, and your own suggestions, may have brought you false information with respect to my character; it is very possible that the man whom you now regard with detestation may inwardly burn with grateful resentment. It is very possible that, upon a second perusal of the letter I sent you, you may see the workings of a mind strongly agitated with gratitude and jealousy. If such circumstances should appear, at least spare invective till my book with Mr Dodsley shall be published, and then, perhaps, you may see the bright side of a mind, when my professions shall not appear the dictates of necessity, but of choice.

You seem to think Dr Milner knew me not. Perhaps so; but he was a man I shall ever honour; but I have friendships only with the dead! I ask pardon for taking up so much time; nor shall I add to it by any other professions than that I am, sir, your humble servant,

OLIVER GOLDSMITH

P.S. — I shall expect impatiently the result of your resolutions.

Griffiths had several months to wait for the *Inquiry into the State of Polite Learning*, the book which Dodsley had in preparation, and took the author's attack on his craft as a personal affront. Though the quarrel was patched up Griffiths never forgave him. In 1760 Goldsmith's *Citizen of the World* ran through John Newbery's *Public Ledger* as the *Chinese Letters*, and was republished by him in two volumes, anonymously, in the following year. For this the author was paid five guineas; for *The Life of Richard Nash* fourteen guineas; for *The Traveller*, the first of Goldsmith's books to bear his name, twenty guineas; and for his anonymous *History of England*, £21. 'Newbery', says Washington Irving, 'was a worthy, intelligent, kind-hearted man, and a reasonable, though cautious, friend to authors, relieving them with small loans when in pecuniary difficulties, though always taking care to be well repaid by the labour of their pains.' During the period between the publication of the *Citizen of the World* and the year of his death (1767) Newbery lived in apartments at Canonbury House, Islington, where, in the upper story, he also provided a temporary home for Goldsmith, paying quarterly for his board and lodging, and getting his author to square the account in the shape of 'copy' — *Goody Two Shoes*, perhaps, and other things. How long Goldsmith remained at Canonbury House, and how much of *The Vicar of Wakefield* was written there, it is impossible to say. As Charles Welsh remarks in his life of Newbery,* 'there are probably few points of literary history of the last century more obscure and involved than the story of the writing, and the sale of the copyright, of this book'. Johnson's own picturesque story is the best known:

I received one morning a message from poor Goldsmith that he was in great distress, and as it was not in his power to come to me, begging that I would come to him as soon as possible. I sent him a guinea, and promised to come to him directly. I accordingly went as soon as I was drest, and found that his landlady had arrested him for his rent, at which he was in a violent passion. I perceived that he had already changed my guinea, and had got a bottle of Madeira and a glass before him. I put the cork into

* *A Bookseller of the Last Century*, 1885.

the bottle, desired he would be calm, and began to talk to him of the means by which he might be extricated. He then told me that he had a novel ready for the press, which he produced to me. I looked into it, and saw its merit; told the landlady I should soon return, and having gone to a bookseller, sold it for sixty pounds. I brought Goldsmith the money, and he discharged his rent, not without rating his landlady in a high tone for having used him so ill.

Whoever the landlady was, and whether John Newbery was at the back of his arrest or not, the fact remains that it was first published in 1766 in the name of 'Honest John's' nephew, Francis Newbery, who, apparently with his uncle's assistance, had been set up in business at the Crown, in Paternoster Row. It seems probable that the elder Newbery had a common interest in the *Vicar*; but if that were so he did not live to see any returns for his investment. His biographer shows that it was not until after the fourth edition had been sold — eight years after the first — that the publisher received any profit from the work. Family disputes broke up the house of Newbery after the founder's death. His nephew opened a new shop at 20 Ludgate Street, while his son, also named Francis, summoned from Oxford on his father's death, carried on the business at the old address in partnership with his stepbrother, Thomas Carnan.

Francis Newbery, the son of the founder, appears to have continued the intimate relations which existed between Goldsmith and his father. 'Being pressed by pecuniary difficulties in 1771–1772', writes James Prior in his life of the author, 'Goldsmith had at various periods obtained the advance of two or three hundred pounds from Newbery under the engagement of writing a novel, which, after the success of the *Vicar of Wakefield*, promised to be one of the most popular speculations. Considerable delay took place in the execution of this undertaking, and when at length submitted to the approval of the bookseller, it proved to be in great measure the plot of the comedy of *The Good Natur'd Man*, turned into a tale. Objections being taken to this, the manuscript was returned. Goldsmith declared himself unable or unwilling to write another, but in liquidation of the debt now pressingly demanded, said he should require time to look round for means of raising the money, unless Mr Newbery chose to take the chance of a play coming forward at Covent Garden. "And yet, to tell you the truth, Frank", added the candid poet in making the proposal, "there are great doubts of its success." Newbery accepted the offer, doubtful of being otherwise repaid, and the popularity of *She Stoops to Conquer* gained, according to the recollection of the narrator, above £300 more than the sum advanced to the author.'

Newbery the younger and Thomas Carnan continued their joint imprint until about the year 1782, when Newbery appears to have retired in order to devote himself to the still flourishing medicinal branch of the business. Carnan remained at the old address until 1788, but all the old copyrights passed at some time or other to the rival house started by the founder's nephew, now, however, carried on by his widow, from whom it subsequently passed to John Harris and his successors.

Carnan deserves to be remembered for breaking down the Stationers' ancient monopoly in the matter of almanacks. He dared to publish almanacks of his own, whereupon the Stationers' Company not only anathematized them as counterfeit, but sent him to prison on a summary process as regularly as he issued them. 'A friend of his family', wrote Charles Knight in 1865, 'told me, some forty years ago, that this incorrigible old bookseller always at this season kept a clean shirt in his pocket, that he might make a decent appearance before the magistrate and keeper of Newgate. But Carnan persevered till the judges of the Court of Common Pleas decided against the validity of the patent, and an injunction which had been obtained in the Exchequer was immediately dissolved. The Stationers' Company then induced Lord North to bring a Bill into Parliament to revest in them the monopoly which had been declared illegal. In 1779, Erskine, in a speech which remains as one of the great triumphs of his oratory, procured the rejection of this Bill by a large majority.'

Another venerable custom shattered about this time was that based on the supposed perpetuity of copyright, the London booksellers believing that they held this right under the Common Law for property not falling within the terms of the Copyright Act of 1709. It was Alexander Donaldson, from Edinburgh, who disillusioned them. A keen pioneer of popular reprints, Donaldson, as already mentioned, had extended his business to London, starting a bookshop in the Strand, and issuing cheap editions of the most popular English books, to the no small discomfiture of his London brethren, who looked askance at his underselling prices. He brought matters to a head by reprinting Thomson's *Seasons*, the statutory copyright of which, under the Act of 1709, had expired in 1758; but which, under what Johnson described as 'an equitable title from usage', was still supposed to possess perpetual copyright, Andrew Millar having bought it in that belief from Thomson, and Millar's executors having sold it to Becket, Sterne's publisher, after the original publisher's death in 1768.

The whole trade, indeed, had lived under that superstition since the passing of the Act of Anne. Publishers had bought and sold such property for large sums, honestly believing that they were dealing in copyrights which held good for ever. When, therefore, Donaldson violated this custom by reprinting the *Seasons*, action was taken against him, and, what is more, Lord Chancellor Bathurst upholding the supposed Common Law right, gained a perpetual injunction against him. The decision was based on an earlier verdict in the similar case of *Millar* v. *Taylor*, where the matter had been allowed to rest; but Donaldson carried the case to the House of Lords, where, in February 1774, he won the day, the House deciding by twenty-one votes to eleven, that no such Common Law right existed.* This was very largely due to a speech from the great Whig lawyer, Lord Camden, who combined Pope's opinion of the generality of booksellers with his own aristocratic scorn of the man who made his living by his pen. 'Knowledge', declared Lord Camden, 'has no value or use for the solitary owner: to be enjoyed it must be communicated. *Scire tuum nihil est, nisi te scire hoc sciat alter.* Glory is the reward of science, and those who deserve it scorn all meaner views: I speak not of the scribblers for bread, who tease the press with their wretched productions; fourteen years is too long a privilege for their perishable trash. It was not for gain that Bacon, Newton, Milton, and Locke instructed and delighted the world; it would be unworthy such men to traffic with a dirty bookseller. When the bookseller offered Milton five pounds for his *Paradise Lost*, he did not reject it and commit it to the flames, nor did he accept the miserable pittance as the reward of his labour; he knew that the real price of his work was immortality, and that posterity would pay it.'

After the decision in the House of Lords an unsuccessful attempt was made to render copyright perpetual, the Bill passing the House of Commons in 1774, but being rejected by the Lords, and so the matter was left until 1801 and 1814, when the Act of 1709 was altered, the copyright term being extended to cover the length of the author's life, or twenty-eight years from the date of publication, whichever was the longer.† Notwithstanding the unsuccessful attempt to secure a Bill for perpetual copyright, the London booksellers, as Boswell tells us, continued — for a time at all events — to preserve their ancient usage by mutual compact. They had an exclusive club of their own, dining once a month at the Shakespeare Tavern, where many a big undertaking was first suggested, chief among them being Johnson's *Lives of the Poets*, the story of which is told in the letter written by Edward Dilly, the

* Alexander Donaldson left a considerable fortune at his death. His son, James Donaldson, who became proprietor and editor of the *Edinburgh Advertiser*, was even more successful, founding Donaldson's Hospital, Edinburgh, and leaving £220,000 for the maintenance of 300 poor children.

† This remained in force until the Act of 1842, which made copyright endure for the author's life, *plus* seven years; or should the two terms not amount to forty-two years, then for forty-two years from the date of first publication. Under the Copyright Act of 1911 the period was extended to cover the life of the author and fifty years after his death; with the proviso that after he had been dead for twenty-five years anyone could reproduce an author's work on certain terms specified in the Act.

elder of the two brothers who were Boswell's 'worthy booksellers and good friends', to Bozzy himself, dated September 26th, 1777:

Dear Sir,

You will find by this letter, that I am still in the same calm retreat, from the noise and bustle of London as when I wrote to you last. I am happy to find you had such an agreeable meeting with your old friend Dr Johnson ... When he opens freely, every one is attentive to what he says, and cannot fail of improvement as well as pleasure. The edition of the Poets, now printing, will do honour to the English press; and a concise account of the life of each author, by Dr Johnson, will be a very valuable addition, and stamp the reputation of this edition superior to anything that is gone before. The first cause that gave rise to this undertaking, I believe, was owing to the little trifling edition of the Poets, printing by the Martins at Edinburgh, and to be sold by Bell in London. Upon examining the volumes which were printed, the type was found so extremely small that many persons could not read them; not only this inconvenience attended it, but the inaccuracy of the press was very conspicuous. These reasons, as well as the idea of an invasion of what we call our Literary Property, induced the London booksellers to print an elegant and accurate edition of all the English poets of reputation, from Chaucer to the present time.

Accordingly a select number of the most respectable booksellers met on the occasion; and, on consulting together, agreed that all the proprietors of copyright in the various poets should be summoned together; and when their opinions were given, to proceed immediately on the business. Accordingly a meeting was held, consisting of about forty of the most respectable booksellers of London, when it was agreed that an elegant and uniform edition of *The English Poets* should be immediately printed, with a concise account of the life of each author, by Dr Samuel Johnson: and that three persons should be deputed to wait upon Dr Johnson, to solicit him to undertake the Lives, viz. T. Davies, Strahan, and Cadell. The Doctor very politely undertook it, and seemed exceedingly pleased with the proposal. As to the terms, it was left entirely with the Doctor to name his own; he mentioned two hundred guineas; it was immediately agreed to; and a farther compliment, I believe, will be made him. A committee was likewise appointed to engage the best engravers, viz. Bartolozzi, Sherwin, Hall, etc. Likewise another committee for giving directions about the paper, printing, etc., so that the whole will be conducted with spirit, and in the best manner, with respect to authorship, editorship, engravings, etc., etc. My brother will give you a list of the poets we mean to give, many of which are within the time of the Act of Queen Anne, which Martin and Bell cannot give, as they have no property in them; the proprietors are almost all the booksellers in London of consequence. I am, dear Sir, ever yours,

EDWARD DILLY

Johnson's moderation in demanding so small a sum is extraordinary, says Malone in remarking on this letter. 'Had he asked one thousand, or even fifteen hundred guineas, the booksellers, who knew the value of his name, would doubtless have readily given it. They have probably got five thousand guineas by this work in the course of twenty-five years.' But Johnson, according to Boswell, paid little attention to profit from his literary labours. John Bell, who thus indirectly helped to father the *Lives of the Poets*, was not only, like Alexander Donaldson, a pioneer of cheapness. Full of ideas, he was the first man to set the fashion of discarding the long f (s), which he did in publishing his *British Theatre* — intended to supersede the old octavo editions of single plays and the large collected editions of the dramatists. He was the first publisher, also, of English pocket classics. Charles Knight calls him 'the very Puck of Booksellers'. His editions of the *British Poets* ran to over a hundred volumes, issued from his busy shop in the Strand from 1777 to 1789. Notwithstanding the prejudiced criticism of the reactionaries quoted in Edward Dilly's letter, the books were beautifully printed and deserved their success. It was not until the present century that justice was done to John Bell's many enterprises, not only in printing technique and publishing method, but also in the English newspaper press — to say nothing of his activities as correspondent with the British Army in Flanders in 1794.* The present house of Bell — the story of which is told on a later page — is of younger growth, and has no connection with John Bell, who died in 1831.

Only two of the twenty-six houses which continued to publish the first edition of Johnson's *Lives of the Poets* (1779–1781) have been continued in direct succession down to the present day — Thomas Longman and John Murray. The first Thomas Longman had died in 1755, only two months after the publication of Johnson's *Dictionary*, in which he held a considerable number of shares. His nephew and successor, Thomas Longman II, to whom reference is now made, controlled the affairs of the firm until towards the end of the eighteenth century, developing the business both at home and abroad on sound if uneventful lines. The first John Murray, at the same date, had only been in business ten years, but long enough to find mention in Boswell's comprehensive gossip:

* See *John Bell, 1745–1831: Bookseller, Printer, Publisher, Typefounder, Journalist, etc.*, by Stanley Morison. 1930.

Somebody mentioned the Reverend Mr Mason's prosecution of Mr Murray, the bookseller, for having inserted in a collection of Gray's *Poems* only fifty lines, of which Mr Mason had still the exclusive property under the statute of Queen Anne; and that Mr Mason had persevered, notwithstanding his being requested to name his own terms of compensation. Johnson signified his displeasure at Mr Mason's conduct very strongly; but added, by way of shewing that he was not surprised at it, 'Mason's a Whig.' MRS KNOWLES (not hearing distinctly): 'What, a prig, Sir?' JOHNSON: 'Worse, Madam; a Whig! But he is both.'

The feud between Whiggery and the House of Murray, as Knight suggests, might thus have had a remote origin.

II

The End of the Eighteenth Century

After Johnson's death in 1784 the chief honours of 'the Trade'* belonged to Thomas Cadell, who, it will not be forgotten, was associated with him in the *Lives of the Poets*, supporting his partners, William Strahan and Tom Davies, during the momentous interview on behalf of the 'Chapter'. Many years earlier Cadell had started life as an apprentice to Andrew Millar, who took him into partnership in 1765; and two years later, on Millar's retirement—to die in the following year—the old apprentice became his successor. Cadell still occupied the house in the Strand at No. 141, 'over against Catherine Street'—where the first Jacob Tonson had hung out his sign of the Shakespeare Head, to be hauled down when the devoted Scot, Andrew Millar, replaced it with that of Buchanan's Head. Many memories clustered round this long forgotten bookshop, haunted by a whole century of illustrious authors—Swift, Addison, Steele and Pope, Johnson and his faithful Boswell, Fielding and Thomson and the authors who made history popular in their day, Hume, Robertson and Gibbon—until the site was obliterated by one of the wings of Somerset House.

Cadell, like his predecessor Millar, had been associated with William Strahan in his literary enterprises up to this period of his career, but Strahan, now in his seventieth year, did not long survive his friend, Dr Johnson, for he died in 1785. Cadell and Strahan together had been worthy leaders of their craft who preceded them. 'There will be no books of importance now printed in London', wrote Hume to his countryman Strahan, on receiving a presentation copy of the first volume of Gibbon's *Decline and Fall* in 1776, 'but through your hands and Mr Cadell's.' And they did, indeed, succeed in gathering round them a remarkable group of men—not only Hume, Robertson, Gibbon and the other authors already mentioned in this connection, but also Thomas Somerville, Adam Smith, Blackstone, Mackenzie—*The Man of Feeling*—and many others.

Boswell tells the story of the plagiarism of *The Man of Feeling* by a young Irish clergyman, named Eccles, who was afterwards drowned near Bath. This impudent impostor had taken the trouble to transcribe

---

* 'As physicians are called "the Faculty", and Counsellors at Law "the Profession",' wrote Boswell, 'the booksellers of London are called "the Trade". Johnson disapproved of these denominations.'

the whole book, with blottings, interlineations and corrections, afterwards displaying it as his own original work. The belief in Eccles as the author became so general that the original publishers, Strahan and Cadell, were compelled to issue an advertisement contradicting the claim, and declaring that they had purchased the copyright from Henry Mackenzie. Five years after the first appearance of *The Man of Feeling* came the splendid success of the first volume of Gibbon's *Decline and Fall*. The historian himself—M.P. for Liskeard at the time—has told us something of the fluctuating fortunes of this book:

> The volume of my History, which had been somewhat delayed by the novelty and tumult of a first session, was now ready for the press. After the perilous adventure had been declined by my friend Mr Elmsley, I agreed upon easy terms with Mr Thomas Cadell, a respectable bookseller, and Mr William Strahan, an eminent printer; and they undertook the care and risk of the publication, which derived more credit from the name of the shop than from that of the author. The last revisal of the proofs was submitted to my vigilance; and many blemishes of style, which had been invisible in the manuscript, were discovered and corrected in the printed sheet. So moderate were our hopes, that the original impression had been stinted to five hundred, till the number was doubled by the prophetic taste of Mr Strahan ... I am at a loss how to describe the success of the work, without betraying the vanity of the writer. The first impression was exhausted in a few days; a second and third edition were scarcely adequate to the demand; and the bookseller's property was twice invaded by the pirates of Dublin.

An illuminating document survives to show us the kind of accounts which passed between author and publisher in this case.* A thousand

* 'State of the Account of Mr Gibbon's *Roman Empire*. Third edition. 1st Vol. No. 1000. April 30th, 1777.

	£	s.	d.
Printing 90 sheets at 1*l*. 6*s*. with notes at the bottom of the page .	117	0	0
180 reams of paper at 19*s*.	171	0	0
Paid the Corrector, extra care	5	5	0
Advertisements and incidental expenses	16	15	0
	£310	0	0

	£	s.	d.
1000 books at 16*s*.	800	0	0
Deduct as above	310	0	0
Profit on this edition when sold . . .	£490	0	0
Mr Gibbon's two-thirds is	326	13	4
Messrs. Strahan and Cadell's	163	6	8
	£490	0	0

Errors excepted.'

copies had been printed of the first edition of the first volume, fifteen hundred of the second edition and another thousand of the third edition. It is to this last that the account refers, from which it will be seen that Gibbon took two-thirds of the profits, and that Strahan and Cadell shared the remaining third between them. No wonder Gibbon was satisfied with his publishers! His second and third volumes did not appear until 1781, and the fourth and completing volume until 1788— three years after Strahan's death—when the day of publication was delayed in order, writes the historian, 'that it might coincide with the fifty-first anniversary of my own birthday; the double festival was celebrated by a cheerful literary dinner at Mr Cadell's house; and I seemed to blush while they read an elegant compliment from Mr Hayley'. Peter Elmsley, who must have been very sorry for himself as he watched the golden harvest being reaped from the very work which he had declined, lived to see the more enterprising publisher made Alderman and afterwards Sheriff of London, and then—like Tonson and Lintot in the earlier days—followed him to the grave in the same year (1802).*

Many gaps were created in the book markets of London in this last quarter of the eighteenth century. John Rivington, continuing the orthodox traditions of his father, kept his house at the head of the religious trade until his death in 1792. True to his principles in private as well as in his business life, he always put up his shutters at the sign of the Bible and Crown in Paternoster Row on January 30th—the anniversary of the execution of Charles I. His more speculative brother, James Rivington, had published Smollett's *History of England* with James Fletcher in St Paul's Churchyard: a work which yielded £10,000, the largest profit ever made up to that time by any one book. This stroke of luck, unhappily, did James more harm than good. Racing and gambling led to failure; and then to various ups and downs at home and in America before he started his *Rivington's New York Gazette* in 1777. John was succeeded by his two elder sons, Francis and Charles, who, in the following year, established the *British Critic* in partnership with William Belloe and Archdeacon Nares.† John Rivington had added greatly to the prestige of the firm by his appointment in 1760 as publisher to the Society for Promoting Christian Knowledge, an appointment which remained in the house for more than seventy years. Burke also made him his publisher after Robert Dodsley's death.‡

* Peter Elmsley's bookshop in the Strand was a favourite haunt of literary men and booklovers in the second half of the eighteenth century. It was here that Gibbon first met Porson.

† Nares acted as editor, and with Belloe's help continued the *British Critic* as a monthly periodical down to 1813, when a new series was begun under the editorship of Dean Lyall. A third series was started in 1825, but ceased at the end of the third volume. Several attempts were made to revive it, but without any lasting success.

‡ Rivington's published the first complete edition of Burke's works in 1853, in eight volumes, edited by Francis Rivington, then head of the house.

Edward Dilly, who gave Boswell the inside history of the *Lives of the Poets*, and was so fond of a gossip that he is said to have talked himself to death, dealt in books which probably caused the Rivingtons to raise their hands in pious horror. Both Edward, and his younger brother Charles, whom he took into partnership, were dissenters, and not only published in England many theological works of that school, but exported great quantities to America. Edward Dilly died in 1779, but his brother—Boswell's publisher—lived until 1807, four years after becoming Master of the Stationers' Company.

When Dr Johnson died—to return to the year 1784—the house of Longmans had not yet achieved the high distinction which it first earned with the reign of Thomas Longman III. John Murray II was only six years old—Byron himself was still unborn; and Archibald Constable was but four years the senior of the great John Murray. But away on the hills of Ayrshire was a 'heaven-taught ploughman', racked with troubles which, though largely of his own making, drove him at times to the very border-land of insanity, yet scribbling, between-while, some of the finest poems that were ever written. Robert Burns was in the midst of his 'Highland Mary' romance and the distractions which followed the natural consequences of his relations with Jean Armour, when he arranged with John Wilson, a printer of Kilmarnock, to publish the first edition of his poems. He had resolved to leave the country for a post as bookkeeper on a West Indian estate, and he only hoped to provide his passage-money out of the profits from the poems. The little volume, issued at the subscription price of three shillings, appeared in July 1786. Few perfect copies are known to exist. One, preserved in the Burns Cottage Museum at Ayr, cost the trustees £1,000. Another copy was sold at Sotheby's in 1925 for £1,750. The price rose to £2,450 for the late James Mann's copy on July 4th, 1929. This was considerably higher than any other price paid for the book, before or since.

> I threw off six hundred copies [wrote Burns in this connection], for which I got subscriptions for about three hundred and fifty. My vanity was highly gratified by the reception I met with from the public; and besides, I pocketed, all expenses deducted, nearly twenty pounds. This came very seasonably, as I was thinking of indenting myself, for want of money to procure my passage. As soon as I was master of nine guineas, the price of wafting me to the torrid zone, I took a steerage passage in the first ship that was to sail from the Clyde; for
>
> Hungry ruin had me in the wind.
>
> I had been for some days skulking from covert to covert, under the terrors of a jail; as some ill-advised people had uncoupled the

merciless pack of the law at my heels.* I had taken the last farewell of my friends; my chest was on the way to Greenock; I had composed the last song I should ever measure in Caledonia, *The gloomy night is gathering fast*, when a letter from Dr Blacklock to a friend of mine overthrew my schemes by opening up new prospects to my poetic ambition.

This led to the visit to Edinburgh, where Burns found himself the literary lion of the day, and also to the second edition of his poems. Wilson, the Kilmarnock printer, had declined to undertake this unless the poet would advance the price of the paper required for it—which Burns was unable to do. In Edinburgh, however, he found a publisher in William Creech, then the chief bookseller in the Scottish capital, through whom the second and enlarged edition was issued by subscription in April of the following year. Burns had good reason to be proud of his subscription list, including as it did many of the most distinguished names of the Scottish aristocracy, some of whom subscribed handsomely, Lord Eglinton, for example, taking as many as forty-two copies. Unfortunately, Burns had to wait a long time for his money, and he abuses Creech heartily in his letters to his friends at that time. But there was a pleasant surprise for him when at length the accounts of his dilatory bookseller were made up, for instead of the £200 or so which he told one of his patrons he hoped to gain by this edition, he found himself, on the day of reckoning, in possession of £500, if not of £600.

At the close of the eighteenth century another national poet was spending the last few years of his life in Norfolk. William Cowper was not only more fortunate than Burns both in popular and official recognition during his own time, but voted himself—for a while at all events—more than satisfied with his publisher. This worthy, Joseph Johnson, had held an honourable place in the ranks of the leading London publishers since the days of Dr Johnson's *Lives of the Poets*, in which he had a share. In close sympathy with the advanced thought of his day, he issued the scientific writings of Priestley, was bookseller and publisher for Horne Tooke and John Newton, and counted Erasmus Darwin among his other notable authors. It was John Newton who introduced Cowper, with their joint *Olney Hymns* in 1779, to 'my old friend Joseph Johnson, in St Paul's Churchyard', as he calls him in a letter to John Thornton, of Clapham, who had promised to bear the risks of publication. 'He printed my *Narrative* and volume of *Sermons*', he adds; 'and though he is not a *professor*, I believe him a man of honour and integrity.' Newton proved uncommonly useful to this 'old friend',

* The truth being that Jean Armour's father, though he refused to accept Burns as a son-in-law, notwithstanding his daughter's unfortunate condition, was pursuing him at law in order to extort money from him.

for when Cowper handed over to him the entire matter of the publication of his own first volume of poems he not only took them straightway to the bookseller, but, on his promising to take the whole charge
upon himself, made him a present of the copyright. Cowper was
perfectly satisfied. He had already told Newton that he only wrote for
amusement, as something 'towards diverting that train of melancholy
thoughts'; and when Johnson suggested to him that the preface which
Newton had contributed to the book—well-meant, no doubt, but alluding unnecessarily to the poet's painful malady and making too much of
the religious value of the volume—should be omitted he at once agreed.

Cowper pays another tribute to his publisher, whose interference
with his text would have roused a more spirited poet to furious indignation. 'I have reason to be very much satisfied with my publisher', he
writes. 'He marked such lines as did not please him, and, as often as I
could, I paid all possible respect to his animadversions. You will
accordingly find, at least if you recollect how they stood in the MS, that
several passages are the better for having undergone his critical notice.
Indeed, I do not know where I could have found a bookseller who could
have pointed out to me my defects with more discernment; and as I
find it is a fashion for modern bards to publish the names of the literati
who have favoured their works with a revisal, would myself most willingly have acknowledged my obligations to Johnson, and so I told him.'

He continued in Cowper's good books at least until 1786, and the
poet was evidently satisfied with the payments which he received for
most of his later books. 'Johnson behaves very handsomely in the
affairs of my two volumes', he writes in that year to Lady Hesketh. 'He
acts with a liberality not often found in persons of his occupation, and
to mention it when occasion calls me to it is a justice due to him.' Poet
and publisher unhappily did not continue these cordial relations to the
end. There was a decided rift in their dealings over the translation of
Homer, which Cowper, like Pope, issued by subscription. His printed
Proposals brought in a list of subscriptions which he believed need not
fear any comparison with Pope's—'considering', he adds, 'that we live
in days of terrible taxation, and when verse, not being necessary to life,
is accounted dear, be it what it may, even at the lowest price'. Cowper,
by this time, had become as keen a bargainer as the most mercenary of
authors. 'I devoutly second your droll wish that the booksellers may
contend with me', he writes to Joseph Hall in 1790. 'The more the
better. Seven times seven, if they please; and let them fight with the
fury of Achilles:

> Till every rubric-post be crimson'd o'er
> With blood of booksellers, in battle slain
> For me, and not a periwig untorn.'

The two volumes were to be issued at the price of three guineas—
which worked out, in the poet's own reckoning, at less than the seventh
part of a farthing per line—and by July 7th, 1791, he complains of his
head 'being filled with the cares of publication, and the bargain that I
am making with my bookseller'. How the affair was settled he tells in
his own way in a letter written four days later to Lady Hesketh:

> My dearest Coz,—I am not much better pleased with that
> dealer in authors than yourself. His first proposal, which was to
> pay me with my own money, or in other words to get my copy for
> nothing, not only dissatisfied but hurt me, implying, as I thought,
> the meanest opinion possible of my labours. For that for which an
> intelligent man will give nothing, can be worth nothing. The con-
> sequence was that my spirits sank considerably below par, and have
> but just begun to recover themselves. His second offer, which is to
> pay all expenses, and to give me a thousand pounds next mid-
> summer, leaving the copyright still in my hands, is more liberal.
> With this offer I have closed ...
>
> As to Sephus' scheme of signing the seven hundred copies in
> order to prevent a clandestine multiplication of them, at the same
> time that I feel the wisdom of it, I feel also an unsurmountable
> dislike of it. It would be calling Johnson a knave, and telling the
> public that I think him one. Now, though I do not perhaps think
> so highly of his liberality as some people do, and as I was once
> myself disposed to think, yet I have no reason at present to charge
> him with dishonesty. I must even take my chance, as other poets
> do, and if I am wronged, must comfort myself with what somebody
> has said,—that authors are the natural prey of booksellers.

In justice to Joseph Johnson it is only fair to add that he left a
reputation which is more in accordance with Newton's judgment
of him as 'a man of honour and integrity' than the impression made by
Cowper's last letter. He held the political and religious views of his
more revolutionary authors, and suffered nine months' imprisonment
for publishing prohibited works of Gilbert Wakefield. But he could
afford to temper his suffering by living in style in the Marshal's House,
where he was free to entertain his literary and political friends as handsomely as he pleased. He was also a generous subscriber to Fuseli's
Milton Gallery, and from 1788 to 1799 published the *Analytical Review*.
More interesting than either of these enterprises was his association
with William Blake, who found in him, in 1791, a sympathetic publisher
for his unfinished work on *The French Revolution*. This was no more
successful than his first volume of verse, the *Poetical Sketches*, printed in
1783 at the expense mainly of the sculptor Flaxman and his friend the
Rev. Henry Mathew. The *Poetical Sketches* were followed in 1789 by

the *Songs of Innocence*, Blake in this case not only writing and illustrating the book himself, but printing it by a process of his own, and finally superintending its binding at the hands of his devoted wife. Five years later, and by similar means, came the companion book, *Songs of Experience*, afterwards bound up with the other in a volume for which Blake received, at various periods, prices ranging from thirty shillings to five guineas—occasionally even more. Blake issued most of his works in this way, the exceptions including his illustrations for two little books by Mary Wollstonecraft, published, like his *French Revolution*, by Joseph Johnson, who, with Fuseli and others, made 'great objections', he writes in connection with his memorable association with Hayley in the *Life of Cowper*, 'to my doing anything but the mere drudgery of business, and intimating that, if I do not confine myself to this, I shall not live.' Blake did a trifle better in his dealings with Edwards of Bond Street, who only paid him, however, at the rate of a guinea a plate for his designs for a new edition of Young's *Night Thoughts*.

But the one publisher of all others remembered in connection with Blake is the notorious Robert H. Cromek, who was more a printseller and engraver than a dealer in books. Cromek not only paid him the lowest market value for his matchless illustrations of Blair's *Grave*—twenty guineas for the series—but broke the agreement by which the artist was also given the engraving to do. Worse still, he stole from Blake the idea of his *Chaucer's Pilgrims* for the oil-painting which he afterwards commissioned from Stothard.

It was the day of the 'horrid' Gothic novelists satirized by Jane Austen in *Northanger Abbey*. The bookshops and libraries were full of tales of terror like Mrs Radcliffe's *Mysteries of Udolpho*—though Walpole, with his *Castle of Otranto* in 1765, had been first in the field— 'Monk' Lewis's *Ambrosio*, and their host of followers. The popular taste was largely fostered by William Lane at 33 Leadenhall Street, where, following the prevailing fashion for classical titles, he called his publishing house the Minerva Press. Lane spread the vogue with the help of circulating libraries which he established in the more fashionable of the country towns, as well as by means of the great central library which he ran in London. Leadenhall Street in those days would be thronged with fashionable women, with their carriages and books, on their way to and from the Minerva Press.

If London had not been first in the field with the circulating library that institution was firmly established there by the middle of the eighteenth century. Simon Fancourt's catalogue of his lending library, which he issued in 1748, ran to two stout volumes. By 1777, when Sheridan's *Rivals* was produced, the new fashion had made such strides that the dramatist was driven to make Sir Anthony Absolute declare: 'A circulating library in a town is as an evergreen tree of diabolical knowledge. It blossoms throughout the year. And depend upon it that they who are so fond of handling the leaves will long for the fruit at last.'

An ambitious, unscrupulous publisher, Lane thought nothing of reprinting forgotten books with fresh titles and issuing them as new. By these and other methods he earned the contempt of his more scrupulous rivals. Yet he did good service as an officer of the H.A.C. and became a partner in the Stationers' Company.* Like James Lackington, he made a fortune which enabled him to drive about town in a magnificent carriage accompanied by cockaded footmen complete with gold-headed canes, before he died in 1814.

The end of the eighteenth century found the book trade still struggling with the problems which, though changed with time, were fundamentally the same as in the days of the old monopolists. The French Revolution, with its universal reassessment of values, had given an added impetus to the movement towards individual liberty which had been part of the history of the Stationers' Company almost from its birth. There was now open war between the more conservative booksellers on the one hand and those rebellious booksellers who declined to bow their heads to old-established usages. The rebels formed themselves about the end of the eighteenth century into an independent band of 'Associated Booksellers', among them Thomas Hood—the bookseller of the Poultry, where his son, Thomas Hood, the poet, was born—and James Lackington. Lackington, though an arrant egotist, was a man of many ideas, and great independence of character. He sold for cash down only; no one—not 'even the nobility'—was allowed any credit; and in spite of all the ridicule which the trade as a whole heaped upon this experiment, and the low prices which Lackington charged for his books, he retired with a large fortune from the 'Temple of the Muses', as he called his once famous bookshop at the corner of Finsbury Square. This building was so vast that a mail-coach and four were driven round the counters at its opening, which took place not long after Lackington, in 1793, sold a fourth share of the business to Robert Allen, who had been brought up as a boy in his shop.

Lackington was the first bookseller, we believe, who speculated systematically in the 'Remainder' trade, the last refuge of the literary failures, and of books that have had their little day of success and died. He tells, in his curious *Memoirs* and *Confessions*, how hard a fight it was to live down the trade prejudices of his time. 'I was very much surprised', he writes, 'to learn that it was common for such as purchased remainders to destroy or burn one-half or three-fourths of such books, and to charge the full price, or nearly that, for such as they kept in

---

* Much light has been thrown on Lane's career and the book trade of his time in Dorothy Blakey's study of 'The Minerva Press', issued by the Bibliographical Society in 1939.

hand.' Lackington changed all this, but it was some time before he forced the trade to yield. And he made many enemies in this way, 'some of whom ... by a variety of pitiful insinuations and dark innuendoes strained every nerve to injure the reputation I had already acquired with the public, determined to effect my ruin, which indeed they daily prognosticated, with a demon-like spirit, must inevitably speedily follow.' Perhaps it was the recollection of this opposition which made him so boastful in his hour of triumph. He built a chariot, on the doors of which he had a motto inscribed: 'Small profits do great things', and in this carriage, attended by his servants, he drove round the kingdom in state.

Lackington has left us some valuable sketches of the book trade as he found it in different parts of the country. Travelling from London to Edinburgh by way of York and Newcastle-on-Tyne, and returning through Glasgow, Carlisle, Leeds and Manchester, he was both surprised and disappointed, 'at meeting with very few of the works of the most esteemed authors; and those few consisted in general of ordinary editions; besides an assemblage of common trifling books, bound in sheep; and that, too, in a very bad manner. It is true, at York and Leeds, there were a few (and but very few) good books; but in all the other towns between London and Edinburgh nothing but trash was to be found; in the latter city, indeed, a few capital articles are kept, but in no other part of Scotland.'

A year or two later he tried the West of England, and found matters just as bad; London was the 'grand emporium of Great Britain for books, engrossing nearly the whole of what is valuable in that very extensive, beneficial, and lucrative branch of trade'. Lackington had been a journeyman shoemaker at Bristol and other places in the West of England, and he amused himself when he made his tour as a successful bookseller by calling on his old masters and addressing each with 'Pray, Sir, have you got any occasion?' which, he explains in his autobiography, was the term then used by journeymen shoemakers when seeking employment. 'Most of these honest men had quite forgotten my person, as many of them had not seen me since I worked for them; so that is is not easy for you to conceive with what surprise they gazed on me. For you must know that I had the vanity (I call it humour) to do this in my chariot, attended by my servants; and on telling them who I was all appeared to be very happy to see me.'

Had Lackington postponed his tour he might have been more favourably impressed with the work that was being done in at least one of these West of England towns, for it was within the next few years that Joseph Cottle, of Bristol—who was something of an author himself as well as a bookseller—became acquainted with Wordsworth, Southey and Coleridge, assisting all of them on the road to fame when they needed a helping hand. In his *Biographia Literaria* Coleridge refers to Cottle as 'a friend from whom I never received any advice that was not wise, or a remonstrance that was not gentle and affectionate'. Cottle undid some of the good he had done when he published his volume of recollections a year or so after Coleridge's death, giving to the world his self-righteous details of the poet's opium habits. Before the end of the eighteenth century the House of Longmans bought the copyrights belonging to the Bristol bookseller, but made him a present of Wordsworth and Coleridge's *Lyrical Ballads*, the first edition of which he had been obliged to 'remainder'. Although the *Ballads* were then set down as being of little pecuniary value, Cottle, who, in turn, handed the copyright back to the authors, described the gift as having been made with Thomas Longman's 'accustomed generosity'. After giving up his Bristol business, Cottle devoted more of his time to writing indifferent verse, drawing upon himself in consequence the contemptuous satire of Byron.

Southey's tribute is better worth remembering: 'Do you suppose, Cottle, that I have forgotten those true and most essential acts of friendship which you showed me when I stood most in need of them ... Sure I am that there never was a more generous or kinder heart than yours, and you will believe me when I add that there does not live a man upon earth whom I remember with more gratitude and affection.'

12

The Romantic Revival

Our story of the English book trade during the early nineteenth century revolves for the most part round the work of those authors who, sometimes in spite of themselves, were largely children of the Revolution: Wordsworth, Coleridge and Scott; Byron, Shelley and Keats. The same influence stirred the book trade to its depths. Demands increased for greater freedom of individual liberty from the laws of established authority.

One who fell under the revolutionary influences of the time was 'the dirty little Jacobin', as 'Christopher North' called him, who lived to become Sir Richard Phillips. Like other booksellers and publishers before and since, Phillips combined the sale of patent medicines with that of books and stationery when he abandoned the hosiery business in Leicester for literary wares and journalism. Not long after starting the *Leicester Herald* in 1792 he was sentenced to eighteen months' imprisonment for selling Paine's *Rights of Man*. But Dr Priestley helped him, and he succeeded in editing the *Herald* from Leicester goal, afterwards starting a magazine which he called the *Museum*. Then came a ruinous fire, which not only put a stop to both those journals, but ended his publishing career so far as Leicester was concerned.

Fortune favoured him, however, when he came to London and opened a shop in St Paul's Churchyard. Here, in 1796, he started the *Monthly Magazine*, and made a small, but temporary, fortune by the sale of cheap educational books and the kind of popular literature on which were built the later houses of Chambers and Cassell. Apparently he outlived his republican views, for in 1807, when serving as Sheriff of London, he acted as the bearer of an address from the City Corporation to George III, from whom he then received his knighthood. Phillips is remembered more for his eccentricities than for his services as a pioneer of cheap literature. His vegetarianism invited the ridicule of Tom Moore who scoffed at his 'Pythagorean diet'; and furnished George Borrow with his character of the vegetarian publisher in *Lavengro*.

At the beginning of the nineteenth century the house of Murray had been in existence some thirty odd years, long enough, as stated on p. 174, to find mention in Boswell's *Johnson*. The founder's original name was MacMurray, but he dropped the prefix when retiring on half-pay as a lieutenant of Marines, and adopting as his emblem a ship

in full sail, he bought the old-established business of William Sandby
in 1768, on the site in Fleet Street later occupied by the publishing
business of Messrs George Philip and Son. His modest beginning may
be illustrated by the shop-card which he printed at the time:

JOHN MURRAY (successor to Mr Sandby),
Bookseller and Stationer,
At No. 32, over-against St Dunstan's Church,
in Fleet Street,
London.

Sells all new Books and Publications. Fits up Public or Private Libraries
in the neatest manner with Books of the choicest Editions, the best
Print, and the richest Bindings.

Also,

Executes East India or foreign Commissions by an assortment of Books
and Stationery suited to the Market or Purpose for which it is destined:
all at the most reasonable rates.

The first John Murray was only moderately successful, though well
supported by his old brother officers. With many of his customers in
distant lands, and England at war with France, Holland, Spain and the
American colonies, money came in slowly. It was a hazardous age for
the trade in many ways. Consignments of books from the Edinburgh
publishers for whom he acted as London agent had to be shipped under
an armed convoy: especially when Paul Jones was sweeping our east
coast with his small ships of war. Ill health also handicapped the founder
of the firm in his later years, when he published some of his best books,
including Mitford's *History of Greece*, and the first volume of Isaac
d'Israeli's *Curiosities of Literature*. When he died in 1793 Samuel Highley,
his 'faithful shopman', as he was termed in his will, was admitted into
patnership with the second John Murray, then a promising schoolboy
of fifteen.

Highley was more interested in selling books issued by other publishers than in running risks himself. The partnership became impossible
when John Murray II, full of a romantic spirit of enterprise at the very
outset of his career, came of age in 1801. 'The truth is', he wrote to
Colman, the dramatist, 'that during my minority I have been shackled
to a drone of a partner.' Two years later the partners separated,
agreeing to draw lots for their house in Fleet Street. The old address
fell to Murray, who, now free to run his unfettered course, embarked
on the career which was to earn for him the title of 'Glorious John', or,
in Scott's phrase, 'Emperor of the West'.

In his early days of freedom London was no longer acknowledged as the undisputed arbiter of English letters. Archibald Constable, who began his eventful career in Edinburgh in the closing years of the eighteenth century, was the first publisher, as Sir Walter Scott afterwards bore witness, to break in upon 'the monopoly of the London trade'. A man of rare sagacity and enterprise, Constable gauged the public taste to a nicety, and paid generously for his books. Gradually collecting the best authors about him, he raised the prestige of the publishing trade throughout Scotland, and made Edinburgh a centre of scholarship and literature. This was after he had established the *Edinburgh Review* in October 1802. It was not long before Scott joined his brilliant band of contributors, and a few years later the publisher issued *Sir Tristram* and *The Lay of the Last Minstrel*. With Scott and the Edinburgh reviewers as names to conjure with, Constable became a power with whom the English publishers had seriously to reckon. The London sale of the *Edinburgh Review* was taken over by Longmans, with a half share in the property, but owing to differences between the two houses the London publication of the review was transferred for a time to John Murray II.

At this time the head of Longmans was Thomas Longman III, Thomas Longman II having died in 1797 — a year before Cottle's publication of Wordsworth and Coleridge's *Lyrical Ballads*, which heralded so unobtrusively the English contribution to the romantic revival. Like Constable and Murray, the third Thomas Longman was destined to play a considerable part in a renaissance which for a time regained for poetry the paramount interest of the English reading public. He took Owen Rees into partnership, and, as mentioned at the close of the last chapter, bought Cottle's copyrights when the Bristol bookseller retired in 1799. In the summer of 1802, Thomas Longman III paid a visit to Scott, when he secured the copyright of the *Border Minstrelsy*. Three years later his firm was associated with Constable in the publication of *The Lay of the Last Minstrel*, Scott standing in on the profit-sharing system. As soon as the first edition was exhausted, Longmans offered £500 for the copyright of the work, an offer which Scott accepted; but, as the introduction says, the publishers afterwards 'added £100 in their own unsolicited kindness. It was handsomely given, to supply the loss of a fine horse which broke down suddenly while the author was riding with one of the worthy publishers'. The worthy publisher, adds Lockhart, was Longman's partner, Owen Rees.

Longmans might have drawn Byron, as well as Scott and Wordsworth, into their comfortable net had they not declined his *English Bards and Scotch Reviewers*, because of its onslaughts on their own poets. The place which Byron might have filled was taken by Tom Moore, who, with the exception of his *Life of Byron*, published all his later books through Longmans. Much might be written of the mutual esteem which marked all the business relations between Moore and his publishers, who set the seal on their connection by offering the poet £3,000 for *Lalla Rookh* before a line of the book was written. 'There has seldom occurred any transaction in which trade and poetry have shone so satisfactorily in each other's eyes', wrote Moore, who, when he found that *Lalla Rookh* was taking him much longer to write than he had anticipated, offered to show his publisher a portion of the work. 'We are certainly impatient for a perusal of your poem', replied Thomas Longman; 'but solely for our gratification. Your sentiments are always honourable.' Happily *Lalla Rookh*, when it appeared in 1817, proved an immediate and memorable success.

It was not until John Murray II had done his utmost to promote a reconciliation between Longmans and Constable that he would undertake the publication of the *Edinburgh Review* in London. Not many years elapsed before Constable's relations became as strained with Murray as they had been with Longmans. Before the Edinburgh potentate established a London branch of his own for the sale of his *Review*, however, the two houses had arranged a joint interest in many books, and Murray had been brought into personal touch with those forces which presently led him to establish the *Quarterly* in 1809 as an antidote to the Whiggism of the older *Edinburgh*.

His long association with Byron had begun at 32 Fleet Street, while *Childe Harold* was being printed. The poet had made a present of the first two cantos to Robert Charles Dallas (whose sister married Captain George Anson Byron), and was highly pleased when he heard that Murray had agreed to publish them. He used to look in at 32 Fleet Street, on his way from the fencing rooms of Angelo and Jackson, and amuse himself with making disconcerting thrusts against the bookshelves while Murray read passages from the proof sheets of the poem. No wonder the publisher afterwards admitted that he was often glad to get rid of him. Both had reason to be satisfied with the success of *Childe Harold*, Byron waking one morning to find himelf famous. The first edition of five hundred copies was exhausted almost at once. Dallas, to whom the poet had presented these cantos, benefited to the extent of £600 — the sum which Murray eventually paid him for the copyright.

It fell to John Murray II to do more than any other publisher to raise the dignity of his craft when authorship was becoming fashionable. He reminded Byron on one occasion — though their relations generally were of the happiest description — that he forgot in writing to his publisher that he was also addressing a gentleman. Shortly after the production of the first cantos of *Childe Harold* in 1812, Murray moved to 50 Albemarle Street. The house had been occupied by William Miller, who had declined to publish *Childe Harold*, and was now retiring from business. Murray took over his copyrights as well as his house, and turned the drawing-room into one of the most famous literary haunts of the age. Here, he wrote to a relative, 'I am in the habit of seeing persons of the highest rank in literature and talent, such as Canning, Frere, Mackintosh, Southey, Campbell, Walter Scott, Madame de Staël, Gifford, Croker, Borrow, Lord Byron, and others; thus leading the most delightful life, with means of prosecuting my business in the highest honour and emolument.'

Murray's words illustrate the changed relations which he had so argely helped to bring about between authors and publishers. Instead of the eighteenth-century custom of, say, Dr Johnson's lifetime, when the literary lion of the day would be surrounded by an association of publishing-booksellers, the publishers' drawing-room was now the centre of an appreciative crowd of authors.

It was in the drawing-room at 50 Albemarle Street that Murray brought about that 'mighty consummation of the meeting of the two bards', Byron and Scott, in the spring of 1815. The publisher's son, afterwards John Murray III, described in his recollections the odd sight presented by the two greatest poets of the age—both lame—as they stumped downstairs side by side after ending their conversation in the drawing-room. They met there again every day during Scott's visit to London, remaining together for two or three hours at a time.

In the same room, seven years later, took place the dramatic conference of Byron's relatives and executors, at which, after Moore and Hobhouse had nearly come to blows, the manuscript of the unpublished *Memoirs* of the poet was irrevocably burnt. The very fireplace remains today in which the book was destroyed. Tom Moore had to borrow £2,000 from Longmans to refund the sum which Murray had given him for the manuscript—Byron having made him a present of the copyright but four years later Murray not only paid off Moore's debt, amounting, with interest, to over £3,000, but gave him, in addition, £1,600 for his life of the poet. He also bought in the remaining copyrights of Byron's poems in order to issue his complete edition of the works.

Meanwhile Murray, having withdrawn from the Ballantynes, who succeeded Constable as his publishers in Edinburgh, had transferred the whole of his Scottish agency to the house of William Blackwood. The founder of that firm had set up for himself in his native Edinburgh in 1804 when that city—as Mrs Oliphant says in *The Annals of William Blackwood and Sons*, with which she fittingly closed her long and honourable connection with the house—was at its highest glory as a centre of intellectual life and influence. He had won something more than a local name as an antiquarian bookseller, having had some useful years of experience in London and Glasgow, as well as in Edinburgh; and had already established his reputation as a publisher on his own account when Murray transferred his Scottish agency to him. Murray, on his side, issued Blackwood's books in London, and thus became the London publisher for Hogg's poems.

In 1816 Blackwood, then thirty years of age, stepped to the front by securing with Murray the publication of the first series of *Tales of My Landlord*. Two years previously Scott, turning to prose when he found his poetry losing some of its vogue after Byron's arrival, had founded the nineteenth-century school of romance with *Waverley*. Published anonymously through Constable, it opened up at once the new career which was to eclipse Scott's reputation as a poet and, for a time at least, restore his embarrassed financial affairs. Abbotsford was now making dangerous inroads into his income, and the demands for more capital from his printing and bookselling partners, the Ballantynes, were insatiable. How deeply involved were his affairs, even when he was drawing something like £15,000 a year as the author of the Waverley Novels, no one knew. If his anonymous authorship had been his only secret Scott would have been a far happier man financially. The more dangerous secret—unknown even to his family—was this fatal partnership with the Ballantynes. It began with his friendly interest in his old school-fellow, James Ballantyne, who printed his *Minstrelsy of the Scottish Border* in 1802. This led to the printing business which Scott, with financial assistance, encouraged James to establish in Edinburgh. Six years later, after certain differences with Constable, he was induced to combine publishing and bookselling with the printing concern under the name of John Ballantyne and Co., the only solid capital in which was furnished by Scott himself. No one outside, however, had any inkling of this. The new venture was foredoomed to failure.

With his native chivalry Scott afterwards took the blame on himself for saddling the firm with unsaleable stock and impracticable ideas. But with an improvident partner like James's younger brother John in charge of the bookselling branch there was never a fair chance of success. With all his whimsical and lovable qualities personally, John was the last man in the world to succeed in any business; and James, excellent printer though he may have been, and as devoted as his brother to Scott, was hopeless at accounts. Scott called the elder Ballantyne Aldiborontiphoscophornio; the younger he nicknamed Rigdum-Funnidos; and was fond of them both; but too often had reason to exclaim: 'For heaven's sake, treat me as a man; not as a milch cow!'

It was in the midst of these struggling years of 'John Ballantyne and Co.' that William Blackwood and John Murray secured the first series of *Tales of My Landlord*. Blackwood's association with the anonymous author did not extend beyond this series. He always took the literary side of his business very seriously, and, when he first saw the sheets of *The Black Dwarf*, ventured boldly to suggest a different conclusion to the story—an alteration probably inspired by Gifford, who seems to have seen the work in proof at Murray's. Scott was furious. 'Tell him and his coadjutor', he wrote to James Ballantyne, who was acting as his agent in the matter, 'that I belong to the Black Hussars of Literature, who neither give nor receive criticism.' The storm appears to have blown over with the rapid success of the book, but Blackwood's relations with 'plausible James' were never very cordial, and with the fifth edition the publication was carried into the hands of Constable. 'This', writes Mrs Oliphant, 'was one of those tragically insignificant circumstances which so often shape life apart from any consciousness of ours. Probably ruin would never have overtaken Sir Walter had he been in the steady and careful hands of Murray and Blackwood, for it is unlikely that even the glamour of the great Magician would have turned heads so reasonable and sober.'

The break with Scott with its temporary triumph for a rival house, and the soreness left by the offensive announcement of the fifth edition long before Blackwood had exhausted the fourth spurred the rising publisher to take the step which soon led to abundant compensation for the loss even of such a tower of strength as the Laird of Abbotsford. Scott was a giant, but he was not the only literary genius in Edinburgh in those days; and Blackwood, who had just moved from Old Edinburgh to the more fashionable Princes Street in the New Town, resolved to make use of this talent in a new Tory magazine which should conteract the Whig influence of the *Edinburgh Review*. The *Quarterly*, which Murray had founded with a similar object in 1809, was not dashing enough for the young bloods among the Scottish Tories. In *Maga*, which Blackwood started in 1817, they found a ready outlet for their high and irresponsible spirits. A false start was made, under the title of the *Edinburgh Monthly Magazine*, with two incompetent editors; but with the seventh number Blackwood himself took over the editorship, and changed the name to *Blackwood's Edinburgh Magazine*. With 'Christopher North' (Professor John Wilson) and John Gibson Lockhart (soon to become Scott's son-in-law) as his chief supporters, he launched out with a number which at once became the talk of the day.

The chief cause of the commotion was the 'Chaldee MS', the kernel of which was contributed by James Hogg, though Lockhart and Wilson, who were both, as Lockhart himself says, 'sweeping the boards of the Parliament House as briefless barristers', interlarded it with a good deal of devilry of their own. The 'Chaldee MS' was a *jeu d'esprit* which shocked many good Scotsmen as much by its biblical phraseology as its extravagance of satire. Friends and foes alike were made to figure in this daring production. Blackwood himself was included — 'and his name was as it had been the colour of ebony' — as well as the rival power, Constable, known already as 'the Crafty', and 'that great Magician which hath his dwelling in the old fastness hard by the River Jordan, which is by the

Border'. Many of the jokes have lost their point for the present generation, but on the day on which the 'Chaldee MS' appeared, Edinburgh
woke up, Mrs Oliphant tells us, 'with a roar of laughter, with a shout of
delight, with convulsions of rage and offence'. Scott, when he read it,
was almost choked with laughter, but others had less cause for merri-
ment, and did not hesitate to say so. Lockhart and Wilson discreetly
betook themselves to 'Christopher North's' home in the Lake District as
soon as the storm burst. That was the way with these young lions when
they had done their roaring; but their editor and publisher faced the
storm undismayed, standing like a rock, 'writing letters to all concerned,
replying at once to indignant publishers, injured authors and severe
lawyers, with a civility and steadiness that never varied—and covering
the real culprits with his ample shield'.

The 'Chaldee MS' was not the only source of trouble in Blackwood's
sensational first number. It also contained an offensive attack by Wilson
upon Coleridge and his *Biographia Literaria*; and the first of a series of
virulent assaults upon the 'Cockney School of Poetry'. Keats, who was
branded with the same epithet through his intimacy with the leaders of
the so-called 'Cockney School', was similarly attacked in a subsequent
number, four months after Crocker's cruel review of *Endymion* in the
Quarterly.

Keat's first volume of poems, published by the brothers Charles and
James Ollier in 1817, had proved a melancholy failure. The Olliers
published much of Shelley's work, and it was through Shelley that
Keats had been introduced to the firm. He blamed them for their
inactivity, and they parted in anger. Keats was more generously
treated by Taylor and Hessey, in whose periodical, the *London Magazine*, as will presently be seen, Lamb's *Essays* made their first appearance.
Taylor and Hessey not only undertook to publish *Endymion* before it was
finished, but allowed Keats to draw upon them in advance. The Olliers,
it should be added, also published for Leigh Hunt and, through that
author's introduction, the 1818 edition of Charles Lamb's *Works*; but
they never prospered, and a few years later the business was wound up.

In the meanwhile, to return to the fortunes of William Blackwood,
that worthy could afford to view with composure the storm of abuse
which had been roused by the early numbers of his magazine. From
Blackwood's point of view the storm was worth all the writs and threats
that were hurled at his head. It had sent up the circulation of *Maga* by
leaps and bounds, and Blackwood had become a power in the land.
Murray, who had taken a share in the reconstructed magazine, grew
nervous for his reputation, but, shrewd enough to see the unexpected
possibilities arising out of his excellent, if questionable, advertisement,
presently paid a thousand pounds for a half-share in the undertaking.
The first 'Blackwood gang', however, soon proved too much for the

great John Murray. 'My hands are withered by it', he complained to his partner, and in January 1819, matters coming to a crisis, his name disappeared from the magazine.

Blackwood stood to his guns without flinching, keeping as firm a hand as he could meanwhile on his unruly lieutenants. He was also developing the book side of his business, taking shares, as was the custom in those days, in several volumes of Byron, Shelley and other poets; sharing Susan Ferrier's novels along with Murray; and issuing independently such works as Lockhart's novels, the *Edinburgh Encyclopaedia* and many volumes reprinted from the magazine.

One worthy who fell out of the ranks at the beginning of the nineteenth century was George Robinson, who earned the name of the 'King of the Booksellers', from the fact that he built up a wholesale trade in Paternoster Row which became the greatest known in the country up to that time. He also bought many sound copyrights, and did a considerable business in publishing. Robinson was succeeded by his son and brother, whom he had taken into partnership in 1784, but the business was 'so immensely large', says Timperley, 'as to exceed their strength, when the grand pillar of the house was removed.' Apart from other misfortunes, their exertions in trade were baffled in a single night by the destruction by fire of a printing office in which they were largely concerned, and they went into bankruptcy: but their assets proved so valuable that they not only settled all their creditors in full, but re-established themselves with flying colours, though neither of the partners lived long afterwards. The copyright of Vyse's *Spelling Book* alone sold for £2,500, with an annuity of fifty guineas to the author.

The 'King of the Booksellers' is apparently associated with 'Peter Pindar's' epigram on the publishers' hypothetical habit of drinking out of authors' skulls; for, when John Wolcot made his name by the vast circulation of his early pieces, Robinson, in partnership with another bookseller named Walker, negotiated with him both for his published and, on certain conditions, for his unpublished works. While this treaty was pending, according to Timperley, the ingenious doctor developed an attack of asthma, which was always at its most distressing stage whenever the publishers were present. Anticipating his early death — though he was then only fifty-seven — they agreed to pay him an annuity of £250 instead of a lump sum down:

Soon after the bond was signed the doctor went to Cornwall, where he recovered his health, and returned to London without any cough, which was far from being a pleasing sight to the persons who had to pay his annuity. One day he called upon Mr Walker, the manager for the parties, who, surveying him with a scrutinizing eye, asked him how he did. 'Much better, thank you', said Wolcot,

'I have taken measure of my asthma; the fellow is troublesome, but I know his strength, and am his master.' 'Oh!' said Mr Walker gravely, and turned into an adjoining room, where Mrs Walker, a prudent woman, had been listening to the conversation. Wolcot, aware of the feeling, paid a keen attention to the husband and wife, and heard the latter exclaim, 'There now, didn't I tell you he wouldn't die? Fool that you've been! I knew he wouldn't die.'

Wolcot was not more rabid in his views of the 'Great Trade' than his Scottish contemporary, the poet Campbell, who once drank Napoleon's health because he had ordered a publisher to be shot!* The booksellers, he complains bitterly to Scott, are 'ravens, croakers, suckers of innocent blood, and living men's brains'; but Campbell's words are a libel on his own publishers, for, almost invariably, they treated him not only justly, but generously. The cause of the trouble—by no means rare when we come to analyse such cases—was that he rated his works far higher than their market value. In the present instance he had demanded £1,000 for his *Specimens of the British Poets*, and the publishers told him that they could not afford so much. Scott, though he knew how to criticize the trade, took a more lenient view of what he once described as 'the most ticklish and unsafe and hazardous of all professions, scarcely with the exception of horse-jockeyship'.

The sale dinner and the Chapter Coffee House were still flourishing at the beginning of the nineteenth century, as well as the custom of sharing in the production of the more important works. These were sometimes divided into as many as 100 or even 200 shares, which were often sold by auction. Early in the nineteenth century, for example, there was a sale of nearly 1,000 shares of the kind, one 26th *Tom Jones* fetching £8; one 100th Johnson's *Lives of the Poets* £11; one 160th Johnson's *Dictionary* £5, and so on. Increasing competition gradually brought this custom into disuse, though it lingered for many years, the last conspicuous instance of partnership publication being Dr Latham's edition of Johnson's *Dictionary* which appeared in 1866.

Although some of these pleasant social conditions survived the eighteenth century, the cooperative age of bookselling was already passing. Competition increased every year. While the record of new books in the first half of the eighteenth century—not a complete record, be it added, but enough to illustrate our point—yielded an average of but ninety-three a year, the annual output during the first twenty-five years of the nineteenth century increased almost to six hundred—a modest total, it is true, when compared with the twentieth-century

* The publisher was Johann Philipp Palm, of Nuremberg. He had issued a pamphlet which roused Napoleon's ire. The death sentence was clumsily carried out on August 26th, 1806. Campbell's malicious toast has also been attributed at different times to Balzac and Southey.

totals shown on pp. 569–71, but sufficient to introduce increasing stress among competitors. There was a tragic reminder of this in 1814 when William Nelson Gardiner, a Pall Mall bookseller and engraver who had taken his degree of B.A. at Cambridge, committed suicide, leaving a letter declaring that his sun was set for ever—that his business had nearly declined—his catalogue failed—his body covered with disease—and that he had determined to seek the asylum 'where the weary are at rest'. Gardiner's downfall was doubtless largely of his own doing, for Timperley says that he was 'a man of great eccentricity of conduct, regardless of all the forms of civilized life, both in his dress and deportment'.

A more noteworthy venture of the early nineteenth century was that of William Godwin, who, like a later apostle of revolt—Robert Buchanan—started to publish on his own account. In Godwin's case the scheme was only intended for juvenile books, to include the works which Godwin himself had written under the name of Edward Baldwin. It was begun in 1805, and the prime mover in the business seems to have been his wife—not Mary Wollstonecraft, but her successor, Mrs Clairmont—the 'Mrs Priscilla Pry' of Charles Lamb's little sketch in the *New Times*, in 1825. Though there was never much love lost between the Lambs and Mrs Godwin, it must not be forgotten, as Mr E. V. Lucas observes in his standard life of Lamb, 'that had she not insisted upon becoming a publisher of books for children—to help out the precarious Godwin finances—those exquisite things, Charles Lamb's story of *The Sea Voyage*, and Mary Lamb's story of "The Sailor Uncle" (in *Mrs Leicester's School*) might have remained unwritten.'

Their joint *Tales from Shakespeare* came from the same publisher in 1807, their *Poetry for Children* in 1807; and two years later they issued *Prince Doris*, the fairy-tale which Charles Lamb wrote in rhyme from the French. The Godwin venture lasted considerably longer than Buchanan's, but with no greater measure of success in the end. Precaution was taken in the first place to omit Godwin's name from the firm, lest this, with its taint of heterodoxy, should alone be sufficient to damn such an enterprise. An unpretentious start was made in Hanway Street, off Oxford Street, with a manager named Thomas Hodgkins to serve as figurehead. Lamb's first literary effort for children, the tiny picture book known as *The King and Queen of Hearts*, must, according to E. V. Lucas, have been among their earliest ventures. It was only in 1891, when the first copy came to light, that Lamb's share in the work was proved; and the value of the discovery was attested by the fact that this copy realized no less than £226. Its original price, in the 'copperplate' series, was a shilling plain, and eighteenpence coloured.

For a time the publishing business gave some promise of success. By the year 1809 Mrs Godwin, putting her own name to her publications, had moved with the whole concern, together with Godwin's strangely assorted family, to roomier quarters in Skinner Street, Snow Hill. Here they were living when Shelley first addressed his impetuous letter in 1812, to be followed by his elopement with Mary Godwin and their subsequent marriage. Godwin himself, rarely free from financial embarrassments during all these years, and not above extorting money from his generous if unconventional son-in-law, received little help from the publishing business in its later years, and in 1822 became bank-rupt. It is pleasant to find the name of John Murray as a subscriber of £10 towards the fund which was then raised, thanks largely to Charles Lamb, in the unsuccessful effort to set the worn out philosopher on his feet again.

A few years before he broke with Blackwood, in 1819, John Murray added Jane Austen to his list by publishing *Emma*, the last of her novels to be issued during her lifetime. This was her fourth to appear, all anonymously, but with nothing like the popularity of the anonymous novelist across the Border, who gave *Emma* a warm-hearted review in the *Quarterly*. According to Smiles the profits of the four novels published during Jane Austen's lifetime did not exceed £700. The first three, *Sense and Sensibility*, *Pride and Prejudice*, and *Mansfield Park*, were all published at the Military Library, Whitehall, by T. Egerton, whose reluctance to take a reasonable risk with new editions may, Geoffrey Keynes suggests in his bibliography of Jane Austen, have determined her to forsake him and turn to John Murray as her publisher. Her two posthumous books, *Persuasion* and *Northanger Abbey*, were also issued by Murray. *Northanger Abbey*, though one of the last to be printed, was the first of the six to be written. After keeping it in manuscript for years, its unassuming author sold it in 1803 for £10 to Crosby & Co., of Stationers' Hall Court. That firm, however, never ventured to publish it, and after waiting in vain until 1816, Jane Austen bought it back for the same sum.

The one outstanding mistake of the second John Murray's life was his ill-advised venture in daily journalism. Encouraged by the success of the *Quarterly*, and no longer holding a share in *Blackwood's*, he happened to mention to young Disraeli one day that he would gladly interest himself in some journal which appeared more frequently than his own review. The Murrays and the Disraelis had been intimate friends since the founder of the house published Isaac d'Israeli's *Curiosities of Literature* in 1791. The elder d'Israeli had been one of the second John Murray's marriage trustees, and the younger members of both families met on the friendliest terms. When Murray mentioned the matter of another journal, Benjamin Disraeli was dabbling in high finance, and full of ambition. The remark at once suggested the idea of planning a daily newspaper with Murray in the Conservative interest.

He was little more than twenty at the time, but he carried Murray with him by his infectious enthusiasm — or 'unrelenting excitement and importunity', as the publisher afterwards put it. Murray himself had high hopes at first that he could run a paper which should rival *The Times*.

'You know well enough', he wrote, in explaining the 'Great Plan' to Scott, 'that the business of a publishing bookseller is not in his shop, or even in his connection, but in his brain.' Murray's brain was perhaps, somewhat turned at this time by dazzling pictures of potential profits, and promises of support that remained unfulfilled. After indefatigable efforts in the preliminary arrangements both at home and abroad, young Disraeli suddenly dropped out of the scheme, together with the financial partner whom he had brought into the venture. It was a period of grave crisis in the city, culminating in December 1825 in panic. The crash came which had for some time been unavoidable, 'spreading disaster far and wide', to quote from the standard memoir of the future statesman by W. F. Monypenny and G. E. Buckle, published by John Murray IV, 'and burying Disraeli's hopes in the general ruin'. The publisher, however, was now so far committed to the enterprise, with printing offices, editorial staffs, and the like, all engaged, that he decided to carry on alone.

The *Representative* made its first appearance on January 25th, 1826. It was a failure from the beginning. In six months, after sinking £26,000, and breaking down in health under the strain, Murray cut his losses and brought the paper to an end. 'I have cut the knot of evil which I could not untie,' he wrote to Washington Irving whose *Bracebridge Hall* and other works he published, 'and am now, by the blessing of God, again restored to reason and the shop.' Here his sounder instincts and common sense enabled him to tide over the troubled year which saw so many other publishing and printing houses tottering in the financial crisis, selling their stocks for whatever they would fetch to save themselves if possible.

The 'extraneous' Thomas Tegg made some of his best 'remainder' bargains during this panic. He bought the pick of Scott's novels, for instance, at fourpence apiece, afterwards reselling at a handsome profit. 'I was the broom that swept the booksellers' warehouses', he wrote in his autobiography. The panic in the city was the sequel to several years of wild speculation recalling the times of the South Sea Bubble. Booksellers and publishers, like other men of business, had been infected with the fever, risking their resources in mines, hops and all manner of ventures foreign to their regular calling. 'Persons of any foresight who knew the infinitely curious links by which booksellers, and printers, and papermakers (and therefore authors) are bound together, for good and evil', wrote Lockhart in his Life of Scott, 'already began to prophesy that whenever the crash, which must come ere long, should arrive, its effect would be felt far and wide among all classes connected with the productions of the press.'

The prophets proved dismally true. Neither Constable nor his London agents, Hurst, Robinson & Co., whose traffic in bills and counter-bills had long since undermined their stability, could save themselves. With them collapsed James Ballantyne & Co., thus involving Scott, and for the first time revealing the secret of his financial interest in that printing firm, as well as the authorship of the Waverley novels. John Ballantyne had not lived to see this day of reckoning. He died in 1821, bankrupt; yet so ignorant of the state of his finances that he left a worthless will, bequeathing his old friend and patron £2,000 towards the completion of his new library at Abbotsford. The wretched bookselling business, which brought Scott to the verge of bankruptcy, had long since been abandoned, Constable—cunningly persuaded by John that it was the only way to prevent his rivals, Murray and Black-wood, from securing the second series of *Tales of My Landlord*—buying the whole of the remaining unsaleable rubbish of 'John Ballantyne & Co.' in 1818 for £5,270. Once before he had come to the rescue of the firm in a similar manner, thus healing the breach with Scott which had started this ill-conceived concern. Although John's death a few years later removed some of Scott's responsibilities—he was giving his services as editor of Ballantyne's Novelist's Library, which he had planned solely for that bookseller's benefit—it filled him with a sense of deep personal loss. 'I feel', he whispered in Lockhart's ear at the graveside, 'as if there would be less sunshine for me from this day henceforth.' It was only when the storm burst in 1826 that he realized the extent to which Constable's affairs had by degrees become bound up with those of the great printing concern in which Sir Walter had all along been James's predominant partner. Scott so prided himself on his shrewdness in smaller points of worldly interest that his ignorance in this connection remains, in Lockhart's phrase, as 'the enigma of his personal history'.

There is no need to repeat the heroic tale of how nobly the novelist faced the situation, determined to pay off every penny of Ballantyne's debts as well as his own: some £130,000 in all; and how at long last—though not in his lifetime—he succeeded. Constable died in the following year, ultimately paying 2s. 9d. in the pound on much heavier debts than Scott's. His colleague, Robert Cadell, who had dissolved partnership in the bankruptcy, now became Scott's publisher. Together they bought back for £8,500 his principal copyrights, which had been put up to auction. When, a little later, Scott asked Murray if he would sell his fourth share of *Marmion*, that publisher rose handsomely to the occasion: 'So highly do I estimate the honour of being, even in so small a degree, the publisher of the author of the poem', he wrote, 'that no pecuniary consideration whatever can induce me to part with it. But there is a consideration of another kind, which, until now, I was not aware of, which would make it painful to me if I were to retain it a moment longer. I mean, the knowledge of its being required by the author, into whose hands it was spontaneously resigned in the same instant that I read his request.' Long before the crash in 1826, Murray had frequently remonstrated with the Edinburgh firms on the risks they were running in trading beyond their capital. Gladly as he would have shared in issuing the later works of the author of *Waverley*, he had abandoned that ambition rather than involve himself further in an alliance which he foresaw could only lead to disaster.

Baldwin, Cradock & Joy, who first published the new *London Magazine* in which *Elia* was born, appear to have been shamefully backward in their payments. When their successors unsuccessfully opposed the publication by Moxon of the *Last Essays of Elia*, Lamb mentioned that he should have received £30 profit out of the publication of the first volume, but that he never received the money. Though he could rail against the trade at large, he was uncommonly kind to certain of its members. There was William Hone, for instance, remembered now chiefly for his *Every-day Book*, and other miscellanies of the kind, but known in the early nineteenth century as the bookseller-satirist of the Regency.

The *Every-day Book* was not very successful; his debts increased until he was thrown into the King's Bench; and it was during his three years' imprisonment that he not only finished the first miscellany, but wrote and issued the *Table Book*. Hone found a good friend in 'Elia', to whom, as well as to Mary Lamb, he dedicated the *Every-day Book*; and whose enthusiastic admirer he remained for the rest of his life. Lamb was prominent among those who endeavoured to give Hone a fresh start in business on his release from the King's Bench, abandoning bookselling as hopeless in his case, and setting him up at a coffee house in Gracechurch Street. But Hone was no more successful here than among his old books and newspapers, and struggled on mainly by the help of his pen, Thomas Tegg giving him £500 for his *Year Book*, and also buying the copyright of his *Every-day Book*. Hone finally came under the influence of Edward Irving, by whom he was converted, his last public appearance being made as an occasional preacher at the Weigh-House Chapel, Eastcheap.

Thomas Tegg who made large sums by Hone's miscellanies, had travelled as a bookseller with an auction licence in his early career, and his nightly auctions when he settled down in Cheapside attracted crowds of bidders. After Trafalgar he sold 50,000 copies at sixpence each of *The Whole Life of Nelson*, which he rushed through the press at a few hours' notice. When Tegg—the original of Twigg in Hood's novel *Tilney*

Hall—abandoned the 'auctioneering way', and settled down to publishing in the Old Mansion House, he made a fortune with his cheap reprints and abridgments of popular works. Another contemporary who prospered in the same way was John Cooke, to whose edition of the British poets in sixpenny parts, Leigh Hunt pays tribute in his autobiography. Cooke learnt his trade with Alexander Hogg, whose cheap 'Paternoster Row' numbers were among the first reprints to appear in weekly parts. The popular reprinters took little heed, as a rule, of the authors whose works had helped to make their fortunes. Carlyle drove this point home in his petition to the Commons on the Copyright Bill: 'May it please your Honourable House', the petition concluded, 'to forbid all Thomas Teggs, and other extraneous persons ... to steal from him his small winnings, for a space of sixty years, at shortest.'

The publisher who owed the deepest debt of gratitude to Charles Lamb was Edward Moxon, whose house in Dover Street became one of the literary landmarks of London. There are points of strong resemblance between Edward Moxon and Robert Dodsley. Both had volumes of their own verse published before they set up in business for themselves, making a point in each case of their humble origin. Moxon issued his first book, *The Prospect, and other Poems*, in 1826, while learning his business at Longmans, as the work of 'a very young man, unlettered and self-taught', and, like Dodsley, was helped to a shop of his own by the generosity of an elder poet. 'Elia' took an interest in Moxon when the future publisher was still at Longmans, who, in 1808, had issued Lamb's *Specimens of English Dramatic Poets*. 'Moxon is but a tradesman in the bud yet', he writes in a characteristic letter introducing him to Wordsworth in 1826, 'and retains his virgin honesty.'

Samuel Rogers, to whom young Moxon had also been introduced by Lamb, and to whom he had dedicated his first volume of verse, was practical in his advice, lending him the £500 with which he was presently established in a business of his own at 64 New Bond Street. That was in 1830. The new publisher's first venture, appropriately, was Charles Lamb's *Album Verses*, dedicated to Moxon himself, who had paid a similar compliment to Lamb in the previous year, in another of his own poems, entitled *Christmas*. Rogers further proved his confidence in his protégé by entrusting him with the elaborate edition of his last book, *Italy*, which cost its author £10,000 to produce. *Italy* was a failure, but Rogers subsequently recouped himself—and through the same publisher—with the sumptuous edition of his works, in two volumes, at a cost of £15,000, with illustrations by Turner and Stothard.

The *London Magazine* was first published by Baldwin, Cradock & Joy, under the editorship of John Scott, who was mortally wounded in the duel with John Gibson Lockhart's second, as a result of the squabble between *Blackwood* and the *London* magazines. Following Scott's tragic death the new magazine was taken over by Taylor and Hessey, who took additional quarters, when they bought the magazine, at 13 Waterloo Place.

Rogers launched another literary bookseller in business—Thomas Miller, who wrote a number of novels and children's books as well as poems. He was granted a pension by Disraeli, and lived until 1874. There was an earlier bookseller of the name of Thomas Miller (1731–1804) who not only combined grocery with bookselling, but formed a remarkable collection of Roman and English coins. It was his son, William Miller, who started publishing in Albemarle Street, where, as recorded earlier in this chapter, he was succeeded in 1812 by John Murray.

13

The Mid-Nineteenth Century

Crabbe's last volume had been issued by Murray in 1819, and it was by the publisher's advice that the original title, *Remembrances*, had been changed to *Tales of the Hall*. For this collection and the remaining copyright of Crabbe's earlier poems Murray had paid Crabbe the handsome sum of £3,000. The poet's joy on receiving such unexpected wealth was so great that he insisted on setting out to Trowbridge at once in order to show the bills for that amount to his son John. 'They would hardly believe in his good luck at home if they did not see the bills,' wrote Tom Moore to Murray in describing the incident. The publisher lost heavily by the deal; but his wholehearted appreciation of genius and its works not infrequently, as in this instance, raised him in Smiles's phrase, 'above the atmosphere of petty calculation'. Nevertheless he was forced by circumstances in his declining years to look 'with rather a jaundiced eye on poetry and fiction', as George Paston remarks in the *Cornhill*.* He transferred the copyright of all his novels—even Jane Austen's—to Bentley, and, for poetry, contented himself with the works of the blameless Crabbe. So discouraging was the demand for Wordsworth's verse that it took four years to exhaust the collected edition of five hundred copies issued in 1820 by Longmans, who had republished the *Lyrical Ballads* in 1800, and brought out the later volumes of his verse. The poet himself told Moore in 1835 that his works had not up to that time earned him above £1,000.

When young Borrow came to London to seek his fortune with his box of manuscripts and his letter of introduction to Sir Richard Phillips—once the 'dirty little Jacobin'—that publisher set young Borrow to the hack work which resulted in the six volumes of *Celebrated Trials*, for which he paid him £50, a sum which had to include the purchase of all books and other expenses in which the author was necessarily involved. Borrow also contributed to Phillips's short-lived *Universal Review*, but the hardest task of all, and one which brought their unhappy association to a close, was that of attempting to translate into German the publisher's own philosophical work. He fell into safer hands later, when John Murray became his publisher.

While the barren years were passing, the seeds of the rich harvest of mid-Victorian verse were being sown in various scattered fields. Some

* *From the Archives of Albemarle Street*, August 1930.

of the first-fruits were produced by Edward Moxon in Dover Street, where he still carried on his business after the death of Charles Lamb. It was to Moxon that the pioneer and founder of the new school, Tennyson, sent his 1833 volume of poems, the publication being negotiated by Arthur Henry Hallam on the understanding that author and publisher should share in the risks and profits. His earliest verse, in *Poems by Two Brothers*, had been issued in 1827 in Louth, by J. & J. Jackson, and brought him £11. After the 1833 volume of poems, Tennyson's association with Moxon remained unbroken until the publisher's death in 1858. So little was poetry appreciated in his younger days, however, that Tennyson had to wait ten years or more before he could afford to marry.

Robert Browning also profited little by his poems at this period. He became associated with Moxon eight years after Tennyson with *Sordello*. The poet was still without honour in his country. Moxon now suggested that Browning should issue his poems in pamphlet form, at a cost which should not exceed £12 or £15 each; and Browning agreed, the *Bells and Pomegranates* appearing in this form, in a series of eight numbers, beginning with *Pippa Passes*, and extending from 1841 to 1846. They were issued at Browning's expense, but yielded no profit, apparently either for poet or publisher. Moxon also published *The Statue and the Bust*, but when Browning offered him the collected edition of his works in 1848—on the understanding that it was to be issued at the publisher's risk—he declined; upon which Browning went over to Dickens's publishers, Chapman & Hall, who accepted the proposal. Twenty years later Smith & Elder became Browning's publishers, the poet forming an intimate friendship with George Smith which closed only with his death.

Moxon's other authors included Southey, Barry Cornwall, Monckton Milnes. Wordsworth was beginning to come into his own when he transferred his allegiance to Moxon, who paid him £1,000 for the new edition of his works which he issued in six volumes in 1836–7—more than the poet had hitherto received for his verse in the whole of his career. The venture appears, however, to have proved a poor investment from the publisher's point of view. He was also associated with Disraeli, publishing his *Revolutionary Epick* in 1834, and even receiving an offer from that versatile genius—then thirty years old—to be taken into partnership, an offer which Moxon declined, 'not thinking', as he told Greville in 1847, 'that he was prudent enough to be trusted'.

Moxon died in 1858, shortly after issuing Hogg's *Life of Shelley*, and Trelawny's *Records of Shelley, Byron and the Author*. In his later years, realizing how hard it was to live by poetry alone, he developed a department for what has been called the 'household stuff' of literature, among his more notable ventures being Haydn's *Dictionary of Dates*.

A story is still told of a woman writer who called at Longmans in the early '40s of last century, and offered the publishers a book of poems. Verse had long since lost its vogue. 'My dear madam,' said the reigning head of the house, Thomas Longman IV, 'it is no good bringing me poetry; nobody wants poetry now. Bring me a cookery book, and we might come to terms.' He spoke more in jest than in earnest, but Eliza Acton took him at his word, and in due course returned with her *Modern Cookery*, which was first published in 1845, and, brought up to date at various periods, sold steadily until the early years of the twentieth century.

Thomas Longman IV, whose taste for good 'household stuff' has just been mentioned, succeeded to the title on the death of the third Thomas Longman in 1842. The imprint of the firm had now changed to Longman, Brown, Green, & Longman, with the fourth Thomas Longman and his brother William, who enjoyed a considerable reputation as a historian and mountaineer, at the head of affairs. To this reign belongs the great Macaulay epoch, beginning in 1842, only two months after the death of the third Thomas Longman, with the publication of the *Lays of Ancient Rome*. Macaulay, little suspecting their pecuniary worth, had made a present of the *Lays* to Longmans, merely stipulating that they should publish them. The publishers returned the copyright as soon as the small first edition had been taken up, and the work must eventually have brought Macaulay and his heirs very considerable sums. In 1843, though hard at work on his *History*, and very dubious as to the permanent value of what he regarded as his ephemeral work, Macaulay was forced by the pirated editions in America to authorize Longmans to publish a collected edition of the essays which he had contributed to the *Edinburgh Review*. The result as everyone knows, was a book which at once made a place for itself as a classic.

Sir George Trevelyan's life of his uncle shows by many references how close and cordial was the long association between Macaulay and his publishers. The best-remembered incident in their business dealings was the signing of the cheque for £20,000, dated March 13th, 1856, which Longmans paid the author as his share, merely 'on account', of the profits of the third and fourth volumes of his *History*.

In the meantime there had been the inevitable dynastic changes in the house of Murray. 'Glorious John' had died in 1843, to be succeeded by his son, John Murray III, who was only four years old when his father moved in 1812 to Albemarle Street, where, twelve years later, he witnessed the burning of Byron's *Memoirs*. Many precious relics of these and later days are preserved at No. 50—the Byron manuscripts, the silver urn which the poet sent to his publisher from Greece, containing some hemlock seeds gathered by Byron at Athens in 1811—they were the direct descendants, he said, of the hemlock which poisoned

Socrates—the manuscript of Scott's *Abbot,* Burns's Commonplace Book, Southey's article on Nelson in the *Quarterly,* with the additions which transformed it into one of the masterpieces of English biography, and other treasures.

It was the third John Murray who inaugurated the guidebooks which carried the name of Murray all over the globe. He started the series in his father's lifetime with the *Handbook of Holland,* which he wrote himself in 1836, following this up with three other volumes from his own pen—*France, South Germany* and *Switzerland.* When pressure of business prevented him from writing further volumes he continued the series with the help of various distinguished authors, some of whose works, such as Ford's *Spain,* have since become standard books. The series was so successful that the publisher was able to build his home, Newstead, at Wimbledon, out of the profits. Hence it was nicknamed *Handbook Hall.*

The reign of John Murray III is also associated with the fine series of illustrated travel books which includes such names as Livingstone, Humboldt, Du Chaillu, Bates, Yule and Mrs Bishop. He also published Darwin's *The Origin of Species* and *The Descent of Man*; Borrow's *Lavengro* and *Wild Wales*; the great series of dictionaries associated with the name of Sir William Smith, and a host of other works which were sound and scholarly but without the glamour attaching to so many of the volumes issued by his father. Borrow's first books, *The Gypsies of Spain* and *The Bible in Spain,* were both brought out in the lifetime of John Murray II. His treatment in the Albemarle Street house was very different from that which he received at the hands of Phillips, some seventeen years before, as described on p. 204.

Piccadilly was one of the highways of the book trade long before Moxon and Murray settled in its neighbourhood. John Hatchard started business there in 1797, almost next door to Wright's shop, where the *Anti-Jacobin* was published, and where Wolcot took his revenge on Gifford, the editor, for his insulting *Epistle to Peter Pindar,* striking him on the head with a stick, and being himself thrown into the gutter for his pains. It was at Wright's, too, that the *Intercepted Letters* of Bonaparte made their sensational appearance. Hatchard's became a fashionable meeting place for booklovers and politicians soon after it was started. Here Isaac d'Israeli, as described by his son, was introduced to the much-abused Laureate, Pye:

> In those days when literary clubs did not exist, and when even political ones were very limited and exclusive in their character, the booksellers' shops were social rendezvous. Debrett's* was the chief

* John Debrett had succeeded John Almon, the bookseller and journalist, who gave loyal support to the Whigs while in opposition, and the close confidant of Wilkes, who had reason for calling him his 'friend, and an honest worthy bookseller'. He compiled, among other

haunt of the Whigs, Hatchard's, I believe, of the Tories. It was at the latter house that my father made the acquaintance of Mr Pye, then publishing his translation of Aristotle's *Poetics*, and so strong was party feeling at that period, that one day walking together down Piccadilly, Mr Pye, stopping at the door of Debrett, requested his companion to join, adding that if he (Pye) had the audacity to enter more than one person would tread upon his toes.

Hatchard's, like the rival shops, dealt largely in pamphlets, for the vogue of that class of literature had not yet given way before the rising tide of newspapers and magazines. Nearly all Canning's publications in this form bore Hatchard's name, and many notable books of the day were published by the same house. The founder had a reputation for piety which leaned towards the Low Church School, and brought him the useful patronage of the Clapham Sect — Wilberforce, Zachary Macaulay and Henry Thornton — among whom circulated the *Christian Observer*, of which he had become publisher. Young Macaulay did his precocious book-buying here, and Hannah More, who took such an interest in his intellectual welfare, also made Hatchard her publisher.

More successful than any of their other publications was the *Proverbial Philosophy* of Martin Tupper, the first of the four series of which ran through no fewer than sixty editions. This while Wordsworth, Tennyson and Browning were a drug on the market! Tupper's first volume, *Sacra Poesis*, was published by Nisbet in 1832, and a hundred years hence, says the complacent author in his autobiography, 'may be a treasure to some bibliomaniac'. Tupper's 'chief authorial work', as he describes his best-known volume of platitudes, began its appearance in serial form in 1838, through Joseph Rickerby, who issued his volume of *Geraldine and other Poems* in the same year; but Tupper left him as 'an unfruitful publisher', and began his connection with Hatchard — 'with whom', he writes, 'I had a long and prosperous career, receiving annually from £500 to £800 a year, and in the aggregate benefiting both — for we shared equally — by something like £10,000 apiece. When that good old man, Grandfather Hatchard, first saw me he placed his hands on my dark hair and said with tears in his eyes, "You will thank God for this book when your head comes to be as white as mine." Let me gratefully acknowledge that he was a true prophet.'

Things did not work so smoothly after 'Grandfather Hatchard's'

---

works, *The Remembrancer: a monthly collection of Papers relating to American Independence*, and *The Correspondence of Wilkes and his Friends*, in five volumes (1805). He also published *The New Peerage* in three volumes, but this was apparently not his own work. Debrett improved upon it with his own *Peerage of England, Scotland, and Ireland*, which made its first appearance in two volumes in 1802. His *Baronetage* followed six years later.

death, and Tupper went over to Moxon's, where his third series was published. This, however, was not a financial success, so the fourth series went to Ward and Lock, with better result, though Tupper's popularity was now on the wane; and when Cassell presently produced the complete edition of the work in one volume it had to be remaindered.

John Hatchard's association with poets was not confined to Pye and Tupper. Crabbe's connection began after the death of his earlier publisher and friend, James Dodsley, to whom he had been introduced by his generous patron Burke. His first venture from the new address was *The Parish Register*, which appeared in 1807, bound up with *Sir Eustace Grey*, *The Birth of Flattery*, and other minor pieces; and its success, writes the poet's son and biographer, 'was not only decided, but nearly unprecedented'. This was in no small measure due to Jeffrey's generous tribute in the *Edinburgh*, the whole of the first edition being sold off within two days of the appearance of that review. *The Borough* also came from Hatchard's, but with his last volume, and the collected edition of his works Crabbe, as we have seen, made the greatest bargain of his life with John Murray II.

Another literary landmark in Piccadilly was Henry Sotheran & Co. Thomas Sotheran, the founder, belonged to an old family of booksellers in York, but, after serving his apprenticeship there, he left for the larger scope of London, serving for a time with the Quaker booksellers of Cornhill, John and Arthur Arch. Here also was apprenticed William Pickering, who subsequently combined antiquarian bookselling with publishing, and adopting the familiar device of the Aldine Press—an anchor and dolphin entwined—which at a later date became the trademark of the Chiswick Press. Pickering's 'Diamond Classics', with which he scored his first success soon after starting for himself in Lincoln's Inn Fields in 1820—removing four years later to Chancery Lane—were so called from the 'diamond' type: 'the smallest edition of the classics ever published', in the words of the publisher's own advertisement. His beautifully printed Aldine edition of the poets ran to fifty-three volumes. J. M. Dent was, later, to revive the name of Aldus in his own reprint series. In 1842 Pickering followed Sotheran to Piccadilly, where, at No. 177, he remained till his death.

Thomas Sotheran, to return to our earlier reference to John and Arthur Arch, left the Quaker booksellers some eight years earlier than Pickering, launching out on his own account in 1812. It was not, however, until he was joined in partnership by his son Henry that the firm assumed its prominent position in the trade. In 1856 a new partner was found in George Willis, whose valuable stock increased their total number of books to about half a million, with a catalogue running to over six hundred pages. On its publishing side the firm has been chiefly interested in works on antiquarian subjects and art, as well as natural history, their most important venture being in connection with the ornithological and other books of John Gould, which were taken over in 1881. Henry Sotheran, who retired in 1893, died twelve years later. At one time the firm had several branch shops in London, but gradually concentrated in its West End headquarters. The Tower Street branch, after being transferred to Queen Street, Cheapside, made its name there under the partnership of Jones & Evans.

Moxon's business in Dover Street survived its founder's death by a considerable number of years, but its best days were over. The chief interest attaching to its last phase, when Bertrand Payne was in control, was its chequered association with Swinburne, beginning with his first book, containing the two plays, *The Queen Mother* and *Rosamund*. That volume was to have been issued in 1860 by Basil M. Pickering, of Piccadilly, William Pickering's son and successor. Before the first twenty copies had been circulated, the book, for some mysterious reason which has never transpired, was withdrawn on the very eve of publication and transferred to Moxon's, who gave it a new title-page. 'Of all still-born books', Swinburne confided to his future biographer, Sir Edmund Gosse, '*The Queen Mother* was the stillest.' Not a copy was sold until long afterwards. Five years later came *Atalanta in Calydon*, with which Swinburne, in Gosse's phrase, 'shot like a rocket into celebrity'.

Here again Moxon's were the publishers, as in the case of *Chastelard*, which followed in the same year. Then came the first series of *Poems and Ballads*, with the 'libidinous songs' which caused such a storm of censure in 1866. Lord Houghton, without the poet's knowledge, had offered this collection to the third John Murray, who refused them, says Gosse, 'in terms which stung the poet to fury'. Moxon's decided to risk it, but the storm proved so violent, and threats of prosecution became so ominous, that the publishers only breathed freely again when they had washed their hands entirely of the offending book. The result was that Swinburne transferred all his works to John Camden Hotten, 'that somewhat notorious tradesman', in Edmund Gosse's phrase, being now the only one who would run the risk of publishing his books. The new alliance however, was far from satisfactory, ugly disputes occurring regarding the number of copies printed and sold, and the like; and it was a happy release for Swinburne when Hotten died in 1873, three years after all personal relations had ceased between them. Hotten's business was taken over at once by Chatto and Windus, who remained Swinburne's publishers till the end of his life.

Songs before Sunrise in the meantime had found another publisher in F. S. Ellis (1871), but this book subsequently made its way, with the rest of Swinburne's works, to Chatto & Windus. F. S. Ellis was a great friend of the Pre-Raphaelites, and, as Edmund Gosse testifies, 'a man of the highest integrity'. Swinburne would have transferred his earlier books to him in Hotten's lifetime, but Hotten refused to surrender them and tried in vain to prevent Ellis from publishing *Songs before Sunrise*. F. S. Ellis, who died in 1901, was head of the house at 29 New Bond Street, which remained a bookshop for upwards of two hundred years. John Brindley started there in 1728, to become joint publisher, seven years later (as mentioned on p. 149), of the first book to be issued by Robert Dodsley in Pall Mall, and the second volume of Pope's Works.

If the great Victorian poets had long to wait before receiving their due reward, Dickens proved that dazzling prizes were to be won in fiction in the middle of the nineteenth century. Not many of the myriads of people who hurry along the Strand today are aware that the corner of Arundel Street is intimately connected with Dickens's early days. Here, at No. 186, stood the little publishing house which first gave *Pickwick* to the world — a house then recently established by Chapman & Hall, two energetic young men whose names are as closely allied to Dickens and his works as that of John Murray is to Lord Byron. The story of Dickens's first piece of literature to find its way into print — *A Dinner at Poplar Walk*, afterwards included in *Sketches by Boz* as *Mr Minns and his Cousin* — how he dropped it by stealth 'in a dark letter-box in a dark office up a dark court in Fleet Street', and almost wept with pride when it appeared in all the glory of type, is one of the familiar anecdotes of literary history. That was in 1833, in Dickens's reporting days, and the man who sold him the momentous number of the magazine was none other than William Hall, one of his future publishers.

How firmly the incident was stamped on his memory is shown in the fact that when William Hall called at his chambers in Furnival's Inn some two years afterwards, with the proposal which was to lead to the immortal *Pickwick*, he recognized the bookseller at once, though he had never seen him either before or since. Young Hall — or 'little Hall', as he was more intimately called — was the junior partner in the publishing firm established with Edward Chapman in 1830. As publishers they began with a number of enterprises which John Forster describes as inglorious rather than important, including a library of fiction, which had for its editor the wayward genius, Charles Whitehead. Whitehead, himself an *Old Monthly* man, was a great admirer of Dickens's contributions to that journal, collected with similar articles from the *Chronicle*, and published early in 1836 as *Sketches by Boz* — and had secured from him for his own series *The Tuggs at Ramsgate*.

In November 1835, Chapman & Hall published *The Squib Annual*, with plates by Robert Seymour, and anxious to follow this up with a similar series of Cockney sporting pictures in shilling numbers had asked Whitehead to write the letterpress. Whitehead, records his biographer

Mackenzie Bell, declined the commission on the ground that he was not equal to the task of producing the copy with sufficient regularity, and it was on his recommendation that Dickens was chosen in his stead. Hence the famous interview at Furnival's Inn, resulting, as everyone knows, in Dickens's acceptance on the understanding that he should have a free hand in the choice of subjects and characters, and that the sketches should illustrate the text—not, as suggested by the publishers, that the text should merely be a running commentary on the pictures. Dickens was only twenty-four when the first part appeared in April 1836. He considered himself on the high road to fortune with the addition to his journalistic income of the £14 which the publishers had agreed to pay for each monthly instalment.

But *Pickwick* was not at first the great success which its author and publishers had hoped. Seymour died by his own hand before the second number appeared, and it was some time before his place was filled by the fortunate choice of Hablot K. Browne ('Phiz'). Forster tells us that it was not until the fourth and fifth numbers (Sam Weller makes his first appearance in the fifth) that *Pickwick*'s importance began to be understood by the trade. From that time, however, all doubt was removed, and the publishers, whose chief difficulty now was to cope with the demand, were so satisfied with their bargain that eventually they paid the author a considerable sum over and above the terms agreed upon.

Richard Bentley, the enterprising publisher of New Burlington Street, quick to grasp the potential value of the rising star, engaged him as editor of a new monthly magazine—*Bentley's Miscellany*—for which Dickens was also to write his next work, *Oliver Twist*; and, not long afterwards, secured him still further with an agreement by which Bentley should also publish his third and fourth books.

The result was that the novelist, while finishing the last half of *Pickwick* for Chapman & Hall, had to turn out similar monthly instalments of *Oliver Twist* for Bentley, edit and write occasional papers for the new magazine, prepare *Barnaby Rudge*, which he had engaged to supply in a complete form at an early date, and, in addition, edit the Memoirs of Grimaldi for the same publisher. Truly an amazing programme, even for that astonishing young genius. No wonder, as the time approached for beginning *Nicholas Nickleby*, which Dickens had undertaken to write for Chapman & Hall as a successor to *Pickwick*, that he complained of a sense of 'something hanging over him like a hideous nightmare'.

It would take too long to tell how he at length succeeded in escaping from the net in which he had been too ready to become entangled. Much negotiating and not ungenerous concessions by Bentley led to the novelist's retirement from the editorial drudgery of the *Miscellany* and his recapture by Chapman & Hall, who advanced the £2,500 which enabled Dickens to purchase from Bentley the copyright and stock of *Oliver Twist,* and cancel his engagements with that publisher not only for *Barnaby Rudge,* but for the third tale which he had agreed to write for him. Chapman & Hall still further strengthened their hold upon Dickens by helping him out of his entanglements with Macrone, the young publisher friend to whom the novelist had sold the copyright of *Sketches by Boz* for a conditional payment which Forster puts at £150 — though Percy Fitzgerald estimates it, all told, at £350 — and who threatened to reissue the work in monthly parts as soon as the author made his great name with the serial publication of *Pickwick* and *Oliver Twist.* Chapman & Hall shared with Dickens the £2,000 which Macrone demanded as a sort of unearned increment before he could be bought out.

Some years later (in 1844) it was the turn of Chapman & Hall to be bought out by Bradbury & Evans. There had been a strange falling off in the sales of *Martin Chuzzlewit*—probably due, to a certain extent, to the author's recent absence in America—and an indiscreet suggestion by Hall, whose premature fears made him speak too openly of safe-guarding the interests of the firm, so wounded the sensitive Dickens that he lent a ready ear to the advances of Bradbury & Evans. Further disappointment with his profits from the enormous sales of the *Christmas Carol,* published but a few days before the following Christmas, settled the matter. On June 1st, 1844, he signed an agreement with Bradbury & Evans by which, upon advance made to him of £2,800, he assigned to them a fourth share in whatever he might write during the ensuing eight years, though no obligations were imposed as to what works, if any, should be written, except that a successor to the *Carol* should be ready for the Christmas of 1844.

Dickens remained with Bradbury & Evans until 1859, when a bitter personal dispute with them sent him back to the publishers associated with his first success. It is sad to think that the younger partner, William Hall—the man who had sold him the historic copy of the *Old Monthly*—should have died during this long business estrangement. His funeral in the spring of 1847 was attended by Dickens, whose personal regard for the publisher had survived the temporary cloud, leaving remembrance only of much kindly intercourse. From 1859 all his copyrights were reserved for Chapman & Hall, and there was never any further question of a separation.

Edward Chapman retired in 1864—by which time the business had been removed from 186 Strand to 193 Piccadilly—and was succeeded as head of the firm by his cousin Frederic Chapman, who had joined the staff in 1841, and taken William Hall's place on the death of the junior partner six years later. Frederick Chapman became the moving spirit in a vigorous and far-seeing policy, which vastly improved the firm's position. 'An excellent fellow he was,' writes Percy Fitzgerald, 'somewhat blunt and bluff, but straightforward and good-natured. He had a small but delightful house in Ovington Square, to which someone had added a billiard-room, which he turned into a charming dining-room. What tasty Lucullus-like dinners were given there! I cannot say how he managed the firm, but when Dickens was alive he tried to meet his wishes in every conceivable way. Forster, too, he looked up to almost reverently ... I recall my first visit to the firm in Piccadilly. John Forster was with me, who strode in all important, "as though the whole place belonged to him." I was struck with the general stately look—the bustle—the number of clerks hurrying about. Forster was received with infinite respect, for he dictated all things.' Dickens's biographer continued as literary adviser to Chapman and Hall until 1860, when he was succeeded by George Meredith, then only thirty-two.

In 1858 Anthony Trollope, after publishing *Barchester Towers* and other early novels with Longmans, *The Three Clerks* with Richard Bentley, and some discouraging experiments elsewhere, settled down, like Dickens, with Chapman & Hall. He soon became intimately associated with the fortunes of the firm. *Framley Parsonage*, which made its first appearance in Smith & Elder's recently established *Cornhill* about this time, suddenly raised him to the rank of a 'bestseller', but did not shake his new allegiance. He dictated his own terms long before he became—for a brief period—one of Chapman & Hall's directors. In his history of the house, *A Hundred Years of Publishing*, Arthur Waugh, for many years its managing director, gives us a vivid sketch of the 'rough, emphatic, clamorous figure who became a terror to the staff'. Trollope, like Frederic Chapman, was one of the founders of the *Fortnightly Review*: chairman, indeed, of the separate company which brought it into being. The founders lost heart in their offspring too soon. In eighteen months they sold it to Chapman & Hall, who had published it from the start, and under whom it gradually became an enviable success. The first editor was George H. Lewes, who was succeeded by Lord Morley—then, of course, plain John Morley—in 1867, when the fortnightly publication became a monthly event. Lord Morley's memorable editorship—broken only by his absence in America, during which his place was filled by George Meredith—lasted until 1883, when he was succeeded in turn by T. H. S. Escott, Frank Harris and W. L. Courtney, the last of whom maintained the best traditions of the *Fortnightly* for thirty-odd years.

George Meredith's association with Chapman & Hall began with the publication by them of *The Shaving of Shagpat*, and after succeeding Forster as literary adviser in 1860, he was for over thirty years a ruling personality of the firm. An article in the *Fortnightly* on 'George Meredith as Publisher's Reader', written by B. W. Matz, shows not only how ready was Meredith always to help and encourage an author whenever a manuscript pleased him, but also how extremely high was his standard of merit. 'To say he was difficult to please is to understate the fact. His standard was tremendously high, and from that pinnacle his judgment was right and sound. But some doubt may be expressed as to whether the standard was the right one to judge a book for commercial purposes.' His rejection of *East Lynne* — one of Bentley's greatest successes — is perhaps the strongest case in point, though to the other side of his account must be placed such discoveries as Olive Schreiner's *Story of an African Farm*. His own novels, with three or four exceptions, were all issued by the same house until 1895, when they were transferred to Constable's.

The story of Thackeray's publishers, which follows naturally on that of Dickens's, recalls the history of another celebrated house — now merged in John Murray's. It was under the second John Murray that the founder of Smith & Elder, as the firm was originally called, served part of his apprenticeship. Like the first John Murray, and many another publisher whose name has become a household word — Blackwood, Macmillan, Blackie, Black, Nelson, Chambers and the rest — George Smith was born on the other side of the Tweed. The son of a Morayshire farmer, he was twenty-seven when, in 1816, he launched out as a London bookseller and stationer in partnership with a brother Scot, Alexander Elder.

Three years later the partners embarked in a modest way as publishers, and in 1824 moved to 65 Cornhill, adding to the firm a third member, who brought a business connection with India which for a considerable time played a larger share than the publishing department in the flourishing affairs of the firm. Those were still the days of the old East India Company, and the fortunes of the Cornhill house were built up mainly on its export trade to India and the Colonies. Officers of the East India Company not only ordered their books and stationery and other things through Smith, Elder & Company, but gradually came to use them as general agents and bankers. It was a profitable but curious assortment of enterprises.

All this is little more than the introduction to the history of the house on its literary side. The first chapter really begins with the entry into the business of the second George Smith, towards the end of the 'thirties. Hitherto the publishing output, though considerable in bulk, and not undistinguished in some of its items, had languished for lack of a steady policy and proper organization. George Smith was barely twenty when, at his own request, he took over this department in 1843, and had the modest sum of £1,500 placed at his absolute disposal to see what he could do to improve matters. His first venture was Horne's *New Spirit of the Age*, the series of essays in which Mrs Browning and Robert Bell both had a hand. Then in 1846 came a book which, as the publisher afterwards related in some reminiscences in the *Cornhill Magazine*, brought him in touch with Leigh Hunt in rather a strange way:

> I went to Peckham to dine with Thomas Powell, who, as well as being a confidential clerk in the counting-house of two brothers who are wealthy merchants in the City, dabbled in literature. The merchants were supposed to have suggested to Charles Dickens the Cheeryble Brothers, in *Nicholas Nickleby*. While I waited in Powell's little drawing-room for a few minutes before dinner, I took up a neatly written manuscript which was lying on the table, and was reading it when my host entered the room. 'Ah', he said, 'that doesn't look worth £40, does it? I advanced £40 to Leigh Hunt on the security of that manuscript, and I shall never see my money again.' When I was leaving I asked Powell to let me take the manuscript with me. I finished reading it before I went to sleep that night, and next day I asked Powell if he would let me have the manuscript if I paid him the £40. He readily assented, and having got from him Leigh Hunt's address, I went off to him in Edwardes Square, Kensington, explained the circumstances under which the manuscript had come into my possession, and asked whether, if I paid him an additional £60, I might have the copyright. 'You young prince!' cried Leigh Hunt, in a tone of something like rapture, and the transaction was promptly concluded. The work was *Imagination and Fancy*. It was succeeded by *Wit and Humour*, and other books, all of which were successful, and the introduction was the foundation of a friendship with Leigh Hunt and the members of his family which was very delightful to me.

There is a letter in Ruskin's correspondence which shows that George Smith sent a copy of *Wit and Humour* to the then unknown author of *Modern Painters*, the first volume of which had been published anonymously, and with disappointing results, by Smith, Elder, & Company. 'I ought before to have thanked you', writes Ruskin, 'for your obliging present of *Wit and Humour*—two characters of intellect in which I am so immensely deficient as never even to have ventured upon a conjecture respecting their real nature.' Ruskin's business relations with the firm lasted for thirty years, and led to a close personal friendship with George Smith himself. It was about this time—in 1846—that the first George Smith died, and the other partners withdrawing not long afterwards, the founder's son, still only twenty-two, found himself sole head of the firm. Young Smith faced the crisis with characteristic courage, and proved himself equal to the task. By force of character, and a rare combination of business acumen and literary instinct, he made a great success of each department.

In 1853 he took into partnership Henry S. King, the Brighton book-seller, whose business was taken over by Messrs Treacher. By 1868 both sides of the house had developed in so many directions that Smith decided to devote himself entirely to the publishing branch, relinquish-ing the other department to the firm which became H. S. King and Company, bankers and East India and Colonial agents. George Smith moved to Waterloo Place in 1869. Long before this separation, he had made a circle of literary friends. His happy association with Charlotte Brontë began in 1847, when the manuscript of *The Professor* arrived at the office from an unknown writer, who gave the signature of 'Currer Bell.' The story of how the manuscript was declined with a letter which, as the novelist afterwards said, was 'so delicate, reasonable, and courte-ous, as to be more cheering than some acceptances': how, on this en-couragement, she sent Smith the manuscript of *Jane Eyre*; how the mysterious author subsequently came to London with her sister and revealed her identity in the publisher's office; and how the rare friend-ship which resulted stood firm — will always remain one of the brightest chapters in the history of publishing. Charlotte Brontë praised her publisher in the most graceful way by making George Smith the original of her Dr John in *Villette*. It was through Smith that Charlotte Brontë came to know Thackeray and George Henry Lewes, and she was able to return the compliment by introducing her publisher to her friends Harriet Martineau and Mrs Gaskell, whose works, as a consequence, soon found their way to the same generous hands.

Thackeray's connection with the house was closer even than that of Charlotte Brontë. It began with the introduction to him which Smith obtained on Charlotte's behalf. At the close of her visit to London in 1850, Thackeray asked him to publish his next Christmas book, *The Kickleburys on the Rhine*. This the publisher did, and in the following year cemented the connection by paying him £1,200 for the first edition of 2,500 copies of *Esmond*. As in his dealings with other authors, Smith's business relations with the novelist ripened into something equally close and lasting on the social side. The intimacy led to the *Cornhill Magazine*, which was originally planned merely as a medium for the serial publi-cation of a novel by Thackeray, though it had long been one of Smith's ambitions to establish a great periodical.

The *Cornhill* — so named by Thackeray after its original publishing address — made its first appearance in January 1860, with Thackeray as its editor at a salary of £1,000 a year. The magazine not only proved an unprecedented success in itself — Smith thereupon doubling Thackeray's salary — but proved a means of bringing to the publishing house many of the illustrious writers and books with which the firm subsequently be-came identified — the Brownings, George Eliot, for whose *Romola* in its serial and book rights the publisher offered £10,000; Anthony

Trollope, John Addington Symonds, Matthew Arnold, whose niece, Mrs Humphrey Ward, like Thackeray's daughter, Lady Ritchie, carried down to the twentieth century the old association with the same publishers, and a host of others — and artistic celebrities, too, for the *Cornhill* in those days was illustrated.

Ever ready for fresh conquests, the publishers some five years later ventured into the thorny paths of evening journalism. With the help of Frederick Greenwood, who became its first editor, he established the *Pall Mall Gazette*, so named after the journal invented by Thackeray for the benefit of Arthur Pendennis. The story of the *P.M.G.*, with its brilliant band of contributors, and of Smith's gallant struggle to place it firmly on its feet, would take up much more space than we can spare.

His old partner, Henry S. King, it should be added, continued the publishing department at Cornhill for a time under his own name. Tennyson, for whom he published in the 'seventies, had the highest opinion of him. 'With none of the publishers into whose hands circumstances had thrown my father', wrote Tennyson's son in his Memoir of the poet, 'was the connection so interruptedly pleasant as with Messrs Macmillan — unless perhaps that with Mr Henry King.'

The house of Macmillan, just mentioned in Lord Tennyson's tribute, first made its mark in London, like Smith, Elder, & Company, in mid-Victorian days. Its history began in the earlier years of Queen Victoria's reign, after its founder, Daniel Macmillan, had mastered his craft in Scotland, first in the town of Irvine, on the Ayrshire coast, and afterwards in Glasgow. His apprenticeship over, Daniel found it impossible to settle down in Scotland. He sought an outlet for his zeal in London, like so many other young Scotsmen, including his friend MacLehose, who afterwards established the well-known business of MacLehose & Sons, publishers to the University of Glasgow, as well as general publishers on their own account. It was to MacLehose, after his first experience of London life at Seeley's, in Fleet Street, that he explained his lofty ideal of what a bookseller's calling should be:

> ... We booksellers, if we are faithful to our task, are trying to destroy and are helping to destroy, all kinds of confusion, and are aiding our great Taskmaster to reduce the world into order and beauty and harmony ... At the same time, it is our duty to manage our affairs wisely, keep our minds easy, and not trade beyond our means.

When he wrote this letter Daniel was himself a bookseller's assistant, earning £80 a year. He had ventured to London in 1833, but finding nothing suitable there had accepted a post at Cambridge, beginning at £30 a year, and boarding with his master, Mr Johnson. London, however, still held out greater attractions for him, and the spring of

Queen Victoria's accession year found him in his situation at Seeley's who then had their publishing address in Fleet Street. Here his salary rose in six years from £60 to £130, his younger brother Alexander meantime joining him in the same house. Always fretting for independence, Daniel at length embarked with his brother in a small bookseller's shop in Aldergate Street. This venture led, in the autumn of 1843, to the purchase of a more promising business in Trinity Street, Cambridge—'just opposite the Senate House'.

That was the turning point in the career of the two Macmillans, largely brought about through the influence and material help of Archdeacon Hare, one of the authors of *Guesses at Truth by Two Brothers*—a book which made so deep an impression on Daniel Macmillan while he was still a shopman at Seeley's (now Seeley, Service & Co., Ltd of 196 Shaftesbury Avenue), that he wrote to the anonymous writers expressing his keen appreciation. The letter pleased the Archdeacon, and presently young Macmillan received an invitation to visit him at Hurstmonceaux. It was the Archdeacon and his brother who lent the Macmillans the £500 which enabled them to buy the business in Cambridge. Here Daniel was at once on the best of terms with the undergraduates and other university men, and, though handicapped by dreadful illnesses, the affairs of the firm prospered exceedingly. It was not long before the brothers were able to take over the business of Stevenson, the ablest of the older Cambridge booksellers, and to think seriously of the possibilities of running a successful publishing branch in conjunction with the bookselling department. 'Our retail trade', wrote Daniel to MacLehose in 1855, 'will chiefly be valuable as bringing about us men who will grow into authors.' The scheme worked splendidly. A business was developed which justified the saying that it was 'founded on Broad Church theology and Cambridge mathematics'. In the more venturesome field of fiction the Macmillans were equally fortunate in publishing for Charles Kingsley, whose *Westward Ho!* shared with Thomas Hughes's *Tom Brown's Schooldays* the chief honours of those early days.

When Daniel Macmillan died he had the satisfaction of leaving a flourishing business in the able hands of his brother Alexander, and knowing that, whatever happened, he had provided for his wife and children. To the last, his biographer tells us, he retained 'a joyousness and playfulness in his intercourse with his family and friends which made it impossible to realize upon how frail a thread his life hung'. The next phase in the fortunes of the house begins with the establishing of a branch in London, and will be discussed later.

While London had become more than ever the centre of the book-publishing trade in Britain, and the old co-operation between the booksellers of Edinburgh and the metropolis no more than a memory long before the death of Daniel Macmillan, some of the leading firms still retained their headquarters in Scotland. Besides the Blacks and Blackwoods, there were, among others, the two vigorous firms of Nelson & Sons, founded by Thomas Nelson as far back as 1798, and Chambers, established by William and Robert Chambers in 1832 with the success of their familiar journal: both concerns flourishing to this day with their popular libraries of reprints, gift-books, encyclopaedias dictionaries, and other works of the kind. When Adam Black laid the modest foundations of his firm in 1807—four years after William Blackwood had started business on his own account—Scott, by his partnership with the Ballantynes, had already taken the luckless step that was to lead to his undoing. It was the younger of these new publishing firms which was destined ultimately—years after Scott's death—to become possessed of some of the most valuable copyrights that ever found their way to the open market.

Like Daniel Macmillan in later years, Adam Black sought the greater possibilities of London after serving his time in Scotland. He described his apprenticeship in John Fairbairn's shop in Edinburgh as 'a dreary disgusting servitude, in which I wasted five of the best years of my life with associates from whom I learned much evil and little good'. He had little money to spare when he started to look for work in London. He was almost at the end of his resources when he earned his first half-guinea from Thomas Sheraton, then regarded only as a worn-out cabinet-maker and encyclopaedist.

After little more than a week with Sheraton—almost ashamed to take his half-guinea from the poor man—Black secured a more lucrative post at the 'Temple of the Muses', Lackington's immense bookshop at the corner of Finsbury Square, which in those days, with its quarter of a million volumes constantly on sale, was one of the sights of London. Here young Black remained until the time arrived to start in business for himself. For this he returned to his native Edinburgh, and, in his twenty-fourth year, opened his unpretentious shop at North Bridge. His pronounced Whiggism and independence in religion—though he was always a man of the sincerest piety—might have affected his prospects in Edinburgh in the early years of the nineteenth century, but he was wise enough not to meddle openly in politics for at least ten years, by which time the foundations of his business were well and truly laid.

Meanwhile, for a few years, he had been associated with an old shop-mate, Thomas Underwood, in a small London bookshop which they had bought up between them. This presently led to their purchase of the Fleet Street business of the second John Murray on his removal to Albemarle Street. Adam Black was forced into this deal rather against his own judgment, and had to fall back on his father for financial support, as well as on his brother Charles, whom he persuaded to leave the building trade and take an active share in the bookselling business. Having put £1,000 into the concern, Charles Black proceeded to London, and John Murray's old place in Fleet Street was taken over by the new firm of Underwood & Black. Only for a short time, however, for Underwood proved an impossible partner to work with. In 1813 both brothers were glad enough to sell out.

All this time Adam Black's Edinburgh business had been developing on sound if unsensational lines. He was gradually expanding the publishing as well as the bookselling side. When the crash came in 1826, involving the fall of Constable & Ballantyne, and overwhelming poor Scott himself, he was ready to jump to the front by acquiring the copyright of the *Encyclopaedia Britannica,* which had been the property of Constable since 1812. The actual purchase was concluded in 1827, when Adam Black succeeded in completing the necessary capital for this ambitious undertaking by securing three fresh partners, whose shares, however, were all bought in by Black within the next ten years, so that by 1837 the *Encyclopaedia* became his sole property. Heedless or unconscious of impending disaster, Constable before his bankruptcy had made all arrangements for a new edition (the seventh) of the *Encyclopaedia,* under the editorship of Macvey Napier, who was to receive for his services a total salary of £6,500, to be paid by instalments on the publication of each half-volume. This plan was carried out by Adam Black and his partners in all its details, Dr James Browne being also engaged as sub-editor, by whom, indeed, the bulk of the editorial work was done.

The next landmark in the publishing career of Adam Black was the purchase from Robert Cadell's trustees of the copyright of Scott's Waverley novels and other works for the sum of £31,000.* This was in 1851, and in the same year Messrs Adam & Charles Black—for by that time the founder had taken his nephew Charles into partnership—moved to larger quarters, on the opposite side of North Bridge. No further move was made until the firm shifted its headquarters to London in 1889, taking possession of the fine building which has since been its home in Soho Square and adding considerably to their laurels in 1861 by the acquisition of the copyright of De Quincey's works. Adam Black lived to be twice Lord Provost of Edinburgh, and, incidentally, to decline the honour of knighthood for his services in that connection.

It was Adam Black who introduced Macaulay to Edinburgh, and when Macaulay was made a peer in 1856 it was Black who succeeded him at Westminster, where he represented his native city until 1865.

---

* Robert Cadell, who as stated on p. 201 became Scott's publisher in 1826, and his partner in the re-purchase of the Waverley novels in the following year, lived to make a fortune out of these golden copyrights. His finest edition was the illustrated Abbotsford Series which cost him some £40,000 to produce.

After his death in 1874—in his ninetieth year—the services of the publisher-politician were recognized by Edinburgh in the erection of a bronze statue, to the memory of 'one of the noblest citizens she ever possessed', in East Princes Street Gardens. In 1870 he retired from the business over which he had ruled for sixty-three years, handing it on to three of his sons, James, Francis and Adam.

While the first Adam Black was thus building up the fortunes of his firm, the slightly senior house of Blackwood was also continuing its flourishing career. Its founder, William Blackwood, was not so long-lived as Adam Black. He died in 1834, a few years after moving his business from Princes Street to 45 George Street, which has since remained the headquarters of the firm. On his death the management passed to two of his sons, Alexander and Robert. The dual reign led to a less eventful but equally prosperous period. The circulation of the magazine rose to 8,000 a month; Barham and Bulwer Lytton were enlisted; and a London branch was established in Pall Mall—to be transferred five years later (1845) to the corner house in Paternoster Row, destined to disappear nearly a hundred years later in the London blitz. It was in 1845 that Alexander Blackwood died, and a more interesting chapter began with the return to Edinburgh of John Blackwood, the founder's third son, to succeed his elder brother in the editorial chair. John had been managing the branch in London, where his friends included Delane and Thackeray, though Thackeray, like Shorthouse in his experience with Smith and Elder, had once enjoyed the distinction of being rejected by the Edinburgh house, and never became one of its authors. In 1849 John was joined by his brother, Major William Blackwood.

The reign of John Blackwood was also notable for Kinglake's *Crimea*, the long list of novels by Mrs Oliphant, tales by Charles Reade, Blackmore, Trollope and many another popular novelist. The crowning glory of all was the association with George Eliot, begun anonymously through George H. Lewes with *Amos Barton*, which started its serial course in *Maga* in January 1857. The mystery surrounding the identity of the author, the part played by Lewes and Blackwood in encouraging her to write and the firm friendship with the publisher which sprang therefrom, fill a familiar page in literary history.

In mid-Victorian days, round which most of the present chapter is written, the Glasgow houses of Blackie and Collins were steadily building up the businesses which have continued to the present day; while the firm of MacLehose, founded many years before by James and his younger brother Robert MacLehose, were now printers to the University. The oldest of the group are Blackie & Son, who, though their books bear their London imprint, still have their headquarters in Glasgow.

At first the publishers confined their attentions to the literary needs of Scotland, but they soon widened their sphere of influence, and by 1830 had their own office in London. A year previously the first John Blackie, a man of rare mental and physical vigour, had taken over the works of Andrew and J. M. Duncan, then printers to the university, and from that time the publishers have done all their own printing and binding. In due course the founder was joined by his three sons—the second John Blackie (afterwards Lord Provost of Glasgow); Dr W. G. Blackie (afterwards Lord Dean of Guild of Glasgow), who took the Ph.D. degree at Jena, to which his native University of Glasgow subsequently added the honorary degree of LL.D.; and Robert Blackie, all of whom helped their father to develop the business on sound, scholarly lines.

The house of Collins dates back to 1819, when it was founded in Glasgow by William Collins in partnership with a brother of the famous divine, Dr Chalmers. Under the second William, afterwards Sir William Collins, the Glasgow business developed into one of the largest manufacturing stationers and publishers in the world.

One of the 'lettered booksellers' of the Victorian age, George Henry Bohn, retired during this period. His father, John Martin Bohn, was a younger son of a noble Westphalian family, and was at school in Germany with the great Count Metternich. Here young Bohn learnt bookbinding, while Metternich took up shoemaking, in accordance with the old German custom that every German schoolboy, whether the son of a prince or pauper, must learn a trade of some sort. 'Who would have thought you would turn your craft to such businesslike account?' said Metternich to Bohn when he met his old schoolmate in London a good many years later. The truth was, apparently, that Bohn, like many another younger son, had to make his own way in the world, and turned to the readiest means of doing so. Coming to London in 1795, he soon won no little reputation by his bindings, inventing what were termed 'spring backs' and introducing other improvements. Having moved to 17 and 18 Henrietta Street, he also started a second-hand book business, and received the appointment of Court bookseller. Meantime he had married Elizabeth Watt, a niece of James Watt, of steam engine fame, Henry George Bohn being born early in 1796.

The son was educated at the expense of George III, and entered his father's business when he was sixteen. His German ancestry and linguistic accomplishments stood him in good stead when he travelled through Europe in search of book bargains for the London business. It was a fortunate period for an ambitious and far-seeing young bookseller. While Napoleon was ravaging the Continent whole libraries were being dispersed by ancient families and religious institutions lest they should fall into the Emperor's hands, and many treasures were picked up in this way by the Anglo-German bookseller. Leipzig was then in its prime as the book mart of the world, and while the guns were booming there in the historic battle of October 18th, 1813, an auction sale was taking place in the market, at which young Bohn was practically the only bidder. He happened to be attending another auction sale at Leipzig while the battle of Waterloo was being fought.

Bohn's knowledge of languages was turned to good account in literature as well as in trade, for he published in London, on his own account, before he was eighteen, an English translation from the German of the romance of *Ferrandino*. Serving merely as his father's right hand did not satisfy his ambition, and shortly after his marriage, in 1831, as his father would not admit him into partnership, he started on his own account at 4 York Street, Covent Garden—a house which had already played a part in English literary annals as the home of De Quincey when he wrote *The Confessions of an English Opium Eater*.

Bohn's business was founded with £2,000, half of which was lent by his father-in-law, William Simpkin, of Simpkin, Marshall & Company. At first he contented himself mainly with developing a profitable connection with rare and valuable old books, and gradually built up an excellent reputation among bibliophiles. Ten years after starting for himself he was able to issue a guinea catalogue of his treasures, containing 1,948 pages and 23,208 items, together with one hundred and fifty-two pages of remainders. Scenting greater profit in the remainder trade than in rare old books, he devoted himself to this branch of the business with the shrewdness and energy which characterized all his undertakings. He began to buy the copyrights of his remainders as well as the surplus stock, reissuing at a popular price any book that appeared to be worth the risk.

It was not Bohn, however, who started the cheap libraries of standard reprints, a distinction which belongs to Charles Tilt and his partner and successor David Bogue. Tilt made his name as a successful book and print seller at 86 Fleet Street, where he issued his illustrated classics and Miniature Library of cheap but elegantly printed volumes. On his retirement in 1842 Bogue bought his business and remainders and had already inaugurated his European Library (in 1845), when Bohn came along with a similar series. Unfortunately for Bogue, he had included in one of his reprints (Roscoe's *Life of Lorenzo de' Medici*) a number of illustrations the copyrights of which had previously been bought among his remainders by Bohn. A lawsuit followed which resulted in an injunction against Bogue, and his rival followed up this success by developing his own library so rapidly and skilfully that Bogue at last was forced to retire from the field. Bohn completed his conquest by taking over Bogue's copyrights. The European Library was thus incorporated in Bohn's Standard Library, which succeeded so well that it was followed in 1847 by the Scientific, the Antiquarian, the Classical and other series. Some six hundred volumes altogether—standard works of every country in Europe—were added by Bohn before he retired, after doing 'as much for literature', said Emerson, 'as railroads have done for internal intercourse'. Bohn himself selected most of the volumes, and the list furnishes striking proof of his immense knowledge of European literature. His linguistic accomplishments—he could speak five modern languages, besides being a Greek and Latin scholar—were here of the utmost service to him, and also enabled him to translate several of the volumes included in the series of Foreign Classics. He contributed in various ways to many other additions to his libraries, besides writing for the Philobiblon Society *The Origin and Progress of Printing* (1857) and *A Biography and Bibliography of Shakespeare* (1863). He was also responsible for a *Dictionary of Quotations* (into which he ventured to put several of his own unpublished verses), and a number of other handbooks.

Bohn's knowledge of old books—well displayed in his edition of Lowndes' *Bibliographer's Manual*—brought him in touch with many distinguished men. His advice was often sought by such great collectors as the Duke of Hamilton and 'Vathek' Beckford, and on more than one occasion he was consulted on everyday matters by the Prince Consort. He was chairman of the committee appointed for the Printed Books Department of the 1851 Exhibition. Gladstone, who had a high opinion of Bohn's abilities, offered him a baronetcy, but we are told that the publisher declined the honour on principle. Bohn tired of his success in 1864, when his sons preferred other professions to following in his footsteps, and sold the whole stock and copyrights of his libraries to Bell & Daldy for about £40,000. His principal copyrights in other departments were taken over by Chatto & Windus for another £20,000, while his second-hand books, which subsequently took forty days to dispose of at various auction rooms, realized a further £13,000. We are not here concerned with the later career of Henry George Bohn; nor with the wonderful collection of art treasures which he accumulated and catalogued in a work that took him, with his daughter, over two years to complete; nor the rose fetes in the garden of his fine old house at Twickenham, attended by Dickens, Cruikshank, Rosa Bonheur and many other celebrities. He lived to the ripe old age of eighty-nine, vigorous and industrious to the last.

The advent of Bell & Daldy brings us to the story of the house in which Bohn's Libraries now belonged. The firm itself dated back to 1838, when George Bell, after serving his apprenticeship with Whittaker & Company, booksellers and publishers, of Ave Maria Lane, began business for himself in Bouverie Street. Like H. G. Bohn, George Bell, who was a native of Richmond, Yorkshire, was the son of a bookseller, and a man of scholarly tastes. He started his publishing career with the annotated series entitled Bibliotheca Classica, in which his old employers,

Messrs Whittaker, had a share. The series did well from the first, and the publisher followed it up with books of educational, architectural and religious interest. He was joined in 1855 by F. R. Daldy, from Rivington's, and together they took over many of the joint publications of William Pickering and the Chiswick Press, including the Aldine Poets, Pickering himself—to whom reference is made on p. 209—having died in 1854, his last days harassed by financial difficulties through standing security to a friend.

George Bell launched out in other directions by starting a business in Brighton, and becoming proprietor (for some years) of the business of Deighton, Bell & Company of Cambridge, whose well-known mathematical connection helped him to start the 'Cambridge Mathematical' series. The crowning event in the firm's career, however, came with the purchase of Bohn's libraries in 1864. Bell & Daldy had already moved from Bouverie Street to 186 Fleet Street. They had now succeeded Bohn at his York Street address, where they not only extended their own business, but revised and enlarged the libraries which had made their predecessors' fortune.

It was while serving in Bohn's bookshop that Bernard Quaritch saved up the £10—from his salary of twenty-four shillings a week—with which he founded an equally celebrated business. Though Quaritch's funds were low, his aims were high, and his spirits undaunted. When Bohn asked him where he was going he told him frankly that he meant to set up in opposition to his old employer. Bohn laughed. 'Don't you know that I am the first bookseller in England?' he said. 'Yes,' came the reply, 'but I am going to be the first bookseller in Europe'—a vow which was in due course fulfilled. Taking out naturalization papers in 1847—for he was a native of Prussian Saxony—he made his modest beginning in the same year with a little corner shop in Castle Street, Leicester Square. Thirteen years later he was able to move to No. 15 Piccadilly, where he reigned as the prince of antiquarian booksellers until his death in 1900. The centenary of the firm was celebrated in 1947.

No mention of Quaritch is complete without some reference to his share in the adventures of FitzGerald's version of *Omar*. FitzGerald handed over his translation in the first place to Parker of the Strand, who had asked him for something for *Fraser*, but, as he made no use of it for over a year, FitzGerald took it back and published it at his own expense in 1859, through Quaritch, as a slim quarto in brown paper. Everyone knows the story of how Quaritch, finding that no one would pay a shilling each for the remainders, of which FitzGerald made him a present, dumped them into the outside box at a penny apiece; and how they were discovered there by Rossetti and his friends.

In the years following Bohn's retirement died two of the nineteenth-century pioneers of cheap literature—John Cassell and Charles Knight. Cassell, who was the first to go (in 1865), owed his success to his own untiring energy. He began life seriously as a carpenter—after two false starts in a cotton mill and a velveteen factory—and was then swept into the teetotal movement. 'Young, bony, big and exceedingly uncultivated', as he is described by Thomas Whittaker, one of the pioneers of the movement, he took up the cause with his whole heart and soul. He was only twenty when he left Manchester. In London, fortunately, he fell among Friends, and the Quakers helped him materially after he had been enrolled among the lecturers of the National Temperance Society.

At the end of his teetotal lectureship Cassell, now a happily married man, started a tea and coffee business in the City, with headquarters successively in Coleman Street and Fenchurch Street, and a sideline in patent medicines.

Two years after embarking on this scheme Cassell turned his thoughts to a plan for helping the temperance cause by means of cheap and enlightening publications for the people. With his wife's encouragement, and the substantial help which she was able to bring with her own inheritance, he started the *Teetotal Times* and the *Teetotal Essayist*, when the fortunes of the movement were none too flourishing. On July 1st, 1848 he launched the first number of a fully equipped weekly journal, the *Standard of Freedom*, published at fourpence halfpenny a copy. This was succeeded in 1850 by a penny weekly called the *Working Man's Friend and Family Instructor*. He now had his own printing office, and from the first the new paper was his own production, with his address for the time being at No. 335 Strand. Then came in steady succession the popular serials and periodicals like *Cassell's Popular Educator*, the *Magazine of Art*, the *Illustrated Family Bible*, the *Family Paper*, the *History of England*, the *Natural History*, *Cassell's Magazine*, the *Quiver*, and illustrated editions of *Don Quixote* and other standard works in weekly parts—all helping to develop a healthy and popular taste in art and letters. But in 1855 he was unable to repay a large loan called in at short notice, and was forced to sell to the printers Petter & Galpin, who retained his services, admitted him into partnership in 1858 and financed the rebuilding of the premises in La Belle Sauvage Yard, Ludgate Hill, into which Cassell had moved in 1852.

The origin of the sign of La Belle Sauvage has given rise to many romantic theories, but the truth seems to be that the inn was originally called the Bell, and presently came to be known also as Savage's Inn, with the result that somehow the two names became inextricably mixed. After many vicissitudes the old inn was demolished in 1873 to provide for the growing needs of the printing and publishing firm—until German bombs demolished it in the Second World War.

John Cassell, who died in 1865, ranks as a pioneer of cheap literature with the brothers William and Robert Chambers, and Charles Knight. Knight, who survived Cassell by eight years, had a passion for cheapness which was more profitable to the public than himself. His first business came to grief in the financial crisis which ruined Scott and his publishers and spread disaster among many smaller houses. Some of his chief ventures after that event, such as the *Penny Encyclopaedia*, were issued when he was acting as publisher to the Society for the Diffusion of Useful Knowledge, organized by Brougham and others. He held this post until the society itself came to grief in 1846 over the *Biographical Dictionary*, winding up with a loss of nearly £5,000. Other works more closely identified with his name were his *Popular History of England*, his *Pictorial Shakespeare*, his *London* and his Shilling Volumes for all Readers —running to nearly two hundred volumes in all and beginning with his life of Caxton. Among his own books, either written or edited by himself, the most popular included his *Half-hours with the Best Authors*, and *Shadows of the Old Booksellers*.

Other publishers whose enterprise left its mark on the reading habits of the people are half forgotten today or remembered no more. Alexander Strahan, for instance, who, eager to follow pioneers like Knight and Chambers by supplying, in his own words, 'such literature as will not ignobly interest nor frivolously amuse, but convey the wisest instruction in the pleasantest manner', founded *Good Words* under Dr Norman Macleod's editorship in 1860.

In all too rapid succession *Good Words* was followed by the *Sunday Magazine*, *Good Words for the Young*, the *Argosy*, and the *Contemporary Review*, Strahan at the same time developing a book-publishing business with equal energy. Unfortunately his financial gifts were not as shrewd as his literary judgment, and he was at length forced to acknowledge defeat. With all his unbusinesslike habits Strahan seems to have been a lovable character. Although somewhat reserved, he drew men by a fascination àll his own, as Professor Blaikie, who became editor for a time of the *Sunday Magazine*, testifies in his *Recollections of a Busy Life*:

> What Archibald Constable had been at the beginning of the century, Alexander Strahan aimed to be further on. It was his generosity to authors, joined to a lack of financial insight, that led him into difficulty. Sanguine and buoyant to a degree, he never seemed to fear any exhaustion of resources. To Tennyson it is understood that he promised £4,000 for the right to publish his books. But he found, like Constable, that you cannot allow to generosity an unbounded sphere.

The first Richard Bentley, who became Publisher in Ordinary to Queen Victoria, and one of the stalwarts of the three-volume novel days, is also little more than a name to the present generation. Bentley started a printing concern early in the nineteenth century with his brother Samuel, and in 1829 was taken into partnership by Henry Colburn, whose publications had already included the Diaries of Evelyn and Pepys. In addition to publishing new books, Colburn not only ran a fashionable library in New Burlington Street, but speculated at different times in at least half a dozen periodicals, among them the *New Monthly Magazine*, whose editors included Thomas Campbell, Bulwer Lytton, Theodore Hook and Harrison Ainsworth.

After three years' partnership Colburn sold his business in New Burlington Street to Bentley, who, equally enterprising in periodical speculations, started, among other ventures, *Bentley's Miscellany* (1837), with Charles Dickens as editor. *Oliver Twist*, as mentioned on p. 212, made its first appearance in the pages of this magazine, which was subsequently merged in *Temple Bar*. Bentley, whose famous Red Room in New Burlington Street had been the meeting place of such men as Dickens and the Disraelis, Cruikshank and Leech, also made a big success of his library of Standard Novels, which ran to 127 volumes. He was succeeded by his son, George Bentley, who edited *Temple Bar* until his own death in 1895.

In the meantime Henry Colburn, repenting of the bargain which he had made with Bentley, to the effect that he would not start publishing again in London, or within twenty miles of it, had retreated to Windsor. The call of the town, however, was too much for him. Sacrificing his guarantees, he made a fresh start in Great Marlborough Street. Here he rivalled Bentley in helping to fill the libraries with three-volume novels at a guinea and a half the set, and issuing, besides, such weightier works as Burke's *Peerage, Baronetage, and Landed Gentry*, and Strickland's *Lives of the Queens of England*. This last was one of Colburn's most profitable ventures. He paid £2,000 for the copyright, which, after his death, was sold again for no less than £6,900. Among the popular novelists who gathered round Colburn in those palmy days of the old three-decker were G. P. R. James, Captain Marryat, Lord Lytton and Theodore Hook. Some of these authors published with him before his partnership with Bentley. Another celebrity associated with Colburn during the same period was Benjamin Disraeli, whose first novel, *Vivian Grey*, he issued in 1826, his second tale, *The Young Duke*, following in 1831. When Colburn retired he was succeeded by Hurst and Blackett, though he retained certain copyrights, which, after his death in 1855, realized £14,000—including the £6,900 for Strickland's *Lives*.

The name of Routledge follows naturally upon that of Colburn, for the popular novelists of the one house were largely exploited by the other for the Railway and other libraries which, in the mid-nineteenth century, formed the bulk of W. H. Smith & Son's bookstall business.

George Routledge founded his own firm on second-hand books and remainders at a little shop in Ryder's Court, Leicester Square. Then, starting the Railway Library and moving to larger quarters in Soho Square, he took into partnership his brother-in-law William Warne, and subsequently — on making a fresh move to Farringdon Street — Frederick Warne, who, on the death of his brother and the dissolution of the partnership, established a new business.

The supremacy of the three-decker novel in the 1860s and 1870s was an artificial vogue largely created by the circulating libraries headed by Charles Edward Mudie. Mudie was a stationer-bookseller, with a modest little shop in Southampton Row, before he started to lend books in 1842. The library grew with sound business methods and a sure perception of what the reading public wanted. It was soon sufficiently established to publish Lowell's poems in England and move into its first vast storehouse in New Oxford Street. Mudie's guinea subscription for new books greatly increased the circulation of the three-volume novel. The short-lived but suicidal opposition of the Library Company, which endeavoured to undermine Mudie's with a half-guinea subscription, created a boom in fiction which, from the publishers' point of view, was too good to last.

In his *Random Recollections of an Old Publisher*, William Tinsley, of Tinsley Brothers, whose business was founded in 1854, bears witness to the phenomenal sales of those days. According to this authority W. H. Smith & Son, which started in 1792 at 4 Little Grosvenor Street, would not have ventured into the booklending business had Mudie come to terms with them when they secured their contracts for selling books and newspapers at most of the principal railway stations in England. In one of the contracts there was a special stipulation that books should be lent, as well as sold, from the different stalls on that line. Smith's, apparently, had no desire to add that branch to their business, and offered Mudie a very large subscription for the loan of a certain number of books in order that they might fulfil this contract. 'But Mr Mudie was then in the full tide of his popular guinea subscription, and he refused Smith & Son's offer', little dreaming that very soon afterwards they would not only be lending books on that particular line, but on almost all the important railways in the kingdom. Nevertheless, Mudie's library continued to grow by leaps and bounds until it migrated to New Oxford Street, where in remained in the stuccoed Regency building for some seventy or eighty years.

W. H. Smith's, it may be added, had inaugurated their railway bookstall station at Euston Station on November 1st, 1848. When the library department was born the firm endeavoured to meet the demand for light literature by themselves printing popular reprints of fiction in yellow covers — the originals of the 'yellow-backs'. Though these were very successful, the firm presently withdrew from a field which they did not feel they were entitled to exploit, and restricted their activities to the distributing side which was suffering severely as it had been for some decades, from the ever-increasing evils of underselling.

The rebellious booksellers had been the chief thorn in the sides of their more conservative brethren for generations. Some sixty years before, as already mentioned, they formed themselves into an independent body under the title of 'Associated Booksellers'—or 'Associated Busy Bees', as they came to be called from the device of the beehive which they used in their books. How long this society lasted we cannot say, but the first association of the protectionists appears to have been formed in 1812 and remodelled about 1828, when underselling, as ordinarily understood in the discount system of the nineteenth century—not the cheapening remainder trade as practised by Lackington—first seriously threatened the well-being of the trade. The 1828 association was not much more effective than the earlier organization.

It was not until another association of London booksellers was established twenty years later, and a new 'trade ticket' prepared in 1850, that war was formally declared against all booksellers who did not abide by its rules and regulations. Sampson Low, then editor of the *Publishers' Circular*, was the secretary of the committee elected to manage the business, and so thoroughly was the work done while it lasted that the undersellers, or Free Traders, had to call for assistance. Public feeling was largely on the side of Free Trade, and nearly all the leading authors of the day condemned the protectionists in what they considered their arbitrary practice of keeping up prices. 'My answer to this question, for my own interests, and for those of the world, so far as I can see them', wrote Carlyle, 'is decidedly "No" ... and, indeed, I can see no issue, of any permanency, to this controversy that has now arisen, but absolute "Free-trade" in all branches of Bookselling and Book-publishing.'

Dickens presided at a meeting of protest against restriction held in May 1852 at John Chapman's bookshop in the Strand, and declared himself, on principle, most strongly opposed to any system of exclusion holding that every man, whatever his calling, must be left to the fair and free exercise of his own honest thrift and enterprise. Gladstone, who declared that the state of the bookselling trade as then existing was a disgrace to civilization, felt so strongly in the matter that he personally supplied certain of the nonconforming booksellers with his pamphlets on Italy, which his publisher, being a member of the Booksellers' Association, could not sell to them. In the face of all this influential opposition the Booksellers' Association appealed for an opinion from a board composed of Lord Campbell—it was seven years before he became Lord Chancellor—and two distinguished historians, George Grote and Dean Milman. In the deputation from the booksellers the chief spokesman was William Longman, himself an author as well as a partner in the great publishing house, and his evidence went to prove that force, or coercion of some kind, would alone prevent one bookseller from underselling his neighbour.

The arbitrators, however, decided against coercion of any sort. 'Such regulations', said Lord Campbell, 'seem *prima facie* to be indefensible, and contrary to the freedom which ought to prevail in commercial transactions. Although the owner of property may put what price he pleases upon it when selling it, the condition that the purchaser, after the property has been transferred to him, and he has paid the purchase money, shall not resell it under a certain price, derogates from the rights of ownership which, as purchaser, he has acquired.' Thereupon this Booksellers' Association dissolved, and the effort made in 1859–60 to form a fresh society to safeguard the interests of the trade in the same matter—for underselling was now unrestricted and unashamed—collapsed for lack of unanimity. It was not, as we shall presently see, until the end of the nineteenth century that the different branches of the trade succeeded in binding themselves together in protection of their separate interests.

Part Two

1870–1970

Ian Norrie

Introduction

In 1870 there was no Net Book Agreement, and underselling was rife. Booksellers in London and Glasgow had, earlier in the century, three times formed trade associations, but doubts of their legality, inflamed in one instance by a threat of deportation, had led to their disbandment. Publishers had not yet found it necessary to organize an official body representing their interests; authors, although complaining, as always, about the rewards of writing and aware of the need for collective action, did not found their society until 1884. Literary agents scarcely existed, the royalty system was almost unknown and foreign authors had no copyright in the United States of America.

Few publishing houses had taken advantage of the Companies Act of 1862 which allowed limited liability. Most were still partnerships, and the separation of bookselling from publishing was as nearly complete as it was to be at any time in the next hundred years. Direct links between the two remained — Blackwell, Heffer and Zwemmer, for instance, were in 1970 members of both trade associations — but some, like Batsford, underwent complete metamorphosis. In 1970 Batsford were solely publishers; in 1870, they had been booksellers who had occasionally also published. At that date the formation and dissolution of partnerships made regular news but there were few mergers or takeovers involving firms of long standing. Publishing was still a business in which individuals had financial, as well as editorial, control of their own destinies. American influence was negligible, although it was well understood on both sides of the Atlantic that there was a ready-made market across the water. George Haven Putnam had had a London office since 1841 and Macmillan had opened in New York in 1869. Neither of the great university presses, nor Longmans, nor Macmillan had as yet set up branches in India or what were then the colonies, but the S.P.C.K. (short for the Society for Promoting Christian Knowledge), the third oldest publisher in the country, had long been distributing its publications to agencies in most parts of the world, by no means confining themselves to those foreign parts where English was spoken.

Names familiar in publishing today already flourished: John Murray, of course; Adam & Charles Black; Hodder & Stoughton; George Routledge, and his brother-in-law Frederick Warne — once in partnership but now each with his own imprint; William Collins; Chapman & Hall; Thomas Nelson; Blackie & Son. The medical houses of Baillière & Tindall (with Cox about to join them) and Churchill in London, and Livingstone in Edinburgh, were well established. Crosby Lockwood and Spon were active in the technical field, and Sweet & Maxwell and Butterworth in the legal. Bacon, Bartholomew and Johnstone were all established map publishers. Allman, Nisbet, George Bell, Rivington and others were issuing school books, and E. J. Arnold, a printer in Barnstaple, moved in that year to Leeds to found his educational supply business. Forster's Education Act in 1870 gave all these firms hope for new business, and Cassell's, then trading as Cassell, Petter & Galpin, had more than one eye open for the new literacy. J. M. Dent was already in London as printer and binder, but was not yet a publisher. Chatto & Windus still issued books under the name of its founder, John Camden Hotten. Hurst & Blackett and Jarrold's had advertised in the first *Bookseller*, in 1858, but George Hutchinson (first an apprentice to Alexander Strachan, afterwards a traveller for Hodder) was not to take them over for several decades, and had not yet established his own imprint.

In the columns of the twelve-year-old *Bookseller* (the other trade paper, *The Publishers' Circular*, had been founded in 1837) the debate about underselling and how to prevent it continued monthly. There were also demands, repeated ever since, that booksellers' assistants should receive better training. Although many booksellers apparently relied increasingly on the sale of stationery, and even sewing-machines, to keep their businesses going, new shops were opened, some surviving today. Some shops had already existed for upwards of seventy years. John Smith of Glasgow—still trading under the same name today— was founded in 1751. Hatchard's of Piccadilly, Ruddock's of Lincoln and the A.P.C.K. in Dublin all dated back to the eighteenth century, as did the fast-growing organization of W. H. Smith & Son. And Macmillan & Bowes (which now claims to be the oldest bookselling business in Britain) could trace its existence as a bookshop in Trinity Street, Cambridge, back to 1581, through many changes of name and ownership.

King's of Lymington, and the House of Andrews in Durham, had begun in the first decade of the century; Duffy of Dublin, and Menzies of Edinburgh, had started in the 1830s; so had George Philip (Son and Nephew to follow) in Liverpool, and Henry Walker in Leeds. In 1840 John Colbran had started what was to become Goulden & Curry of Tunbridge Wells, and six years later Benjamin Harris Blackwell opened in Oxford, though the now-famous booksellers of Broad Street were not there in 1870, when the first B.H. had been dead for fifteen years and his son was apprenticed to another Oxford shop. William George had started in Bristol, and his successors were to be saved by a third generation of Blackwell some sixty years later.

James Thin had passed more than two decades in Edinburgh; Henry Young was well established in Liverpool, Mowbray in Oxford,

H. M. Gilbert in Southampton. Anthony Brown had started in Hull in 1860, the same year as Ernest Gait founded his family business across the Humber in Grimsby. Hill's doors were open in Sunderland; Wells's in Winchester; Wyllie's in Aberdeen; the McDougall Brothers in Paisley, and Filleul's in St Helier, on Jersey. These firms are, happily, still trading today despite—perhaps because of—the profound changes which have affected society and despite the cries of doom which have been uttered by each new generation of booksellers. Sometimes, in the hundred years under review, desperate measures appeared necessary for survival; when they were taken at all they were often taken too late, but there are half-a-dozen major instances of the trade saving itself by the skin of its teeth and, by 1970, bookselling, at least, was certainly in a healthier state than it had been a century earlier, and all the riper for takeover as a consequence.

Publishing in 1970 was also healthy, in as much as many more books were sold than ever before, and a cottage industry had become an important part of the nation's export trade. Books were selling in quantities undreamed of in 1870; traditional export markets, developed throughout our period, were still absorbing an increasing annual number of British books despite the growth of indigenous publishing and American competition. But the number of individually owned houses was on the wane. Some, like Collins and Black, had become public companies but remained under family direction; others, like Longmans, Cassell's and Sweet & Maxwell were now units in huge organizations financed by British or American capital. Names unknown in 1870—Heinemann, Methuen, The Bodley Head, Hutchinson, Hamlyn, etc.—were integral parts of large groups. Publishing had become big business and most issues of the now-weekly *Bookseller* carried news of American money being poured into the British market.

The paperback revolution had occurred, bringing a new public to the bookshops and bookstalls; international publishing, successfully tried by William Heinemann before the First World War, had caused the rapid growth of, in particular, Thames & Hudson and Paul Hamlyn. The pioneer work done in the 'twenties and 'thirties by Stanley Morison, Wren Howard, Ian Parsons, Charles Prentice, Richard de la Mare and others had taken the design of books away from the printers' factories and into the publishers' offices. Production departments, advertising and publicity sections and sales hierarchies proliferated, creating a need for larger offices. But two world wars had inflated the cost of accommodation in central London, and many publishers had moved their warehouses and even, in some instances, their editorial departments, to new towns in Essex, Hampshire and Hertfordshire. Problems of distribution exercised the trade as obsessively as underselling had in the nineteenth century. The Net Book Agreement had been twice upheld. The Publishers' Association, now a strong unifying force even in a trade of rampant individualists, provided its members with services such as none but the smallest of publishers could do without. The Booksellers' Association, membership of which was essential for any bookseller who wished to sell and exchange book tokens, levied an increasing amount in return for services about which some of its members were still in doubt. The Society of Authors, with the backing of the P.A., continued to fight for a public lending right which would give authors a royalty on public library issues of their books, while the Library Association continued to resist the idea and to raise periodically the bogey of higher discounts from booksellers. Some local education authorities demanded the right to buy direct from publishers at trade price, and there were unfortunate precedents which gave them a case. Numerous other organizations had come into being, either to promote the distribution of books (the Society of Bookmen, the National Book League, the Book Development Council, the Charter Booksellers Group of the B.A., the Educational Publishers' Council) or to encourage social and intellectual exchange between individuals engaged in the trade (the Whitefriars', the Galley Club, the Paternoster's, the Society of Young Publishers, the Book Publishers' Representatives' Association, the Publishers' Publicity Circle, The Publishers' Circle). The trade reflected mid-twentieth-century life in becoming highly organized and intensely committee-conscious, and, in addition to its own clubs and associations, it was represented on the Arts Council of Great Britain and much involved in the work of the British Council. It had learned something of cooperation. The Book Centre undertook warehousing, accounting and distribution for 120 publishers, and statistical services and parcels-delivery through a clearing-house for many more. For booksellers it operated an orders clearing-house, saving them time and money in addressing and stamping hundreds of envelopes each week. But none of these services, valuable as they were, filled the gap left by the collapse of the great wholesale house of Simpkin Marshall in 1955.

The trade mirrored the ethos of the time also in attempting to practise new sales and advertising techniques with armies of business consultants, public relations officers, marketing managers and field sales managers joining in the act. And their salaries had, finally, to be met by the persons and institutions purchasing the books they promoted.

Public libraries had grown to become, with the various educational authorities, very large customers on the home market, thus creating a new type of middleman in the library supplier, who was not concerned with the retailing of books and, therefore, did not have a shop — or sometimes, even a showroom. In the educational contract business, booksellers learned to supplement books with furniture, stationery and other schools' equipment.

During the hundred years I am concerned with, the commercial libraries were extended to every town, including the smallest, in the country and reached a peak of prosperity between the wars; but after 1945 their decline was rapid, and by 1970 they were all but extinct. The market in modern first editions had enjoyed a brief boom during the 'twenties until the American slump killed it. Private presses, sometimes concerned with this trade, sprang up at the same time, and a few remained at the end of our period. Reprint book clubs, which had come in in the 'thirties, did not suffer the same fate as the commercial libraries but their heyday was long past by 1970, although simultaneous book club publication of new potential bestsellers had been introduced from America two years earlier.

Booksellers, despite the protection of the Net Book Agreement, had passed through various doldrums. Hit by the depression of the 'thirties and by the soaring property values of the late 'forties and 'fifties, many firms went under, often because they refused to modernize their premises and accept new techniques of display; sometimes, perhaps, eased into bankruptcy because publishers kept down prices for too long. But by the mid-1960s, there was increasing acceptance of the sale-or-return, or see-safe, system of holding stock, more and more booksellers practised stock control, and there was a boom on the home market which was helped, rather than hindered, to everyone's surprise, by the spread of television. There were those who regarded the retail side of the trade as an occupation from which they might expect 'to retire from on a competency', as Mr Newton of Liverpool was quoted as saying in *The Bookseller* of 1861. Booksellers concentrated increasingly on selling books, having for long carried other lines such as greetings cards and stationery, and, latterly, gramophone records. They were helped by the growing demands of students of all ages, whose requirements led to the establishment of separate university bookshops in towns and on campuses. This brought about new groupings, and some booksellers voluntarily joined U.B.O. (University Bookshops Oxford, financed by Blackwells and O.U.P.) or Bowes & Bowes (owned by W. H. Smith) to reach this market with adequate resources.

By 1970 British authors were protected by the Universal Copyright Convention (although our government had dragged its feet before signing it), and had won tax concessions from a chancellor of the exchequer who allowed writers to spread their taxable income over a perod of three years. Yet far too many authors continued to write too many books, and these were published by far too many publishers. Booksellers complained when they surveyed their already bulging shelves; reviewers grew distraught (but were mollified when they thought of the amount to be earned from the sale of their free copies); public librarians indented for larger book funds, and, when they didn't receive them, bought review copies on the cheap. Most publishers defended their rising output by citing the turnover theory (overheads are X, therefore turnover has to be Y, therefore Z titles must be published); some wiser and smaller publishers deliberately restricted their output and remained prosperous and independent.

Small or large, however, they met and mingled with booksellers, authors, literary agents and journalists at parties, at conferences and at the Frankfurt Book Fair, an annual junket which gained momentum from the 'fifties onwards. As it produced more, the book trade became ever more sociable, the love-hate relationship between printer, publisher, bookseller, literary agent, reviewer, author, growing blurred if only because so many involved wore more than one hat.

How and why these changes took place is the subject of this second section. It brings in famous names in publishing and bookselling which have not featured so far in these pages—Swan Sonnenschein, Grant Richards, the Foyle Brothers, Stanley Unwin, E. F. Hudson, H. W. Keay, J. G. Wilson, Basil Blackwell, Jonathan Cape, Harold Raymond, Victor Gollancz, Geoffrey Faber, John Baker, Allen Lane, Frank Denny, Henry Schollick, Una Dillon and so on. It is a history concerned with the details of the trade, but anyone who studies it should remember that books, even in 1970, still began with authors. Publishers and literary agents often put up the idea for a book but a computer still had not actually written one by itself—though, no doubt, that will come.

The student of book trade history should also remember that in this particular hundred years, advances in science and technology brought about fundamental changes in society altering the whole process of communication. Far-sighted publishers had anticipated the advantages of film and tape and taken steps to exploit the market. In 1480, in 1870 and even in 1960 printers employed the same basic foundation of manufacture, (as J. A. Cochrane observed in his address to the Manchester Bibliographical Society in 1967), but by 1970 they were adopting processes of computer-setting which seemed as dangerous to some as the introduction of the motor-car had to late-Victorians. At the risk of triteness, it has to be emphasized, that between the years 1870 and 1970 the telephone, radio, television, the motor-car, the aeroplane and the computer all came into general use. The book trade may sometimes have taken a more Luddite attitude to such inventions than did other industries, but alongside them came social changes which could not be resisted. Education became a right not a privilege. Trade unions became strong, and although they did little for those directly concerned with books (apart from printers) the side effects were telling. The standard of living rose and the population increased, which meant not only that the home market for books multiplied but also that those supplying it rightly expected a proportionately higher reward for their labours.

And there was a revolution in public taste. The most advanced reader of 1870 would have been astonished, even shocked, by some of the volumes published in 1970 without printer, author, publisher or bookseller being prosecuted. In the nineteenth century no publisher issued a book dealing freely with sexual matters without risking court proceedings; a hundred years later, homosexuality, masturbation, abortion and drug addiction were everyday subjects for novels and non-fiction, and bookshop buyers had long been accustomed to judge the sales potential of a new novel on whether or not it was what was popularly called 'dirty'.

The booksellers' buyer, by 1970, might be a man or a woman. At the start of our period women played little part in the book world, except as authors. In that role they excelled, especially as novelists and poets, and still do, although their achievements in music and the plastic arts have never equalled men's. Similarly, women have been amongst the most gifted of booksellers in the twentieth century but have seldom, as yet, been permitted the same opportunities to rise to the top on the other side of the trade, except as editors of children's books.

In 1870 the book trade was organized individually and, according to the standards of the time, individual enterprise rewarded the few rather than the many. The printing and distribution of books was quick and efficient. By 1970 individual enterprise was often confined by the dictates of the organization's accountants, and efficient distribution was certainly affected by the claims for a living wage of the less gifted and less enterprising. This reflected the evolution of society in Western democracy. But even in 1970, some publishing houses and some booksellers contrived to equate acceptable standards of employment with effective service to customers. Not many, but some: hopeful words with which to embark on this part of the history.

I

Trade Affairs

The trade starts to organize itself—Frederick Orridge Macmillan; the fight against underselling—formation of the Associated Booksellers and the Publishers' Association—Net Book Agreement; literary agents—A. P. Watt; international copyright; International Congress of Publishers; decline of three-decker novel; censorship.

The three-decker novel was on the way out, and perhaps no one foresaw that a hundred years later the three and even five-volume autobiography would have come in. In 1870, Charles Dickens died, Henry James was twenty-seven, Bernard Shaw, fourteen, and John Galsworthy, three. The works of Marx and Freud were unknown; Joyce, Proust and T. S. Eliot were unborn. Leonard Woolf (1880–1969) and E. M. Forster (1879–1970) span most of my period; Bertrand Russell (1872–1970) even more of it. These gifted men contributed much to the history of their time and there could be no worthier examples, from publishing and writing, of the civilizing force in *Homo sapiens*, the encouragement of which is the basic business of the British and every other book trade. But the British book trade had other business, almost as basic, in the second half of Victoria's reign: namely to commence the vast task of organizing itself.

Of those who were centrally involved in this process, Frederick Orridge Macmillan stands out. He was the son of Daniel, one of the founders of the House of Macmillan, who died at the age of forty-four in the room in Trinity Street, Cambridge, which, in 1970, was the office of Esmond Warner, then chairman of Bowes & Bowes. Frederick was six at the time and, with his mother, two brothers and a sister, he went to live with his uncle Alexander, the other founder of the dynasty. He received early training as a bookseller in the family shop in Cambridge and, as a publisher, in Henrietta Street, Covent Garden. There followed five years in the New York office, opened in 1869, and when he returned to England he travelled the Macmillan list, thus embarking on his career with a thorough knowledge of publishing and some, at least, of bookselling. His experiences alerted him to the demands of both *The Bookseller*, and booksellers, to put a stop to the practice of underselling which had plagued the trade for many decades. His uncle, Alexander, had tried to net the Macmillan Shakespeare as early as 1864, and four years later had written to William Ewart Gladstone that whereas booksellers had once made a living by keeping good stocks of solid, standard works, these were now, through underselling, so profitless that books were nothing but appendages to toyshops and Berlin-wool warehouses. 'Intelligence and sympathy with literature has gone out of the trade almost wholly,' he wrote, and went on to emphasize his view that an intelligent bookseller in every town in the kingdom was almost as valuable as an intelligent schoolmaster or parson. We do not know how Gladstone, who in 1860 had described English books as abominably dear, reacted to this; we do know that Alexander's nephew continued the fight against underselling, often finding himself in opposition to booksellers themselves.

It must be stressed that price-cutting, the practice of selling books at less than their advertised price, was not a wicked invention of the reading public. It was introduced by individual booksellers with an eye to capturing more of the market for themselves. The public merely shopped around to buy at the most advantageous price, as it does today in supermarkets, stores and off-licences. Far-sighted booksellers and publishers saw a danger in this which led them to work for the Net Book Agreement. Before they could achieve this, however, it was necessary for them to sink some, though not very much, of their individuality into collective action.

Bookseller-publishers had been organized as early as the fifteenth century, when the Stationers' Company was formed (see p. 39) but it was not until 1812, when publishing was already becoming a separate trade, that London booksellers attempted to found an association of their own in order to prevent underselling. This failed, as did another attempt in 1828. Six years later the Glasgow Booksellers' Protection Association was more effective, but also short-lived, thanks to the publication of a pamphlet suggesting that membership of the association was a conspiracy rendering members liable to transportation for seven years. London booksellers made another bid in 1848, but 'Free Trade' was the cry of the time, and in 1852 a weighty legal opinion — employing, as so often with English law, an argument that had nothing to do with justice — persuaded the booksellers to disband voluntarily.

More unsuccessful efforts were made, in London in 1859, and in Bradford in 1867. Meanwhile in most issues of *The Bookseller*, the self-styled 'Organ of the Book Trade' (Whitaker had taken over from *Bent's Literary Advertiser* in 1858), there were calls for corporate action. One correspondent complained of sales to public libraries at up to 50 per cent discount in 1862; a year later booksellers were exhorted to form an association to prevent similar recurrences; in 1865 at the London Coffee House, in Ludgate Hill, another meeting was held at which a Mr E. Blackwell of Reading called for associations to be formed in London and in the country 'to devise an efficient remedy for the evils of underselling'. During the 1870s the pleas were renewed and Eyre and Spottiswoode announced that for some years they had been closing accounts with booksellers who refused to sell at recommended prices. But booksellers still undersold, and the public could not be blamed for taking advantage of bargain offers. Lewis Carroll attempted his own remedy in the 'eighties by insisting that his books be supplied at not more than twopence in the shilling discount to the trade, thus leaving no margin for underselling. Ruskin, who became his own publisher, adopted similar tactics a few years later. *The Bookseller* continued to campaign for a union, and in 1889 no less than 136 booksellers signed a 'memorial' to publishers calling upon them to discontinue supplying anyone who sold books at a greater discount than threepence in the shilling.

In 1890 Frederick Macmillan wrote a momentous letter to *The Bookseller*. In his twenty-three years in the trade, he said, underselling had been a burning question, but it had recently assumed such proportions that a bookseller dealing in current literature could not make a living. It was up to publishers who wanted to see well-stocked bookshops to take the initiative. He echoed his author Lewis Carroll in advocating twopence in the shilling discount to booksellers and no discount whatever to the public. 'I have no doubt', he wrote, 'that with the hearty cooperation of the retail trade the *net* system could be introduced.' The cooperation was not there. *The Bookseller* sent out thousands of forms to assess opinion and, receiving only 450 replies, assumed that Macmillan's suggestion did not meet with approval enough to justify its adoption.

In the same year, the London Booksellers' Society was formed, but it was soon sadly recording that although the system of net books adopted by one or two publishers was well meant (Macmillan's had 16 net books in 1890, including significantly Alfred Marshall's *Principles of Economics*, and 136 in 1897), it was making life difficult for those booksellers whose businesses were based on giving discounts. They therefore recommended that only high-class publications of limited circulation should be netted.

The path of the reformer is difficult indeed, but Frederick Macmillan persevered, and closed the account of one large City chain (Stoneham's probably, but the official history does not say) which refused to conform. Meanwhile the views of the London Booksellers' Society had widened, and by 1894 they were inviting their colleagues in the country to join them, with the result that the Associated Booksellers of Great Britain and Ireland was formed on January 23rd, 1895, and was dedicated to the introduction of the net book system. Publishers were invited to meet them, but this time the fencing came from the other side. William Heinemann, who had won cheers when he told the booksellers that he had closed more than one account with persistent undersellers, wanted a meeting to take place but C. J. Longman opted for caution, citing the legal opinion of 1852, and suggested at an informal gathering at John Murray's house that publishers should fix a wholesale price and then leave it to the retailer to come to terms with his customers. Back to square one, except that this meeting had the curious result of organizing the publishers. John Murray proposed the formation of an association, and a committee of nine were elected to draw up rules. They represented Messrs Longmans; Macmillan; Murray; Routledge; Heinemann; Sampson Low; Bentley; Blackwood and Smith, Elder. In the same year the Association of Foreign Booksellers in London was formed. (For the record it should be noted that the Publishers' Association did not officially exist until January 23rd, 1896, when the Associated Booksellers was a sturdy one-year-old.)

Macmillan hoped that the formation of the P.A. would lead to the general introduction of the net system, but the request of the booksellers for a joint conference was repulsed by the first secretary of the P.A., William Poulten, who said that the subject of discounts was a matter for arrangement by individual publishers. In 1897, however, the associations did officially confer, and they agreed that net books should not be sold at less than published price and that non-net books should be subject to not more than twopence in the shilling discount, provided that the Society of Authors, formed in 1884, agreed. However, the Society of Authors refused to ratify the P.A.'s proposals, and it was not until 1899 that the three organizations agreed the terms and conditions of the supply of net books to retail booksellers. John Murray remarked austerely that it was not the publishers who wanted the agreement but the booksellers; he hoped, however, that publishers would honour it, despite pressures from the lending libraries, and that booksellers would recognize the endeavours that had been made to help them. It is dangerous nowadays to invite gratitude from the patronized, but he was on firm ground in 1899, both economically and socially. On January 1st, 1900, the Net Book Agreement came into being. Serious underselling was to have only one more significant challenge in the decade ahead, and to many the prosperity of bookselling seemed assured in the foreseeable future.

In the late-Victorian era the first literary agents began to establish themselves. The London Literary Agency had advertised from 23 Tavistock Street, Covent Garden, in 1870, but seems not to have lasted long. 'Agents, Literary', were listed in the post office directory for the first time in 1874, but for the next twenty years there are never more than six at any one time, and none at all appears in two London telephone directories for 1884 and 1885. Given the increasing complexity of trade organization it was inevitable that literary agents should start to appear on the scene. The growing division between publishing and bookselling earlier in the century had made it increasingly difficult for publishers to remain their own middlemen between author and public. John Forster had acted as unofficial agent between Dickens, Thackeray and other writers and their publishers, as had G. H. Lewes for George Eliot, and Watts-Dunton for Swinburne. None of these gentlemen accepted payment for their efforts, and Arthur Waugh, later head of Chapman & Hall, described Forster as having bridged the gulf between the patron of the eighteenth century and the literary agent of the nineteenth.

The introduction of international copyright, with its often incomprehensible ramifications, made an agent all the more necessary. Besides, authors had long needed the services of agents because although publishers sometimes acted generously towards them, at least as often they were miserly. Books were published for outright payment, or leased from authors for agreed periods, or brought out on a part- or half-profits basis or on commission, the latter meaning that the author kept his copyright but paid for all the production and promotion, the publisher being merely the salesman and distributor. The royalty system was almost unknown; so, usually, were advances.

The outright payment (like the commission system not entirely dead today) benefited the author of a work which failed to sell and the publisher of one which was popular, although when a work was reprinted the publisher sometimes paid the author an additional sum. The half- or shared-profits scheme should have worked but didn't, because it was too easy for publishers to cheat. Profits did not accrue until overheads had been covered, and it was for the publisher to assess these, so an unscrupulous publisher could extend his costs over an entire edition until there was no profit to share. Sometimes, of course, such costs might extend themselves without help. Trollope made nothing from his first two books and only £20 from his third; thereafter he sometimes sold outright, sometimes agreed to share. *Three Clerks* went to Bentley for £250 and *Dr Thorne* to Chapman & Hall for £400, yet by 1876 he had earned on half profits over £700 from *The Warden* and *Barchester Towers*. Trollope insisted that *Dr Thorne*, however, was his bestselling novel so, as James Hepburn pointed out in *The Author's Empty Purse**, he would presumably have done better with it if he had not sold it outright.

* Where details of publication are not provided, they may be found in the Bibliography.

In considering Trollope we are dealing with success, and in seeking more favourable terms authors tended to look at the rewards gained by writers in popular favour rather than the pittances earned by those whose public was small. This is understandable if one realizes that most authors in any age have a spark of vanity in them without which they would probably never set pen to paper: There goes Trollope; there, *with* the grace of God, go I! It is little wonder that the demand for a royalty system grew. (Although, curiously, as late as 1890 the Society of Authors was still recommending its members to publish on commission if they could afford it.)

The key figure here is undoubtedly Alexander Pollock Watt, whom modern literary agents think of as the father of their profession. Watt was born in Glasgow, was self-educated and became a bookseller in Edinburgh. Later he partnered the publisher Alexander Strahan, but when the latter got into difficulties Watt became first an advertising, then a literary, agent. He represented Wilkie Collins, Rudyard Kipling, Bret Harte, Conan Doyle and Walter Besant, amongst others. In 1883 he had solicited testimonials from his best-known authors, but by 1892 he was loftily claiming that he had never advertised his services. This was soon after William Heinemann's outburst in *The Athenaeum* castigating the literary agent as a parasitic middleman who flourished on the publisher's efforts to bring unknown authors to fame. For such a job one needed neither capital nor special qualifications, according to Heinemann, who kept up his vendetta against agents till the end of his life despite the fact that he, in common with Cassell and Sampson Low, employed Paul Revere Reynolds to act for him in New York. Perhaps he did not appreciate that Reynolds was also an agent for American authors — a double agent, in modern terms.

Watt survived Heinemann's attack. Andrew Chatto, Senior, was on his side, and the agent also had testimonials from Bentley and Longmans. The literary agent had obviously come to stay; he established himself as, at worst, a necessary evil, at best, as a friend of author and publisher, and his power grew with each decade. A. P. Watt's firm prospers to this day, as does that started by Curtis Brown, who came to London in 1898 as a freelance journalist and within a year had been appointed head of the International Publishing Bureau in Henrietta Street. Pinker, the third of the great trio at the turn of the century, has not lasted, but the first Pinker left £40,000, while his client, Arnold Bennett, left £36,000.

Nevertheless, individual authors still had to come to terms with individual publishers, with or without an agent as intermediary; even Sir Walter Besant, founder of the Society of Authors, which advised authors against signing contracts that ignored sources of future profit, continued to sell his books, with one exception, outright to Chatto &

Windus.* Despite his excellent relationship with Chatto, Besant was still complaining in 1892 that no worker in the world was more help-less, ignorant or cruelly sweated than an author—a claim difficult to uphold, one would have thought, in view of the living conditions of manual workers at that time. The Society of Authors never became effective as an agency or a publishing imprint, but its membership increased rapidly from its original sixty-eight, so that its weight was sufficient, by the late 'nineties, to make the Publishers' Association consider its views before inviting booksellers to ratify the Net Book Agreement.

Before the days of international copyright agreements there were no foreign rights to be sold. And prior to the popularization of Colonial editions authors did not need the protection that an agent could offer them in what is now the Commonwealth; their books were pirated freely, and their only hope of redress lay in costly litigation which might, anyhow, go against them.

I do not propose to examine in any detail the intricacies of the law relating to copyright because, like so much of law, it is almost meaning-less to laymen. Simon Nowell-Smith's *International Copyright Law and the Publisher in the Reign of Queen Victoria* is an admirable and easily readable analysis of its subject. For the purposes of this book, it is sufficient to comment on the main innovations of international copyright as they affected British publishers.

In 1838 foreign authors were given the same copyright in Britain as they would have enjoyed as natives, provided the arrangement was reciprocal. Thus the first agreements came about between Britain, Prussia and France, heralding the International Copyright Act of 1844. Two years earlier, in 1842, a new Copyright Act, repealing all previous ones from the 1709 Statute of Anne onwards, prolonged the period of copyright to forty-two years from first publication or until seven years after the author's death, whichever was the longer. This was the first time that the duration of copyright was related to the lifespan of the author. (It was also a condition that a copy of every new book seeking protection must be delivered free to the British Museum. Only, let it be noted, if the publisher and author *sought* protection; they were not to be protected against their will. Compulsion had preceded this act, when each and every new book had to be submitted to the Stationers' Company for registration; compulsion was to follow, when not only the British Museum but other deposit libraries were to receive free copies of all new books, whether or not the donor wished to make the gift,

* The exception was the *Eulogy to Richard Jefferies*; Besant arranged for two-thirds of the profits on this to be paid to Jefferies's relatives.

and without these gifts conferring copyright protection in the U.S.A.)
The United States and Russia were not involved in these agreements—
probably because Great Britain was much less of a market for their
authors than vice versa—much to the bitterness of British authors.
Charles Dickens, not surprisingly, led for the authors, and during his
visits to the States spent much time campaigning for a just deal, which
his fellow writers did not begin to enjoy until twenty years after his
death. What is known as the Chace Act (from the Senator who introduced it) at last gave protection to foreign authors, provided their
work was printed in the United States, a condition which did not
please British printers or publishers. There were, in due course, modifi-
cations of this.

During this period the market for British books boomed in the newly
colonized territories of Australia and New Zealand, and in Canada
outstripped trade with the United States. Figures quoted by Mr
Nowell-Smith show an increase between 1870 and 1876 of £200,000 in
books exported to Australia from this country (over 150 per cent), and
to Canada of £17,000 (33 per cent). But in these 'colonies' British
authors had no copyright protection until further legislation was introduced, and even then legal decisions contradicted each other, and the
Australasian and Canadian markets were flooded with pirated editions
printed in America or home grown. To counteract this, British publishers invented the Colonial cheap edition, on which authors usually
received a standard royalty of 3d. The Colonial edition led to further
complexities of copyright, Gilbertian in their absurdity, but on the
whole it worked, and one Edward Augustus Petherick who ran the
Colonial Booksellers Agency in Paternoster Row, claimed to have
spent £180,000 with British publishers in his seven years there. (In
1894 he unfortunately went bankrupt for £50,000 of this, and George
Bell [one of his creditors] took over the Petherick Collection of Favourite
and Approved Authors and began a rapid expansion of his own colonial
business.) Petherick, an Australian, had previously worked for George
Robertson of Melbourne who had opened a London office in 1870.
This Robertson also employed two young Scots, another George
Robertson, who was not a relative, and David Mackenzie Angus.
Angus opened his own shop in Sydney in 1884 and was joined by the
younger Robertson two years later. In 1888 they started their own
publishing house, which meant more work for Alexander Pollock
Watt and his fellow agents.

Amid all the piracy and acrimony of these times the Leipzig publisher
Christian Bernhard Tauchnitz stood out, saint-like. When he made his
rather pompous approach to British authors inviting them to appear
in his cheap English language editions for sale on the Continent, he
made it clear that he was not required to ask their permission; he did

so only because he believed in furthering the advancement of a reciprocal copyright agreement between Britain and Prussia. He asked
for the right to publish on the Continent, promised not to send his
edition to Britain or to her colonies and accepted the fact that the
ordinary English edition would still be allowed into Europe. Tauchnitz
and his son published most British authors of standing, and dealt
honestly with them, but there is no way of knowing now what their
files would have revealed in the way of publisher-author relationships
because they were destroyed, along with their stock and printing plant,
when the R.A.F. bombed Leipzig in 1943—one of the many ironies of
war. But we do know that Dickens sent a son to Christian Bernhard to
learn German, and that Harrison Ainsworth dedicated a novel to him.
There was less need for an agent in dealing with so straightforward a
man than there was in coping with some of those on the international
scene. A. & C. Black were to suffer from loopholes in the law over the
Encyclopaedia Britannica; their adventures in the courtrooms of the
U.S.A. will be dealt with later.

What other subjects were exercising the book trade during these years,
when Gladstone and Disraeli alternated as prime minister for so long,
when the empire expanded apace, when farmers faced ruin, and everyone had the right to receive some schooling?

   There was a further instance of the desire for international cooperation with the inaugural session of the International Congress of Publishers in Paris in 1896. This was held in various capitals until 1914.
British publishers opened offices in India, Australia, Canada, South
Africa, etc. (some details of these operations will be found in the next
chapter). The three-volume or 'three-decker' novel was in decline
throughout the period, and by 1894 the circulating libraries were
refusing to take any more. Free public libraries, cheap reprints and an
ever-increasing demand for the latest novel made the three-deckers
uneconomic for them, and they plumped instead for the one-volume
6s. novel which remained at the same price, with some exceptions,
until 1918.

   Censorship, of course, exercised the book trade; censorship has never
been less than an irritant at any time. Today it does not cause as much
nuisance as it did, but even now obscenity has not been satisfactorily
defined so that the trade is still not free from prosecution. In the late-
Victorian period, and for long after, publishers, printers, authors and
booksellers lived in the shadow of Chief Justice Cockburn's finding
that the test of obscenity was 'whether the tendency of the matter
charged as obscene is to deprave and corrupt those whose minds are
open to such immoral influences, and into whose hands a publication

of this sort may fall'. Were they to publish only such literature as would not shock an innocent child? (The unblemished schoolgirl of fourteen was the usual image evoked when this vexed subject was debated.) A lot of worthwhile books were published in spite of the risk—which is not to sanction for one moment the essential absurdity of censorship, but to applaud the ingenuity and courage of authors and publishers.

Other trade matters will be dealt with as they fall naturally into place with the activities of the particular publishers and booksellers who are the subjects of the next chapters.

2

Oxford University Press; Cambridge University Press; S.P.C.K.

In recording the history of the two great university presses which existed in 1870 it is necessary, for the reason given in the Preface, to go back a further four centuries.

It was in 1478 (the year after Caxton printed his first book at Westminster) that Theodoric Rood travelled to Oxford from Cologne and printed there a *Commentary on the Apostles' Creed*. Controversy raged for long in scholarly circles about the date of this work, which bore, in Roman numerals, the year 1468, but it is now thought that an X was omitted in error and that Caxton, therefore, does not lose his place of honour as the first to print in England.

Rood continued to print in Oxford for about seven years, after which there is a gap until 1519, when for a brief period printers were again at work. Then there was a long interval, lasting for most of the century. The Convocation set up a committee in 1585 and the Earl of Leicester, chancellor of the university, was asked to intercede with the Queen. He appears to have been successful because the imprint of Joseph Barnes at Oxford, as Printer to the University, was in use from 1585 until 1617. Barnes was a local bookseller and it was he who first printed entire books in Greek and Hebrew (although Thomas Thomas, at Cambridge, used Greek characters before he did.) The Star Chamber restricted the number of presses and apprentices at each university to 'one at one tyme at the most', and it was not easy to oppose the Star Chamber, which was to remain a force until far into the following century, when one tyranny gave way to another during Cromwell's Protectorship. The London trade undersold university publications by printing their own unauthorized editions. The universities retaliated by forbidding retailers in Oxford and Cambridge to sell books printed in London, or anywhere else in England, if either of the presses had produced an edition of the same work, or had announced its intention of doing so. Students were ordered not to buy such books, and both shopkeepers and undergraduates were threatened with perpetual banishment if they transgressed.

Joseph Barnes's successors, following his retirement in 1617, were small-time traders who were not much approved of by William Laud, who became chancellor in 1629. Laud, later Archbishop of Canterbury, and later still beheaded by Cromwell, spent his few years in Oxford raising the status of the Press by securing royal charters entitling the university to exercise direct control over printing, and to print the Bible. This latter privilege was delegated from 1637 until 1672 to the Stationers' Company for £200 a year.

The university first appointed Delegates of the Press in 1633, but soon after that Charles I moved his court to Oxford, the Civil War raged, Cromwell ruled, and there were other things than literature to occupy men's minds (although the press was busy running off pamphlets). The modern history of O.U.P. really begins in 1671, by which time Charles II was firmly on the throne. In that year Dr John Fell ('I do not love thee, Dr Fell'—that one) took a lease, with three friends, of the university's right of printing. Six years earlier he had presented the Press with sets of types bearing his name which are still cast from the punches and matrixes he collected. Fell, who was a bishop and vice-chancellor of the university, and his associates worked as a private company printing in the Sheldonian Theatre. They issued the first Oxford Bible in 1675 which, as we have seen (p. 120), led to prolonged and bitter quarrels with the Stationers' Company about whose prerogative it was to print the holy book. Fell died in 1686 and four years later his executors made over the printing and type-founding plant to the university, whose delegates thereafter managed the business, although until 1780 the Bible press continued to be sublet.

The next important figure in Oxford publishing was the second Earl of Clarendon, who presented the press with the copyright of his father's *History of the Rebellion*, a gift seconded by an Act of Parliament which made the copyright perpetual. From the proceeds the Clarendon building, designed jointly by Hawksmoor and Vanbrugh, was erected and there the Press remained until 1829 when it moved to Walton Street where it still is.

Learned publishing fell into decline in the eighteenth century until 1755 when Sir William Blackstone, later the first professor of English law, was appointed a delegate. The Bible press, however, constantly expanded its activities and opened a London warehouse in Paternoster Row. In the following century the activity in both departments was intense, the philologist W. W. Skeat and the Cambridge librarian and scholar William Aldis Wright, particularly, editing with great accuracy numerous volumes of classics and several important works of reference. And for the Bible press there were two outstanding events.

The romantic story surrounding the introduction of India Paper is mainly legend according to Harry Carter, the Oxford archivist. A graduate of the university is supposed to have brought home from the Far East in 1841 some extremely thin but tough paper which was used to print twenty-four copies of the Bible, one of which was presented

to Queen Victoria. No one could trace the origins of this paper. Mr
Gladstone's advice was sought to no avail, but in 1896 a papermaker
said it was machine-made, of hemp origin and known as 'pottery
tissue'. Much earlier the Press had come to an arrangement with
Thomas Brittain in Hanley to manufacture 'Oxford India' for them,
and for them alone. In 1874 an edition of 250,000 Bibles was printed
on it and sold out within a few weeks. In the following decade, an
official Revised Version of the Bible was published jointly with Cambridge, and a million copies sold in twenty-four hours. American
publishers attempted to secure advance sheets with a view to pirating,
but the *Chicago Times* beat them to it by issuing the complete New
Testament as a supplement, the entire text having been telegraphed
to them immediately copies arrived in New York.

Alexander Macmillan became publisher to O.U.P. in 1863 and
handled their general list until 1880, when Henry Frowde, who had
been manager of the Bible warehouse in Paternoster Row for some
years, became the first Publisher to the University. Three years later
the minority shareholders in the Bible Press were bought out, and the
Learned and Bible Presses became one.

During Frowde's reign at O.U.P., publication of the *Oxford English
Dictionary* was begun in 1884, the New York branch was opened in
1896 and *The Periodical*, one of the earliest house journals, was started.
But it should be remembered that at the turn of the century numerous
bread-and-butter lines, which, in 1970, made Oxford books indispensable to every bookshop in the land and to many thousands of
others overseas, were not then invented: the World's Classics and the
Dictionary of National Biography were created by other publishers and
still in their possession, and there was no *Oxford Dictionary of Quotations*
or *Companion to Music*; no *Concise Oxford Dictionary*, no illustrated
Dickens or *Dictionary of Modern English Usage*.

Publishing at Cambridge did not commence until 1521, when John
Siberch was the first man to print there. He is thought to have come
from Cologne, as did Rood of Oxford, but not much is known of him
except that he was a friend of Erasmus, and that he worked his press
for under two years at the sign of the Arma Regia, facing St Michael's
Church (now part of Gonville and Caius College). According to the
Dictionary of National Biography, Bullock's *Oratio* to Cardinal Wolsey was
his first book, and there were about eight or nine others, including
Galen's *De Temperamentis*, translated by Linacre, the prescribed textbook for the medical course. Siberch borrowed £20 from the university
and never repaid it. In fact, the debt was not honoured until 1971,
when the Press reimbursed the university in full, although without
the compound interest of £68,000, which the faculty kindly waived.

Although printing activities started later than at Oxford, Cambridge received a royal licence to print in 1534 when Henry VIII granted to the chancellor, or his deputies, the right to approve books to be printed by three stationers of their appointment. Evidently they deemed it wiser in those troubled times not to exercise the right, because there is no record of another Cambridge book until 1585, by which time Thomas Thomas had been made first Printer to the University. Thomas, a fellow of King's, was a scholar, and he compiled a Latin dictionary, which members of the Stationers' Company instantly pirated when it appeared. The line remains unbroken to this day and includes several distinguished names.

In Thomas's first year, 1582, the Bishop of London authorized members of the Stationers' Company to seize his plant. The faculty appealed to Lord Burghley, who was already on record as being against the restoration of a printing press in Cambridge, and to the Bishop of London, who was unrepentant and described Thomas as a 'man utterlie ignorant in printing ...' The Stationers, of course, backed the bishop, and argued that as there were no less than fifty-three printers in London there was no need for one in Cambridge. It took some months to establish the validity of Henry VIII's charter and to have Thomas reinstated.

The Press continued to print in the homes of its various printers until John Field leased ground near Queen's College in 1655. Field succeeded John Lydgate the younger in that year, but it was Richard Bentley, soon to become Master of Trinity, who persuaded the chancellor, the Duke of Somerset, in 1696, to appeal to the university to make the Press at Cambridge worthy of 'those great and excellent writings ... soe frequently published from ye members of yr own body'. Eight hundred pounds had been subscribed by public-spirited gentlemen; the Duke offered a further £200 on loan, and Bentley was granted powers authorizing him to take responsibility for renovating the Press. Another building was added to Field's. New types were ordered from Holland, and with them came Cornelius Crownfield, who became first 'Inspector' of the Press at £26 a year, and then, in 1705, Printer. A governing body was appointed which was the forerunner of the Syndics of 1970 — a committee of senior members of the university which formally accepted all books published under their imprint, a procedure which perpetuates the position of the Press as a department of the university.

In the eighteenth century an overall manager with no other responsibilities than to the Press was needed. But Richard Bentley was Master of Trinity, with numerous additional obligations, and he probably took on too much. He certainly made an unfortunate deal with an Oxford bookseller, John Owen, to print the *Suidas Lexicon*. Owen became insolvent and the university had to bear the outlay on the book which was eventually jobbed off to booksellers for cash or in exchange for other books. Bentley was often at odds with his colleagues over minor infringements of university law; he was summonsed and convicted, but no one dared to implement the judgment. Bentley died in 1742, still Master of Trinity, but the building he had acquired for the press was disposed of in 1716 as part of a prolonged economy campaign when the rights in certain school books were sold, and the privilege of printing the Bible was sublet for £100 a year (half what Oxford leased their similar rights for) in order to pay for the lexicon.

The next prominent figure in Cambridge publishing was John Baskerville, a self-educated man from Worcester, where he started his working life (like Robert Dodsley) as a footman. Dodsley, as we have seen became the most celebrated publisher-bookseller of his time; Baskerville became the finest printer of his. In 1758 he was one of the stationers and printers who were elected to serve Cambridge for a ten-year period. He transferred his types from Birmingham and produced the Bible which Thomas Frognall Dibdin, the bibliographer, referred to as 'one of the most beautifully printed books in the world'. Baskerville, however, felt himself exploited, and complained bitterly of the heavy premium he had to pay to the Syndics for the right to print at Cambridge. Players, fiddlers, dancers, he said, lived in affluence and amassed fortunes but he, excelling in the most useful art known to man, was a pauper. He did not stay ten years but walked out after five. He tried to sell his plant to his old friend Benjamin Franklin, and eventually succeeded in disposing of it to Beaumarchais who used it for his complete edition of Voltaire. It changed hands numerous times thereafter but eventually came into the possession of Deberny et Peignot, the Paris typefounders, who generously returned the original punches to Cambridge in 1953.

In 1833 Cambridge University Press moved into a Gothic building on Trumpington Street, with the help of surplus subscriptions for a statue to William Pitt in Hanover Square, London: hence the Pitt Press of later years. They had previously acquired additional ground on the Silver Street site purchased in 1762 for a warehouse, and here a new printing plant was completed in 1827.

Until 1873 various agencies were arranged for the distribution of Cambridge books — then chiefly Bibles and prayer books — to the trade. In that year a London office was opened in Paternoster Row and C. J. Clay, appointed printer in 1854, managed it. Clay remained printer to Cambridge until 1894, and his sons succeeded him.

At the time of the opening of the London office Cambridge University Press were not seriously engaged in general publishing. The Macmillan brothers had creamed off many of the secular books written by the Cambridge faculty which might otherwise have gone to C.U.P. It was

G. R. Browne, the secretary of the Local Examinations Board Syndicate, who pushed the Syndics of the Press into the school book world when he invited them to issue editions of various set books in foreign languages. This, in 1874, was the basis of the Pitt Press series known to many generations of students. Expansion, once undertaken, was rapid, reaching far beyond school texts to Doughty's *Arabia Deserta* and Acton's plan for the Cambridge Modern History. There were 30 titles on the Cambridge list in 1860; by 1900 there were over 500.

The third oldest publisher in the United Kingdom, the Society for Promoting Christian Knowledge (S.P.C.K.), was founded in 1698 by Thomas Bray, D.D., and four laymen. Their purpose was 'the great duty of Disposing and Dispersing of Good Books among the People'. In 1700 they were already planning books in Arabic and French. S.P.C.K. claimed to have introduced one of the earliest planned-distribution systems; all methods of transport then invented were used to convey its own publications, and others of which it approved, to many parts of the world. Churches, charity schools, hospitals, almshouses, workhouses, prisons, etc., were numbered amongst its members in places as far away as the hinterland of America and the Coromandel coast. In Tsarist camps in Russia, Persian prisoners of war received parcels of the Society's Arabic publications.

In 1757 the Society was helped by the introduction of book grants for those studying for the ministry. At the start of the nineteenth century there was a rapid rise in the Society's membership from two thousand in 1800 to fifteen thousand in 1822, and in 1832, the year of the first reform bill, the S.P.C.K. took the bold step of including general literature on its list. Three years later it opened its own printing works and its own shops, in the form of book rooms, in various provincial towns and cities (see also pp. 286, 294).

In 1837 S.P.C.K. issued just over two million Bibles, prayer-books and works of a religious nature as against 136,000 'other books'. By 1897 sales of Bibles, etc., had reached nearly four million, but 'other books' had overtaken them to the extent of eight and a half million.

3

The Established Publishers: Fathers and Sons

Longmans; John Murray; William Collins, Sons & Co; Blackie & Son; A. &. C. Black; Thomas Nelson & Sons; Oliver & Boyd; E. & S. Livingstone; T. & T. Clark; J. & A. Churchill; Baillière; E. & F. Spon; Crosby Lockwood & Son; Sweet & Maxwell; Stevens; Butterworth; W. Green; Epworth Press; Burns, Oates & Washbourne; Bailey Brothers; Eyre & Spottiswoode; Sampson Low; Chapman & Hall; G. Bell & Sons; Putnam; Routledge; Frederick Warne; Macmillan; Cassell: Ward & Lock; Chatto & Windus; Allman & Son; James Nisbet; Hodder & Stoughton; Tinsley; Smith & Elder.

There is a dynastic ring to this section which will not sound again so clearly.

Longmans of the fifth generation entered the partnership during the 1870s, Thomas Norton becoming head of the firm when his father died in 1879. Thomas IV outlived his brother William by only two years; each of them provided two sons to carry on the family tradition.

The decade began with the success of Disraeli's novel *Lothair*. The author had resigned as prime minister in 1868 and been offered £10,000 for a novel by another publisher. The offer was declined but the novel written and submitted to Longmans. Disraeli earned over £6,000 from it in four years, and in 1877, by which time he was again premier, he sold the copyright in all his novels to Longmans for £2,100.

However, it was not a Longman who was responsible for the most radical change in the firm's publishing policy in this period, but J. W. Allen, an elementary schoolteacher who was invited to join them in 1884. Longmans had always included educational books on their list, but they were of less importance than the general works. Allen completely altered the balance of business by building up the school book side and developing markets in India (the Bombay branch was opened in 1895) and elsewhere. Then in 1890 came the amalgamation described in *The Bookseller* as the most important since Longmans had taken over John W. Parker, Son & Bourne in 1863. The sole proprietor of the house of Rivington, Francis Hansard Rivington, announced his retirement and the sale of the oldest private publishing business in the land to the second oldest. Confusingly, Rivington's seventh son,

Septimus, had started his own list, also using the family name, in the previous year. This remained independent of Longmans, who by their purchase of the older firm acquired more of the *Annual Register* (a shareholding publication in which Rivington held a majority) and considerably strengthened their theological list.

For the House of Murray the late-Victorian era was one of consolidation, apart from a couple of ill-advised ventures into magazine publishing. John Murray III was in control until his death in 1892, which came shortly after the publication of Samuel Smiles's two-volume biography of John Murray II. In fact John Murray III wrote some of this work himself, as he had also written a number of the Murray handbooks to various countries. Travel was a passion of his and the list reflected it, with books by David Livingstone and other explorers, amongst them the indomitable Isabella Bird who, although a chronic invalid, took up travel in search of better health at the age of forty-one and stuck at it for a further thirty-one years. Besides publishing her, John Murray III taught her to ride a tricycle, the lessons taking place in Albemarle Street with Miss Bird, daringly for the time, dressed in trousers. John Murray III, who published Darwin's *The Origin of Species* and Samuel Smiles's *Self-Help* on the same day in 1859, did not live to see the 13-volume edition of Byron's letters and poems which his son issued in 1895.

The custom of holding trade sale dinners died out during his time although in 1881 Murray's was still as well attended and attractive as ever according to the trade press. Only the cream of London booksellers was invited, and on November 4th, 2,500 copies of *The Speaker's Commentary* were offered and bought in ten minutes. But a few years later Mr Murray announced that he would discontinue trade dinners and subscribe books through a traveller in future, which left only Bentley and Quaritch still practising a custom which was as agreeable a way for a bookseller to purchase his stock as any that has been thought of since. (It was revived in 1965 when Cedric Dickens, great-grandson of the novelist, invited a number of booksellers to roast beef and claret at the George and Vulture in the City of London, and subscribed his edition of *A Christmas Carol*, produced to raise funds for the upkeep of Dickens's house in Doughty Street.)

In Glasgow the house of Collins had passed its golden jubilee by 1870, and its founder had long since dissolved his partnership with Dr Thomas Chalmers, who had transferred all his literary interests and goodwill to Oliver & Boyd in a fit of temper in 1846. Collins had been built partly on Chalmer's religious writings, although from the start Collins himself had quickly developed the trade in school books and printing, and had been responsible for the Select Library of Christian Literature. The first William Collins died in 1853, and the business was continued by his son, also William, who combined his work as a publisher with civic duties in Glasgow, where he became Lord Provost, and was reviled as 'Water Willie' because of his strong teetotal views.

Collins were appointed Queen's Printer for Scotland in 1862, by which time their editions of the Scriptures were already well known. 'Water Willie' applied himself indefatigably to publishing the Bible, and claimed that by 1860 he had printed 17 different types and sizes and issued them in some 300 styles of binding, achieving an annual sale of nearly 300,000. His sons, William Collins III and Alexander, became partners in 1870, and the three of them, at dynamic pace, expanded all sides of the business. William Collins III had scientific leanings, and invented a machine which folded, gummed and dried envelopes so that 180,000 could be produced in a day, thus enabling Collins to meet the current demand. Forster's Education Act provoked them to publish more and more school books and, with a typical tycoon touch, they bought out the Scottish School Book Association in 1875 (they had been its official publisher for more than a decade) and put its staff on their own payroll. In that year they had more than 1,200 employees.

The Collinses, father and sons, worked with fantastic energy to widen their markets at home and abroad, and the mind reels at what they achieved. In 1862 they opened an office in Edinburgh (they had already been operating in London, from various addresses, for many years). Permanent representatives were established in South Africa and Canada, and within a few weeks of the outbreak of the Franco-Prussian War in 1870 Collins had a map on sale showing the railways, roads and fortified towns involved. In 1876 a warehouse and showroom were opened in Sydney, and New Zealand was colonized twelve years later.

William Collins II died in 1895, having converted the partnership into a limited company sixteen years earlier by buying out the various partners, including his sons, for a total of £75,000. His grandsons were made directors soon after his death. One of them, William Collins IV, son of Alexander, was taken from school, to his regret, and apprenticed in the London warehouse at 5s. a week although, for some reason, he received only 3s. 6d. net. The Collins children and grandchildren were expected to inherit but first they had to learn the business the hard way. William Collins IV learned quickly, and in 1897, aged twenty-four, having been ordered to take a holiday in India, Australia and New Zealand and to take a box of samples with him (it was a Collins-type holiday), he was rewarded with a directorship. There was little doubt that the Collinses were ready for the twentieth century, which they greeted with unflagging enthusiasm.

Turning to the other great nineteenth-century Scottish publishers after trying to keep up the breathless pace of the Collinses is like listening to Vivaldi's *Seasons* after hearing the Choral Symphony.

Blackie, founded ten years earlier than Collins, was emerging from what its official history calls its 'quiet years'. A fine list of religious, technical and historical works had been built up and a printing works operated successfully. John, Junior, the eldest son, died in 1873, predeceasing his ninety-year-old father by a year, and the firm was continued by his brother Dr W. G. (Walter) who had already made plans for entering the school book market. The Blackie educational representative, John Nichol, that year attended a conference at Bristol and exhibited their school list which 'occupied a single chair in the vestibule'. And the chair, added Nichol, also supported the exhibitor. Modesty indeed.

A third generation of Blackies built up the school list, profiting especially from their association with Vere Foster, a philanthropist who devoted his life to furthering education and social conditions in Ireland. Foster had designed writing- and copying-books for children which he insisted should be printed in Ireland in order to provide employment. The agency to print them was with the firm of Marcus Ward in Belfast, and when John Ward withdrew from his family business Vere Foster's books went with him. An agreement was made with Blackie's who then set up a printing works in Dublin.

Blackie also widened their juvenile list in this period, with titles from G. A. Henty and George Macdonald, and, in a quieter way, they expanded as Collins did, opening a London office in 1837 and becoming a limited company in 1890. They were for a long time associated with subscription publishing (direct sale to the public), and in 1898 they formed a subsidiary, the Gresham Publishing Co. Ltd, for this purpose.

Adam Black retired in 1870 from the publishing house he had founded sixty-three years earlier. During the century he had acquired the copyright of the Waverley Novels and of the *Encyclopaedia Britannica* (see pp. 221–2), and he retired as a protest against what he considered the extravagant plans made by his sons for the *Britannica*'s ninth edition. The sons, James, Francis and Adam, justified themselves by selling nearly half a million sets between 1875 and 1888. But they met severe trouble in the States where although they sold some sets through their agents Little, Brown of Boston, two American firms sold more pirated editions than Black's sold throughout the world. The Black's attempt to obtain justice in the American courts was overruled, and rival encyclopaedias, based on theirs, were printed and sold by promotional campaigns that urged the American people to buy American. America did not sign the International Copyright Act of 1891, so the situation did not ease for Black and their agents.

In June 1889 the Blacks moved into offices in Soho Square which had formerly been a factory for the making of munitions. Their descendants still occupied them in 1970. At the end of the 'nineties, with his two brothers dead, and himself feeling the urge to retire, James Tait Black sanctioned a deal over the *Britannica* with Horace Everett Hooper, an American who, on behalf of James Clarke and company, negotiated successfully with *The Times* to promote a new sale of the ninth edition. Hooper, aware of the financial difficulties of *The Times*, averred that the newspaper needed him more than he and his associates needed it. He was right. *The Times* agreed to offer the encyclopaedia to its readers provided Black guaranteed delivery of stock. *Times* readers gratefully took the opportunity of buying the *Britannica* at half price, and a year later Hooper and an associate bought out Clarke and became sole proprietors of the *Encyclopaedia* on payment of £5,000 to A. & C. Black, who had already received £46,500 from Clarke. Thus a work of British scholarship was sold to America on the eve of the new century, a deed very much heralding the pattern of things to come. (It is perhaps worth recording that at Frankfurt in 1968 I met a German employee of Encyclopaedia Brittanica Ltd who assured me that I was quite wrong in supposing the encyclopaedia to be of British origin!)

Another great encyclopaedia of Scottish origin, Chambers's, was on sale in these years. It appeared in 520 weekly parts from 1859 to 1868, and new editions were issued from time to time. Thomas Nelson's, established in 1798, had also weathered the storms of the nineteenth century and moved into a 'grand, new building in Paternoster Row' in 1870. Most of the Scottish publishers had either opened London offices or moved entirely to the English capital by the end of the century.

One which remained firmly based in Edinburgh was Oliver & Boyd, whose history properly began when Thomas Oliver, who had set up as a printer in 1778 using the hearth in his mother's house as an imposing stone, took George Boyd, a bookbinder, into partnership. This was in about 1807, and in 1812 they commenced publication of the *Edinburgh Almanac*, a compendium of civil, political, municipal and legal affairs which was to last for 120 years. In the 1820s all sides of the business were moved to Tweeddale House, a late-sixteenth-century building at 16 High Street, Edinburgh.

Oliver & Boyd became the largest wholesale booksellers in Scotland, according to James Thin, having the agencies for Murray, Charles Knight and Simpkin Marshall amongst others. In 1843 Oliver retired and Boyd died. The business was continued by Boyd's brother and three sons until, in 1896, the Edinburgh booksellers Thin & Grant bought it. By then it had a considerable reputation for educational and reference books, and was still publishing the *Edinburgh Medical Journal* which had been taken over from Simpkin's in 1862. This was to pass out of Oliver & Boyd's hands in 1897, but it returned to them in the twentieth century.

Edinburgh is closely associated with medical publishing, and its importance as a training centre for doctors and nurses was well established when Edward Livingstone opened his first bookshop at 57 South Bridge in 1863. At that time 131 firms in the city were listed as engaged in selling books and stationery, and of these 32 were publishers. A year earlier, the first Medical Officer of Health, Henry D. Littlejohn, had been appointed, and his appointment had far-reaching results which were reflected in the list of E. & S. Livingstone as it quickly grew. S. was for Stuart, Edward's younger brother who joined him in 1865. Five years later the partners were building up their list of nursing books following sweeping changes in nursing techniques initiated by Miss Barclay at the Edinburgh Royal Infirmary.

The Livingstones were not solely concerned with medical publishing, however, for in 1871 they issued the *Edinburgh University Magazine* with the young Robert Louis Stevenson as editor. It ran for only four numbers, but R.L.S., in his *Memories and Portraits*, has left us a neat picture of Edward and Stuart: 'A pair of little, active brothers ... great skippers on the foot, great rubbers of the hands, who ... had been debauched to play the part of publishers.'

On one Christmas Day in the late 1890s the Livingstone staff might well have been rubbing their hands and skipping, in consequence of a benevolent decision by the brothers. It was not customary then to close shops on Christmas Day in Scotland, but Edward announced that they would shut early on the 25th, adding that there would, therefore, be no need to light the fires. By one o'clock there wasn't a penny in the till and Edward went to lunch. Returning at three to his pinched and frozen employees, who had still failed to effect a single sale, he exclaimed cheerfully, 'Well, well, we must not work any longer on such a day as this.' (Normal working hours were from 8.30 a.m. to 8 p.m.)

Another Edinburgh publisher of that time still in business in 1970 was T. & T. Clark. Both Clarks, uncle and nephew, were named Thomas; the elder had been the chief law bookseller in the City and publisher to the university.

Medical publishing in London was represented chiefly by J. & A. Churchill of Burlington Street, and by Baillière. John Churchill founded his firm in 1825 and retired in 1870, handing on to his sons, John and Augustus, who, in turn, made their sons, John Theodore and Augustus William, partners in the business in 1901. Jean-Baptiste Baillière started in Paris in 1818 and opened an English branch eight years later, placing his younger brother Hyppolyte in charge of it. Albert Alfred Tindall, already experienced in this field of publishing, joined Hyppolyte's widow in 1869, and William Cox entered the partnership a year after that. Baillière, Tindall & Cox were pioneers of veterinary publishing and also became prominent for their nursing aid series.

Technical publishing became important in the nineteenth century, and apart from those general publishers who developed technical lists on the side there were the specialists: Charles Griffin, who started his family firm in 1820; Baron de Spon, founder of E. & F. Spon, who set up ten years later; and Lockwood, grandson of Benjamin Crosby, proprietor of the first Simpkin's. Lockwood worked with Mark, his father, at Simpkin's for seventeen years before establishing his own imprint in 1858, and in 1876 he adopted Crosby as a Christian name.

The great names in legal publishing have not changed. In 1870 Sweet & Maxwell were seventy-one years old; Stevens, whom they were eventually to take over, were sixty, and Butterworth, fifty-two. The latter was founded by Henry Butterworth of Coventry at No. 7 Fleet Street, in which thoroughfare his father had worked as partner in a law bookshop since 1780. There is the usual dynastic tale to relate—Henry's son Joshua inherited Butterworth and was appointed Queen Victoria's law publisher—but the family connection ended with his death in 1895, when Stanley Shaw Bond became the owner. A great period of expansion followed, and new premises were taken in 1897 in Bell Yard. W. Green, the Edinburgh law publisher, began in 1884.

In sectarian religious publishing the name of the Epworth Press had been known since 1739; it operated from what had been John Wesley's house in the City Road. In the 1830s James Burns started what became the great Catholic publishing house of Burns & Lambert, then Burns & Oates and, after that, Burns, Oates & Washbourne. He was a convert, and had first set up as a high Anglican who published the theological work of Edward Pusey, of Oxford Movement fame. Then, two years after John Newman's conversion, Burns also turned to Rome, a change of faith which nearly ruined his publishing business. Newman came to his rescue with the manuscript of *Loss and Gain* and followed it up with *The Dream of Gerontius*, setting Burns on his feet again.

Bailey Brothers began as a Bible bookshop in Seven Sisters Road, Holloway, in 1825. Its proprietor, Frank Evans Bailey, subsequently left his brother to mind the shop and opened a bindery, later to become associated with Oxford University Press, in nearby Highbury.

For the next imprint founded as a specialist religious firm it is necessary to return to the eighteenth century. The granting of patents to print the Bible and Prayer Book was a complicated matter, and it so happened that a certain Mr Baskett bought up one which was on offer in 1719 from Benjamin Tooke (who sold books at the sign of the ship, in St Paul's Churchyard, before the first Longman) and John Barker. This cost more than he had, so he borrowed a total of £32,000 from John Eyre over the next five years, which resulted in the transfer of the patent to the lender. John Eyre might seem to have had more money than sense, but his successors benefited from his faith in Baskett's business ability. Charles Eyre, the son, went into partnership with

William Strahan, who kept his own printing business running separately. Their descendants were able to renew the patents periodically, although it was a near thing when successive select committees were appointed by Parliament to investigate this monopoly, and in 1820 they made a record profit of £19,448. When Strahan's son died, his nephews Andrew and Robert Spottiswoode inherited his share of the patent—hence the Eyre & Spottiswoode which in due course became printers to the government and which, in 1901 after the Queen's death, were again given renewal of their patent.

So much for the specialists. There remain upwards of a dozen names in general publishing whose imprints, or those of their successors, survived in 1970. One of the oldest of these was Sampson Low. The first Sampson Low, printer and publisher from 1766–98, died when the second was only two. Sampson Low II worked at Longmans for some years before opening a bookshop and stationers' in Lambs Conduit Street in 1819. In the year of the Queen's accession, 1837, a group of publishers who had become dissatisfied with the existing trade journals financed the *Publishers' Circular* (the *P.C.*) and invited Low to manage it. Thirty years later the manager bought out the publishers and remained editor of the journal until 1883. Meanwhile, with his son, Sampson Low III, he had begun publishing. The second Low had a distinguished career indeed, not only as bookseller, publisher and editor, but also as author of *Low's Comparative and Historical Register of the House of Commons* 1827–41; 1841–47; as an early sponsor of the Booksellers Provident Institution (later the Book Trade Benevolent Society); and as secretary of the ill-fated London Booksellers' Association of 1848–52.

Edward Marston, earlier associated with the bookselling business, returned from Australia in 1856 and became a partner, and it was his son who succeeded Sampson Low II as editor of the *Circular*. Edward Marston, too, made a valuable contribution to publishing. He enjoyed a long and close friendship with R. D. Blackmore, whose *Lorna Doone* he brought out in 1869. 'But for you,' wrote Blackmore years later, '*Lorna Doone* might never have seen the light. All the magazines rejected her and Smith & Elder refused to give me £200 for the copyright.' Marston's relations with Hardy were less happy. He published many of his novels after taking over *Far From the Madding Crowd* from Smith & Elder, but was obliged, regretfully, to part with them to the American company of Osgood, M'Ilvaine. Osgood M'Ilvaine opened in Albermarle Street in 1891, succeeding Sampson Low as English representatives of Harper's, and issuing a complete uniform edition of Hardy.

The sons of Low and Marston encountered strong competition for their *P.C.* when Joseph Whitaker, who had been a bookseller with J. H. Parker in Oxford and London, and had edited the *Gentlemen's Magazine*, started *The Bookseller* in 1858. His intention was to provide a monthly journal which covered the activities of the entire book trade, and published regular lists of new titles, an intention admirably realized ever since. In 1868 he also started *Whitaker's Almanac*, and six years later the first *Reference Catalogue of Current Literature* was published. Then he handed on the editorship of *The Bookseller* to his son Vernon. Vernon remained editor for twenty years, during which time 'the organ' ceaselessly campaigned to stop underselling and to start an association of booksellers. Vernon died at fifty, and Joseph survived him by only four months, leaving his younger son, George Herbert, to carry on the business.

Which other names might readers of *The Bookseller* and the *P.C.* have seen advertising in the trade papers in 1870?

It was the year of Charles Dickens's death, and also the year in which Frederick Chapman bought the novelist's copyrights. Dickens had had what might seem a typical author-publisher relationship with the Chapman cousins and Hall; one minute protesting his affection and his belief in their utter integrity, the next bursting with fury and accusing them of swindling him. Hall was dead by the time Dickens had quarrelled with Bradbury & Evans as well and returned to his first publishers, and George Meredith had long displaced John Forster as the firm's reader. In 1880 Chapman turned the partnership into a company with Anthony Trollope and others on the board, whereupon they all settled down to twenty years of apathy, living on the proceeds of former glories. When Meredith asked for a rise of £50 to make his salary £300 a year and was refused, he resigned and went off to Ward, Lock. Chapman died in the same year, and Dickens's copyrights were gradually running out. At this time it is said that one director of the company could not understand why if they had made a profit of x thousand pounds that amount of money wasn't in the bank. However, the misfortune of that gentleman's chairmanship was somewhat offset by the acquisition of the Wiley agency, and the appointment, at the turn of the century, of Arthur Waugh as managing director. Another successful era lay ahead.

George Bell and F. R. Daldy's seventeen-year-old partnership was dissolved in 1872, and the former continued with his two sons, Edward and Ernest. It has been seen already how they grasped the opportunity of exploiting the Colonial cloth edition market and this was typical of the energy with which the sons applied themselves to the expansion of the firm.

George P. Putnam, who in 1841 became the first American publisher to open a London office, died of apoplexy in New York in 1873 and was succeeded by his son, Dr George Haven Putnam, who continued the father's disinterested work for international copyright. An early American takeover of an English imprint had occurred the previous year when Samuel French of New York, who had been issuing playscripts since 1854, bought his friend Thomas Hailes Lacy's similar business in Wellington Street, Strand. Lacy's acting editions had been on sale for over forty years. He and French had become friends when the latter visited London because the climate was good for his asthma. French lived on until 1898, and in 1901 the firm moved out of the ancient premises off the Strand and into an early-eighteenth-century building in Southampton Street, on the edge of Covent Garden market.

George Routledge, who had dissolved his partnership with his brother-in-law Frederick Warne in 1865, remained with his business until his death in 1888. By then it had already fallen upon bad times and it did not recover until the takeover of 1902, which will be dealt with in the next section. Warne inherited Nuttall's *Dictionary* from the dissolution, and with this and his Chandos Classics—154 titles comprising most of the then standard authors in prose and poetry in 1s. 6d. paper editions and 2s. cloth, which sold over five million copies—he built a solid foundation for his list. Warne, lucky man, lived in Bedford Square where so many publishers later worked or conferred. He kept open house at No. 8, where he had the eccentric habit of calling all his men-servants 'John' and all his maids 'Mary'. He opened a New York branch in 1881 and retired in 1894, by which time his three sons, Harold, Fruing and Norman, were in the firm.

The death of Daniel Macmillan in 1857 has already been noted. His brother Alexander published in London as well as Cambridge from that year, and in 1863, despite the latter address, he became publisher to the University of Oxford. By 1870 all publishing activities were transferred to London, the premises in Trinity Street, Cambridge, being devoted thereafter to retail trade, and Alexander took George Lillie Craik into partnership. Craik was husband to the author of *John Halifax, Gentleman,* but in his publishing life he was more concerned with administration than literature. Daniel's sons Frederick Orridge and Maurice, and Alexander's, Malcolm and George, had all become partners by 1883. One of Frederick's earliest recorded acts in the company was to accept a volume of essays sent in by Henry James, although the reader, probably John Morley, considered these mediocre, 'honest scribble, and no more'; and indeed Macmillans did not grow rich on James. Thomas Hardy's first book was looked on even less favourably and rejected but he, modest man, accepted their assessment of his work and came to them again. Bernard Shaw submitted a number of novels which Macmillan, correctly from a short-term view, turned down. Every publisher has rejected manuscripts which have become bestsellers on other lists but, broadly speaking, Macmillan's published for the future and they were right enough, often enough, to survive.

In 1881 Alexander ceased to act as publisher for O.U.P., and he received an honorary degree for his services. He lived on until 1896, when a limited company was formed and Frederick became chairman. Soon after, the imposing new offices in St Martin's Street, which the Macmillans were to occupy for some sixty-eight years, were ready, and they applied themselves to steady expansion; the Bentley List was purchased in 1898 for £8,000, and the Bombay branch opened in 1901.

Cassell and Ward & Lock are linked historically through Thomas Dixon Galpin of Dorchester, who received his early education at the hands of the poet William Barnes. Galpin's aunt Eliza married a farmer called George Lock. When the son of this marriage, also George, came to London in 1854, he sought his cousin's advice about a future career. Galpin was then a printer in partnership with George Petter, and he introduced George Lock to Ebenezer Ward, then working for the publisher Herbert Ingram. Ward was correctly apprehensive about the financial viability of Ingram's business, so Galpin arranged for some capital from George Lock, Senior, and the firm of Ward & Lock opened at 158 Fleet Street, where David Nutt had once sold foreign books.

In 1855 Petter & Galpin bought Cassell's, and four years later made John Cassell a partner (see p. 227). This infuriated Ward and Lock, who recognized the dangers of direct competition, and many rows ensued, especially when both houses issued *The Vicar of Wakefield* simultaneously. However, personal relations between George Lock and Dixon Galpin remained friendly, and when eventually Herbert Ingram failed, Ward & Lock and Petter & Galpin jointly bought up his copyrights and stock, which included Webster's *Dictionary* and *Spelling-Book*.

In 1866 the City of London endured its worst financial crisis since the South Sea Bubble. One of the discount houses which failed was Overend, Gurney & Co., who had unwisely sold bills representing deposit savings. Thus Samuel Orchart Beeton, widower and publisher of the famous cook, became 'a licensee in bankruptcy' to Ward and Lock and their recently acquired partner, Charles Tyler. Poor Beeton, still suffering from the loss of his Isabella the year before, agreed to hand over all his copyrights in exchange for £400 a year and one-sixth of the profits. This arrangement worked well until, in the following decade, he began to write anti-royalist parodies of Tennyson, and broke his agreement with his employers by using his name on other publishers' books. Beeton was dismissed, and Ward & Lock kept *Beeton's Book of Household Management*, *Dictionary of Every Day Cookery*, the *Boys' Own Magazine* and other valuable properties.

Throughout our period Ward & Lock were vastly acquisitive. In 1870 they bought Edward Moxon. Moxon himself, probably the greatest poetry publisher of his time, had been dead twelve years but there were still numerous plums on his list. W. Tegg & Co. were purchased in 1881 by which year George Lock's younger brother John, and James Bowden, who had come originally to the firm with the Beeton takeover, were partners. Tegg was an eccentric who held nightly auctions of books in Cheapside, until he began a brisk trade in cheap reprints which were published from the address of the old Mansion House. A year later the New York office was opened, and in 1883 Ebenezer Ward retired. George Lock died in 1891.

Bowden and John Lock continued in partnership for two years and then formed a limited company known as Ward Lock & Bowden, which in 1896 began to issue the well-known guides, at the start in green paper boards, for 1s. each. In 1900 A. D. Innes, which had a fine list of sports books, was bought up and the company faced the new century very confidently indeed.

The fortunes of Cassell, Petter & Galpin went the opposite way after a period of furious expansion ending in 1888. An office in Paris was opened in 1871, one in Melbourne in 1884, and John Cassell himself had started the New York branch way back in 1860. The staff increased from five hundred in 1865 to nearly twelve hundred in 1888, in which year Petter died, having retired five years earlier. Galpin was succeeded as chairman by Robert Turner, once a small printer-bookseller in Islington, who had been made a partner ten years before. In that year also Thomas Teignmouth Shore resigned; he had boasted that 'under my editorial control that great publishing house reached its highest point of prosperity and success'.

No publisher worked harder through propaganda and its own publications to help create the climate of opinion which led to the passing of Forster's Education Act in 1870. Yet it is one of the ironies of publishing history that that same firm failed to keep abreast of its competitors in the 'nineties, by which time a whole generation had benefited from compulsory education. It is even more ironical that by then the secretary of the company was H. O. Arnold-Forster, the adopted son of the author of the Act. Arnold-Forster and his colleagues were more interested in politics than in publishing, and the new century dawned not at all bright over La Belle Sauvage Yard.

The death of John Camden Hotten, one of the more colourful figures in nineteenth-century publishing, occurred in 1873 (see p. 210). Hotten began in 1855 in a bookshop on the site of what became the Ritz Hotel in Piccadilly. He subsequently moved to other addresses in the same thoroughfare, from which he published numerous American authors, including Bret Harte, Mark Twain, Edgar Allen Poe, Walt Whitman and Oliver Wendell Holmes. It has to be recorded that he was as unscrupulous on this side of the Atlantic about the absence of international copyright agreements as were American publishers on the other. Mark Twain not only complained of receiving no payment for his English editions, but had to protest that his books were quite bad enough as they were without Mr Hotten adding half a dozen chapters of his own. When he read these additional chapters he felt, he said, like knocking the man's brains out—'Not in anger, for I feel none. Oh! Not in anger; but only to see, that is all. Mere idle curiosity.'

Hotten had a hand in many books apart from Mark Twain's, and there is no complete record of all his pseudonyms. On his death Mrs Hotten sold the business to his partner Andrew Chatto for £25,000, whereafter relations with Twain and other American writers improved. W. E. Windus, a minor poet, became Chatto's partner but never took a very active part in a business which grew, from 1876, under the inspiration of Percy Spalding as well as of Chatto. Andrew Chatto subscribed his own books to Smith's and Mudie's. Spalding, according to Frank Swinnerton, their reader for many years, 'did not pretend to any literary taste but put his hands in his pockets, jangled his keys and coppers, whistled *Meet Me Tonight in Dreamland*, and said to all authors, whatever their pretensions, "Nce, give us a rattling good story." ' Like Ward & Lock, Chatto & Windus looked to the future optimistically, and were not to be disappointed.

Many others could be mentioned, among them the educational firms of Allman and Nisbet, dating back to the beginning of the century; W. H. Allen, which claimed an even earlier birth: and Pitman, founded in 1849. A comparative newcomer was Hodder & Stoughton, which grew out of Jackson, Walford & Hodder, and was formed in 1868 when Matthew Henry Hodder, described by one friend as a white-bearded patriarch, was joined by Thomas Wilberforce Stoughton, who had worked at Nisbet's. Both men were interested in evangelical and low church theology, so it was not surprising that they acted for a while as official publishers to the Congregational Union. The list broadened in due course with the arrival of Sir William Robertson Nicoll in the 1880s. He came from Scotland to be literary adviser and editor-in-chief, and launched J. M. Barrie as a novelist; but the chief glory of Hodder & Stoughton belongs to a later period.

All these imprints would have been familiar to booksellers in both 1870 and 1970. However, two other publishers, Tinsley's and Smith & Elder did not survive so well.

The Tinsleys were a curious pair. Their father was a gamekeeper, and they came to London from Hertfordshire riding on a haycart, as Edward Tinsley was wont to say in his cups. George Moore thought little of the younger brother, William, who liked to work in his shirt-sleeves and could be wooed into accepting manuscripts by authors who took the trouble to play with the black cat on his counter. Moore apparently took this trouble, and appeared under the Tinsley imprint. Edward Tinsley was an enthusiastic supporter of Hardy, and in 1871 published Hardy's first novel, *Desperate Remedies*, anonymously in three volumes. The novel introduced ultra-sensational matter, he said, but there was enough of the bright side of human nature in the book to sell at least one fair edition. Or so he thought. There proved not to be, but Edward Tinsley considered that Hardy did not have much to complain about over his first venture, and in the following year he bought the copyright of *Under the Greenwood Tree*, which he thought the best little prose idyll he had ever read. But it failed to sell. When the original two-volume edition did not move, he produced it as one pretty illustrated book; but without success. His third attempt was a 2s. paper edition which, like the others, did not attract the public despite outstanding reviews. Tinsley serialized Hardy's next work, *A Pair of Blue Eyes*, in *Tinsley's Magazine*, and afterwards published it in three volumes; again with disappointing results. He had paid £30 for the copyright of *Under the Greenwood Tree*, and when Hardy came to him saying that George Smith had offered £300 for *Far From the Madding Crowd*, he said he couldn't match it, wished Hardy good luck, and farewell.

The foundation of Smith & Elder has been recorded on p. 215. The second George Smith sold the *Pall Mall Gazette* to his son-in-law Henry Yates Thompson in 1880, but he kept the *Cornhill*. He serialized *Far From the Madding Crowd* in 1874, brought it out as a three-decker later the same year, and reprinted it three times before, as we have seen, Sampson Low took it over.

Smith's greatest contribution to publishing — the most lasting work of scholarship to come from his imprint — began in 1882. *The Dictionary of National Biography* has been an indispensable reference work for generations of writers and journalists, and in 1970 it remained a monument to the man who first published it and to its first editor, Sir Leslie Stephen, writer, mountaineer, critic, sometime editor of the *Cornhill* and father of Virginia Woolf. Stephen was one of the great Victorian scholars who combined intellectual and athletic pursuits; he was ordained, climbed peaks, wrote treatises, gave up holy orders, campaigned for the emancipation of slaves and wrote on political, philosophical and theological subjects. Perhaps, above all, he was the first editor of the *D.N.B.*, although he may live even longer in public estimation as the father of a twentieth-century genius.

George Smith's son, Reginald, joined his father in 1894, having previously been at the bar. Reginald became editor of *Cornhill* in 1898, gained sole control of the firm a year later and settled down to a dis-tinguished but relatively short career. George died in 1901. The year before, William Tinsley had published *Random Recollections*; the next year he, also, died.

4

The New Imprints

John Ruskin; George Allen; Swan Sonnenschein; B. T. Batsford; Hutchinson; Unwin; Iliffe; H.F.L.; Chiswick Press; Collingridge; H.M.S.O.; J. M. Dent; William Heinemann; Methuen; Edward Arnold; Constable; The Bodley Head; Grant Richards; Studio; Gale & Polden; Temple Press; Gerald Duckworth; J. M. Watkins; John Tiranti; Liverpool University Press; Kelmscott Press; George G. Harrap; Ginn & Co.

Many authors have wished to be freed from the bondage, as they see it, of publishers; even more have cried to have direct contact with their public unfettered by publishers or booksellers. There have always been self-published writers, although they have usually had to fall back on the retail trade to achieve any sort of distribution. Most have been chastened, and some embittered, by their lack of commercial success.

In 1871 John Ruskin was in a position to defy both publisher and bookseller, and, certain compromises taken into account, he succeeded magnificently. But he was already a well-known author and a rich man. Ruskin had met a young man called George Allen when he was teaching at the Working Men's College in Great Ormond Street, and this young man became his assistant. They went on geological study tours together in the Swiss mountains, where Allen executed some of his finest steel engravings. Ruskin chose him to oversee his publishing when he set up his own press in Orpington in Kent. The first publication was *Fors Clavigera* (of which Smith & Elder also issued an edition) at 7d. a copy. This went unadvertised and was ignored by the regular book trade. Ruskin told his readers that it cost him £10 to print a thousand copies, and £5 more to give them a picture, and a penny off his 7d. to send them the book. A thousand sixpences were £25. 'When you have bought a thousand *Fors* off me,' he wrote to them, 'I shall therefore have £5 for my trouble, and my single shopman, Mr Allen, £5 for his; we won't work for less, either of us.' And Mrs Allen apparently concurred, because she also stayed up half the night helping them in their enterprise. 'And I mean to sell all my large books, henceforth,' Ruskin further proclaimed, 'in the same way, well printed, well bound, and at a fixed price; and the trade may charge a proper and acknowledged profit for their trouble in retailing the book. Then the public will know what they are about, and so will the tradesmen. I, the first producer,

answer to the best of my power for the quality of the bookpaper, bindings, eloquence and all; the retail dealer charges what he ought to
charge openly; and if the public do not choose to give it they can't get
the book. That is what I call legitimate business.' Which was a fine
gauntlet to fling down at the trade and at the public.

Eventually the Orpington plant took over all Ruskin's works and
made a handsome profit, despite the opposition of booksellers with
whom, in 1882, Ruskin came to terms because he saw that his high
prices made his works prohibitive to the very public he wished to reach.
Yet he maintained that he had little sympathy for working men who
wrote that they could not afford the books he produced; his works
would only be wanted if they were expensively and beautifully presented, he claimed (a presager of the snob market to be exploited
several decades later in the coffee table book), but he made a cool
£4,000 per year from his publishing and writing during the last fifteen
years of his life, partly through lowering his prices and dealing with
retailers. At the same time he gave away much of his inheritance of
£200,000 in acts of generosity.

Meanwhile George Allen had been allowed to acquire other authors,
although Ruskin's works were always the mainstay of his list, and to
open a London office in 1882, in Bell Yard, near the law courts. The
two men remained friends and partners until Ruskin's death in 1900, by
which time Allen had moved to 156 Charing Cross Road and had
published Maeterlinck, and the first of Gilbert Murray's translations
from the Greek.

Next we should take Swan Sonnenschein & Co., because they were
to be associated with George Allen in one of the most distinguished
imprints of the twentieth century.

Sonnenschein's father had come to England from Moravia in 1848
and opened a school in Highbury, in north London. William Swan was
born in 1855, and started his publishing house at 15 Paternoster Square,
at the age of twenty-three. Nine years later he published Shaw's novel
An Unsocial Socialist and J. M. Barrie's *Better Dead*. In the same year,
1887, he took Herbert Wigram into partnership. Sonnenschein was a
young man with considerable flair, advising Shaw that although he did
not regret having published his novel, from which he had made nothing,
he thought the author would do better to write plays. He founded the
Muirhead Library of Philosophy and a whole series of works on the
social sciences. He became a member of the first Ethical Society in
England, publishing Hegel, Bergson, Bradley, Beatrice Webb and others.
In 1887, four years after Marx's death, he published the first English
translation of *Das Kapital*, edited by Friedrich Engels. This appeared
under the imprint of Swan Sonnenschein, Lowrey & Co., as the firm
was known until 1888 when Francis Lowrey emigrated to South Africa,

to be replaced in 1891 by Colonel Philip Hugh Dalbiac, whose *Dictionary of English Quotations* was issued in 1896, a year after the firm became a limited company.

William Swan Sonnenschein was a publisher of marked intellectual vigour and business acumen, who was too ambitious to rest upon his laurels. His further adventures in the book trade, undertaken only when he knew that his firstborn was strong enough to survive without him, will be related in the next part.

Bradley Thomas Batsford, an orphan from Hertford, was apprenticed to his cousin Bickers of Leicester Square, a bookseller who believed in giving the public discounts. Young Batsford did the collecting, and because Bickers was boycotted by some publishers for price-cutting, he had to lurk about near Simpkin Marshall's until after closing hours when he was let in by the back door to get the books he wanted. As closing time was certainly eight p.m., and sometimes nine, Bradley Thomas had precious few leisure hours, but the training no doubt stood him in good stead when he came to run his own business. The first shop, lit by a lamp and candles, opened in 1843 at 30 High Holborn. A few years later Batsford moved to No. 52 where he stayed until 1893 when a further move was made to No. 94 in the same street. He had three sons; Bradley, Henry, who died of typhoid when he was only thirty-one, and Herbert, who gave up studying law when his brother died, and entered the family firm. Publishing had become a sideline as early as the 1850s with James Colling's *Details of Gothic Architecture*. The Batsford sons later gained a reputation for their architectural books, and by 1897, when Harry Batsford, son of the short-lived Henry, joined his uncles and grandfather, they were as active in producing books as in retailing them. There was little formal delegation of duties; each partner was a jack-of-all-trades and their shop was a meeting-place for bookmen from all parts of the world. Harry Batsford recalled in later life that although the principals worked until eight every evening (towards the end Bradley Thomas would knock off at six as a concession to his advanced age) there was a pleasant and leisurely chattiness about their business life. He learned his craft in a very cosmopolitan atmosphere of 'little Japanese, in spectacles, in search of data for the establishment of shipyards and steelworks', and of publishers and booksellers from Paris and Leipzig, and squires building up their country-house libraries. His uncles, he recalled, did not send telegrams or live on the end of a telephone to conduct their day's work, although one of them loved to dictate and had an ambition, unfulfilled, alas, to go a day's railway journey dictating all the way.

George Hutchinson, who had been a traveller for Hodder & Stoughton, founded his imprint in 1880 and issued paperbacks, 'the sixpenny Blacks', some fifty-five years before Allen Lane's similarly priced

Penguins appeared. There were twenty-five titles in the first year, and their success enabled him to move out of his basement office into 34 Paternoster Square. He also pioneered part-work at a halfpenny per issue, another branch of publishing that was to be successfully revived in the late 1960s. His first bound book was *By Order of the Czar*, a novel by James Hatton (1886).

A neighbour of Hutchinson's in Paternoster Square was T. Fisher Unwin, who had also been with Hodder, first as an apprentice with Jackson, Walford & Hodder, later as a senior salesman who travelled the Continent. In 1882 he set up on his own, purchasing the small list of Marshall, Japp & Co. for £1,000, a sum he did not have to pay for six months by which time he was able to meet it from his profits. Unwin's father, Jacob, founded the Gresham Press, and his mother came from a family of printers and booksellers in Dunbar and Haddington, who started *The Cheap Magazine* twenty years before Chambers brought out their journal. Fisher Unwin recognized a growing market, in a better educated public, for the unknown writer who would previously have had to show exceptional promise to have been published for the circu-lating libraries. He started the Pseudonym Library in the brave belief that if a book had the right literary quality it would succeed. Paper-bound volumes by W. B. Yeats, Olive Schreiner and others were issued in this library, and he also brought out the early work of Somerset Maugham and Joseph Conrad. Conrad was the contribution to his list of Edward Garnett, the most distinguished of publisher's readers, who joined Unwin in the unlikely role of packer. As he was totally inept at packing, and indeed at anything except reading, it was natural that he should instead stay to advise on manuscripts, which, after he had quarrelled with Unwin, he went on to do with Heinemann and later with Duckworth and Cape. Garnett married Constance Black who became famous for her translations from the Russian.

It was in the 1880s also that more specialized publishers began to make an impact. Iliffe, of Coventry, opened a London office to cope with the new national enthusiasm for cycling, a recreation which some feared would kill the reading habit, but which developed a whole literature of its own. H.F.L., concerned with accountancy and law, was founded in 1884. F. C. C. Watts, who published on his own behalf and also for the Rationalist Association, brought out the first issue of the *Agnostic Journal* in the same year.

A. H. Bullen, an Elizabethan scholar, rediscovered the poems of Thomas Campion and reprinted them through the Chiswick Press in 1889. He also contracted with J. C. Nimmo to publish a collection of old English plays, and the works of various poets. Later he became a partner in Lawrence & Bullen and, still later, founded the Shakespeare Head Press in premises close to Shakespeare's birthplace in Stratford-upon-Avon. Further north in Bradford, Lund, Humphries & Co. began as printers, but took to publishing as well in 1885. In London, the brothers W. H. and L. Collingridge began publishing their journal *Amateur Gardening* in 1884. It was an obvious step for the Collingridge brothers to supplement magazine publishing with book publishing in their own subject, and their editor, T. W. Sanders, wrote the standard textbook which, updated from time to time, was still selling briskly in 1970.

What was to become the largest specialist publisher of all, Her Majesty's Stationery Office, first became an imprint to be reckoned with — and paid for — by the public in 1883, when it took over the issue of parliamentary papers. H.M.S.O. was established in 1786, but its actual publishing activities did not commence until well into the nineteenth century, when certain departmental publications began to be offered for sale. Before this it was primarily concerned with printing, and it did not become responsible for producing Hansard, the record of parliamentary debates, until 1909.

The most illustrious new names in publishing in the 'eighties came at the end of the decade, when Joseph Malaby Dent, William Heinemann and Algernon Methuen Marshall Stedman set up their respective houses. These three giants founded imprints which wielded enormous influence in popular education and publishing techniques throughout the whole period we are studying.

J. M. Dent was born in Darlington, where he was apprenticed to a book-binder whose business failed. At eighteen, in 1867, he followed his elder brother to London, arrived with 1s. 6d. in his pocket, and took up his trade again in Bucklersbury. Seven years later he opened his own bindery in Great Eastern Street, which he ran successfully for some fifteen years until it was burned down. In the same year his wife died. Rallying from these twin blows he carried on business in new premises and took up publishing because, according to Frank Swinnerton, who worked for him at one period, he couldn't obtain 'satisfactory sheets for the gift market'. Dent's associations with Toynbee Hall, in London's East End, suggested to him the need for a cheap pocket edition of Shakespeare. This was the origin of the Temple Shakespeare which was completed in forty volumes in 1896. Meanwhile he had produced the Temple Library — the first two titles were Lamb's *Essays of Elia*, and *Last Essays* — and earned the praise of Bernard Quaritch for 'the best piece of bookmaking for years'. The public, said Quaritch, would soon want to know more of the man who had made them. The man, according to Swinnerton, was less than medium height, lame, stingy and had a violent temper. 'He never praised; he paid very poorly; he frightened everybody who worked for him.' Swinnerton confesses to having been afraid of him, although Dent liked him, and for some years trusted only him to bring in his meagre lunch of a penny roll, butter, cheese, apple and ginger beer.

It is not an attractive portrait, but he must have appeared in a different light to others. He remarried in 1890, and went to Italy with the Toynbee Travellers Club. This journey suggested the Medieval Towns series of guidebooks to him and he was soon to be 'overwhelmingly, even passionately' engaged in his publishing, as he recalls in his memoirs. So much so that when Macmillan's offices in Bedford Street became vacant he took them over because of the building's associations with Tennyson, Kingsley, Huxley and Tom Hughes. This was in 1898, soon after he had started the Temple Classics, with Sir Israel Gollancz (uncle of Victor Gollancz) as editor for the first five years. Dent also brought out a series of eighteenth-century novelists and Malory's *Morte d'Arthur*, illustrated by Aubrey Beardsley. Beardsley, then nineteen, was introduced to him by a city bookseller, Frederick Evans. The book came out in monthly parts in 1893–4, and the publisher confessed his joy at producing it. He must also have had great satisfaction in seeing a quarter of a million of his Shakespeares selling each year and, very probably, there was already stirring in his mind the idea of Everyman's Library which was to prove his greatest monument.

William Heinemann was born in Surbiton in 1863 of German-Jewish stock. His father, naturalized in 1856, came from Hanover; his mother from Manchester; from them he inherited the positive characteristics of two formidable races. He was tough, cosmopolitan, cultivated, successful in business and had immense energy and single-mindedness. He learned his publishing with Nicholas Trubner, of Ludgate Hill, after finishing his education in Dresden.

Trubner, whose deepest interest was in Oriental subjects, died in 1884 and Heinemann became largely responsible for running the business which was bought eventually by Kegan Paul & Co. Kegan Paul had bought Henry King & Co. of Cornhill in the 'seventies, and when a son of Richard Trench (Archbishop of Dublin, and prolific writer) joined them the partnership became known as Kegan Paul, Trench, Trubner & Co. Perhaps Heinemann saw no future for himself in this firm; more likely, he knew he must operate alone anyway, so in 1889, when Cassell turned down Hall Caine's *The Bondman*, he bought the novel and issued it on February 1st, 1890, establishing an author and an imprint with one blow. His offices were at 21 Bedford Street, where a tailor had the ground floor and the Camera Club the first.

Early publications of his included Whistler's *The Gentle Art of Making Enemies* and *Twenty-Five Years of Secret Service* by 'Major Le Caron', the pseudonym of a British government spy who disclosed the secrets of the Sinn Feiners in America, thereby earning the enmity of various Irish

M.P.s and collecting numerous threats of libel action, none of which matured.

Heinemann persuaded the tailor to give up his shop when the Camera Club vacated the first floor, and took possession of the whole of the Bedford Street building. From there he began to issue, in translation, the works of great European writers of the nineteenth century. This was to be his peculiar contribution to publishing, puncturing the innate chauvinism of most of his colleagues. (Henry Vizetelly, to be strictly accurate, had first introduced Dostoevsky, Tolstoy and Lermontov to the English public in the 'eighties; but he got no thanks for it, and when he had turned to French literature and had had Zola translated, he was prosecuted for his pains.)

By the time Heinemann established himself there was a reading public for the great Russians, and in addition to them he published translations of Björnson and Ibsen (the famous William Archer translations of the latter were first published by one Walter Scott) and of Gerhart Hauptmann, Georg Brandes, Guy de Maupassant and Gabriele d'Annunzio. He offered the British the opportunity of appreciating contemporary European literature and he also, for a time, competed with Tauchnitz by operating on the Continent with English language editions. Sir Edmund Gosse edited his International Library and, later on, his Literature of the World.

Heinemann published the plays of Arthur Wing Pinero but turned down Bernard Shaw's because, he said, the public would not buy plays: he produced a ledger showing Pinero's accounts to make his point. (His own plays, it should be added, were brought out by John Lane.) Swinnerton describes him as above middle height, with a pale, round face and a rather resentful mouth. In addition to his translations he published numerous British authors and was the bitter enemy of literary agents whom he suspected (possibly, with justice) of luring authors away from him. Certainly, amongst the authors he failed to keep were Kipling, Robert Hichens, W. J. Locke and H. G. Wells — but then nobody kept Wells for long.

Algernon Methuen Marshall Stedman was born in 1856, the son of a doctor and descendant of the John Methuen who negotiated in 1709 the trade treaty between Britain and Portugal which bears his name. Stedman, a classical scholar, opened a school in Surrey where, according to a former pupil, he gave the boys 'something to get on with by themselves' whilst he wrote textbooks on his dais. These were published initially by George Bell, but the author had publishing ambitions himself and began approaching well-known writers for books. Not all of them were discouraging, and in 1889 he rented a back room in Bury Street, Bloomsbury, in the premises of one W. W. Gibbins, a remainder merchant. His first book was a novel by Edna Lyall called *Derrick*

Vaughan, Novelist, and it sold 25,000 copies in its first year. Gibbins was appointed trade manager and soon had much to manage, because Stedman bought his school books back from Bell and published them himself. In his second year there were twenty new titles and he rented a second room; two years later he issued Kipling's *Barrack-Room Ballads* which was an overnight success. It begins to read like a fairy story, and it remained like this despite a trade depression in the mid-'nineties. Stedman gave up his school, changed his name to Methuen in 1899 and began to broaden his list. He published E. F. Benson, Stanley Weyman (*Under the Red Robe*), Anthony Hope and, biggest success of all, Marie Corelli. By then he had moved to Essex Street, where the firm was to remain until after the Second World War, and had begun to issue *Methuen's Gazette and Literary Notes,* the first number of which records that 'few books have ever been received with such shrieks of abuse as *Barabbas.* Miss Corelli is fortunately case-hardened, and the darts of the critics leave no wound.' The *Gazette* also announced various volumes dealing with astronomy, botany, electricity and meteorology, in addition to which Stedman himself edited a series of school examination test papers and later promoted a University Extension Series. From its earliest days the Methuen list was a splendid amalgam of fiction, non-fiction and academic works, catering for all brows, but with an eye to building a healthy back list. The schoolmaster-turned-publisher seemed to have intuitively understood the basis of successful publishing; many of the works he commissioned, or wrote himself, were still in print long after his death.*

The 'nineties brought many new names, one of the first being Edward Arnold (not to be confused with E. J. Arnold of Leeds, the West Country printer who had laid the foundation of his huge educational supply business twenty years earlier). Edward Arnold was the grandson of Arnold of Rugby, and a cousin of Mrs Humphrey Ward. Like his namesake of Leeds, his list became noted for standard school-books. A year after he opened he became a neighbour of Heinemann and Macmillan in Bedford Street.

1890 also saw the revival of the house of Constable by the grandson of the great Edinburgh publisher who crashed in 1826. The third Archibald Constable retired quite soon, handing over to his nephew H. Arthur Doubleday after only three years. In 1895 Doubleday took O. Kyllmann (ex-Macmillan in London and New York) and W. M. Meredith as partners. Meredith's famous father, George, fell out with Chapman & Hall at this time, as has been related; the man went to Ward, Lock but his books went to Constable, who subsequently issued his complete works firstly in thirty-two volumes, later in seventeen.

* I am indebted for much of the information about Algernon Methuen to unpublished notes by J. Alan White.

Soon after Constable had an enormous success with the explorer Nansen's *Farthest North*, for which they paid £10,000 (a huge sum for those days), and in 1899 they began publication of the highly ambitious Victoria History of the Counties of England, which Doubleday planned personally. Another of his ventures was *The Complete Peerage*, a work which attracts certain vested interests and has, therefore, been saved by outside money on several occasions.

Although, as we have seen, Dent published Beardsley's illustrated edition of *Morte d'Arthur*, the artist is more familiarly associated with The Bodley Head and John Lane. Lane founded the notorious *Yellow Book* in 1894 and employed Beardsley as art editor. The literary editor was Henry Harland and the magazine, during its brief life, was to epitomize the aesthetic movement of the 'nineties.

John Lane, who began his working life as a railway clerk, persuaded Elkin Matthews, who had a bookshop in Exeter, to open instead in Vigo Street, London W.1. There in 1887 they opened at the sign of The Bodley Head, a name chosen not only because of the famous library, but because its founder had been, like Lane, a Devonian. John Lane, in this brilliant decade, published Richard Le Gallienne, who relates in *The Romantic 'Nineties* how Beardsley tried his publishers' patience by slipping into his drawings minute indecencies which often could only be discerned with the aid of a magnifying glass. John Lane felt it necessary to ask his friends to inspect the drawings thoroughly before he put them into his *Yellow Book*. This problem was resolved when Beardsley left in 1895 and became art editor of *Savoy*, another short-lived production. Also published from the sign of The Bodley Head, which moved across Vigo Street when Lane and Matthews dissolved their partnership, were Lord Alfred Douglas, Francis Thompson, Max Beerbohm and George Moore.

Grant Richards began publishing in the mid-'nineties, and one of his first books was A. E. Housman's *A Shropshire Lad*. He had the curious contractual arrangement with the poet that he didn't have to pay any royalty as long as he kept the book in print at 6d. He also published Bernard Shaw for a while, as well as bringing out his own novels and founding the World's Classics Series at 1s. per volume. Among his successful publications were The Dumpy Books, which included *Little Black Sambo*, one of the most popular children's titles of the century. With others in the series it later passed to Chatto & Windus, and was denounced as 'racist' in a lengthy *Times* correspondence in 1971. Richards was the son of an Oxford don; he left the City of London school at sixteen to work for the wholesalers Hamilton, Adams & Co., who amalgamated with Simpkin Marshall during his time with them. He followed this experience by some years in journalism before starting in publishing on his own account with a guaranteed capital of £1,400.

This proved inadequate, and Shaw said that it was Grant's tragedy that he was a publisher who had allowed himself to fall in love with literature.

Several other houses started in the 'nineties. Among them were the Studio (which remained family-owned for many decades); Gale & Polden (1892), publishers of militaria from an address in Aldershot; the Temple Press (1891); Gerald Duckworth (for whom Jonathan Cape was to work); J. M. Watkins (still a publisher and bookseller in Cecil Court, off Charing Cross Road, in 1970); John Tiranti; and the first of the redbrick university presses, at Liverpool. In Scotland, Glasgow University Press was founded in the seventeenth century (see p. 161), and Aberdeen University Press in 1840. In 1893 William Morris, previously published by Reeves & Turner, started the Kelmscott Press, inspired by Ruskin's example to do-it-himself. He had already decided to auction his books as he produced them, and to do without a publisher for the series of books which was to do so much to revive the art of printing, but Reeves & Turner had continued to be imprinted on them. From 1893, with few exceptions, they bore the legend 'Published by William Morris at the Kelmscott Press'. They became very rare items indeed, and when in 1971 Blackwell's issued a catalogue offering a complete set, plus a few duplicates, of fifty-three items most of them were priced at £100 or over, two at £1,250 and the Chaucer, one of 425 copies, at £1,975.

In 1900 Ruskin, Oscar Wilde and R. D. Blackmore died; *The World's Work Magazine* was started by Heinemann; *Lord Jim, Love and Mr Lewisham* and *The Oxford Book of English Verse* were published; and Arnold Bennett, aged thirty-two, became literary adviser to Pearson's, a popular magazine-publishing company akin to Newnes's, with which it was later to amalgamate.

In 1901, George Harrap was founded, *Kim* was published and Ginn & Co., American educational publishers formerly represented by Edward Arnold, opened up in London. Salisbury was prime minister, the Boer War still raged and Queen Victoria died.

5

Bookselling: London

The booksellers' plight; Hatchard's; Bumpus; Simpkin Marshall; W. H. Smith & Son; Commercial libraries — Mudie's; Stoneham's; Gilbert & Field; Alfred Wilson; Jones & Evans; Alfred Denny; Robert Lamley; Hachette; S.P.C.K.; Wyman & Son; Seager; William Dawson; Edward Stanford; entries under 'Booksellers' in Post Office Directories; Charing Cross Road and Cecil Court become centres of bookselling.

When we turn to the booksellers we find fewer familiar names than amongst the publishers. This is partly because some of the publishers who survived from 1870 to 1970 were in 1870 also booksellers; partly because some of the booksellers had concentrated entirely on antiquarian books by the twentieth century and therefore fall outside the scope of this study; and partly because of the fierce Victorian price-cutting, and the slump between the two world wars.

In no period during this history have booksellers *en masse* presented an especially cheerful image to the public. They have always appeared to be suffering from real or imaginary wounds inflicted upon them by publishers, and they have fallen prey to correspondents to *The Times*, who have attacked booksellers far more readily than other retailers whose suppliers failed to meet delivery dates. In late-Victorian days booksellers, with a few exceptions, were certainly not among the more privileged of shopkeepers, nor were many of them booksellers pure and simple. They sold anything, from patent medicines to packets of envelopes, from sewing machines to ink, to supplement their trade in books. And many of them dealt in secondhand books which did not come labelled with a price, off which they were expected to give the public a handsome discount.

Amongst booksellers, however, there were certain aristocrats. Hatchard's for example (see pp. 207–9), had been established at one or another address in Piccadilly since 1797. The first Hatchard, John, started with £5, and died in 1849 worth £100,000. He was succeeded by his second son, Thomas (the elder had gone into the church), who outlived his father by only nine years, but it was in his time that Edwin Shepherd became apprenticed to the business for seven years, on payment of £200. After Thomas's death, the founder's great-grandson Henry Hudson took over, and very soon the firm lost large sums publishing *Atalanta*, a magazine for girls. Such was the crisis that in the

282

late, 'eighties Hatchard's was offered for sale, and Shepherd, then manager, bought it. In 1881 he had taken on A. L. Humphreys as assistant at £1 per week. Humphreys had been apprenticed to a Bristol bookseller who moved to Paternoster Row where the young man was paid 15s. for his weekly labours. When, after a year, he asked for a rise, this was refused; hence his removal to Hatchard's. He became a partner in 1891, and two years later wrote the first history of the firm. In the same year (1893), Cecil Rhodes visited the shop and announced that he wished to fill one room of an old Dutch farmhouse he had purchased with copies of the books which Gibbon had used in writing *The Decline and Fall of the Roman Empire*. Those volumes which were not already in English were to be translated, no book was to be expurgated, fine bindings must be used and the workers well paid. The task was never completed because of Rhodes's early death, but there are some hundreds of volumes in the library of Groote Schuur, bound as he intended. Shepherd sold the publishing side of Hatchard's to Rivington. Later, his two sons joined him and Humphreys at 187 Piccadilly, where in 1895 Herbert Jonathan Cape, aged sixteen, was employed as an errand boy.

Another pedigree name was Bumpus. The first, also a John, started as a publisher and bookseller in Clerkenwell in about 1790 and later moved to Holborn Bars which was handy for the Hampstead coach. Mrs Bumpus's hospitable back parlour was said to be a familiar haunt for students and booklovers before taking their seats, although one must wonder how many students lived in Hampstead in those days when it was still a village four miles from London. Thomas Bumpus, friend of Dickens, continued the business, and it was his son who started the Oxford Street shop of John and Edward Bumpus. The second John died in 1880, aged sixty-two.

In 1870 the wholesale bookseller was a vital link in the distribution of books and for most of our period the leading name, for the home trade, was that of Simpkin Marshall & Co. Its founder was Benjamin Crosby, who travelled regularly and systematically throughout the country and, according to one handed-down story, showed great enterprise in investing in publishers' stock. He sold his business in 1814 to Mr W. Simpkin and to Mr R. Marshall, one of his assistants, and by 1859 these gentlemen were well enough known for *The Bookseller* to refer to John Menzies, of Edinburgh, as 'the Simpkin and Marshall of Scotland'.

It was in that latter year also that the principal wholesale houses took the magnanimous decision to close on Saturdays, *in the Summer months*, at 2 p.m., in order to give their assistants the opportunity for recreation. On May 7th the assistants celebrated this seasonal release from servicing orders by playing a cricket match at Blackheath. The match ended in a draw; it is not recorded how those assistants who did not love cricket spent their new-found freedom. It is obvious that some people did not approve of the use made of these gained hours; in 1870, *The Bookseller* was offering prizes for bibliographical knowledge because, it was conceded, some booksellers' assistants 'were deficient in precise knowledge'. Considering the 'precise knowledge' that any and every booksellers' assistant is expected to have at any time it is scarcely surprising that similar incentive schemes were regularly advocated and some (without incentives) actually introduced at intervals.

In 1889 three wholesale houses amalgamated to form Simpkin, Marshall, Hamilton, Kent & Co., which was the basis of the twentieth-century Simpkin's, and the firm where so many who later became independent booksellers learned their trade. Frank Hanson, who was a representative for Simpkin's, left them to become a partner with Joseph Truslove of Oxford Street in 1893 — hence Truslove & Hanson, one of the best known of London's smaller bookselling chains in the decades ahead. A year later Joseph Shaylor became managing director of Simpkin's, and devoted his time not only to running the great wholesaling house, but to writing about bookselling and books in the *Publishers' Circular*, *Chambers's Journal*, the *Cornhill*, and numerous other magazines. His subjects ranged from *Bookselling and the Distribution of Books* to *Hymns, Hymn-Writers and Hymn-Books*.*

Some of the early history of W. H. Smith and Son has already been related. The first Smith was not 'W.H.' but 'H.W. — Henry Walton — and he is mentioned in the rate books as being a stationer, at 4 Little Grosvenor Street, in 1792. Possibly, indeed probably, he was there before that because he died in 1792 and his widow took over the business. When she died in 1816 her sons Henry Edward and William Henry succeeded, trading as booksellers, agents and binders, as well as newsagents. Two years later they opened new premises in Duke Street, and three years after that started a reading-room in the Strand. In 1828, Henry, who was apparently more interested in reading books than in selling them (a problem which has beset most booksellers in their relations with their partners and assistants) amicably left his brother, who carried on alone. Thus W. H. Smith; in 1846 '& son' was added. W. H. Smith II entered Parliament in 1868, by which time the family firm had spread amongst the new railways of England and was already becoming something of a national institution. The political success of this Smith had strange repercussions through the Dublin book business of J. K. Johnstone, purchased about 1850. Charles Eason was appointed manager of the shop in 1856, but thirty years later, when W. H. Smith II became chief secretary for Ireland, the new minister correctly decided that his political and business responsibilities were incompatible, and so transferred the Dublin branch to Eason and his son.

* For complete list, see Bibliography.

On this Smith's death in 1891 his widow was made Viscountess Hambleden and their son, the second viscount, entered the business and became its head two years later. Charles Awdry, a friend of his father's, was a partner at this time, but William Lethbridge, whom W. H. Smith II had brought into active participation in 1858, retired in 1886. Alfred Dyke Acland, who had married a daughter of W. H. Smith II, came into the firm in 1885 and remained with it until after the First World War. W. H. Smith III, the second Viscount Hambleden, was joined by Charles Harry St John Hornby, who became a partner in 1894.

It was during the reigns of the early Smiths that wholesale houses were opened in Birmingham, Manchester and Liverpool. The firm's importance was recognized by *The Times*, which announced in 1854 that until 6.45 a.m. daily they would supply only W. H. Smith & Son. Bookselling activities in a large way were to develop later, as the result of a crisis in Edwardian times, but W. H. Smith & Son were already important to publishers through their circulating libraries. The right of W. H. Smith's management to decide what they should or should not stock caused no less controversy in the 1890s than in the 1970s. In 1894 they were in trouble because their buyer, William Faux, refused to take George Moore's *Esther Waters* for Smith's readers; another novelist, T. Mullet Ellis (less well remembered) was so incensed by being denied distribution through W. H. Smith because the title of his book included the word God, that he stood (unsuccessfully) against Smith III in a parliamentary election.

Pre-eminence in the circulating library field belonged not to W. H. Smith but to Charles Edward Mudie. He was the king-pin, and when he died in 1890 he left a thriving business with a world-wide reputation. His fame was to be perpetuated in the works of Oscar Wilde, among others, and by the end of the Victorian era, Mudie's were dictating their terms to publishers, backed up by competitors, and announcing that no more three-decker novels would be acceptable to their circulating libraries. Booksellers since have seldom, if ever, been in a position to influence publishing policy so dramatically.

Stoneham's, the leading City booksellers, were often in dispute with publishers about price-cutting. The firm was started by E. J. Stoneham in 1874. In 1879 he opened his eighth branch at 4 Charlotte Row, Mansion House, in premises which had been a bookseller's under different ownership for many years. Stoneham was said to control his various branches personally, inspecting their stock and accounts minutely and daily, and yet being at his headquarters sufficiently often to buy every item of stock for all branches. Sometimes he would subscribe as many as 10,000 copies of a book. He never, apparently, allowed his own good taste to disturb his judgment about a popular book; he exploited the system of underselling without condoning it, certainly to the disadvantage of his suburban colleagues whose customers travelled every weekday to the City where Stoneham operated. In such a homogeneous area as the City of London—'the golden square mile'—it was possible for him to understand his customers' tastes as in no other place in Britain; certainly there wasn't a comparably affluent public anywhere in the world in so small a market. He was bold, decisive and unsparing of his energy. It is not surprising that he died at the early age of fifty, earning the epitaph in *The Bookseller* 'the well-known underselling bookseller of Cheapside and elsewhere'. He was succeeded by his sons F. and E. Stoneham.

Some of Stoneham's assistants, subjected perhaps to less strain than their master, lasted longer. J. W. White, who began as an assistant in 1885 and eventually became manager of the almost kiosk-sized branch in narrow Cullum Street, retired only in 1939, and then temporarily, because he was recalled for further service when younger men joined the forces. He finally ended his sixty years of bookselling in 1945.

Despite competition from Stoneham, other booksellers held their own in the City. Gilbert & Field started at 18 Gracechurch Street in 1851 and were bought in 1885 by Alfred Wilson, who continued to operate successfully, in a building designed soon after the great fire of London, for many decades after Stoneham died. In Queen Street Frederick Evans, Shaw's 'ideal bookseller', presided over Jones & Evans and, according to Grant Richards, dictated to the City what it should read. Shaw confirmed this view, maintaining that the only reason his *The Quintessence of Ibsenism* sold was because Evans liked it and stood no nonsense from his customers. (This same Evans 'discovered' Aubrey Beardsley — see p. 277.)

Farther west, in the Strand, Alfred Denny took his brother into partnership in 1886, and in Kensington, Robert Lamley (a maternal great-uncle of Harold Sweeten, of Preston and Blackpool, (see pp. 296 and 543) had a shop in Exhibition Road, where later Charles Young was to become a celebrated bookseller, and friend and publisher of Arnold Bennett.

The firm of Hachette, founded in 1826 in France, where it pioneered pocket editions for railway travellers, opened its London branch at 16 King William Street in 1859. During the Franco-Prussian war Hachette's London manager began publishing on his own account, when he could not get supplies from Paris. He would have been applauded by the founder, Louis Hachette, who turned bookseller when the college where he was training to be a teacher was closed for disseminating liberal ideas.

The S.P.C.K. was operating at various addresses in the City and Westminster, fervently selling Christian and other literature. Gordon &

Gotch, exporters, had started as early as 1853: the Army & Navy Stores, founded in 1871, sold books to its members (and for several decades only to its members) usually at 25 per cent discount, apart from books on naval and military subjects which, curiously, were subject to but 15 per cent off the published price. This must have been because the publishers supplied even the Army & Navy Stores at short discounts.

The booksellers who claimed the oldest heritage of all, however, were Messrs Wyman & Son, although they were known by that appellation only from 1872. They traced their descent from the great Jacob Tonson, through the printing firm of John Watts (Benjamin Franklin worked as a journeyman for him in 1728), who was succeeded by Edward Cox, whose progeny formed Cox Brothers & Wyman in 1855. The first Wyman, Charles, was a printer; he became interested in the bookselling side of the business, which later developed from retailing into wholesaling. The connection is tenuous, because the actual book-shop of Tonson III ceased trading in 1767; but genealogists may argue the claim of Wyman, whose name was perpetuated in Wyman-Marshall of the 1960s until it became incorporated into John Menzies, another great name, of which more later.

East of the City, down in dockland, John Seager, an engineer from Nottingham who had worked as a ship repairer in a Blackwall yard, opened a shop in 1868 in East India Dock Road for nautical instruments, charts and marine and technical handbooks. He divided his premises into four small rooms—the Chart Room, the Captain's Room, the Library and the Stationery Shop. He later took over responsibility for supplying ship's libraries, and his grandson still owned the business in 1970.

In 1892 William Dawson's, since 1809 a business similar to W. H. Smith's, moved to Chancery Lane. They had been purchased by Sampson Low a year before. Dawson's became well known in the wholesale export field, which was then an expanding business, because it was beneficial for overseas buyers to channel their orders through one London agent, on a commission basis, rather than open accounts with each individual publisher. Another such was Castle, Lamb & Storr, in Salisbury Square, E.C.4. Here one Frederick Joiner was taken on in 1893, aged thirteen, at 5s per week, hours of work 8 a.m. to 7 p.m. It was more often, Joiner recalled in an article in the *Publishers' Circular* in 1951, 8 a.m. to 9 p.m., during which time he delivered newspapers and carried out other odd jobs well enough to earn a 2s. 6d. increase. More will be heard of him later, when he became one of the eccentrics of the London trade.

At the turn of the century an established London bookseller, Edward Stanford of Cockspur Street, suffering the compulsory purchase of his premises by the London County Council, decided to give up general bookselling and remove to Long Acre, on the fringe of Covent Garden, where he settled down to specialize in the selling and production of maps and allied products. His assistant for nineteen years at Cockspur Street, Hugh Rees, took over the general bookselling and stationery sides and opened in elegant premises in Pall Mall (shades of Dodsley) where he was to remain until more than halfway through the twentieth century.

There were many other London booksellers during this period, and my choice is necessarily limited and eclectic. The actual number of businesses engaged in bookselling in the capital at any particular date is difficult to calculate, because these were the days before the Associated Booksellers issued a handbook of members. In the 1856 Post Office Directory there are some nine hundred entries under 'Booksellers', but they included publishers and stationers as well. Two agricultural booksellers are noted, and three botanical, and there are nine under Architectural, engineering and scientific. Twenty-eight are listed as dealing in foreign books, including the eminent names of James Bain and David Nutt. There are seven medical and sixteen theological.

The 1877 Directory does not give these categories and the total number had by then fallen to around eight hundred, which included Kimpton at 82 High Holborn, and H. K. Lewis at 136 Gower Street, both specialists in medical literature. Bertram Dobell was working from Queen Crescent, Haverstock Hill, in north London, at that date, but by 1893 he had arrived in the newly formed Charing Cross Road, as had Kegan Paul, Trench & Trubner and a number of other antiquarians. In that year Stoneham had nine branches in the City; specialist nautical bookseller neighbours in the Square Mile, established by 1884, were Imray & Son and Norie & Wilson, both in the Minories, and later to amalgamate. Williams & Norgate, experts in Orientalia, were in 14 Henrietta Street, later the headquarters of Victor Gollancz.

The lists in these directories for Paternoster Row include many names already mentioned but even more who were but dimly, if at all, remembered in 1970.

As Charing Cross Road quickly became a centre of bookselling, so did one of the paved ways off it leading to St Martin's Lane. Cecil Court was a thoroughfare long before the more famous artery which it joins at one end, but it was not until the 'nineties that booksellers began to rent small shops there.

6

Bookselling: Scotland

Glasgow: John Smith—also opened a circulating library; W. & R. Holmes; Grant Educational; Edinburgh: Black; Blackwood; Chambers; Livingstone; Murray; Oliver & Boyd; James Thin; John Menzies; Charles Smith; Douglas & Foulis; William Brown; Frederick Bauermeister; Aberdeen: James G. Bisset; Paisley: McDougal Bros.

Bowes & Bowes of Cambridge claimed in 1970 to be the oldest bookshop in the kingdom, as there had been a bookshop on their site since the sixteenth century. But John Smith of Glasgow had the oldest continuous heritage, with its name unchanged since the founder set up shop on the north side of Trongate in 1751. Glasgow then had a population of about 20,000 and Trongate was near its western border. Smith, the youngest son of the Laird of Craigend, Strathblane, was twenty-seven when he became a bookseller; he had previously been a soldier, and had fought and been wounded in Flanders. He moved to New Street in 1757.

There had been a university in Glasgow for three hundred years, and in the mid-eighteenth century Adam Smith, an ex-student, joined the faculty which then included the chemists Joseph Black and William Cullen and, most important of all to us, James Moor, Greek scholar and sometime librarian, who edited the fine books referred to in part one (p. 161). These were printed by the Foulis Brothers and Robert Urie with type founded by Alexander Wilson at Camlachie.

Bookselling prospered in such an ambience. In his third year, John Smith opened the first circulating library in Glasgow and, ten years later, he moved again back into Trongate into premises which measured 16ft × 14ft. and which Smith called 'commodious'. Sometime in the following decade the second John was taken into partnership, and in 1781 the founder retired at the early age of fifty-seven, but lived on until 1814 by which time his grandson had long been in the firm. The first John Smith was pictured late in life as upright, square-jawed, with high forehead and prominent cheekbones—an austere but not unkindly face. He died a nonagenerian, having outlived three wives.

According to custom Smith's sold tobacco, snuff and tea in their early days, but 'other lines', apart from stationery, were gradually dropped, and even the circulating library seems to have been regarded as something of a nuisance for most of its life. In 1828 Smith's tried to sell the library, by now called the 'Select Reading Club' but no one would buy, and in 1892, when the shop was moved for the eighth time, it was given up for lack of space. Publishing had begun in 1808 and became an important sideline. The third John, who liked to refer to himself as 'John Smith, Ygst', was a friend of Walter Scott and of Lockhart. He had a high domed forehead, like his grandfather, but a rounder, more sympathetic face; his literary and antiquarian attainments were recognized by Glasgow University, which awarded him an honorary LL.D. When he died in 1849 the Smith line ended, and David Watson, an ex-apprentice who had become a partner, gained sole control. A year later another ex-apprentice, John Knox, joined Watson, and their sons remained in partnership until the business became a limited company in 1909.

In 1870, when John Smith's were operating from their sixth premises, in St Vincent Street, William and Robert Love Holmes started in Dunlop Street. Five years later William left to form a wholesale newspaper business and Robert, with Peter Kyle as partner, continued to run the steadily expanding book side. From 1897 the ranks of Glasgow booksellers and publishers were extended to include the Grant Educational Co. Ltd, started by Donald Grant, who lived to see its golden jubilee. It was originally intended to supply schools with books and equipment, but soon developed into publishing its own textbooks as well.

In 1863 Edinburgh proudly boasted that it had more bookshops per head of population than any city in the British Isles. When, thirteen years later, a meeting was held to form an association there, the forty-six founder members included such names as Black, Blackwood, Chambers, Livingstone, Murray and Oliver & Boyd, with whom we have already dealt in the publishing section, and others, equally distinguished, who were primarily booksellers. Some idea of the manner in which publishers and booksellers subsequently split their functions may be gathered from this list.

The first James Thin was apprenticed to the bookseller James McIntosh of North College Street before he was twelve years old; he earned 2s. 6d. per week, worked a twelve-hour day, and had to provide his own pen and pencil. He received an annual increase of 6d. per week until his apprenticeship ceased in 1841, when he procured the handsome salary of £35 a year. Seven years later a bookseller called Rickard failed. Thin bought his stock and fittings and a lease of the shop in Infirmary Street, conveniently near to the university. The familiar tale of expansion and removal follows. The twelve-hour day which Thin had worked as an apprentice was increased to twelve and a half now that he was his own boss. He arrived on South Bridge in 1855 and began to absorb properties around him as his business grew. In the 'seventies and 'eighties he took over various other booksellers, and at the turn of the century he remained active in his shop, and married for the second time. In the centenary booklet put out by his descendants, the first James Thin is portrayed as a whitehaired and heavily bearded patriarch wearing a skullcap — a clear brained Scottish Lear whose daughters always knew their place.

Preceding Thin were, amongst others, Robert Grant (1804), John Menzies and Charles Smith all of Princes Street. The latter sold in 1847 to Alexander Edmondston and David Douglas, who subsequently started a Select English and Foreign Library and Reading Club, with subscriptions of one guinea and upwards. When this partnership was dissolved Douglas, with his librarian Thomas Foulis, set up at 9 Castle Street. In the same year William Brown's business was opened.

John Menzies began, also in Princes Street, in 1833. Menzies was then aged twenty-five, and had had the 'stiff and joyless' experience of being apprenticed to an Edinburgh bookseller. This ended, mercifully for him, when his father gave him £10 and advised him to seek his fortune elsewhere, He did so in London, where he found employment with the publisher Charles Tilt. When his father died suddenly he was recalled to Edinburgh to provide for his stepmother and two sisters. Tilt made him Scottish agent for the Miniature Library, and in 1837 he had the good luck to be appointed to act as well for Chapman & Hall, who were bringing out *Pickwick* in 1s. parts at that time. Four years later Menzies also became agent for *Punch*, and the wholesale newsagent had arrived; so too had the publisher, because he began to issue Scottish guidebooks and volumes on the costumes of the clans. In 1843 he married and took his bride to honeymoon in his beloved London, where he introduced her to his numerous trade friends.

Back in Edinburgh he went on expanding his business with renewed energy. The railways attracted his attention because the termini bookstalls in Edinburgh were not in Scottish hands. He made sure in the next decade that on most stations elsewhere in his homeland the nameplate John Menzies appeared. A branch was opened in Glasgow in 1868, a year after he had made four of his loyal senior employees partners. When he died in 1879 his sons John R. and Charles succeeded him.

In 1900 another famous name, later associated with Edinburgh, reached Scotland when Frederick Bauermeister, with experience in Hanover, Paris and London, set up as a foreign bookseller in Glasgow, and boldly hung out a sign stating, AUSLANDISCHE-BUCHHAND-LUNG.

Other Scottish bookselling businesses founded in this period include James G. Bisset of Aberdeen (1879) and the McDougal Brothers, John and James, of Paisley (1865).

7

Bookselling: Provincial, Welsh, Irish

The university towns: Cambridge; Oxford; Durham. Other provincial towns: Nottingham; Bristol; Liverpool; Manchester; Blackpool; Sunderland; Oldham; Chester; Newcastle-on-Tyne; Birmingham; Grimsby; Hull; Lincoln; Rugby; Norwich; Ipswich; Reading; Lymington; Southampton; Winchester; Bournemouth; Eastbourne; Hove; Folkestone and Hythe; Dover; Ramsgate; Canterbury; Tunbridge Wells; Exeter; Cardiff; Swansea; St Helier, Jersey; Dublin.

Bowes & Bowes's claim to be the oldest bookshop in the kingdom is legitimate, despite the fact that the shop has passed through many hands. The first bookseller (also *stacyoner* and binder) at No. 1 Trinity Street, Cambridge, William Scarlett, was hauled before the Star Chamber accused of pirating the Countess of Pembroke's *Arcadia*, but he survived until 1617. In the next two centuries there were eleven different owners. Thurlbourne & Woodyer were the leading Cambridge booksellers of the eighteenth century, and after them came a man named 'Maps' Nicholson, who was said to supply essays and sermons, from an unknown source, for lazy undergraduates.

The next distinguished proprietors were Daniel and Alexander Macmillan, who were to become even more celebrated as publishers. They acquired the bookshop in Trinity Street in 1846 and soon became intimate friends with various dons whose works they published. Daniel recorded, 'We have commenced quite in a small way. If a large tree grows from this small seed we shall be grateful.' By the time of his early death the Macmillans were already established. Tennyson read *Maud* in the first-floor drawing-room above the shop; Charles Kingsley visited and became one of their authors; they gave lunch to Thackeray. When Daniel died they had been in business only eleven years. In 1858, a year later, a nephew, Robert Bowes, was sent to London to open an office for the publishing department. When this required Alexander Macmillan's full-time attention Bowes returned to Cambridge, where the bookshop became Macmillan & Bowes. Robert Bowes was a scholar as well as a bookseller and his researches were recognized by the university when they made him an honorary M.A. George Brimley Bowes, his son, became a partner in 1899.

In 1876 a new rival to Bowes appeared in William Heffer, who started a small post office and stationery shop, with a few books, at

104 Fitzroy Street. This business expanded so quickly that by 1900 the books were installed in premises in Petty Cury, and the stationery in nearby Sidney Street.

Another Cambridge business was Deighton Bell's, established, under another name, at 13 Trinity Street in 1700. Deighton became the proprietor in 1778 and the publisher George Bell, son of a Yorkshire bookseller, was in partnership there with one Mr Wright Smith from 1854 to 1870. Wright Smith's son carried it on until 1896, when Alfred Earnshaw Smith bought it. There was also Galloway & Porter. Galloway had a shop near the Round Church in the 1890s, later joined with Porter, and sold out to him about 1902 when he moved to Aberystwyth.

A character amongst Cambridge booksellers was Gustave David, born in Paris in 1860, and later the owner of a stall in the market-place of the university town. He later acquired the respectability of a shop in St Edward's Passage but his pitch in the market still existed in 1970. David was highly regarded by members of the faculty, who lunched him on one occasion and, after his death, had the university press issue a volume in his honour.

The most famous business associated with the other ancient university, Oxford, was started by Benjamin Harris Blackwell in 1846. However, this date is not strictly accurate, as when Blackwell died young in 1855, his shop died with him. Benjamin Harris was Oxford's first public librarian, and because he was not a freeman of the city, he was obliged to open his shop outside its walls at 46 High Street, St Clement's. At that time there were twenty-one other booksellers in Oxford, including the inappropriately named Fred Trash, who was also a publisher. It was Benjamin Harris's son, Benjamin Henry, who founded the Blackwell's which was to become one of the best-known bookselling businesses in the world. Benjamin Henry began his working life apprenticed to another Oxford bookseller for a 1s. per week. In 1879 he borrowed £150 from an old lady and opened at 50 Broad Street. In the 1880s he added No. 51 to his premises and, inevitably, took on the additional role of publisher.

Between the two 'founding' Blackwells, Alfred Richard Mowbray had opened, in 1858, in Cornmarket Street. Mowbray had intended to become a missionary, but, inspired by the Anglo-Catholic revival, he started a bookshop instead. A historian of the Oxford Movement has referred to the founding of Mowbray's as one of the most significant second generation events of its progress. A friend of various leading churchmen, Mowbray, like Blackwell, soon began to publish as well as sell books. In 1871 he died suddenly, but his widow continued and expanded the business, a London branch being opened in 1873.

In 1899 the Oxford Booksellers' Association held an inaugural meeting, attended by Alden & Co., B. H. Blackwell, Messrs George's Sons, Mr W. G. Grant, Mr Harvey, Mr R. Hill, the Oxford Educational Supply Association, James Parker & Co., Slatter & Rose, Mr James Thornton, Joseph Thornton & Son, Mr Wheeler and Williams & Norgate (who had a foreign branch in Oxford but who, like the others in the above list, bowed later to the growing supremacy of Blackwell's).

Oxford and Cambridge were the main centres of learning in the British Isles, but there were others. Durham University was founded in 1832; the House of Andrews, booksellers, predated it by twenty-four years. George Andrews, freeman of the City and a member of the Drapers' Company, opened his shop in 1808, and a few years later was co-publisher of Surtees's *History of Durham*. When he died his widow and two sons succeeded him, but in 1861 George Andrews, Junior, died and his sister Frances took control as sole proprietor, bringing fresh feminine influence into the trade. She later married and became Mrs Le Keux, but it was not until 1895 that she sold the House of Andrews to her manager, Warneford Smart. It would not be accurate to say that Frances le Keux was a woman bookseller, although she was proprietor of the House of Andrews; she did not, in all probability, sell on the shop floor. But she was the head of a retail business at a time when few other women were.

Another woman who played a more influential part in the book trade was the daughter of a Jersey stationer and bookseller, who had married Jesse Boot, the founder of the pharmaceutical business. Florence Boot started the first Boots' Library in Nottingham thinking that people who were sick in bed would need food for the mind as they lay recuperating. Libraries in London noticed the increasing demand from Mrs Boot in Nottingham and in 1900 a man from Mudie's suggested a much larger operation. Boots' the chemists already had numerous branches; the man from Mudie's became their first librarian.

Nottingham's most notable bookseller, Charles James Sisson, started in 1854 as manager of a S.P.C.K. depot. Thirty years later he took over the financial responsibility and in 1897 moved into premises in Wheeler Gate. The S.P.C.K. were, of course, pioneer booksellers in many parts of the country and had opened depots in Bristol (1813) and Bath (1820).

In Bristol there was also William George, who at the age of twelve, in 1842, had gone to learn the trade with his uncle, William Strong, in Clare Street. Four years later uncle died, and in 1847 George started on his own with £50 capital in Bath Street. As was the way with these nineteenth-century retail adventurers, who lived in an age when property was easily available and cheap to rent, he made several moves before settling himself at 89 Park Street, then the last house in Bristol on the Clifton road, but later to be so easily accessible to the university on the crown of the hill. That was in 1884, when William took his two sons into partnership and himself devoted his remaining years to antiquarian interests. He died in 1900.

In the 1890 Directory for Bristol sixty-four booksellers are listed, only thirteen of them dealing in secondhand books. They included John Wright of Stonebridge (later also publishers of medical and technical books), J. W. Arrowsmith (afterwards taken over by J. M. Dent) and the British and Foreign Bible Society, who turn up in so many towns and cities. Publishers were listed separately, and there were thirteen of them including the same Arrowsmith, and agencies of Nelson and Gresham (Blackie).

In Liverpool, where the first of the redbrick university presses was established before the turn of the century, a long tradition of good bookselling preceded the academics. Henry Young, a Cornishman who had painted railway carriages for a living, was advised by a relative already in bookselling to take up the same pursuit, so he opened a shop in South Castle Street in 1848. This prospered steadily and he handed it on to his two sons in the 'eighties, Harold continuing progress with the new books and Henry with the antiquarian. Nathaniel Hawthorne, when American consul in Liverpool, bought books from them; so did Augustine Birrell, who remarked that it was the custom of a gentleman in Liverpool to belong to the Athenaeum and owe money to Henry Young.

George Philip opened his shop in 1834, and a few years after started a factory to manufacture maps and stationery. He brought his son into partnership and, later, also his nephew—hence Philip, Son & Nephew. Nephew took over the retail and school supply business eventually, and in 1859 the printing works became a separate enterprise. Three years later they opened a shop in London's Fleet Street to sell geographical books and maps, and in 1901 built a model one-storey factory in Willesden, at which time a limited company was formed.

Tom Parry, a retired schoolmaster, founded Parry Books in 1879, and when he died the pattern of widow and sons continuing the business was repeated. In the 1870s, Cornish of Lord Street, a famous name in nineteenth-century bookselling, was still thriving, apparently unequalled as a training-ground for northern booksellers.

In the other great Lancashire city of Manchester there was a branch of Cornish, and it was there that John Sherratt and Joseph David Hughes learned their trade. They opened their own business in a small shop at the corner of St Ann Street and Half Moon Street in 1896. The story goes that an elderly lady, obviously undernourished, called there one day with two first editions of Shelley's poems, and asked a modest £1 for the pair. Hughes sent her to a nearby café, with two shillings to buy sustenance, while he valued the books. When she returned to the shop he told her they were worth £450, and she fainted. Brandy was

ordered, and when she recovered, the booksellers explained that they
had not sufficient capital to make her an outright offer, but, instead,
proposed paying her 30s. per week until the amount was paid off. The
lady accepted—and brandy was always kept on the premises thereafter. At this time Joe Cheetham, senior, who was later to join Sherratt
& Hughes, worked for a Mr Wardleworth. Known as the Discount
Bookseller, Wardleworth bought 6s. novels for 4s. and sold them at
4s. 6d. He later went bankrupt.

Further north, in Blackpool, a bookshop was opened in 1870 by a
Mr Donnelly; he was joined by F. P. Sweeten in 1900. Sweeten, whose
grandfather had published and printed the first newspaper in Penrith
in 1841, and had also sold books there, had learned his trade in Ireland,
Brighton and Bombay before returning to England to form a partnership which was handed on to his son and grandsons. Another
business with which his family were subsequently to be associated was
Robinson's of Preston, which opened about 1890 in Fishergate.

It would be tedious to relate in detail the statistics for all the counties
of England, but some should be lingered over in order to place the period
in proper perspective. Lancashire seems to me a good county to choose
from amongst the northern shires, because it was much affected by the
industrial revolution yet also had certain towns which remained largely
tourist and middle-class, or at least genteel. Thus in 1890 in one bracing
seaside resort, Blackpool, there was a resident population of some
20,000 supporting a list of 19 booksellers and stationers. In another,
Southport, with a population about double Blackpool's, there were no
less than 45 retailers of books and stationery, including a branch of
William Wardleworth's who boasted, in bold type in the local directory,
'the largest stock in Southport, new books added as published', and all
subject 'to 3d. in the 1s. discounts'. But in Burnley, whose population
in 1888 was estimated at 70,000, there were 43 booksellers and stationers; in Preston (96,000) there were 32; in Blackburn (112,574 in 1885)
there were 12, which included the W.H.S. railway bookstall and a
'religious tract depot'; and in Bolton (192,413 in 1881) there were 14.

It would seem that in Lancashire at this time the rule was the larger
the population the fewer the bookshops, and this was still the case in
1957 when Chatto & Windus published Richard Hoggart's *The Uses of
Literacy*. In the large cities the evidence was similar, given the fact that
in any great urban centre there must be a literate minority. Gore's
Directory for Liverpool (1870) lists about 120 booksellers, with or without
circulating libraries, but including such publishers as Blackie, Nelson
and the British and Foreign Bible Society, who had agencies there. The
1873 Directory for Manchester lists 87, including 18 as publishers,
Blackie amongst them.

The Liverpool *Directory* of 1890 has 170 entries but there is no indication as to which are stationers only and which are booksellers. Similarly, in Manchester in 1890 there are approximately 150 entries, but these include many publishers. In both cities there is evidence of the growth of the firm of Cornish. In Liverpool it became James Cornish & Sons, at two addresses; in Manchester, it remained James Edward Cornish, at two addresses, and with a branch in Owen's College at Chorlton-upon-Medlock.

Victorian Lancashire probably epitomized the two nations which a later publisher and prime minister over-confidently pronounced vanished. There can be little doubt that those who had been forcibly educated by the 1870 Act did not buy books in the same proportion as those who frequented the watering-places of Southport and Blackpool. It may be that they did not want to; certainly they could not afford to. (And when the same publisher and afterwards premier represented some of them in parliament in the next century, they still did not have the means.)

To look elsewhere in the north, Henry Walker had started his bookshop in Briggate, Leeds, in 1837, and William Henry Hills his in High Street West, Sunderland, in 1852. Oldham Bookshop commenced business in 1882 when D. W. Bardsley opened, and in Chester Stephen Golder and John Phillipson took over from a stationer and sold books from 1864 in competition with, amongst others, Minshull & Meeson. Gladstone, Charles Kingsley (sometime Canon of Chester Cathedral) and Stanley Weyman were claimed as customers by Phillipson & Golder who, in the twentieth century, took over Minshull & Meeson.

Mawson, Swan & Morgan, in Newcastle-upon-Tyne, had a curious origin. Joseph Wilson Swan was the inventor of the incandescent electric lamp which helped to make mining safer. Swan joined Mawson, who was a chemist, and Sheriff of Newcastle, and it is not certain what they sold in their first shop. Mawson was killed by an explosion while he was supervising the disposal of a quantity of nitro-glycerine. In 1878 Thomas Morgan became partner to Swan, who had acquired Morgan's stationery and book business. After that Mawson, Swan & Morgan was conducted from various addresses, printing and picture-framing were added to the other sidelines and, in 1900, what was later to become the successful store in Grey Street became a limited company with Morgan as chairman. Grey Street is a wide, elegant, thoroughfare curving up a hill, at the top of which stands a statue to the Charles Grey who introduced the first reform bill into the House of Commons. It is fitting that a prosperous bookshop should have functioned for so long in the street named after him.

What was to be Dring's Bookshop in Newcastle opened in 1900, with the object of supplying Sunday school prizes and other requirements to the Brunswick Methodist Church. A Mr and Miss Symons later became the proprietors and developed a general shop, although keeping a close relationship with the church.

In the Midlands the great new industrial city of Birmingham had become (as noted p. 150) a better centre for books than it had been in the days of Samuel Johnson's childhood; Johnson's father, the bookseller of Lichfield, set up a stall on market days in the then small town because no one else offered books there. The firm of Cornish, which I am unable to establish as being linked with the shops of the same name in Lancashire, was founded about 1790, if not earlier. A Cornish sold to Charles Linnell in about 1897, and a year later the twentieth-century owner, William Finch, was apprenticed to him.

The Midland Educational Company was started by a group of teachers in Union Street in 1870. They formed an educational trading organization to issue cheap school books and equipment, and within three years they were celebrating success with a ball. In 1883 they moved into Corporation Street, a new thoroughfare inspired by Joseph Chamberlain's plans for the city. The Midland Educational was to grow into a vast business and absorb, amongst others, the Northampton bookshop Marks, founded about 1700.

The founder of Combridge of Birmingham, begun in 1887, later became an alderman of the city. Before his time, there was a Mr B. Hudson, printer and bookseller of Bull Street, who died in 1875 having done business there for more than forty years. He was not an ancestor of the Hudsons who later became the city's leading booksellers.

There were 50 entries under 'Booksellers, Etc.', in the 1870 directory for Birmingham, and 42 under 'Bookbinders'—some of them overlapping. By 1890 there were 73 under 'Booksellers', 29 of which were also publishers. W. H. Smith had expanded from their branch in Union Street to include station bookstalls at New Street and Snow Hill.

Ernest Gait, in Grimsby, and Anthony Brown, in Hull, opened their shops in 1860 on opposite banks of the Humber. Brown's eldest son worked at Simpkin Marshall before joining his father. During their partnership a school outfitting department was added and proved so successful that new premises were taken in 1877. Hull was to be a university town and to offer more to a bookseller than Grimsby, a fishing port where in the nineteenth century it was necessary to sell patent medicines to offset the poor return on books, and to make sufficient to buy the printing press which Albert Gait correctly saw as the salvation of his tottering business. Even in 1970, 60 per cent of Gait's turnover was in goods other than books, but the family firm survived as such for the whole of our period, and the health of bookselling and the home trade depended at all times on having sufficient outlets for the ever-increasing volume of books. London, Edinburgh, Oxford, undoubtedly sold more books per head of population than Grimsby, but there was still a market in such towns, although it remained largely untapped, for there were few men as persistent as the Gaits in offering books for sale.

In the county town of Lincolnshire there was a bookshop dating from the eighteenth century, and J. W. Ruddock became its sole proprietor in 1884. At Rugby, in Warwickshire, George Over's bookshop had an even earlier origin. In about 1750, Mr Clay of Daventry sold books on market days to boys of Rugby school, and about ten years later his son opened a shop near the George Hotel. George Rowell took over the business in 1792, and ran it for nearly forty years until Dr Arnold requested that a shop be established for his pupils in Sheep Street. There were many changes of ownership and partnership, with apprentices winning their spurs and continuing the business. One of these was George Over, who was certainly in the shop long before 1877.

In East Anglia, Goose's of Norwich was founded in about 1870, and Jarrold's, the printers, who also became booksellers, a century or so earlier. White's *Directory for Norfolk* (1890) lists 21 booksellers and stationers for Norwich, including 9 publishers, among them the ubiquitous Blackie. It also shows 9 each for King's Lynn and Great Yarmouth, and a total of 63 for the whole county. In Ipswich a beautiful sixteenth-century mansion with a priest-hole, carved windows, sloping floors and old beams was turned into a bookshop in 1897 by W. E. Harrison.

Reading has a special place in book trade history because of John Newbery, the first publisher of children's books (see p. 167), who married the widow of William Carnan, publisher of the *Reading Mercury*. Newbery added a bookshop to the newspaper and later moved to London. His grandchildren sold the shop, which passed through several hands until it became William Smith's in the twentieth century. The main premises include a house where William Penn worshipped. James Golder's, a Reading bookshop of religious origins, was founded in 1829.

One of the oldest bookshops in the kingdom is King's of Lymington, in Hampshire. It started in the early nineteenth century, succeeding a printing works begun by John King in Yeovil in about 1735. King's youngest son, Charles, who was a bookseller in Dorchester, moved to Lymington in 1805, and was joined there by his nephew Richard seventeen years later. Richard suffered fierce competition in Lymington, and went to London to purchase remainders from Thomas Tegg. Remainders were a novelty in those days, and he kept the business going until it became an established success. He published and printed local guides, as well as being the leading purveyor of books. His son succeeded him.

Henry Gilbert, a printer and bookseller in Halstead, Essex, since 1825, set up in Southampton in 1859. He was a refugee from his native town, where his Nonconformist beliefs were held against him, and where the Anglicans had set up a rival bookseller. Gilbert died in 1869, handing on his business to his son, Henry March, who had been trained at

Sotheran's in London. After moving about the town, Gilbert settled on premises at $2\frac{1}{2}$ Portland Street, where, at one time, they had a back entrance whose address was $1\frac{1}{2}$ Regent Street. (They once received a letter addressed to $2\frac{1}{2}$d Postcard Street!) In 1895, Henry March's son Owen opened a branch in Winchester, returning in 1899 to take over the main shop. This branch became established permanently in Winchester, but the main bookseller to the school there was Joseph Wells. Wells had been apprenticed to James Robbins, who had purchased the College Street bookshop of Thomas Burdon and his son. Burdon had opened in 1760, and his son sold to Robbins in 1806. Wells's father became beer butler to Winchester College in 1797 and died in his pantry in 1834; his son was made manager of the bookshop by David Nutt, the London bookseller who had taken over the Winchester business in 1844. Nutt made Wells a partner, and after his death Wells became sole proprietor. By then he had built a bindery, which employed several hands, at the back of the shop. His sons joined Wells and succeeded him on his death in 1890.

Bournemouth was one of the new towns of the nineteenth century to arise out of the recently discovered delights of the seaside. Beale's department store, which opened there in 1881, had a book department early in its history, and J. F. Hyams, a buyer for the store in the 1960s, recalled Arthur Ransome telling him that his father had bought him his first copy of *Treasure Island* in the Fancy Fair at Beale's in the 'nineties.

Eastbourne came into prominence as a resort in the same period, and there Mr A. Ryder opened his bookshop in 1875 in South Street. A figure more prominent in trade history also sold books in the town: H. W. Keay, the first president of the Associated Booksellers, was one of those formidable Victorians who combined good works with good business. He trained as a solicitor's clerk, but at the age of eighteen, became manager of W. H. Smith's first bookstall on Eastbourne station. Six years later, in 1872, he opened his own shop in Terminus Road, and prospered so well that he sold it to his former employers in 1905. In the meantime, in addition to his activities with the Associated Booksellers, he had become a member of Eastbourne Town Council, later serving as alderman, and then as mayor for four terms. It is probable that he sold his business because none of his three sons elected to follow him in it; otherwise there might have been another dynastic tale to relate. Keay was obviously an intensely public-spirited man, and it must be surmised that at the age of fifty-seven, with no willing family successors, he preferred to concentrate his energies on local politics, charities and other public service (he was also a magistrate and head of the League of Mercy), and on national book trade affairs, instead of dealing with the day-to-day organization of his own business. In this decision he was much wiser than some mid-twentieth-century booksellers who later put outside interests before their own commercial survival, going bankrupt and doing the trade they wished to serve more harm than good in the long run.

At Hove—the polite end of Brighton—Daniel Burchell Friend started at Church Road. He already owned a shop in Western Road, Brighton, which was bought by Samuel Combridge, a relative of the Brum Combridge, in 1901. In 1892 the shop was described in the local almanack as being 'of such a character as to make the same a library and artistic salon where patrons may have the opportunity of inspecting the extensive stock without crush or confusion'.

At Folkestone and Hythe, on the Kent coast, William Tiffen published local guides and sold books from about 1820 onwards, and in Dover in 1847 there were no less than 13 listed in the town directory as 'Booksellers, Printers and Stationers', 8 of them in narrow Snargate Street, by the docks. At the same date Ramsgate boasted 10 in this category, Canterbury, 9, and Tunbridge Wells, 6, including John Colbran's in the High Street, later linked with Goulden's of Canterbury. Goulden & Nye (1885) and Goulden & Curry (1895) became prominent in Kent as booksellers, stationers, printers and newspaper proprietors.

Wheaton's of Exeter opened in the mid-nineteenth century. Lear's of Cardiff started in 1887 as a small theological bookshop in the Royal Arcade, then, as later, immune from the noise of traffic. In the neighbouring town of Swansea, Alfred Raymond Way took over in 1895 the bookshop started by a Mr Clover.

On the Channel Islands, W. F. Filleul opened in about 1869 in Burrard Street, St Helier, Jersey. And across a wider sea, in Dublin, (now in the Republic of Eire but still linked to the United Kingdom under membership of the Booksellers' Association of Great Britain and Ireland) were James Duffy (established 1830); Charles Eason's, whose emergence from the W.H.S. empire has already been recorded; Browne & Nolan, started as a printing house in 1827 by John Browne, but becoming publishers and booksellers when William Nolan joined the firm in 1870; and the A.P.C.K., founded by William Watson in 1792 as an Association for Discountenancing Vice and Promoting the Knowledge and Practice of the Christian Religion. The A.P.C.K. pioneered schools for both Protestant and Catholic children, and no child received religious instruction without the parents' permission. In 1856, the Association published the Church Hymnal for the Church of Ireland. In that religion-rent Emerald Isle, the A.P.C.K., like Eason's, continued right up to 1970 to sell books in Eire and in Ulster. How this was achieved remains a mystery to those—and they are legion, however many of us may have Irish grandmothers—who fail to understand the Irish character which has contributed so much to English literature and the British book trade.

I

Trade Affairs

Further steps in trade organization—Stanley Unwin; P.A.—school book distribution—Times Book War—piracy of colonial editions; Publishers' Circle formed; copyright; trade-union dispute; price of novels; censorship; literary agents; publishers suspected by authors of earning too much; A.B. expands; increasing numbers of books published between 1911 and 1914; effects of the First World War; A.B. call for all books to be netted; postwar crisis; P.A. criticized by its younger members; Society of Bookmen formed; National Book Council established; joint committee of publishers and booksellers set up; B.P.R.A. organized; industrial strife; pressure for discount from the Library Association; increased printing costs; international copyright; broadcasting and the sale of subsidiary rights; The Bookseller *becomes the trade's official journal; A.B. jubilee; innovations within the trade in the 'thirties— Book Tokens and book clubs—Readers' Union; British Council; P.A. and A.B. joint conference.*

Just as Frederick Orridge Macmillan typified those far-sighted publishers in late-Victorian times who saw the necessity for organizing the book trade, so, in this next period, the figure of Stanley Unwin emerges as the embodiment of a concerted effort towards cooperation.

Stanley Unwin was born, in 1884, the ninth child of Edward and Elizabeth Unwin. He was regarded as so sickly an entrant into the human race that one over-frank friend of his father's remarked, 'If you can't do better than that you'd better stop.' Stanley's parents were fairly typical middle-class Victorian Nonconformists. On his father's side grandfather Jacob had founded a printing works; on his mother's, a Spicer had started a paper-manufacturing firm. When Stanley was in his late teens the printing plant was burned down, the insurance assessors treated the owners shabbily, and funds were short. The sickly child, who had somehow survived, went to work in the City of London at a shipping and insurance brokers' with which employment he was little in sympathy although he retained an interest in insurance to the end of his life. But he was able to save, and, after a comparatively short time, he gave in his notice, knowing that his real career lay elsewhere.

Unwin was born with desire to travel, and later framed his life's work within this urge. On the day he gave notice to the shipping broker he was invited to spend a weekend with his uncle, T. Fisher Unwin. Fisher had no children of his own and had been running his own imprint for nearly twenty years. He was looking for a partner and a successor. Stanley Unwin came through the weekend well and was invited to join his uncle, but the young man was determined to travel, and to learn foreign languages, so it was agreed that he should first spend nine months in Germany, followed by three in France before he became a publisher.

Stanley went to Germany in September, 1903, and soon found himself working twelve hours a day, six days a week, for Hinrich, in Leipzig. He was only absolved from working on Sundays also by protesting, quite truthfully, that his parents would not approve. Hinrich's were theological publishers as well as booksellers, and the keen-minded young Unwin learned much from them. Wishing, however, to widen his experience, he suggested to his uncle that he should visit Berlin, and asked for expenses for the trip. Three pounds was granted, and the nephew did one hundred and twenty pound's worth of business which, he recalled ruefully in his autobiography, sixty years later, would have paid him better had he been operating on the usual traveller's 10 per cent. (He did not recall, in the same volume, that his London traveller in the 1950s, a financially hard-pressed young man, with a wife and family, working on 10s. [50p] per week fares allowance, put in for a 2s. 6d.[12½p] per week subsistence rise but was granted only 2s. [10p]).

Uncle Fisher contrived to curtail the continental trip, and Stanley was brought back to England ahead of schedule, at which point Fisher, capriciously, did not need his services immediately, so Stanley spent valuable time at his father's printing works, near Ludgate Hill, learning about typesetting and the cost of standing type.

In his autobiography, *The Truth About a Publisher*, Stanley Unwin describes Fisher as 'tall, handsome, bearded, with a floppy yellow tie, physically as straight as a dart, a keen mountaineer ... wonderfully good company out of office hours.' When he first joined him he was employed as an invoice clerk, and was later sent on the road to travel the list. Then, T. Werner Laurie, Fisher Unwin's manager, left to start his own imprint, and Stanley returned to the office, first to inaugurate an export drive, secondly to gradually take over the day-to-day management of the firm. His uncle sent him to America and began to lean more and more on him for advice, while preserving the appearance of running the business himself. Eventually it was too much for an ambitious young man who had watched the profits grow from between £600 and £700 a year to between £6,000 and £7,000, while

he was expected to travel Oxford and Cambridge three times a year
on a daily allowance of 12s. 6d. (62½p) rising to 15s. (75p). And meanwhile Stanley was introducing profitable lines into the business himself.
Twice Stanley offered his notice, twice his salary was doubled. On the
third occasion he refused the increase because he saw he would never
gain control of the business, and resigned. He at once planned a journey
round the world with his future brother-in-law, Severn Storr, and they
visited countries to which no British publisher had been before. Stanley
made copious notes about everyone he called upon, and the knowledge
he gained on that trip no doubt gave rise to some of the stories thereafter circulated. According to one of these, when, decades later, Allen
& Unwin published a book with apparently meagre potential, the head
of the house would base his print order on the knowledge that three
would be sold in this capital, ten in that, five in such-and-such a university city in the Far East, fifty in another, and so on. The story is no
doubt apocryphal, as are so many relating to this remarkable man, but
it holds a grain of truth.

When he returned to England in 1913, Stanley Unwin looked around
for a bankrupt list to buy. On January 1st, 1914, a receiver was
appointed to George Allen & Co., who had amalgamated with Swan,
Sonnenschein, in 1911. After a struggle, and some heart-searching,
Unwin, who had been out of work for eighteen months, agreed to
accept the receiver's onerous terms, and took up a life managing
directorship with other managing directors, who were also debenture
holders. This undertaking restricted his powers because, although he
held more shares than any other director, *all* of them had to agree
about each particular book they were to publish. Any one of them could
veto any book, and on the fateful fourth of August of 1914, they entered
into their obligations. In the same year Stanley Unwin was married,
and true to his essential business acumen, commissioned a book from
the officiating cleric in the vestry after the service.

The glories of the Allen & Unwin list will be discussed later; the
particular contribution of Stanley Unwin, to trade politics, through
the Publishers' Association, of which he later became president, and
through the Society of Bookmen, of which he was a founder member,
is noted in what follows.

The detailed history of the first fifty years of the P.A. is most admirably recorded by one of its ex-presidents, R. J. L. Kingsford, in *The
Publishers' Association 1896–1946*. Here we are concerned only with the
main events and policies which attracted its council's attention. The
Publishers' Association, as we have seen, was formed as a direct result
of the Associated Booksellers' demands for a net book system. Where,
before 1896, publishers had been stronger than booksellers only as
individuals, from that date they were able to muster collective strength

when they cared to. By 1900 some sixty-eight publishers showed a willingness to unite by becoming members of the P.A.; ten years later their number had increased to eighty-nine. Collective action was sometimes effective, as in 1903 when booksellers demanded 33⅓ per cent discount on non-net books and the P.A. recommended that the proposal be turned down; sometimes less so, as when in the same year the council of the P.A. advised its members that education boards should make their purchases through booksellers but emphasized that it had no power to force them not to sell direct to local authorities if they wished to.

The Education Act of 1902 created 328 local boards which instantly clamoured to be supplied direct by publishers at full trade terms, the London School Board having established a precedent for this in 1875. Eventually, certain local authorities, apart from the London County Council, were supplied direct, but the majority were refused, and the daft system whereby booksellers gave discount on the books which they bought at the worst terms, but gave none at all on those supplied to them at the best terms, continued up till 1970, when demands for supply from publishers, without the intervention of the middleman-bookseller, to schools and libraries under the jurisdiction of local authorities, were made with increasing raucousness.

Throughout this period, official thought on the supply of books to schools was that booksellers should compete with each other in securing contracts for the supply of textbooks, offering discounts that might involve them in a loss, but recouping on the sale of net books to school libraries and other school equipment. It was not framed in such definite terms as these, but this was the spirit of the publishers' attitude, publishers being happy in the knowledge that the teachers must come to them, one way or another, for the books which they alone published. They were, therefore, in a secure position to leave booksellers to throw out a sprat to catch a mackerel. It was the booksellers' basic refusal to recognize the built-in strength of the publishers that led them into so much prolonged controversy.

Publishers, however, for all their superior status, never wished to do without booksellers because they recognized the advantages of a well-organized retail structure economically viable in its own right. The argument was really about the efficiency of the retail outlet, and it was obtuse of publishers not to realize that such efficiency could only be gained by giving better terms. The wrangle continued throughout the century, with publishers slowly conceding more. It was inevitable that the P.A., if it genuinely wished for a healthy retail distribution, should condone this trend. It had, after all, however paternally, condoned the Net Book Agreement, so that it was logical, when the first real challenge came, that it should close its ranks and fight for the two interested parties in the famous 'Times Book War'.

In the early years of the twentieth century *The Times* was struggling for survival. In an attempt to increase circulation a book club and library was established in the West End of London, and five-year contracts were signed in 1905 with many publishers. It soon became obvious that books were being sold at a discount after being loaned as few as two or three times, and that members of the Times Book Club were able to purchase virtually new books for much less than the advertised published price. The two trade associations protested, but the Book Club maintained that only books which were no longer in a state fit for circulation were sold. A new version of the Net Book Agreement was speedily drawn up with a clause forbidding the sale of a book as secondhand, until six months after publication. Most booksellers signed this readily, but the Times Book Club did not. The Book Club, supported by editorials in *The Times*, attacked the new agreement. The 'Book War' was on.

The Times Book Club was declared 'black' by the P.A. Many publishers at once ceased supply, but those who had signed contracts with *The Times* were bound by them. Messrs Constable had their own problem with their author Bernard Shaw, who, like many a famous writer in the previous century, approved of underselling, and produced his own edition of one of his plays imprinted 'Issued by the author for the Times Book Club'.

The battle continued for some two years and involved many thousands of people, vast numbers of whom signed a petition protesting against the Net Book Agreement on the grounds that publishers sold books at half price to the colonies (Colonial editions in cheaper bindings) but objected to British citizens within the British Isles enjoying the same privilege. It was a good rabble-rousing argument, however much it ignored the difficulties of publishers wishing to increase trade by exporting to the then colonies.

The climax came in the autumn of 1907 when John Murray published *The Letters of Queen Victoria* in three volumes at £3 3s. The Book Club was obliged to buy copies at full price, and a *Times* reviewer complained about the high retail price. He was backed up by a correspondent (actually a member of the Printing House Square staff writing to the editor under a pseudonym) who penned two letters accusing Murray of extortion, going to the length of coupling his name with that of Judas Iscariot. Murray brought an action for libel and was awarded damages of £7,500.

By then several months had passed, the Book Club was losing hundreds of pounds each week, and the new proprietor of the newspaper, Lord Northcliffe, was negotiating peace with the P.A. In September 1908 the Times Book Club signed the new Net Book Agreement and, one month later, *The Times* and Murray's jointly published a cheap edition of the Queen's letters. Underselling had again been stamped out, and, despite apparent infringements of the N.B.A. by the same Book Club in the following year, the agreement, which had been extended in 1905 to cover maps as well as books, was not seriously challenged again until the 1950s, (but see p. 388).

Council members of the P.A. were also concerned, in these early years of collective consultation, with various less dramatic issues, such as the piracy of Colonial editions by indigenous publishers, and the practice of newspapers of quoting excessively from books under the guise of reviewing them. Not all members approved of the council's efforts. In 1907 John Lane suggested improving the Association by opening a central London showroom for new books by issuing a weekly catalogue of new titles, and by introducing an on-approval scheme for librarians and booksellers for all books over 5s. (Heinemann, in 1901, had offered to send books, through a bookseller, on approval to any member of the public.) The council, arrogantly, did not even consider Lane's proposals, but it was partly as a result of this official disdain that a ginger group, the Publishers' Circle, was formed a year later. The Circle was the suggestion of Arthur Spurgeon of Cassell, and it received the blessing of the Association. Arthur Waugh, of Chapman & Hall, was the first president of this luncheon club which concerned itself with those problems which the P.A. chose to ignore.

The International Congress of Publishers continued to meet every two or three years up to the outbreak of the First World War. International copyright was invariably an important item on its agenda, but progress towards a universal agreement was slow, and inevitably made slower by military conflict between the main literate nations, although German copyright was respected by the P.A. in 1914. In the British Isles a new copyright act in 1911 protected an author's work during his lifetime and for fifty years after death, and the National Library of Wales was added to the list of deposit libraries, with certain qualifications—not all new publications were to be theirs free of charge, as was the case with the others. These other deposit libraries were the British Museum; the Library of the Faculty of Advocates, Edinburgh (later the National Library of Scotland); the University Library in Cambridge; the Bodleian, in Oxford; and the Library of Trinity College, Dublin. Some publishers resented this obligation except in the case of the British Museum.

Trade-union troubles were first experienced in 1913, when there was a dispute with binders, heralding some bitter struggles in other workshops in the following decade. And there was the matter of the thirty booksellers' assistants in Oxford who petitioned humbly and politely for the right to have a half-day off each week, but were told by the local branch of the Associated Booksellers (a boss organization) that there was no point even in discussing such a proposition because there would be some employers who would not agree! It was not only the council of the P.A. which had feudal inclinations in those days.

The price of novels was a perennial source of dissatisfaction to all concerned, from those who wrote them to those it was thought should, but apparently did not, buy them, and there were some vehement exchanges on the subject between publishers and booksellers, and between publishers and publishers. Cloth-bound fiction reprints at 7d. upset the sale of 6s. editions. The booksellers officially deplored this state of affairs; so did the publishers. But the associations, separately and jointly, could not stop them, and they ran their course without bringing ruin to the majority of either publishers or booksellers.

Other familiar issues fomented discontent and provided the trade press with correspondents. Censorship was often in the news. The commercial libraries, stamping-grounds for Mrs Grundy as long as they remained a source of commercial gain, banned books by H. G. Wells, Compton Mackenzie, Hall Caine and others, and the Doncaster Free Library Committee burst into the act by ordering copies of *Tom Jones* to be burned. (Decades later another North Country authority sought to protect its ratepayers from *Boswell's London Journal*, but by then sophistication had made certain inroads and no actual incineration was recorded; it is even probable that Boswell made his way back on to the shelves during the period known as the permissive society.)

William Heinemann went on attacking literary agents, some of whom prospered (A. P. Watt died in 1914 worth £60,000), while others failed disastrously, even dishonourably (Arthur Addison Bright committed suicide in 1906 having swindled his friend, J. M. Barrie, out of £16,000; A. M. Burghes and his son were convicted of fraud in 1912).

Publishers, as always, were suspected by authors of earning too much. Conan Doyle, at a Society of Authors' Dinner in 1905, commented that an eminent writer on astronomy had left £1,200, another on zoology a mere £300, but that Smith, of Smith, Elder & Co., had died worth £750,000. (In the fierceness of his feeling he omitted to add that Smith had made most of his fortune from mineral waters.) Conan Doyle joined Shaw and Wells in issuing a prospectus for Bookshops Ltd, a company dedicated to promote the sale of books on behalf of authors, and to be managed on entirely new lines. Nothing seems to have come of the project.

New branches of the Associated Booksellers were started. H. W. Keay became the first president in 1903 (previously he had been chairman) and when he sold his Eastbourne shop two years later the rules of the Association were altered to allow him to remain in office although he was no longer in business. Keay was president until 1923, and gave his members' approval when demands for a discount from the

Library Association were met by a typical P.A. refusal even to discuss them.

The number of books published increased from some 6,000 in 1900 to 11,818 in 1911. It went up again in 1912 to 12,886 but dropped back to 12,046 the following year, while in 1914, predictably, it fell to 8,863.

The war brought a paper and a staff shortage. There was little damage to property but appalling losses in personnel. *The Bookseller*, which had become a weekly in 1909, reverted to monthly publication in 1915, in which year the Associated Booksellers called for all books to be netted. The proposal was not accepted by the P.A., so local agreements came into being in some cities and areas to fix the discount on school books. In 1916 the East Midlands Branch of the A.B. reported that booksellers' profits had fallen from 8·46 per cent net in 1914, to 1·7 per cent. In 1917 the P.A. Education Sub-Committee held its first meeting, but a year later Mr W. M. Meredith, the P.A. president, was complaining of the lack of organization in the trade. His words were not unheeded and there was a reception at Stationers' Hall on November 19th, 1929, to celebrate a decade of cooperation, not only between members of the P.A., but between booksellers, authors and publishers.

The groundwork done since 1895 bore fruit in the 'twenties, in an upsurge of activity prompted by the determination of various individuals to produce a better book trade in the aftermath of a war which had taken terrifying toll of men and created new economic conditions for everyone in Europe. Trade with Germany was at a standstill because of inflation. The reparations demanded by the victorious allies caused the German government to devalue the mark again and again until, by the end of 1923, it was worthless. Other Central European and Scandinavian countries also had to devalue their currencies so drastically that foreign books became prohibitively expensive for them. Britain, too, was in a financial crisis, and could not afford to be represented at the Florence Book Fair in 1922 until the Italian government offered free space and free transport to British publishers. The British government gave a grant to publishers for the 1925 fair, but the crisis at home prevented a similar subsidy in 1928, by which time Germany, with its government's backing, was competing successfully with British books in other parts of the world, notably Japan. International finance is a subject even more complicated than international copyright, and it was as much a matter of luck as of judgment who survived in the economic anarchy of those times.

Against this background of trading chaos in the export markets of the world the council of the P.A. came under heavy criticism from younger members of the Association, who thought that resolutions and recommendations should be binding on all, and not ignored by those who found them personally inconvenient. It was then, and later, idealistic to suppose that the council of the P.A. could impose its will on the membership as a whole; all it could hope to do was influence individual publishers for what it saw as the general good, and, as it became more organized, its recommendations carried more weight. But it was always up against the unfortunate truth that economics is not an exact science but a matter of interpretation of apparent facts. Councils, of publishers or any other body of men, tend to rely on the opinions of experts, and experts are as fallible as popes, so it was correct for the younger publishers to keep up the pressure on their elders. Backbencher irritants are essential to any healthy community to counteract the complacency and conservatism which always prevails in any hierarchy.

To the pre-war ginger group the Publishers' Circle, whose activities continued after 1918 and for decades to come, was added in 1921 the Society of Bookmen, which embraced the whole trade. The Society was founded by Hugh Walpole, as the result of a meeting of another homogeneous group, the Whitefriars. Membership, at first restricted to seventy-five, and later increased to one hundred, was open to men concerned with the creation, distribution and production of books. It held monthly dinners at which papers of interest to the trade were read and discussed freely, on the understanding that nothing said at the meeting would be recorded or reported. From its *in camera* deliberations arose the National Book Council (afterwards the National Book League), the Book Tokens scheme and the formation of working parties to examine the structure of the book trade in other European countries. One of its earliest positive suggestions was for a system of cooperative advertising, paid for jointly by publishers and booksellers, of books as books, and not as individual titles. The project was never adopted by the trade because not enough firms were willing to subscribe to this method of advertising, although other industries took it up in due course. It became a perennial subject of discussion—every year at least one publisher or bookseller commended it to the attention of the trade as a whole.

The National Book Council was not, at first, officially supported by the P.A., but it later appointed three representatives to its executive committee, and thereafter publishers were to be the Council's chief source of revenue. The N.B.C. came into existence on May 14th, 1925, sponsored by a joint committee, representing the P.A., the A.B., the Society of Bookmen, the Publishers' Circle and the Society of Authors. Maurice Marston, who was also secretary to the Bookmen, was made organizing secretary and was given a grant of £750 for the first year's experimental work. By 1928, popular support for the Council was shown by a staggering increase in membership of over 100 per cent in twelve months, the figure standing at 1,575 in the official report for that year.

Marston formed the nucleus of a reference library of books about books, some three hundred of which he presented himself to the Council.

In 1926 the Society of Bookmen sent a delegation to Holland and Germany to study the clearing-house system for the dispatch of orders. On their return a joint committee of publishers and booksellers was set up, to examine existing conditions in the trade, and advise on how they might be improved. The joint committee was not formed without some in-fighting. The P.A., realizing that the Bookmen was stealing its thunder, told the Society in a characteristically high-handed fashion that the creation of a joint committee was none of a dining-club's business. The Society said it didn't mind about this, so long as note was taken of the findings of its delegation, and that it would be absurd for acrimony to arise over the matter because half the Bookmen's membership were also members of the P.A.; but such is pride, and all politics, book trade or otherwise, is governed by men whose dignity must be preserved.

So the committee was appointed jointly by the A.B. and the P.A. It published its findings in three reports in 1928 and 1929, and these were eventually collected, together with the reports of the Society of Bookmen on book trade matters, in *British Book Trade Organisation*, edited by F. D. Sanders.

The importance of the joint committee's research cannot be over emphasized. The work which the individual delegates contributed, in their own and their firms' time, enabled the two associations to produce the first-ever comprehensive anatomy of the book trade in Britain. The document, as it appears in book form, is a concise and lucid description of the actual day-to-day working arrangements of a most complex industry, with recommendations for their improvement. It is a monu-ment of detailed research.

The 1920s also saw the organization of other bodies within the trade. Publishers' travelling salesmen, the 'reps', found collective identity in the formation of the Book Publishers' Representatives' Association (the B.P.R.A.) in 1924. On the initiative of Leslie Munro of Heinemann and William Grant of Nisbet, the reps were invited to a meeting in London in December 1923. From this grew the Association which fostered friendship amongst members and between them and their customers, the booksellers. A samaritan fund was instituted to help those in need of financial assistance, and annual guest nights were arranged which brought a new conviviality to bookseller-traveller relationships.

Publishers looked with favour on the B.P.R.A., but there was less official enthusiasm for the collective action of other workers who attempted to achieve recognition by joining unions. When the packers at Macmillan's struck because their weekly wage was reduced from 70s. to 60s., on the grounds that the cost of living index had gone down, there was no attempt at conciliation. The strike there, and elsewhere, was broken and the packers crept back to their benches to work at the lower rate. John Baker, a young trainee with Macmillan's, engaged to learn the catalogue,* was ordered to join them. He had sided with the packers during their strike, and the uncompromising management informed him that as he seemed so fond of their company he had better stand beside them amongst the corrugated paper and cardboard. Baker, naturally, resigned, and resumed his career at Sampson Low's. (Macmillan's had a distinctly feudal attitude: a boy from the warehouse who dared ascend the director's staircase was instantly dismissed for his effrontery—in comparison, John Baker was quite leniently dealt with. These conditions were not to last much longer, but the consequences were severe for those who infringed the code.) The strike was similarly broken, after three months, at Simpkin Marshall, W. H. Smith's and at Wyman's, where staff had joined the union in large numbers at the end of the war. The General Strike of 1926 soon followed and union members again came out, along with millions of other workers all over the country.

That the book trade suffered less industrial strife than did other trades was owing to the poor organization of the workers rather than to lack of causes. On the retail side bookshop managers and assistants might join a union if they wished, or dared, but membership did nothing to increase their income. Shopworkers generally remained underpaid and ill-organized, even in 1970, when the minimum wages laid down for them were still absurdly unrealistic.

In the late 1920s publishers were also under pressure again from the Library Association who wanted a 10 per cent discount on purchases. Commercial libraries, dealing directly with publishers, received the same discount as booksellers (in most cases they *were* booksellers) and they loaned their books for a fee. The public librarians who loaned theirs free, and were a charge on the rates, were not slow to appreciate this point, but their demands were resisted because the Associated Booksellers, through whom they were supplied, strongly objected, understanding that it would be their 10 per cent, and not the publishers', which the libraries would get. Four years later, however, in 1929, the Library Agreement was concluded and the public libraries got 10 per cent discount openly, whilst booksellers eventually got better terms on single copies supplied to libraries if they wrote their orders on special forms provided by the B.A. The P.A. gave in on this point mainly because there were so many evasions of the net ruling by bookseller suppliers that it was thought better to regularize the situation by agreeing a fixed discount. Booksellers continued to resent this for years, but those of them who were large enough to run public library supply

* See his Introduction to Frank Swinnerton's *The Bookman's London*.

departments, and those who specialized in this exclusively, found methods of giving extra services at competitive (that is, at cost, or below cost) rates. It was stipulated that a library must spend at least £100 a year to qualify for a discount, and that a bookseller was not obliged to give a discount on books bought on short terms ($16\frac{2}{3}+5$ per cent or less).

It was easier for publishers to resist the demands for higher wages than it was for them to beat down printers. By 1920 printing charges stood at 200 per cent above the pre-war level. Printers faced with a 5s. a week increase for their workers slapped 5 per cent on their prices, which enraged publishers; and two years later, when printing workers' wages had fallen by 7s. 6d. a week, prices were reduced by only 3 per cent. The cost of paper, which had soared during the war, fluctuated wildly in the 'twenties, but the average novel settled to retail at between 7s. and 7s. 6d. in 1918 and remained at that price for twenty years. It should also be noted that as early as 1916, printers and binders had begun to charge publishers for storing sheets and bound stock which formerly they had held gratis.

In international copyright, the Indian states in 1923 gave protection to books produced in the British Empire but in 1924 Egyptian publishers grandly announced that they would not pay for any translation they made into Arabic from British books. One step forward, one, even one and a half, backwards. Another irritant in this field came in 1922 when, despite the creation of Eire as an independent country, Trinity College, Dublin, remained entitled to receive one copy free of all British books. That this was a reciprocal agreement hardly brought peace of mind to either the British or the Irish publishers, the latter having to provide five copies of their books to a foreign power.

With the invention of broadcasting there came a new opportunity for selling subsidiary rights in books. There was never any quarrel between the British Broadcasting Corporation and the Publishers' Association about payment for material used on radio, the B.B.C. accepting the principle that it should pay for what it transmitted, but some alarm was felt about the Corporation's own publishing activities, particularly in connection with talks reproduced in the B.B.C. journal *The Listener*. Publishers questioned whether the B.B.C.'s charter gave it any right to publish; the law ruled that it had. Qualms were gradually allayed as it was realized that even broadcasts to schools would not end the demand for textbooks, and not revived until television arose as a further apparent threat to the printed word.

In the 'twenties the P.A., noting the usefulness to the German book trade of its official paper the *Borsenblatt*, was bothered by the absence of a similar journal in Britain. It could not hope to finance a daily paper such as the Germans had, and which had fired the imagination of the young Stanley Unwin on his tour of Germany in Edwardian days, but it cast its eye on what existed. Both the *Publishers' Circular* and *The Bookseller* acted as trade papers; each was privately owned and each willing to be wooed. In 1928 the Whitaker family agreed to transfer their journal into the care of the P.A. and the A.B., as *The Publisher and Bookseller*, reserving the right to keep 20 per cent commission from the sales for themselves and to hand over the remaining profits to the two trade associations. G. S. Williams was appointed editor and the experiment lasted five years, after which Whitaker's exercised their option and terminated the agreement. The title of the journal reverted to *The Bookseller*, and it was edited by Edmond Segrave, who had previously been with Heinemann's. *The Publishers' Circular* then became the joint trade paper until 1938 when, after two profitless years, the arrangement between the trade associations and the Marstons was suspended, and finally lapsed with the outbreak of the Second World War.

The Associated Booksellers celebrated their silver jubilee in 1920 by appointing a paid secretary, W. J. Magenis, for the first time. He was installed in a room in Paternoster Square, donated by Simpkin Marshall, and designated the association's headquarters. In 1923 a three-day conference was held at Nottingham. On this occasion H. W. Keay, president for twenty years, retired and the London bookseller F. W. Denny succeeded him. Thereafter presidents served usually only for two years and long reigns were ended for good. As with the P.A. the A.B. grew subcommittees and considered, along with the publishers, the numerous problems besetting the trade. In 1925 membership stood at 877, and a year later the financial report showed a deficit of £127. Subscriptions were increased and, by 1935, thanks mainly to the introduction of Book Tokens, the membership had grown to over 1,200. Miss Hilda Light succeeded Magenis as secretary in 1930 and the Association moved to larger offices in Warwick Lane, from which Miss Light organized the now annual conference which became more social as publishers began to be invited to take part. The publishers, it should be noted, resisted all suggestions that they should hold a similar conference, or a joint one with booksellers. They always preferred to be present as observers, although as time went by they became participators at joint sessions.

Hilda Light was secretary to H. E. Alden, managing director of Simpkin's, at the time Magenis left the A.B. She was loaned to the Association as a temporary replacement but stayed to harry the enemy, which is how she saw publishers, according to her opposite number at the P.A., Frank Sanders. She captained England at hockey and brought the tough qualities demanded on the hockey field into the secretariat and the conference room. She made many enemies, but Sanders was not one of them. After her death he referred to her as 'that charming but formidable lady'.

The 1930s began with the depression and ended with the outbreak of the Second World War. In this difficult and dark decade the book trade pursued its policy of cooperation and organization against a background of unemployment and mounting international tension.

There were two very important innovations within the trade—Book Tokens and Book Clubs—and one, equally valuable, in the political world—the British Council.

The idea of selling vouchers exchangeable for books in all bookshops was first suggested by Harold Raymond, of Chatto & Windus, at a meeting of the Society of Bookmen in 1926. The scheme did not get under way until 1932, four years after a sub-committee of the National Book Council had investigated it. It should have been discussed at the 1929 conference of the A.B., but more urgent matters left no time for it. For two years little was done (except by Harold Raymond, behind the scenes), then the N.B.C. again approached the booksellers, who approved it in principle at their Chester conference, and invited the N.B.C. to manage it for them. The N.B.C. agreed, but only on the understanding that Book Tokens was the property of the A.B. This arrangement annoyed some publishers, especially Stanley Unwin, and went on aggravating them for years after Book Tokens had proved an unexpected source of extra profits, but it must be admitted that the publishers were slow to take a risk which the booksellers accepted.

The tokens scheme simply consisted of printing stamps of various denominations from 3s. 6d. upwards, which the issuing bookseller was required to affix to a card designed by Book Tokens and costing both the bookseller and the customer 3d. (later 4d.). $12\frac{1}{2}$ per cent of the token value was retained by the bookseller selling it, and the whole cost of the card was handed over to Book Tokens to cover their administrative and production costs. The bookseller exchanging the token received $87\frac{1}{2}$ per cent of the value of the stamp from Book Tokens, so that on the one hand the issuing bookseller received $12\frac{1}{2}$ per cent commission for his pains without risk, and on the other the exchanging bookseller $87\frac{1}{2}$ per cent of the price of the book held in stock or ordered at the usual discount. The scheme at first attracted only 30 per cent of the A.B. membership, but as it became acceptable to the public more and more joined in, so that eventually the right to sell and exchange Book Tokens led scores of tobacconists, stationers and sub-postmistresses to apply for membership, but they were not accepted unless they were already selling some books. This proved, in later years, a mixed blessing to those who wished to organize the actual sellers of books rather than those who applied their commercial expertise to the adhesion of paper to paper. Unexpected profits accrued from tokens which were never redeemed, and this gave the A.B. a hold over its members—a hold which it failed to exert effectively; but that issue belongs to a later section.

In the 'thirties there were other vouchers besides Book Tokens which endeared themselves less to booksellers—cigarette coupons which were exchangeable for 'free' books from fifteen publishers' lists. Books also became a bait with which newspaper proprietors attempted to woo more readers during the circulation war. Sets of Dickens and other classics, encyclopedias, atlases, cookery books, were offered for so many coupons cut out of a newspaper, plus a small cash sum. The *Daily Mail*, for instance, advertised a complete Shakespeare for 5s. 9d., plus six coupons. Basil Blackwell instantly counter-attacked by offering his Shakespeare Head edition of the plays for 6s. and no coupons. Naturally, Bernard Shaw stepped into the ring, once again to Constable's annoyance, and through the *Daily Herald*, his collected plays to date were any reader's for six coupons, plus 3s. 9d. It was a pity that Shaw's natural polemic was never engaged willingly on behalf of the book trade (which he nevertheless enriched); with their joint pertinacity and debating skill, he and Stanley Unwin might have cleaned up for a generation or more of authors, publishers and booksellers. Instead of which they both died rich men in their own right, the one having done considerable service to his fellow bookmen and all authors in the process, the other having contributed to the gaiety of millions. Who is to say which of them conferred the greater blessing?

In any case the system of dangling carrots before newspaper readers died a natural death because it became too costly for the press barons, who agreed a truce. An unsuccessful experiment by the publishers Nicholson & Watson with coupon advertising for one of their books, perhaps proved that booksellers had little to fear from such forms of competition, anyhow.

The introduction of book clubs led to protests from booksellers, who imagined that all their trade would be lost once the public became accustomed to waiting a few years and then buying their books on the cheap, through a club. Foyle's alone among booksellers took action and started their own clubs.

The first book club did not, in fact, undersell. The Book Society, founded by Alan Bott in 1929, sold at full published price by post. A panel of authors—J. B. Priestley and Hugh Walpole were amongst the first judges—made a monthly choice and, as membership grew, the publisher of the selected book was able to reduce its price because he could order a larger run. Later still, he was obliged to reduce it, because otherwise the Society would not choose his book. Many Book Society members were expatriates, or lived in remote parts of the country far from bookshops, and there was no evidence that the Society harmed the retail book world.

The creation of Readers' Union by John Baker in 1937 might have seemed more of a threat, particularly as it enrolled 17,000 members in a year. Baker had been involved in selling new books on the instalment plan (sometimes for as little as 1d. per day) through the Phoenix Book Company, founded in 1928. But even this was too expensive for those on a small income. Readers' Union offered them the same books, in tastefully designed editions, at 2s. 6d. each, a reduction, in the case of the first choice, of 13s. 6d.; but, of course, members had to wait for a period after original publication before getting this bargain. Foyle's formed another general book club, later branching out into numerous specialist subjects as well. The Student Christian Movement Press inaugurated a Religious Book Club in 1937, but the most famous of the specialists was Victor Gollancz's Left Book Club, which started in 1936 and had 60,000 members at the height of its success.

Although booksellers eventually learned to cooperate with those clubs willing to deal with them, and accepted subscriptions on their behalf, it became apparent that the clubs were serving a new market and not poaching on the booksellers' traditional preserves. The size of the cake was not fixed, it transpired, but it took years of suspicion and ill will before the majority of retailers, understandably jealous during a period of difficult trading conditions, accepted the evidence.

The British Council was set up by the government in 1934 for the purpose of selling the British way of life. Books were an important commodity in this propaganda, and Stanley Unwin, who had for years maintained that trade follows the book, was appointed to the executive committee of the Council as early as 1935. The Council established libraries in foreign countries and organized exhibitions of books with increasing cooperation from publishers.

To return to the A.B. and its chronic fear of competition the growth of 'other traders' amongst Twopenny Library owners alarmed booksellers at the 1932 Chester conference. At the end of that year 16 firms, including a chain of tobacconists, had been recognized for trade terms in this activity, and the number increased by 42 in 1933, 73 in 1934 and 91 in 1935, with Foyle's, again, offering the amenity to interested newsagents and stationers in Greater London and the provinces. At a time of economic depression the slightest innovation is bound to cause concern in those who see their livelihood threatened. There was the cinema and radio to compete with; soon there was also to be television, its effects only delayed by the outbreak of war. Rents were rising, overheads going up, and booksellers in northern towns especially were forced out of business as unemployment grew. If for no other reason than raising morale, it was necessary for Basil Blackwell, when President of the A.B., to make rallying noises. As one not accustomed to make noises without good reason, and who found himself representative of

very many much less fortunately placed than himself, he invited
Stanley Unwin, then president of the P.A. (and no two presidents have
ever been better matched) to be joint host with him at an unofficial
weekend conference of fifty publishers and booksellers. Blackwell and
Unwin had already inaugurated fortnightly meetings, at which each
paid for his own lunch, to keep one another informed of the feelings of
their respective members; the Ripon Hall Conference, Blackwell's
idea, was a natural consequence of this, and introduced an element of
frank informality into the unreported discussions. At Ripon Hall those
present were not under the constraint of being guests, since they had
paid 50s. for the privilege of being there, and they spoke and argued
together freely about the important issues of the time, thus enhancing
the work of the joint committee whose deliberations had done so much
to bring them together. Opportunities for such joint discussions were
less frequent at this time than in later decades, when all leading
publishers were invited to attend booksellers' conferences. Friendships
that were to help the trade as a whole were made at Ripon Hall in
1934, and sealed when the experiment was repeated in 1936. The
cooperation resulting from these two between-the-wars decades was to
serve the trade nobly in the harrowing and nearly disastrous early years
of World War Two.

The other important events of the 'thirties were the setting up of a
permanent Joint Advisory Committee (the J.A.C.) of representatives
of the two trade associations; the appointment of Frank Sanders as
secretary to the P.A. in 1934; the prosecution of James Hanley's *Boy*,
when the publishers, Boriswood, were fined £400 and yet remained
liable to further prosecution for the same book in other courts, and the
start of Penguin Books, in 1935.

2

The Dynasties

Longmans; John Murray; Macmillan; William Collins, Sons & Co.; J. M. Dent & Sons; Thomas Nelson & Sons; A. & C. Black; Blackie & Son; William Blackwood & Sons; Frederick Warne; B. T. Batsford; G. Bell & Sons; George G. Harrap; Hutchinson; Hodder & Stoughton; Ward, Lock; Sampson Low; J. Whitaker & Sons; Sir Isaac Pitman & Sons.

In the Edwardian decade a sixth generation of Longman, Robert Guy and William L., both great-grandsons of the third Thomas Longman, became partners in 1909. These two cousins took a leading part in expanding the overseas branches of the house, and William took a particular interest in India, discovering that publishing there in the vernacular was even more rewarding than selling British books. The Longmans tended to live to advanced ages, so that fathers, sons, uncles, nephews and brothers worked side by side for many years, one or other occupying the position of chairman and of managing director at different times. Historically, to one who did not know them, they become an amorphous group but they were, in fact, very much individuals, concerned with trade affairs as well as with their imprint. They were not, however, afraid to call on outside help when this seemed necessary. In 1921, two years after the retirement of Thomas Norton V, one Kenneth Potter, formerly an accountant, joined them and became a director a year later. Potter gave to Longmans the same drive and ability as members of the family had devoted to it for centuries, and understood the traditions of the business and the trade of which he became an influential part. Not all of the accountants who followed him into publishing in later years had the same inherent sympathy with book-making as distinct from book-keeping.

The old-established family of publishers attracted an even more eminent dynasty of authors in the Trevelyan family. Sir George Otto (nephew of Lord Macaulay) was on the list at the turn of the century and his son, George Macaulay, became the most distinguished Longman historian of this period. G.M. wrote a biography of his father, a three-volume work on Garibaldi and the making of modern Italy, and many studies of British history, a dozen of which were in print in 1940. In the 1930s four other Trevelyans, including R.C., whose collected works appeared in two volumes in 1939, graced this imprint.

The 'thirties also brought Longmans the novelists Stella Gibbons, whose *Cold Comfort Farm* is still popular, Mary Renault (*Purposes of Love*, 1939), and the Americans, James Gould Cozzens and Thornton Wilder. *Roget's Thesaurus of English Words and Phrases* was a valuable backlist title often revised and reissued, as was Gray's *Anatomy*, the twenty-fourth edition of which was brought out in 1930. In the ever-important educational department (and publishing was still small enough in those days to have departments rather than divisions) C. E. Eckersley (English) and W. F. H. Whitmarsh (French) embarked on their highly successful textbooks destined to serve several generations.

And in 1938, Mark, the last Longman to become the head of the firm, first reported for duty at the offices in Paternoster Row which were soon to be suddenly destroyed.

There were fewer Murrays than Longmans, but the various Johns of that ilk never allowed the family fortunes to rest upon the laurels of the Byron industry. The fourth Murray, a scholar and author like his father, edited Gibbon's autobiography as well as the correspondence of the poet who meant so much to their early reputation. During his reign Reginald Smith of Smith & Elder died, in the middle of the First World War, and Murray's acquired their list, with the exception of the great *Dictionary of National Biography*, which went to Oxford University Press. With Smith & Elder came the valuable Conan Doyle stories and novels, and the *Cornhill Magazine*, always a source of new authors. From 1916 *Cornhill* was issued alongside the *Quarterly Review*, from 50 Albemarle Street. Sir John Murray IV died in 1928 and was succeeded by his son, who became editor of the *Quarterly*. It was in his reign that Axel Munthe joined the list and John Gibbins joined the staff; the one acquisition was as longlasting as the other, with the *Story of San Michele* a solid backlist title in 1970, and Mr Gibbins, as publicity manager, well down the course towards his gold watch. Murray V had no son, and brought in his nephew, John Grey, who later changed his name by deed poll to preserve the identity of the house. During the 'thirties John Betjeman, Osbert Lancaster, Freya Stark and others added new lustre to a list which always combined economic viability with scholarly standards.

The Macmillans, like the Longmans, though not as old established, produced sufficient offspring to carry on the tradition. Sir Frederick had no direct successor in St Martin's Street, but his nephews Daniel and Harold took over, the former holding the senior position until his death, whilst the younger pursued a political career ending in the highest office. They were joined shortly before the Second World War by Lovat Dickson, a young Canadian who had run his own imprint for a number of years. Dickson has related his experiences in a series of autobiographies, of which the second, *The House of Words*, is of especial interest to students of book trade history.

Macmillan's opened overseas branches in Melbourne (1904) and Toronto (1905), the former American agency being by then already a separate company under George Platt Brett, son of the first manager appointed by Sir Frederick. The home list strengthened and grew, acquiring a marked Irish flavour with W. B. Yeats. Yeats had been rejected in 1900 by the firm's readers Mowbray Morris and John Morley; the former had conceded that Yeats had 'a feeling for literature' and 'a poetical gift ... higher than [Stephen] Phillips', but the latter had thought it 'sheer nonsense'. Yeats was first published by Macmillan in 1916, by which time James Stephens, Æ and others of his country-men were already familiar with the imposing frontage of St Martin's House. Equally illustrious names were to follow them across the Irish sea in the 'twenties and 'thirties, amongst them Sean O'Casey, Frank O'Connor and Lennox Robinson. As the ultra-conservative editors Morris and Morley were followed by younger men, the list became broader-based, bringing in Hugh Walpole, Charles Morgan, A. G. Macdonnell, James Hilton and two of the Sitwells, Edith and Osbert.

Meanwhile the Macmillans expanded their educational list with classical texts still favoured by advanced schools in the 1970s, and with Hall and Knight's algebra books, which continued to earn such vast sums that it became a family joke to name the statues at the entrance to their country seat, Birch Grove, after the two mathematicians. The leaning towards economics became more marked in the 'twenties, when J. M. Keynes, Joan Robinson and A. C. Pigou enhanced this side of the list. The historians Lewis Namier and E. H. Carr published with them, as did the great anthropologist Sir James Frazer, whose *The Golden Bough* at last found a wider public when it was put out in an abridged edition in 1922. For a company which produced a conservative prime minister, Macmillan's had a good record of progressive literature.

Thomas Mark, who joined the company in 1913 and remained with it for forty-six years, should be mentioned, if for no other reason, than for his sympathetic handling of Hugh Walpole, the author of the Herries series, who not only wrote too much but involved himself in too many outside interests, to the detriment of verisimilitude in his novels. Mark was his editor, proof-corrector and patient friend; for a fuller apprecia-tion of his worth to author, publisher and general reader, Charles Morgan's *The House of Macmillan* and Rupert Hart-Davis's *Hugh Walpole* should be consulted.

At Collins, in London, Glasgow and in the Commonwealth, expan-sion was as relentless as ever. William III was an eccentric who dressed in the first garment which came to hand, took his own meat and game into restaurants so that he might be certain of the quality of his meals, and paid his wife £5 every time he failed to attend divine service on a Sunday (which was often). He modernized the printing presses at

Glasgow, established a stationery manufacturing department in Sydney, New South Wales, and proudly brought out Collins's Illustrated Pocket Classics (at first clumsily named Collin's Handy Illustrated Pocket Novels) in the autumn of 1903, three years before the first of Dent's Everyman Library. *David Copperfield* was the first Collins Classic, and it held its place in their top ten selling titles for half a century. The pace at which this Collins, who, unlike his father, was no puritan, conducted his working life added some gaiety to the pursuit of wealth. But he died, as he had lived, in too great a hurry; his impatience led him to unlock the lift gates of his London flat and fall to his death down the shaft.

William IV (the nephew, not the son, of the previous chairman) succeeded in 1906 and had a happy working relationship with his younger brother Godfrey. William supervised stationery and office affairs; his brother became the publisher, and, in competition with Nelson's, produced the 7d. reprints of novels which caused such heartburn in official circles. Godfrey became a liberal M.P., and served in the First World War along with his brother and 275 of their employees. After the war he became secretary of state for Scotland in the National Government first under Ramsay MacDonald, then under Stanley Baldwin. But before his admission to the cabinet necessitated his removal from business life, he had successfully created a fiction and general list which brought Collins well into the twentieth century ahead of most of their competitors. Rose Macaulay, a stray from her dynasty which published with Longmans, was one of Godfrey's first post-war authors, and she adorned the Collins list from *Potterism* (1920) until her last novel, *The Towers of Trebizond* (1956). Walter de la Mare's *Memoirs of a Midget* came his way in 1921, and in 1922 it was his year to bear the loss on a new work by H. G. Wells — a volume of political essays, long forgotten. In 1926 came Collins's first Agatha Christie thriller, *The Murder of Roger Ackroyd* (she had previously been published by John Lane), and four years later the long-lived Crime Club series was inaugurated.

The Collinses, numerous and energetic though they were, could not do without outside help. Sir Godfrey brought to London in 1926 F. T. Smith as chief editor, R. J. Politzer as publicity manager and Sydney J. Goldsack, in charge of sales. Goldsack, who had opened the New York office for the company in 1923 and then made two world trips, was a Collins in spirit if not in name, and he spent his life selling their list. Politzer, working in a field where it is difficult to judge what success or failure is due to the actions and inspirations of the individual concerned, was revered. Certainly, until the Hamlyn marketing adventures of the 1950s and 1960s no books were promoted with more zest and belief in the product than when Politzer was in charge of publicity and Goldsack ran the sales force.

When Sir Godfrey joined the government, William V—W. A. R. ('Billy') Collins—assumed more responsibility and guided the publishing side of the firm through further years of expansion, with Rosamond Lehmann, Howard Spring and Peter Cheyney, amongst others, joining the list. William V was matched on the printing and Bible side by his cousin, William Hope, and by his brother, Ian, although William IV was still in the chair. Sir Godfrey never returned to active publishing, dying in office in 1936.

Joseph Malaby Dent's finest contribution to publishing was the institution of Everyman's Library. When he issued the first title— Boswell's *Life of Johnson*, published in two volumes in 1906—he had the clear idea that he wished to publish a cheap library of the greatest works ever written. Not just the greatest novels, but the most important classical works, biographies, religious and philosophical treatises, political and social theses, plays, poems and chronicles of travel and adventure. The knowledge to be derived from the series would benefit not only men like J. M. Dent himself, who had little formal education, but anyone, of whatever standard of education, who was willing to continue learning.

Dent had the simplicity and imagination to see what he was doing as both a cultural benefit to his fellows and as a business enterprise. In the note that Ernest Rhys, first and foremost editor of Everyman, added to many of the volumes, he quoted Victor Hugo as saying that a library was 'an act of faith'. Everyman's Library was precisely that, with its decorative endpapers embellishing the words

> Everyman I will go with thee
> and be thy Guide
> In thy most need
> To go by thy side.

Everyman's Library, at 1s. a volume, paid off at every level. Dent had started it at the age of fifty-seven. Seven years later he published the first encyclopaedia issued exclusively through the trade. This work was often revised, and formed part of a library of reference works under the general Everyman imprint.

Dent lost two sons in the First World War, but the family retained control through a surviving child, Hugh, who arranged the purchase of Aldine House in Bedford Street, the premises which his father had leased from Macmillan's in the 1890s. Hugh Dent died in 1938 and was followed by W. G. Taylor, president of the P.A. from 1935-7, and one who entered publishing after embarking on a different career. Joseph Malaby died in 1926, and his *Memoirs* were published two years later. He was not, perhaps, the most loveable of men, but he stamped his particular vision on publishing as few have done before or since, and made his name synonymous in many minds with the search for learning.

Nelson's, of Edinburgh, also issued a series of classics which were steadily successful throughout the century, but, like Collins', they never grew to the range of Everyman. Nelson's were rivals to Collins in the 7d. reprint market before the First World War, and even succeeded in publishing their first titles several days before their Glasgow competitors. In 1906 John Buchan joined them as advisory editor in Parkside, Edinburgh, after which district a series of their classics was called. It is scarcely credible that so prolific a writer as Buchan should also have been involved in the daily job of publishing, but in fact he probably wrote some of his bestselling works in his time with Nelson's. He remained with the firm until long after the First World War, the history of which he wrote for them, recording amongst many other deaths that of Captain T. A. Nelson, whose promise as a publisher was not allowed to flower. Ian Nelson, his younger brother, succeeded to the business, and Buchan gradually became absorbed in his writing and politics to the exclusion of publishing. He was a conservative M.P. for some years and ended his life in 1940 as Lord Tweedsmuir, Governor-General of Canada. In 1938 H. P. Morrison joined Nelson's as managing director, and his bent for philosophy soon showed itself in the list. John Hampden, known as a writer, followed Henry Scheurmier as head of the London office for many years and was succeeded by Mervyn Horder, who later bought Gerald Duckworth's business.

Another great Scottish firm, A. & C. Black, began the century at low ebb. The last of the founder's sons, James Tait, had retired in 1899, and the *Encyclopaedia Britannica* had been sold off, the principals of the sale being Adam Rimmer Black, and W. W. Callender, who had joined the firm as a boy in 1876. It was the latter who realized the potential of three-colour printing, and inaugurated Black's highly successful series on Venice, Brittany, India, Alpine flowers, Birds of Britain and other suitable subjects, some eighty titles in all produced over fourteen years. *Who's Who*, established as an annual once it had been purchased in 1896, was broadened to include the eminent in all fields, and not just the rich and noble, thus extending its market immeasurably. *The Writers' and Artists' Year Book*, first published in 1906, became an important reference work for all engaged in writing for books and periodicals, and Black's *Medical Encyclopaedia* also became an authoritative volume. With these three, the *Encyclopaedia Biblica*, and other publications, A. & C. Black became a good, though modest, second to Oxford University Press in the field of reference books.

Albert Schweitzer joined the list in 1910 with *The Quest for the Historical Jesus*, and this at present unfashionable twentieth-century saint published most of his books from Soho Square. The fiction list had been allowed to die, but in 1919 they published Charles Morgan's *The Gunroom*, the author having sent it to Black's because they published *The Writers' and Artists' Year Book*. It did not subscribe well because the imprint was not noted for fiction, but such copies as were sold mysteriously disappeared from shops and libraries in a curious suppression thought, by some, to be inspired by the fact that the Admiralty frowned upon a story about the navy written from a junior officer's viewpoint. It was not until 1968, when Morgan had been dead for several years, that it became available again through Chatto & Windus; the lords of Admiralty may have frowned still, but they did not, apparently, interfere with circulation.

J. D. Newth joined Black's in 1925, learned his trade under Callender and became a director in 1935, a year before Adam Black died suddenly one morning on his way to Soho Square. Archibald, son of Adam, then became chairman.

At the start of the century Walter, Dr W. G. Blackie, second son of the founder, was still in the chair, but he had retired from active participation, and died in 1906 only three years before the firm's centenary. His sons and nephews succeeded, and the business prospered quietly, producing sumptuous volumes for children and adults in an age accustomed to elegance at the highest echelons. John Alexander, who took the chair on his father's death, suffered the loss of his only son in the First World War, and died himself in 1918. (A Nelson, two Dents, a Blackie, a nephew of Heinemann, and so many others who might have graced the publishing scene of the twentieth century died in that senseless war.) Blackie's, like other family businesses, rallied from the blow and the Bisacres, related by marriage, took the place of those who were lost in battle, and carried on the imprint. Frederick Bisacre, nephew-in-law to John Alexander Blackie, joined in 1919, and his experience as an engineer leant practical value to the expansion of the technical side of the list. Meanwhile the market already established in educational books and children's 'rewards' was consolidated, with G. A. Henty catering for generations of boys, and Angela Brazil, from 1907, for girls.

Black, Blackie, Blackwood, might almost be a conjugation. The house of Blackwood, which had published much of George Eliot's work in the nineteenth century, entered the twentieth under George William Blackwood, great-grandson of the founder. He edited *Blackwood's Magazine* until his death during the Second World War, and it was in his time, in 1911, that Ivy Compton-Burnett's first novel, *Dolores*, came out under his imprint, fourteen years before any of her other work was published.

The London dynasties also prospered. Frederick Warne's introduced one of their most successful and eminent authors in 1902 when Beatrix

Potter's *The Tale of Peter Rabbit* was published. Miss Potter, whose twenty-three small books sold millions in the decades to come, was engaged to Norman Warne, youngest son of the founder, when he died in 1905. She remained loyal to the family, and made a fortune for herself and them.

In 1903, Frederick Warne Stephens, grandson of the founder, joined the firm, which was made into a limited company in 1919, with Fruing Warne, son of Frederick, as managing director (Fruing's brother Harold left to start his own stationery business). Fruing died in 1928 and Arthur L. Stephens became managing director. By then Arthur's son Cyril was already in the business, and the family connection and succession firmly sealed. In 1938 the popular Observer series of genuinely pocket-sized guides to birds, trees, architecture, cars and larger moths, etc., was successfully launched.

Bradley Thomas, first of the book trade Batsfords, died at the age of eighty-three, in 1904; it was his practice, until quite late in life, to walk daily most of the way to his shop in Holborn from his residence in Kilburn, in north-west London, and he did not, in fact, give up regular work until the end of 1903. His eldest son, Bradley II, outlived him by only two years, leaving the direction of the firm in the hands of his youngest brother, Herbert, and his nephew, Harry. Herbert built up the architectural side of the list, earning the tribute, in an obituary in the journal of the Royal Institute of British Architects, that he 'combined the functions of editor and patron, and encouraged architects to record their own impressions of the meaning of architecture'. Herbert died in 1917, leaving Harry much more committed to publishing than bookselling than the firm had been in its earliest days. Harry was now the sole surviving Batsford in the business, although Aunt Florence had travelled the list in the First World War and may well have been the first woman book representative.

Under Harry, Batsford's not only endured, but actually thrived through the hard times of the 'twenties and 'thirties. Charles Fry joined in 1924; working hours, he was told, were 9 a.m. to 6.30 p.m. On the first day, on the dot of nine, he rang the bell in High Holborn, and after a long time an 'elderly crone', as he later described her, opened the door and invited him in, saying, 'Mr 'Arry's not 'ere yet; 'E's out with some bird, I suppose.' It transpired that 'Mr 'Arry', and others, were wont to appear nearer to ten o'clock than nine, which must have made Bradley Thomas I turn over in his grave. But the founder could scarcely have failed to admire the industry of his grandson and Charles Fry, who were joined, in 1927, by Francis Lucarotti, eventually to become production manager, and, in 1928, by Brian Cook, son of Harry's sister, who subsequently changed his name to Batsford. Brian Cook entered the family business as an enthusiastic artist with a predilection for gaily coloured jackets which became the image of the imprint within a short time.

On the very eve of the great slump Batsford's moved west to North Audley Street in Mayfair, taking their bookshop with them. That they survived the depression was entirely due to their adaptability. They specialized, when in Holborn, in fine editions, sumptuously illustrated, less expensive than their pre-war productions, but still quality books in comparatively small editions. Fry and Cook realized that they must produce cheaper books if they were to stay in business, and Harry Batsford not only listened to their youthful suggestions but entered zestfully into the planning of the British Heritage Series, which aimed to provide a text of 40,000 words plus upwards of 130 illustrations per volume. To achieve this at a popular price it was necessary to think in terms of first editions of 10,000 copies. So they did exactly this, and most of the titles had to be reprinted. A similar series on the Face of Britain was then launched.

Batsford, Fry and Cook not only published these books; they also wrote and illustrated many of them. Both series became a joyous crusade for the three of them; they would set off in an old motor-car, leaving their business cares behind them in Mayfair, and tour around whichever part of the British Isles was to be their next subject. Publishing can seldom have provided more pleasure for those who lived by it, even though Charles Fry complained about some of the primus-stove conditions he was expected to endure. It was into this atmosphere that Sam Carr, having first deliberately gained post-graduate experience in a London bookshop, first entered upon his editorial career. He was just in time to savour these joys vicariously before the Second World War put an end to such frolics, though not, happily, to the Batsford list which was adapted, with the usual ingenuity, to the times.

It is improbable that such frivolity would have been countenanced within the austere, even mausoleum-like, portals of York House, Portugal Street, where the descendants of George Bell, who had started in the same decade as Bradley Batsford, continued to prosper steadily, not least from the sale of school texts. Edward, son of the founder, was an early president of the P.A., and Colonel A. H. Bell, a grandson, who had been in the Royal Engineers for thirty years, joined the board in 1927, becoming chairman in 1936. Outside the family there were Guy H. Bickers, managing director for many years, and A. W. Ready, who came from Cambridge University Press in 1921 and was elected to the board in 1936. Ready was a leading figure in educational publishing for over forty years, and Bell's books went by the million into many schools and colleges, notably the mathematics books of C. V. Durell.

Harrap's, a newer dynasty than the others, also forged ahead in educational publishing. Walter, second son of George G., joined the firm in 1912 aged seventeen, and returned after war service. Noting that publishers worked too much in isolation, and following the Unwin line of greater cooperation, he formed the Advertising Circle, later the Publishers' Publicity Circle. When George G. Harrap died in 1938, G. Oliver Anderson succeeded to the chairmanship of the company, with Walter and the new chairman's son, R. Olaf, in active participation. Premises were acquired in High Holborn in 1935, about the time Winston Spencer Churchill's four-volume *Marlborough: His Life and Times* was published. The vast stone building survived the blitz of the Second World War; it seemed made to endure all onslaughts. Any bookseller's collector who was also a theatre-goer must have felt he was making his way to the 'gods' as he climbed to Harrap's second-floor trade counter, labouring up the clanging steps to sign for his daily order, and passing the entrance to Charles Fox, Wig-Makers, on his way.

Walter Hutchinson succeeded his father in 1926 as head of a company which, between the wars, absorbed so many lists that no complete tally of them is known. Certainly the old imprints of Rider (established c. 1700), Hurst & Blackett (1812), Skeffington (1840), Stanley Paul (1908) and Jarrold's (1916), were amongst those amalgamated with Hutchinson's of Paternoster Row. When the young Robert Lusty joined in 1928 he asked to be given charge of an imprint and had two bales of books dumped into his office, one labelled 'Selwyn', the other 'Blount'. Selwyn & Blount was founded by Roger Ingpen, a Shelley scholar who had learned his publishing with Smith & Elder. After leaving Hutchinson's, who had acquired his list, he became an antiquarian bookseller in Museum Street and started another imprint, Ingpen & Grant, which took over the publication of Edward Thomas's complete poems from Selwyn. Lusty, after leaving Hutchinson's for the new list of Michael Joseph in 1935, returned as managing director in 1956, after Walter's death. Walter always inspired controversy, and in 1969 there was correspondence in *The Bookseller* about the reading fees he paid, J. C. Reynolds recalling that he received 2s. 6d. per manuscript read in the 1930s, while Humphrey Wilson countered with 5s.

The grandson of Matthew Hodder, Ernest Hodder-Williams, joined Hodder & Stoughton in 1902, and his enterprise led to the company publishing for London Universities Press in 1904, the name being changed to University of London Press six years later. U.L.P. was the precursor of the English Universities Press, whose Teach Yourself series started in 1935 under Leonard Cutts, grew eventually to over 350 titles, becoming standard stock in every bookshop in the English-speaking world. When Ernest Hodder-Williams died in 1927, his brothers Percy and Ralph continued the business, which had developed on the fiction and general sides since the days of its founders, although the original tradition remained very much alive. The Moffatt translation of the New Testament came out in 1913, and the complete Bible in his version in 1926. Paul Hodder-Williams and John Attenborough, both great-grandsons of Matthew Hodder (who died in 1911, at which juncture his partner T. W. Stoughton withdrew from the firm), began their careers with the company in the 1930s and were destined to preside over changes which might well have shocked the two congregationalists who started it all.

Of the other family businesses Ward, Lock were guided by various Locks throughout the period and acquired such authors as Edgar Wallace, Dornford Yates and E. Phillips Oppenheim. The famous Wonder Books, with comic endpapers familiar to the children of several generations, were started in 1905. Colonel Eric Shipton, a great-grandson of the founder, entered the firm in 1914. At that time there was one female employee on the staff, described in the official history as a 'critic'. Eric Shipton soon went to the war, and by the time he returned to publishing there were more than sixty women on the payroll.

Sampson Low & Marston, proprietors of *The Publishers' Circular*, continued the book side of their enterprise under Fred Rymer, who received authors with his own brand of informality. He was wont to preside over Sampson Low's affairs in shirtsleeves, waistcoat and bowler hat.

Whitaker's, who owned *The Bookseller*, continued to produce their own editors until 1933 when George Herbert Whitaker's son Haddon became head of the firm. Edmond Segrave was then appointed the fourth editor of the journal.

Sir Isaac Pitman's two sons brought their list into the twentieth century, the founder having died in 1897. Men of very different stamp, one preferred to work on idealistic lines, the other said he would as soon manufacture and sell beer if that made more money. The former's son, James (after Sir James) inherited his father's outlook and was later to become head of the firm. Pitman's was always in the forefront of educational publishing, as befitted it as the pioneer of shorthand and typewriting books, which Sir James believed did as much to emancipate women as giving them the vote. Pitman's took over Isbister & Son during the Edwardian decade, and the technical house of Whittaker (not to be confused with the proprietors of *The Bookseller*) in about 1920, at the same period in which they moved into offices in Parker Street where they long remained.

3

The University Presses

Oxford University Press; Cambridge University Press; Manchester University Press; University of Wales Press; University of London Press.

Oxford and Cambridge publishing evolved differently, although the presses of the two leading universities remained linked through their common interest in the official state rights in the Bible.

The Delegates of the Press at Oxford remained a committee responsible to the university and in overall control of both Oxford University Press and of the Clarendon Press (see p. 253). The former maintained its publishing headquarters in London, where the publisher to the Press organized the broadly commercial side of the list. The Clarendon Press continued to operate from offices in Oxford, where it dealt with works of a purely learned and educational nature, but the sales and distribution forces for both were centred on London.

Humphrey Milford succeeded Henry Frowde as publisher to O.U.P. in 1913, and remained in command during both world wars. Milford, in addition to his work as publisher, edited volumes of verse by Robert Browning and William Cowper, amongst others. It was under his aegis that the World's Classics, taken over from Grant Richards, were expanded, that *The Oxford Dictionary of Quotations* was compiled, and the Oxford History of England series, originally planned in fourteen volumes, was started. During the same period *The Oxford English Dictionary*, under the wing of the Clarendon Press, was completed. The *O.E.D.* was first suggested by Dean Trench in 1857, and the first volume was issued in 1884. It gave rise to a number of smaller dictionaries—the *Shorter*, in one and two volumes, the *Concise*, the *Pocket* (the pocket in mind being, apparently, that of a somewhat voluminous overcoat) and the *Little*.

During this period overseas branches were opened in Toronto in 1904, Melbourne in 1908, Bombay in 1912 and Cape Town in 1915. In the 'twenties there was further expansion in several directions, and the New York branch started to publish autonomously, as well as continuing to distribute books originating in London and Oxford. In 1926 O.U.P. began to cater specifically for schools abroad by instituting the overseas education department, heralding the time when books would be published locally in some three dozen African and Asian languages and dialects, in addition to English-language texts. The London office was moved to Amen House, Warwick Square, in 1924, and six years later a warehouse was built at Neasden, near London's North Circular Road.

The breadth and depth of Oxford publishing knew no limits. A children's books department was started in 1907, an International Series of Monographs in Physics in 1931, there were medical and musical offshoots, Medieval and Early Christian texts, and the Oxford Standard Authors series. The O.S.A. consisted of definitive editions of the works of major and minor poets, and it spilt over, in time, to include some prose works.

Alongside O.U.P., the Clarendon Press developed in the early decades of the twentieth century under Charles Cannan, R. W. Chapman (a Jane Austen scholar) and Kenneth Sisam. The great dictionary was its prime consideration, but *The Dictionary of National Biography* also came under its control when Reginald Smith of Smith & Elder died in 1916. To the general public, and indeed to the book trade, O.U.P. and the Clarendon Press were one, and it is probable that the fine distinctions between the two were appreciated only by those intimately connected with their direction. The Delegates of the Press controlled both, and were responsible only to the university. There were no shareholders in this huge enterprise, and the profits from its commercial ventures were used to sponsor research and to underwrite the cost of producing academic works which did not enjoy large sales, or could not earn their subsidies.

There were many distinguished writers involved in editorial work for the press, none more so than Gerard Hopkins, who joined in 1919 and remained for thirty-eight years. He was a translator of note and chairman of the Society of Bookmen for many years.

Cambridge publishing continued to be controlled by the Syndics in Cambridge, with a manager in London who did not originate any books of his own but was concerned solely with sales and promotion. Whilst the Delegates at Oxford were happy to see their list grow, and to establish branches in distant parts, Cambridge were content to expand more slowly, and, in particular, to dwell upon the quality of their printing and production. Their success was due to two remarkable men, neither of them academics — Walter Lewis and Stanley Morison. Their unique contribution is recorded in a beautifully simple piece of bookmaking, *Two Men*, issued by Brooke Crutchley in 1968, when Printer to the University. Walter Lewis was Crutchley's predecessor as Printer, and Stanley Morison was typographical adviser to the Press from 1925 to 1945, historian of *The Times*, author, typefounder and leading light of the Monotype Corporation for many years. Their story belongs to the history of printing, but such was their devotion to producing not the

Book Beautiful, but books that were beautiful because they were so easy to read and handle, that they must be mentioned in passing in any history of publishing and bookselling.

The administration of C.U.P. underwent radical changes at the beginning of the century, when official recognition was given to the status of Printer and of publishing manager. It will be recalled that C. J. Clay, Printer from 1854, was first manager of the London office. His sons, John and C. F. Clay, shared these functions subsequently, but in 1905 the elder was officially appointed Printer, and the younger, London manager. At this time R. T. Wright was secretary to the Syndics. He was succeeded by A. R. Waller in 1911. Not, however, before he had contracted with Horace Hooper for the Press to publish the eleventh edition of the *Encyclopaedia Britannica*. Eyebrows were raised at high table on publication — the encyclopaedia had not been revised with the same degree of academic excellence as before and after — and the twelfth edition was not issued by C.U.P.

John Clay died in 1916; his successor as Printer, J. B. Peace, survived only until 1922, the same year that Waller died. Thereafter Lewis took over the printing, and the publishing side revived alongside it with a remarkable list of scientific bestsellers in the works of Sir James Jeans, A. S. Eddington and others. The Cambridge Modern History, born earlier in the century, grew as planned, and although C.U.P. did not open any overseas branches during this period it enjoyed a time of solid growth. R. J. L. Kingsford, a former assistant secretary to the Syndics, became London manager in the 'thirties, and was in charge when the offices in Fetter Lane, taken at the time of reorganization in 1905, were vacated in 1937 for the new building in Euston Road appropriately named Bentley House.

Until 1912 the University of Manchester published occasionally through the local booksellers Sherratt & Hughes, but in that year their own press was founded and H. M. McKechnie was appointed secretary. Longmans at first undertook distribution, but from 1931 they handled it for themselves. The University of Wales Press, in Cathays Park, Cardiff, commenced publishing in 1922, but other universities did not establish their own imprints during this period. As noted the London Universities Press changed its name to University of London Press in 1910 and leaned heavily on Hodder & Stoughton, who subsequently became its sole owners.

4

Other Nineteenth-Century Publishers

William Heinemann; Methuen; Chapman & Hall; Routledge & Kegan Paul; George Allen & Unwin; Cassell; Chatto & Windus; Grant Richards; Gerald Duckworth; Constable; The Bodley Head; Eyre & Spottiswoode; Putnam; Edward Arnold; Crosby Lockwood & Son.

Some publishers entered the twentieth century with their initial impetus unimpaired; others limped into it in urgent need of a blood transfusion. Amongst the former were William Heinemann and Algernon Methuen, both comparative newcomers as yet, but firmly established in their first, and only, generation.

In the new century John Galsworthy, Somerset Maugham, John Masefield and William de Morgan, among many other native authors, not only joined Heinemann, but stayed with him. De Morgan, whose *Joseph Vance* was accepted when the author was past sixty, was recommended to Heinemann by Bullen, of Lawrence & Bullen, whose firm had not sufficient resources for so long a novel. Lawrence felt so enthusiastic about *Vance* that he literally staggered round to his fellow publisher with the heavy manuscript, some of which was written on torn envelopes and odd scraps of paper. Heinemann published this unkempt offering, and all of de Morgan's subsequent work.

Heinemann had a habit of over-editing, and occasionally infuriated his authors. However, as he didn't always remember what he had added, a tactful writer could delete what wasn't his own in proof. Publishing as an international activity continued to absorb Heinemann and he spent as much time travelling and discovering authors as he did in London, where in his absence his office was presided over by Sydney Pawling, who had come to him from Mudie's. His travels once brought him a wife as well as an author, and an unhappy marriage ensued. His domestic life had been more felicitous in the days when the painter Whistler, a desperate widower, had in his grief taken over the publisher's home to such an extent that, on one occasion, he inquired as to the whereabouts of 'my guest, Heinemann'.

The Ars Una series was inaugurated with Saloman Reinach's *Apollo*, and it was Reinach who introduced Heinemann to James Loeb, who was pursuing the idea of a classical library with original texts on one page and a sound translation on the opposite. Loeb said of Heinemann that he displayed real interest and the utmost deference to his, Loeb's, wishes, although he had no hesitation in making it clear when the scholar's ideas did not conform with those of the practical publisher's. They met several times, and Heinemann advised Loeb that there was no need to advertise so excellent a venture because the library would find its own level. Loeb fell ill when only five volumes had been issued, and by the time of his recovery in 1917, although publication continued, William Heinemann was already threatened with blindness, and low in spirit from the loss of his nephew in the war.

On a less academic level than the Loeb series was Heinemann's publication, arranged simultaneously in nine European languages, of the explorer Shackleton's *Heart of the Antarctic* (1910). This feat of organization pre-dated the work of Walter Neurath and Paul Hamlyn by nearly fifty years.

These were Heinemann's last real achievements. The war, for one of Anglo-German origins, was a particularly unhappy period, and there was the added frustration of seeing his work for international copyright and the International Congress of Publishers come to a standstill. He was left a divided man, without the consolation of wife and family, and soon after the Armistice of 1918, he died. In his thirty years of publishing he had issued new books by over five hundred writers, half of whom were novelists.

In 1920, Doubleday, Page & Co. of New York bought Heinemann's, but the English company was continued with Theodore Byard as chairman and Charles S. Evans as managing director. It was at the latter's suggestion that nine novels by Galsworthy were turned, with the interpolation of bridge passages, into *The Forsyte Saga*, *A Modern Comedy*, and *The End of the Chapter*. Alexander Frere joined in 1923, and by the end of the 'twenties Heinemann's had been sold back to British ownership. In 1928 the company's offices were moved from Bedford Street to 99 Great Russell Street, a William and Mary mansion in which some of the incidents recorded in *Boswell's London Journal* took place. William Heinemann Medical Books was formed in this era, as was Heinemann & Zsolnay, a practical form of help to Paul Zsolnay, a refugee from Hitler's occupation of Austria in 1938.

J. B. Priestley, D. H. Lawrence and others made Heinemann's amongst the most distinguished fiction lists between the wars. Charles Evans became chairman on Byard's death in 1931, and saw his son, A. Dwye Evans, already at work within the firm.

Methuen's list rivalled Heinemann's in fiction, with Henry James, Joseph Conrad and Arnold Bennett providing the quality, while the big sales came from Marie Corelli and Anthony Hope. The 1911 autumn list was headed by Corelli's *The Life Everlasting*, with a subscription of over 100,000 copies. The vulgar authoress of this work set up her home in Stratford in order to become on literary terms with Shakespeare and succeeded in becoming known as 'The Swan of Avon'.

James took second place to Marie Corelli on that 1911 list, but never earned the advances of between £150 and £300 on the six novels which Methuen's published. Arnold Bennett fared better, with a first printing of 10,000 of *Hilda Lessways*; Conrad did less well, with 3,000 of *Under Western Eyes*, but he broke through to bigger sales a year or two later with *Chance*. Edgar Rice Burroughs, with his Tarzan series, brought immediate reward to Methuen and himself. D. H. Lawrence, with *The Rainbow*, brought only trouble, that fine novel being prosecuted for obscene libel at Bow Street. The magistrate who made this decision was Sir John Dickinson, one of a long line of narrow-minded legal pontificators whose judgments deserve the contempt of later generations.

Methuen suffered a curious publishing failure in 1904–5, when his Standard Library of Classics (1s. cloth, 6d. paper) were greeted with paeons of praise from the reviewers and indifference from the public: the same public, presumably, which shortly afterwards took Dent's Everyman's Library to its hearts. Methuen fared better with his Sixpenny Library—reprints of current and classical authors—which appeared some thirty years before Allen Lane's similarly priced Penguins. He also established the Arden edition of Shakespeare and the Little Guides to the counties of England.

The children's list received a fillip, at first unnoticed, from Kenneth Grahame's *The Wind in the Willows*, in 1908. The book began to sell, inexplicably to the publishers—perhaps by word-of-mouth publicity, always the best and cheapest form of advertising—some two years after first being issued with a single illustration by Graham Robertson. Grahame had asked for Arthur Rackham as illustrator, but did not get him. Long afterwards, Ernest Shepard made the drawings which several generations identified with the characters in the book; Grahame had to wait thirty years for Rackham's.

It was Methuen himself who secured the first prose book of T. S. Eliot, *The Sacred Wood*, which had appeared anonymously as contributions to *The Times Literary Supplement*. Methuen got the book by the simple means of writing to the author c/o *The T.L.S.* When Eliot had become a director of Faber & Faber, who published most of his later work, Faber's asked to buy the rights in *The Sacred Wood*. The request was, reasonably, refused, and Eliot himself did not demur. By then Methuen had died, leaving £250,000, but missing the huge new fortunes which would have boosted his estate from the publication of A. A. Milne and H. V. Morton. Milne's four famous books for young children* made an instant appeal, and joined *The Wind in the Willows*

---

* *When We Were Very Young*; *Now We Are Six*; *Winnie-the-Pooh* and *The House at Pooh Corner*.

as standard backlist titles which sold by the tens of thousands, in various editions, for decades to come.

A year before he died, Methuen appointed E. V. Rieu as an editor of academic books. Rieu continued in that position until the late 'thirties, despite a lack of enthusiasm shown for his efforts by the directors who were put into office by the peculiar terms of Sir Algernon's will. The sales manager, C. W. Chamberlain, learned at Methuen's funeral that he had been bequeathed the managing directorship, and an editor, E. V. Lucas, inherited the chairmanship. In 1928, Methuen's went public and fell into the hands of Sir George Roberts, a biscuit millionaire, who did not take a seat on the board but regularly interfered from a distance, a habit which led to wholesale resignations from the board and E. V. Rieu's short-lived appointment as managing director. He was succeeded by Andrew Dakers for only a year, by which time Roberts had jeopardized the firm, in the interests of property speculation. Lloyd's Bank took over, nominating Philip Inman, then proprietor of Chapman & Hall, as chairman but not as publisher. In a decade when finance was short, only a company as broadly based as Methuen could have rallied from such disasters. Eventually it did, and in the early years of the Second World War it was under the financial backing of Nutcombe Hume (head of Charterhouse Trust), James Pitman and Stanley Unwin. During all these upheavals, J. Alan White, who had joined in 1924, stayed the course and became a director, contributing the necessary qualities of man of business and man of literary taste to a great tradition of publishing.

Methuen's experience in this period ought to have warned others of the perils of going public and falling into the hands of the City, but all it did was to foreshadow a regrettable pattern which the book trade largely failed to counteract, perhaps because economic conditions made it so very difficult to do otherwise. But the study of that unhappy situation belongs to later chapters on mergers and takeovers.

Life at Methuen's for the lower orders in the immediate postwar period was recalled by John A. Ford in his retirement speech in 1969. In April 1919, aged fifteen, he had been employed as an order boy at 15s. per week, plus 7d. for tea money. His job was to hand-write invoices under the guidance of Frederick Muller (later to found his own imprint). The staff worked on high stools at sloping desks; speaking tubes had only just been made obsolete; and wet-letter presses and spiked files were still in use.

Chapman & Hall serves to bridge the gap between those who rode triumphantly into the twentieth century and those who faltered a little. The Dickens copyrights were running out, the great house had lost most of the momentum given it by its founders, and when Arthur Waugh joined as managing director in 1902 he was told two things: 'If it wasn't for Dickens we might as well put up the shutters tomorrow,' and, 'Mr Chapman always said that you can't make money out of miscellaneous publishing.' Waugh cleverly ignored both warnings, noted the increasing success of the John Wiley technical list for which the company held the agency, and produced two sons who became highly successful novelists.

He claimed an Arnold Bennett success with *The Old Wives' Tale*, although, of course, that author did not remain with him. Bennett, in addition to his own novels and stories, was writing other novels and serials with Eden Philpotts, plays with Edward Knoblock and a journal —not to mention hundreds of letters, many of them to his agent, J. B. Pinker, who was badgered endlessly to find the right publisher for his client. Chatto & Windus fell into disfavour when they failed to advertise one novel to the author's satisfaction, and poor Alfred Nutt, who had inherited the business started by his father in the nineteenth century, was criticized for asking when the work he had commissioned might be ready. Bennett's letters to Pinker (see the Bibliography) contain much to interest the student of book trade history.

To return to Chapman & Hall, Arthur Waugh's eldest son, Alec, precociously wrote a bestseller about public school life in his eighteenth year, but *The Loom of Youth* went to Grant Richards. The next novel, *The Prisoners of Mainz*, came out under the Chapman & Hall imprint, but most of his subsequent work went to Cassell's, although Alec joined his father in office hours, and was elected to the board. Father and son worked happily together during the 'twenties, but by the centenary year of the firm the elder had retired to write the history of the house and the younger to write the novels which were to be his living. By then, the second son, Evelyn, had matured, and with *Decline and Fall* (1928), *Vile Bodies* (1930) and *Scoop* (1938) established himself as the foremost satirical novelist of his age. No other author was to shed such lustre on the Chapman & Hall list for the next forty years. Meanwhile Arthur Waugh became chairman in his semi-retirement, and Ralph Straus, later a distinguished reviewer, took Alec's place. The financial control of the firm passed quickly in the 1930s into the hands of Philip Inman, who took over Methuen (see above) and sold Chapman & Hall to that company in 1938. Arthur Waugh returned briefly as chairman until his death in 1943.

George Routledge & Co. crept tentatively into the new century, no new impetus being felt after the founder's death in 1888. In 1902, however, William Swan Sonnenschein, one of the more adventurous spirits of late-Victorian publishing, chose to leave his own imprint in the hands of Colonel Dalbiac and Herbert Wigram, and to set about reviving the fortunes of Routledge, partnered by Arthur E. Franklin, a banker. Why he chose to abandon his own successful creation (from which he divorced

himself entirely four years later) to breathe life into a moribund list is
perhaps explained by his lust for work, although that had already found
an outlet, which would have been enough for most men, in the compilation of *The Best Books*, a bibliography aimed at recording all that
was worthwhile and available in the literature of all subjects. So formidable an undertaking could have been a full-time occupation in
itself, but Sonnenschein pursued it as a spare-time hobby, leaving his
long working-day free to act as senior managing director of Routledge,
for whom he bought up the valuable copyrights of J. C. Nimmo, in
1903, and the company of Kegan Paul, Trench & Trubner, in 1911.
The latter was run as a separate business, and after the first war C. K.
Ogden joined it to create, with Sonnenschein (who took his mother's
maiden name, Stallybrass, in 1917), an incomparable series of books,
the International Library of Psychology, Philosophy and Scientific
Method. Ogden, a pacifist, who had run the Cambridge Bookshop
during the war, was a man of business as well as of scholarly discernment, and he arranged for a small royalty to be paid to himself on every
work he introduced. (And his authors included C. G. Jung, Alfred
Adler, Ludwig Wittgenstein and I. A. Richards!) As well as being a
brilliant editor he was exceptionally industrious out of office hours,
using his spare time to compile a system of Basic English which reduced
the vocabulary of the language to 850 simple words.

Into the antiquated premises of Broadway House, Carter Lane, just
off Ludgate Hill, Frederic J. Warburg was introduced as an apprentice
publisher in 1922. Warburg had graduated from Oxford, after fighting
in the trenches, and entered publishing by accident. He belonged to
the banking family but had no taste for that profession, and as he
wished to get married and needed to earn his living, he looked around
for a likely occupation. His brother-in-law worked at that time for
Routledge, but wished to leave. Feeling, curiously, that he should
supply a successor, he arranged for Warburg to meet Stallybrass. An
interview took place, Stallybrass duly engaged the soldier-graduate, and
set him to work at a desk in the office which he shared with Cecil
Franklin, the son of Arthur Franklin. The initial encounter and subsequent day-to-day affairs of Routledge in the 'twenties are recorded
in Fred Warburg's eminently readable and entertaining autobiography,
An Occupation for Gentlemen. The apprentice greatly admired his Master,
describing Stallybrass as 'the greatest scholar-publisher of his day', and
as 'modest, shy, a trifle puritanical, learned, energetic, with broad
interests, humorous and honest ... ' For all the adulation, Warburg
nevertheless shocked his Master by suggesting translations of bawdy
Greek and Italian classics; some were sanctioned, but others were permitted publication only in the original tongue—a nice compromise,
making alleged pornography available only to those of classical learn-

ing. The Broadway translations were a successful series, and were widened to include the literature of France and other nations. They were, wrote Warburg, 'lively, unconventional and scholarly. They were *mine*, my first creative effort in publishing, and in some ways my best.' But when the *Casanova Memoirs*, first issued by John Rodker (candidate for Pornographer Royal in Warburg's estimation) through the Casanova Society, were bought for Routledge, Stallybrass panicked. These were days when a publisher of the old school did not lightly risk prosecution for obscene libel, and the Master sold off the entire edition as a remainder to Grant's of Edinbugh, who cleaned up handsomely on the deal and were never brought to court.

Stallybrass, too eager to return to work after an illness, died in 1931, aged seventy-five, and Fred Warburg, now a director, felt the urge to bring the Routledge list up to date in a new way, which included introducing fiction. His efforts were not appreciated by the Franklins who, with some justification, saw their solidly built academic list as entirely suited to their purpose. The inevitable rift occurred and is humourously related by Warburg in his memoir, a volume now out of print but which I strongly recommend as the most diverting piece of personal book trade history of the period. Routledge survived, and in 1939 even took to fiction with the works of Georges Simenon; so, by the skin of his teeth, did Fred Warburg, but the tale of his further adventures belongs to the next section.

When he went to Routledge, Sonnenschein, as he still was then, took the initiative away from his own firm and it is not surprising that it faltered and finally failed. George Allen died in 1907, soon after completing a memorial edition of Ruskin, and his sons, who acquired in 1909 the old imprint of Bemrose (a Derby printer who had started publishing in 1865 from Paternoster Row), amalgamated two years later with Swan Sonnenschein & Co. But the spark had gone out of both ventures and they became George Allen & Unwin Ltd on the eve of the First World War.

Something has already been said of the importance of Stanley Unwin's work for the book trade, and also of his relationship with his uncle T. Fisher Unwin. The latter, it will be recalled, handed over the daily management of his list to Stanley, who looked about him for new authors. H. G. Wells boasted that none of his publishers had made a penny out of him, and it was well known that he had unearned advances with several houses. Stanley persuaded Fisher to write to Wells, who responded by offering his new novel, *Ann Veronica*, outright for £1,500. Stanley countered with a proposal that Wells should have three instalments of £500 each, on condition that the serial rights could be sold by the publisher with whatever cuts in the text might be demanded. Wells agreed, *Ann Veronica* was denounced as 'poisonous' which turned the book into a bestseller; the American rights were sold for £525 and Stanley was vindicated.

Soon after, the nephew arranged a similar success with Robert Service's *Songs of a Surdough*, and followed up by securing an agency for Baedeker Guides and for Ordnance Survey Maps, but Uncle Fisher never willingly increased Stanley's salary, and this caused the final breach between them, leading to the younger man's absence from publishing for some eighteen months, until the formation of Allen & Unwin.

Allen & Unwin started business with Stanley Unwin in charge of trade matters, in a tiny office on the ground floor, from where he could see all approaching visitors; his co-directors were established in more splendid, but also more remote, accommodation on the upper storeys. C. A. Reynolds, a solicitor, became company secretary, and soon incurred Unwin's displeasure by vetoing the publication of Marie Stopes's *Married Love*, apparently in retaliation for Unwin's vetoing a novel which he knew would be thought obscene. *Married Love*, untroubled by the law, eventually sold at least a million under another imprint; the novel was published by C. W. Daniel, who was successfully prosecuted for his pains.

The other two directors were E. L. Skinner, who controlled advertising, and Colonel Dalbiac, who took over the accounts — at which he was, apparently, charming but incompetent — and became chairman. Dalbiac and Reynolds were called up and went to the war; Unwin was classified B3 and stayed behind to publish Bertrand Russell (who was imprisoned for his pacifist views and became a pillar of Allen & Unwin's fortunes) and Ramsay MacDonald (a Hampstead neighbour), and to reissue *Praeterita*, of which there was a warehouse full of unsellable copies, under the new title *Autobiography of Ruskin*, which was a sell-out.

Unwin built up his list scientifically, and Frank Mumby claimed in an earlier edition of this book that Allen & Unwin made a bigger contribution, in proportion to its size, to the common stock of knowledge, than any other publishing house in the country. This assessment would certainly have appealed to Stanley Unwin as the only reasonable conclusion of a fair-minded historian. He had little humour in his make-up (he even boasted of this during his eightieth-birthday celebrations, perhaps implying that there was more than he was suggesting) and his autobiography is riddled with earnest Pooter-like anecdotes of how his list was built. 'I have always maintained', he wrote, 'that if it was by a recognized authority, and was the best on the subject, my firm would publish any book regardless of whether it was particularly in our line or not.' And he went on to illustrate this by instancing his publication of books on the biochemistry of malting and brewing, of Lady Wentworth's *Thoroughbred Racing Stock* and of J. R. R. Tolkien's *The Hobbit*.

'My younger son, as a boy, must have read *The Hobbit* eight or nine times, so absorbing did he find it. Many years were to elapse before the publication of its sequel—not addressed to children though they will enjoy it—*The Lord of the Rings*, in three large volumes.' Yes, there was the authentic voice of Pooter, and also the true voice of a publisher who had absolute belief in what he was doing.

After the first war Unwin gradually acquired debentures, as well as more shares in Allen & Unwin, which took over the Swarthmore Press and Maunsel & Co., published Gilbert Murray's translations of the classics, and Freud's *A Young Girl's Diary*. He got into trouble about the last-named, but, in court, he wore down the public prosecutor and finally won the case, as was his wont.

In the 'twenties he began to travel extensively again, and wrote *The Truth about Publishing*, which William Swan Stallybrass said was foolish, because it helped his competitors to know their job better, and which the bookseller Frank Denny derided because, he said, no one would want to read it. Jonathan Cape, one of Unwin's new competitors, dubbed it 'the publisher's bible', however, and this it has remained.

But Stanley Unwin had not yet disposed of all of his fellow managing directors. E. L. Skinner remained until 1934, when he and the imprint of Williams & Norgate, purchased in 1928, went together, leaving Unwin master of his own house at last. It was appropriate timing because he was on the brink of the presidency of the Publishers' Association and soon to become president, also, of the International Publishers' Congress.

'Uncle Stan' as the trade called him—though never to his face—had a happier working relationship with his nephew and sons than Fisher had had with him. After the war the childless Fisher, who had married Richard Cobden's daughter, brought his great-nephew, Philip, into the business, and there is a vivid description of the office in the Adelphi in the latter's memoir, *The Publishing Unwins*. But Fisher Unwin's was less sound than the new recruit imagined, and in 1926 the list was sold to Ernest Benn in return for an annuity for Unwin and his wife.

Philip Unwin remained for the rest of his publishing life, seeing Allen & Unwin prosper as the list broadened in all directions, and met with the bestsellers which every general publisher needs periodically. Amongst these were Lancelot Hogben's *Science for the Citizen* and *Mathematics for the Million*, Stanley having wisely laid claim to that author's future works when he sold Williams & Norgate to Skinner. When *Mathematics* was offered in 1936, C. A. Furth, a much respected colleague, 'pronounced it as quite outstanding and all of us who looked at it agreed with him'. Furth became a director and had the fortitude to withstand the rigours of travelling abroad with the Chief.

Stanley Unwin was an absolute professional, who knew his business from the packing-floor upwards. It was said of him that when he was not on a foreign tour, or on the holidays that he rightly considered essential to maintaining his extremely good health, he always opened the morning post himself, and vetted every outgoing letter before it left the office. Certainly, credence is given to this story by the strong probability that he was the first person in his office after the postman had called, but in any case, the head of a business who is not too sluggish to appreciate the experience knows that to open the post is the best way of knowing what is going on.

Cassell's, like Routledge's, we left in the doldrums. Their recovery was delayed until 1905, when Arthur Spurgeon became general manager on the death of Sir Wemyss Reid. Spurgeon started by making drastic cuts in staff, which hit some of the older established employees hard, but probably saved the firm from liquidation. At that time Cassell's were more prominent as magazine than as book publishers and Spurgeon, in his first years, concentrated on increasing circulations and putting that side of the house in order. He and the shareholders were soon rewarded, and a dividend was paid in 1908 for the first time for many years. He then turned his attention to books, forming the Waverley Book Company (1909) to sell expensive illustrated volumes on the instalment plan directly to the public. A. Bain Irvine was put in charge of this operation.

Three years later Newman Flower, who had been brought in by Spurgeon in 1906 to edit the *Penny Magazine*, was given the task of reviving the trade book department which languished almost hopelessly —only two books were announced for the spring list. Flower used the now successful magazines under his control to attract authors, pleading with them to give him books, promising that if he failed to sell them he would not appeal again. Over several years of list-building, the gamble worked. G. K. Chesterton obliged with the Father Brown stories, and H. G. Wells, for once a benefactor to his publisher, with *Mr Britling Sees it Through*. Later the Wells connection led to *The Outline of History*, originally issued in parts. Arnold Bennett joined Cassell's in 1916, at last ending his wanderings amongst various publishers, and remaining loyal to Flower until his sudden demise in 1931. He gave Cassell's *Riceyman Steps*, a gripping narrative about a secondhand bookseller who starved himself to death, *Imperial Palace*, and other fictional items, during the decade when he became the most influential reviewer of his time. Ernest Raymond, whose first novel, *Tell England*, was one of the foremost bestsellers of the 1920s, and remained in print in 1970, was to be loyal for an even longer period, outstripping even Warwick Deeping's length of service, which began uneventfully in 1907 but reached a high-point of success with *Sorrell and Son* in 1924. Sheila Kaye-Smith was another novelist who had a long connection. It must be emphasized that these relationships were built on friendship, as well as mutual respect, enduring all the upheavals of company finance, which were frequent in La Belle Sauvage Yard, Cassells' headquarters in the 'twenties.

At the start of the decade the Berrys (later the newspaper barons Camrose and Kemsley) bought all the shares and Spurgeon became chairman, holding office for two years. In 1923 Cassell's went public again, and a few years later the Berrys decided to close down the printing works because of continued industrial disputes. This was followed by the sale of the magazine interests to the Amalgamated Press and, finally, of the book side to Newman Flower. Desmond Flower, Newman's son, entered the firm in 1930, by which time H. Aubrey Gentry (ex-Newnes) had been there for seven years. The Flowers and the Gentrys presided over some distinguished publishing in the years to come, acquiring Louis Bromfield and Robert Graves in the 'thirties, and the British rights in the Knopf list, that American publisher having decided to close his London office. Dashiell Hammett, Guy de Maupassant, André Gide and others, thus came Cassell's way.

Chatto & Windus also acquired a new broom in 1905, although the need there was not nearly as acute as at Cassell's. Indeed, he was not strictly necessary at all, for Percy Spalding, whom we left in the previous section happily singing 'Meet Me Tonight in Dreamland', was by no means over the top. He published at a pace more leisurely than was becoming fashionable, but the list was not fraying at the edges. The ball of fire in St Martin's Street was one Philip Lee-Warner, an eccentric who lay flat on his back on the floor to dictate letters. His contributions during a brief partnership were to set a high standard of production and to inaugurate a series of costly art books. He lasted five years before going on to the Medici Society and leaving Andrew Chatto, Senior, to enjoy the renewed peace of his offices for the remaining year left to him. Chatto's son (also Andrew) remained a not over-interested partner until 1919, and *his* son, Tom, defected to the antiquarian book trade. Meanwhile Frank Swinnerton and Geoffrey Whitworth had joined as editors, and with Charles Prentice, Harold Raymond and Spalding, Chatto & Windus had a good blend of age and youth at the top to see them through the first post-war years of boom and depression. When Spalding died Prentice became chief partner and continued to issue books of what Ruari McLean later described as 'a quiet and unpretentious excellence', and which included the Phoenix Library, pocket-sized, clothbound reprints, the first of which appeared in the late 'twenties. The tradition of good design was carried on by Ian Parsons, who joined on coming down from Cambridge in 1926 and, on Prentice's retirement, shared the partnership with Harold Raymond and J. W. McDougall. Ian Parsons was also a notable critic of poetry in the 'thirties, an attribute which was very strongly reflected in the list.

Chatto's moved into William IV Street, into a building of no great elegance but where evidence of industry was apparent on every floor and in every passage. Publications ranged wide and deep before and after the move, and the new authors of the postwar period included Lytton Strachey (*Eminent Victorians*, etc.), Wilfred Owen (posthumous editions of the war poems), Aldous Huxley (all of whose novels came from Chatto) and the C. K. Scott Moncrieff translation of Proust's *À La Recherche du temps perdu*, a monumental piece of scholarship and publishing which the translator, alas, did not live to complete. Another remarkable, but utterly different, publication in the 1920s was Daisy Ashford's *The Young Visiters*, a highly sensational novel (to use that adjective in its 1920s sense) written when the author was nine, and since enjoyed by several generations of adults and sophisticated children. The Constance Garnett translations of Chekhov's plays and stories also went to Chatto, because Heinemann had turned them down. They proved a good buy, once the theatre-going public had been coaxed by the drama critic James Agate, in print and on radio, to accept the Russian dramatist as an entertainer of rare genius. The lit. crit. list was enlarged with controversial and original works, ranging from the tempestuous F. R. Leavis (*New Bearings in English Poetry*), and the scintillating William Empson (*Seven Types of Ambiguity*), to the rather earnestly erudite Clive Bell (*Civilization*). And hanging over the firm, until Harold Raymond sold them off, were the three quarters of a million or so of 6d. reprints of once-popular novels which remind historians of the trade yet again that Allen Lane was not the first in the field with these. (Not the first, but the first to *remain* in business with them.)

Grant Richards's fortunes vacillated, with two bankruptcies amid much fine publishing. His business failure was due not so much to lack of acumen about what to publish, as to his inability to scale down his style of living to match what he could take out of the business: not, according to Alec Waugh, that he was unduly extravagant; he was a victim of the economic climate of the 'twenties. Certainly Richards loved to entertain at his house in Cookham Dean, where it was his practice to introduce one author at a time into his parties. He also loved to travel, and was never an office-bound publisher. He called regularly on booksellers in both London and the provinces, and on one momentous occasion accompanied the American author Theodore Dreiser to the Continent, a fictionalized account of which subsequently came from that writer's pen.

Richards was something of an innovator in publishers' advertising methods, taking a half-column in the *T.L.S.* each week in which he chatted in a gossipy fashion about his books and authors, much as Cape's Anthony Colwell was to do fifty years later. In his memoirs,

Author Hunting, he admitted to a weakness for publishing 'firsts', and the authors who made their maiden appearance under his imprint included John Masefield, Alec Waugh, Ronald Firbank (whom he considered much overrated), G. K. Chesterton, Philip Gibbs, Warwick Deeping and Cecil Roberts. By his first bankruptcy he lost the World's Classics to O.U.P., and then traded for some years under his first wife's name. His eldest son was killed in an accident whilst still a schoolboy, and his first marriage broke up. His second was happier and saw him through his next two failures and his retirement, much of which was spent on the Riviera. After his second crash, in the 'twenties, he became for a time chairman of the Richards Press, but he resigned when he realized that the appointment carried little real authority. He was an incorrigible optimist and rode his failures, and at least he did not live to be taken over by an American publisher and fêted for a short time before being jettisoned, as happened to some natural heirs of his type of publishing in later decades. (Corvo portrays him amusingly, but with undoubted malice, in *Nicholas Crabbe*.)

Another literary imprint of the late 'nineties was Gerald Duckworth, which was to survive without making a sensation, in an orderly and quiet fashion. Duckworth had learned his publishing with J. M. Dent, and met there A. R. Waller, who was to become his first partner until he left him to join Cambridge University Press. He had the good fortune to engage Edward Garnett as his reader, and, later, Jonathan Cape as his town traveller. He was the stepson of Sir Leslie Stephen and, therefore, the natural publisher of Virginia Woolf's early works. Garnett brought him Hilaire Belloc, and he also published the plays of Galsworthy and Strindberg. Cape did not return when he was demobilized in 1919, and it was said that Duckworth would not make him a partner because he was not a gentleman. But it is doubtful if anyone of Cape's ability would have rested for long without his own imprint, and when he started on his own he took Garnett with him.

In 1921 Thomas Balston joined Duckworth, and in this decade they published most of what the three Sitwells wrote. The list was always small, but distinguished by works which built up a solid backlist. In the 'thirties Duckworth started his Great Lives series, potted biographies which eventually ran to over a hundred volumes. Balston left in 1936 and Duckworth died a year later. In 1938, Mervyn Horder, ex-Methuen and Nelson, joined the board and soon concluded a trade agreement with Nelson's whereby they distributed for Duckworth's, although both firms retained their separate identity, financially and editorially. George Milsted, who started with Duckworth in 1899, was a link between the founder and the later ownership.

The revived house of Constable had Bernard Shaw as its chief author and irritant during the first half of the century. Shaw published through

Constable, paying them a commission, but he was a valuable property to them none the less. Under W. M. Meredith (the son of the novelist George Meredith), until his health broke, then under Michael Sadleir who was also a novelist, the firm acquired other authors of distinction such as Harold Nicolson, Damon Runyon, Patrick Hamilton and James Bridie. They also began to build a technical list. Sadleir, who added an 'i' to his name to distinguish himself from his father, in due course engaged a young writer, Ralph Arnold, as an apprentice, adding the inducement of a directorship if he proved satisfactory. Arnold's memoirs, *Orange Street and Brickhole Lane*, aptly describe the rather bleak-looking office building which belied the homely atmosphere within. He gives pen sketches of Sadleir and the other principals, among them Martha Smith, who was one of the first women to achieve executive status in British publishing. After seventeen years with the company as publicity manager and associate editor, she was elected to the board in 1937. She was a formidable woman who quickly scotched the young Arnold's suggestions for modernizing Constable's advertising.

John Lane's heyday at The Bodley Head was, perhaps, brief, but in the new century he introduced two important French authors to the English reading public—Anatole France and André Maurois—and also the endearing Canadian humorist, Stephen Leacock. Perhaps more importantly he brought in his nephew, Allen, in 1919, and soon appointed him a director. John Lane died in 1925, and for the next ten years The Bodley Head kept afloat but scarcely in the forefront of positive publishing. After Allen Lane had launched Penguin's, the first titles of which bore The Bodley Head imprint, he severed his connection with his uncle's firm and it passed into the joint control of Allen & Unwin, Jonathan Cape and J. M. Dent in 1937.

Eyre & Spottiswoode continued to live, primarily as printers, on their Bible concession, but in 1928 Douglas Jerrold became manager, gaining Charles Friend as a colleague a year later, and the fine art publishing side of Eyre & Spottiswoode was separated from the printing side. The first two books were novels by Frances Parkinson Keyes and Malcolm Muggeridge; the latter was deemed libellous and had to be burned. Apparently there were not, at this stage, any profits, and soon after the outbreak of the Second World War the offices were burned, at which point Jerrold made an instantly successful bid for Thornton Butterworth's, and changed the company's fortunes. Douglas Jerrold also became chairman of the Roman Catholic publishing house of Burns, Oates in 1939, when it sold out to the Eyre Trust. (Walter Hutchinson had had an interest in Burns, Oates, as in many other firms.)

At Putnam's, the last of that name died in 1930, leaving control to Constant Huntington, a compatriot and relative who had worked with him for many years—and also against him, for he was instrumental in introducing John Galsworthy not to his uncle, but to William Heinemann. When James MacGibbon joined in 1929 as a teenager, he was just in time to take part in the publication of a huge success, Erich Maria Remarque's *All Quiet on the Western Front*. The office was somewhat chaotically run then, and a number of review copies of the book were not sent out, but the novel sold, as with so many before and since, by word of mouth. Another in this class was Charles Sale's *The Specialist*, an incomparable comic masterpiece about an American backwoodsman building himself a privy. James MacGibbon maintains that that pillar of New England rectitude, Constant Huntington, held deep within him a desire to shock the public, which was why he published *The Specialist* and also the works of the evangelist birthcontroller, Marie Stopes. When MacGibbon left publishing for advertising in 1936 in order to earn sufficient to keep a wife and family, Marie Stopes suggested he should manage her business organization. In 1970 he reflected that he might have had a more affluent life if he had accepted her offer; fortunately for the book trade he did not, nor did he record if any conditions were laid down as to the size of his family if he had.

By 1970 the novels of E. M. Forster looked oddly out of place on the Edward Arnold list, but earlier in the century fiction was not uncommon under this imprint. Arnold was not, in fact, the first publisher of *Where Angels Fear to Tread* (1905) or *The Longest Journey* (1907); these were issued by Blackwood. But the other three fine novels published during the writer's lifetime bore, from the start, the imprint of the firm with which he was associated for so many years. When *A Passage to India* came out in 1924 Arnold arranged with Blackwood to take over the first two novels and include them in a standard edition, but the short stories went, some years later, to Sidgwick & Jackson, perhaps because by then there was already an increasing concern in Maddox Street with academic works catering for a broad market from secondary school onwards, and fiction was overshadowed. Nevertheless, Forster, one of the least prolific of great twentieth-century writers, otherwise remained mostly faithful to his second publisher and gave him the occasional biography or critical work, not least *Aspects of the Novel*. He was an undemanding author and seems to have enjoyed the happiest of relations with his publishers. Edward Arnold retired in 1930 and was succeeded by Brian Fagan, who had become his partner in 1921, both as head of the firm and friend to Forster.

At Ginn's, whom Arnold had once represented before the American company opened its own office, the famous Beacon Readers, first published in the U.S.A. about 1912, were brought to Britain in 1922, and retained their popularity with teachers and parents way beyond this period. Feminism was even more rampant here than at Constable's for there were two senior working female directors, Miss M. Williams and Miss E. Grassam.

Lastly, in this section, I must mention the technical publishers, Crosby Lockwood & Co. In the early 'thirties they found themselves affected adversely by the depression, and in 1933 the last Crosby Lockwood sold the major part of his copyrights and stock to a new company, the Technical Press Ltd, so that none of his creditors, mainly his authors, should be the losers. The balance went to Simpkin Marshall, who continued to operate the company under the management of Harold Paroissien.

5

The New Publishers

Martin Secker; Medici Society; Architectural Press;, Shakespeare Head Press; Concrete Publications; Macdonald & Evans; Kingsgate Press; Faith Press; Sidgwick & Jackson; Mills & Boon; Herbert Jenkins; Christopher's; Evans Brothers; James Nisbet; James Brodie's; Country Life; Hogarth Press; Jonathan Cape; Faber & Faber; Victor Gollancz; Hamish Hamilton; Michael Joseph; Secker & Warburg; Ernest Benn; A. Zwemmer; Phaidon; Golden Cockerel; Scholartis; Cresset Press; Geoffrey Bles; Peter Davies; Frederick Muller; Robert Hale; Lindsay Drummond; Andrew Dakers; Lovat Dickson; Herbert Joseph; Nicholson & Watson; Blandford Press; Wills & Hepworth; Penguin Books.

The years from the turn of the century to the outbreak of war did not produce any new publishers on the scale of Heinemann, Methuen and Dent, although there were many new imprints, some of which endured. (George Allen & Unwin was in fact established on the very day of the outbreak of war, August 4th, 1914.) Some of those who were to be the great between-the-wars publishers were already at work with other firms, and one can almost sense in them a waiting for the worst to be over.

Martin Secker might perhaps have been the exception. He first worked for Eveleigh Nash (formed 1902) and read Compton Mackenzie's *The Passionate Elopement*, which he strongly recommended. Nash got a second, less favourable, opinion, and turned it down. About a year later, in 1910, Secker set up on his own, had an instant huge success with Mackenzie's novel, and went on to publish Norman Douglas, J. E. Flecker, Kafka, Thomas Mann and D. H. Lawrence. For a time he became the most fashionable publisher in London for works of originality and high literary quality. But whether as a result of the financial climate of the 'twenties and 'thirties, or because Secker pursued what interested him without sufficient regard for making money, or both, in 1935 he failed. The Lawrence titles were sold to Heinemann to clear pressing debts, and a few years later the list was revived under Frederic Warburg as Martin Secker & Warburg Ltd. Secker remained with it for only a short while, leaving to continue his own personal style of publishing with the Richards Press which grew out of Grant Richards' last crash. It would be interesting to evaluate the qualities which turned the literary enthusiasm of a Heinemann, say, into a successful commercial publisher, and compare them with the attributes of a Martin Secker, whose discernment and flair led him to issue the works of some of the most notable authors of his time. Such an evaluation might only end with the finding that luck played its part. Certainly Secker, like Grant Richards, lived to enjoy his old age in tranquillity, whereas Heinemann died in his fifties, sick and disillusioned by the war. Coincidentally Heinemann left a wealthy publishing property which was later to be associated with Secker & Warburg, though owned by interests outside the trade.

The Medici Society, to which Philip Lee-Warner turned his talents after he had broken with Chatto & Windus, set up as specialist art publishers in 1908. The Architectural Press (1902) served another specialist cause, and Percy Hastings, one of the original directors, was still in office in 1940. The Shakespeare Head Press, started by A. H. Bullen in 1904, issued the Stratford Town Shakespeare during its first three years, thus achieving its founder's ambitions. Over in Dublin Elizabeth Yeats, sister of the poet, founded the Dun Emer Press (1903), which became the Cuala Press (1908) and published most of the leading Irish writers apart from Joyce. On the technical front, Concrete Publications and Macdonald & Evans began in 1906 and 1907 respectively, and in the religious field the Kingsgate Press (Baptist) started in 1903, and the Faith Press (Anglo-Catholic) two years later.

Most notable of the new non-specialist publishers were Sidgwick & Jackson (1908), formed when Frank Sidgwick left Lawrence & Bullen. Sidgwick was primarily a publisher of poetry (Rupert Brooke and John Drinkwater were amongst his authors) and he issued *Poems of Today*, compiled for schools by the English Association, in editions running into six figures. He also brought out the plays and criticism of Harley Granville-Barker during the first great era of the Royal Court Theatre in Sloane Square. In his latter years he apparently lived largely on the copyright in Rupert Brooke's work. He died in 1939. With luck, he might have been one of the great publishers, but at least his imprint survived him and took on a new lease of life thirty-one years after his death.

Mills & Boon began in 1909, both of the original directors, Gerald Mills and Charles Boon, having worked previously for Methuen, as educational and sales managers respectively. Mills & Boon turned over £16,650 in its first year's trading, and before 1914 Hugh Walpole, P. G. Wodehouse, Padraic Colum and Robert Lynd had all graced its list. In the 'twenties the firm failed to prosper with its 1s. cloth editions, of which it held a stock of a quarter of a million. Gerald Mills died in 1928 and fresh capital had to be raised. Charles Boon had always included romances in his list, and was thus able to exploit the suddenly rising market of the commercial libraries in the late 'twenties and early 'thirties, so giving the company its best years since the war.

Herbert Jenkins was a novelist-publisher who had his early trade experience with John Lane. He began to publish for himself in 1913, his own Bindle tales bringing him almost as much fortune as the works of P. G. Wodehouse, whose books he was issuing by the end of the first war. Unfortunately, his health broke and he died in 1923 having willed his business, and his own copyrights, to the Royal Society for the Prevention of Cruelty to Animals, who, not knowing what to do with something so far removed from their own good works, sold them to J. Derek Grimsdick, whose son later joined him in the business.

Bertram Christian, described in a 1940 reference book as 'sole partner', started the educational house of Christopher's in 1906, in the same year as Robert Evans began Evans Brothers (and he was 'sole brother' until Edward joined him in 1908) in one room in Newgate Street. Five years later the brothers took over *Teachers' World*, and Robert was knighted for his services to education. Christian, to his chagrin, never received the accolade, but was a hardworking president of the P.A. and also had an interest in James Nisbet's whose board he joined in 1913. John Mackenzie Wood sat on the board with him from 1932, and it was Wood and his wife who created the world-famous Janet and John readers. James Brodie's, a firm devoted to helping teachers and pupils achieve better examination results, started in 1907, and its notes on chosen English texts remained heavily in demand over sixty years later.

Country Life magazine had started in 1897, but the book list did not emerge until 1903. For the remainder of this period high quality illustrated books reflecting the interests of *Country Life* readers — antiques, architecture, gardening and furniture, for instance — were regularly issued. From the start George Newnes was associated with *Country Life* (although it was Edward Hudson's idea), and his family firm was its part-owner for the first eight years. In 1905 Sir Edwin Lutyens designed a grand new building on the edge of Covent Garden from which the magazine has been edited ever since. In the late 'twenties the Collingridge list of gardening and horticultural books was purchased, and by 1940 the chief directors were Sir Frank Newnes and Sir Neville Pearson.

Nothing could illustrate more forcefully the notion of fact being stranger than fiction than the history of the Hogarth Press. The most famous poem of the twentieth century, T. S. Eliot's *The Waste Land*, was set by hand by Virginia and Leonard Woolf, in the dining-room of their home in Richmond, Surrey. No work of genius was ever so cradled by the hands of another creative genius in the twentieth, or any other, century. How it came about deserves a chapter to itself.

Leonard Woolf, a Cambridge undergraduate at the turn of the century, when Russell, Whitehead and G. E. Moore were fellows of Trinity, left the academic atmosphere, where Lytton Strachey was one of his closest friends, to become a minor administrator of colonial government in Ceylon. Returning to England in 1912 he married Virginia Stephen, who was on the threshold of her writing career and was already prone to the fits of nervous depression which temporarily unbalanced her during much of her life. It was her custom to work on the current novel or short story during the morning, and on critical work for *The Times Literary Supplement* and other papers during the afternoon. Woolf, perceiving that she would benefit from a different kind of activity, and wishing to learn the art of printing, bought a small hand-press, plus a book of instructions, from a shop in Farringdon Street. This was installed at their home, Hogarth House. The Woolfs applied themselves to the task of learning how to print, and a month later issued a thirty-two page booklet containing a story by each of them. The edition ran to 150 copies. It was announced to friends, and others who it was thought might be interested, and eventually 134 copies were sold. Encouraged by this success, the Woolfs, in the following year, printed and bound *Prelude*, a long short story by Katherine Mansfield. In 1919 came another slender volume from Mrs Woolf and three other books, including some poems by T. S. Eliot, whose *Prufrock* had already been published by the Egoist.

It was Harriet Weaver, editor of the *Egoist*, who brought to Richmond the manuscript of the first part of James Joyce's *Ulysses*. The Woolfs knew that they could not handprint this work themselves and, reluctantly, let it go when they could not find a printer willing to undertake it. Meanwhile they brought out Maxim Gorky's *Reminiscences of Tolstoi*, and Clive Bell's *Poems*. They sent out very few review copies and had little direct contact with the retail trade, which on the whole was not sympathetic. The Hogarth Press remained a spare-time occupation but, nonetheless, it paid for itself and never after had to call for more than the £35 initial capital which Leonard Woolf sank in it.

In 1922 Virginia Woolf's *Jacob's Room* was ready, and Gerald Duckworth, her half-brother, who had published her first books, had an option on it. The idea of printing it themselves appealed to them because Virginia Woolf had a horror of submitting her work for approval to others. This is a common enough feeling, and to publish on one's own account can be a dangerous road to self-indulgence, but it was not so for Virginia Woolf, who had immense powers of self-criticism. She did not help to set her own book—it was farmed out to a commercial printer—but it was published by Hogarth, as were all her subsequent novels.

The press grew, and in 1923 there were thirteen new books, including

The Waste Land and E. M. Forster's *Pharos and Pharillon*. The Woolfs engaged a succession of young men to help manage the press for them, and often they were tempted to give it up entirely, as it became more and more of a call upon their time, but their commitment to their authors held them. T. S. Eliot became a director of Faber & Faber, taking his books with him, but there were always others who needed encouragement and practical backing. And there was the increasing importance of Virginia's own work. Heinemann's and others made overtures, but Leonard Woolf would not sell or accept the umbrella of a larger publisher.

In 1924 he took over the publications of the International Psycho-Analytical Library, and thus came ultimately to publish the entire works of Sigmund Freud, and others associated with him. Relations with the trade broadened, and in his autobiography Woolf pays tribute to J. G. Wilson and a few other booksellers who cooperated with him. In 1931 John Lehmann joined him as manager, and Hogarth published forty books, including V. Sackville-West's *All Passion Spent* and Virginia Woolf's *The Waves*. Apart from the principals who worked part time, the staff numbered five, plus one traveller who in the 'twenties, was Alice Ritchie, the first official woman representative of a British publishing house. Lehmann left in 1932, but returned six years later, by which time Christopher Isherwood (*The Memorial* and *Mr Norris Changes Trains*) and C. Day Lewis, among others, were established as Hogarth authors.

The press moved from Richmond to a house in Mecklenburgh Square, Bloomsbury, and although they did less and less printing, the Woolfs continued to take part in the invoicing and dispatching of books; the therapy of packing helped Virginia unwind from the rigours of writing. It is doubtful if the operation could have been maintained on its amateur-professional basis had not Leonard Woolf been so balanced and able a man. A British-born Jew of remarkable intellectual stamina, he combined administrative efficiency with an enormous capacity for detailed work, and a rare understanding of original genius. Had he not married, loved and understood Virginia it is probable that she could not have survived as long as she did to contribute so fully to English literature. Had he not had innate business acumen and commonsense, the Hogarth Press could not have made the contribution it did to English publishing. His unique gift was not only to love and guide a genius through the often agonizing years of her maturity, but to defy all twentieth-century business axioms and maintain, and *contain*, a highly successful commercial operation for fifty years. His last three volumes of autobiography are essential reading for all students of the book trade who wish to place their research in correct perspective. Leonard Woolf was always a part-time publisher because he was also involved in writing, editorship and politics. He never built an ivory tower to shield himself or Virginia from reality; he claimed that he did not suffer fools gladly, but he was not quick to label any man or woman 'fool' because they did not have his own cultural and intellectual attainments. There was no snobbery, social or intellectual, in his make-up, and no one could have been farther removed than he was from the popular conception of Bloomsbury elitism.

His conclusions about life were largely stoical and pessimistic, and this is not the place to consider his findings on the nature of life and civilization. However, his comments on the optimum size of a publishing house, and the supposed necessity for chasing turnover, are very relevant to today's trends in publishing, and should be remembered when the last sections of this book, on the years 1945–70, are read.

In the twenty years between the world wars a number of other gifted men established imprints under their own names. They had the temerity to start in times of economic crisis and growing unemployment, but those who began in the 'twenties fared better in the long run than those who began in the following decade. In 1970 Faber and Gollancz were still privately owned, and Cape was part of a private merger with Chatto, although the creators of all three were dead; but Hamish Hamilton, Michael Joseph and Secker & Warburg had joined bigger brothers, with Hamilton and Warburg still alive and in active management.

Jonathan Cape issued his first list in 1921. His first job in publishing was as traveller for the American firm of Harper & Brothers, which had a London office. In 1904, aged 24, he moved to Duckworth's where, after seven years on the road, he became manager. He and Gerald Duckworth appear to have taken it in turns to go to war, one looking after the business while the other was at the front. Cape was demobbed in 1919 and shortly afterwards decided to set up on his own. While casting around for a partner he took a temporary appointment with the eccentric Philip Lee Warner at the Medici Society, and also started a one-room publishing company, Jonathan Page & Co., with Vida James (later his second wife) as assistant. He advertised for a partner and Geoffrey Faber replied, but as both men needed capital, they had to look elsewhere. Cape found his through a colleague at the Medici Society, G. Wren Howard, who borrowed £5,000 from his father. Cape contributed £2,000, and it was agreed to value the Page stock at £5,000, so that Jonathan had a majority holding of 7 to 5.

Cape and Howard became as perfect a combination as any in twentieth-century publishing. They were both shrewd, and believed in a high standard of book production and they enjoyed mutual esteem. Cape was tall, slim, handsome, with a gentle charm for his authors and friends, and a cool, hard stare for booksellers. Howard, the younger and shorter of the two, was as smart in mind and appearance as he was shy. Jonathan got the books; Wren Howard produced them. Cape was not, however, a natural discoverer of literary talent and relied much on the advice of others, particularly of Edward Garnett, who, as I have said, followed him from Duckworth's (via The Bodley Head) as reader. Garnett and Cape often bickered over the years, but the publisher finally admitted gracefully what he owed to the reader. Three weeks after opening his offices in Gower Street on the first day of 1921, Jonathan set off for America, the first of his regular trips made, by preference in slow ships, in search of books and authors. His list was strong in American writing from the start, including, amongst others, Sinclair Lewis, Eugene O'Neill, Hugh Lofting and Ernest Hemingway, although he first met the latter in Paris, as Michael S. Howard (son of Wren) described in *Jonathan Cape, Publisher*, an historical memoir which does not idealize either of the founding partners.

Strong as was the American bias, native writers were not neglected. One with whom Cape persevered was Mary Webb, whose *Precious Bane* was published in 1924 but did not become a bestseller until two years later, when the prime minister, Stanley Baldwin, praised it at a Royal Literary Fund dinner. Such is, or was, the power of politicians that Mary Webb's reputation was made, although too late for her own enjoyment; she had died in 1927. Robert Graves, a year later, was permitted the satisfaction of commercial success in his own lifetime with *Goodbye to All That*, perhaps the most nightmarishly gripping of all accounts of the horrors of the First World War and certainly one of the most damning indictments of public school life, of which Cape sold 30,000 in a few weeks.

The list was broad-based. Despite the partners' lack of enthusiasm for verse, there was the poetry of Robert Frost and A. E. Housman, whose brother, Laurence, published his plays with Cape (although both Housmans also published with other houses). There were the children's and adventure books of Arthur Ransome. There was J. E. Neale's *Queen Elizabeth*, a work which upset the author's fellow academics because it did away with footnotes. Neale became an adviser to the firm, which inaugurated the Bedford Historical Series in 1939. Other series were the Traveller's Library, pocket editions in neat format running to over two hundred titles by 1940, and the Florin Library of 2s. cased reprints of contemporary and nineteenth-century writers.

Several novelists made their reputations on the Cape list, among them Eric Linklater, E. Arnot Robertson, Walter Greenwood and H. E. Bates—one of Garnett's finds. Christopher Isherwood's first novel, *All the Conspirators*, did not bring either author or publisher success—only 290 copies were sold—and he moved on to the Hogarth Press.

One of Cape's most important authors of this period was T. E. Lawrence. To some a fascinating enigma; to others, a pulverizing bore; to Cape's, Lawrence was a highly saleable author who, maddeningly, wrote little and then prevented publication of much of it. Wren Howard claimed that on him the foundations of the firm were built; he was referring to Cape's first book, a nine-guinea reprint of Doughty's *Arabia Deserta*, published jointly with the Medici Society, for which Lawrence wrote an introduction. A few years later came *Revolt in the Desert*, condensed from a privately printed edition of *Seven Pillars of Wisdom*, the complete edition of which was not published until after Lawrence's death in 1935. This was an instant success, but *The Mint*, Lawrence's diary of his R.A.F. experiences at Uxbridge, was kept in cold storage too long and when it was finally published in 1955 it was a damp squib, having been outdated by Norman Mailer's *The Naked and the Dead* and other equally frank records of life in the armed services. But even so it sold 40,000 copies.

In his first year Cape bought the A. C. Fifield list, which brought him Samuel Butler's books and Bernard Shaw's praise. A more important purchase, in 1924, was that of The Egoist Press, Harriet Weaver's small concern, which had been the first publisher of Eliot's verse. Thus James Joyce came to Cape—*A Portrait of the Artist as a Young Man, Chamber Music* and *Exiles*, but not *Ulysses*, which was still a hot property, 499 out of the 500 numbered edition published by the Egoist Press having been seized by the customs at Folkestone in 1923. It was reissued by Shakespeare & Company, Sylvia Beach's Paris bookshop, in 1924, but Jonathan, wisely, did not touch it.

When the premises in Gower Street became too cramped for the successful new firm, a lease was taken of 30 Bedford Square, an elegant terrace house on the west side of the most perfectly preserved square in London which provided as fine a setting for good publishing as it once had for good living.

In the 'thirties expansion brought in new faces. Rupert Hart-Davis, formerly with the Book Society and Heinemann's, was allowed to buy some shares, and joined with instructions from Jonathan that, as he was to be a director, he must direct. Hart-Davis did so, though not always according to Cape's wishes, but despite skirmishes between them he remained, until the second war took him away, and introduced Peter Fleming, C. Day Lewis and others to the list. When Garnett died, William Plomer succeeded him as reader, and at about this time Guy Chapman, ex-Knopf, was appointed an editor. Daniel George, a later reader and editor, arrived on the list but not yet on the staff.

Wren Howard, known as 'Bob' to his friends, supervised contracts and book-design, but his shyness prevented him from establishing deep relations with any but a few of his authors. Perhaps the greatest compliment to his work came from a new young publisher of the 'fifties, Anthony Blond, who sent typescripts to printers with the instruction, 'Make it look like a Cape book'. Blond was sneered at for his naivety by other young publishers, but printers understood him.

Neither Cape nor Howard took much part in the social life of the book trade, although the latter spent much time working for the P.A., of which he was president (1937–9) and on whose council he sat for thirty-five years. Cape did little for the P.A., and even less for booksellers, except, as he would have claimed, publish books that they could sell. His terms of sale, however, were not attractive, and discounts fell behind those of other general publishers. When *Seven Pillars* was published, a bookseller had to order a hundred copies to receive 33⅓ per cent discount! Jonathan wanted the reader to have the benefit of the cheapest possible prices, and he didn't believe the bookseller deserved any more than he got. He did not seek to sell his books direct to the public, or through other channels—he relied, in fact, on the bookseller—but wilfully refused to understand the economics of the retail trade. So there grew up, quite understandably, the notion that Jonathan Cape was stingy, and it took years of persuasion and practical change after the second war to dispel this belief.

From 1924 to 1969 Arthur Child, a dapper little cockney and a great personality, operated a personal delivery service for Cape. Child took it upon himself to be salesman as well as deliverer when he thought occasion demanded it, and his cry, uttered with immense buoyancy, as he thumped down parcels on to booksellers' floors and counters, 'Ree-marrrrk-ab-le weather for the time o' the yee-ar,' deserves inclusion in any compilation of London street cries. Standardization of distribution was to denude the trade of men like Arthur Child, but his irrepressible good humour lightened the days of many a harassed bookseller.

Faber & Faber grew out of the Scientific Press, which published the *Hospital Newspaper* and the *Nursing Mirror*. The Scientific Press belonged to Sir Henry Burdett, after whose death it passed to his daughter, Lady Gwyer. Geoffrey Faber came into the picture in 1924, when it was reorganized as Faber & Gwyer. It sounds an unpromising start for a leading publisher of poetry and general literature, but it suited Geoffrey Faber. He had had some experience of publishing with O.U.P. before serving in the First World War, some experience of commerce as a director of his family's brewery, and he had been called to the bar and appointed Estates Bursar of All Souls College in 1923. Faber sold the *Nursing Mirror*, bought out Lady Gwyer, and in 1929 established Faber *& Faber*—although in fact there was only himself. By then Richard de la Mare and T. S. Eliot were already directors, and Frank Morley, Morley Kennerley and C. W. Stewart (who had been with Faber at Scientific Press, and at Faber & Gwyer), also joined the board.

The scientific side was continued, but other branches of literature, usually indicating a particular director's special interests, were reflected in the growing list. Young poets of the 'thirties were an obvious draw, but it was not only Eliot's presence which attracted such writers as W. H. Auden, Ezra Pound and Stephen Spender. Geoffrey Faber was himself a poet, and shared with Frank Sidgwick and Ian Parsons an abiding interest in issuing volumes of verse by new authors. He also demanded from his production staff that his books should appeal to the eye and the touch, thus identifying himself also with Leonard Woolf and Jonathan Cape. (It is interesting to note that the books of Christopher Isherwood catalogued as in print in 1940 bore the imprints of Cape, Faber and Hogarth.) Geoffrey Faber sought excellence in all departments of publishing and gave his colleagues their heads. Richard de la Mare was allowed to indulge his passion for art and gardening; Morley Kennerley, his for sport; W. J. Crawley, who joined as sales manager in 1934, his for children's books. Sales and editorial have often been regarded in publishing as almost watertight compartments, but in Faber's, the sales executives always had some say in editorial policy. This may be why they achieved such a broadly based list, ranging over almost the entire field of creative, specialist and technical publishing. During their early years Faber published the novels of Forrest Reid, Joyce's *Finnegans Wake*, R. H. Wilenski's volumes of critical works on painting, Alison Uttley's children's books and Edith Sitwell's *The English Eccentrics*. He published 60 books in 1930, in which year he employed only 13 people, including Ethel Swan whose voice, uttering the one word 'Fay-ber', was to be familiar to thousands of telephone inquirers for several decades. In 1940 he published 177 titles.

That the major poet of the English-speaking world should have sat on the board of Faber & Faber for over forty years is a fact worth considering briefly. Eliot was, of course, never an employee of Faber's in the ordinary sense. He was a director from its inception, and not expected to be a full-time working executive. A legend grew that he wrote the blurbs for all of Faber's books. This was not so, although he wrote most of the blurbs for the books of poetry, but he did attend at 24 Russell Square on most days, and joined the regular Wednesday book committees when future titles were decided. He edited *The Criterion* from Faber's headquarters, and introduced many poets of outstanding quality to the book-reading public. Because of his position in English literature as poet and critic, Faber & Faber must be regarded as the foremost poetry publisher of at least the first seventy years of the twentieth century, although, of course their range extended widely, and the name of Faber guaranteed quality whatever the subject.

The third outstanding new publisher of the 'twenties was Victor Gollancz, who served his apprenticeship with another notable individualist, Ernest Benn. (Benn actually founded the Society of Individualists, so this was a good start for V.G.)

Gollancz, a Jew of Polish origins, was unfit for service in the first war and became a master at Repton, working there under Dr Fisher, later Archbishop of Canterbury. He gave up teaching for publishing soon after the war, and joined Benn Brothers to reorganize their trade magazines department. In 1923 he became managing director of Ernest Benn, Book Publishers, and responsible for Benn's Sixpenny Library and Sixpenny Poets, as well as overseeing publication of more grandiose volumes such as Stanley Morison's *Four Centuries of Fine Printing*. Inevitably it was necessary for him to have his own imprint and this he started in 1928 when he moved into Williams & Norgate's old premises in Henrietta Street, Covent Garden. Here he reigned for the rest of his life in offices which made no concession to modernity. On the Henrietta Street frontage a drab, bare-boarded window was lit up by his glaring yellow jackets; at the Maiden Lane trade entrance, booksellers' collectors were liable to have the counter bashed into their backsides as V.G. came clattering down the uncarpeted stairs on some errand of his own. It happened to me in the 'fifties; the impact must have been even greater in the 'thirties.

The stark austerity of the offices utterly belied the image of the new firm as it was projected in the press. Publishers' advertising took on a new note with V.G. It was vulgar and eye-catching, like his yellow jackets. It was also splendidly arrogant and did not play down to any supposed lower level of literacy. If his copy boldly stated SAYERS'S LATEST or THE NEW CRONIN, the reader was assumed to know who those authors were and what they had written. Often he did not bother to append his own name; that was implicit in the style of the advertisement, and he took it for granted that anyone could recognize a Gollancz-paid eight-inch double. He spent lavishly on advertising where other publishers invested in three- and four-colour jackets. His bindings were almost invariably black, his paper often greyish-white, but his typography was acceptable and he drove printers and binders mad by increasing his print orders in derisory quantities. 'You mean of course, seven fifty?' one printer dared to say to him, hardly able to believe his ears, 'No,' replied V.G., 'seventy-five.'

He got his authors by paying large advances and guaranteeing them publicity and wide sales. He believed in big sales potential because he believed in himself as a salesman, accrediting himself with a *mana* which he defined, via the *Encyclopaedia Britannica*, as a 'wonder-working power'. He confused his colleagues at sales meetings by stopping to listen to Moses, the voice which told him what to do. He was a latter-day St Joan, with all the conviction and single-mindedness of Shaw's saint. The fact that he was often wrong never deterred him, probably because he was always too busy to notice it. He didn't work scientifically, like Stanley Unwin, laying one brick neatly upon another with absolute certainty of his course, he worked emotionally and explosively, always one hundred per-cent committed to whatever he was involved in. V.G. did not know the meaning of half-heartedness. He was a large man in every sense, and often a tiresome one, but his socialism was based on humanitarianism and he did more than most to live up to his beliefs. He adored music and food and was as much a glutton for them as for work. He often announced he was taking a holiday and then didn't, to the dismay of his staff who were all ready for a breather. An impossible but loveable man, for those who could live at his pace and in his manner; there were those who fell by the wayside.

When he started publishing, V.G. had luck with him and found it with, of all things, a play. R. C. Sherriff, a man as mild as Gollancz was headstrong, wrote a drama called *Journey's End* about life in the trenches. It came at the correct psychological moment, as *Goodbye to All That* had; it was an instant success in the West End and for the new publisher. While he built up his list of bestselling authors—Daphne Du Maurier came to him from Heinemann in the 'thirties—he indulged his passion for politics. Extremely left wing himself, he saw the menace of Hitler as few on the left or right did. He started the Left Book Club to make the public aware of the threat of fascist totalitarianism. It achieved immense success in publishing terms but did not stop the drift to war. However, with V.G., publishing was always a crusade—he published what his convictions told him he must publish and he made what money he made. He was as complicated and sincere a man as many another who has published for the twin reasons of seeing his beliefs in print and earning himself a living. There is no simple explanation of such a man and we must await a definitive biography; his own essays in autobiography are too self-indulgent, and do not give the answer. One of his monuments is Dorothy L. Sayers, whose detective novels earned vast sums for V.G. and their author. She was also a scholar—she translated Dante—and a devout Christian who wrote plays about the message of Jesus. Nothing perhaps highlights more the lifework of V.G. than this combination of religion, popular appeal and scholarship in the work of one of his most successful authors. He was religious in the broadest sense, robustly scholarly and knew a business trick or two.

The first prominent new publisher of the dark decade of the 'thirties was Hamish Hamilton, who started in 1931 with Sidney G. Davies as co-director. Hamilton had learned his publishing with Cape at the same time as reading for the bar, and, like Cape, managed Harper's London Office for six years before throwing his own cap into the ring. He was half American, and wanted to publish books which would contribute to greater Anglo-American understanding in the face of the growing menace of renewed German aggression. Hence such works as John Gunther's *Inside Europe*, the first of a series which became popular reference books of contemporary events. But despite such political works, and a subsidiary company to handle law books, Hamish Hamilton's was an essentially literary list with an early bias towards biography, in which category Hesketh Pearson supplied approximately one study a year. James Thurber was on the list by 1935, heralding a London home at 90 Great Russell Street for numerous contributors to the *New Yorker*. In popular fiction Angela Thirkell provided a necessary financial prop from 1933 onwards, and the basis of a healthy thriller list was laid from the beginning with John Dickson Carr's crime stories. (Carr wrote similar books for Heinemann under a pseudonym Carter Dickson, and produced at least one a year for each publisher.) These solid foundations, laid in difficult years, provided the basis for an even more distinguished and varied list after the war.

Michael Joseph, who had been a literary agent, published his first list in 1935 with the secret backing of Victor Gollancz, who withdrew his support when Joseph brought out a book of which he disapproved politically. This estrangement meant that Joseph had to leave the shared offices in 14 Henrietta Street, so in 1937 he moved to Bloomsbury Street, where he gave Robert Lusty, who had been with him from the start, the larger first-floor front office and took the quieter, smaller room overlooking the garden for himself. Victor Gollancz had provided Joseph with one salesman, Charles Pick; the other, Peter Hebdon, joined as office boy and rose to be managing director.

When war broke out, Michael Joseph's was a struggling four-year-old, but already with some healthy roots: C. S. Forester had moved from The Bodley Head, and Captain Hornblower, R.N., had made his first impact on the public; and a great-granddaughter of Dickens, whom Charles Pick met at a dance, was persuaded to write down her experiences as a maidservant in *One Pair of Hands*, which appeared in 1939. This bestseller was joined in the same year by another, Richard Llewellyn's *How Green was my Valley*.

Secker & Warburg was a year younger and somewhat less healthy. Frederic Warburg, in the memoirs already quoted from, noted a loss of £3,197 in 1938 on a turnover of £11,358. But, he insisted, it was a distinguished loss, and his list of twenty-six general books and nine novels was something he felt proud of. Frank Swinnerton wrote of the young firm that 'they published what they liked, and did their weeping in private.' The loss, however, had to be covered. Warburg started with £1,000 borrowed from an aunt, and with rather more capital put in by his partner, Roger Senhouse, a young man who had had some business experience in dockland and had been an assistant to Lytton Strachey. Together they bought up the bankrupt firm of Martin

Secker. Secker remained on the board for a short while but resigned in 1938, by which time Warburg was acquiring some fame as a left-wing publisher. As more capital was required he again went to Aunt Agnes who, fortunately, was impressed by his list and found a further £5,000, although she regretted that he published 'so many of those horrid Socialist books, and attacking dear Mr Chamberlain too ...' So Secker & Warburg approached the unexpectedly boom years of wartime publishing with fresh heart and a backlist which already included Thomas Mann (taken over from Martin Secker), George Orwell, Gabriel Chevallier's *Clochemerle* (their first bestseller) translated from the French by an official in the Lord Chamberlain's office, Jomo Kenyatta's *Facing Mount Kenya*, and, inevitably, H. G. Wells. Such was Wells's fame by then, however, that the young publisher sought out the writer in order to obtain the bestseller his firm needed to survive. *The Fate of Homo Sapiens* was published in August 1939, sold 13,000 copies and helped considerably to reduce the annual loss by half.

Many others gave their names to new firms during these two decades but there was little that was singular enough about them to warrant mention here. An exception is Ernest Benn Ltd, which grew out of the merger between T. Fisher Unwin and Benn Brothers. Victor Gollancz was assisted as manager by Douglas Jerrold, an odd enough combination for any house, but perhaps necessary for one which Ernest Benn said was interested in good literature of every class 'from fiction to works on synthetic rubber or early Chinese pottery'! Neither V.G. nor Jerrold stayed long, and the former took with him the young novelist Joyce Cary, whom he was later to hand over, ungratefully, to Michael Joseph. Glanvill Benn joined in the year of V.G.'s departure and he and Keon Hughes were elected to the board in 1928. Three years later Muirhead's Blue Guides, perhaps the most detailed of guides to individual countries, were launched, which was bad timing because the government was trying to encourage the idea that it was unpatriotic to travel abroad and spend sterling. Benn's, however, persevered, knowing that people continued to go abroad if they could afford to and twenty-two titles were in print in 1940. They published little else in the 'thirties, concentrating more and more on their journals. Ernest Benn himself, was a considerable character, and vigorously pursued various causes, mostly concerned with the freedom of the individual.

Anton Zwemmer is another exception. A Dutchman who settled in England, he managed Jaschke's bookshop in Charing Cross Road while the proprietor, a German, was interned. He bought the shop in 1924, specializing from the beginning in books on the fine arts. Amongst his first customers were Kenneth Clark, Herbert Read and Henry Moore. Publishing commenced in 1925 and continued spasmodically until the mid-'thirties. He brought out the first book on Giotto (by Carlo Carra) since Ruskin's, the first ever in English on Matisse, by Roger Fry, and the first ever on Picasso, by Eugenio d'Ors. In 1934 came Herbert Read's *Henry Moore* for which the trade subscription was thirty-six — no wonder Zwemmer complained that the English would not buy art books. Japanese booksellers saved him on this title and most of the edition was sold to them. The publishing side received a boost when in 1936 Zwemmer became agent for Albert Skira of Geneva, thus introducing a fine new series for which the public, on the whole, were not ready.

Bela Horovitz was another pioneer of fine art books. Horovitz and Ludwig Goldscheider started the Phaidon Press in Vienna in 1923, and moved hurriedly to England fifteen years later when Hitler annexed Austria. By then the press was officially owned by Allen & Unwin, who had bought its stocks and assets so that it should be free from the taint of Jewish blood when the Nazis marched in. Unwin and Horovitz parted company in 1950.

The 'twenties was a time of boom for what were called the private presses, small publishing imprints mostly operated on a shoe-string from the owners' houses. They specialized in sumptuously produced limited editions which were sold mostly to Americans. The bottom fell out of this market with the Wall Street slump and the private presses never thereafter regained their former buoyancy, although many continued to eke out an existence. The names of Golden Cockerel and Scholartis stand out in this category. Apart from obvious commercial gain when times were good, the best justification for private presses is that they helped to raise the standards of book production. But as Stanley Morison, Wren Howard, Ian Parsons and others achieved this with unlimited editions, it may perhaps be true to say that private presses were a byway of publishing and that as far as writers and readers — though not book-collectors — were concerned, they might never have existed.

The Cresset Press, formed by Dennis Cohen in 1927, was also concerned with the first-edition market, but when the slump came it adapted quickly to the general market and survived the bad years. Geoffrey Bles tempered a learned list, including such writers as Berdyaev and Stanislavsky, with bread-and-butter thrillers; Peter Davies and his brother Nicholas (who were brought up, along with other brothers, by J. M. Barrie when they were orphaned). Frederick Muller, Robert Hale, Lindsay Drummond, Andrew Dakers also followed a middle path. Lovat Dickson had some spectacular successes, notably with works by Grey Owl, a bogus half-caste Indian from the Far North, but did not remain independent for long. Herbert Joseph, cousin of Michael, found a profitable line in cookery books by the Countess Morphy. And Ivor Nicholson and Graham Watson had a winner with Lloyd George's memoirs, for which they paid £15,000, an enormous sum for that time.

Most of the above named survived the second war, as did the Blandford Press, which was established in 1919 and passed its golden jubilee without, as far as I know, any public celebration. That no more is said of them here is not to imply any contempt for their activities. The firm of Wills & Hepworth should perhaps extend this paragraph because although it does not appear in Whitaker's Reference Catalogue of Current Literature for 1940 in the list of publishers, it was a company from 1924 onwards. Its origins in the nineteenth century are obscure, but the trademark for the famous Ladybird series was taken out as early as 1916 when it was a private business owned by Mr W. S. Hepworth. The story of this remarkable adventure in children's books comes later, as does that of its Leicestershire neighbour, the Brockhampton Press.

I have saved until last the most famous of all new publishing companies to emerge between the wars — Penguin Books.

Allen Lane left school in 1919 at the age of sixteen to join his uncle John's publishing firm, The Bodley Head. He commenced his apprenticeship by being a looker-out; when orders came into the house from booksellers it was his job to go to the warehouse and find the titles required. He next went to the packing-bench, and, having worked in various departments of the business, became a director at the age of twenty-one. A year later John Lane died and he was appointed managing director, an honour not as great as it may seem because The Bodley Head was no longer the bright star it had been. The brilliant publisher of the *fin-de-siècle*, once the thorn in the side of the P.A. establishment, had suffered eclipse in the post-war years. Allen Lane spent his 'twenties finding out just how difficult it was to sell case-bound books and, in view of his subsequent career, it is surprising that he remained patient for so long. He was a man who loved things to happen, who could not stand still, so he must have been waiting for the right moment; in any case he played along with his colleagues at The Bodley Head for ten years and did few things they could have thought rash. An exception was a volume of cartoons by Peter Arno which he had bought on a trip to New York. These were regarded as quite undesirable, so Allen improvised an imprint of his own and sold 8,000 copies. Another independent experiment was a 2s. 6d. juvenile of Walt Disney's *Three Little Pigs*, later sold through Woolworth's. Then, always ready to do battle with the law, he went to Paris and posted himself in London a copy of *Ulysses*, in a package clearly bearing the message THIS CONTAINS A COPY OF ULYSSES BY JAMES JOYCE. It reached its destination without being opened, and The Bodley Head published the book in a 63s. limited edition in 1936, a trade edition following later.

It was obvious that The Bodley Head could not contain Allen Lane for much longer, particularly when he had witnessed the success of Jonathan Cape and Victor Gollancz. By 1935 he was ready to risk everything and gamble on 6d. reprints of popular books in paperback—not an original idea; as I have mentioned, various publishers had tried it before with their own backlist titles. The difference was only one of conception. Lane was not relying on Bodley Head titles; he proposed to take in other publisher's books, and he planned ten titles every three months for an indefinite period. He went to Jonathan Cape first because, he said later, Cape was the publisher of the moment. He asked for ten titles, offered £25 down payment for each against a ¼d. royalty, and settled for £40 against ⅜d. (Cape confessed later that he thought the venture doomed, and anyway he disliked paperbacks, but didn't see why he shouldn't make something out of it).

The name Penguin was suggested by Allen Lane's secretary, Joan Coles. Edward Young was sent off to Regent's Park Zoo to make drawings of Penguins for the colophon, numerous versions of which were subsequently used, giving cheerful animation to a shelf of the thin orange and white books. Penguin, Lane declared many years later, had 'a dignified flippancy', which is what he had sought. He launched the series on £100 capital and the trade did not respond kindly, so he wooed Clifford Prescott, the chief buyer at F. W. Woolworth who, with some misgivings, gave a first order for 34,000 books. Prescott's wife, Blanche, deserved as much credit for backing Penguins as he. She called at his office whilst Allen Lane was there pressing for an order and was asked to put herself in the position of 'ordinary member of the public'. She came down heavily in favour of the new series and the impressive initial order was followed by an even larger repeat.

Penguin's took offices, if such they could be called, in the crypt of Holy Trinity Church, in Euston Road. The petty cash was kept in one empty tomb, the invoice book in another. The packers pinned up nudes above their benches and the management arranged for blinds which could be quickly pulled down to obscure them when the Vicar paid a call to 'see how the dear boys were getting on'. The new venture had an air of improvisation and fun which it always, to some extent, retained whilst Allen Lane lived, but in the early years he led it zestfully himself, transporting the entire staff to Paris for weekends when the mood took him, and encouraging some to make men of themselves for the first time. Nothing quite like it had happened in British publishing before, and Joseph Malaby Dent, not to mention Hodder & Stoughton, must have turned in their graves.

The first batch of Penguins included André Maurois's *Ariel* and titles by Ernest Hemingway, Eric Linklater, Mary Webb, Agatha Christie and Dorothy Sayers. As the demand increased, booksellers began to stock, and even to welcome, them. Lane soon looked around for possibilities of expansion. Nonfiction had already engaged his attention when, at King's Cross bookstall, one day, he heard a woman inquiring for 'one of those Pelican books'. He knew there was no such series, did not like the idea of a rival with a name so akin, and instantly arranged for works by Shaw, Wells, Julian Huxley, Leonard Woolley, G. D. H. Cole, etc., to appear not as Penguins, in orange covers, but as Pelicans, in blue. New works were commissioned, and so, from an early date, there was some independence of other publishers.

The first Penguins appeared bearing The Bodley Head imprint as well, but the name of the older firm soon disappeared from their covers, and Allen Lane severed his connection with it, his uncle's company passing, as I have recorded, into a consortium owned by Allen & Unwin, Cape and Dent.

Soon another series, the Penguin Specials, was established, born of the same desire that motivated Victor Gollancz and Hamish Hamilton —to alert public opinion to the dangers of what was happening in totalitarian Europe. The first Special was Edgar Mowrer's *Germany Puts the Clock Back* (November 1937), and Lane commissioned a French-woman, Geneviève Tabouis, to write *Blackmail or War?* in the light of Hitler's bullying of small states. The hardback publisher who had turned to paperback reprints as a means of salvation was already, in two years, a publisher of important original work.

The pace of Penguin publishing was always dazzling. It was as though the pent-up frustrations of fifteen years spent at the Bodley Head had exploded. They went on exploding, and there was to be no rest, apart from those wild weekends across the Channel. By 1939 there were already 18 volumes of the Penguin Shakespeare, 6 guides to English counties, 10 classics (Jane Austen, Defoe, Browning, Swift, etc.) illustrated with woodcuts, and the first two King Penguins, volumes with short texts and numerous colour plates, in stiff jacketed boards; they later became collector's items.

In the early days the other directors were Allen's brothers, Richard and John (who was killed in the Second World War), and they were assisted by, among others, Edward Young, Eunice Frost, William Emrys Williams and Krishna Menon (later a senior member of the Indian government). The extraordinary exploit soon outgrew the crypt of Holy Trinity Church, where stock was delivered down a chute from the graveyard, and moved to a modern factory near the present London Airport, in Harmondsworth, Middlesex. And yet Penguin's remarkable success was microscopic compared with what was to come.

Penguin Books reflected the concern of contemporary casebound publishers with presentation and production. They were impeccably printed and designed, for all their cheapness, and this played a big part in their instant success. They sold to those who wanted the best they could afford, and when Pelicans came along they appealed at once to those who—like Allen Lane himself—had not received higher education but were interested in learning. In later years Lane told an interviewer that Pelicans were introduced to compensate for his own lack of university training; but by then he had become so accustomed to being told that he had created a social revolution singlehanded that he may well have invented this reason on the spot, with the customary wicked twinkle in his eyes.

Allen Lane was a complex person, and efforts to label and pigeonhole him caused him great amusement. It did not suit some academics and educators to suppose that a man could create Penguin Books without having clearly before him the ideals of social usefulness and the betterment of mankind. The earnest evaluators often overlooked the nature of the man behind the movement, either because they wished to idealize him, or because they found him as puzzling as I did. He liked to claim something approaching illiteracy for himself and he put it about that he did not read books but he always took careful note of any advice or recommendation offered him. Some of his colleagues say that no pose was involved, he really wasn't a bookish or a cultured man; but they all expressed great loyalty and friendship to him, and none of them denigrated him or suggested his success was due to others. I have never heard anyone claim that they could have done the same thing given the opportunity. He was a man of action in a world of words, an assessment which he would have found altogether too solemn. He might have recognized it as being partially true, but he would have laughed at it because there was nothing pretentious or pompous about him. According to Robert Lusty, when Lane was told he had been offered a knighthood, he took to his bed for a day in sheer disbelief.

6

Bookselling: London

W. H. Smith & Son; Wyman & Son; Simpkin Marshall; Bailey Brothers; Angus & Robertson; Whitcombe & Tombs; William Jackson; Times Book Club; commercial libraries — Harrod's, Army & Navy Stores; Mudie's; J. & E. Bumpus; Hatchard's; A. & R. Mowbray; Alfred Wilson; Barker & Howard; Dobell; W. & G. Foyle; Beaumont; Luzac; Poetry Bookshop; Red Lion Bookshop; Gutman; David Archer; W. J. Bryce; A. Zwemmer; Miller & Gill; Pioneer Bookshop; Student's Bookshops; G. Heywood Hill; Michael Williams; Collet's; Dillon's; International University Booksellers; Wimbledon — Hill Bookshop; Enfield — Don Gresswell; Banstead — Ibis Library; Brentwood — Burgess's Bookshop; entries under 'Booksellers' in Post Office Directories; the wages of bookshop managers and assistants.

The retail book trade's major battle against underselling during the Edwardian decade, provoked by the Times Book Club, has already been noted. W. H. Smith & Son faced as big a crisis in 1905, when their contracts for railway bookstalls were cancelled in bulk. This led to the extraordinary feat of their opening two-hundred shops in ten weeks, all situated, for obvious reasons, as near as possible to railway and London Underground stations. (It would have been impossible to make so swift a comeback later in the century, when obtaining planning permission from local authorities alone would have delayed opening new shops.)

As well as catering for the newspaper and periodical trade, these new shops developed their retail bookselling side, of which David Roy eventually emerged as head, succeeding J. G. Metcalf in 1920. (Roy joined in 1911 and became manager of the publicity department in 1914.) He won for himself not only the respect of his employers, but the high regard of publishers. In latter years, long after his death, I have seen the face of Stanley Unwin take on a mellow, wistful look as he recalled the great Roy of Smith's. Presumably Roy bought the books which Unwin and other publishers thought he should buy, and in satisfactory quantities. He must also have sold them, because his reign at Strand House lasted throughout the 'twenties and 'thirties, and he survived the transition of W. H. Smith into a limited company after the second Viscount Hambleden's death in 1928. It was in 1923, during Roy's early years as book buyer, that the small Truslove & Hanson chain was purchased. The three branches, all in fashionable shopping streets in south-west and west London, were precursors of the later Bowes & Bowes group, and one of them in fact became part of it. In 1924 a second-generation Hornby (Michael) became a partner.

As W. H. Smith lost bookstall contracts, Wyman & Son gained them, the first in 1906, and then 349 more over the years. Both companies opened wholesale houses in provincial towns and cities to cope with their trade. Wyman's followed Smith's into retail bookselling in 1930 when they opened the first of many branches at Acton, West London.

Most wholesalers remained centred on London, including Simpkin Marshall, who formed a special company to take over the Stoneham group of shops which went bankrupt in 1907. During these years Simpkin's were an essential part of the distribution structure, booksellers having far fewer direct accounts than were forced upon them when wholesaling broke down after the Second World War. Simpkin's operated on small margins and paid low wages — they could not do otherwise — but many later successful booksellers gained their knowledge of the trade working for Simpkin's, which handled all publishers' books and dealt with most of the retail outlets in the kingdom. Throughout much of this period Arthur Minshull, who joined Simpkin Marshall, Hamilton & Kent in 1908, played an increasingly important part in the affairs of the great wholesaler.

Edward Swinfen looked after Simpkin's publishing activities until he joined Alex Bailey, of Bailey Brothers in 1929. Swinfen persuaded Bailey to allow him to visit the Continent, where he bought distribution rights in various German publications which provided a necessary extra string to their bow when the slump came. At about this time Oxford University Press closed down their bindery, and Bailey's Highbury headquarters became too small for the increased flow of Oxford Bibles and Prayer Books, so the wholesale import department moved (fatefully — they were blitzed in the Second World War) to Paternoster Row. At this time Humphrey Milford joined Bailey's board, on which the Publisher to O.U.P. has sat ever since.

It was the custom for large Australian and New Zealand booksellers to have their own buying agents in London. Angus & Robertson, of Sydney, who had been represented by the Australian Book Company owned by Henry George for many years, bought that concern in 1938. G. A. Ferguson, grandson of the co-founder George Robertson, was sent to London to convert the Australian Book Company into a branch of the family business. He arrived four days before Henry George, who was over eighty, died, and was thus not able to enjoy what had been planned as a gradual handing-over of responsibility.

One who came earlier and stayed longer than Ferguson, was Maurice Cameron of Whitcombe & Tombs, of Wellington, New Zealand. Cameron spent half of his working life in the London office, and it was said that he arranged to work in Britain rather than New Zealand because of his passion for cricket. Certainly he arrived at the antiquated offices in Addle Hill, near St Paul's Cathedral, in 1930 for a proposed stay of two to three years, but stayed until his retirement in 1957. And when a rep. had a cricket book to subscribe, a queue of other travellers would form outside his glass-walled office whilst he gave the volume detailed attention and reminisced about his favourite sport. But waiting is an occupational hazard for representatives, and Cameron was popular amongst them.

Wholesale exporters also flourished in this period, charging overseas customers a commission, 5 or 10 per cent on invoice price, and sometimes making their business more profitable by buying at colonial rates and invoicing at home, as well as adding surcharges for insurance which they took the risk of underwriting themselves. The firm of William Jackson (Books) Ltd was started by Frederick C. Joiner in 1918 while he was still employed by another wholesaler, William Dawson, as a collector. The wily Joiner made contacts with his employer's customers and gained some accounts for himself. Hence the use of the pseudonym. He soon began to specialize in the American market, which did not expect colonial terms on fiction, so that he could buy a 7s. 6d. novel for 3s. 9d., and invoice it out at 5s. plus 10 per cent commission, still making it worthwhile for the American bookseller to undersell the American edition.

Joiner flourished into the 'fifties on this basis, but also had accounts in the then colonies who expected to have the colonial rates passed on to them. Probably he was only tolerated by publishers because he paid his bills promptly, and, although there were outcries from time to time because English editions were rather too prominently displayed in shops in New York and Chicago, he was seldom effectively challenged. What gave him real annoyance was the custom of some publishers who stamped their colonial editions with violet ink. Joiner, a man of uncouth tongue and habits, would then demand eradicating liquid and attempt to remove the marks. When he failed, his language heralded the permissive society of which he would certainly have disapproved.

In 1927 he turned William Jackson into a limited company, and his first co-director was Alan Steele, a young man who had started in the trade as a W. H. Smith trainee and gone on to run Macfarlane & Steele, a chain of bookshops in Sussex. (Macfarlane later joined Nelson.) Steele went to Took's Court, off Chancery Lane, from which address Joiner conducted his business, which included dabbling in pornography. Jackson's were agents for Pino Orioli, in Florence, and for various small firms in France. D. H. Lawrence's poems, *Pansies*, were ordered by Jackson's to be sent direct from Sylvia Beach's bookshop in Paris to a customer in Montreal. The correspondence referring to this order was intercepted by the Home Office, and Alan Steele, to whom Joiner had delegated the responsibility for dealing with anything likely to excite the attentions of the law, was called before Sir Archibald Bodkin, whom he remembered as 'a terrifying little man with a wizened, yellow face, wearing a pair of steel-rimmed spectacles', who threatened to prosecute him if he continued to deal in such literature. A few weeks later forty bags of registered mail containing *Lady Chatterley's Lover* turned up in Took's Court from Orioli! Such were the excitements and hazards of wholesale bookselling in London between the wars. Joiner once told me how he successfully evaded the customs with copies of *Ulysses* illicitly imported from Paris and then dispatched to the new world. He was always game to take a risk and, if possible, to ease the responsibility on to someone else. For many years that someone was Alan Steele, who could have borne it longer but for interference from Joiner's wife Ethel, who would not tolerate anyone who appeared more brilliant than her husband. This was rating human attainment rather low but the junior director took the hint and gave more and more of his attention to their publishing imprint, Joiner & Steele, issuing the Furnival books of short stories, an illustrated *As You Like It* and developing some of William Jackson's overseas agencies.

Whilst Steele was travelling a book called *Tender Buttons*, published by a small press in Paris, he was once again accused of outraging public taste. He subscribed it to Frank Denny in his long, dark bookshop in the Strand where travellers were received in a confessional-like cubicle. Denny leafed through the book until his eye alighted on the word 'knickers'. In shocked tones the sometime president of the Associated Booksellers read the young publisher a lecture on where he was likely to end up if he continued to circulate such filth, and ordered him from the shop. But, inevitably, it was Ethel, and not the public prosecutor, who forced the final separation between Joiner and Steele which occurred when the latter was offered the position of export manager at The Times Book Club.

The Times Book Club was reorganized, after the famous 'war', and in 1911 the library was thrown open to the general public at a subscription rate of £2 12s. od. for three volumes. (Mudie's and Smith's subs were £1. 17s. od. by comparison). Three years later, ever the innovator, the book club went further and invited the public to browse amongst the actual books on the shelves, a hitherto unheard of privilege. As a result of this, and of the wartime boom, the accumulated loss of the company had by 1918 been turned to profit, and four years later new premises in Wigmore Street, W.1, were taken.

Harrods were already selling books when the century began; other London stores soon followed them. In 1918 the Army & Navy in Victoria Street, previously only seeking the patronage of officers of the armed services, opened its doors to all, with the result that the book department and library became a substantial account for most publishers. In the Strand, the Civil Service Stores had a book department in 1920, and at Selfridge's in Oxford Street books eventually came under the management of 'Jock' Elliott, who succeeded S. J. Manning when the latter was called up in 1940. Thomas Joy joined Harrods in 1936, having worked at Denny's and been an antiquarian bookseller in Oxford, and a year later bought for them the bankrupt stock of Mudie's. He was promoted manager of the book department in 1939, when R. Cadness Page, the head librarian, was called up.

Mudie's had become very much a London, even something of a national, institution. Shortly before he died in 1945, Edgar Gladwin, who succeeded to the business of Frank Denny, recalled in an address to the Society of Bookmen that assistants at Mudie's, for whom he started to work about 1900, were sometimes invited to stay with customers, and were brought gifts of game. F. T. Bell, who went to work for Mudie's (in regulation black coat and striped trousers) in 1929 for £2 a week, believed that their failure was due to their moving away from the fashionable New Oxford Street premises to another building in Kingsway, where it was not possible to keep more than 80,000 volumes in stock. The remainder was in a warehouse across the river, and subscribers, exasperated at having to wait whilst the books they wanted were fetched from two miles away, transferred their patronage to the Times or to Harrods.

Of the older established firms mentioned in previous chapters, Bumpus's and Hatchard's entered the twentieth century as London's two main pedigree shops, and were the focus of fashionable book buying for much of this period. J. & E. Bumpus moved from Holborn Bars to Oxford Street in 1903 and, some ten years later, acquired the services of John G. Wilson, perhaps the most distinguished of London booksellers in the twentieth century. 'J.G.', a Scot, had his training with John Smith's of Glasgow, but when he came South he entered publishing, at Constable's. Bookselling, however, proved the stronger attraction, and in 1909, he joined Jones & Evans, in the City, a business still commanded by his son-in-law George Downie in 1970. Wilson soon moved on to Bumpus, and the shop over which he ruled for many decades became a paradise for booklovers and for publishers' representatives. These were the days before sale-or-return, when booksellers operated on small overheads, paid starvation wages and took on apprentices. In the 1920s J.G. found himself training the son of the man who had trained him: John Knox II came to England for part of his apprenticeship before returning to Glasgow and John Smith's.

Bumpus in those days had the patronage of the post-war version of the carriage trade, and Ian Parsons, himself a trainee at the time, remembers that when Harold Nicolson's *Some People* was first published, J.G. stood at the door of his shop, beside a pile of copies of that book, handing it out enthusiastically to customers (or perhaps they were clients then) saying, 'I'll charge it to your account.' One must admire Wilson's drive and influence with his public, but a cautionary rider should be added: when Bumpus's passed into new ownership in the 1950s the incoming managing director discovered customers' credit accounts which had not been settled since before the second war. J.G. operated in a climate very different from that of forty years on. Between the wars, taxes, like wages, were lower, and businesses could salt away their profits against lean times, and subsidize customers who wished, in their lordly way, to settle their accounts annually, if at all. Bumpus did not, fortunately, rely solely on the carriage trade, and in a symposium, *The Book World Today*, J. G. Wilson emphasized the importance of the tourist and visitor to the London bookseller. He sold to them for cash, and lured them into his premises by operating on a main shopping street. Even so, although seasonal changes were less marked in central London than elsewhere, between 20 and 25 per cent of his annual trade was done in December.

At this time most of what a bookseller bought was a firm purchase, as I have said, but J. G. commented on the absurd fact that for this reason many excellent books were not in bookshops but in publishers' warehouses. He was confident that London booksellers could reverse this state of affairs if the then little-used sale-or-return system was extended. It is interesting that he was not apparently affected by Jonathan Cape's harsh terms on *Seven Pillars*; he noted enthusiastically that this bestseller stimulated trade all round and brought back customers who had stopped buying books. He believed very strongly in the personal relationship between the bookseller and his customers, and thought that young people were reading hard, and with a purpose—to change a world with which they were not over-pleased. He already foresaw the effects of increased leisure, and of women entering business life. During most of his reign at Bumpus he had on his staff Dickie Bland, who was still active at Hatchard's in 1973 at the age of eighty-three. Mr Bland began his career with The Times Book Club in 1905, but four years later joined the navy and stayed at sea until 1923 when he returned to his first love. He had a prodigious memory for authors, titles, publishers and prices which made him an invaluable stock-keeper. Another notable colleague of J.G.'s was Dr Homeyer, a refugee from Nazi Germany, who became head of Bumpus's foreign department.

A. L. Humphreys remained at Hatchard's, in Piccadilly, until 1924, occupying much the same position of respect amongst publishers and customers as J. G. Wilson. The two sons of Edwin Shepherd carried on the business after his departure, but it deteriorated. In 1938 Sir Thomas

Moore, then a Member of Parliament, campaigned for the release of Clarence Hatry, who had been convicted of fraud. Moore succeeded when fresh evidence came to light and asked Hatry what he proposed to do with his freedom. Hatry replied that he would like to run a bookshop so Sir Thomas looked around and visited Hatchard's where he found the shelves half empty of books. 'The place was filthy,' he told me, 'the lights were bad, and there were several elderly gentlemen who had evidently grown up with their arms folded, but no business.' Moore and Hatry bought Hatchard's, cleaned it up and opened a meeting-room on the first floor where distinguished political and literary figures addressed customers and the general public. This was rather more in the tradition of John Hatchard, and it was popular.

Amongst other survivors from the nineteenth century were A. R. Mowbray's and Alfred Wilson's. Mowbray's moved from Great Castle Street to Margaret Street, north of Oxford Circus, in 1908 and under their chairman and managing director, E. A. Judge, still mainly concentrated on theological works. Alfred Wilson's was in Gracechurch Street in the City, in premises which dated from the Great Fire of London. Alfred died in 1928 and was succeeded by his son Hubert, who rebuilt 7 Ship Tavern Passage and moved there in 1930. It was a wise move because the ancient edifice, with a front wall 13 inches and a back one 18 inches from vertical, was condemned by the City Surveyor a year later. Hubert Wilson also bought a shop in Victoria Street, near the station, and another in Hampstead High Street, which A. F. Mason had acquired from one Hewetson just after the first war. At this stage Alfred Wilson became a limited company, with Maurice Hockliffe, a Bedford bookseller, as associate director.

Also in the City, in Fenchurch Street, was Barker & Howard, which inhabited a narrow building on several floors, teeming with activity that had as much to do with newspapers and periodicals as with books. And in Charing Cross Road there was Bertram Dobell, whose sons took over when he died in 1914. Dobell began life as a grocer's assistant and bought books from stalls in markets and from bookshops' bargain trays. His fame rests partly on his rediscovery of lost poets, amongst them Thomas Traherne, whose manuscripts he bought for a song. He edited and published them between 1906 and 1908. Dobell wrote verse himself, and was a friend of the poet James Thomson, to whom he brought comfort in his last unhappy years.

The bookshop primarily associated in the public mind with Charing Cross Road is that of Foyle's. The brothers William and Gilbert Foyle, aged nineteen and seventeen, failed their civil service examinations in 1904 and discovered there was a market for used textbooks. They sold their secondhand books from the kitchen of their parents' house in Hoxton, achieving a turnover of £10 in their first year. When more space became necessary they moved to 5s. a week premises in Islington, then on to slightly larger offices costing 10s. a week in Peckham. Within a short while they had leased a shop in Charing Cross Road, and in 1929 their success was such that the Lord Mayor of London officially opened the new five-storey premises at one corner of Manette Street, facing the older shop on the opposite corner. William's son and daughter, Richard and Christina, joined the business, and the latter inaugurated in 1931 the series of literary luncheons which were still held in 1973. Distinguished authors talked about their books and signed copies of them after the lunch, and members of the public were delighted to pay for their lunch *and* buy the book. Christina Foyle also started the book clubs previously referred to.

Foyle's was always a mixture of new and secondhand books, and ever favoured bold advertising. The banner across their frontage proclaimed them The World's Largest Bookshop, and they attracted both customers, who knew there was a good chance of finding what they wanted as they rummaged among the vast accumulation of titles on shelves and floors, and those who, like the original Foyle brothers, wished to sell their own books.

Lower down Charing Cross Road, opposite Zwemmer's, was from 1910 a small shop plus a basement workroom run by Cyril Beaumont. He specialized in books on ballet and the dance, some of which were not only written and published by the bookseller, but even handprinted by him on his press in the cellar. Beaumont became interested in the ballet by accident, when he reluctantly agreed to accompany his wife to see a Pavlova performance. He was the complete bookman—author, printer, publisher, critic, bookseller and, frequently, his own delivery boy as well. There is a graceful tribute to him in Osbert Sitwell's *Laughter in the Next Room.*

Other specialist shops included Luzac & Co., already thirteen years old when H. B. Knight-Smith became its proprietor in 1903 and took charge of its bookselling and publishing activities in Orientalia, and the Poetry Bookshop, which opened at 35 Devonshire Street, off Theobalds Road, Holborn, in 1913. The latter was Harold Monro's idea and was dedicated to the sale of verse and books and pamphlets on poetry. Lascelles Abercrombie was invited to perform the opening ceremony, but modestly suggested that an older poet should be given the task, so Sir Henry Newbolt ('Play up! play up! and play the game!') officiated instead. Monro was a poet himself and edited an anthology for Chatto. (His collected poems were reissued by Duckworth in 1970.) He created a *salon* which was a meeting-place for poets and intellectuals, but he was never far from financial ruin. The stock was moved to 38 Great Russell Street in 1926, and again, some years later, into a back room of the same premises when lack of cash obliged him to sublet the shop to

Kegan Paul. Monro died in 1932 and his widow, Alida, closed the business three years later.

Meeting-places were provided by other booksellers in the 'twenties. One was Charlie Lahr's tiny Red Lion Bookshop, described by H. E. Bates as 'a rabbit-hutch', which could accommodate no more than four or five at a time. When there were more callers—and they tended to be callers, in search of literary gossip and intellectual stimulation, rather than customers—latecomers had to sit on ladders. Lahr came from Germany in 1904 and never took out naturalization papers. He remained a stateless citizen until his death in 1971 and was interned in both world wars. Such commercial success as he had was built on the chance acquisition of a first-edition Kipling, which he sold for £325. He specialized in first editions, and published early work by Bates, Rhys Davies, Liam O'Flaherty, etc., and the unexpurgated edition of Lawrence's *Pansies*, in return for which D. H. drew a self-portrait and presented it to him. An eccentric in the anarchist tradition, Charlie Lahr always wore sandals, usually without socks, and bicycled around central London unperturbed, even as an old man. He was a natural iconoclast and plastered his shop with pictures cut from newspapers of famous people, which he embellished with blasphemous and unlikely comments coming in balloons from their mouths.

Across the Thames, at 89 Bermondsey Street, Ethel Gutman opened the Bermondsey Bookshop in 1921. Her object was 'to bring books, the love of books and the allied arts into the lives of the working men and women of Bermondsey'. She was open from 5 p.m. to 11 p.m. from Monday to Friday, and again on Sunday. She sold books on the instalment system for as little as a penny a week, and she attracted people of all classes from many parts of London. She organized play-readings, which led to the formation of a local repertory theatre, and she published a quarterly review to which famous authors were glad to contribute. Tragically, she died in 1925 and five years later her successors closed the still flourishing shop. Nothing of its kind appeared again on the south bank of the river.

The gap left by the closing of the Poetry Bookshop was at least partly filled by David Archer's opening a similar shop in Parton Street, off Red Lion Square. From this address Archer published the first books of many poets, including Dylan Thomas. He made no profit from these and returned the copyrights to the authors. An eccentric with little business acumen, he used money inherited from a property-owning family to support poetry which he personally did not read. He preferred thrillers, but claimed that he could recognize the poetry in people.

In 1917 William Jackson Bryce opened a shop in High Holborn, but moved in 1931 to the corner of Museum and Little Russell Streets in

the shadow of Allen & Unwin—very much in the shadow, for Stanley
Unwin rescued the business when a receiver was appointed. In his
autobiography Sir Stanley related how he thought it would have been
a tragedy if Bryce's services 'and those of his quite outstanding colleague, I. P. M. Chambers' had been lost to the book trade. Ivan
Chambers joined Bryce in 1925, after working as a commercial translator. He had long been determined to become a bookseller, to which
calling he brought a unique wit and the highest standards of personal
service. In later years Chambers recalled W. J. Bryce putting one of the
shortcomings of bookselling into a nutshell. Chambers asked for a 5s.
a week increase in wages. 'No,' said Bryce, 'the shop cannot afford it.
Your reward will be in the hereafter.'

The reconstructed business prospered. In 1971 Angus Wilson recalled that there were many bookshops around the British Museum
when he went to work in the library there in 1936, but that the booksellers in most of them seemed intent on cultivating the impression that
they had stepped out of the pages of W. J. Locke. Ivan Chambers was
the first he encounterd who *knew* about books.

Amongst other new shops opened in London in the 'twenties and
'thirties were Zwemmer's (already mentioned on p. 362) and Miller &
Gill, which was originally owned by Simpkin Marshall and operated
from a shop in Cambridge Circus, but later moved to 94 Charing Cross
Road and subsequently became Better Books. Eric Norris was a junior
assistant there in about 1925, when customers would be kept waiting
while he was dispatched to nearby publishers' trade counters to collect
their special orders. Decades later, Norris was to become the proprietor
of the Pioneer Bookshop, Woolwich, and this early training in collecting
persisted for the benefit of his customers. The Pioneer was opened by
George Goodchild in 1927 on behalf of the Woolwich Labour Party.
The Pioneer Press had operated from the same premises (later described
in guidebooks as 'next to the jellied-eel shop'), printing left-wing
literature. Quite soon Goodchild leased it from the labour party on a
weekly basis, and broadened the stock.

A similarly socially orientated venture was Student's Bookshops Ltd,
started by the Workers' Educational Association in its London headquarters in 1910, and moved into Tottenham Court Road in 1926. A
shop was also established inside the London School of Economics in
Houghton Street. This was managed very successfully by O. H. H.
Jermy until the outbreak of war, when it was evacuated to Cambridge,
never to return.

In the West End, Heywood Hill's elegant Mayfair emporium, with
its Queen Ann bow window, opened in Curzon Street in 1937. His
future partner, Handasyde Buchanan, another erudite bookseller, was
then a partner in the nearby shop of Michael Williams. Hill, joined by

Buchanan at the end of the war, established a market for current new books and a rare books department which attracted collectors.

In 1931 Frank Ward opened the 'first modern bookshop' in London at 3 Baker Street. Ward set out to challenge the image of the traditional bookshop, with its window displays built up so as to obscure the inside of the shop from the street (plenty of examples still extant) and its sanctified air of an old, dusty, ill-lit library. His shop had light oak shelves, fittings by Heal's, and fitted carpet, and its window was low and open, attracting the customers in to the books which they could see so alluringly arranged in the interior. His was a pioneer bookshop in a different sense from the one at Woolwich, which in 1969 still remained totally uninfluenced by Ward's innovations.

In 1934, Eva Reckitt, daughter of a rich industrialist, bought what was known as 'The Bomb Shop' at 66 Charing Cross Road. The name derived from the socialist-anarchist leanings of its owner, Mr Henderson. Miss Reckitt, although not privy to acts of violence during her long reign at Collet's, as she named her business, opened her shop to promote the sale of progressive literature. She was a natural supporter of V.G.'s Left Book Club, and of Allen Lane's Penguins. Collet's expanded considerably in later years, as we shall see.

Another woman bookseller made a humble beginning in Store Street, Bloomsbury, three years after Eva Reckitt. Una Dillon had a science degree from Bedford College, and had worked for the Central Association for Mental Welfare, when she started her small shop at the age of thirty-five, on £800 capital. She took over a short lease from a library supplier, Ronald Burns, and bought some of his stock. Two years later she pursued her student and academic customers at London University to Cardiff, Leicester and Knebworth House, in Hertfordshire, when the evacuation of 1939 took place. But the Store Street shop survived those grim years, and her greater glories as a bookseller were in the postwar decade.

Already supplying London University students when Miss Dillon began were International University Booksellers, of Gower Street, for whom Norman Askew, later sales director of Cape's, was apprenticed in 1936 for 10s. per week, rising to £1 5s. od. after four years.

At Wimbledon, Harold Cook took over the Hill Bookshop in 1935, and on the edge of Greater London, bookshops at Enfield, Banstead and Brentwood warrant mention. Don Gresswell's enterprise began on a small scale at Enfield in 1938. A trained mechanical engineer, Gresswell decided to give up science for commerce, and purchased a stationer's and tobacconist's where he soon began to sell, with increasing success, Penguins and other books. In the same year, at Banstead, Irene Babbidge and Evelyn Folds-Taylor opened the Ibis Library, enrolling a hundred members on their first day, and provided a small bookselling department in a shop that was to become very well known to the trade. At Brentwood, Alec Bunch, who had been with Alfred Wilson's, bought Burgess's Bookshop and survived the perils of suburban bookselling which had not prospered overmuch between the wars and was to decline further thereafter.

There were many other London booksellers during this period and my selection is probably altogether too invidious but, at least, I hope it may be broadly representative. For the statistical record, according to the Post Office Directories, the number of booksellers in the Greater London Area was approxiamtely 400 in 1914 and roughly the same number at the end of the first war. In 1919 the list took up some five columns against four and a half, but some entries were much longer, Beazley's of Belgravia, for instance, who claimed they could 'supply any book wanted', taking up one quarter of a column. Ten years later they were still as noticeable but had tempered their advertisement to read 'can supply *the* book wanted'. In 1929 the figure of all booksellers was nearer to 500, as it was also in 1939, but these lists are not 100 per cent accurate and include a number who traded only in secondhand books.

It is less easy to record even as approximately the wages paid to managers and assistants who worked in these shops. H. F. Johns joined Hugh Rees in Pall Mall, in 1927, at the age of fifteen and was paid 12s. (60p) per week. By 1935 this had increased to £1 and he worked of an evening on the tote at Wimbledon to supplement it — if he could get to the race track in time because all work at the shop had to be completed each day, although the official hours were 8.30 a.m. to 6.30 p.m. Small wonder that Johns, and many others, changed sides and became publishers' reps. Thomas Joy was more fortunate at Denny's, where in the 1920s he earned the princely sum, for those days, of £3 a week.

7

Bookselling: Provincial, Welsh, Scottish

Electricity, telephones and typewriters are taken up by booksellers; booksellers receive by-return service from suppliers; Blackwell's denunciation of unworkable terms; provincial towns: Oxford; Cambridge; Birmingham—entries under 'Booksellers' in Kelly's Directory for 1913 and 1939—the activities of Hudson and Woolston; Nottingham; Middlesbrough: Sunderland; Newcastle upon Tyne Sheffield; Leeds; Hull; Manchester; Blackburn; Liverpool: library supply— James Askew and Holt-Jackson; Chester; Bangor; Colwyn Bay; Ellesmere Port; Chesterfield; Lincoln; Coventry; East Anglia and the east Midlands covered by Countryside Libraries; Welwyn Garden City; Exeter; Penzance; Winchester; Reading; Bristol; Cheltenham; Ely; Maldon; Wokingham; Lyme Regis; Worthing; Brighton; Reigate; Aylesbury; Tunbridge Wells; Crowborough; Scottish towns: Glasgow; Edinburgh.

Bookselling, not the most forward-looking of retail trades, was nevertheless affected by the revolution in communications brought about by railways, motor transport and the advance of technology. In 1901 the provincial bookseller may well still have lit his shop by gaslight. He may not yet have had a telephone installed. Possibly he owned a typewriter. By 1939, few, if any, shops were not electrically lit, only the most eccentric still eschewed the 'phone, and although the handwritten letter was still much favoured, most shops had typewriters and some even calculating-machines. Publishers' reps, who at the turn of the century travelled country areas on buses and trains, gradually acquired cars. Delivery to provincial, Scottish and Welsh booksellers was made by train and carrier, or by post, and carriers soon exchanged their nags for motor-driven vans.

Despite the First World War and the industrial upsets of the following twenty years, booksellers received a by-return service from publishers and wholesalers. The number of books published annually more than doubled between 1918 and 1938, but they could still be handled efficiently, and overheads were low enough to permit first-class service to the cutomer.

Not that provincial booksellers were happy with their lot, or regarded their trading terms with publishers as ideal, or even as fair. In *The Book World*, from which I have already quoted J. G. Wilson on London bookselling, Basil Blackwell succinctly denounced the seven deadly paradoxes of provincial bookselling. He maintained, for instance, that the better the bookseller the less likelihood was there of his surviving, because he carried a representative stock, none of which was returnable, and he and his assistants spent too much of each day on unproductive research for customers. A draper selling children's books at Christmas, on the other hand, was not expected to have any knowledge of them beyond their selling price, and reaped the reward of quick turnover coupled with minimal risk of bad stock. Another paradox illustrated the inane practice of offering better terms for journey orders (those taken by the representative on his quarterly or half-yearly call) than for repeat orders for titles which sold quickly. Either the bookseller waited three to six months for the traveller's next visit in order to buy at best terms, or he reordered immediately at the lower discount. Ernest Heffer's epitaph on one of his own calling was 'Died waiting for the traveller to call', to which Basil Blackwell added, 'Also he may die waiting for a customer to call', for he saw the provincial bookseller as doomed to extinction in non-university towns of about 40,000 people.

Blackwell's own company, however, far from failing, was the means of saving others. Basil Blackwell joined his father in Broad Street, Oxford, just before the first war, and continued the tradition of publishing poetry and other items, as well as retailing other people's books. In 1920 he acquired the Shakespeare Head Press, which led to the publication of several ambitious multi-volumed projects, and nine years later he was invited to take over responsibility for William George's of Bristol. George's had hit hard times and been reduced to a staff of five; Blackwell's backing ensured its survival through the slump, and it was about this time that Raymond Haynes, later a director, joined the firm. In his opinion bookselling was an enjoyable and leisurely occupation until about 1938. Closer to home, indeed almost on their doorstep, Blackwell's took a deliberately non-controlling interest in Parker's of Broad Street in 1930, and on the eve of the second war, F. A. Wood's Oxford shop was purchased.

Something has already been said of Basil Blackwell's work for the Associated Booksellers; a colleague who joined him in 1932, Henry Schollick, also combined his working day as bookseller/publisher with voluntary duties for the Association, believing that a man must serve the trade he lives by. Blackwell and Schollick became two of the best-loved personalities of the book trade in their time, and although they practised bookselling under conditions more advantageous than many enjoyed, they did not withdraw into an ivory tower. They did not neglect their own company to take leading parts in trade politics, but were men of such prodigious energy that they successfully contrived to combine both tasks.

In Cambridge, Ernest W. Heffer (see above), son of William Heffer,

developed the family shop in Petty Cury and added printing to his
activities when he bought the Black Bear Press in 1912. His son Reuben
joined him in 1931. Other established Cambridge booksellers were
Macmillan & Bowes, which became Bowes & Bowes in 1907—George
Brimley Bowes was also an activist in trade affairs—and Deighton, Bell
& Co., where the Earnshaw Smith family remained in charge. Both
firms absorbed other local businesses between the wars, but not that of
Gustave David, whose small shop in St Edward's Passage (and his stall
in the market place) were taken over by his son, Hubert, when he died
in 1936. Galloway & Porter also remained independent; although it had
effectively become only Porter by 1902, when Galloway set off for
Aberystwyth for the sake of his daughter's health. There he started
Galloway & Morgan in 1903, and at Bangor Galloway & Hodgson in
1919, with Miss M. E. Hodgson, who had been his assistant at
Aberystwyth, as manageress.

Perhaps the most significant new provincial business in the first half
of the century was that of Hudson & Woolston, which opened in New
Street, Birmingham, in 1906. Ernest Foster Hudson, who had
started bookselling with Hamilton's, at Saltburn-on-Sea in Yorkshire,
and Walter Percy Woolston met as assistants at Combridge's, in Birmingham. These two energetic Edwardians lasted precisely three years together before their partnership was dissolved, and Woolston went off to
Nottingham. After the split, each traded under his own name. Hudson
subsequently married a member of his staff, and the eldest of their
three children, Pat, joined the business in 1936.

There were 79 booksellers listed in *Kelly's Directory* for Birmingham in
1913, 29 of whom also rated as publishers, although 2 of them were
branches of George Newnes and the Temple Press. By 1939 approximately 100 booksellers were recorded, and Hudson was advertising in
Kelly's, rather grandly, as 'The World's Booksellers, Wholesale and
Retail … ' The figures for both dates include branches of W. H. Smith's
and of Boots Booklovers Library. There were also other older established
businesses—Combridge and Cornish, and the Midland Educational
which, in 1927, when R. E. Hearne (later managing director) joined,
had only one branch, in Leicester.

When he left Hudson, Woolston took another partner for the first
year and traded as Sinclair & Woolston, but he was soon on his own. It
was his intention to have a chain of retail shops. Directly after the
Armistice he opened branches in York and Lancaster, and started
wholesaling. By 1921 he had had second thoughts and decided that
retailing didn't pay. Having increased his capital from £5,000 to £20,000
in the previous year he closed his shops, including the one at Nottingham, and concentrated on supplying libraries. In 1931, in search of
further expansion, Woolston opened an office in Dublin, but this lasted

only seven years. Before this F. Crosby had been appointed his joint managing director.

Woolston's neighbours in Nottingham, Boot's Pure Drug Co. prospered, not only as manufacturing and retailing chemists and druggists but also as commercial librarians and booksellers. They enjoyed rapid growth in the inter-war years and by the early 1940s there were some 460 libraries operating within their stores.

Elsewhere in the industrial North and Midlands conditions were not as good for bookselling or any other trade once the Armistice was signed. In Middlesbrough, on Tees-side, Boddy's, founded in 1904, was almost alone in surviving the depression. George William Boddy had learned his trade at Bailey's in Darlington Horse Market, and later worked in Belfast, Louth and Wigan, before taking over Bell's Library and renaming it. His apprenticeship almost certainly taught him to be resourceful and resilient, and he was able to hand on the structure of a business to his son, whereas three other booksellers in Linthorpe Road alone closed between the wars; a fourth, a branch of T. & G. Allen, a small north-eastern chain, was taken over by W. H. Smith in about 1930.

Hill's, in nearby Sunderland, also remained solvent when four or five neighbouring booksellers went under; only the toughest remained in this region, grimly hanging on until the war brought relief from unemployment. Life in Newcastle-upon-Tyne was marginally less severe than in many neighbouring towns and cities; the small store of Mawson, Swan & Morgan got by and T. Robson Dring even dared to buy the Book Room, in Saville Row, in 1936, and develop it along general bookselling lines. And in southern Yorkshire there were others game to fight against serious odds. Alan Ward, son of an industrialist and brother of Frank Ward, opened in Chapel Walk, Sheffield, in 1929, and also took a small shop in Leavygreave, close to the literally redbrick university which then had only eight hundred undergraduates. Neither shop showed a profit until 1942. W. Hartley Seed, an older established Sheffield bookseller, also carried on through these years and the S.P.C.K. opened a branch in 1936.

In Leeds B. L. Austick opened the first of what were to become a chain of shops in 1928. Richard Jackson's, in the same city, was taken over by Mowbray's, who made several attempts to sell books in Yorkshire. At Hull, Frank Bacon, who began as an assistant in the book department of Brown's, subsequently became manager, director, and then managing director. His son Arthur joined him in 1933 in a business which had, for long, been a public company with enormous educational contracts in all school equipment, apart from books, and with a large export trade. In York, in 1906, T. C. Godfrey founded a new and antiquarian business in Stonegate, in the narrow complex of streets near the minster; this subsequently changed hands several times.

In the larger cities bookselling was protected to some extent from the worst effects of the depression because there were sufficient middle-class and other non-manual workers who did not suffer the same privations as those who were laid off at the factories and shipyards. Sherratt & Hughes enjoyed supremacy in Manchester and took an extra shop in 1905. Until 1912 they were publishers to the University of Manchester, and also issued books of local historical and topographical interest. Their star title was, however, the Ellesmere Chaucer, in two volumes, at £50 the set. J. D. Hughes was in charge of the book side of the business during the whole of this period. He was gifted with a prodigious memory, which often appeared even more formidable than it was because he took the trouble to keep a daybook in which he entered the purchases of all the customers with whom he dealt personally. Many authors sought his advice, as Arnold Bennett mentions in his diaries, and Miss Horniman, of the famous Gaiety Repertory Theatre, was a constant visitor to the shop. It was at this time that Manchester was a cultural as well as a commercial centre, and the questionable belief arose that 'what Manchester thinks today, London will think tomorrow'.

Many of the more eminent citizens preferred to shop out of hours because they disliked crowds, and for them Sherratt & Hughes would be opened, by appointment, in the evenings and, for one great surgeon, on Sunday mornings. The business was owned in these years by the two who gave their name to it, but within it there grew up the unofficial partnership of Joe Cheetham and William Bullock. Bullock who was one-armed, went straight to the new premises on the corner of St Ann and Cross Streets, near the Royal Exchange, in 1905, when he left school at fifteen. Three years later Cheetham became his colleague (Mr Wardle-worth, the discount bookseller for whom he had worked for twenty years, having bankrupted himself at last). His son, also Joe, joined the firm in 1916. Joe, Junior, recalls that in the first thirty years of the century 50 per cent of the annual business was done during November and December.

Cornish, the Manchester bookseller for whom both Sherratt and Hughes worked before starting on their own, declined in the twentieth century. After the first war the lease of his shop in St Ann's Square fell in, and he declined to renew at double the old rent. He moved into a side street, and as his faithful old customers died there were few new ones to replace them. The business was finally absorbed into Kendal Milne's department store. Meanwhile, William Henry Willshaw had opened in John Dalton Street in 1920 where he remained until 1946 when Frank Gabbutt, who had started Seed & Gabbutt in Blackburn in 1907, bought him out. (Miss Mary Seed and Gabbutt had both worked for a bookseller in the same town who had failed.) At Blackburn, Gabbutt's son John took over when his father bought Willshaw's.

In Liverpool, Henry Young's, A. E. Parry's, Philip, Son & Nephew and Cornish's branch were all active at the turn of the century. Of these only Cornish foundered, his goodwill being bought by Philip's whose ramifications were manifold by then. Philip, Son & Nephew became a separate business from George Philip's in London, but each remained firmly in the control of the family.

After the first war the Youngs of Henry Young sold their shop, on the instalment plan, to three assistants, one of whom died in 1925. Another retired in the 'thirties and the third, Mr Thomas, remained in sole charge, running the business with the aid of two experienced assistants, Arthur Jones and Arnold Wilson.

A. E. Parry, the son of Tom Parry, died in 1922 and his daughter Amy inherited the shop which still dealt in secondhand books only, and those of a primarily educational nature. Amy Parry married another Liverpool bookseller, Arnold Yates, whose partner was a Mr Ward. When Ward died that business went not to Parry's but to Charles Wilson who had started in 1929 and who also took over Edward Howell's shop in 1932. Those who thrived in Liverpool seemed to do very well indeed; there was certainly no lack of candidates to absorb those who failed or died.

Lancashire became a stronghold of library supply. James Askew's were already at Preston in 1913, and were listed in Kelly's as publishers as well. The market increased in the early 'twenties, when the county libraries began to operate, and the Holt-Jackson Book Company began in the early 'thirties and after a few difficult years was turning over £15,000 a year by 1939 and employing two representatives to call on public libraries, one of them being F. T. Bell, ex-Foyle, ex-Mudie, who was to manage the business in later years. William Holt-Jackson had been a librarian in various parts of the country before he turned to selling. His wife played an active part in building up the business at Lytham St Anne's.

Liverpool also first housed another enterprising bookseller who started between the wars. Mr and Mrs H. J. Elsley's first shop was officially opened in 1935 by the romantic novelist Denise Robins, which emphasized the fact that it was more concerned with lending than with selling, this being the high noon of the commercial circulating library. Elsley eventually sold the Liverpool shop to Charles Wilson, and concentrated on the others which he had bought in Chester, Bangor, Colwyn Bay and Ellesmere Port. The main shop in Chester (there were two there) was an early example of two-level shopping. It was in Chester Rows, and boasted a cobbled floor and stable-type door at the rear, but it was later modernized. It is evident that these towns were at least good potential venues for bookseller-commercial librarians, and in 1938 another branch was opened at Wallasey. But southwards, at

Stafford, where there had been four booksellers in 1851, and even one in the 1790s, there was none in 1928.

Chester already had the old established business of Phillipson and Golder, which had absorbed the even older-established Minshull & Meeson in 1927, when the Elsleys arrived. At Chesterfield, in neighbouring Derbyshire, a town remarkable for the crazily crooked spire of its church, Mrs Edith Ford founded a family shop in 1905. She was joined by her son, who came straight into the business from school, in the mid-'twenties.

One of the provincial shops which felt a need for modernization well ahead of its time was Ruddock's, in Lincoln. A new shop-front with spacious arcade windows was put in in 1928, and four years later B. J. Field, who later took charge of the book side of the firm, joined them.

In the Midlands, G. J. T. Collier opened the Church Bookshop in Coventry in 1921, having learned his bookselling at Rugby, mostly with George Over. Over's is a shop with a lengthy lineage and really demands the attentions of a trade genealogist, if that word can be applied in a non-family sense. The Northamptonshire poet Norman Gale wrote a pamphlet about it called *A Famous Bookshop*. George Over already owned another book shop in the town when he took over the business inspired by Arnold of Rugby, and he ran both shops until 1935. When he died in 1937 control passed to C. E. Pearce who had been with Warren of Winchester. The webs of provincial bookselling are very complex and there is room for a study of them in depth.

East Anglia and the East Midlands were starved of bookshops and good libraries during the early 'thirties, and this inspired Basil Donne-Smith, a Stoneham's manager in London, to start Countryside Libraries in 1935, in conjunction with Lord St Davids and J. S. Austin. Countryside Libraries was an enormous success and catered instantly for the book-hungry in the towns and surrounds of Hitchin, Letchworth, Bedford, Hertford, St Albans, St Neots, Coventry, Kettering, Northampton, Rushden, Hanley, Dunstable, Camberley, Guildford, Sudbury, Chatham, Windsor, Maidenhead and elsewhere—there were eventually twenty-five shops and libraries extending southwards across the Thames. Countryside Libraries, in which Mrs Audrey Donne-Smith also took an active part, was financed by a group of investment trust companies and provided a pay-as-you-read service to readers who had neither bookshops nor public libraries of the quality they needed. Countryside Libraries was also a great boon to authors whose works the Donne-Smiths literally took to the people on a commercial basis. In Hayes, Middlesex, Ray Smith, a printer, also catered for this market, opening premises in the main street and offering books at 2d. per week and no deposit. There was a queue fifty yards long on the day he opened.

Another who pinned his faith on 2d. libraries was Christopher Barclay, who started a travelling library in Surrey in the mid-'thirties, and later helped to form Pelican Bookshops Ltd which had three retail outlets by 1939.

There was argument beyond 1970 on how much the lending of books, either by direct payment, or paid through the rates, deterred book-buying but certainly when B. L. Langdon-Davies took over the Book Department of the Welwyn Department Store in 1929 he found a market. Welwyn Garden City, and the Hampstead Garden Suburb, were prototypes for urban-rural development and were studied by experts from all over the world. Welwyn had pleasant houses, detached, semi-detached and terraced, with gardens, in quiet streets, a shopping and community centre flanked by a railway station with a fast service to London, and a factory belt. At one end of the shopping enclave the Welwyn Department Store's stock of books and other goods made it unnecessary for shoppers to journey to London. Langdon-Davies, who had had a varied career, became a bookseller late in life, having been a hotel manager in Calcutta and a publisher with Williams & Norgate, amongst other things. But he was a natural, soon to become a pundit, and author of a textbook on the subject.

In the South of England, always more protected economically than the Midlands and the North, business at Penzance and Exeter, in the south-west, prospered sufficiently to attract those looking for an entry into the trade. At Exeter, Wheaton's, which had opened in the nine-teenth century and became a limited company in 1906, had Pitt's as competitors from 1935. In Winchester, the Wellses succeeded one another in the course of time, and during the First World War Miss Wells, who had joined the back room staff in 1908, was allowed to appear in the shop during opening hours for the first time. In 1925, Wells's took over the shop at Charterhouse School.

William Smith's of Reading became known under that name when William Long sold the business and its historic building. Twenty-five years later H. W. Brown, related to Smith, bought it. At Bristol, where the S.P.C.K. were not yet represented, Miss Dorothy Higgins and Miss Doris Prince opened the Pied Piper Bookshop at 72 Park Row in 1930, as a small children's shop with a few general books. At elegant Cheltenham, Ernest Williams started the Promenade Bookshop in the High Street at about the same time.

In the Home Counties A. F. Mason spent the between-wars period practically supporting provincial bookselling. In terms of actual turn-over he may have added little to publishers' profits, but he was prepared to take risks to provide outlets in small towns. In 1933 he took over an old established business in Ely, with Bernard E. Dorman as partner, and bought others in Maldon, Wokingham and Lyme Regis. He sold his Hampstead, London, shop (see p. 374) and went to live in Worthing, where he partnered Stanley Hodges (ex-Over's of Rugby) in turning what had been the Grove Circulating Library into a bookshop. The year before, Frank Ward had started a shop in East Street, Brighton, with Kenneth Bredon. They ran at a loss until the war, and the wages bill for their staff of four was under £10 per week. But the boom time was to come.

At Reigate, Surrey, Arthur A. Cole started the Ancient House Book-shop in 1931. Ten years earlier, Frank W. Weatherhead had opened in Folkestone, Kent. The civilian population of Folkestone was to become even smaller through evacuation during the war, and soon after hostilities began, Frank Weatherhead wisely moved to Aylesbury, then a small Bucks town with a population of 18,000 but no bookshop.

On the Kent-Sussex border, only seven miles apart, two of the most remarkable personal booksellers of their time established themselves between the wars. They were Thomas Rayward and Elise Santoro. Thomas Rayward, a miller's son, left school at thirteen and joined Goulden & Curry, booksellers and stationers, in Tunbridge Wells High Street in 1905. The book department was then only a small side-line of a business whose headquarters in Canterbury (there were branches in Ashford, Dover and Deal as well) boldly advertised in Kelly's 1913 Directory as follows:

> PIANOFORTE MANUFACTURER
> BOOKSELLER
> AGENT FOR ORDNANCE MAPS
> *3d. in the 1s. discount for cash off books in stock*

So much for the armistice following The Times Book War. At Tun-bridge Wells the book department did not develop seriously until 1919 when Rayward returned from the real war, having lost an eye. His health was otherwise unimpaired, and he set himself the task of making the people of Tunbridge Wells and district come to Goulden & Curry's to buy books from him. Eventually his department occupied the whole of the first floor, apart from the library at the rear. The actual space it occupied was far from ideal, but had the advantage of being on split levels with several short flights of steps and an occasional cubbyhole to delight the browser. The shelves were high and packed with books, there was little open display space and no concession to modernity.

Rayward had a flair for buying, and knew how to sell; the local population came to accept his recommendations. An assistant of his has recorded that he would sometimes start the day by placing on the counter a volume which had stayed too long in stock, and would invariably have sold it by closing-time. Tom Rayward was both shy and yet, to some, rather intimidating. He exercised a charm over women customers which made him an outstanding master of the soft sell, but he did not abuse this talent because he had a high standard of literary appreciation and was not interested in disseminating trash. As a buyer he took little notice of what travellers told him of their wares, but made up his own mind quickly and unalterably. He learned his bookselling on the floor of the shop, read widely and had a wealth of anecdotes for his chosen customers, who were, according to Marcus Crouch, the Kent librarian and an author of excellent topographical works on the home counties, also his friends. A colleague of Rayward's has it that he would never visit his customers' homes, despite pressing invitations, because he never overcame his feelings of social inferiority—information that came as a surprise to one who, as a boy, haunted his shop several times a week after school but never dared to approach him. I dealt instead with his assistant, Miss Elizabeth Woodhams, who was the model of all that a bookseller's assistant should be. Helpful, serious and understanding, and also a very good businesswoman, she gave me my earliest lessons in good bookselling, although neither of us knew that at the time. She was the perfect assistant, working harmoniously with an inspired bookseller/buyer; together they gave Tunbridge Wells, a town of some 35,000 inhabitants, the sort of bookshop which every town and suburb should have but all too few actually enjoy. Neither of them became rich, except in the knowledge of what they had given to the booklovers they served.

Miss Elise Santoro would not have bought the Book Club, Crowborough, had she been aware of Thomas Rayward's authority and standing in Tunbridge Wells only seven miles away. The Book Club was started by a Miss Lea in 1932, in what she called a cultural desert—the lovely hilly countryside to the north of Ashdown Forest. She took an old cottage in Crowborough's Broadway, and began to woo the locals. Her health broke after a year and it was then that Miss Santoro, who worked at the American Embassy in Rome, bought it in partnership with Miss Frampton. Neither of these ladies had had any experience of the trade, but each felt a missionary zeal to make people buy or borrow and read books. Thirty years later Miss Santoro still believed that stock-holding booksellers created their own reading public, and by then she had the proof. She and Miss Frampton bravely put the theory to the test, and by 1939 they were established with a library delivery service over an eight-mile radius, and with branches in the small towns of Mayfield and Uckfield. The 'thirties brought some formidable women into bookselling—besides Miss Santoro, Miss Dillon, Miss Reckitt and Miss Babbidge all made the grade in the man's world of commerce. Miss Santoro's is perhaps the most remarkable achievement, because Crowborough is a small country town which even in 1961 had a

population of only 8,000. Both she and Tom Rayward based their success
as booksellers on a high standard of personal service and on confidence
in their product. They believed that people needed books, and would
buy them if only they were made available.

In Glasgow, the oldest established booksellers, John Smith's, went
steadily ahead in the early years of the twentieth century, opening
branches in the university area of the city. Smith's became a limited
company in 1909, and John M. Knox succeeded David James Knox as
managing director in 1927. A year later the business of Alexander
Stenhouse was purchased, but during the 'thirties they hit lean times
when the loss on books and stationery in one twelve months was made
up by the profit on the sale and manufacture of medical instruments.
However, the hard times did not prevent John B. Wylie from opening
in 1935. He had been an assistant at John Smith's and decided to go it
alone, a measure in which he received practical support on his day of
opening by ten customers who each deposited a £100 against future
purchases. He built up a small, personal business with library and
university connections. W. & R. Holmes, already well established, took
advantage of the boom in public spending through libraries to enlarge
their own business.

The best-known personal bookseller in Glasgow during this time was,
perhaps, Alan Jackson, who became president of the Associated Booksellers in 1939. He ran the Western Book Club from his neo-renaissance
building in West George Street, and supplied books to those outlying
parts of Scotland which could not hope to support bookshops.

Frederick Bauermeister moved from Glasgow to Edinburgh in 1924
when he bought Wilson, Ross & Co. (formerly Otto Schulze & Co.) and
four years later moved to Bank Street, the Mound, where he became
firmly established as one of the leading booksellers in the City. His main
competitors were Menzies, who became a limited company in 1906 and
built up their wholesale organization in the 'twenties, and Thin's, the
founder of which died in 1915 at the age of ninety-two.

In Scotland, as in Ireland, the established names weathered the
trying conditions of these years without drama. The less favoured went
to the wall; the hardy Smiths, and Menzies and Thins, in one country;
the Easons and Browne & Nolans, and Duffys and A.P.C.K.s, in the
other, survived. And to do that was to do well.

P.A. collects trading figures; publishers and wholesalers stay in London; paper rationing; fight against imposition of purchase tax; many publishers and book-sellers casualties of the blitz; Simpkin Marshall destroyed; home sales and exports boom; Macmillan and Batsford centenaries; Neurath and Britain in Pictures series; new wartime imprints: Allan Wingate — Pleiades — Mac-donald & Co. — Hollis & Carter — Edmund Ward — Mercier Press — Pan — Panther — Ian Allan; new wartime bookshops: Pelham Bookshop in Havant — S.P.C.K. in Salisbury; shops in Paris selling English books; Simpkin Marshall resuscitated; creation of National Book League; war ends but austerity continues; new titles proliferate and turnover increases; P.A. and A.B. increase membership; defence of the N.B.A.; Frankfurt Book Fair; Society of Young Publishers formed; television; increased complexity of publishing; Longmans state that extra discount will result in higher prices; Collins becomes a public company; Penguin's expansion continues; international copyright; obscene libel; the vogue for war books and science fiction.

The declaration of war on September 3rd, 1939, led to compulsory national service which eventually left only the old and the unfit in most publishing offices and bookshops. Air raids brought loss of life and property and dislocation of trade, war risks insurance had to be borne once again, paper was rationed and rose drastically in price, and many important books went out of print for the duration, and for some time after.

Yet under wartime conditions the book trade grew to know itself better. Statistics collected by the P.A., at Geoffrey Faber's instigation, proved that a total of 33 per cent of home-produced books were sent abroad, figures which surprised many publishers and were of vital importance in the fight against the imposition of a purchase tax on books. According to *The Bookseller*, in February 1940, the figures also indicated that the percentage of export business usually increased in proportion to the size of the firm. It was evident that a trade depending so much on export, and the extended credit that implied, needed a healthy home trade to back it, so that the wartime trend towards greatly increased reading amongst all sections of the population was doubly welcome.

During a war it is easier than it is in peacetime to persuade people to cooperate for the common good. The P.A. official report for 1939–40 noted the benefits of collective action, and while it never suggested that all who published should be forced to join the Association, it did, quite justifiably, point out that non-members received benefits gained for and by members, a potent argument dear to all shop stewards and one which is difficult to answer except on the grounds of the individual's supposed right to choose for himself.

The continuity of paper supply was the trade's main concern throughout the war, and not only during the early period when there was little military action. Civilians evacuated from London and other cities tended to drift back to their homes when the expected holocaust did not happen. Most publishers did not leave in the first place, a mistake for which they were to pay dearly, and the two largest wholesalers, Simpkin Marshall and W. H. Smith & Son, never apparently thought of moving to the country. Harry Batsford and some of his staff went at once; Macmillan's took the conscious decision to remain in St Martin's Street where the basements were strengthened for the use and shelter of the staff during attacks. Booksellers could not very well leave town centres without taking their customers with them although, as we have already seen, Miss Dillon pursued her teachers and students to various addresses, and the Student's Bookshop moved to Cambridge. The others opened hopefully for 'Business as Usual' and for those who were neither bombed nor burned out of existence the war years were not unprofitable.

Plans for the official training of booksellers' assistants were held up by the war and the annual conference was centred on London for several years. There was otherwise little immediate change for booksellers. Christina Foyle's literary lunches went on almost uninterrupted. In November 1939 Dr Beneš, the exiled president of Czechoslovakia, and H. G. Wells spoke at a Grosvenor House lunch attended by over seven hundred people (the demand for tickets was even greater), and the speeches were broadcast on the Home and Overseas programmes of the B.B.C. The following month Lord Halifax was chairman and Anthony Eden, a leading Tory politician and a later Prime Minister, was one of the speakers. (Four years later Wells again spoke at a Grosvenor House meeting, this time sponsored by the Society of Authors, and called for the burning of all textbooks as soon as they were ten years old, a curious demand to make at a time when books were in such short supply, but otherwise not at all a bad idea for several reasons.)

The calm of the phoney war was broken in the spring of 1940, when German troops invaded Denmark and Norway, but a more immediate cause for concern amongst publishers was the announcement that books were not to be excluded from paper rationing. The allocation for book publishers was fixed at 60 per cent of their consumption during the twelve months before August 1939. The percentage fluctuated with the fortunes of war but the terms of reference remained standard. Later the Moberley Pool was introduced to supply paper to publishers who were short of it for what were deemed essential books, which provoked fears, on the part of a few, of a hidden censorship. These could not be taken very seriously because new publishers were allowed to purchase on the open market, a lunatic anomaly which led to the birth of new imprints, some of them unashamedly offshoots of existing publishing houses bound by the quota rules. Publishers who already existed were allowed their ration and no more; new entrants could have all they could get; but that was an irritating situation to be faced later in the war.

In 1940 the fight for a larger allocation was overshadowed by the threat of books becoming liable to purchase tax. The chancellor of the exchequer at that time was Sir Kingsley Wood, a politician of exceptionally thin credentials even by the standards of the Chamberlain administration. He refused to recognize that books were in any way different from soap or radios, and once again it was Stanley Unwin who took up the cudgels on behalf of the trade, blasting off a letter to *The Times* in which he pointed out acidly that purchase tax was not being levied on food for the body and that it should not be on food for the mind; books were not a luxury, and there should be no tax on knowledge. 'It would be humiliating', he wrote, 'if, in a war for freedom of thought, the sale of books in which man's highest thoughts are enshrined should be hampered by taxation.' Kingsley Wood remained implacable, and worked out (rather like the woman who said she didn't want a book for Christmas, thank you, because she already had one) that there were sufficient books in the country to be getting along with. He reckoned, however, without Stanley Unwin and the P.A. which, under its president Geoffrey Faber, mobilized a formidable body of opinion, headed by the Archbishop of Canterbury, and including representatives from Parliament, the universities and literature, to support its case. In the House of Commons two M.P.s, Kenneth Lindsay and Henry Strauss, opposed the tax on books; outside, Hugh Walpole, J. B. Priestley, John Masefield and other highly articulate citizens kept up the pressure. Belgium, Holland, Luxembourg and, finally, France fell. In the exceptionally hot summer of 1940 the remnants of the British Army were evacuated from Dunkirk, but the energies of those fighting for the survival of books were undiminished. It was what historians would call a peculiarly British situation. Europe was disintegrating around them, at any moment each and every one of the people concerned with the fight against purchase tax might be fleeing for their lives from the Gestapo, but they were able to concentrate their minds on this important issue. And they won. For once the priorities were right, however extraordinary it may seem to later generations that anyone could take time off from war to organize public meetings against a tax on books. Sir Kingsley unexpectedly caved in and books were omitted from the list of those commodities subject to tax. The matter was not debated in Parliament, the concession was made without further argument.

Perhaps someone showed the Chancellor a book and he thought he should have one.

Those who had campaigned felt a sense of anti-climax as well as of relief, and took further time off for a celebration lunch.

This victory was the last occasion for general rejoicing in the trade for some time to come. The long hot summer was nearly at an end, and in September the blitz broke on London and many provincial cities. The drastic effect of this prolonged bombardment was summed up in a typical shaft of Shavian wit. 'The Germans', recorded Bernard Shaw, 'have done what Constable's have never succeeded in doing. They have disposed of 86,701 sheets of my works in less than twenty-four hours.'

The raids reached their climax for the book trade on the night of December 29th–30th, when Paternoster Row and surrounding streets and alleys were nearly all demolished. Longmans could supply between five and six thousand titles on December 28th, but only twelve on the following Monday. Whitaker's were burned out, with all their records, but even so *The Bookseller* appeared on January 2nd, 1941, as usual, in Geoffrey Faber's phrase, 'without a hair out of place'. Simpkin's premises and total stocks were destroyed, a disaster from which the trade never completely recovered.

The City bookseller Hubert Wilson, who contributed a column to *The Bookseller* under the pseudonym 'Petrel', described the desolation in a memorable article:

It is the eve of the new year — and the hub of the English book trade lies in smoking ruins. Such a scene of destruction I have never seen or imagined ... With many others Simpkin's, Whitaker's, Longmans', Nelson's, Hutchinson's and, further afield, Collins' and Eyre & Spottiswoode, are gutted shells. In their basements, on Monday afternoon, glowed and shuddered the remnants of a million books. Gusts of hot air and acrid smoke blew across the streets, and around the outskirts of the devastation played the jets from the firemen's hoses.

This would have been bad enough by itself. But these famous houses, and the streets in which they stood, marked only the boundaries of a scene of destruction so complete, so utterly irre-trievable that it held me spellbound. Nowhere were pavements or road surface to be seen. From Warwick Square on the west to Ivy Lane on the east, from the Row nearly to Newgate Street, there lies now an undulating sea of broken yellow bricks. As I picked my way gingerly across from brick to brick, hot gouts of sulphurous fumes from buried fires seeped up between my feet; desultory flames played in the remains of a rafter here or a floor joist there, and on either side the smoking causeway fell sharply away into

cavernous glowing holes, once basements full of stock, now the
crematories of the City's book world. I looked around me in what
was Paternoster Square and recognised nothing but a pillar box,
the top beneath my feet; there was nothing left to recognise. Here
and there half a wall still stood in dangerous solitude, two or three
stories high, giving form and significance to the desolation, and that
was all. I was quite alone (for I had found my way in through a
passage unsuspected by the police) and no living thing was to be
seen.

Others whose premises went that night included Ward Lock; Sheed
& Ward (a Roman Catholic publishing house started in 1926 by
F. J. Sheed and Maisie Ward); Sampson, Low; Bailey Brothers; and
Stoneham's bookshop on Ludgate Hill where the gold lettering on the
spines of charred books temporarily survived the blaze, gleaming eerily
amongst the burned remains.

In Coventry, Collier's bookshop was destroyed, and in Liverpool,
both Philip, Son & Nephew's and Henry Young's. Provincial cities
suffered more than once, but London was under almost continuous
attack for many months. Cassell's, in La Belle Sauvage Yard, who
escaped the great fire raid, were obliterated the following spring, and
in the same alert a quarter of a million books were lost through incen-
diaries at Harrap's in High Holborn, although the building itself
remained mostly intact. Jones & Evans's bookshop in Cheapside was
gutted, and Hodder & Stoughton, who had taken over evacuated school
premises at Bickley, in Kent, were bombed out there as well. The list is
longer but must be curtailed here.

Most publishers suffered, but reacted with a resilience that kept their
imprints alive under conditions which were worse than any they had
hitherto encountered, or were to meet in the vastly changed structure of
trade in the next twenty-five years.

Amidst this chaos the demand for books increased, and those booksellers whose shops remained intact found themselves in the novel
situation of being rationed by publishers. They also discovered that
almost anything would sell, and the risk of bad stock was, therefore,
considerably reduced. New books were printed under wartime economy
regulations; wide margins were out, the quality of much of the paper
was inevitably poor and the use of small typefaces became essential, but
sales rose. Book Tokens also prospered, selling a record one and a half
million stamps in 1943. Tokens solved the gift problem for thousands,
and introduced the book-buying habit to sections of the population who
had never bought a book before.

Exports also boomed, stimulated by the demands from British ser-
vicemen overseas. It is an unfortunate fact that nothing seems to

concentrate people's minds so effectively on the appreciation of the arts as a total war — although not all the literature which was consumed came under the heading of art. The British Council and the P.A. agreed a scheme under which publishers supplied books on sale or return to customers in the Balkans and other countries, and the Council then bought any that were returned. The percentage was very low, and John Hampden (ex-Nelson's), who became head of the Books Department of the Council in 1941 in succession to Egerton Sykes, adjudged the scheme a success, although publishers were less happy to cooperate when it spread to other countries, encroaching on their traditional markets. Nor were they pleased when war-time production limitations meant that certain overseas customers (Canada, for instance) were understandably tending to buy the more attractive-looking American editions of books of British origin.

As the war lengthened and produced long periods of comparative inactivity in the battle zones life returned to something like normal for many, and the history of the book trade in this period must, therefore, be recorded without always referring to the blitz. The second war was not six years of hourly waiting for the outcome of this battle or that; for much of the time business was as usual, unaccompanied by screaming sirens or the descent of high explosive.

There were two important centenaries in 1943, both celebrated by the publication of commemorative histories. Charles Morgan's *The House of Macmillan*, a small-crown volume produced without undue austerity, and with a good stout cloth binding, recorded that Harold Macmillan gave up his directorship in the company when he joined the government in 1940 and that Lovat Dickson became a director soon after. However, it is in Dickson's second volume of memoirs, *The House of Words*, rather than in Morgan's official history, that there is a vivid description of Richard Hillary, the young airman whose remarkable book *The Last Enemy* became and remained a bestseller on the Macmillan list; Hillary, tragically, did not survive the war.

Macmillan collaborated with O.U.P. to produce a single volume edition of Tolstoy's *War and Peace*, a work to which the British reading public responded more positively than ever before. There were never sufficient copies of the book available in any edition until well after the war. Macmillan's were also faced with the problem of finding sufficient paper for reprints of Margaret Mitchell's *Gone With The Wind*, a not especially distinguished epic of another war, demand for which was stimulated by the arrival of the long-heralded Hollywood film. A cautious first printing of 3,000 was ordered but the reprints soon added a nought to this figure, and the largest was 100,000

A Batsford Century ignored all wartime restrictions and appeared in a quarter leather binding, with hundreds of illustrations, some in colour, and lavish margins. Just how they got round the regulations is obscure; according to the official P.A. report for 1942-3 it was necessary for all producers of books to sign the Book Production War Economy Agreement before getting their paper allocation. No doubt Harry Batsford was a firm believer that rules were made to be broken; in any case it is not recorded that his company was penalized or officially castigated. Batsford spent the war divided. Mr Harry and some of his staff remained at Malvern, although one packer could not stand the silence and darkness of the countryside and returned to London before 1939 was out; Charles Fry and the others stayed in North Audley Street, except for a brief period when an unexploded bomb lay under the boiler in the basement of a nearby bookseller. During these few days a stock room in Mount Street was used for business, and members of Batsford's staff were allowed to pay quick visits to their premises to get books or look up records. Brian Cook was called up into the R.A.F., and the joyful trio who had produced their bestselling travel books in the 'thirties was temporarily split up. Harry Batsford in fact marked the declaration of war by retiring, with his elderly mother, into the damp and inconvenient solitude of Llanthony Abbey, in a deserted Welsh valley, in order to write the 30,000 words of *How to See the Country* for the Batsford Home Front Series, in ten days. His sole complaint was of having to climb fifty-nine steps up to his bedroom in a turret.

One of the finest publishing ventures of the war was the Britain in Pictures Series, published by Collins but produced by Adprint Ltd. They were the inspiration of Walter Neurath, who recalled twenty years later that he had to create 'art books in disguise'—like Anton Zwemmer, Neurath was cynical about the reaction of the British public to this category. He had been a publisher in Vienna, like Horovitz, before Hitler marched in, and along with many another refugee from the Continent he found the business of publishing books in London highly profitable. The Britain in Pictures Series was edited by W. J. Turner; each title ran to 48 pages, with 8 colour plates and 12-20 black and white illustrations. The aim was to represent the British way of life, with subjects such as *The English Poets*, *The English Diarists*, *The Londoner*, *Life Among the English*, *Children's Illustrated Books*, etc., and the authors included Rose Macaulay, Lord David Cecil and J. B. Priestley. The first titles were published on March 21st, 1941, and Viola Garvin wrote in *The Observer*: 'These books manage to distil "the glories of our blood and state" and with neither vanity nor pomp to make clear to ourselves, as well as the rest of the world, the full and serious nobility of our heritage.' Walter Neurath was to publish bigger and better art books in terms of size and quality of reproduction, but these modest volumes (price 2s.6d.) were very much to the taste of the book buying public, who were not as innately philistine as the Austrian supposed.

Another refugee publisher was André Deutsch, a Hungarian Jew, who began his career with Nicholson & Watson in 1942. He was fairly quickly frustrated by not being permitted to buy Orwell's *Animal Farm*, and at the end of 1944 he announced the formation of Allan Wingate Ltd and his first list, which appeared a year later. Nicholson & Watson were not alone in turning down *Animal Farm*. Victor Gollancz was the first to do so, but he had already quarrelled with Orwell so would probably have needed no official dissuasion. Jonathan Cape would like to have taken it, and indeed would have done so had not a senior official of the Ministry of Information made it very clear that the government would find publication a severe embarrassment in its relations with Soviet Russia. Neither Cape nor Fred Warburg, who did finally publish it, cared for censorship by an appeal to patriotism, but the issue was decided by the allied victory, although Warburg had already taken the decision to publish.

There were many new imprints during wartime, some of them as I have said brought into being purely so that paper could be bought. Pleiades, a subsidiary of the Cresset Press, was one of these; Macdonald & Co., belonging to the Purnell Group, was another. J.Murray Thompson was in charge of the latter from the beginning, and was joined by John Foster White in 1943. They were able to find the paper for Kathleen Winsor's *Forever Amber*, a sensational (by 1943 standards) historical novel which no other publisher would take because they wouldn't risk part of their quota for it. It must be said for Macdonald that thereafter they did many, many better books. Hollis & Carter started in the same year; its board included Christopher Hollis, historian and later politician, and Douglas Jerrold of Eyre & Spottiswoode. A year earlier Edmund Ward had begun publishing children's books from Leicester which was becoming a good centre for juveniles. The Brockhampton Book Co. (later the Brockhampton Press) had been started by Percy Hodder-Williams on the eve of war as a subsidiary of Hodder & Stoughton, and was managed by E. A. Roker from Leicester. From the neighbouring town of Loughborough the remarkable series of Ladybird Books, in the format which was to remain standard for over thirty years, first appeared in 1940 at 2s. each (the price was increased to 2s.6d. a year later). Also, outside the United Kingdom but still within Mumby's province, there began in Dublin in 1944 the Mercier Press, devoted to the production of Catholic theological texts. It was started by John M. Feehan, an Officer of the Irish Army, in which service he remained until it was apparent his publishing had become successful enough to support him. Nineteen forty-four also saw the birth of both Pan and Panther, which were later to become major paperback publishers. Pan began as an independent subsidiary of the Book Society; Panther was founded by Hamilton & Co. of Stafford. Earlier in the war the British Publisher's Guild had been formed by a consortium of general publishers to produce paperbacks of quality in competition with Penguin's.

A specialist publisher who began in war time in a small way was Ian Allan. Allan had lost a leg when he was eighteen and was ineligible for military service. This accident also stopped him from pursuing the career he wanted with Southern Railway, whose chairman found him a job for the duration instead in the Public Relations Office at Waterloo Station. There the young man quickly became a mine of information about the Southern Railway and collected his facts into a notebook which he suggested the railway company should publish for profit. They declined the offer, so he published it himself at 1s. per copy with a first print of 2,000. The orders poured in through an advertisement in the *Railway Magazine*. Certain officials of Southern Railway were furious because they had not been consulted and demanded that the book be withdrawn. Allan quickly appealed to higher authority, and was congratulated on his enterprise. When direction of labour finished, Ian Allan Ltd already had a small, but sound foundation.

There were also some new bookshops. Irene Babbidge opened the Pelham Bookshop in Havant, Hampshire, mainly as a library in 1941, the same year in which S.P.C.K. started a branch in Salisbury. In 1943 W. Hartley Seed's of Sheffield, the oldest-established bookseller in the City, was sold to the Duffield's, who were perhaps encouraged by the fact that the tide had at last turned for Alan Ward, who had been operating there since 1929 without making a profit.

In Paris in 1940 there were four bookshops selling English books, three of them with British managers—the branch of W. H. Smith; Brentano's and the Galignani Library. The managers of the first two escaped when the Germans overran France, but F. Moulder, manager of Galignani, did not. He was not at first interned by the Nazis, but after Field-Marshall Goering (Hitler's second-in-command) visited his shop he was imprisoned for three months. When released he was forbidden to sell any British book published after 1870. Moulder, although in fact already very ill, continued to trade in books published long after that date, under the counter and under the eye of the occupying forces. He died in 1944 before the liberation of France. The fourth shop was Sylvia Beach's renowned Shakespeare and Company. Miss Beach spent six months of the war in a concentration camp, but survived.

After the destruction of Simpkin's, a group of publishers, headed by Sir James Pitman, took over the famous wholesaling firm from the Miles family and formed Simpkin Marshall (1941) Ltd. Stoneham's bookshops were sold to Hatchard's and, at first, the revived Simpkin's was run from Book Centre in the North Circular Road. Later premises were found in the basement of Rossmore Court, a block of flats near Regent's Park.

Finally, the most notable joint trade effort of the war, after the fight against purchase tax had been won and the bombing had ceased to bind the two sides together, was the creation of the National Book League out of the old National Book Council. Geoffrey Faber and Sydney Goldsack particularly campaigned for this and it was also a cause dear to Stanley Unwin. It was felt that it should involve the book reading public as well as those who wrote, produced and sold books. To this end John Hadfield, then with the British Council in the Middle East, was recalled and given the post of director. The brave new book world was before us.

The fighting was over but austerity went on. The newly elected Labour government of 1945, committed to create a welfare state out of a bankrupt exchequer, was forced to continue rationing many commodities for some years after the atomic bombs had burst over Hiroshima and Nagasaki. For publishers this meant no quick return to prewar conditions when as much paper was available as could be afforded—indeed, in one bleak postwar winter the quota was again reduced from 90 per cent to 60 per cent of 1938 consumption. Strikes and shortages hit the nation, and in 1946 J. G. Wilson reported that five out of every six requests for particular books made by eager would-be book-purchasers, in his Oxford Street shop, had to be met with a regretful 'No'. Alan Steele returned from a Japanese prisoner-of-war camp and now with Butler & Tanner, printers, wrote in an article in *The Author* that when his firm were given a manuscript by a publisher, twelve months would elapse before they could print it. Such was the paucity of manpower and raw materials in printers' workshops and binderies. Strawboard was in short supply and this hampered exports. Exports were also affected by the voluntary continuance of the War Economy standards of book production, which gave many British books a sad 'utility' appearance although grateful allowance must be made for those publishers who strove to maintain high standards with poor materials. Urgent recommendations had to be made to the Board of Trade about this particular issue because overseas markets, the Australian especially, which was already accounting for a disproportionate amount of U.K. exports, were showing signs of preference for America's more attractively produced and more durable products; this was a bitter pill to swallow for the British publishers who had done so much in the inter-war years to improve standards. Fortunately the U.K. government allowed relaxation of restrictions, which permitted our publishers and printers to produce books they could be proud of, but it was not until 1949 that the War Economy Agreement, along with paper rationing, finally lapsed.

In the transition from war to peace, the boom period in which anything that was published could be sold was soon over. Stock in publishers' warehouses and on booksellers' shelves began to accumulate unhealthily again, so that there was an inevitable renewal of the demand for an on sale or return basis of supply.

New titles proliferated. In 1945, 6,747 titles were published, as against 14,904 in 1939, but by 1949 there were 17,034 new books. New editions and reprints took longer to regain their pre-war figure, and in this was reflected the constant complaints of a shortage of school and university textbooks. It was not until paper rationing ended, with its attendant anomalies which had allowed mushroom publishers to start up and bring out new books without any responsibility for a back list, that established publishers were able to plan large reprint programmes for their important involuntarily out-of-print titles.

Actual turnover rose from just over ten millions in 1939 to almost twenty-seven millions in 1946, and by 1950, this figure had risen to thirty seven millions, of which 30.7 per cent represented exports. Yet the percentage of exports in the immediate postwar years did not catch up with the 1939 figure, so that the home market was as important as ever. The apparently large increase in the home trade figures was partly due to higher prices, which reflected rising overheads, and it was this aspect which troubled all parts of the trade, although later the emphasis was to turn on to too slowly increasing prices.

Membership of the P.A. rose continually as publishers appreciated more and more the benefits of belonging to a trade organization. In 1939 there had been only 124 members; in 1945 there were 214, and in 1950, 272. Penguin Books did not become full members until 1950, and Hutchinson's who had withdrawn from the association in 1942, only returned in 1952, when Walter Hutchinson died (and earned himself perhaps the worst obituary notice ever printed in *The Bookseller*, see p. 495).

The Associated Booksellers also gathered new members (there were 2,400 in 1945) which brought protests that there were too many bookshops, the popular belief being that the cake was of unalterable size and that if anyone new tried to share in it there would be fewer crumbs all round. It is not certain that that view had been altogether dispelled twenty-five years later. Miss Hilda Light retired from the secretaryship in 1946 and was succeeded by Gordon Smith, who in turn was replaced by Bruce Hepburn, an ex-Blackwell's bookseller, in 1948, in which year the name was changed to the Booksellers' Association of Great Britain and Ireland. Both associations occupied premises at 28 Little Russell Street,

next door to Allen & Unwin's, where Book Tokens also had their
offices. The P.A. had been given sanctuary there during the war when
Stationers' Hall was bombed. The premises soon became too cramped
to hold them all and in 1949 the publishers moved their secretariat into
more splendid accommodation on the north side of Bedford Square.

As membership of each trade association grew, so did the activities of
both the paid officials and the members who searched for magic for-
mulas which would renew wartime prosperity. The first public manifestation of this came at the 1947 A.B. Conference when Sydney
Goldsack, sales director of Collins, blasted into the attack in typical
fashion, denouncing the 'general bickering' which he thought had
characterized the joint publisher-bookseller session, and proposing the
formation of a committee, representing both sides, which would discuss
the terms of supply. The proposal was accepted and in October 1947,
fifteen publishers and seventeen booksellers met at Rottingdean, in
Sussex, to talk about the problem. As a result of this weekend conference,
held on the property developers' desecrated cliff top, the 1948 Book
Trade Committee came into being. After sitting for four years, and
allowing a further two for digestion and printing-trade gestation, it
produced a document of considerable tedium, amounting to 94 pages
plus a further 76 of appendices and index. It is scarcely surprising that
those who met in Bedford Square in 1970 to form yet another book trade
working party should have immediately rejected any idea of emulating
their predecessors.

One does not question the integrity of those who filed the 1948
report. Some of the recommendations made therein had been suggested
by earlier committees; some were to be made again, by subsequent ones;
but events overtook them. Whilst they beavered away, those publishers
and booksellers, their colleagues, and authors and printers, went on
with their pursuits, because none of them could await the deliberations
of a committee. Especially it was useless to hope for much from a committee which had no power anyway because neither the P.A. nor the
B.A. could command their members to do anything; they could only
persuade and exhort. And everyone went in for exhortation. Almost
everyone, it seemed, had a remedy for the ills of the trade, and it wasn't
so much that none of them could agree on what ought to be done, but
that their official organizations had no teeth.

So everyone settled down to defending the Net Book Agreement,
which began to be threatened as early as 1949 when a report of the
Committee on Resale Price Maintenance was published as a white
paper. The N.B.A. and all other trade agreements were endangered and
hardly any were upheld by the Registrar of Restrictive Trading Agreements whose court was subsequently set up by the government.

It was generally agreed, however, before any such cases had been heard, that the Net Book Agreement was worth preserving if only because most people in the trade could not remember a time when it had not existed, and few wished for any more basic changes. There had been sufficient of them to endure in the past ten years, so that to defend the N.B.A. provided something to cling on to in a world where values and beliefs had been turned upside down. Christianity had been found wanting once again; communism had deteriorated into Stalinism; a Labour government with a huge majority was nationalizing the country's most cherished (and sometimes least efficient) industries; the British Empire was disintegrating fast; family life was threatened from all sides; but the Net Book Agreement was still there, having suffered no more erosion than the average chunk of granite during its nearly fifty years of existence.

This, of course, was not the official attitude. Officers and staff of the two trade associations had to take a totally serious view of the situation and play the legal game, amassing evidence and economic argument, as will be seen in the next chapter.

Meanwhile life went on. The Associated Booksellers devised and started the Booksellers Clearing House in 1947, instituting a simple and effective method by which most accounts for purchases could be settled by the issue or receipt of one cheque. Not all schemes were as clear-cut and useful. Book Tallies, an idea of Harold Raymond's, taken up by Book Tokens Ltd, for extending the token principle to appeal to a child's collecting instinct, did not catch on, probably because it became subject to purchase tax. Tallies were priced at 6d. each, the intention being that children should buy them whenever they had a tanner to spare, and accumulate sufficient to buy the book or books they desired. The scheme was officially wound up in 1952.

A National Book Sale was recommended by a majority attending the B.A. Conference in 1949 but was not actually instituted until 1955. It did not gain maximum support, or anything like it, from booksellers, some of whom preferred to go on organizing their own sales at their own time, and some of whom didn't want a sale at all, but publishers supported the efforts of Thomas Joy, Cadness Page and others which led to its establishment as an annual event. All department stores had sales which the public expected at regular intervals, so it was natural that the bookshops within the stores should have them and that the lead, supported by the P.A., to the trade for a National Book Sale should come from a Thomas Joy.

Meanwhile the immediate attentions of publishers turned to the Frankfurt Book Fair which was to replace in importance the one held annually before the war at Leipzig. Germany was now divided, permanently it seemed, and Leipzig was in the communist-dominated eastern part. Western Germany was on the threshold of economic

recovery, and its always well-organized book trade grasped the opportunity which British publishers missed, through government inaction,
to establish an annual world book fair in their own country. Frankfurt,
the venue of medieval fairs, had been devastated by bombing, and a
vast area was allotted to building an exhibition site which could house
trade conventions of all types. It could have been done in London, or
elsewhere in Britain, but it wasn't, and subsequent generations of publishers, who found it increasingly important to spend ten days in a city
of surpassing squalor, described by one of them as 'the anus of Europe',
were to regret it, although it must be admitted that the annual pilgrimage to the Rhine was sometimes turned to advantage by using it
as the excuse for an extra holiday afterwards in France or Luxembourg.

The Society of Young Publishers was formed in 1950, reflecting the
postwar determination of the new generation to make a better job of
things than their fathers had. The Society provided a regular platform
for the new entrants into the trade from which they could air their
grievances and make, in their turn, recommendations for curing its
chronic sickness. Their speeches were faithfully recorded in the trade
press and the subjects of their meetings had an almost nostalgic flavour,
dealing as they did with the necessity for more and better bookshops,
cooperative advertising, the death of fiction (like Charles II it had been
an unconscionable time dying), broadening the market for books, and
so on.

At official level the two associations also threw themselves into a
frenzy of activity, resulting in rather too many hours being spent in
committee meetings at the expense of the working day. In 1945 the P.A.
had representation on fifteen committees; by 1950, the figure had
doubled. Some of the talking achieved results but few reckoned the cost
in terms of man hours. The whole process of identifying work and industry with groups of people talking round a table was symptomatic of
mid-twentieth century society, when there was an earnest desire to
make democracy effective but when almost everyone confused work
with talk.

The motives behind all this were usually good, but in practice it often
exasperated those who discovered that the most effective committee
work was done outside the council room by unilateral decision or private
agreement. The book trade was caught in the universal dilemma—
trying to make democracy work because no one had thought of a better
system, for even in a benevolent dictatorship benevolence can be one-
sided.

Individual firms, perhaps fortunately, continued to be dominated by
individuals who took decisions without excessive consultation. Books
were not, on the whole, written by committees—an exception being
that turgid 1948 Report—nor were they often bought by them, or

read by them, except when twelve good men and true were required to decide whether or not a work was obscene.

Commonsense and the instinct to survive commercially, resulted in the continued publication of huge amounts of literature. The growth, once wartime restrictions were shed, was alarming. As early as 1947 there was a *cri-de-coeur* from the Hon. Andrew Shirley, manager of The Times Book Club (where, under his successor books *were* bought by a committee) who complained that during the war it was nothing for publication dates to be postponed by a couple of months and couldn't voluntary postponement be introduced? But publishers, like the rest of commerce and industry, were already caught up in the turnover syndrome, producing more titles in order to pay the overheads incurred in producing past titles.

Television came back during these years after the enforced closure of transmission during the war, and there was immediate alarm about its possible effects on the sale of books. In fact, its re-introduction meant a new market for authors and further squabbles between publishers, literary agents and writers about subsidiary rights. Constantly, during these and other controversies the P.A. deplored the fact that literary agents had no organized association to represent them; wisely, no doubt, from their viewpoint, the agents refrained from diluting their highly individual personalities within a corporate body. This left them in a strong position, seemingly for a long time to come, and some modern publishers ruefully wished that their forefathers had treated authors less meanly, thus forestalling perhaps the conditions under which literary agencies had arisen. But the clock could not be turned back and most publishers concentrated on cementing their own particular love-hate relationships with agents, relying on the schisms which from time to time shook the agency business to yield some benefits.

Television failed to kill the book, to everyone's expressed surprise. It certainly damaged the cinema and the provincial theatre, and finished the commercial libraries, but it did not adversely affect the sale of books or the use of public libraries. Indeed, the improvement of public libraries may, along with T.V., have been responsible for the demise of the commercial libraries. The book trade found a new ally in television, and learned to exploit and be exploited by it. Booksellers were soon happy to feature the book on which the latest screen serial was based, or to sell the book written by, or ghosted for, the latest television personality. The new medium presented excellent opportunities for publicity for books, and the possibilities were instantly seized upon by the public relations industry, a new force in modern society, which had to be reckoned with and paid for.

The end of the 'forties saw the beginnings of complex publishing. Only the smallest firms, content to remain small, could continue to float a list by bringing out a book or two, issuing review copies, subscribing titles to the trade through shared travellers, and distributing the resulting orders, hand-packed, perhaps by the directors. For the medium or large-sized, a network of experts came to seem essential. Sales managers had long been regarded as desirable to integrate the work of travellers in the field selling to booksellers. Production managers had become necessary as publishers had thought it important to challenge printers with their own expertise. Advertising and publicity managers had crept in to offer advice on which newspapers and journals were worth taking space in. Inevitably public relations officers, who really duplicated the work of both advertising and publicity managers, and the individual efforts of editorial men, soon came to be indispensible as well. And the web didn't stop there. With a growing market for subsidiary rights it became important to employ managers who would concern themselves with disposing of foreign rights and fight for serialization in leading newspapers, although the literary agents often did this work for them, and not, by any means, always to the publishers' satisfaction because a book gutted in extract in the *Observer* or the *Sunday Times*, could suffer in bookshop sales. Sales managers began to require assistants as export markets opened up and sales organizations had to be re-shaped, demanding the existence of an overall sales director, to whom were responsible the home sales manager and the export sales manager, and their assistants and secretaries. Sometimes the new personnel were genuinely needed, in the interests of expansion and efficiency, often they were brought in only to bolster-up the self-importance of an executive who felt his position might be shaky if he did not exert his authority. In the long run, this whole new army of administrators was accepted because efficiency and credibility (a new word which gained approval as efficiency itself ceased to be a credible one) had to be maintained. There even came to be appointed dignitaries known as Customer Relations Officers, their chief duty being, it appeared, to explain to booksellers why their orders were not filled, or had been serviced incorrectly. The cost of all these new people had, inevitably, to be shown in the price of each book.

At this point it is worth looking at the declared profits of an old established publisher—Longmans, Green. In 1941, after the disastrous fire, profits before tax were £10,870. By 1942 a rapid recovery increased them to £40,396, and by 1947, they had grown to £207,027. A year later Longmans became a public company, and quite soon its chairman, Kenneth Potter, informed the trade that if terms to booksellers were to be improved then the extra discount could only result in higher prices. Booksellers, faced with dwindling profits, gross and net, could perhaps be forgiven for thinking that publishers could afford to offer better terms whether or not book prices went up.

Collins, also, became a public company, in 1949, although the family retained a majority of the shareholding. Other old established publishers saw the need to form limited liability companies against the demands of death duties; this process had started in the nineteenth century but was accelerated after the second war until by the late 'fifties scarcely any 'pure' partnerships remained. All publishers needed fresh capital to finance expansion; some, like Collins and Longmans, found it by selling shares to the public; others allowed themselves to be taken over by commercial enterprises formerly outside the book trade, or to merge with other publishers, but this metamorphosis did not get under way until the next decade.

Penguin's, already firmly established by 1939, grew considerably during the war and their success prompted others to publish for the paperback market. The paperback revolution was but a few years off and some of its potential was revealed in 1946 when Allen Lane celebrated Bernard Shaw's ninetieth birthday by issuing a million copies of ten of his plays. The National Book League held an exhibition which was attended by the great man himself. At the opening Shaw toured the stands, enthusiastically commenting on this and that, and lecturing everyone within earshot. Then, after half an hour, he announced in his rich brogue, 'Now, ladies and gentlemen, you have seen the animal,' and strode out into Albemarle Street. There were immediate thunderclaps and flashes of lightning as London was hit by one of the worst electric storms of the century.

Penguin's also looked to the future by making agreements with Chatto, Faber, Hamish Hamilton, Heinemann and Michael Joseph, for exclusive publication, under a joint imprint in paperback, of titles originally on those publishers' case-bound lists. This, in effect, gave Penguin first call on a great many important contemporary works and was a safeguard against immediate competition from Pan and other new paperback imprints.

International copyright and obscene libel continued to be vexatious problems. Some progress was to be made on the former and will be dealt with in the next section. 'Progress' was hardly a suitable word for the attorney general's announcement in the House of Commons, in 1949, that it was important that no publication should be permitted to deprave or corrupt morals, exalt vice or encourage its commission. He added, however, that it was also important that there should be as little interference as possible with freedom of publication, and that objection to frank portrayal of sordid and unedifying aspects of life simply on the grounds of offence against taste or manners was not enough. Nor was it enough to help publishers to decide what they might or might not publish without fear of prosecution. In fact, they had to go on taking risks. In 1948 the new firm of Allan Wingate decided to stick its neck out by publishing Norman Mailer's lengthy war novel *The Naked and the Dead*. Its exceptional outspokenness so upset the octogenerian editor of the *Sunday Times* that he devoted a whole column on his front page to denouncing it. The book became an instant bestseller and no action was taken against the publisher; others were to be less leniently treated in the 1950s. Meanwhile, the law remained as obscure as ever.

War books came back into fashion in the late 'forties. Eric Williams, ex-book buyer of Lewis's, a department store with branches all over the country, wrote *The Wooden Horse*, the story of his escape from a German prisoner-of-war camp, and had it accepted by Collins, after another equally distinguished publisher had explained to him precisely why it could not be expected to sell. Many booksellers were as sceptical, refusing to place orders for the book, until the public came clamouring into their shops for it. The same public had actually queued up to make sure of their first editions of *The Gathering Storm*, the first volume of Winston Churchill's war memoirs, when it appeared from Cassell's a few months before. This took the trade by surprise, but in retrospect it is not surprising because Churchill was already then a creature of mythology. He was widely regarded as having won the war single-handed and Conservative voters took it very personally, on his behalf, that the electorate should have spurned him and his party in 1945 and voted Labour to power. It was a point of honour almost, crossing party barriers even, to buy his history of the war. How many of those who bought it actually read it it would be instructive to know; certainly, as was always the case, ardour wore a little thin as the succeeding five volumes appeared but even so the individual sale of each volume was enormous, and they were still selling in hardback and paper in 1970.

Another pronounced literary trend was towards science fiction — S.F. as it became universally known. Jules Verne, H. G. Wells and others had long had successes in this genre, but S.F. was to become after 1945 a permanent section of literature in most bookshops; it proved to be not a passing fad of the public and attracted the attentions of other distinguished writers.

British society recovered slowly from the effects of six years of total war, and Attlee's first Labour administration (1945–50) governed during a period which was, for most of its duration, an extension of the national state of emergency. The story of modern publishing and bookselling, therefore, properly begins at 1950.

I

Trade Affairs

The collapse of Simpkin Marshall—problems of supply which followed; introduction of computers; surcharging; service charges; staff problems; I.S.B.N.s; attempts to improve ordering; improved terms of supply; credit control; London trade counters close as publishers move out; costs rise, as does executive expenditure; takeovers; rationalization; co-editions; international copyright; British publishers open overseas branches; educational publishing; technical and scientific books; paperback revolution; simultaneous publication; The Penguin Press; old-fashioned bookshops die out and a new breed of book-seller emerges—Tony Godwin; Charter Group of Booksellers; economic difficulties; other specialist groups within the B.A.—university bookselling; B.A. conference; Book Tokens; Book Trade Improvement; booksellers' assistants; publishers' reps; salaries in the trade; B.A. and P.A. affairs; defence of N.B.A.; activities of Society of Bookmen; Whitefriars Club; Paternosters; Publishers' Publicity Circle; Society of Young Publishers; Galley Club; B.P.R.A.; N.B.L. Council; Arts Council—the Public Lending Right; Book Festivals; National Book Sale; National Library Week; the Library Association; Book Development Council; the British Council; Book Fairs; obscene libel; Book Clubs; trade journals; the honours list; literary prizes; increased output.

In the years 1950–70 the book trade underwent important changes, and no single event affected its structure as radically as did the demise of Simpkin Marshall Ltd in 1955.

Simpkin's was an old-established wholesale house which held in stock (some of it on consignment) sufficient supplies of all important publishers' lists to meet daily single-copy and small stock orders from booksellers, thus benefiting both their customers and their suppliers. To make a living for themselves, however, Simpkin's had to diversify and to act as comprehensive stockists for certain small publishers whose books could not be obtained except through them. They also had to promote their own quantity sales by putting travellers on the road to persuade booksellers to buy in bulk through the wholesaler instead of from the publisher. They were thus placed in the position of working both for the publisher, by syphoning off his unwanted single-copy

409

trade, and against him, by soliciting the stock orders which his own
travellers were employed to obtain. Simpkin's also had a department
for wholesale export which buttressed publishers against small, long-
term credit orders from overseas, and another for selling off publishers'
remainders. They were, or should have been, the middleman *par
excellence*, performing numerous tasks for publishers which would have
been, and proved to be, so much more expensive without their existence.

After their destruction in the blitz, Pitman's, together with other
publishers, refloated the company (see p. 399). Simpkin Marshall
(1941) Ltd soldiered on until 1951, with publishers still showing a
marked reluctance to offer realistic discounts, and it then passed into
the hands of Captain Ian Robert Maxwell, a Czech-born Jew who had
fought with distinction against Hitler, and who had already established
publishing connections in this country. He moved Simpkin's from its
makeshift premises in Rossmore Court, St John's Wood, where it
occupied the garage floor of a block of flats, into a warehouse in the
nearby Marylebone Road which he grandly named, with a splendid
indifference to its instant-coffee overtones, Maxwell House. (Captain
Ian Maxwell will later reappear in these pages as Mr Robert Maxwell,
erstwhile M.P. for Buckingham.)

Maxwell was confidently expected to put the trade's wholesale house
in order, but late in 1954 it was apparent that Simpkin's was in difficulties, and consultations went on at the P.A.'s headquarters. The
trouble, basically, was that publishers were not prepared to allow
sufficient discount for the major wholesaler to operate profitably.
Simpkin's were buying at between 33⅓ per cent and 40 per cent, and
selling to booksellers at 25 per cent, or, for quantity orders, 33⅓ per
cent. It didn't require an economic wizard to understand that the margin was totally inadequate, especially considering the service expected
in reporting on non-available items. So Simpkin's went into the hands
of the official receiver with an estimated deficit of £475,000. Macmillan's
petitioned for a compulsory winding-up order, against the wishes of the
creditors as a whole who had called for a voluntary liquidation.
Macmillan's demands were upheld on May 2nd, 1955, and later in the
same month the name, goodwill and Maxwell House, together with the
export department and other adjuncts, were purchased by Theodore
Cole, then managing director of Hatchard's of Piccadilly. But Simpkin's
never operated again as wholesaler for the British book trade, despite
various schemes put forward for the establishment of what a bookseller,
Basil Donne-Smith, dubbed a 'single-copy house'.

Piers Raymond, son of Harold, was a notable campaigner for saving
Simpkin's, and was rare amongst publishers for instantly understanding
what its end would mean economically. He had the foresight to formu-
late a plan for a non-stockholding wholesaler but, alas, other publishers,

who had all lost by the on-consignment standing stock they had kept at Maxwell House, were not prepared to accept his proposals. J. Neilson Lapraik, Managing Director of the Book Centre, favoured a single-copy house on the Dutch Boekhuis pattern working alongside a central clearing house for orders, and as a practical step, Book Centre started, at the B.A.'s request, an orders-clearing service at Pitman's Kingsway trade counter which booksellers and publishers were soon to regard as invaluable for efficient distribution.

However, in the long and the short term, publishers were not willing to gamble on creating a single-copy house (and finally all realistic discussion ended when booksellers made it clear that they would not accept 25 per cent discount and a charge for carriage); so Simpkin's died, its export department being taken over by Messrs Wyman, and its assets finally paying its creditors but a small dividend. The immediate effects were alarming. Publishers were inundated with tiny orders from booksellers, the cost of servicing which made for instant resentment on both sides. Yet the fault lay with no one but the publishers, who had been cheese-paring about what they were willing to give Simpkin's to do their single-copy work for them.

The problems of supply which followed on the untimely failure of Simpkin's (and W. H. Smith's eventual withdrawal from wholesaling) set the scene for the widespread introduction of the computer. In 1955 automation was still reverently regarded by every progressive person as a means of emancipating workers from unnecessary drudgery, and as leading to a shorter working week. And, in fact, the working week became curtailed to an average five-day thirty-five to forty hours. But many people put the extra leisure hours gained not into creative pursuits, for which few had any leaning, but into working overtime at increased rates of pay. The results of automation were, therefore, not as utopian as had been hoped, nor did automation make working life easier or more efficient for anyone, perhaps because the input of a computer demanded more intelligence than anyone had bargained for.

It is worth noting here that in the 1955 edition of the *Shorter Oxford English Dictionary* the word 'compute' is described as 'now rare', and the word 'computer' actually appears only in a sub-entry as 'one who computes; *spec.* one employed to make calculations in an observatory, etc.' Few, if any, publishers had observatories in 1955; by 1970 most of the larger ones made use of computers which were invented as a substitute for the human brain and human labour. Any experienced bookseller could tell you before decimalization, without a moment's thought, that $33\frac{1}{3}$ per cent discount off 35s. was 11s. 8d., and that 25 per cent off 25s. was 6s. 3d. The computer could tell you that 85 copies of a 42s. book, at 30 per cent discount, less charter terms of $2\frac{1}{2}$ per cent was £121 16s. 7d. (give or take a decimal point) without more than a slight whirr—provided it was properly programmed and fed. It could also tell you, more interestingly, that one-third off 121 books sold at 10s. each to the bookseller was not £60 10s., as one might have expected, but £60 10s. 0·1d., a result fiercely contested with me as correct by a very senior official of the Oxford University Press.

Computers, however, entered more quickly into the public consciousness than was allowed for by the dictionary, and by 1970, they had become a way of life, for the book trade as for everyone else. They had also established themselves as the universal excuse for things going wrong, and a great many things went wrong every single working day because those who programmed computers saw that they remained as imperfect a 'brain' as the human kind; indeed, more so, because they hadn't the human ability to correct error as it was perceived. When the computer input was incorrect, as sometimes happened, mistakes were made that were so wild as to be comical; for example, the sales manager of one small company received five hundred copies of a book which he had asked to have sent to Australia, invoiced to him personally at full price (£750), at his own small office. However, booksellers opening parcels in 1970 did not find it so amusing when anything between 10 and 50 per cent of them produced queries of non-delivery without a report, wrong books, or wrong editions of the right books, the rectification of which added to everyone's overheads and should have produced a vast profit for the government-owned post office, but that department always resolutely maintained that its services operated at a loss and regularly put up the charge for handling mail.

Nevertheless it was believed that the volume of business in the book trade, which increased from £37 million in 1950 to £153,677,000 in 1970, could not have been handled effectively without computerization. It is certainly true that if the operation had been left to a roomful of invoice typists Penguin Books could not have serviced their orders from booksellers (averaging 2,838 per week in 1971 for singles and multiples of over one thousand stock titles in print) and invoiced and dispatched them in the same week. Similarly with Book Centre, which invoiced and dispatched for 10 publishers with an annual combined turnover of £1,300,000 in 1950; for 50 with a total turnover of £3 million in 1960; and for 120 in 1970, by which time they also invoiced for an additional thirty through their Publishers' Computer Service, making for a combined turnover of £21·5 million. When the computer input was correct it operated at a work rate which no human brain could equal.

Another striking result of the computer age was the proliferation of mostly unnecessary bumf (a word *not* excluded from the *Shorter Oxford*). Before automation, publishers often complained about wholesale exporters who demanded five or six copies of invoices; but once computerization got under way, publishers sanctioned the delivery of one book to which was attached voluminous documentation, at the same time as protesting about wickedly rising overheads. It also became the custom to dispatch several invoices by post to the same booksellers, on the same day, in separate envelopes, each costing four old pence, plus stationery and labour.

Surcharging became a vexed subject. It seemed reasonable to some booksellers that large casebound and paperback publishers should charge for servicing small orders which could easily have been made up to £3 invoice value without stock risk to the retailer, but this did not answer the problem of small publishers dealing with small booksellers, or even of small publishers dealing with medium-sized and large booksellers. Where there was not the range to make a stock order to supplement a customer's particular requirement, the publisher often imposed a surcharge and the bookseller stood the loss or passed it on. Some booksellers passed it on from as early as the 1950s, but many more were loth to do so for fear of losing trade to their competitors. It should be added that publishers very often got scant support from booksellers for the books they chose to publish, and didn't see why they should reward non-stockholding retailers with full terms.

Achieving adequate profits was not made easier for booksellers by previously unheard-of publishers advertising their one and only publication as 'available from all booksellers' at a stated price. The bookseller was expected to obtain the book, having probably had to research about the actual publisher whose name was unlikely to appear in Whitaker's *Publishers in the U.K. and Their Addresses*, and then had to face an outraged customer if he requested a few shillings more than the labelled price of the book to cover his expenses. So that the traditional notion that booksellers must be prepared to get any book or pamphlet, advertised anywhere, at the price quoted in the advertisement (Vaughan's of Tottenham Court Road proudly proclaimed on their shop fascia in the 1940s and 1950s SPECIALISTS IN ALL BOOKS) began to be challenged by 1970 (by which time Bill Vaughan was in publishing, anyhow). This was reasonable because by then any householder knew that to call an electrician or a plumber to his home was to incur an immediate service charge of up to £1 before any actual work was done, and that to send his car for service was to make him liable to labour charges of several pounds per day. Only very gradually did the bookseller wake up to the fact that he must charge for *his* services.)

Publishers were driven to use the computer because they believed it would produce the statistics which modern methods of management regarded as vital, and because it was so difficult to get invoice clerks; and there was no evidence that staff engaged to do manual invoicing would be more efficient than those employed to operate the machine.

Gone, very soon, were the old retainers who had been with a firm since they left school at an early age and were prepared to spend their working lives sitting at high stools writing out charges to booksellers. There was growing unemployment in the 'sixties, but on the whole it did not affect London, where most publishers still operated, and good office staff became expensive. So automation prevailed and the public, which did not expect delivery of a suite of furniture, a dinner service or a new car within weeks—or even months—of ordering it, but did expect the much lower-priced item, a book, to be obtained in twenty-four hours, vociferously blamed the book trade for its inefficiency.

A side result of the vastly increased number of titles handled by frequently changing staff was inaccurate answering. O/P (out of print) meant precisely that—order cancelled, title will not be reprinted—until some years after the second war, but it came to mean O/P/P (out of print at present); T/O/P (temporarily out of print); RP/ND (reprinting, no date); or even that the book would reappear in vast quantities within a few months, or, in the case of paperbacks, a few weeks. And new answers crept in which were meaningless to everyone. Of these D/R (due recorded) and O/S (out of stock) were amongst the most maddening. Due from where? Out of stock where? The proliferation of unhelpful reports grew in proportion to the increased employment of public relations officers and customer-liaison staff.

The requirements of the machine led also to the introduction of Standard Book Numbering (I.S.B.N.s) in the 1960s. There was international agreement about this, the computer's need to identify books for cataloguing purposes overcoming, in no time at all, all the ethnic, political, linguistic and temperamental differences which stood in the way of international agreements at more important levels. Every book was given a number which every computer would recognize; joint publications were given two numbers, because incorporated in every S.B.N. was a digit or two which denoted the publisher. It was quite clearly hoped that booksellers would come to use numbers instead of authors and titles when ordering, despite fierce denials that this was the intention, but Penguin Books, for instance, went to the bother of producing a monthly list by number only and asked booksellers to use it, for preference; and I.S.B.N.s began to appear with increasing prominence on the spines of books and in publishers' advertising. Nineteen eighty-four was uncomfortably near, and those who held the strange, old-fashioned belief that a title and an author were easier to remember than nine or ten digits were clearly due for sacrifice to the machine. In the field of distribution, publishers were exasperated, and made more inefficient, by receiving orders from booksellers written, perhaps typed, on scraps of paper, on postcards, on order forms of infinitely varying dimensions, bearing curious instructions as to delivery and charging. So P.A.C.H. (Publishers Accounts Clearing House) was introduced by Walter Harrap and others in 1958, providing a fairly simple form to use for up to ten titles and carbonized to five copies, one of which the publisher could use as his invoice. At the 1958 B.A. Conference it was enthusiastically adopted by many booksellers, who gained preferential terms by using it: preferential terms, that is, from the 84 publishers who accepted it by September of that year. Meanwhile efforts to devise a more lasting standardized form for booksellers continued, and P.A.C.H. was killed off abruptly in 1971. Little progress however was made in persuading publishers to standardize their invoice forms, which were an increasing nuisance to booksellers who had to cope with fifty or more different shapes to file into their bought ledger systems.

Terms gradually improved during these twenty years; but not quickly enough for stockholding booksellers. Some publishers—Collins, for instance—recognized that their own overheads could be decreased by simplifying terms; others went on creating their own eccentric conditions, even after the inauguration of the Charter Group of Booksellers. The Charter Group came into being in 1964, but by 1970 there were still many publishers, particularly those trading in the academic and technical spheres, who wished to supply their books for stock at 20 per cent, 25 per cent and 30 per cent discount, when all the evidence suggested that booksellers could not afford to stock books at less than $33\frac{1}{3}$ per cent.

Terms of supply was one problem; terms of credit another, and it gave rise to a breed of faceless beings called credit controllers. These persons sent duplicated monthly letters to their customers pointing out that accounts had not been paid at thirty days, which was the officially recognized settlement time. The letters were impersonal and crude and endangered the goodwill which had been established between publishers' sales staff and booksellers, thus creating the absurd situation where one part of a company was working against the other: a salesman would call on a bookseller urging him to buy fifty of a new title, which he certainly would sell over six months, but the credit controller wanted settlement for the whole consignment after thirty days, by which time perhaps only twenty had been sold. This situation was further aggravated as more and more publishers elected to have their invoicing done through the Publishers' Computer Service, so that the largest account any bookseller had to pay each month was the Book Centre's, and this proved embarrassing to many. It also proved embarrassing to Book Centre on occasions when the machine 'stopped' an account which was, in fact, up to date.

For booksellers near enough to London the problems of distribution were eased by the continued existence of some trade counters from which stock could be collected. Trade counters had existed for as long as publishers had been selling to other publishers and booksellers. In London, it was an obviously easy way of dealing with day-to-day orders. The public got the books they wanted quickly (sometimes, as we have seen, actually waiting in a shop whilst a runner was sent to the publisher), the publisher did not have to concern himself about methods of dispatch; the bookseller could compete with his rival round the corner. Booksellers' collectors were always an under-privileged minority, traipsing by foot about the City and Bloomsbury through all weathers, with heavy bags slung over their shoulders, but the larger booksellers gradually acquired vans. Yet for many years following the second war most publishers maintained counters, manned sometimes by helpful individuals with a built-in knowledge of their lists dating back to the time they had joined their firms from school, but sometimes by underpaid awkward cusses, who showed their disgruntlement by taking the maximum amount of time to supply any book demanded.

On the whole, however, it was found beneficial to both sides of the trade to keep counters open, until the great exodus of publishers' warehouses from central London began in the late 'fifties. The foot collectors could still make a living—if it could be called that—and the fairly harmless rackets of their calling made the job worthwhile until terms improved. The collector for William Jackson (Books) Ltd, of Southampton Row, Holborn, earned £2 10s. od per week in the late 'forties. His employer, Frederick Joiner, did not expect him to live on this meagre wage but knew, as an ex-collector himself, about the system of 'doubling-up'. If two or more collectors had single copy orders for the same publisher who gave only 25 per cent discount on one copy, but 33⅓ per cent on two or more, then collectors would pool their orders, obtain a third off cash paid, and split the difference between them. Thus, there would be 1s. 3d. on each 15s. book ordered as a single copy for each collector, and in those days that meant several cups of tea, a pint of beer, or even something more to take home to the wife. It was a rough-and-ready economy which enabled the bookseller to underpay his collector, and still receive the poor terms which he barked about when he met the publisher's representative.

The cost of maintaining these trade counters became increasingly painful to publishers as rents and overheads rose, and more and more of them elected to close down in central London and operate a theoretically better service from their warehouses, by their own transport. But some were cautious enough to keep their trade counters open as a side door for distribution. Booksellers who gave up hand-collecting in the early 'sixties because it wasn't economic to collect so little, or humane to expect any member of staff to collect more, acquired their own vehicles and discovered it was at least worthwhile to make a weekly collection, although by then many trade counters had shut down, apparently for ever. Those that remained open were busy, and through them grew up a vital comradeship enabling booksellers to promise some customers the books they required within a specified short time.

Exemplifying the best in trade-counter management was Heinemann's in Gower Mews, formerly the stabling area for those who lived in Bedford Square. Here collectors were received by the well-informed George Chapman and Pat Morris, who welcomed them, through a barrage of two-finger typing, with choice items of good-humoured badinage. George and Pat were first to be encountered (Chapman joined in 1940; Morris, in '41) down the area steps of 99 Great Russell Street, from which address they operated until their editorial and sales colleagues moved into new offices in Mayfair. They were transplanted to Gower Mews, where they had more daylight but no relaxation from visiting booksellers, for many of whom they were the essential contact with the actual books. In fact Chapman and Morris were salesmen, although not officially designated as such, and any bookseller who did not behave in a hoity-toity manner could be their friends, and receive useful tips about new titles and backlist stock.

The weekly excursion to the various trade counters sometimes resembled a trip for tourists around the remains of Dickens's London, so antiquated were the premises, and even some of the individuals, visited. As leases fell in on property ripe for development many publishers moved out of London and into the new towns. Faber and Longmans moved to Harlow, as did the Educational Supply Association, once on the corner of High Holborn and Drury Lane, publishers of old examination papers and manufacturers of school equipment. Macmillan and Pan Books went to Basingstoke; Methuen and Eyre & Spottiswoode (under their new title, Associated Book Publishers) to Andover; Batsford, to Braintree; Hutchinson, to Tiptree; other publishers, as yet unheard of in these pages, to other country venues, which migration brings us to the next subject: mergers and takeovers.

Publishing, and subsequently bookselling, like many other industries, became group-minded under the pressures of the time. In some cases individual firms could not provide sufficient capital to finance necessary growth in a suddenly expanded market; in others the alternative to gobbling up others was to be gobbled up oneself. In the world of banking this showed itself very clearly when two of the five major clearing banks in the United Kingdom—each of which was utterly viable economically in its own right—joined forces to maintain some sort of theoretical independence lest any two or more of the remaining three should first achieve dominance and take them over. It made little sense to those who ran accounts with either big bank, except that they had, after the merger, a choice of two local branches. It did not lead to lower bank charges or to increased efficiency. The merger was seen as protection for the banks, not for the customers they served.

It is scarcely surprising that in publishing, where much smaller sums of money were involved than in banking, the same uneasy need for protection was felt. Thus by the end of 1970 Longmans, who had already absorbed several other imprints, had merged with Penguin's; Tillings, a transport company, owned Heinemann and its various satellites; and such conglomerate titles as Associated Book Publishers Ltd, the British Printing Corporation (B.P.C. Publishing Ltd), the International Publishing Corporation (I.P.C.); Granada, the Thomson Group and others concealed the names of numerous once independent imprints, whilst in the field of American infiltration the Crowell Collier-Macmillan Company had bought bookselling businesses and library suppliers as well as famous publishing houses.

Some firms which sold their shares to larger publishers, or allowed themselves to be taken over by American interests, did so because they urgently needed more working capital. Previously the cost of expansion had been met out of the trading accounts, by ploughing back part of the profits. This was possible in times of low taxation and wages, and before literary agents were able to drive hard bargains in a competitive market for large advances not only on the original casebound editions but also on the basis of increasing sales of paperback and other subsidiary rights. Everything, it seemed, contributed to the vastly increased cost of publishing not least the very real rise in the standard of living. The middle classes, into which publishers fell, became accustomed to own cars, and even yachts, to holiday abroad and to maintain centrally heated houses with every possible modern convenience. Business running costs had also risen because it was deemed necessary to make regular and frequent trips abroad, not only to buy books but to sell them, so that at any given time an army of British publishers would be flying about the world in the interests of cementing their African, Australian, Far Eastern, American and other connections, and adding extensively to their overheads by each and every rev of the jet engines which propelled them hither and thither. Some of these journeys were no doubt really necessary and did actually promote the sale of British books in far off territories, but I suspect that a great many of them were undertaken only because they became the fashion. Miss Phyllis Alexander, who ran the World's Work (1913) Ltd imprint, owned by Heinemann, and dealing almost exclusively in books of American origin, managed it successfully for several decades without ever paying a visit to the United States during her professional life. And John Murray's, the publishers of *Parkinson's Law*, should perhaps be singled out at this point. Their emissaries were not often mentioned in the columns of *The Bookseller* as being about to depart on extensive overseas tours, nor, as late as 1971, had any rumour been heard about their ripeness for takeover. A few others fell into the same category, but by and large most medium-sized and big publishers had become vulnerable to the takeover-merger procedure by 1970, and many had succumbed. At January 1st, 1971, Dent, Faber, Gollancz, Macmillan, Murray and Warne were still unmerged and independent, but most other big names had news of projected mergers, even if they had not already taken place.

Rationalization, once again, was the fashionable word used to denote takeovers, particularly when the capital came from the U.S.A. Those being bought usually expressed some guilt, and the City of London was sometimes blamed for not being willing to back home publishing, its reluctance usually being attributed to the poor returns expected on capital invested in the book trade compared with that risked in other industries. Yet it didn't deter Tillings, for instance. The American publishers who were so willing to invest in British publishing were regarded as saviours until, as was so often the case, the New York presidents began to interfere with their London satellites; then it was the common formula for the man who had sold out and been retained as head of his American-owned company to resign in pique, and for the investing interloper to reign supreme. In one instance, at least, this did not happen, and Mark Goulden, who owned the old-established firm of W. H. Allen, conducted several transatlantic sales, contriving to remain very successfully in charge of his own outfit whoever happened to hold the controlling shares.

Just as in mergers and takeovers two or more units joined together to make a financially secure group, in international publishing the cost of producing the illustrations was spread over numerous different editions for various countries, the text being set independently as dictated by language requirements. Thus a book of reproductions of paintings in colour which would have been impossibly expensive in a run of even 5,000 in an English edition, not only became viable when 100,000 or 200,000 could be produced for a world market, but very often a bargain for the customer at the same time. Paul Hamlyn's *World Architecture*, edited by Trewin Copplestone, ran to 348 pages of Super Royal Quarto (10in $\times$ 13$\frac{1}{2}$in) with 32 pages of colour plates and 1,038 black and white illustrations, and cost £4 4s. when first published in 1963. William Gaunt's *The Impressionists* (same size) published by Thames & Hudson in 1970, had 108 colour plates and extensive text for £5 5s. It was Hamlyn and Walter Neurath of Thames & Hudson who first seriously exploited this world market, which lent itself particularly to the production of art books and illustrated children's books, but was also a channel for historical works. It was a rare instance in the twentieth century of bigger really meaning better and not the opposite. The numerous meretricious books published according to the same system earned the contemptuous apellation 'coffee-table books', by which was meant expensive-looking volumes which could be casually left about in living-rooms to impress guests. One might flick through them looking at the pictures, but fairly certainly no one would read much of the text—because, for one thing, the layout made that difficult.

International publishing possibly eased the way for those working for more cooperation on international copyright. There were two important steps forward. In August 1954 the United States Senate passed an amendment modifying its country's copyright law in such a way as to allow for membership of the Universal Copyright Convention. The practical result of this was that publications in English, by non-American authors, no longer had to be manufactured in the U.S.A. to enjoy protection. In fact British authors did not benefit from this until 1957 because the United Kingdom government did not ratify the U.C.C. until then.

Ironically, some ten years later, all the good work patiently achieved over a century was threatened when the newly created countries of Africa and the East demanded less stringent rules for themselves. What they really wanted was to reprint textbooks without paying royalties. Many of these new countries were poor, and were receiving aid from the U.K. and the U.S.A., so it would have been hard on British authors and publishers who contributed already to foreign aid through their taxes if they had also had to bear with piracy. There were instances of this but, by and large, the new governments of Africa and Asia realized that if textbook authors were not paid for their work they would cease to write them, so there would be no books to pirate anyhow. Instead, they sought relaxation of some of the rules of the Berne Copyright Convention which was revised for the sixth time in 1948, in Brussels (there were then 34 member countries), again in Stockholm in 1967 and yet again in Paris in 1971. In 1969 there were 59 members, of whom 34 were also signatories of the Universal Copyright Convention. The U.C.C. had been formed in 1952, under the auspices of UNESCO, in the hope of reconciling the Pan-American system, which required works to be registered before copyright became effective, and the Berne (mostly European) method, which recognized that copyright applied automatically as soon as a work existed.

Soviet Russia and some other communist countries treated copyright with capricious contempt. Sometimes Western authors were accredited royalties, but had to go to the U.S.S.R. to spend them; sometimes they were not. There was no apparent logic about the selection. British authors and publishers often visited Poland to spend assets which were frozen in that country. In the Far East, on the island of Taiwan, pirated editions of textbooks were produced by sweated labour, thus adding to the headaches of the trade.

International copyright is a subject which few have mastered. Ronald Barker, Secretary of the P.A., became the acknowledged expert in Britain, and his pamphlets *International Copyright: the Search for a Formula for the '70s* and *Copyright: the New International Convention* are recommended further reading.

As we have seen, British publishers began to open overseas branches before the end of the nineteenth century. Their number grew steadily in the first half of the twentieth, and after 1945 not only were more branches opened by most major publishers, but separate subsidiaries were formed in Australia (which in 1953 accounted for 27 per cent of all British book exports), Canada and elsewhere. These subsidiaries began to publish original books once they had become firmly established as sales points for the parent companies' lists. This vast new activity, which added to the travels of principals and sales executives, took place against a background of educational and political upheaval, especially in Africa. As new countries were formed out of the lost empires of the British, French, Belgians, Dutch and Americans, the men and women who had led the clamour for independence now devoted part of their energies to spreading education, which meant a demand for more textbooks both in English and in the vernacular. The competition amongst publishers to dominate this lucrative new market was not confined to rival British firms but became an issue between the U.K. and the U.S.A. who had begun, during the second war, to break into the British publishers' traditional market. The Russians also sought to influence the emergent peoples of the Far East by printing heavily subsidized (and of course pirated) editions of British books, in English, which they distributed at give-away prices. British publishers had to fight hard to persuade successive governments that British books must also be helped if British influence and trade were to be maintained and increased. Too often government refused to intervene, at the same time as cutting down on British Council estimates and causing that worthy institution to close many of its overseas libraries. It says much for the industry and initiative of our publishers that despite a general lack of support officially, they continued to prosper in the export market — they were even able to spare some time to slitting each other's throats, as a change from those of the Americans and Russians.

That our publishers were able to hold the market was, of course, partly because their product was a good one. Educational publishing improved not only in turnover in this period but also in quality, and it was to promote the educational lists that so much foreign travel was undertaken. There were times when one had the impression that the surest way of eventually meeting up with everyone of importance in this field would be to sit in the arrival and departure lounge of Nairobi or Delhi airport. Certainly Alan Hill would have turned up in them fairly frequently; he was the inspiration behind, and later chairman of, Heinemann Educational Books Ltd, and it was men such as he, and Roy Yglesias, first of Ginn, then of Longmans, who understood that a new generation needed new text books, and that these should be attractively designed and written. Many schools continued to use books published in the Edwardian era (and bearing every appearance of having been bound up then, too), either because they were thought to be still the best works in their field, or because there weren't sufficient funds to buy alternatives; but many others threw out the tattered and disintegrating volumes which had been preserved by sticky tape and faith to last through the war, and replaced them with more up to date titles. Many more would have done so if educational book grants had been more generous. A secondary school teacher writing to *The Times Educational Supplement* in 1970 pointed out that in 1959–60 he had been allocated 6s. per pupil per annum for books, and that not only had this amount not been increased ten years later but the total sum involved, £150, now had to be spread over one hundred additional pupils. Small wonder that educational publishers formed a council in 1969 to bring pressure to bear on the government and local authorities to spend more on books. At that date some grammar-school children being crammed for O and A level examinations, in the manner favoured in our forced-farming educational system, were still learning geography from atlases published in 1957, when Africa was still largely governed by Europe.

Another rapid growth area was in technical and scientific books. Nuclear fission, cybernetics, automation, space projects, plastics and numerous other developments each called for a literature of its own, and competition to sell such books in the export markets of the world was especially keen, once again, between Britain and the U.S.A.

But the greatest growth of all was in paperbacks. The word 'revolution' has been applied unstintingly in this connection, but it was almost 'evolutionary' in that it took so long, even if one dates it only from 1935 when Penguin's started. Allen Lane had a sufficiently clear field for twenty years so that when the major impact came in the late 1950s he thrived on the competition and expanded at a rate which made his early progress seem trivial by comparison. He was still indisputably in the lead in 1970.

Alongside the popular paperbacks, mostly fiction, romance, crime and war stories, were soon ranged non-fiction series, which, because of their highbrow nature, came to be known as 'eggheads'. At first these were imports from the States—Harper Torchbooks, Ann Arbor's, and so forth—but the university presses in England soon took to the idea and issued their own academic works in paper covers. Other publishers, such as Faber, Methuen and Routledge, followed suit. It became the general opinion that there were no limits to what might be paper-backed, so in due course, everything thought saleable in that form was given the treatment, even large-format art books and dictionaries, neither of which was really suited to it because the page size of an art book made it floppy to handle and reference books need stout bindings if they are to endure everyday use. (The format was often determined by the original hardback size, the same sheets being used for both editions; there was thus little uniformity of appearance as with purpose-made paperbacks.)

The appearance of bookshops changed more rapidly than ever before to accommodate the paperback phenomenon, and publishers vied with each other to provide free fittings for their own ranges. Once again Penguin's took the lead, with Penguin Bookshops either in separate premises, as at Heffer's and Collet's, or inside existing shops, and by 1970 they were undertaking to put in other paperback pub-lishers' fittings for them and persuading their rivals to meet some of the booksellers' costs. It was a novel situation for the bookseller, being wooed. He had already become accustomed to buying almost all paper-back stock on a completely returnable basis (there were some excep-tions amongst the egghead publishers) which had led to a collapse of the publishers' traditional attitude to accepting back casebound books for credit or exchange. As the paperback boom gathered force it was increasingly difficult to sell new novels and biographies and travel books by unknown writers. Therefore, if the publishers wanted them at the point of sale, against the possibility of favourable publicity, they had to supply them on the booksellers' conditions. What was known as the 'see safe' system (titles which did not sell could be swapped for those which did) was adopted and its benefits extended to anyone whom the publisher, or his sales manager or rep., regarded as an outlet worth fostering. This did not mean every member of the Booksellers' Associa-tion by any means, nor did it exclude those who were not members.

Simultaneous publication in both cased and paper editions also became a fashion; Thames & Hudson, for instance, regularly issued most of their World of Art series in this way. Usually, new fiction appeared first in hardback, as in the past, although there were occasional exceptions.

Famous series such as Everyman and the Arden and New Cambridge editions of Shakespeare gradually took to appearing also in paperback because, as Allen Lane had noted in the early years of Penguins, they had a greater appeal to the young—and not just because they were cheaper. Very often a paperback edition at only a few shillings or pence less than the original would sell enormously more copies; in some instances the paperback even sold more at a higher price than the cloth edition. Price resistance at times seemed non-existent and the 6d. (2½p) pre-war Penguin novel was soon accepted at anything up to 10s. (50p) and beyond. In non-fiction, and especially in academic categories, paperbacks were anything but cheap, but they were often staggeringly cheaper than the bound version, and here the purchaser with a small book grant, much of which was spent on other goods, or on rent, was interested in buying the lowest priced edition.

An important consideration in the paperback revolution was that there were no taboos regarding how they should be handled. Previously children had been taught not to illtreat books, which were regarded as examples of craftsmanship whose bindings should not be broken, whose pages should not be dog-eared or annotated, and which should only be touched with clean hands. It was not so with paperbacks. They could be stuffed into pockets, left lying open and upside down, or bent back at the page last read. They were also expendable, and not part of one's luggage through life. Coffee cups and beer glasses could be placed on them, and they were eminently suitable for use on sandy beaches and in the bath. As their price soared this became less true of the more expensive ones, but the general attitude that they could be knocked around during the course of use remained popular.

Not all paperbacks sold by any means, and this created a still unresolved problem in remaindering; often pulping was the only answer.

All trends being reversible, even by the setter, Penguin's once again took the lead in 1967 when Allen Lane announced the formation of The Penguin Press to publish original hardbacks from the offices in Vigo Street where his Uncle John had run The Bodley Head. The Penguin Press was created partly, perhaps mostly, to ensure that Penguin Books would have first call on worthwhile non-fiction for its Pelican and Peregrine imprints in the event of traditional publishers keeping their bestselling titles for their own paperback series. Until the late 1950s Penguin had automatically had the choice of the majority of non-fiction published, and had also been able to compete effectively for almost any novel. Pan, Panther, Fontana (owned by Collins), Four Square, Corgi and other new firms became serious competitors for saleable fiction, but there was always sufficient to go round, and, for most authors, to be put into Penguin was a very real honour conferring the probability of large financial reward. Gradually the advances for paperback rights increased to astronomical heights and were often fixed before the hardback edition was published. Mostly it was a case, once the pressure was on, of a title going to whoever made the largest bid and often it was found that a title would do better in an established paperback list rather than in the original publisher's own paperback series. But that was not necessarily the reason why the rights were sold;

selling the paperback rights to another house was a way of limiting possible loss and of recouping on the amount paid in advance for the hardback edition.

There were other pressures, apart from the paperback revolution, which altered the appearance of British bookshops, although a lingering minority of traditionalists still remained happily immersed in the nineteenth century right up to 1970. It can be assumed, however, that death, leases falling in and reduced turnover will have seen most of them out by the time this is published. Their passing should not go entirely unmourned because they symbolized an approach to life which was messy but humane, and their proprietors were imbued with a wish to give service in a world that had decided to apply the criterion of profitability to everything. The old-fashioned bookshop, ill-lit, overcrowded with dark-brown high shelving, some of which was quite inaccessible without a ladder, and with notions of window-dressing that would have seemed pleasingly familiar to a Tonson or a Dodsley, had an atmosphere to which many a bibliophile responded warmly, so there must be some regrets for its banishment. The personal grocer who cut ham from the bone, and offered forty different types of cheese all lovingly touched by human hand, was also due for extinction and the supermarket was, in the opinion of some, a poor substitute.

Yet the bookshop always operated on the self-service principle. It was a supermarket to be browsed in, and the less its stock was classified or the more it was incorrectly signed (as in most supermarkets) the greater likelihood there was of stumbling on the unexpected. The new, modernized bookshops accepted the principle, without insisting on the wire trays, and learned something about displaying goods attractively from supermarket techniques. However, there was one vital difference: in the supermarket you could not order one tin of peaches canned by a company with whom Tesco or Waitrose did not trade; the bookseller, traditional or modern, was expected to deal with all publishers and, moreover, to be willing to deal with any and every association, institution or crank organization choosing to bring out a book or pamphlet.

So there grew up a more ruthless breed of bookseller, impatient, as youth always is, with the ways of the previous generation. The dark, bookish atmosphere of their fathers' shops held little nostalgia for them. They had lived with and seen through the charming muddle on the literary bookseller's counter to the inefficiency and wasted opportunities beyond. They were determined to be at least as good businessmen as was necessary to stay in bookselling, and some swung to the other end of the pendulum and prided themselves on being nothing but businessmen, expressing a contempt for the intellectual approach; it was an understandable reaction but did not marry quite happily with the product which, as they would probably have put it, they were merchandising.

(Merchandising and marketing were very 'in' words in the 1960s, as were 'sales-potential' and 'dynamic-sales-integration'.)

The new approach was inevitable and essential, the old shops had to be spring-cleaned, and the younger generation needed to be a little brash and insensitive in carrying out its ideas. In London it was led by Tony Godwin, who took over Better Books (opposite Foyle's) a small shop with a basement, referred to earlier as Miller & Gill. He did such daring things as ordering one-tenth (1,000 copies) of the whole edition of Christopher Fry's play *Venus Observed* and filling his window with it, whilst his huge competitor had subscribed only twenty-four, most of which went on the first day on staff sales. Godwin had a fascia board designed, after Mondrian, by John Sewell, and got himself talked about by advertising amusingly on London Transport and in the *New Statesman*, using such artists as Ronald Searle and André François. But behind the talk was substance, and booklovers flocked to Better Books to buy poetry, contemporary fiction and philosophy in surroundings which were bright and unfusty. It became the leading avant-garde bookshop in London, although only a fraction the size of Bumpus, Hatchard's or Dillon's.

When Alfred Wilson's collapsed in 1956 Godwin took over its City branch in Ship Tavern Passage, gutted it and turned it into a beguilingly attractive shop in which individual books stood out. This was in stark contrast to the effect made under the previous management, when it was necessary to pass through two doors before gaining access to a veritable forest of books in which the trees could not be easily detected, although previous years' leaves could. Godwin next became managing director of Bumpus, at the request of the consortium of publishers who owned it, and organized the move from Oxford Street to Baker Street, where he gave rather too much prominence to statuary and seating at the expense of the books; success was also hampered by the refusal of the landlords to allow him to hang a shop sign. Next he acquired premises adjacent to Better Books and dreamed up a horror of a bookshop where the walls were used not for books but for notices and posters, and the stock was held on snaky aluminium stands which could be removed when poetry evenings were held. And everything, as I recall it, was painted silver. It was, however, a reflection of contemporary taste and of his desire to make his shop a social centre; it also had a coffee bar.

Godwin subsequently went into publishing and sold his shops. He is mentioned at length here because his influence was important. His was not the first modern bookshop in London, as was sometimes claimed, any more than Penguins were the first paperbacks, but like Allen Lane, with whom he worked for seven years, he was a doer rather than a talker, and he did many things, especially at Bumpus, which upset people because they overthrew cherished traditions. To many of us younger booksellers of the time Tony Godwin blew a vital wind of change through the trade, and his success encouraged others to have their shops re-designed inside and out. The effect on turnover was often staggering. Even Ivan Chambers, a fine, traditional bookseller of marked efficiency and order, was surprised when Bryce's, having been purchased and modernized by the Bowes & Bowes Group, attracted sensationally more custom than before. Shopfitters found the book trade a new outlet for their services. Many booksellers, large and small, used the old established firm of Wiltshier's, of Canterbury; others preferred to work with their own architects. Indicative of a new prosperity, which booksellers hotly denied, was the amount of money spent on refitting in all parts of the U.K.

Much of the change was due to imitation, but it was also stimulated by the formation of the Charter Group of booksellers in 1964. The need to separate the real booksellers from those who dealt mainly in stationery and other goods had long been thought desirable. Booksellers argued that they would never get the terms they needed for survival and expansion if they were to be identified with the fancy goods shops which sold a few paperbacks and juveniles and were only members of the Association in order to obtain the right to sell (rather than exchange) Book Tokens. The number of real booksellers in the B.A.'s total of about 3,200 in 1963 was thought to be rather less than one thousand, and some jaundiced publishers put it as low as one hundred. It came to be recognized as the result of various surveys that approximately 80 per cent of a publisher's home trade was done with 20 per cent of his outlets. Publishers, therefore, became interested in differentiating between the 80 per cent and the 20 per cent, provided that the 20 per cent would put their houses in order, establish effective staff training schemes, spend a proportion of their budgets on improving their premises, maintain a bibliographical service and contribute data to an annual economic survey. In return, booksellers in the group received better terms than those outside it.

Those concerned to be in it, or to keep others out of it, were much occupied, officially or unofficially, with the qualifications for membership. If the minimum turnover to qualify were fixed at too high a figure, many good, small country bookshops would be excluded, and they were amongst the very retailers which both Associations wished to help; if it were fixed too low it would open the floodgates to many small businesses who could not hope to carry out the conditions of membership, and to whom publishers would not be willing to give extra discount. Eventually a minimum stock of £1,000 (later £2,000), and floor space of 150 square feet devoted to books, was agreed. A packed inaugural meeting was held in Church House, Westminster, at which Harold Hitchen, a

Harrogate bookseller who was then president of the B.A., was elected chairman, and a committee of ten was voted in. Publishers were co-opted to the committee which instantly spawned sub-committees, and booksellers uninvolved at this level sat back and waited to see who would give what.

Predictably, publishers indulged their built-in talent for spreading non-conformity. O.U.P. and Longmans issued blocks of tickets, to be attached to the monthly stock orders, which entitled the bookseller to a higher discount. But only on the monthly orders. This discouraged the bookseller from replacing his stock as he sold it, which many thought to be a retrograde step. Other publishers announced varying improved discounts and bonuses on increased turnover, some to be paid by cheque, others by credit note, and target figures for future trading years. At the same time service charges were imposed on small orders. As an exercise in non-rationalization it was masterly, but it left the Charter bookseller in a daze of incomprehension. When the dust settled he looked around, and then asked for more. A few kept up the pressure for 35 per cent all round and no service charges, and this, in due course, was followed by a demand for 40 per cent, carriage free, see safe, no handling charges. Publishers did not concede these terms in anything like the majority of cases, and certainly never with any uniformity.

Strong emphasis on staff training was a condition of membership of the Charter Group, and it was encouraged by the Distributive Industries Training Board, a government-sponsored organization which added yet another dimension to bureaucracy without noticeably increasing the efficiency of anything. Courses were arranged for managers and assistants, and booksellers who did not send their staff were threatened with expulsion from the Charter Group. This led to considerable ructions. Some booksellers maintained that the shopfloor was the place to learn bookselling, and that assistants could not expect a five-day working week, three week's paid holiday annually, sick pay, *and* be spared for a week's training course. They were, however, in a minority in a country which had become quite drunk by new notions of education, and it was not fashionable to oppose the Charter Group's training schemes.

The creation of the Charter Group accelerated the progress towards better terms without which many businesses would have foundered during the period when the Labour Government held office, 1964-70, when bills authorizing Selective Employment Tax, Corporation Tax and the distribution of 60 per cent of all profits were made law. These measures jointly overtaxed small companies, leaving them with little or nothing over to plough back for future expansion; often they had to borrow from their banks to pay their tax, which was a ludicrous situation, particularly as the banks were not supposed to lend to them. There were signs of alleviation in the 1971 Tory budget, which left a sour taste in the mouths of those left-wing booksellers who did not believe a Conservative administration was good for the country.

Apart from the Charter Group, within the B.A. there were many other specialist groups concerned with university bookselling, school books, technical books, export, library supply and so on. Of these the most significant proportional increase in representation came in the University Bookselling Group. Although there was never any great government enthusiasm to found new universities, fashion overtook what was deemed practical politics and, in Westminster, the ladies and gentlemen who passed through the lobbies in support of or opposition to this and that approved the extension of the higher and further educational institutions. In addition to new universities in places such as Canterbury, Falmer (Sussex), Colchester and Norwich, existing universities were expanded and Birmingham gained a second one. There were also new colleges of further education, teachers' training colleges, technical schools and many more art and drama schools than were ever likely to prove necessary to meet the demand for actors and artists, or for more teachers to teach more actors and artists. But in America nearly everyone apparently went to university or college of some sort, so in the United Kingdom it was thought proper to follow the pattern. The whole vast process added markedly to the number of books both bought and stolen.

To cater for these thousands of extra students new bookshops were opened. At Leicester there was a furore because the university decided to run its own bookshop, which was so successful that it contributed to the overheads of the publishing side, Leicester University Press. Most other faculties were content to allow a bookseller on to or near the campus to do the job for them, although they often attempted to impose unacceptable conditions. This led to the formation of two large groups, Bowes & Bowes, and U.B.O. (University Bookshops Oxford), the former belonging to W. H. Smith & Son and based on the famous Cambridge bookshop, and the latter being financed jointly by Blackwell's and O.U.P. The Bowes & Bowes group bought many famous bookselling businesses, U.B.O. acquired at least an equal holding in those willing to join, and sometimes purchased outright. In London the university authorities invited Una Dillon to move from Store Street into large and expandable premises on the corner of Malet Street and Torrington Place, and there Dillon's University Bookshop opened in 1956. In Birmingham the Hudson brothers and sister remained independent of the large groups and opened two university bookshops of their own at Edgbaston and Aston, as well as extending their premises in the city centre.

The main problem of university bookselling was a seasonal one. The university terms were short, but it was not practical to keep a bookshop open for little more than half the year, particularly as there were often people doing courses at colleges during the vacations. It didn't matter to those who operated from sites in the centre of urban areas, as in Oxford and Cambridge, because they served two publics anyhow, but away on the campus at Wivenhoe, five miles from the middle of Colchester, the bookshop manager found his shop more or less deserted for weeks of the year, and had little hope of attracting people there from the city. At the other end of the spectrum, as the start of the main term approached, there had to be an enormous build-up of stock, which surpassed even the heavy ordering indulged in by most booksellers immediately before Christmas. The rush subsided at the end of October, with brief revivals at the commencement of each term and in May, just before the exams. It was a tricky timetable to cope with as a management operation, but it had to be done.

Whether or not it was being done profitably was questionable in a number of cases at the time of writing, while at all times the profitability of bookselling as a whole was questioned by leading and lesser booksellers who flocked to the annual Booksellers' Association conference to bemoan their fate and enjoy the company of their colleagues, and of publishers who, from the late 'forties onwards were represented in increasing numbers and took part in joint sessions, although their votes were not required. The Conference was often held in a watering place far from London. Such venues as Thurlestone on a tip of Devon, down a single-track railway to Kingsbridge, and then by coach, were favoured, but even by 1956, when it was held there, many of the delegates came in their own cars so it hardly mattered. It was always a long conference, delegates leaving their homes in time to gather on a Thursday evening, spending Friday, part or all of Saturday in session, and the rest of the weekend at private parties or on excursions, then reforming for further sessions on Monday, followed by a banquet (evening dress) at which mostly execrable food was served, at its best tasteless, at its worst, actually poisonous. After a late night they packed their bags on Tuesday morning and made for home. It was a five to six day event, and many looked forward to it as one of the treats of the year. It was undoubtedly a social success and provided an excellent opportunity not only for booksellers and publishers but also for their wives and families to meet. Many friendships were founded on these occasions and for some this was the chief value of the conference which, otherwise, represented hours of speeches and discussion, late nights, too much to drink and, at the end of it all, a brain reeling with all that had been said and repeated over and over again. Booksellers voted on resolutions put forward by the council or various branches, but nothing they decided could be binding on all of the membership and, as with any other annual conference, the argument tended to centre around the same old vexed issues.

At its best it could be said that the conference hall was a good place in which to sound out opinion. In 1957 the indefatigable Sydney Goldsack, having heard H. E. Bailey's comparative analysis of book-selling profitability with that of other retail trades, typically took the bull by the horns once again and said that Collins would give booksellers $33\frac{1}{3}$ per cent discount off all net books, but would booksellers be pre-pared for the price of books to rise? Yes, chorused those booksellers present, they would. Prices were rising anyhow, and there was already a feeling that they should have been forced up in the book trade much earlier instead of being deliberately kept down. From that moment prices soared and there is still no sign of an end to the inflationary spiral that had become a major national issue long before Labour took office in 1964. The name H. E. Bailey was a new one in trade politics, but he was to be heard of repeatedly thereafter. Stepson and successor of Mr Lear of Cardiff, Bailey became unofficial statistician to the trade, impressing and sometimes baffling his readers and listeners with figures of great complexity accompanied by intricate explanations, the accept-ability of which depended on one's economic outlook. He took his figures very seriously, and his object in presenting them to the trade was to prove to publishers that booksellers were living on the breadline, a state of affairs which they did not exactly confirm by their appearance and behaviour at the annual conference which was as expensive as it was long. Some booksellers sported luxurious cars, perhaps paid for out of the profits of other business interests or from private means, but they made the psychological mistake of driving them to those very con-ferences at which they pleaded poverty. The Blackwells even brought their yacht on one occasion; but they were always an exceptional case, never pretending to be anything but affluent, and always on the side of their less fortunate colleagues.

An annual item on the conference agenda was the report from Book Tokens. It was usually presented by Henry Schollick, who was chairman of Book Tokens for twenty years, and added to by Humphrey Tenby, who became manager of the scheme after the war and whose businesslike methods transformed a rather amateurishly run office into one of the most smoothly organized in the trade. Having done this he gave his attention to administering the Booksellers' Clearing House and Book Trade Improvement Ltd. Working with him in a voluntary capacity for most of this time was the above mentioned Oxford bookseller and publisher; Schollick watched over the emergence of Book Trade Improvement Ltd, a company formed to lend money to booksellers wishing to improve their premises or to open new shops with, partly, their own capital. Book Tokens accumulated capital through the unexpected non-cashing of stamps and by wise investment, and was thus able to finance, on the accruing interest, the development of good outlets, and assist in the promotion of advertising schemes for books in general. The use made of the assests of Book Tokens was questioned in 1970 by some booksellers, who thought that the company should come more directly under the control of the B.A., but there was never any suggestion that the funds were improperly handled, and many booksellers had reason to be grateful to Henry Schollick and his co-directors of Book Tokens, who, with a minimum of red tape, gave help, when required, through the services of Book Trade Improvement Ltd.

Book Trade Improvement was often of vital importance to those bookselling businesses — and they were many — which were not profitable enough to attract investment, except from private sources, and which could not usually support sleeping partners (publishing, on the other hand, became the happy hunting ground of big business interests on both sides of the Atlantic). Eric Bailey's persistence in pointing this out was, perhaps, his most important contribution to the argument.

At a lesser level Bailey and nearly everyone else were concerned to raise the wages of booksellers' assistants in order to attract better qualified staff into bookshops. A good bookseller's assistant was expected to have a wide general knowledge, a particular knowledge of English and other literatures, a trained and retentive memory for titles, authors and publishers; to be quick at mental arithmetic; to like his fellows sufficiently well to be welcoming to all customers, and to suffer fools gladly; to appreciate the economic relationship between stock on the shelves and capital tied up; to be willing to tackle every job from buying and selling to dusting the stock and making the tea; to love books yet not to spend his/her time reading them when there were no customers; and to have the physical stamina to spend much of the day standing up. It called for a breed of superbeings, and it is not surprising that there were few who could match up to such standards or even would have done if they had been paid handsomely, which they were not.

In 1970 a Charter Group liaison sub-committee researched into the actual salary structure and commented that their findings made one of the grimmest and most depressing documents ever to emanate from B.A. headquarters. Only 2 per cent of managers were likely to earn more than £2,500 a year; only 7½ per cent more than £2,000. Of 94 cases sampled, 6 managers earned £800 or less, 34 between £1,200 and £1,600, and 22 between £1,600 and £2,000. Only one exceeded £3,000. For assistants it was even worse, new entrants outside the London area being unlikely to earn more than £11 per week before they were twenty and, unless they rose to middle or top management, only a few pounds more at twenty-five. Senior assistants and middle management had almost as much chance of earning less than £800 at the age of twenty-five as of earning more. Of 129 booksellers sampled in all parts of the country, only twenty-five offered £14 per week and above to a twenty-one-year-old assistant—ten of these were in London. These were the actual rates; the official scale laid down by the Wages Council in March 1970, *as a proposal*, provided £10 3s. (£10·15) per week minimum for a female assistant aged twenty-two or over in the London area and £12 15s. (£12·75) for a male. The rates were even lower in the provinces. The minimum for a London manageress was £12 12s. 6d. (£12·62½), for a manager, £14 9s. 6d. (£14·47½).

So there was no improvement in real terms on what the situation had been in 1950, when Thomas Joy had quoted the minimum wage of £4 5s. (£4·25) for a woman assistant of twenty-four in the London suburbs as disgraceful. At that time one suburban bookseller said that he personally could not afford to pay more.

It was scarcely to be wondered that young men and women of ability did not remain in bookselling in any great number, and either left to take up some completely different occupation or became publishers' representatives, in which capacity they could, and did, earn three or four times what they had been paid as booksellers. Reps sometimes earned more than the sales managers who were their immediate superiors, and also enjoyed greater security of employment. The rep. who carried out his task faithfully, subscribed new books, took repeat orders and delivered stock at moments of crisis (which were frequent) was able to justify his salary more easily than a sales executive who was often, in practice, little more than an office clerk dealing with queries from booksellers. Many were the instances of sales managers and their assistants receiving the chop because a publisher's expected swans for the season turned out to be geese. Despite this, some reps pined to get off the road and become sales managers, and a number of those who achieved the enhanced status bitterly regretted it later. (It is worth emphasizing that sometimes the rep. could not afford to go inside behind a desk. Reps paid on commission could earn in excess of £4,000 a year by 1970, although these were the exceptions.)

Inside publishing houses the white-collar workers were poorly rewarded in comparison with their fellows in commerce and the civil service. Staff accepted this as a condition of being employed in something more interesting than routine office work, but the door was wide open for trade union activity. In 1970, Clive Jenkins, general secretary of A.S.T.M.S. (Association of Scientific, Technical and Management Staffs), began to enrol members in his publishing section, and publishers were faced with having to reckon with one of the most vocal and successful bargainers in twentieth-century trade-union history.

Although the financial situation was not grim for many on both sides

of the trade, for most booksellers relatively high salaries—£4,000 a year
and above—came only when they achieved ownership of the businesses
in which they worked, or if they were appointed to the managing
directorships of one of the comparatively few large companies. Top
executives in publishing were more numerous, and ranked amongst
that 2 per cent of the population which lived far above the breadline.
Actual salaries were rarely revealed, and certainly not for publication,
but it was safe to assume that the nation's needy were not to be found in
the dining-rooms of the Garrick and the Savile, both of which clubs had
a high proportion of publisher members. The chairmen and managing
directors of some of the larger groups had chauffeur-driven Rolls-Royces
on their companies, and were able to claim liberal expenses for their
overseas tours, in addition to salaries in the £8,000–£11,000 bracket.
Publishing and bookselling, like so many occupations, were fine for those
who reached the top, but the disparity between those whose ability (or
in some cases luck) made them leaders and those in middle management
and below was too wide for a healthy society.

For all the bickering about terms and the hardships resulting from
low wages, the book trade remained an essentially friendly one, and this
was often the deciding factor for those who remained in it. It was a
close community in which there was an air of everyone knowing everyone else, but it was not exclusive. Newcomers were welcomed and
helped and it was a characteristic of those involved that they were willing to reveal figures about their trading and turnover, either to illustrate
their poverty or prosperity, or in order to help a better economic
understanding of what they were doing. Conference apart, there was no
lack of opportunity for publishers and booksellers to meet. At official
level there were the various committees and sub-committees of the trade
associations, and those who valued these organizations and who wanted
to take office in them spent many hours in Buckingham Palace Gardens
or Bedford Square discussing the problems of the trade.

At the B.A. Bruce Hepburn continued as general secretary until 1954,
and then joined Penguin's as sales manager. He was succeeded by
G. R. Davies, a librarian from Cambridge, who, like his predecessor
quickly established numerous friendships on both sides of the trade.
Gerry Davies eventually became director of the association, and Mary
Curtis, who had joined the staff in 1960 as his personal assistant was
renamed secretary. In effect she became acting director during Davies's
illness in 1965 and after his resignation the following year, when he
became managing director of the Bowker Company of New York's
British subsidiary. (He returned as director of the B.A. in 1970.) There
was never anything but respect and affection for these officials of the
B.A., but there were those who felt that the secretariat had grown too
large, so that when Davies's successors had come and gone in a short

while, some booksellers thought that the position should go to Mary Curtis. Council opposed this, on the grounds that a woman would not be able to stand up to ministers of education as a man might, and that in case the Net Book Agreement had to be defended again a lawyer was essential. So John Newton, from the Photographic Suppliers Association, who had the legal qualifications, was appointed, only to resign three years later. By that time the Registrar of Restrictive Practices had announced that the Net Book Agreement had been reprieved once again, and that there would be no further hearing. It is perhaps relevant to observe that not the least formidable member of the Wilson government was Mrs Barbara Castle, which did not exactly support the official line on the necessity for a male director.

At the P.A. Frank Sanders, who had been an outstanding secretary for twenty-five years, resigned in 1958 to become managing director of the Book Centre. He was succeeded by R. E. Barker, who had been deputy secretary for many years but had left Bedford Square in 1956 to join Curtis Brown. Ron Barker was also an author of novels and detective stories, and as export secretary in the years immediately following the war he had alerted publishers to the growing importance of the Frankfurt Book Fair. Soon after his appointment as secretary, R. C. Gowers became assistant secretary; the third member of the triumvirate, which was to survive for many years, was Peter Phelan. It is doubtful if any association anywhere ever had three better respected and liked senior officials.

It fell to Gerry Davies and Ron Barker to guide their respective associations through the defence of the Net Book Agreement, which was successfully conducted at a cost exceeding £40,000, during a hearing lasting twenty-four days during June and July 1962. The two associations had collected evidence since 1948 to prove that the Net Book Agreement did not work against the public interest. The Restrictive Practices Court had been set up because politicians thought that there were too many trade agreements to fix prices thus disallowing fair competition, and that if, for example, there was a company willing to manufacture electric light bulbs to be retailed at 1s. (5p) it was not right for those who monopolized the market to agree to sell them at 1s. 6d. (7½p). In the Net Book Agreement case the judgment stated that 'no two literary works are the same or alike in the way in which, or the extent to which two oranges or two eggs may be said to be', and expressed the belief that if the agreement were not upheld the number of stock-holding bookshops in the country would be reduced, and the extent of stock held by those who survived would present less variety; that fewer titles would be published and that the retail prices of books would go up. In the summing up Mr Justice Buckley, referring to trade terms, stated that they were not uniform or immutable, that net profits earned by booksellers were modest compared with other branches of commerce and that 'in the competitive state of the book trade publishers have so far been able to resist pressure by booksellers for higher rates of discount'.

When, after four months of waiting, this judgment was announced the book trade heaved a sigh of relief and booksellers began demanding higher discounts, and reducing the extent of their stock in the interests of turning it over more quickly. They also soon began to experience lower net profits, whilst publishers went on producing more and more books and prices reached a level unthought of ten years before. There were dissenters from the accepted view of the value of the N.B.A., but some doubters came to accept it as security against the type of anarchy which, in 1970, reigned in the wine and spirits trade where undercutting was so fierce that off-licences closed down in considerable numbers.

Philip Andrews was the P.A.'s economic adviser in the defence, assisted by Miss Elizabeth Brunner. The legal team was led by Arthur Bagnall, Q.C., supported by D. A. Grant, Q.C., and Jeremy Lever, all instructed by Michael Rubinstein, of Rubinstein, Nash & Co., solicitors specializing in book trade and literary matters. The witnesses, in the order in which they gave evidence, were Peter du Sautoy (Faber), Ian Parsons (Chatto & Windus), R. W. David (Cambridge University Press), Miss Irene Babbidge (Pelham Bookshop, Havant), Richard Blackwell, J. E. M. Hoare (London and ex-Canadian bookseller, and also ex-publisher), I. P. M. Chambers (W. J. Bryce, Ltd), Norman Tomlinson (Gillingham Public Library), Clifford Currie (then Librarian at the Imperial College of Technology), H. G. T. Christopher (Librarian to Penge Urban District Council), F. T. Bell (Holt Jackson, Library Suppliers), F. D. Sanders, W. Balleny (Chalmers Wade, accountants), John Attenborough (Hodder & Stoughton) and Philip Andrews. The entire proceedings and the historical background were published by Macmillan in *Books are Different*, a vast volume edited by R. E. Barker and G. R. Davies.

The Agreement defended was an amended one drawn up and approved on January 17th, 1957, which allowed for individual publishers taking action against breaches concerned with their own books, thus making an important legal distinction between corporate action by all members of the P.A., and that of one publisher against one bookseller.

W. Balleny, the P.A. auditor mentioned above, was a principal partner in a large firm of City accountants who, in a report on the book trade, published in 1953, said that a stage might already have been reached when £50,000 capital would not be enough initial finance for a publishing firm, and that a turnover of £100,000 would not necessarily produce a reasonable profit.

To return to the opportunities which booksellers and publishers had for getting to know each other outside their shops, here is the place to record the continued existence of the Society of Bookmen, which gave a public lunch to Stanley Unwin, to celebrate his eightieth birthday in January 1965, and entertained a visiting delegation of overseas booksellers at the Banqueting House, Whitehall, in the same year, as well as holding its usual dinners. At one of its meetings in 1961 proposals were made for Charter Bookselling, and in 1959 Robert Lusty made a suggestion for sampling the reading habits of Londoners which was taken up by the Society of Young Publishers the following year. The Whitefriars Club, with its curious and wordy ritual welcome which was a torment to each chairman who had to recite it, went on meeting at the Cock Tavern, Fleet Street; the Paternosters, a lunchtime club with a large membership, attracted national figures to address it at the Connaught Rooms; the Publishers' Publicity Circle also met at lunchtime, thus effectively keeping numerous publishers and booksellers away from their work for several hours every month; and there were the Society of Young Publishers who among other activities in 1964 hired a bus and took it to the bookless areas of Luton and elsewhere with discouraging results; the Galley Club, like the Double Crown, mostly concerned with printing and production; and the B.P.R.A., whose annual guest night at the Connaught Rooms each September was a curious mixture of formality and schoolboy prankishness. The toasts, which were numerous at this event, were called out at intervals during the dinner — 'Mr President, My Lord, gentlemen, your president will now take wine with all past presidents', etc., interrupting conversation and making for rude comment. After dinner there would be speeches, often of great tedium, but occasionally of sparkling brilliance, when the speaker luckily happened to get the measure of his difficult audience, and after them, a cabaret, almost always of the standard holidaymakers at British seaside resorts would expect to find at the end of the pier. The ladies were catered for at an evening dress dinner-dance held in January.

There were other organizations which led to publishers and booksellers meeting on neutral ground. The National Book League Council and Executive Committee had representatives from the P.A. and B.A., whose members largely financed it, but not adequately — the League was in financial difficulties during most of this period. (The deficit in 1965–6 was £17,116.) The first two presidents were John Masefield and Sir Norman (later Lord) Birkett. J. E. (Jack) Morpurgo became director in 1954, taking over from Herbert Howarth who in his turn had succeeded John Hadfield. Morpurgo was compelled to spend too much time worrying about raising money, but despite this he travelled all over the world spreading the gospel of British books, whilst the League's exhibitions, latterly under the control of Clifford Simmons (formerly of Allan Wingate), travelled even more widely, both in the U.K. and

overseas. The League did much undercover work, persuading local educational authorities of the necessity to provide more money for books.
Most of what was done was insufficiently known outside Albemarle
Street, however, and there were many who regarded the N.B.L. as a
waste of time and money. Public relations were never good because no
one had time to attend to them. Morpurgo, Simmons, Mrs Joy Heiseler
and others worked long hours for comparatively low rewards, against a
background of increasing insolvency.

In 1969 Morpurgo resigned, and resumed his academic and literary
career. Clifford Simmons was acting director for nearly a year and then,
Martyn Goff, a Banstead bookseller, was appointed, to the apparently
unqualified delight of the entire trade. By then the financial position
seemed to be easing, and from the first few months of renewed activity
it seemed that the League would extend its reputation and influence
during the Goff regime. 1971 saw a splendid celebration of books in
the Bedford Square Book Bang, an open-air and under-canvas exhibition in the centre of London to which were attracted many, old and
young, who had never before been exposed so positively to books. But a
year later, although continuing its inestimable good work with exhibitions and poetry readings, the League still had severe monetary worries
which could easily have been solved by more support from publishers
and booksellers.

The Arts Council of Great Britain had set up a literature panel in
1965 on which distinguished authors served, alongside a sprinkling of
publishers and a bookseller. It was one of the many bodies, among
them the Society of Authors, which championed the cause of a Public
Lending Right to provide authors with a royalty on public library
issues of their works. Authors had clamoured for this, as of right, from
1951 onwards when John Brophy put forward proposals which subsequently became known as the 'Brophy Penny'. A. P. Herbert, a lifelong
fighter for seemingly lost causes, became a prominent crusader. The
principal opposition argument was that authors were fortunate in
having such a large public library system to buy so many copies of their
books. It was well known that many novels, especially, would never
have been published had the publisher not had a reasonable expectation
of recouping a large slice of his outlay from public library sales. And
there was no evidence that the public, even had it been deprived of its
so-called 'free libraries', would have besieged the bookshops to buy all
the books they couldn't borrow. The arguments for P.L.R. are summed
up in a symposium of that title published by André Deutsch in 1970.

Other trade events during this period were the *Sunday Times* Book
Exhibitions, discontinued in the 1950s; the Nottingham Book Festival
of autumn 1954, organized by Brian Batsford for the Booksellers'
Association with the active assistance of Tony Godwin and others; the

World Book Fair at Earls Court in 1964; and the Children's Book Show, an annual event in London from 1957 onwards, attended in 1969 by 22,000 adults and children. The Nottingham Festival was an experiment in cooperative promotion. It lasted for three months, which many thought too long, but everyone, both publishers and booksellers, agreed that they had learned much from the activities sponsored at the festival which, like all joint book trade efforts, was supported by some and carped at by others.

The World Book Fair came in for even more adverse criticism, some of it justified. Held in the bleak, concrete exhibition stadium at Earls Court, it is doubtful if it attracted many who were not already accustomed to buy or borrow books. However, 80,000 people attended it, and Philip Unwin, who was chairman of the organizing committee, believed it had potential as a regular event. In his autobiography he referred to 'certain complexities of trade politics' which prevented this. The Children's Book Show, after initial bursts of opposition from booksellers who thought, once again, that the bread was being taken from their mouths, was more popular with the trade. After some skirmishes it was allowed that books should be sold at the exhibition, the idea of refusing money from a would-be purchaser and directing him/her instead to the nearest bookshop being clearly too silly even for a committee to uphold.

The National Book Sale, mentioned earlier, became an annual event from 1955. It lasted for some ten days in the early part of the year, during which the shops of participating booksellers looked as though they had been the object of large-scale looting. Book purchasers who behaved with reasonable care when browsing or buying during the rest of the year became the victims of jumble-sale fever as soon as the words National Book Sale appeared, and indeed jumble many of the 'bargains' were, consisting mostly of publishers' unsold stock, which would otherwise have been remaindered. The rules of the sale stated that the books reduced had to be offered at their original price when normal trading was resumed, which made life confusing for both booksellers and customers. However, for better or worse a lot of previously slow-moving stock was disposed of during National Book Sale weeks and no one who didn't wish to was forced to participate, except perhaps some chain-store managers.

The main effect of National Library Week, the first of which was held in 1966, was to make for more friendly relations between booksellers and librarians (and publishers, too, but they didn't officially then have a relationship with librarians). As public servants, public librarians had tended to remain somewhat aloof from the social activities of the book trade, and to behave with formality even when attending conferences and receptions. N.L.W., with its local committees composed of authors, publishers, booksellers, librarians and literary critics, broke many barriers and revealed librarians to the book trade as human beings, who after all had Christian names. (Perhaps the reverse process also worked; one hopes so.) It is not certain that much else was achieved, although the event was repeated in 1968 and 1969. Plans, as at present formulated, are to transform it, under the auspices of the N.B.L., into National Book Week, the first of which took place in November 1972.

The Library Association was fairly undemanding of publishers during this time, although there were occasional rumblings about the need for larger discounts. One Islington councillor, Mrs Sandra Bron, who was also editorial director of Vision Press, a small publishing house, tried to rally support for an overall buying authority within the Greater London Council to buy direct from publishers at the same discount received by booksellers. She obtained little support from librarians and less from publishers, but it is possible that in the foreseeable future the various large local authorities, with their enormous buying power, will force publishers to sell to them direct, or at least to insist on a larger discount through booksellers (who will then need a larger discount from publishers). Various educational authorities had already been successful in this, the precedent having been set way back at the beginning of the century when the London School Board, subsequently the L.C.C., was permitted to make its purchases direct at trade prices.

It was proper that booksellers and publishers should be as much concerned as librarians were with N.L.W. because it was really an attempt to promote the sale as much as the lending of books. Another promotional body with the same object as the N.B.L. was the Book Development Council, sponsored by the P.A. and founded in 1965. Its object was to foster the spread of British books overseas in recognition of the fact that books carried a knowledge and understanding of British achievements and values, and could, therefore, both promote all aspects of the export drive and enhance the country's standing overseas. The fourteen founder publishing houses provided the original finance and some sixty others then came in as member firms. A £10,000 non-recurrent grant was received from the Foreign Office in 1966, and there were others from the Board of Trade, diminishing over three years from £20,000 to £10,000. Philip Harris was director general until February 1970, when the P.A. took over the Council, appointing Reg Gowers in his place. The latter was seconded to Gordon & Gotch in 1972, and was succeeded by Martin Ballard, a former teacher who had been director of the Educational Publishers' Council for some three years. The first two chairmen of the B.D.C. were distinguished non-trade figures: Patrick Gordon Walker, foreign secretary from 1964 to 1965, who, on his return to office in the second Wilson administration, handed over to the economist, Sir Eric Roll. The B.D.C., like the British Council, took the initiative in organizing overseas exhibitions of British books, in training booksellers from the developing countries and in holding seminars on publishing techniques.

The head of the books department of the British Council from 1941–63 was John Hampden, a distinguished author who had a long career in publishing behind him. On his retirement John Barnicot and Richard Goffin succeeded him, the latter becoming head of the book exhibitions department, which was detached from the main books department. In 1968 the British Council held 143 exhibitions, and issued five and a half million books from its libraries, to 300,000 members, from a stock of two million volumes. The Council had a long-standing association with Longmans, who distributed their pamphlet series, Writers and their Work, and other, mainly medical, publications. It published *British Book News*, giving regular information about new publications, and liaised with other government departments about the production of low-priced books for foreign markets which were, at last, sanctioned in 1960 as part of aid to underdeveloped countries. Under this scheme more than three million books were sold in the first five years.

The British Council was constantly attacked by the gutter press, and its grant was cut too rigorously by successive governments who didn't appreciate its very real value in promoting the British way of life. Not all bureaucracies are totally bad, and the British Council deserved more support than it got both officially and from Fleet Street. Like the B.D.C., it organized courses and regularly brought booksellers from all over the world to London to hear lectures by British publishers and booksellers, and to be conducted around printing works and publishing offices and warehouses. After John Hampden's retirement the courses were organized by Una Dillon and Frank Sanders, who were supposed, by then, to be retired themselves.

Apart from the Frankfurt Book Fair there were annual pilgrimages by publishers of juveniles to the Bologna Children's Book Fair, and by 1970 some interest was beginning to be shown in the Nice Book Festival, possibly not so much because anyone, except the French, thought it likely to prove as important as Frankfurt, but because the Riviera in May was more attractive than the Rhine in the autumn. There were also junketings in many other parts of the world—Toronto and Tokyo, for example—but Frankfurt remained the largest annual attraction and at the twentieth fair in 1968 three thousand publishers from over fifty countries exhibited in two vast halls, in neither of which could one see from end to end. Stands of varying size—the British Council's, as always, the largest of all—lined each and every aisle, with oases at certain points where vastly expensive drinks and food could be bought and consumed out of cardboard and plastic containers. Wherever one looked there were more books and more publishers, and although it was possible to talk to the publishers, the last thing one could possibly concentrate on doing at that mammoth feast of the written word was to actually open a book and read it. At the first fair in 1949 205 publishers were represented; five years later there were 1,000. Not all British publishers exhibited, Gollancz falling out early and allowing W. H. Smith to represent him, as they did many others, on their stand. But each year the number of exhibitors grew. There were too few hotel rooms in Frankfurt, and there were always stories of leading publishers who had had to sleep in baths or passages, or spend whole nights in armchairs. (Some spent all night talking anyhow, and George Weidenfeld even invited those who wished to do deals with him to breakfast.)

In the 'sixties the fair became a focal point for undergraduate unrest, and in 1968 it had to be closed one afternoon when some protestors were arrested and brutally treated by the German police. Several British stands closed down in protest, and there seemed at one stage a real risk of the whole fair being abruptly terminated. It was not an easy task to run it smoothly, and Dr Sigfred Taubert, a bibliophile who directed the fair so efficiently, had the sympathy of most of those who attended, which always included a few booksellers who had managed to convince themselves that it was in the interests of their foreign books department to be there. Printers and journalists were to be found there also, but very few authors. It was not really a literary occasion.

At home publishers had to contend with the continued irritation of obscure laws on obscene libel. In the early 'fifties there were a number of prosecutions, and in 1954 Fredric Warburg elected for trial by jury when accused for publishing *The Philanderer* by Stanley Kauffman. He was found not guilty, and in the summing-up Mr Justice Stable uttered these significant words: 'Are we to take our literary standards as being the level of something that is suitable for the decently brought-up young female aged fourteen? Or do we even go further back than that and are we to be reduced to the sort of books that one reads as a child in the nursery? The answer to that is: of course not. A mass of literature, great literature, from many angles, is wholly unsuitable for reading by the adolescent, but that does not mean that the publisher is guilty of a criminal offence for making those works available to the general public.'

Wise words, and to printers, publishers, booksellers and authors, all of whom were liable to prosecution, it seemed possible that the law had at last acquired some common sense. Unfortunately Mr Justice Stable's strictures did not bind other learned judges. Mrs Webb, Hutchinson & Co., of which she was chairman, and the printer of *September in Quinze*, by Vivian Connell, were all heavily fined when found guilty of publishing an obscene work. A. S. Frere of Heinemann was more fortunate over Walter Baxter's *The Image and the Search*, although he had to endure three trials before the Recorder of London required a jury to return a verdict of not guilty because of insufficient evidence. At the two previous trials the jury had not agreed.

But the most celebrated case of all occurred when Allen Lane announced his intention, in 1960, of publishing the unexpurgated text of D. H. Lawrence's *Lady Chatterley's Lover* in Penguin at 3s. 6d. (17½p). The book was set up and proofs sent out to some booksellers, which was not Penguin's usual practice, and in August the police demanded a copy and decided to prosecute. Penguin's called thirty-five witnesses, including many distinguished authors and critics, who expressed their opinion that Lawrence was a great writer and that no passage in the book would tend to deprave or corrupt anyone. The case received wide publicity, and the jury found that the book was not obscene. Two hundred thousand copies were awaiting the decision in Penguin's warehouse, and as it became apparent that there were people willing to buy this book who had never bought any printed literature except a newspaper before in their whole lives, a further 300,000 were ordered three days after the verdict. Lorries stopped outside bookshops with their engines throbbing as rough-handed drivers strode inside to buy *Lady C.* without even having to say what it was they wanted. There never can have been so many disappointed readers, because *Lady Chatterley* was far from easy for those who did not read regularly and was not, despite what the distinguished witnesses had said at the trial, anywhere near being Lawrence's best work.

The acquittal brought another glow of optimism to the trade. The obscene libel nonsense really did seem to be over at last. The trade turned, once again, to Allen Lane with gratitude, and every novelist who wished to be with it began to sprinkle the word 'fuck' liberally about his typescript. But it was not all over at all, because British justice does not work that way—and anyhow, no allowance had been made for what publishers would dare to offer in an increasingly permissive society. So from time to time more prosecutions took place, inevitably with the result that a book for which there had been little demand before someone screamed that it should be banned was turned into a bestseller. Those who prosecuted seemed incapable of learning to ignore that which they regarded as so harmful. At the same time there was no evidence of a diminishing taste for what the public, despite all the acquittals, persisted in thinking of as desirable pornography. If they hadn't thought of it as obscene, where would have been the fun in reading it? It was always overlooked that the taste for what was called obscene or pornographic was a normal, even a healthy one; certainly a very common one, although Pamela Hansford Johnson put a strong humanist claim for considering an opposite opinion in her compassion-ately written *On Iniquity* (Macmillan, 1967).

Book clubs can scarcely have been said to prosper during the greater part of this period, but most of them at least survived. There were no longer cries about unfair competition from booksellers, who gradually ceased to deal in subscriptions for them and so never handled book club editions except at secondhand. The advent of simultaneous book club publication (another American import) in 1968 produced some alarm from the B.A. at first, but once again no harm was done. Bookshop trade was also unaffected by the direct selling of such sponsored titles as the Reader's Digest *Book of Birds* and the A.A. *Treasures of Britain,* which were offered to huge membership lists at a reduced price, but enjoyed large and continuing sales through the shops when appearing on the Collins list. *The Good Food Guide* was an even more striking example; started in 1949 by Raymond Postgate with a band of voluntary helpers, it was subsequently distributed by Cassell and then by Hodder for the Consumers' Association, who offered it at about 20 per cent reduction to the armies of people who sent in reports about hotels and restaurants. Each issue became a larger seller for publisher and booksellers.

All the matters discussed in this section, and many others, were fully reported and commented upon in *The Bookseller*, which established itself as the leading trade journal, earning the right to its sub-title, *The Organ of the Book Trade*. There were others: the *Publishers' Circular*, which became the monthly *British Books*; the official B.A. magazine *Bookshop*; an independent journal called *The Publisher*; and W. H. Smith's *Trade News*, in which a Fleet Street journalist called 'Whitefriar' (later revealed to be Eric Hiscock of the *Evening Standard*) wrote a column of gossip and speculation which was widely read and quoted in publishers' advertising. *Trade News* was edited by Charles Down, who succeeded John Burt in the late 1950s. It was, however, to *The Bookseller* that all publishers, booksellers, librarians, printers, literary journalists and others interested had to turn each week to know what was going on. It was the one publication they could not afford to overlook, and as this became more evident so the amount of advertising in it increased, and its circulation grew to 14,550 per issue.

During the whole of this period the editor was Edmond Segrave, who died in 1971. He had been in charge of the Whitaker magazine since 1933, when he was sacked from Heinemann's for reasons he never dis-covered (his salary there had once been doubled on the spot because he perspicaciously noticed that Soames Forsyte's child, Fleur, had suddenly changed sex at the start of Galsworthy's latest instalment of the saga). Segrave built up the circulation of *The Bookseller* by opening its columns to trade controversy and encouraging everyone in the trade to send in items of news (and always news rather than gossip). He started features, invariably with a pseudonymous byline, many of which he wrote himself, but the hands of Gerry Davies, Colin Eccleshare of C.U.P., Hubert Wilson and others were also there. These became regular columns of comment on what had been reviewed in the papers the previous week ('Henry Puffmore'), the weekly trials of a bookseller (The Brightfount Diaries), and so forth. In 1945 Philothea Thompson joined the staff and became assistant editor, and there was an occasional other hand; but between the two of them, Segrave and Miss Thompson put the paper to bed each week with untiring devotion to detail. On press night—and it was night because the editor and his assistant found it conducive to work away from the publishing office and the phone—they would be at the printer's correcting proofs and filling-up columns with an absolute professionalism which was apparent in each and every issue; it was rare to find a literal in *The Bookseller*.

Edmond Segrave was a short man of Anglo-Irish Roman Catholic stock, who had been intended for the priesthood. He was a perfectionist, who would spend hours worrying a sentence into shape. If he received a letter for publication whose sense struck him as obscure, or the phrasing of which seemed to him ugly, he would often phone the writer and tell him how he proposed to alter it; in his more arrogant moods he would just alter it! He seldom wrote letters, or replied to those he received, except for his annual stylized note to selected booksellers asking them to comment on aspects of Christmas trading. He never acknowledged articles or poems sent in for publication, but if he published them, prompt payment followed. If he rejected them they were not returned to their authors, but joined the mass of printed matter which accumulated over the years in his room on the second floor of 13 Bedford Square, an office which resembled nothing so much as a second-hand bookshop. Around three sides of his desk were stacked, two or three deep, and up to its top, books which had been sent to him over the years. On three sides of the room there were shelves similarly crammed, with bound-up runs of *The Bookseller*, in no particular order, lying across them. It was difficult to reach these shelves because against their lower parts were more books, two and three and even four deep. This was his way, and as John Hadfield, who edited the magazine at one stage when Segrave was on holiday, recorded in his long obituary in *The Bookseller*, he always kept a small area of his desktop clear for work on the current number. He had many close friends and also a number of enemies whom he cherished almost as much. He didn't suffer fools at all, let alone gladly, and did not go out of his way to be seen at this function or that. As the whim took him he went to some trade parties and dinners, but stayed away from most. If he wanted to talk to you he would decide when and where, and when he talked he could be witty, indiscreet and fascinating because he probably knew more about the contemporary book trade than anyone else. Philothea Thompson, deservedly, succeeded him.

At the end of each year *The Bookseller* published a résumé of the events of the previous twelve months which was an invaluable guide to the historian. It would include the twice yearly honours list, which did not neglect literature and the book trade. O.B.E.s, C.B.E.s, M.B.E.s and other chivalric emblems of an empire which no longer existed were liberally sprayed around. Knighthoods were harder to come by, but it seemed that anyone who hungered sufficiently after one eventually got it. Stanley Unwin, no doubt to illustrate that he was more equal than others, was awarded two, by some quirk of the system beyond my comprehension. Noble lords were thin on the ground, but as 'Sirs' became two a decimal penny no doubt the day of the publisher life peer was not far off. Curiously the one publisher who could have sat in the upper house, Harold Macmillan, preferred to remain 'Mister', and sat at home plodding away at his apparently interminable memoirs. (Lord Longford took his ermine before he became a publisher.)

Also reported were the awards for the various literary prizes, the most rewarding of which, in financial terms, was the Booker, started in 1968. The winner received £5,000 in cash and a blaze of publicity, which led to the sale of paperback rights if they had not already been taken. Older prizes, such as the Somerset Maugham, the James Tait Black, the Duff Cooper and the John Llewelyn Rhys, earned their winners less, and some of them brought no more than prestige amongst a coterie of literary and book trade folk.

During these twenty years publishers' output grew, faltering only in the year of a printers' strike, when one large book printer, at least, had record net profits because for several weeks he had no wages bill, and for several months after the resumption of work his machines were never idle, catching up on the backlog. Details of titles produced, and of home and export turnover, together with the rolls of those who were presidents of the P.A. and B.A. will be found in the appendix. In the next two sections, concerning individual publishers and booksellers, the trends noted in this long chapter will be underlined, and some others, not already introduced, noted.

2

The University Presses

Oxford University Press; Cambridge University Press; Manchester, Liverpool, Leicester, Edinburgh, Bradford university presses; Athlone Press; Irish Universities Press; Scottish Academies Press; Sussex University Press; American university presses.

Humphrey Milford retired as publisher to the Oxford University Press in 1945 and was succeeded by Geoffrey Cumberlege, who had been manager of the Bombay and New York branches during his thirty-two years of service. When Cumberlege retired in 1956, John G. Brown, who started with the Press in 1937, had also worked in the Bombay branch, and had been sales manager since 1949, took over. At the Clarendon Press A. L. P. Norrington was succeeded as Secretary to the Delegates, in 1954, by Colin Roberts. Norrington then became president of Trinity College and gave his name to the magnificent extension to Blackwell's bookshop which will be referred to later.

The size and authority of Oxford publishing expanded apace during this time, and by 1970 equally responsible to the Secretary of the Delegates were the Printer, the Controller of the Wolvercote Paper Mill, the publisher to the Clarendon Press, the Publisher to O.U.P., London, and the president of O.U.P., New York. Below them were the heads of the cartographic and music departments, and the twenty managers of the overseas branches—seven in Africa, ten in Asia and one each in Australia, New Zealand and Canada. It was a formidable organization, publishing about 850 new titles each year and handling 600–700 titles originated by other university presses. Seventeen thousand titles were listed in the 1970 catalogue, and at the Neasden warehouse, which was extended in 1961, there were usually three million volumes in stock. The annual turnover exceeded £13 million, and no wonder the Hebdomadal Council of the university thought it necessary in 1967 to investigate the entire organization. Amongst those appointed to a committee under the chairmanship of Sir Humphrey Walcock (professor of Law at Oxford), was R. J. L. Kingsford, a former Secretary to the Syndics of Cambridge Press. When it reported in 1970, the committee suggested, in its thirty-eight recommendations, that senior executives of the Press should receive salaries comparable to those paid by other publishers rather than remuneration on a par with university appointments.

Oxford books remained important to all stockholding booksellers, whose basic lines were increased by the publication of the *Oxford Junior Encyclopaedia* in thirteen volumes, by various other reference works for adults and children and by a splendid juvenile list headed by Eleanor Farjeon, Rosemary Sutcliffe, Edward Ardizzone, Ronald Welch, Edward Blishen, Brian Wildsmith and others. In addition to the constant hidden bestsellers such as the Bible, the dictionaries and the companions to literature, theatre, art and music, there were also popular scholarly works such as A.J.P. Taylor's *English History*, 1914-45, an additional volume in the Oxford History of England, which first appeared in 1965. It was an instant success, Taylor being a well-known television celebrity, and a reviewer who expressed inflammatory opinions in a rollicking prose style, as well as being an impeccable scholar. Such was the demand for it that the tyranny of the computer was, for once, overridden: when the first repeat orders were placed the trade was informed that the several thousand copies in the warehouse could not be released until it was their turn to trundle into the pipeline—delay of up to seven days. Fortunately, common-sense prevailed and the computer was programmed to release Taylor against orders for that book only. For this rationalization, which was, for once, actually rational, the trade had to thank A.T.G. (Tony) Pocock, his then assistant, Michael Hosking and the manager at Neasden, J. Y. Huws-Davies, three men who had sufficient personality to control the machine for the benefit of the consumers. Tony Pocock, as sales manager, made many friends amongst book-sellers all over the world, and held down a crucial position with good humour and intense hard work.

His sales force also acted for other publishers in parts of Africa and Asia, and, despite its size, the O.U.P. organization kept a personal contact with its customers, large and small, at home and overseas. It often handled books which many an ordinary, non-academic publisher would have been pleased to promote—the plays of Christopher Fry, for example, and the three-volume biography of Trotsky by Isaac Deutscher. But the largest bestseller of all was the new translation of the Bible. The New Testament, published jointly with Cambridge, appeared in 1961, and the Old, under the same sponsorship, in 1970. (It should be noted that Eyre & Spottiswoode had to be restrained by court order from printing it as well.) Few books have received better promotion than the New English Bible, and six million copies of the New Testament had been sold by 1966. The publicity was brilliantly handled by John White, a charming and scholarly man, who was a devoted servant of O.U.P. until his death in 1968. By then Amen House, in Warwick Square, with its section of preserved Roman Wall in the deep basement, had been vacated to allow for the extension of the Central Criminal Court. O.U.P. moved to Ely House in Dover Street, Mayfair, where offices were taken in a fine eighteenth-century mansion which had once been the town house of the Bishops of Ely. Amongst the editors during this period was Derek Hudson, author of many biographies, and editor of the *Periodical*, the occasional O.U.P. publication which printed extracts from forthcoming books, and had a circulation of 25,000.

In 1966, O.U.P. employed nearly three thousand people at home and overseas.

That there was no serious rivalry between the two great university presses is illustrated by R. J. L. Kingsford's appointment to the Waldock Committee. He remained as London manager at Bentley House until 1948, when he went to Cambridge to succeed S. C. Roberts as Secretary to the Syndics. Kingsford held that office until 1963, when R. W. David, who had taken over from him in London, followed him to Trumpington Street. At this point Colin Eccleshare, who had become assistant to David in London in 1948, became manager at Bentley House, and Kingsford became free to write his excellent history of the P.A. (In 1964 the latter also became educational advisor to Rupert Hart Davis Ltd.)

Until the 1960s Cambridge University Press issued about 150 books per year, but by 1966 this number had doubled, with the introduction of an extensive paperback list, including The New Shakespeare, begun in 1921 by Sir Arthur Quiller-Couch and J. Dover Wilson. C.U.P. was slower to establish overseas branches than Oxford, but in 1949 the first was opened in New York, under the management of Ronald Mansbridge. Twenty years later an Australian office was established when the former agent's business was acquired. The Cambridge list remained more exclusively academic than Oxford's and did not overlap into children's book publishing, for instance, but development in the 1960s made its paperback imprint, particularly, of increasing importance to booksellers. The maintenance of a trade counter behind Euston Road, and the excellence of its service during the 1960s, gave it the edge on O.U.P. for Bible delivery and, on the purely educational side, the sponsorship of the School Mathematics Project, a new series of textbooks designed to make maths more easily learned and taught, developed its trade enormously. The tradition of fine production was also upheld, and relations with the trade were friendly at every level. Colin Eccleshare was a member of many official P.A. delegations to various parts of the world, and a witty speaker at home trade functions also.

In 1967 the two leading university presses joined with Longmans and Associated Book Publishers to provide a computerized mailing service to teaching and research staff in the U.K. and Ireland in all institutions above secondary level. University Mailing Service Ltd was the inspiration of Michael Hosking who, regrettably, did not remain in the trade.

The activities of the lesser university presses must seem puny by comparison, but that is not to say that they did not also do good work. At Manchester, H. M. McKechnie was succeeded as secretary, in 1949, by T. L. Jones; at Liverpool, in 1954, J. G. O'Kane became his opposite number. Leicester, Edinburgh, Bradford and others also had presses; Birmingham and Hull contented themselves with publications officers. In London, in 1948, the Athlone Press was formed by a resolution of the Senate and named after the chancellor. W. D. Hogarth became secretary to the board of management until his death in the 1960s; subsequently, in 1968, a complete edition of Jeremy Bentham, in thirty-eight volumes, was inaugurated to mark the two-hundredth anniversary of the political philosopher's birth.

In 1967 the Irish University Press was founded to 'publish primarily source material for use in universities and research centres throughout the world'. Two years later a sale of shares to the First National City Bank of New York was announced, but did not take place, and in 1971 a property tycoon, William Stern, took over the company, which printed and bound books on its own industrial estate in Shannon and opened offices in Dublin, London and New York, with plans for others in Rome and Sydney. I.U.P. reprinted the entire Cuala Press list (see p. 350).

The Scottish Academies Press Ltd was formed in 1969 by the Universities of St Andrews and Dundee, in association with Chatto & Windus, whose chairman, Ian Parsons, was a member of the board. From 1971 Chatto also published and distributed for the Sussex University Press.

American University presses tended, for long, to be represented in the U.K. by Oxford or Cambridge, and Harvard continued to be so in 1970, but others opened their own London offices—Yale and Columbia, for example—or joined the American University Publishers Group Ltd (Texas, Washington, Wisconsin, Indiana, Illinois, etc.). Their books were not popularly dispersed amongst U.K. booksellers but they established a selling point for Europe and often used the Book Centre in Neasden for distribution.

3

The Older Independent Publishers

John Murray; Macmillan; William Collins, Sons & Co.; Chatto & Windus; Hogarth Press; Jonathan Cape; Hodder & Stoughton; Brockhampton Press; Wills & Hepworth; B. T. Batsford; Routledge & Kegan Paul; Constable; J. M. Dent & Sons; Sir Isaac Pitman & Sons; George G. Harrap; A. & C. Black; Blackie & Son; Frederick Warne; W. & R. Chambers; Gerald Duckworth; Sidgwick & Jackson; Mills & Boon; Robert Hale; Evans Brothers; George Allen & Unwin; Whitaker; Faber & Faber; Victor Gollancz; Ernest Benn.

In the autumn of 1968 John Murray's, a limited company since 1951, celebrated its double century with a series of four parties at the Albemarle Street house famous for its Byron associations. Sir John Murray V had died the previous year, but had lived to see another generation enter the firm in 1964 when John Grey ('Jock') Murray's son, John, joined after a lengthy apprenticeship in printing, binding and bookselling. In the bicentenary year father and son continued a family tradition which defied any suggestion that genetic strains wear out by the sixth and seventh generation.

'Jock' Murray was ever a complete bookman, living his work as much in his Hampstead house, where authors often stayed, as at his office, at home equally with writers, other publishers and booksellers. So much so that he was as happy to turn delivery boy on receiving, one day in 1956, a message from his local bookseller—'Will you ask Mr Murray to bring in twelve *Nudes* on his way home?'—as he was to be publisher of Sir Kenneth Clark's book of that title. Even allowing for the industry of some nineteenth-century publishers, none worked harder at their calling than Jock Murray. Under the fifth Sir John and himself the company remained relatively small, although publishing many big sellers by Freya Stark, Arthur Grimble, John Betjeman, Philip Magnus, Kenneth Clark, etc. Betjeman's *Collected Poems* (1958) proved the existence of a wide market for light verse; C. Northcote Parkinson's *Law*, and other titles, showed, unusually, that a right-wing satirist could also be amusingly acceptable to men and women of differing views; and Clark's *Civilisation*, issued under a joint imprint with B.B.C. publications, could hardly have failed after a fifty-minute commercial on television once a week for thirteen weeks. Never had a new book received such gratis publicity before, although *The Forsyte Saga* had had twenty-six weeks of similar exposure, for the second time, immediately before it. Clark's personal view of Civilisation was the 'Pelican' of television, a guide for the intelligent layman, and it was the runaway bestseller of Christmas 1969.

Murray's developed their educational list in the 'fifties and 'sixties under Kenneth Pinnock, and became one of the publishers of the Nuffield Mathematics Project. Less characteristically, in 1955 they introduced Françoise Sagan, considered a very daring young French novelist at the time, to Britain.

The *Cornhill* continued to appear under Murray's auspices, although not enjoying the vast circulation it had in had the nineteenth century, because it attracted new authors. The *Quarterly* died with Sir John, but the backlist did not, Conan Doyle, P. C. Wren, Axel Munthe and, of course, the wittiest of architectural commentators, Osbert Lancaster, still contributing to the well-being of the imprint, and of booksellers. Senior non-family directors in addition to Pinnock were Kenneth Foster and Simon Young.

Macmillan's, younger than Murray's, but larger for many years now, grew still more; the family retained control, some giving their working lives to publishing, other dividing their time between Westminster and St Martin's Street. The image became one of keen big business with a strong bias towards educational publishing, on which the firm had built its fortunes in the days of Hall and Knight. The remaining interest in the Macmillan Company of New York was disposed of in the early 1950s, and in the following decade there was much activity in Africa and the East. The Australian Branch at Melbourne became a separate company in 1967, while, despite Harold Macmillan's 'Wind of Change' speech in Cape Town, which scarcely endeared him to those who ruled and maintained apartheid, a new company was formed in South Africa in 1966. Elsewhere on the same continent agreements were made with the new states to sponsor local publishing of school books. Other publishers hotly resented these because they appeared unilaterally to condone the infringement of their copyrights for Macmillan's benefit. Accusations, denials and dignified statements were issued all round and the storm was a long time dying.

At home there was a reconstruction following the retirement of Daniel Macmillan (grandson of the first Daniel) in 1964. He was succeeded by his brother Harold, who had resigned as prime minister the previous year. Harold's son Maurice was also active in the firm when he wasn't in office as a Conservative minister. Non-family senior executives were 'Rache' Lovat Dickson, a director from 1941 to 1964; Thomas Mark, who retired after forty-six years in 1959, although remaining a literary adviser until his death; R. C. Rowland-Clark, on the educational projects front (Macmillan's did not overlook the importance of audio-visual aids and cassettes in teaching and, therefore, school equipment); N. G. Byam Shaw, sales, and later deputy managing director; and F. N. Whitehead, who became managing director in 1965.

The solid Victorian building in St Martin's Street was sold in 1965 and pulled down for redevelopment a year after the warehouse had been moved to Basingstoke. The editorial departments moved to Little Essex Street, Strand, until they too could be housed in Hampshire.

A half-share in Pan Books (Collins had the other) was purchased in 1962; the Cleaver-Hume Press was acquired in 1964, and with it P. J. Edmonds, its managing director, and in 1968 Gill & Macmillan Ltd, of Dublin, was floated to take over the former list of M. H. Gill and to market Macmillan titles in Ireland.

The accountants were powerful in Macmillan's long before they dominated most other firms. Few, if any, booksellers were allowed to exceed the statutory thirty days credit, warehouse space at Basingstoke was costed down to the last square inch and prices increased accordingly if slow-moving stock did not pay its way. This caused comment in the trade press, the not illogical thought being expressed that such stock might pay its way better by being reduced in price and sold. But Macmillan's wouldn't budge; as always they were adamant and dignified about it.

On the general side the list continued to be broadly based, particularly strong in economics, history, poetry and, of course, fiction. The Lewis Eliot novels of C. P. Snow were immensely popular with the public but drew the fire of F. R. Leavis. Sides were taken up and hurtful things said, but Snow completed his series, even calling one later volume *The Corridors of Power*, which readers and reviewers had already identified as the world in which his hero watched the great or would-be so, and listened to their outpourings. Lady Snow, Pamela Hansford Johnson, was also on the Macmillan list, having transferred from Michael Joseph; she was a more creative and amusing novelist, but did not enjoy quite such large sales. Muriel Spark fared better, after a quick rise to fame from the unlikely springboard of winning a Sunday newspaper short story competition, with such engaging titles as *The Ballad of Peckham Rye*, *The Prime of Miss Jean Brodie* and *The Girls of Slender Means*. By 1970 she was one of the handful of gifted novelists whose books actually sold respectable numbers in hardback. Osbert Sitwell's autobiography *Left Hand, Right Hand!* established a fashion for multi-volumed memoirs, his own running to five fascinating tomes in which there was as much biography of others as self-revelation. Not all his imitators were so unegotistical.

The backlist was still worth a fortune. It was augmented by popular works by such writers as Mazo de la Roche (a kind of Canadian log cabin was erected on the grand staircase of St Martin's House when a party was thrown for her in 1961) and Rumer Godden. And, inevitably, Macmillan's introduced a softcover series called Papermacs.

The Collinses also remained active in their family firm, as much after it became a public company in December 1949 as before. Billy Collins succeeded his father, who died in 1945, as chairman, and led the new company with his brother Ian as vice-chairman, his cousin W. Hope as managing director and the forceful Sydney Goldsack, who was also on the board. Goldsack was the first chairman of the National Book League from 1944 to 1945, and was much associated with its work and social activities. He or Billy Collins usually captained the League's cricket XI in an annual fixture, played on the Westminster School ground in Vincent Square, Victoria, against the authors. The 'authors' often included famous test match players who had, in most cases, not actually written the books bearing their names.

Collins's continued in the big time throughout this period with one resounding success after another — *The Wooden Horse* by Eric Williams (nearly half a million sold in hardback); *Rommel*, Desmond Young's biography of the German general (210,000 in hardback); Chester Wilmot's *The Struggle for Europe*; Arthur Bryant's *The Story of England*; Boris Pasternak's *Doctor Zhivago*, a novel in the great Russian tradition chiefly important for what it revealed about its writer after he had lived through thirty years of Soviet rule; Lampedusa's *The Leopard*, another remarkable novel; Teilhard de Chardin's *The Phenomenon of Man* and Joy Adamson's Elsa the lioness saga, starting with *Born Free* of which 170,000 copies were sold in eleven months. The firm seemed capable of finding bestsellers in any category and Sir William Collins (the sword fell on him in 1970) retained a firm belief in the saleability of casebound fiction long after many of his competitors in that field had begun a policy of severe retrenchment. Billy Collins inherited all the family energy and enthusiasm and actively enjoyed the business of publishing, taking each day as it came with a never-lost boyish excitement for launching a new book or series on the market. He revelled in the ever-increasing sales, and despite the largeness of his organization, kept in touch with those he employed and published. His delight in the great project which was Collins was infectious to those who worked beside him and could stand the pace.

There were splendid original series of books such as the New Naturalist Library; the Companion Guides (amongst the most readable guides ever published and yet suitable for field work) and the Fontana paperbacks, which, after a start all too slow for the impatient men of St James' Place, eventually flowered and began to sprout their own sub-series, such as the Modern Masters, thought up by Michael Turnbull, a

New Zealander to whom Billy Collins gave the job of building a list of egg-head paperbacks which would sell. The ordinary Fontanas were a natural home for the ever-popular Agatha Christie and Ngaio Marsh detective stories, and also for the new storytellers, such as Hammond Innes and Alistair MacLean, whom Collins promoted with enormous enthusiasm and success. Innes, MacLean, Christie, *et al.* at one end of the fiction list; Rose Macaulay, Bryher, Simone de Beauvoir, Rosamond Lehmann and other richly gifted women novelists at the other; and Howard Spring somewhere around the middle. No wonder Collins prospered, and became acquisitive.

Geoffrey Bles Ltd was bought in 1953 and Jocelyn Gibb retained as managing director. Bles himself was dead, but Gibb was allowed to control the list until his own retirement nearly twenty years later. Notably successful during this time were the works of C. S. Lewis, both the theological treatises and his children's books, especially the Narnia series.

Harvill Press was the next purchase. This had been started in 1946 by Mrs Manya Harari and Mrs Marjorie Villiers, and they concentrated on introducing European writers to the English market. Mrs Harari, who died in 1969, was Russian-born and it was through her that *Doctor Zhivago* fell into Collins's lap.

Hatchard's in Piccadilly was bought in 1956, thus saving an historic bookshop and preserving an outlet for Collins's and other publishers' books, and Better Books, of Charing Cross Road, was owned for a few years in the 1960s.

There were many deaths and new faces as is inevitable in any large concern, but Collins had more than their fair share of losses during one period of eight years when Sydney Goldsack and Ronald Politzer, most respected of publicity men, and their managing director, W. Hope Collins, all died. Goldsack was succeeded in 1959 by his second-in-command, Ian Chapman, who joined the firm in 1941 and eventually became managing director. No one outside the family had ever climbed so high before. Mark Bonham-Carter was a leading editor (R. T. Smith retired in the 'sixties), and so was Sir William's son-in-law, Philip Ziegler, who was also an excellent historian. Lady Collins edited the religious titles which went into Fontana, which series came under the complete control of her second son, Mark.

The sales force was large and world wide. Collins's travellers expected to be, and were, sent at short notice to new territories thousands of miles away. They were controlled by a brigade of sales managers and field sales managers, who often hunted in packs, with trainee reps tagging along beside them. They were given regular sales drill in London and Glasgow by the chairman, managing director and others; some did not stay with Collins, but I never heard of a publisher interviewing a prospective rep. who didn't hold it to the applicant's credit that he was Collins-trained.

Collins were one of the first to recognize the need for larger discounts and to offer 35 per cent all round on general books, with additional bonuses for Charter and other booksellers. After Goldsack's death (and it must have happened even had he lived) the rather illiberal no-returns policy was abandoned, and, at least for those booksellers who were able to collect from York Way, King's Cross, doing business with Collins was painless and fast. (It was not so good ordering school books from Glasgow.)

In 1969 the 150th anniversary was celebrated in Glasgow Cathedral with a Thanksgiving Service attended by Collins's own industrial chaplain and addressed by William Barclay, one of their theological authors, who referred to the company as benefactors of society and mankind.

The published profits after tax, for 1969, were £963,974. In 1970 turnover rose by a further £1 million to £12,825,000 and profits after tax to £1,836,000. More than sixteen million books were housed in the Glasgow warehouse, opened by another author, Field-Marshal Montgomery, in 1962. And in Jamaica a subsidiary was formed in 1968 to cope with local publishing demands, especially in the educational sphere, without any of the uproar which greeted Macmillan's similar projects the year before.

Chatto & Windus remained firmly undominated by accountants, P.R.O.s or marketing men, its destiny guided masterfully by the senior editorial directors, who were also wise in business. Harold Raymond retired in 1956, the partnership having been converted into a limited company in 1953, leaving Ian Parsons in command, with Norah Smallwood, Piers Raymond and Peter Calvocoressi as his colleagues on the board. The trade responsibilities and management of the Hogarth Press were taken over when John Lehmann left Leonard Woolf, for the second time, to start his own imprint, but the stoical Mr Woolf remained in editorial command of his small and ever distinguished list to the end. The educational company of Christopher's was acquired when Bertram Christian died, and C. Day Lewis became a literary adviser from 1946, later being elected to the board and remaining on it after he became Poet Laureate in 1968. Piers Raymond, who had been responsible for sales, left in 1960 to join Methuen, by which time a senior editor and director Peter Cochrane (whose wife, Louisa, contributed to the children's list as editor and author) had gone into printing with Butler & Tanner. The juvenile list of Oliver & Boyd was purchased in 1968.

The Chatto list remained during the whole of this period a prime example of quality publishing as the art of the possible in terms of over-

all economic viability. Many books, particularly of verse, were published at a loss, but the commercial balance was always held on the
right side, and most Chatto authors felt it an honour to be published
from William IV Street. The list was distinguished, particularly in
fiction, literary criticism and poetry, and there were regular plums:
some, like Richard Hoggart's *The Uses of Literacy* (an historical-
sociological survey which proved to be a seminal work) took a few
months to ripen; others, like Laurie Lee's autobiographical *Cider with
Rosie*, paraded all the signs of bestsellerdom before they were actually
published. When these two, and many others besides, were announced,
the dominance of the editorial directors was evident, Parsons and Mrs
Smallwood sparing no efforts to persuade their sales staff, booksellers
and literary journalists of the importance and saleability of what they
were about to publish. This wholehearted approach made their working
lives exciting for them and for those booksellers who were prepared to
take notice of their hot tips. And they were often right.

Aldous Huxley and William Faulkner continued to publish with
Chatto until their deaths, and Chatto's new novelists included such
prize stock as Iris Murdoch, who got critical acclaim as well as large
sales, and who became ever more fashionable as her books grew
kinkier. On the Hogarth side the same indefatigable promotion was
applied (Leonard Woolf being liked and respected by the Chatto
salesmen) and the books of Laurens Van Der Post, William Sansom
and Woolf himself proved extremely popular. One new work by
Virginia Woolf was a selection made by her husband from her private
diaries. To avoid offending people who were still alive, *A Writer's
Diary* contained only part of the author's comments on being a novelist,
essayist and publisher. No doubt further volumes will eventually
appear.

In Lit. Crit. the Leavis school was well represented, and many of the
titles Chatto published formed the basis of the Penguin Peregrine
series which was launched in the early 'sixties. In the reprint market
Chatto made two other important contributions: the Zodiac Library
of British and American novels (Eliot, Austen, Trollope, Twain, etc.),
handsomely produced editions using typefaces large enough to make
for restful reading of long books; and the Landmark Library, which
reprinted novels, mostly by twentieth-century writers, which had been
allowed to go out of print although there was still a demand for them.
But Ian Parsons, who took a particular interest in these two series,
kept poetry as his first love. He published many new poets and produced
his own excellent anthology of First World War verse — *Men Who March
Away*.

Creative publishing needed its Chattos and needed them of the size
that could compete in the market for books which attracted large

advances. It was good news for British publishing, therefore, when it was announced in 1969 that Cape and Chatto had arranged to merge under a joint holding company while remaining editorially autonomous. Ian Parsons and Norah Smallwood were approaching retirement, and the merger seemed to allow for the continued independence of each house and to diminish the possibility of American takeover. So it is logical to consider Jonathan Cape Ltd next before writing about other still-independent imprints which began in the nineteenth century.

Jonathan Cape had always been rather high-handed in his dealings with booksellers. Take it or leave it, was his attitude, and as the bookseller had no alternative but to take it when a title was in demand, since no one else published Cape's books, Jonathan could scarcely fail to be the winner. After the war, however, with Wren Howard's son, Michael, returned from military service, the new generation began knocking at the door. Cape and Wren Howard had tended to secretiveness about their publishing, only the readers and editors, Veronica Wedgwood (also a distinguished historian on the list), Daniel George and William Plomer, having advance knowledge of what was to be in the next autumn and spring lists. This was not so much because the two founders wished to hide what they were doing from inquisitive eyes, as that it did not occur to them to suppose that it was any business of their underlings until the time to sell arrived. And, when that moment came, the booksellers were lucky to have such good books subscribed to them! Michael Howard persuaded Jonathan of the value of regular meetings within the house, and had the support of Norman Askew, his London rep. (later sales manager, then sales director) whose difficult task it was to woo booksellers away from their belief that Cape's terms were stingy. That he succeeded was due to his utter integrity, to both his customers and his company. He never oversold, and took endless trouble to help those who were prepared to promote his books.

There was a marking-time period for Cape's in the 'fifties, after the initial post-war successes when the rich American connections continued to bring top-selling books to Bedford Square—Hemingway's *The Old Man and the Sea*, Irwin Shaw's *The Young Lions* and Herman Wouk's *The 'Caine' Mutiny*, to name but three. Although *The Wooden Horse* was rejected because of a misunderstanding, other war books proved very lucrative (e.g. Popski's *Private Army* and Fitzroy MacLean's *Eastern Approaches*) and Elizabeth Bowen's *The Heat of the Day* was a particularly distinguished English novel, new on the list. But H. E. Bates went to Joseph's and William Golding was turned down. And Cape and Howard were getting old. Jonathan had a stroke, but recovered sufficiently to make further trips to America. He died in 1960, having outlived three wives and borne the disappointment of his son, David, deciding to quit publishing and return to the army. There was not to be a second-generation Cape-Howard partnership, and Michael Howard's active participation did not long outlast his father's death in 1968. Robert Knittel joined the board as an editorial director in 1956 but it was with Tom Maschler's appointment as an editor in 1960 that the renaissance began. Maschler had been with André Deutsch, MacGibbon & Kee and Penguin's (where he had started the New Dramatists series), had been chairman of the Society of Young Publishers, and as editor of the anthology *Declaration* became identified with new philosophies in literature. He had written a book himself with Frederic Raphael (*The S-Man*, by Mark Caine, if you please, S standing for success). A few months after his appointment as a special director he survived an attempted *coup d'état*, when three directors of Michael Joseph, with the backing of Allen Lane, made an offer for Jonathan's shares. The firm's accountant, William Balleny, who was also Cape's executor, strongly advised the Howards to accept. There was, apparently, no room for Maschler in the proposed new set-up, so the offer was refused, and eventually Sidney Bernstein of the Granada cinema and television group bought a minority interest, a few months after another special director, Graham C. Greene, had been appointed. Graham, son of Hugh Carleton Greene, then director-general of the B.B.C., and nephew of the novelist Graham Greene, had been with Secker & Warburg as sales manager.

Under Maschler and Greene, now chairman and managing director, Cape's had had by 1970 nearly a decade of spiralling success, with British and American and German authors particularly, with fiction, history, popular science and philosophy, and with juveniles; also with what might be termed the 'non-book', chief amongst which were the Jackdaw series. These folders, containing facsimiles of documents illustrating a subject (usually historical), sold so well that they warranted the formation of a separate company in 1968. Other 'non-books' included *The Teach Your Baby to Read Kit*, a box of pieces of cardboard with letters and words printed on them, designed as visual aids. Despite these symbols of a new approach to literature, Cape's remained mostly concerned with actual books. At the popular level Ian Fleming's sadistic spy stories, first taken on in Jonathan's day, entered households where books had never gone before; some of them became equally popular films and all sold by the million in Pan paperbacks. From America came Joseph Heller's *Catch-22* and Philip Roth's *Portnoy's Complaint*, two of the biggest bestselling novels of the 'sixties, while in popular science Desmond Morris's *The Naked Ape* earned the author so much money so quickly that he fled to Malta to avoid paying away most of his sudden fortune in tax. This problem faced other authors who found themselves overnight successes; some formed themselves into companies to combat the tax collector's demands.

A Maschler innovation was Cape Editions—'Books which are too long for an article and too short for a book', as they were described in the trade press on their appearance in 1967. They were thin and pocket-sized and included fiction, verse, philosophy, drama and science. Maschler and Greene also started Cape Goliard, a subsidiary issuing gaily produced volumes of new verse in curious formats, and ran a bookshop near Primrose Hill for a number of years. The full story of Cape's has been admirably written by Michael Howard, in one of the most highly praised books on the book trade. It was published on the firm's fiftieth anniversary in January 1971.

To return to the nineteenth century and Hodder & Stoughton is a far cry from Cape's permissive publishing in stately Bedford Square, but until 1962 the essential spirit of Hodder's belonged more to the previous than to the present century. In that year Anthony Sampson's *Anatomy of Britain* was published and augured the subsequent involvement of Hodder's in contemporary fiction with a capital F. Encouraged by Robin Denniston, who joined from Collins, authors whose novels would never have made the list in the days when the criterion for this imprint was suitability for the shelves of the most polite of circulating libraries were soon attracted to Hodder's. Not that the old fiction was jettisoned; indeed, it continued to satisfy a large market, and at least one new practitioner of marked talent was added in Mary Stewart. The family continued to be represented at high level on the board, with Paul succeeding Ralph Hodder-Williams (who had succeeded brother Percy) as chairman in the early 'sixties, and with John Attenborough as deputy chairman. John's son Philip became sales director, but by 1968, the centenary year, 70 per cent of the directors were not descended from the founders. Leonard Cutts, the guiding spirit behind the ever-flourishing Teach Yourself Series and the religious list, retired in 1969 having served the company for forty-seven years and earned himself the citation 'one of the greatest publishers' editors of our age'. But even the theological list reflected the changing times when, in 1970, a book by John Allegro attacking traditional Christian viewpoints was published amidst wide publicity. (Robin Denniston joined Weidenfeld in 1973.)

Brockhampton Press, a subsidiary company started in 1940, grew to become one of the most important children's lists of the time under the guidance of Ewart Wharmby. He operated from the top of a pleasant three-storey building close to Leicester University, and the offices were so designed that every worker could look out and see sky and trees.

It was just as convenient for most Brockhampton authors to visit Leicester as to journey to London, which in fact Wharmby and his editorial director, Antony Kamm, did regularly to keep contact with the parent firm. Brockhampton was entirely devoted to publishing

for children of all ages and varying tastes. It was a list which deter-
minedly set itself against cultural snobbery without glorying in phili-
stinism. Two especially successful series were the Junior Reference
Books and the French strip cartoons, *Asterix*, which followed in the
wake of the popular *Tintin*, published by Methuen. Brockhampton also
issued titles by the prolific Enid Blyton, who was suspected of employing hacks to assist in her huge output. Many children adored her books
and would read nothing else; some read her and passed on to other
books; most teachers, reviewers of children's books and literary booksellers regarded her as a pernicious influence whose works stunted the
imagination. In fact there were other equally bad or even worse writers
for children; the menace of Blyton, if such it was, was her prodigious output; once they had become hooked on her many of her readers thought
literature began with Mary Mouse and Noddy and ended with the
Secret Seven. For all the feeling against her, Miss Blyton had numerous
publishers and provided bread and butter for all of them; from the
light and airy office in Leicester Messrs Wharmby and Kamm were
happy to publish her and felt no need to excuse themselves for doing so.
(Kamm left in 1971 to join the Commonwealth Secretariat.)

At Loughborough, not many miles away, the policy of Wills &
Hepworth, publishers of the Ladybird series, was extended from producing books of pure amusement to include others of an informative
and often historical nature, and school books such as the Key Words
Reading Scheme. Except for a brief spell soon after 1945, the price did
not change for the whole of this period. It was 2s. 6d. (12½p) when the
war ended, and still so on December 31st, 1970. (It was increased to 15p
in June 1971.) How the publishers achieved this with these remarkable
little books, with their excellent texts but rather gaudy pictures, during
a period of intense inflation can only be explained by soaring sales
which kept down the unit cost. (They were bought by the Pearson
Longman group at the end of 1971.)

The colourful Harry Batsford died in 1951 and was succeeded by his
nephew, Brian Cook, who changed his name at his uncle's request.
Brian Batsford became Conservative M.P. for Ealing South in 1958,
but, being a man of vast energy, contrived to combine his duties both as
a publisher and a politician, working at his office until lunchtime and
then going to the House for the rest of the day and perhaps some of the
night as well. When he became a government whip Sam Carr became
managing director and chief editor, but this did not mean that the
politician had entirely ousted the publisher. Batsford's style of publishing did not alter a great deal and the actual production improved.
Books entitled *Britain* or *England* or *London in Colour* continued to appear
at frequent intervals. The authors varied, so usually did the actual
illustrations, but the subjects were dictated by the demands of the

tourist trade. What was the use, to a visiting American, of a picture book on London which did not include shots of the Tower, the Abbey, various palaces and the pigeons in Trafalgar Square? Batsfords were past masters at offering the public what it wanted, and many of the books were superbly made. New series on British Battles were introduced, and the Everyday Life range was greatly expanded, and there were hidden bestsellers in volumes such as Mitchell's *Building Construction,* a set book on many courses and a stock line even in some literary bookshops. In London and the home counties Batsford's were represented by Mr H. F. Johns, who had started working life as an underpaid assistant with Rees in Pall Mall in the early 'thirties (see p. 379). Mr Johns (and I never knew anyone in our almost over-familiar trade who knew what either the H. or the F. stood for) always made appointments with booksellers, as much to conserve his own time as his customers'; was a reliable checker of stock, which he would take unobtrusively if he happened to arrive early; was one of the first reps to take back unwanted volumes with a minimum of fuss ('Send them back as arranged with me, old chap'), and had the perfect knack of seeming to relax and enjoy his visit whilst taking half the time that many of his more garrulous colleagues did. His favourite catch-phrase, delivered with a twinkle in his eye, was, 'Batsford don't have customers; they have friends.'

Batsford's ceased to be booksellers in the 1960s. Until the beginning of that decade, when they stopped retailing, their own publications could be purchased in their shop in South Audley Street, Mayfair. The rare and secondhand departments were sold and transferred to Blackwell's a few years later. By then the publishing side had been at 4 Fitzhardinge Street for over a decade and it was from there that the warehouse was removed to Braintree, in Essex.

The Batsford warehouse went in one direction; the Routledge in another, to Henley-on-Thames, in Oxfordshire. Routledge remained an independent family business, although in 1969 a deal was done with the American Crowell, Collier-Macmillan Company who subscribed some £350,000 for unsecured loan stock convertible into ordinary shares in 1974. Routledge were by then short of capital following expansion and the move to Henley, and their trading profit before tax had fallen from £132,383 in 1968 to £18,491. However, the results for 1971–2 showed a pre-tax profit of £144,508, and in the following year Routledge bought back a majority holding of the Crowell, Collier loan stock.

The Franklin family and John Carter governed the firm from 1953, when John Harvard-Watts resigned and took with him the Tavistock list, until 1965, when three new directors, Brian Southam, Richard Bailey (sales) and Robert Locke were appointed. John Carter died in office the following year, and Norman Franklin, who succeeded him, noted that no head of Routledge had ever retired. If they had not expired on the job, they had gone bankrupt. (Cecil Franklin died suddenly in 1961.)

The Routledge list became more and more academic during this time. In 1954 there was a quarrel with Madame Simenon which led to her husband's later books going to Hamish Hamilton, and with that, the decision was made to cease publishing fiction altogether. Eight years later the small firm of Cohen & West was bought — an important acquisition, because it brought Routledge a number of anthropological titles which they had coveted. Like all of the other publishers so far mentioned in this section Routledge took to paperbacks, being one of the first British firms to issue 'eggheads' — by I. A. Richards, Jung, Ruth Benedict, Erich Fromm and others. Later they put some volumes of their excellent Muses Library into a paper edition; poets such as Andrew Marvell, Rochester and some of the minor Victorian versifiers were often available only in this series.

Michael Sadleir retired from Constable in 1957, in which year he died, leaving his son Richard, Ralph Arnold and D. F. Grover in charge. Under Grace Hogarth, a cheerful children's list was built, and eventually sold to Longmans, when she retired. Meantime the company had been bought in 1962 by Ben Glazebrook, who had been with Heinemann, and Donald Hyde, an American bibliophile. Grover was made chairman, but was succeeded by Glazebrook six years later by which time Richard Sadler had left and Hyde had died. Paul Marks (sales) and Miles Huddleston (publicity) later joined the board, which also included two nominees of Hutchinson's, which bought a minority holding in Constable. The premises at Orange Street became too cramped for expanding activity and the warehouse was moved to Tiptree, where Hutchinson's had established a distribution company for their own and other publishers' books. Important on the Constable list during this period were the American Dover paperback series which covered most fields of publishing; amongst the more remarkable native works were numerous volumes by Harold Nicolson (although the three volumes of diaries and letters, edited by his son, Nigel, went to Collins); Lord David Cecil's *Max* (Beerbohm) and a magnificent travel book, *Journey Through Britain*, by John Hillaby, the record of a walk from Land's End to John O'Groats which earned a permanent place of honour beside Cobbett on the national bookshelf, and was acclaimed as a classic by David Holloway, the literary editor of the *Daily Telegraph*. (Holloway, incidentally, was one of the few journalists to take an active part in the social life of the book trade. He read for and advised many publishers and wrote a monograph on John Galsworthy.)

The chief events at J. M. Dent were the publication of Dylan

Thomas's *Collected Poems*; the promotion of a subsidiary company, Phoenix House, and the gradual emergence of Everyman's Library in a paperback format. Thomas came to Dent through Richard Church, their reader, a poet himself, though of a rather different style. Church did not like Thomas's poems but listened to the advice of Ralph Abercrombie and his brothers, and bought them. Thomas, on the verge of middle age, died from alcoholism; his poems sold by the tens of thousands and he became the idol of other young poets. His radio play *Under Milk Wood*, the script of which was left in a taxi but luckily retrieved, was equally successful on the air, on the stage and in print. Phoenix House was started for John Baker in 1948 and he was given absolute freedom to publish what he wished to, which included the first Shell books. These were inaugurated when Baker went to the Shell Petroleum Company to seek permission to use some of their advertisements in a book on wild flowers. From this stemmed the Shell subsidies for many beautifully illustrated books published by Phoenix, Dent, Faber and Michael Joseph. The first thirteen had a total initial printing order of 145,000 copies. Baker, who continued to run the Readers' Union Book Club during this time, went to Dent as sales director from 1959 to 1963, when he bought The Richards Press and Unicorn Press from Martin Secker and started John Baker Ltd in quaint offices in the Royal Opera Arcade, behind the massive New Zealand House block in the Haymarket. This little company which kept alive some attractive books from early Grant Richards lists, and was supplemented by new volumes on archaeology and London history, etc., was merged into A. & C. Black, Ltd in 1970. (Baker died in 1971.) Dent's issued the thousandth Everyman (Aristotle's *Metaphysics*) in March 1956, and the famous encyclopaedia was revised and reset twice in this period. W. G. Taylor, who was inspired by Everyman to become a publisher in middle life, died in retirement in 1969 having been succeeded as chairman by Joseph Malaby's grandson, F. J. Martin Dent. A. E. Pigott became joint managing director with this Dent in 1967.

Pitman's remained large, mostly educational, publishers with R. H. Code Holland (a most active worker for the P.A.) as publishing director for many years. He was later managing director. Sir James Pitman, whose idea the Book Centre was, left the company in 1964 and thereafter concentrated on spreading the Initial Teaching Alphabet from the Initial Teaching Foundation's offices in Pitman's College, Southampton Row, Holborn. His brother Christian left at the same time. Subsidiaries of the company included Pitman Medical and Scientific Publishing Co., C. A. Watts & Co. and the Focal and Museum Presses; the latter formerly belonged to Robert Hale, and was managed for many years by Desmond Vesey who, in his spare time, translated Brecht.

David Patrick gave long service to Pitman's in these years and became a consultant to the company on his retirement. A sale to America for eight and a quarter million pounds was announced in 1970, but this was not followed through.

Sir James Pitman (a Tory M.P. for many years), grandson of the founder, invented the 44-character alphabet which became known as I.T.A. (the Initial Teaching Alphabet). Recognizing that it was hopeless to try to persuade teachers to use the I.T.A. when there were no books using the system, Sir James instead first persuaded publishers, including of course Pitman's, to take a chance and produce the books as an act of faith. In doing so he gave away his own copyright in the alphabet, but had the reward of watching the system catch on so that by 1970 there was a very large literature available to help the many children who first learned to read by this method. Sir James retained the residual copyright in I.T.A. and was chairman of its Foundation.

At Harrap's George Kamm returned as publicity manager after war service but did not remain with the firm for long, perhaps because the Harrap list, although full of solid bread-and-butter, wasn't exciting to promote. Walter Harrap continued as actively as ever in trade affairs, and when things went wrong in his warehouse, and orders were piling up, he would be down on the packing floor, defying union regulations, and making up parcels himself. Enormously energetic, given to writing extremely long letters to *The Bookseller* and personal correspondents, he never spared himself in promoting cooperation within the trade and in furthering the family business. In 1961 he was given a dinner at Stationers' Hall to celebrate his first half-a-century in the trade. He survived for only another six years, dying suddenly in 1967, and being succeeded, as chairman, by R. Olaf Anderson, another formidably likeable individualist. The other Harraps of this period were Walter's two nephews, Paull and Arthur, and his son, Ian, who resigned to become a bookseller in 1971. Paull, in due course, succeeded Olaf Anderson, Arthur having gone to Australia in 1947 to manage the Australasian Publishing Company. Harrap's were pioneers in audio-visual language courses and were always pre-eminent in the field of French dictionaries and texts, thanks to the masterful editorial direction of René Ledésert.

Of many old-established companies there is little to say except that they continued quietly and profitably to publish and sell their books. A. & C. Black did so so successfully that they became a public company in 1965. Their business doubled between 1957 and 1968 and half of their turnover was in educational books. Archibald Black's son, Charles, great-great-grandson of the founder, joined his father on the board, on which also sat J. D. Newth, who celebrated forty-five years with the firm in 1970. Jack Newth was one of the most devoted of

workers for the P.A., whose president he was from 1949 to 1951, and
for the Book Trade Benevolent Society, as it came to be called, which
administered the leading trade charity and maintained the Booksellers'
Retreat at King's Langley, in Hertfordshire, where retired members of
the trade and their dependents lived either in the original Victorian
house by the side of the railway track, or in new and excellently designed bungalows. The latter were donated by various publishers and
booksellers and named after them. Others who could not afford to
underwrite the cost of building maintained social connections with the
Retreat by taking part in an annual garden party to raise funds, or by
organizing outings for the residents.

Blackie's policy remained largely unchanged although they sold
their printing works and bindery in Bishopbriggs, Glasgow, to Collins
in 1966. Warne's, also, did business as usual in numerous established
bread-and-butter lines, and the Beatrix Potter market remained a huge
source of revenue. Other books grew around the Potter titles, including
Margaret Lane's biography, an edition of the *Journal* decoded by Leslie
Linder, and an illustrated fat volume of *The Art of Beatrix Potter*. Mr
Linder made a collection of Potter manuscripts, drawings and curios
which became a permanent exhibition based on the National Book
League. Warne's expanded the Observer books series, but published
relatively few other new titles. Dick Billington became managing
director in 1946 and was succeeded by Cyril Stephens in 1960. David
Bisacre joined from Blackie in 1967. (In 1972 they returned to Bedford
Square, but not to the house where their founder had lived.)

W. & R. Chambers of Edinburgh ceased publishing their famous
Journal in 1956, after 134 years, thus emphasizing a trend in magazine
publishing. Ten years later their equally famous encyclopaedia passed
by lease, via Newnes, Odham's and the Hamlyn empire, to Robert
Maxwell's Buckingham Press, and was put on sale to the public through
the trade at normal terms, thus providing a welcome £40 in discount
per set to any bookseller who sold it. Chambers continued to publish
modestly, and to keep their excellent dictionaries in print; in 1967 they
joined with Murray's in the maths part of the Nuffield Foundation
Project. J. E. Allen, another activist in P.A. affairs, continued as
manager of the London branch until 1950 and stayed on the board for
a further twelve months, having served the company, for which his
father had also worked, for fifty-one years. He died in 1971.

Mervyn Horder, who became a lord on the death of his eminent
physician father, took the chair at Duckworth's in 1949 and ruled over a
small but valuable list, with the inestimable help of A. G. Lewis
(manager 1923-50) who, extravagantly, perhaps, claimed to have
taught Stanley Unwin all that gentleman knew about publishing whilst
they were at Fisher Unwin's together. If this was so the debt is certainly

not acknowledged in Sir Stanley's memoirs, which make no reference to Lewis. Lewis joined Duckworth in 1923 and died in 1969 soon after Lord Horder had handed over the management of the company to Colin Haycraft and Timothy Simon, at which juncture the archaic terms structure which had been operating for decades was revised.

Sidgwick & Jackson was under the direction of J. Knapp-Fisher during most of this period, and it was he who made the suggestion that his firm should take over Jonathan Cape's which drew the tart reply from Jonathan that he thought the boot should be on the other foot. Charles Forte, the catering industry magnate, bought Sidgwick's in 1970, and Lord Longford, most members of whose family were furiously writing books for other publishers, was installed as chairman in 1970, with Stephen du Sautoy (son of Peter du Sautoy of Faber), ex-joint managing director of Jackdaws, as sales director. The list immediately began to show signs of renewed life and attracted extra attention because of the activities of its noble chairman, who took it upon himself to campaign against over-permissiveness, earning himself the nickname 'Lord Porn'.

Mills & Boon, who lived off the commercial libraries for many a year, saw that market dwindling in the early 'fifties and made plans for expanding in other directions. Their first general book for twenty-five years, *Discovering Embroidery* by Winsome Douglas, was issued in 1955 and was an instant success. They later built strongly on the arts and crafts side, and also on the educational side, a development reinforced by the purchase of the old company of Allman in 1961. As the commercial libraries closed, Mills & Boon readers were deprived of their favourite romances, and the company received touching letters from thousands of them, some of which were reproduced in an article in *The Bookseller* in 1968 when John Boon, who had become managing director in 1964, explained why M. & B. romances had appeared in paperback. By so doing the market for bookbuying was widened, and it was proved that those who had formerly borrowed now bought. Mrs Joan Bryant, an editorial director of the firm, was one of the few women who reached senior executive status in publishing, and she had a pleasantly shrewd and undogmatic approach to the market which she was helping to cater for. Mills & Boon, by providing practical books for those who read their romances, encouraged the practice of owning books amongst people who had not formerly felt the need for a bookshelf. Also in the romance market in a large way, with their authors working at top speed to provide two new titles a year at least, were Robert Hale.

Evans Brothers, noted mostly for their school texts, woodwork manuals and play scripts, had enormous sales in the post-1945 boom in war books, chalking up success after success with *The Dam Busters, The*

White Rabbit and others. *My Memories of Six Reigns* by Princess Marie Louise, grand-daughter of Queen Victoria, also became a bestseller in 1957, reflecting, perhaps, more a taste for vicarious rubbing of shoulders with royalty than for great literature. Leonard Cottrell wrote books of popular archaeology for Evans, and there were other general books of wide appeal, but by the late 1960s they were again concentrating on the juvenile and educational lists with particular success in overseas markets, although their young managing director, Robin Hyman, found time amongst his arduous duties to compile his own book of quotations and to contribute some titles to the attractive Zebra series of paperbacks for young readers. Hyman became managing director in 1969 when John Browning, a qualified lawyer and son-in-law of Sir Robert Evans, became chairman. Noel Evans, a son of one of the founders of the firm had died tragically young in 1964, two years after the acquisition of the second Rivington educational list (see p. 258).

At 40 Museum Street, Stanley Unwin, knighted in 1946, and honoured throughout the book world, remained in control until his death in 1968. On the board with him were his nephew Philip, who retired in 1970, and his son Rayner, who succeeded as chairman. Geoffrey Cass, who had already reorganized the Cambridge Press trade department, came in as managing director until 1971 and the trade department moved to Hemel Hempstead with a minimum of fuss and no kow-towing to a computer. Charles Knight, who had spent most of his forty-five years with the company in increasingly important positions in the accounts department, subsequently became managing director at Hemel.

Of the many bestsellers which Allen & Unwin had during this time *The Kon-Tiki Expedition* overshadows them all, more than two million copies being sold in the British edition alone. At the height of its success Sir Stanley refused to give a third off to any bookseller who ordered less than six copies, thus forcing the retailers to keep adequate stocks if they wanted best terms. It was hardly a practice to be favoured by booksellers in principle, but it was difficult to object to at the time. Allen & Unwin continued to give less than the best terms, even in 1970; but against this they gave splendid and usually accurate service.

More success came with Bertrand Russell's monumental *History of Western Philosophy* and with his autobiography. During their fifty years' association, Stanley Unwin and Russell met infrequently and hardly ever socially, yet each respected and enjoyed the company of the other. Huge sales were also notched up with J. R. R. Tolkien's *Lord of the Rings* trilogy, which appealed to both adults and children; the notorious Indian handbook of erotica, the *Kama Sutra*—published, under this respectable imprint, without so much as a hint of public prosecution— and James Pope Hennessy's biography of Queen Mary. These, and

Thor Heyerdahl's *Aku-Aku*, about his discoveries on Easter Island, were the highlights, but there was so much else; the list was weak in fiction but strong in almost every other category. All of the Unwins also wrote books, including David, who did not stay in publishing, perhaps because he found himself no more of a match for his father in that sphere than his brother Rayner did on the tennis court, where Uncle Stan's prowess was famous to an advanced age. Rayner gave up tennis but, happily, not publishing, from which occupation he found diversion in writing, the best of his books being *The Defeat of John Hawkins*, an absorbing essay in history which found its way into Pelican paperback. Philip also, not to be outdone, wrote a manual for new entrants to publishing, but Hamish Hamilton published this, whilst his excellent memoirs of the two uncles for whom he had worked, *The Publishing Unwins*, came from Heinemann.

A new Whitaker appeared in the Bedford Square offices in the early 1950s in the person of David, son of Haddon, and his advent emphasized the strong family nature of the firm which continued to publish the leading trade journal, *The Bookseller*, and the two almanacks, one bearing their name and selling at least 50,000 copies annually, and the other under the Sporting Handbooks imprint that of John Wisden, cricketer and maker of bats and balls. Sir Cuthbert Whitaker, editor of the first almanack for fifty-five years, died in 1950, at which date his nephew Haddon became chairman. The board was widened in 1956 to include Edmond Segrave, editor of *The Bookseller*, and in 1958 the centenary of the magazine was celebrated with a reception and party at the Dorchester Hotel. On the publishing side they remained content to record the statistics of their fellows rather than increase by more than a few the number of their own publications, which included the annual issue of *Publishers in the U.K. and Their Addresses* and *British Books in Print* and the occasional, and usually much delayed, *Paperbacks in Print*.

The growth at Faber's was controlled. In 1940, 177 new books were published; in 1950, 216; it had gone up to 268 in 1960, and reached 276 a year ten years later. The staff grew from 109 in 1950, to 220 in 1970. As always, the list reflected every side of publishing, and was especially strong in poetry under the influence of T. S. Eliot. Amongst the new poets introduced were Thom Gunn, Sylvia Plath, Philip Larkin (his first volume had come from the tiny Marvell Press), Seamus Heaney and Ted Hughes, the latter's *Crow* being a bestseller in some bookshops at Christmas 1970. The first paper covered editions were brought out in 1958 as an attempt to revive the old Faber library reprints. They caught on quickly, boosted by Lawrence Durrell's *Alexandria Quartet*, at first in four separate volumes, later in one, which sold as quickly as any Penguin, and encouraged Faber's to take back the rights of *Lord of the Flies*, William Golding's highly successful novel, from Harmondsworth, and to issue their own soft cover edition.

Peter du Sautoy, having previously been at the British Museum, and worked as an assistant education officer, joined Faber at the start of 1946 and rose to be vice-chairman in 1971. In 1947 W. J. Crawley's son Peter also arrived at 24 Russell Square and eventually succeeded his father as sales director. There was considerable development of the play library following Charles Monteith's purchase of John Osborne's *Look Back in Anger*, production of which play heralded a revival of British playwriting and caused Faber to compete vigorously with Methuen, Penguin's and Heinemann Educational for the rights to publish the new dramatists. Faber got Samuel Beckett and Jean Genet amongst others. Music publishing was undertaken with Donald Mitchell in charge and Benjamin Britten a member of the board of Faber Music Ltd.

Geoffrey Faber — by then Sir Geoffrey — died in 1961 and T. S. Eliot, four years later, and in 1970 there were two more deaths — David Bland, production director and author of the *History of Book Illustration*, and John Oliver, the forty-nine-year old educational manager. Fortunately Faber did not lack talent in any department, and these grievous losses were withstood, although, as always, the actual list continued to reflect the particular bents of those in control. The warehouse moved out to Harlow in Essex, in 1960, and the offices to Queen Square in 1971.

Victor Gollancz remained in control of his affairs until his death in 1967, although by then his energy had been diminished by a stroke. For most of the period, however, he was as active as ever in politics as well as publishing, and he also found time to write a great many books, some of them in the form of a diary for his godson, Timothy. When he died, his daughter Livia took over, with John Bush, who might be described as the one who survived, as her joint managing director. Amongst those who did not survive were V.G.'s son-in-law, Hilary Rubinstein, who left to join the *Observer* and, later, the literary agency of A. P. Watt, and James MacGibbon, who had left another literary agency to join his old friend in 1962 but who resigned soon after the great man's death, followed in 1972 by Giles Gordon, a lively young editor who had served with Secker, Hutchinson's and Penguin's. Amongst the achievements of these two erstwhile directors, who went on to enjoy other senior positions, were the discoveries on Rubunstein's part of Kingsley Amis, whose *Lucky Jim* humorously ushered in the anti-hero to Eng. Lit., and on MacGibbon's part of the Soviet novelist Solzhenitsyn, whose *One Day in the Life of Ivan Denisovitch* revealed a great new Russian talent to English readers. (Gollancz subsequently lost Amis to Cape, and Solzhenitsyn to Collins and The Bodley Head.) A later editorial director who also resigned was Alec Bartholemew. He went to America where he bought a bestseller (*Jonathan Livingstone Seagull*) with which to start his own British imprint in 1972. Other new Gollancz authors of this period were Colin Wilson, who had an enormous success with a semi-philosophical work called *The Outsider* in 1956, and John Le Carré, whose *The Spy Who Came in From the Cold*, his third novel, was quite remarkably turned into a big bestseller several months after publication. The latter's sudden sales were partly due to high commendation from Graham Greene in a Books of the Year column, but equally to the persistence of V.G. and John Bush, who lost no opportunity to get behind the publicity the book received long after the reviews had appeared. Le Carré's next book went to Heinemann, which made for raised eyebrows and V.G.'s comment, 'In my own good time I shall tell the whole story of the Le Carré affair, an affair of the greatest import to every publisher in the land.' In fact he never did, and Heinemann maintained that there was no bidding for *The Looking-Glass War*, the book in question.

The importance of the end-of-the-year puffs by famous citizens, not necessarily authors, in the *Observer* and the *Sunday Times* was measured by the number of mentions a book received. If it was commended highly by more than three contributors to either paper, increased sales fairly certainly followed; if it got half-a-dozen, the book was often given a whole new lease of life. This happened to John Gross's *The Rise and Fall of the Man of Letters*, published in the spring of 1969 by Weidenfeld with little success. The following Christmas it was mentioned several times and the sales, once a reprint had been rushed through, continued through much of 1970. The Sunday papers also played a part in making books during the rest of the year, although not perhaps so much as in the past. Nevertheless, V.G. once remarked at a dinner that but for the lucky chance of Cyril Connolly reviewing a two-volume anthology of poetry edited by Edith Sitwell, which he had published a few weeks before, the book would have remained a total failure. After the Connolly review the edition was sold out.

The house of Gollancz continued to have great success with popular novelists such as A. J. Cronin and Daphne Du Maurier, to extend its philosophical and music sides and to build a good children's list. Its publications were often eccentrically jacketed with blurbs which not only extended around the whole of the outside of the cover and up and down the fly leaves, but occasionally continued on the inside as well. By contrast, sometimes there weren't any blurbs at all, only boldly printed commendations from eminent persons. V.G. himself became increasingly relentless in discovering the most exciting (yet again) book of his lifetime and trying to convey his enthusiasm for it to his staff and to booksellers. But for all his mistakes, he was a great publisher and was held in affection by all who cared, as he did, for people and the apparently lost causes they supported. It should never be forgotten that he, a Jew, was amongst the first to sponsor help for the broken German nation after the second war. His humanitarianism may not always have been apparent to his senior colleagues during the day-to-day course of their business lives, but he was a big man in every sense, and well enough loved by most of those who worked for him.

V.G.'s old firm of Ernest Benn took over a number of other imprints —Williams & Norgate (who had already absorbed Home & Van Thal) and Lindsay Drummond amongst them—during this period when they lived mainly off their famous Blue Guides, revised as often as possible and invaluable to so many travellers, and the children's list (E. Nesbit, etc.) which came to be the province of John Denton. Denton, who had himself written a popular juvenile novel for Collins, became managing director in 1964. That great individualist, Sir Ernest Benn, who once tore up his wartime ration book without apparently starving thereafter, died in 1954, and in 1970 there was little trace either of him or of V.G. on the list.

4

The New Publishers

Weidenfeld & Nicolson; Thames & Hudson; André Deutsch; Souvenir Press; Anthony Blond; Blond & Briggs; Peter Wolfe; Peter Owen; John Lehmann; Calder & Boyars; Falcon Press; Grey Walls Press; Dennis Dobson; Elliot Right Way Books; Merlin Press; Scorpion Press; Marvell Press; Fortune Press; Fulcrum Press; Stuart & Watkins; J. M. Watkins; Rapp & Whiting; Arlington Books; Leo Cooper; Seeley, Service; Maurice Temple Smith; Arms and Armour Press; Darton, Longman & Todd; Search Press; Evelyn, Adams & Mackay; Adams & Dart, Hugh Evelyn; David & Charles; Bailey Brothers & Swinfen; W. H. Freeman; Mitchell Beazley; Paul Elek; Centaur Press.

It was Ernest Hecht, a Jewish refugee from Czechoslovakia and founder of the Souvenir Press, who told me of the visiting American publisher's remark, 'It's lovely to come to London and meet English publishers.' 'Sure,' gagged Ernest, 'Like Mr Weidenfeld, Mr Neurath, Mr Deutsch ...'

George Weidenfeld's first publishing venture was a magazine, *Contact*, shortly after the Second World War. In 1949 he started a publishing company bearing his name and that of Nigel Nicolson, the younger son of Harold Nicolson and sometime Tory M.P. Weidenfeld & Nicolson (and it was always Weidenfeld who was the active one) started modestly, and in the early days published children's books for Marks & Spencer. As fresh capital was injected, however, Weidenfeld began to expand as vigorously as any rising Victorian publisher, and by 1968 he was issuing 250 titles a year under his own imprint and that of Arthur Barker, which he had absorbed. Barker went into voluntary liquidation at the beginning of the war, much of which he spent in a Japanese P.O.W. camp. When he re-started he was a sick man and soon handed over the running of his business to Herbert Van Thal, spending six months of each year himself in Spain. Bertie Van Thal had had publishing experience with Peter Davies and others in the 'twenties and 'thirties, and post-war for a brief period on his own account (Home & Van Thal), reissuing a few of Gissing's works and some pleasing series of *belles-lettres*, not the least of which was his own *Recipe for Reading*. When capital became tight he organized the sale of Arthur Barker to Weidenfeld (without Barker's entire approval) and

473

stayed to manage the list for a while; but, as he related in his memoirs, *The Tops of the Mulberry Trees*, he was not built to work for long with the tycoon temperament of a Weidenfeld.

Weidenfeld also had an educational list, which he sold to Granada in 1969, and sponsored the World University Library in hardback and paper, a widely based academic series which Colin Haycraft edited until he left for Duckworth's. Tony Godwin joined (as joint managing director with Halfdan Lynner) after he had broken with Allen Lane, and he attracted many novelists from other lists as well as keeping such best-selling Americans as Saul Bellow and Mary McCarthy, and of course Vladimir Nabokov, whose *Lolita* had appeared in the late 'fifties. It had been strongly supposed that *Lolita* would be prosecuted, but at an eve of publication party the rumour spread that Weidenfeld had received a phone call from 'official sources' saying it would not be. And it wasn't. Weidenfeld's also published many historical biographies and art and coffee-table books, and numerous thick volumes on Jewish history and culture. It was impossible for a bookseller not to feel that Weidenfeld & Nicolson published too much, and altogether too much which was ephemeral, but that was also the case with most large publishers. Lynner, who had come via Methuen and others, left in 1968 to join a new subsidiary of Hutchinson's which produced a vast encyclopaedia, taken from a weekly part-work. On the sales side he was succeeded by Geoffrey Howard, who had been sales director of Hutchinson's for many years. In the same year Encyclopaedia Britannica acquired 39 per cent of Weidenfeld's shares. Two years later, Nicolas Thompson, a joint managing director, left to take over from R. H. Code Holland at Pitman's, which left Godwin as undisputed second-in-command until 1973, when Robin Denniston became group deputy chairman. Godwin stayed as a 'senior editorial director'.

Walter Neurath has already appeared in these pages. He established his company, and himself as chairman of it, in the same year as Weidenfeld started. He took a Highgate bookseller, Trevor Craker, as his sales manager and used Constable's for representation and dispatch, but the tail was soon wagging the dog and Constable reps had to decide whether or not to stay with their parent firm or move over to Neurath's exclusive employment. Most of them chose Thames & Hudson, and cannot have regretted it, because Neurath proceeded to produce so many saleable books that there were 800 in print in 1969 and 180 new titles each year. The staff by then numbered 160. It was a remarkable achievement in twenty years, but Neurath did not live to celebrate his firm's coming of age.

His first book was *English Cathedrals*, by Martin Hurlimann, which set the pattern for high-class art and photographic volumes. The first title in the World of Art series, *Picasso*, appeared in 1956. In 1970 the series had become so established and the public for art books had so grown that an English painter, Turner, was introduced for the first time. The argument against books of reproductions of English painters had always been that the world market would not tolerate them; it was popularly supposed amongst foreigners that English painting was beneath their notice. Happily this notion, like the one that the British public is totally philistine, was breaking down by the 1960s, and this was partly due to Neurath and his ambitious publishing programme. His greatest monument was probably the History of Civilization Library, edited by his friend Max Parrish, who joined Thames & Hudson in 1960 after his own imprint had been taken into the Purnell group. The eight volumes in this series started with the *Dawn of Civilization* and ended with *The Twentieth Century*. The first printing of the first volume, at £8 8s., was 200,000 copies.

On Neurath's death his widow became chairman, and his son, Thomas, managing director. The editorial inspiration behind many Thames & Hudson books was Tom Rosenthal, who left in 1970 to become managing director of Secker & Warburg. The same positive approach to selling was maintained after the founder's death in 1967, and sales staff were required to arrange and man displays in colleges of art as well as selling to booksellers. Neurath, like Allen Lane, had the pleasant custom of sending specially prepared editions of literary curiosities to friends in the trade to mark anniversaries. A particularly efficient trade department operated from Aldershot from 1967, but the editorial and sales offices remained in Bloomsbury Street where a mosaic of a dolphin, the firm's colophon, was impressed on the top step of No. 30.

André Deutsch was always a trade-minded publisher, and celebrated the birth of his own imprint in 1951 with a symposium, *Books are Essential*, with contributions from prominent publishers, booksellers and authors. His co-directors included Diana Athill, author of a remarkably honest autobiography published by Chatto, and winner of the *Observer* short story competition in 1958, and Nicolas Bentley, cartoonist and humorist.

Deutsch was primarily interested in creative publishing, and established many American and British novelists—John Updike, Brian Moore, Roy Fuller, V. S. Naipaul, amongst them. He also bought back from Allan Wingate (the firm he started at the end of the war, and from which he was forced to resign) the works of the satirist George Mikes, a fellow Hungarian, whose *How to be an Alien* became a classic view of the English. (Wingate went into the receiver's hands in 1959 and was bought by William Kimber, a small publisher, who thus gained the popular Jewish novelist Leon Uris). Deutsch's subsequent acquisitions were the short-lived Derek Verschoyle list, which enabled him to move into premises just off Soho Square, and Grafton's (in 1961), specialists in the literature of librarianship. He started the Language Library, edited by Eric Partridge and Simeon Potter, and, overseas, created the African Universities Press in Nigeria and the East African Publishing House in Nairobi. The last two he claimed as his proudest achievements, although he lost money on one of them, and thought that their success would contribute significantly to the development of their respective countries.

As he grew, Deutsch entered the big time in bidding for American bestsellers, and there were moments when he seemed to be stretching his resources; however, he stayed independent. Often his gambles came off, and his list always reflected high literary standards. As a publisher he was an enthusiast, caring, like the Collins family, for the books he took and never wasting time crying over his mistakes. He had a reputation for running through sales managers rather more swiftly than most publishers, and he was undoubtedly a hard task master, working long hours himself and expecting his employees to be equally devoted. Perhaps he overlooked the fact that those on his payroll could not take holidays as often he did, and had wives and families to look after. But publishing for him was always an exciting crusade. There may have seemed to be injustice, sometimes, in his dealings, but there was never boredom or sustained ill will, because he cared passionately about all that he did, and sponsored some very worthwhile books. And to his credit must stand the fact that he was one of the first to accept returns from booksellers who were prepared to make a show of his books, believing correctly that it was worth having books at the point of sale at the moment when they might be in demand.

Ernest Hecht published at a lower cultural level, until the 1970s, and with a happy knack for making money. A fanatical sportsman, on leaving Hull University he failed to get the job he wanted of secretary to the Universities Athletic Association, and filled in time doing free-lance publishing work. His first book was a 2s. paperback about the England cricketer, Len Hutton. He borrowed £250 from his parents and worked from home for years establishing the Souvenir Press, with a staff consisting of himself and a secretary. He later moved to offices in Bloomsbury Street, where he displayed the announcement of a bullfight in which he was falsely billed as a toreador, and proceeded to publish quiet bestsellers about sportsmen and pop singers in between trips abroad to see every important sporting event which took his fancy. He sold hundreds of thousands of copies of *Meet the Beatles* and *Meet Cliff* to pop music fans and, when distinguished educational publishers had turned down the *Trachtenberg Speed System of Mathematics* (which taught human beings how to do incredibly complicated calculations with computer-like skill) he bought it and sold 100,000 copies within a year. He expanded cautiously on the staff side, taking on Ronald Payne (who died tragically in a traffic accident a few years later) as a partner and also an author. This doubled his staff, since Payne was also allowed a secretary. When, because he had published some fiction, Arthur Hailey came his way, he had the sense to understand that his sales organization could not cope with a popular novel of huge potential, so he published jointly with Michael Joseph. *Hotel* and *Airport* were enormous bestsellers in hard and paperback.

Ernest Hecht was important in this period of publishing not so much for the books he produced, although there was literary merit in some of them, as for the way he disproved the theory that a publisher starting in the 'fifties had to have large resources of capital. He had no such backing, but by keeping his overheads to a minimum he remained independent and able to enjoy the life he chose, travelling to South America for the World Cup, or just to sun himself on the beaches at Rio, to Australia, for test matches, to Japan and Mexico for the Olympics, and to anywhere that Real Madrid happened to be kicking a football around. It is probable that he gained more actual enjoyment from publishing than did any of his contemporaries.

Anthony Blond was another enthusiast who started his list in 1958 recklessly with several first novels of doubtful sales potential. Subsequently he found success with Simon Raven, Jennifer Dawson and Harold Robbins, and also turned his attention to vast reference books about Africa and Asia. Always impatient to break new ground, he decided to enter educational publishing and took himself off to a school in Doncaster to teach English for a short spell. Horrified by the textbooks he was expected to use, he commissioned Emmens and Rowe to produce new ones, and launched Blond Educational. This was a huge success but ran him short of capital, and when he failed to raise the necessary backing in the City of London, he sold out to Columbia Broadcasting System and Holt, Rinehart of the United States, retaining the managing directorship for himself, and the sales directorship for Desmond Briggs, who had joined him from Angus & Robertson in 1960. There will be those who think that had he been less lavish in the advances he paid for general books, he could have financed his own expansion into the educational market. (Needless to say, the period of working for his new American bosses was barely the prescribed two years, and he and Briggs broke amicably from them in 1971 and started their own new imprint using their two names.)

Peter Wolfe, having had sales management experience with Methuen and Deutsch, and having published books for the *Sunday Times*, went it alone in 1962, beginning with books for sales promotional purposes. Two years later he began to publish for the trade, specializing in books which appeared to be humorous but which were, in fact, fundamentally serious. The Bluffers Guides (to English Literature, Music, Marketing, etc.) made their appeal through witty jacketing but contained sound advice; similarly with the Awful series, on driving, cooking, spelling and so on. Wolfe also made his mark in *The Bookseller* with whole-page ads of facsimile typewritten letters to booksellers about his publications, which provided a welcome Saturday morning giggle. George Hayward, doyen of London reps, a freelance for Edward Arnold and others for many years, was on the Wolfe board, a distinction enjoyed by few if any other travellers.

There was always humour in the approach of Hecht, Blond and Wolfe; other small and smaller independent publishers were more earnest, though not necessarily more purposeful, in their attempts to woo the trade.

Peter Owen, like Ernest Hecht, proved that publishing could be done on a shoestring. He started at twenty-three in 1951 with £900, and built a distinguished list which included Cocteau, Gide, Sartre, the German novelist Hermann Hesse and other European writers, such as Cesare Pavese, who were greatly esteemed in their own countries but little known elsewhere. He tended towards the experimental in fiction, but by 1970 he was protesting about high production costs and threatening not to publish any more novels. His non-fiction included Marc Chagall's autobiography, the *Complete Poems of Michelangelo*, and various theatrical textbooks.

John Lehmann, who became an independent publisher in 1946, also had a strong leaning towards contemporary European writers, but he lost control of his firm six years after starting it; perhaps because he believed in trying to expand too quickly with insufficient capital; perhaps, as Leonard Woolf suggests in his last volume of autobiography, because he took himself too seriously. In any event Purnell's took over his firm but not him, and Lehmann started *London Magazine*, with the backing of the *Daily Mirror*. He ran this for several years before selling it to the poet and sports writer Alan Ross, who subsequently began to publish books on a modest scale.

The third smallish publisher much identified with European literature, especially of the avant-garde, was John Calder, who began in 1949. Marion Boyars joined him in 1961, acquiring a substantial interest, and four years later the firm became known as Calder & Boyars. They were the first publishers in Britain of the playwright Ionesco; of the French school of anti-novelists (Marguerite Duras, Nathalie Sarraute, Robbe-Grillet, etc.) and, as the permissive climate grew, out came Henry Miller's *Tropic of Cancer* and *Tropic of Capricorn*, which no one had previously dared to publish for fear of prosecution. They remained clear of the law with these, and with the works of William Burroughs, but with *Last Exit to Brooklyn*, by Hubert Selby, Jr, action was taken and they went on trial in 1967, several distinguished literary figures giving evidence against the book. The court found Calder & Boyars guilty of publishing an obscene libel, but the decision was reversed on appeal and the book, thereafter, was freely on sale. Amongst those who gave evidence against the book was Sir Basil Blackwell, whose son Richard had in fact provoked the whole case by sending a copy of it to a Tory M.P. When the appeal was won, Calder & Boyars put in hand a reprint of 20,000 copies, interest in the book having been much revived by those who wished to suppress it. An old, old story.

It is not possible to mention all the new imprints of this era. Some, such as the Falcon and Grey Walls Presses, run by the late Peter Baker, another Tory M.P., who managed to defraud Barclays Bank of some £40,000 and was imprisoned for seven years, are almost forgotten now. Others, like Dennis Dobson, who have brought out individual books of merit, particularly in musicology, S.F. and children's literature, have not altered the face of the trade and are not, therefore, as yet, historically important, although Dobson ranks a mention for laughter-raising by publishing the eccentric cartoons of Gerard Hoffnung and some of the best goonish work of Spike Milligan. Milligan was difficult to tie down, and appeared on several lists.

There were other imprints which lasted through much of the period. Andrew George Elliot's Right Way Books, for instance, instructional manuals on a wide range of subjects, including publishing, which he cornily called Paperfronts. He claimed to love single-copy orders and serviced them by return, giving booksellers a third-off discount postage free. He turned his limited company into a partnership with his two sons, and believed he was starting a trend away from the fashion of the twentieth century. An industrious Scot, who insisted on clearing each day's orders before he finished his work, Andrew George Elliot wrote some of his own books under pseudonyms, as well as taking a practical part in the construction of the new warehouse which his swiftly expanding business required by 1963. He was a phenomenon who proved, if such proof is necessary so late in this work, that there are no hard and fast rules for success in publishing.

The Merlin Press was started in the late 'fifties by Martin Eve, who had been a rep. with Weidenfeld & Nicolson, Michael Joseph and others. For many years he published from his home with another quite different type of publisher, Neville Spearman (hugely successful with the literature of U.F.O.s and amusing erotica, etc.) as his warehouse and trade counter. Some of Stendhal's books were published in English for the first time by Eve, who also re-published classic works on medieval farming, and other scholarly subjects, for a small but known market. The works of Georg Lukacs, the Marxist Hungarian critic, came his way, and it was with one of these that he made his first paperback sale to

Penguin's. He also started a new left-wing book club, and produced a solemn volume each year, in both hard and paperback, entitled *The Socialist Register*; on the lighter side he had a series of books of cartoons about monks. In time Martin Eve took a small office in Fitzroy Square and attended to his own distribution. His activities, over fifteen years, were further proof of the viability of going it alone on limited means.

Jack Hobbs and John Rolph had similar success with the Scorpion Press, which set out to prove that poetry by unknown writers could be published profitably. They ran their press as a sideline, each travelling for a large publisher to earn the main part of their income. Some of the poets whom they first published were later taken up by established publishers, a transition which they accepted philosophically as a measure of the success of their pioneer work. Hobbs later began to publish mainly humorous books and posters under the imprint of Jack & Margaret Hobbs, and Rolph ran Scorpion from a secondhand bookshop in Suffolk.

Small poetry presses abounded, many of them producing inferior work, often messily cyclostyled and usually paid for by the poets so published. In some cases the poets were also required to sell their pamphlets to booksellers, an embarrassing exercise for all concerned. Most literary bookshops had a corner of litter which was the final resting-place of many tiny muses thus thrown upon the harsh commercial market. They were the bane of many booksellers' lives and became nothing more than a repository of lost hopes. Rising above these piteous booksellers' grave-yards of humble vanity were the books produced by such small firms as the Marvell Press and the Fortune Press. The Fulcrum Press, which began in the late 'sixties, published in good cloth and/or pleasantly designed paper-covered editions.

Stuart & Watkins, which started as Stuart & Richards in 1948, published the five volumes of Commentaries on Gurdjeff and Ouspensky, and several other books by Maurice Nicoll, which enjoyed a great vogue for a number of years. Their policy was to publish books concerned with 'the real, inner meaning of man's life', and also volumes on ecology and natural resources. They merged with J. M. Watkins, of Cecil Court, Charing Cross Road, in 1963.

Rapp & Carroll began in 1966, when Georg Rapp, who had retired young from the metal business, decided to indulge his taste for poetry and for publishing. He did not issue his own verse, although he recited some of it publicly in company with Roy Fuller, but brought out many volumes by others both before he parted with Donald Carroll and after. The company's name was changed to Rapp & Whiting when Ronald Whiting joined him. Whiting had had twenty years of sales and editorial experience with Allen & Unwin, Hamlyn, Michael Joseph and Dobson, and latterly with his own imprint of Ronald Whiting &

Wheaton, (bought over his head by Robert Maxwell before he had issued his first book). Whiting's trade know-how, and bread-and-butter contributions of S.F. and children's books to the new list, made a splendid balance with Rapp's less easily saleable poetry, but the partnership was doomed because Rapp had a serious heart attack in 1969 and had to settle for publishing as a part-time occupation. André Deutsch undertook distribution for Rapp, and Whiting joined B.P.C. to promote the sales and publication of *Jane's Fighting Ships* and *All the World's Aircraft*, and other similar volumes which had been acquired through Sampson Low

Desmond Elliott, who had been a publicity manager with The Bodley Head, Hutchinson and others, and also a literary agent, started Arlington Books in the 'sixties. He caused raised eyebrows, and disarmed his critics, by printing on the jackets of his books a note to the public beginning, 'Your bookseller is a friendly person who wants to help you ... ' He had early success with the *I Hate To Cook Book*, and its sequel *I Hate To Housekeep Book*. When the Society of Young Publishers produced an annual revue in the late 'fifties, Elliott was a leading performer, creating with Michael Turner of Methuen a hilarious double act, Rosencrantz and Guildenstern (Publishers of Good Books) Ltd.

It became the fashion for senior executives to leave large publishing houses (sometimes the larger publishing houses left them) and to start on their own. Leo Cooper, ex-publicity at Longmans and Hamish Hamilton, gave his name to an imprint devoted to military history, and later merged with the old established Seeley, Service, a rather staid firm which had for a long time specialized in sporting and military matters. It had been founded in 1744, a date connected with both subjects as the year of the first notable cricket match, when Kent played an All England XI on the Honourable Artillery Company ground at Finsbury, an event celebrated in verse by the son of the architect George Dance.

Maurice Temple Smith, too, put his own name on his books, after distinguished service with Eyre & Spottiswoode and Secker & Warburg. Lionel Levanthal left the Barrie & Rockliff group, which he had entered with Herbert Jenkins, to join Hamlyn's for eighteen months before starting his own Arms and Armour Press, and T. M. Longman broke away from the family firm in the 1960s to begin Darton, Longman & Todd, issuing mainly religious books. After the collapse of many Roman Catholic publishers, following the papal encyclical which did away with missals, Longman also published for the Search Press which took over 238 titles formerly on the Burns, Oates list.

And there was Hugh Evelyn, which became Evelyn, Adams & Mackay (Cory Adams & Mackay had been small art publishers), and later split into Adams & Dart, based on Bath, and again, Hugh Evelyn.

Behind all this activity was Hugh Street, who had a nice line in large colourfully illustrated books on old cars and sailing ships, traction engines, ceremonial barges and like subjects. These could be sold as books or taken apart and marketed as individual prints. Jack Hobbs joined him in the early 'sixties and threw himself enthusiastically into selling both books and prints, later making his own impression on the firm by introducing curios of Victorian literature such as *The Language of Flowers* and *A Manual of Etiquette*, republished in facsimile. In 1969, when Hobbs left, the new firm of Adams & Dart acquired all the list except the original large format monographs which Hugh Street retained. Adams & Dart devoted part of their list to facsimile reprints, a fashion which, as we shall see, played a large part in the expansion of David & Charles.

It was Frank Cass, a Bloomsbury bookseller who in 1958 began to reprint famous scholarly books of the past in small editions, who first opened up the market for reproducing old books. The Scolar Press, founded by R. C. Alston in 1965, followed. Operating first from rat-infested premises in Leeds, they began to issue facsimiles of learned works which won support from universities all over the world. They soon moved to healthier surroundings in the Yorkshire village of Menston, and in the 'seventies began to seek additional sales through the retail trade. David & Charles began modestly enough in the mid-'sixties with offices actually on Newton Abbot railway station, an important junction in Devonshire. Intending passengers passed the publisher's door, which was opposite the ticket collector. David was David St John Thomas, and Charles, Charles Hadfield, an author of books on railways. The former was the more active force in the firm, which was interested at the beginning mainly in railway and boating literature and in local history. Growing out of the railway books came the facsimile reprints of some of Bradshaw's early timetables. The success of these led to the reproduction of early telephone directories, the Army & Navy Stores catalogue for 1907, various editions of Jane's *Fighting Ships* and *All the Worlds Aircraft*, a complete first edition of Ordnance Survey maps of Great Britain, newspapers of the First World War and numerous other items. By 1970, with Robert Hale, Kingsmead Reprints and others on the bandwagon, the whole fashion seemed in danger of being overdone and it was possibly only a matter of time before some publisher or other got in with *Whitaker's Almanack* for 1945, the 50,000th edition of *The Times*, or even a typical Second World War Economy Standard first novel. By then David & Charles had taken additional accommodation for their invoicing and warehousing, although the editorial department remained on the railway station. This, and the vast output—about 150 titles a year—took some of the romance out of their story, and each issue of the *David and Charles Gazette*, a regular back-page advertisement in *The Bookseller,* described by one correspondent to 'The Organ' as having a 'self-congratulatory tone', added pomposity to the image of the firm. The *Gazette* had a complacent air, and the layout irritated some people with its suggestion of a small-time provincial newspaper whose editor had turned his back on the appeal of modern typography. More and more the weekly ad. tended to make the point that only David & Charles books really mattered, and booksellers were admonished for not trying harder to sell them, only W. H. Smith (always a satisfactory pupil at the Newton Abbot academy) receiving plaudits for installing D. & C. stands in their stores. But in so young a firm perhaps these were merely growing pains; one hopes so because St John Thomas produced many admirable books.

Also operating from outside London were Bailey Brothers & Swinfen. They moved in the 1960s into a light, modern factory on a new industrial estate, in the Kent port of Folkestone. Edward Swinfen retired in 1960, after seventy-one years in the trade, and John Bailey, a descendent of one of the founders, continued the company with other non-family directors. They were mainly importers, notably of dictionaries, from Europe and America, and were agents for many years of W. H. Freeman, American scientific publishers. To allow for the progress of both firms, Freeman registered as a separate British company in 1959.

Much controlled in output was the Mitchell Beazley list, which concentrated on producing a very few titles a year and promoting them thoroughly, although not without a certain tendency towards executive deification on the part of the two clever young men who were the brains behind it. James Mitchell, who had both publishing and bookselling experience, met John Beazley while at Nelson's. Together they planned a small list for the international market, starting in 1969 with two lavish atlases, and following it up with *Persia: The Immortal Kingdom* which they contracted to sell to the Iranian government for well over £100,000. More modestly they ended 1970 by producing a witty volume of cartoons and potted biographies of English monarchs by Nicolas Bentley. *Golden Sovereigns*, priced at £1, was a worthy successor in apocryphal history to the classic *1066 and All That,* and indicated that Mitchell and Beazley had not lost their souls to international money-making.

Another general publisher who kept his imprint intact, with some variations of official company nomenclature, was Paul Elek. Elek produced some handsome topographical books during the late 'sixties, and indefatigably brought out an annual volume of *Plays of the Year*, edited by J. C. Trewin, as hard-working and honest a drama critic as ever sat through thousands of first nights. (Trewin also wrote scholarly but readable biographies of actors, ranging from Macready to Robert Donat, for Harrap and Heinemann.)

There were others, medium and small, who stayed the course for many years, and I must be guilty of omitting to mention some of those who attended the annual conference of the Small Independent Publishers at the Spa Hotel, Tunbridge Wells. One who on grounds of longevity must be included is Jon Wynne-Tyson, of the Centaur Press, who was an early practitioner in reprinting, at high prices, scholarly works of an earlier age. Wynne-Tyson was a fierce correspondent to *The Bookseller*, and on one occasion recorded amusingly his experiences of publishing almost single-handed from a semi-farmhouse in the countryside. He and his like contributed to the infinite variety of personal publishing without adding much to the daily sales in most bookshops, but they kept alive a tradition worth cherishing.

5

British-Owned Groups

Longmans; Heinemann; Methuen—Associated Book Publishers; Paul Hamlyn; Granada; Hutchinson; The Bodley Head; Barrie & Jenkins; B.P.C.; First National Finance Company; Pergamon; W.H. Allen; Kaye & Ward; Book Centre.

Longmans' independence came to an end after 244 years in 1968, when they accepted a bid by the Financial and Provincial Publishing Company of between sixteen and seventeen million pounds. Mark, the last of the family still working in the company, remained chairman, and Longmans became the chief publishers in a group which already included the medical houses of J. & A. Churchill and E. & S. Livingstone, and the general and educational list of Oliver & Boyd (which had taken over the sixty-nine year old Meiklejohn imprint in 1958), all acquired by the *Financial Times* (F.P.P.C.) earlier in the decade. Later in 1968 Constable Young Books were bought and amalgamated with the Longmans juvenile list, and the Oliver & Boyd children's titles were sold to Chatto & Windus. In the following year consultations began between Mark Longman and Allen Lane to find a formula for the merging of Penguin's with the Longmans group, to avoid an American takeover of either, and sufficient agreement had been reached by the time of Sir Allen's death in 1970 for the union to be proclaimed on the day after he died. It was a particularly fitting alliance at one level, because the first Thomas Longman, like Lane, was a Bristolian.

Mark Longman joined the company before the war, and along with his second cousin Thomas Michael became a director in 1947. Thomas Longman, as we have seen, later left to start Darton, Longman & Todd. Mark Longman became vice-chairman in 1962 and joint chairman the following year with William Longman, who was by then eighty. Kenneth Potter's sudden demise led to the promotion of John Newsom, sometime senior education officer for Hertfordshire, and an educationalist of controversial opinions whose name was given to the official government report on secondary education, *Half Our Future*. Newsom became a working director of Longmans in 1957 and organized the move of the warehouse, and eventually the editorial offices also, to Harlow New Town in Essex, where a giant new building was erected opposite the railway station. From inside there were views over the gently rolling countryside, and most of the staff seemed to accept the transition from London, although some continued to live in the capital.

Mark Longman and Sir John Newsom led a distinguished team. It included John Guest and Michael Hoare (editorial), both ex-Collins, and the former a winner of the Heinemann Foundation for Literature for his wartime memoir *Broken Images*; P.C.B. Wallis (production), Bruce Hepburn, who went to them from Penguin's succeeding A. L. Stanton (sales), and Roy Yglesias, a former teacher, who had had publishing experience with Ginn, and who came in to take charge of the huge programme of school and university textbooks. The latter were always a dominant feature of the vast Longman organization, whose trading profit approached the £1 million mark as early as 1963.

The academic lists were of paramount importance to the group, but the general side was not neglected. Sales of the novels of Mary Renault and James Gould Cozzens may have looked relatively insignificant beside those for Eckersley's *Essential English for Foreign Students*, but they were welcome properties, as were Stevie Smith's poems and the works of Gavin Maxwell, although the latter had a tendency to involve himself and his publishers in lawsuits. His *Ring of Bright Water*, however, the story of his pet otter, was one of the big continuing sellers of the period, and there were no repercussions from the animal world. There was also G. M. Trevelyan's *English Social History*, a bestseller as soon as it was published in Britain in 1944. It subsequently appeared in a four-volume illustrated edition, later paperbacked by Penguin And in children's fiction, which ultimately became as difficult to sell in hard-back as adult novels, there were Leon Garfields' historical romances (acquired through the Constable purchase) which broke the general rule and were so appealing to young readers that they enjoyed great success in their original editions.

The Longman tradition of serving the trade was very much upheld by Kenneth Potter and Mark Longman, who both served not only as president of the P.A., but also as chairman of the N.B.L., while Sir John Newsom was a member of so many committees and inquiries that the effort undoubtedly contributed to his early death in 1971.

Mark himself died, aged fifty-seven, in 1972, after years of illness courageously borne. The last Longman in the company, he had no sons, and was said to have known before he died that the general list, which bore his name and in which he had particularly interested himself, was to become part of Allen Lane, The Penguin Press, under the managing directorship of James Price. Michael Hoare became redundant in this rationalization, and Bruce Hepburn had already negotiated for an early retirement at his own request.

The Pearson Longman group, as it was by then known, was too huge a concern to be thought of as a family business any more, and it was

thus, also, in the two medical companies which formed part of it.
J. Rivers, who had joined Churchill's in 1907, became managing director in 1947 when Augustus Churchill died, and Charles Macmillan, who
went to Livingstone's as an office boy in 1919, was joint managing
director by the end of the second war, and chairman when he retired in
1968. Oliver & Boyd, which started an important paperback series,
Writers and Critics, remained in the control of the bookselling families
of Thin & Grant until the sale to the *Financial Times*; Michael Wayte
was later appointed its managing director. It was inevitable that family
connections should disappear in a giant modern organization.

Longmans had two major anniversaries during this period. In 1949
they were 225 years old, and the then general manager, N. D. J. Brack,
recalled at a party that at the 200th anniversary his predecessor had
spoken to a staff of only ninety. He addressed 170. The other anniversary was of Gray's *Anatomy*, first published in 1858, and enjoying ever-
increasing sales one hundred years later, even though it was priced
at £6 6s. (£6.30) in 1959.

At Heinemann's, A. S. Frere succeeded Charles Evans as chairman at
the end of the war and reigned during the time when the Boswell
journals, discovered at Malahide Castle, were published with a success
all the more pronounced because from time to time librarians and
teachers denounced them as filth. In the years immediately following
the end of hostilities Heinemann's produced other winners, especially
in their traditional field of fiction. Graham Greene, after years of
patient nursing by Charles Evans, at last came into his own; there was
a D. H. Lawrence revival, which allowed for the crummily printed and
bound standard edition issued in the early 'fifties to be replaced by a
more elegant set; Maugham and Priestley continued to enhance the
list; and Nevil Shute flowered. Amongst the newcomers were Anthony
Burgess, who was immensely prolific, and endeared himself to some
when he was sacked as fiction reviewer of the *Yorkshire Post* for favourably noticing one of his own books written under the pseudonym of
Joseph Kell; Olivia Manning, whose Balkan Trilogy got all the critical
acclaim it deserved but not all the sales; and Anthony Powell, described
extravagantly as the English Proust, whose projected twelve-volume
A Dance To the Music of Time was three-quarters completed by the end
of this period. At a more popular level were the historical romances of
Georgette Heyer and Sergeanne Golon. In non-fiction an outstanding
success came with Michael Holroyd's two-volume *Lytton Strachey*, a work
of great length which extended the known bounds of biography by
embracing in detail the lives of many others of the Bloomsbury group
who had influenced and been influenced by the main subject. Whilst
the quiet bestseller from the back list, year after year, was a philosophical work in poetic-prose, *The Prophet*, by Kahlil Gibran, first

published in 1926. The cult for Gibran grew as the 'sixties gave way to the 'seventies. His other books also enjoyed healthy sales but *The Prophet* was noted as one of the ten most popular books amongst students in a campus survey carried out by *The Times Educational Supplement*.

Nevertheless, by the end of the 'fifties Heinemann's was not, financially, as steady as all this success should have made it, and a controlling interest was bought in 1961 by a public company, Thomas Tilling. Fortunately for publishing, Tilling's were not as philistine as many city companies, and one remarkable executive, W. Lionel Fraser, who recommended the purchase, was a most cultured and literate man as well as being a self-made banking tycoon. (Heinemann later published his autobiography.) Peter Ryder, their managing director, was also sympathetic, and when the group (in the meantime other imprints had been purchased) was once again prosperous, and ripe, in city terms, for takeover, the blandishments of McGraw-Hill and others were resisted. It was said, in 1970, that publishing had become one of the most profitable sides of the Tilling empire. There can be no doubt that the good sense of the city men in leaving the publishers to run their own show paid off.

Frere and his second-in-command H. L. Hall resigned in 1961. A Dwye Evans remained as managing director, and Harry Townshend, sales director of Rupert Hart-Davis, became general manager of the group. In 1962 Charles Pick (ex Michael Joseph) became managing director of William Heinemann with Dwye Evans, Chairman. Tim Manderson (formerly with Allan Wingate) was persuaded back from industry by Lionel Fraser, and became sales director. Nigel Viney joined as production director, and Bill Holden, ex-Collins and others, became publicity director, organizing many parties and luncheons until his resignation in 1970. (Soon after, he bought a bookshop in St Johns Wood, north-west London.) The company moved from an elegant William and Mary mansion in Great Russell Street, into a bleak glass and concrete structure in Mayfair in 1959. The list, which had grown like an unweeded garden, was cut back ruthlessly, prices of the saleable back titles were increased sharply and new authors were attracted. Monica Dickens, Richard Gordon and others followed Charles Pick from Joseph's; John Le Carré came from Gollancz but went on to Hodder; Georgette Heyer and Graham Greene went to the Bodley Head, as did editor James Michie. Agreements and rights, subjects not mentioned much in these pages, were the province of Elizabeth Anderson, a director who began her career as Dwye Evans's Secretary.

From all this upheaval a healthy new list emerged, stimulated by the fantastic success of the *Forsyte Saga* which B.B.C. television filmed for a twenty-six-week serial. This had been shown in the U.K. three times by the end of 1970, and in many other countries, including Soviet Russia, and had led to the sale of over 150,000 volumes in the Heinemann editions and to a million and a half Penguins (in nine volumes) during a two-year period.

In 1946 a young man returned from the forces, deciding to opt for publishing rather than politics, and was given the task of reviving the educational department which had been discontinued during the war. Alan Hill was joined by Edward Thompson in 1947, and by Anthony Beal two years later. By 1961 the turnover of Heinemann Educational Books had doubled every three years. The Drama Library (Thompson's particular baby) and the New Windmill Series were launched, the latter consisting of shortened versions of mostly contemporary works, edited for young readers. H.E.B. became a separate company in 1961, and soon after moved out of the overcrowded Queen Street offices and into a handsome terrace building once the town house of Lord Randolph Churchill, in nearby Charles Street. Subsidiary companies were established in Australia, New Zealand, South East Asia, East and West Africa and Canada; in each case local publishing followed, and Alan Hill was especially proud of his African Writers Series. He had an ever-increasing and extremely loyal staff (Hamish MacGibbon, son of James, amongst them) who rarely moved on to work for other publishers, perhaps because the expansion of H.E.B. was rapid enough to allow for promotion without having to wait to step into dead men's shoes. Perhaps, also, it was because twenty-five years after it had started the company was still conducted as an exciting adventure into publishing, with Alan Hill leading a joyous mission, in the course of which he was once accused, at an African airport, of being a Biafran mercenary. (Nigeria was then in the throes of civil war.) It was a story he loved to tell and embellish.

Secker & Warburg and Hart-Davis were in the group by 1956. Fred Warburg related his recurrent financial crises in his *An Occupation for Gentlemen*. These were eased somewhat when George Orwell became a bestseller with *Animal Farm* and *1984*, but he was glad, all the same, to accept shelter under the Heinemann umbrella, and his style was not cramped in any way. He continued to publish what he wanted to, and in Angus Wilson he discovered probably the most important new British novelist of the period; to date all of Angus Wilson's novels and short stories have appeared under the Secker & Warburg imprint. Warburg, and his senior colleague Roger Senhouse, successfully introduced Günter Grass and other Continental authors to Britain, and equally rewarding for them were the vast tomes of American James Michener. The many Japanese novelists whom they also published were, on the whole, less enthusiastically received. David Farrer (sales and editorial) and John Pattison were other senior colleagues from 1947, but the latter resigned in 1963. It was Farrer who nursed the literary talent of an ex-criminal, Frank Norman, whose first book, *Bang to Rights*, was especially popular.

Fred Warburg was one of the first to increase prices noticeably, and at times he seemed to be several shillings ahead of what seemed acceptable. Events, however, often proved him right, and it is arguable whether Angus Wilson's *No Laughing Matter* would have sold more copies at 35s. (£1.75) than it did at 42s. (£2.10).

Rupert Hart-Davis always claimed that having too many bestsellers lost him his independence. He started his own imprint when he was demobbed, Jonathan Cape having announced in his lordly way that he couldn't even consider Hart-Davis's proposed terms on which he should return to Bedford Square, and in his early days he published Heinrich Harrer's *Seven Years in Tibet*, Edward Young's *One of our Submarines* and J. H. Williams's *Elephant Bill*, all of which were runaway winners, so that the firm expanded more quickly than was good for it and when the following years did not bring equal trios of bestsellers he was compelled to seek financial support from a large group. Edward Young, who had been with Hart-Davis from the start, resigned in 1955, but Harry Townshend, whose family had once owned Simpkin Marshall, stayed on. He was a kindly sales director in as much as he would lunch a bookseller generously but be absolutely adamant in his refusal to take returns. Later he went back to his first love, which was farming.

Rupert Hart-Davis wrote a scholarly life of Hugh Walpole which Macmillan published, and also edited the letters of Oscar Wilde for his own list; but that was after he had left the Heinemann group and had the backing, from 1962 for a short period, of Harcourt, Brace of New York. The American association lasted but briefly, and the firm was sold to Bernstein of Granada, about whom I shall write later.

The other imprints in the Heinemann Group were the World's Work (1913) Ltd; Peter Davies, of which Derek Priestley, sometime sales manager of William Heinemann, became managing director in 1968; the Naldrett Press (sporting books); Heinemann & Zsolnay (see p. 334); and Heinemann (Medical Books) Ltd, operating from an address in Bedford Square and numbering Dwye Evans's son amongst its staff. The Peter Davies imprint was much revived by Priestley, and enjoyed particular success with the works of Margaret Powell, who, after spending much of her life as housemaid and kitchenmaid, discovered she had a rich talent for writing about it. Peter Davies's brother Nicholas was active for many years after the war and fittingly his firm published the definitive book about Barrie and *Peter Pan*. Peter Davies himself died by falling in front of an underground train in 1960.

Two ex-managing directors returned to Methuen during the war years, C. W. Chamberlain, who was re-appointed to his old position and also to the chairmanship, and E. V. Rieu, who interrupted his work on translating Homer for Penguin's, to take on editorial work. (Frank Mumby was also employed as part-time reader.) In 1946 Chamberlain died and was succeeded by Nutcombe Hume, and when the younger editors returned from the war, Rieu became an editorial adviser. Stanley Unwin sold a minority holding in the company which, according to his autobiography, he could have controlled, and J. Alan White, on whom increasing responsibility had fallen in recent years, became managing director. White organized the move of Methuen's warehouse into Book Centre, which also serviced Chapman & Hall. In 1950 Methuen bought a half share in Book Centre and thus became equal principal controllers with Pitman, until they withdrew in the 1960s to form their own trade distribution centre at Andover in Hampshire. By then they had become Associated Book Publishers Ltd, which included the two companies already mentioned and Sweet & Maxwell, Stevens & Son, Eyre & Spottiswoode and Tavistock Publications, not to mention E. & F. Spon and W. Green. Group turnover in 1969 exceeded £7 million, and profit before tax was over £684,000. It was a far cry from the dodgy 'thirties.

Methuen, ever strong in children's books, promoted the French strip cartoon series *Tintin*, by Hergé, and received the approval of many teachers for so doing; they were less successful with their Talking Books series, if only, perhaps, because the finished product was very little different from an ordinary gramophone record. They continued to publish de Brunhoff's Babar books, but not, alas, in the original large format, and introduced the Bruna books and friezes from Holland. Halfdan Lynner, with Peter Wolfe as his assistant for part of the time, was sales manager until he returned to his native Norway: Piers Raymond replaced him, and remained for ten years, during which time overall direction passed to Peter Allsop. When Raymond left, Frank Herrmann the production manager, who had written some successful juveniles, also went, and there were frequent announcements of new management structures within A.B.P. From these Michael Turner, who had been with Methuen for many years on the advertising and publicity side, designing eye-catching copy, emerged as marketing director, and Charles Friend, a long-serving employee of Eyre & Spottiswoode, as sales director. Amongst senior editors there was less change, Peter Wait, John Cullen and Anthony Forster serving from 1945 onwards and building strong general and academic lists, and Olive Jones taking charge of juveniles after Eleanor Graham had departed to edit Puffins.

At Eyre & Spottiswoode Frank Morley, who wrote two memoirs of his publishing life for other imprints, stayed until 1956 as vice-chairman to Douglas Jerrold who remained until 1959 two years after the merger with Methuen. A new recruit was Maurice Temple Smith, sometime

assistant at Bryce's bookshop after graduating, and then for a short
while with Spon before moving sideways into Eyre & Spottiswoode.
There he bought John Braine's *Room at the Top*, which became an instant
success, its *zeitgeist* hero being readily recognizable as a contemporary
phenomenon both fascinating and repellent. Temple Smith also built
up a formidable list of historical biographies during his stay.

In 1961 the Methuen group received an offer from Howard Samuel
(see p. 494) of 50s. (£2.50) for each £1 ordinary share. The offer expired
the day before Samuel's death, after which share prices dropped
sharply. Samuel held 40 per cent of the shares, which were then bought
by Penguin's, Allen Lane joining the board. Col. O. E. Crosthwaite-
Eyre at this time held 56 per cent of the shares, and the Eyre Family
Trust bought back the Penguin holding in 1962, when Lane resigned.

Chapman & Hall, once heavily dependent on Dickens, was again
very much a one-author list (with all due respect to others whose novels
appeared on it) during this period, when Evelyn Waugh dominated the
literary side in talent and sales. The long held Wiley concession in
technical books was lost when the American company set up its own
organization in Sussex, where it fell at once into the Yankee habit
of selling its books at 20 per cent discount. Technical and medical
publishers, A.B.P. excepted, were amongst the last to understand the
necessity of improving their terms to stockholding booksellers. When
university booksellers of one group threatened to refuse to stock their
academic and technical books unless they received improved terms,
A.B.P. graciously applied general terms of 38.3 per cent to all their
publications, apart from the law list, and gave it unasked to all charter
booksellers. (Faber, it should be recorded, gave equally enlightened
terms.) An unsuspected advantage of the merger system, from the bookseller's point of view, was that it became unnecessary to negotiate
separately with the many companies forming the one integrated group.

The Paul Hamlyn story will almost certainly become a wide-screen
musical in glorious colourscope with international rights sold in advance
and a world premiere in space. It has all the ingredients of a Hollywood
epic, although it was not certain at one moment that its incidental
music did not already exist in *The Sorcerer's Apprentice*.

Hamlyn, an assistant at Zwemmer's bookshop, inherited £300 in
1946. He registered Books for Pleasure as a company, bought up remainders and used department stores as his principal outlet. He serviced
the stands he put into the stores and allowed returns. In the early
'fifties he started publishing his own books and printed them, for cheapness, in Czechoslovakia. He also extended his remaindering to the
United States, and acquired several foundering firms, amongst them,
Andrew Dakers, the Batchworth Press and Peter Nevill. He took warehouse premises in Spring Place, Kentish Town, in north-west London,

and set about proving that the great British public would buy books if they were attractively presented at bargain prices. Speaking to the Society of Young Publishers in 1960 he said that most people were terrified of going into a bookshop, and that to change this attitude new outlets must be found. Translating words into action, he did no harm to traditional shops but, on the contrary, brought increased sales to existing booksellers whose shops were brightened by the very appearance of his products. Young people in publishing were eager to work for him as Joan Clibbon, an editor from 1958 onward, recorded in a *Bookseller* article in 1970, because to do so was exciting and stimulating. The editors thought up their own books, and then Hamlyn and his salesmen literally flew around the world selling them and buying others. At senior level he was joined in 1959 by Philip Jarvis, who, when book buyer for Boot's, had become notorious for insisting that books could be sold like soap, and in 1963 by Ralph Vernon-Hunt, who came from Pan Books. Vernon-Hunt returned to Pan later in the decade, by which time Hamlyn had sold out to the International Publishing Corporation, owners of the *Daily Mirror*, for £2,275,000.

Hamlyn was thirty-nine and a millionaire, and retained his job in the deal. He found himself head of a whole division of publishing, because I.P.C. had already bought Odham's Press, thus acquiring Newnes, Pearson, Country Life, Collingridge, Dean's Rag Books (founded in the eighteenth century) and Hulton's annuals. Spring Place had been vacated for offices in Fulham; from there the organization moved to Hamlyn House in Feltham, west London, but Hamlyn himself was based at the *Daily Mirror* building on the edge of Fleet Street, at the centre of power. When his immediate superior, Cecil King, was ousted it was revealed that he individually owned more shares in I.P.C. than anyone else. In 1968 it was announced that the book division, despite vast turnover, was making a loss. There had been a takeover battle with Pergamon the year before for control of Butterworth's, and I.P.C. had won. Two groups were then formed, with the popular books in one and the scientific, including Ginn (acquired through Odham's but later re-sold) and Temple Press (through Odhams-Newnes), in the other. But the distribution machine was creating nightmares for the sales staff and booksellers, and then in the disastrous floods of autumn 1968 hundreds of thousands of Odham's books were washed away. Nevertheless sales increased by £18 million in that year (although the figure also included records and prints). But there were rumours of the employment of eighty or so accountants to get the computer to work properly, and of vast undiscovered stocks of popular titles which the machine had answered out of stock. There were sackings and resignations and reorganization of the sales force, and then Hamlyn himself left in May 1970, followed a few months later by Philip Jarvis. Ken Stephenson had come in earlier in the year from S.P.C.K. and Heinemann, via Gordon & Gotch, as a consultant director, and he planned the further move of the warehouse to Wellingborough in Northamptonshire. The distribution problem was partly resolved through the initiative of Bertram's of Norwich, who became wholesalers of Hamlyn books, giving a by-return service with handwritten invoices enclosed with the goods.

Howard Samuel, a left-wing property tycoon with a genuine interest in the arts, made James MacGibbon an unexpected offer for MacGibbon & Kee in 1956, and it was accepted. MacGibbon, who had started the list soon after the war with Robert Kee, later to become a prominent television commentator, left to go into Curtis Brown's literary agency, where another former publisher, Graham Watson, was already a senior executive. Samuel appointed Reg Davis-Poynter, who had been a bookseller with Denny's and a publisher with Max Reinhardt's H.F.L.(Ltd), as general manager; David Harrison, a Heinemann rep., sales manager; Tim O'Keefe, editor; and Tom Maschler in charge of foreign and subsidiary rights. The backlist included the novelist Colin MacInnes (son of Angela Thirkell), who was to write some saleable books based on teenage and immigrant life, and the new regime secured short stories by Doris Lessing, a South African writer whose novels were becoming popular, and had a *succès d'estime* with a volume edited by Maschler called *Declaration*. Later came the beginnings of the group, with the purchase of Staples Press (mainly dental and business management books) and Arco (started by Bernard Hanison who later became a restaurateur).

In 1961 Samuel was drowned whilst on holiday in Greece. He left £15,000 to Davis-Poynter and £10,000 to Harrison, and the former arranged through a solicitor friend (Arnold, later Lord, Goodman, chairman of the Arts Council) for Sidney Bernstein to buy MacGibbon's and retain the services of himself and his colleagues. The year following saw publication of the first volume of Michael Foot's biography of his friend Aneurin Bevan, one of Labour's outstanding statesmen. In 1963, again at the suggestion of Arnold Goodman, Rupert Hart-Davis Ltd was acquired, and Adlard Coles Ltd (concerned with books on sailing) was bought from the American firm of Harcourt Brace; the Adlard Coles deal was unusual in that it reversed the trend which transferred ownership of so many companies from east to west of the Atlantic. Bernstein, who was in the entertainment world, also bought, as we have seen, some of Jonathan Cape's shares, again at the instigation of Goodman. He was very much concerned to enlarge his new empire speedily, and took over Panther books and another paperback range, Mayflower, which had been founded in 1948 to represent American educational publishers in England. Alewyn Birch moved from Heinemann, where he had been export sales director, to Granada, as Bernstein's group became known, becoming sales director in 1969. In the same year, David Harrison resigned, followed soon after by Davis-Poynter, who then started to plan his own list with the backing of Kingsley Amis, Lord Goodman and others. Tim O'Keefe also departed and founded yet another new imprint.

By the end of 1970 Granada, through the changed image of the Hart-Davis imprint, were selling the first book on women's lib, a new fad of the new decade. *The Female Eunuch*, by Germaine Greer, sold as fast as they could print it, which, until 1971, was not fast enough to meet the demand.

When Walter Hutchinson died in 1950 he was the subject of a number of unflattering obituary notices, one of which occupied a whole page of *The Bookseller*, above the initials of its editor. Segrave referred to his 'uninhibited capacity for self-glorification', which was manifested in a circular he distributed to the trade at the end of the war. In this, Hutchinson told 'with pardonable pride, the story of the greatest achievement in publishing history' which, according to him, was the vital contribution his companies had made to ensure the survival of the book trade. 'If', he proclaimed grandly, 'money alone were the measure of Hutchinson support, the payment of £1,000 a day towards the cost of the war ... would enable us to rest content that through our endeavour we fulfilled to overflowing this responsibility which we so readily accepted.' Segrave said that to many of his fellow publishers Hutchinson was a figure of fun, but that his unpredictable rages made him an object of terror to those whom he sacked without warning. A few days after his suicide an injunction was sought to put the company into liquidation, a firm of electrical contractors having tired of waiting for payment of some £1,400 for work done at Hutchinson House, off Oxford Street, which 'Mr Walter' had turned into a National Gallery of British Sports and Pastimes. When this had been sorted out Mrs K. H. Webb and F. C. Thomas were appointed to administer the company under the chairmanship of Hutchinson's widow.

This management continued until 1956, when Robert Lusty was attracted from Michael Joseph's to become managing director with a reputedly large salary, watertight contract and chauffeur-driven Bentley. He put into action an immediate and much needed policy of rationalization and gave the group an overall new colophon, that of a bull. All the companies which Walter had acquired, and no one knew quite how many there were, had learned to operate autonomously, with the result that three or more of them would often produce books on the same subject at approximately the same time. Bob Lusty straightened out this tangle, settling all the sporting books on Stanley Paul, the romantic fiction on Hurst & Blackett, crime on John Long and so forth. He also, unlike his predecessors, resumed the normal practice of dating his books.

The journalist and ex-editor of the *Spectator*, Iain Hamilton, was an editorial director for some years until 1961, from which date Harold Harris, ex-*Evening Standard*, held the same position. Elizabeth Stockwell had the distinction of becoming sales director, a rare achievement for a woman. David Roy (son of the great Roy of W.H.S.) joined from Longmans to assist first Geoffrey Howard, who had been with Hutchinson for most of his working life, and, later, Miss Stockwell. The old trade premises in Ireland Yard, St Andrews Hill, were abandoned; Walter's 'Museum' in Stratford Place was also vacated and the substitute for the former was found in a new warehouse at Tiptree, in Essex, and for the latter in a vast block in Great Portland Street, from which most staff departed for Radlett in 1971.

Arthur Koestler was one of the leading Hutchinson authors during this period; his *The Sleepwalkers* and *The Act of Creation*, good examples of serious scientific-philosophical works, enjoyed large sales. Dennis Wheatley, Ethel Mannin, Frank Slaughter and other novelists continued to provide bread and butter; the Hutchinson University Library was put into paperback and Arrow Books were promoted for popular softback titles. Robert Lusty also started a New Authors imprint to help first novelists, but the ever-increasing cost of production soon affected the overall success of this and other similar ventures. He paid big money for the book by Stalin's daughter, *Twenty Letters To a Friend*, and also published Svetlana's second book. A regular annual seller was *The Saturday Book*, a glossy chocolate-box of a book for the Christmas market, exotic and romantic in text and illustration, edited first by Leonard Russell, later by John Hadfield. In 1970 he enjoyed unusual success with a book of verse, when Mary Wilson, wife of the ex-premier, published her *Poems* which were much in the Patience Strong tradition and sold almost as well as that other lady's harmless and comforting rhymes. In 1959 R. A. A. Holt, grandson of Sir George Hutchinson, was elected chairman of Hutchinson (Ltd) which controlled both the publishing group and a printing trust.

The Bodley Head was sold by the Unwin-Howard-Taylor triumvirate to Ansbacher & Co., merchant bankers who had backed Max Reinhardt in 1957. Reinhardt had had his own small publishing company since 1949, issuing a few books of quality each year, including the Bernard Shaw–Ellen Terry Letters, and volumes of Paul Jennings's amusing essays from the *Observer*. Reinhardt already owned H.F.L. (Publishers) Ltd (law and accountancy) when he bought The Bodley Head and began to restore its fortunes. (At the suggestion of Sir Francis Meynell he had also revived the Nonesuch imprint, bringing out a four-volume Shakespeare for Coronation Year, 1953.) After The Bodley Head, came Putnam's (1962), including Bowes & Bowes Publishers Ltd (as distinct from the bookshop) and Nattali & Maurice, T. Werner

Laurie (bought in 1957) and Hollis & Carter (1962). Putnam had been owned for several years by Roger Lubbock, a member of the distinguished family of Liberal politicians, and sometime journalist in Glasgow. He and John Huntington, nephew of Constant of that ilk, with John Pudney as part-time editorial director, published some interesting books, among them Caitlin (widow of Dylan) Thomas's autobiography, *Leftover Life to Kill*, and also had a profitable line in aircraft books. John Huntington moved to The Bodley Head with Putnam but Lubbock studied law and later became involved in publishing for the Open University.

Max Reinhardt had an excellent children's editor in Judy Taylor who made the juvenile list one of the best in contemporary publishing, and the general side was expanded with some notable successes such as Charles Chaplin's autobiography, and some of the works of Solzhenitsyn, the Soviet author whose books were frowned upon by his own government. After his retirement from the B.B.C., Graham Greene's brother Sir Hugh Carleton Greene became chairman of a board which included Sir Francis Meynell and the actors Sir Ralph Richardson and Anthony Quayle.

The Barrie & Jenkins group evolved rather tortuously, with frequent announcements of a change of name. There were five companies in it: James Barrie Ltd, which started soon after the war, and was managed by Leopold Ullstein, a refugee publisher from Germany, and, amongst others, John Bunting (son of Daniel George); the Rockliff Publishing Corporation, whose book side was the hobby of a very successful magazine proprietor, R. H. Rockliff, publisher of the monthly *Theatre World*; Herbert Jenkins Ltd, which went on indefatigably publishing the works of P. G. Wodehouse and also a great many volumes on fishing and guns (Barrie acquiring the entire issued capital in 1965); Hammond, Hammond, owned by Peter Guttmann until his death in 1965, and having big sellers in the humorous autobiographies of Betty Macdonald (*The Egg and I, The Plague and I*), and with the novels of Radclyffe Hall; and the Cresset Press, which joined the group when Dennis Cohen retired; Cresset had a distinguished small list, which included the novels of Carson McCullers and John O'Hara, the plays of Arthur Miller, various books by Marghanita Laski, whose husband John Howard was a director of the firm and edited Napoleon's letters for them, and the Cresset Classics, which kept in print many minor works such as the *Autobiography* of Leigh Hunt and the journal of Celia Fiennes. As Barrie & Jenkins settled down it became apparent that its imprint would appear on a great many fine art books, produced under the guidance of Richard Wadleigh, and that the list was to be broad-based including some excellent guidebooks. An editorial director was Christopher MacLehose, whose father had had his own imprint until 1939, when it was sold to Chambers, and whose great-grandfather was printer to Glasgow University (see p. 222).

Another large group belonged to the printers Purnell, and became known as B.P.C. Publishing Ltd. Book publishing was only a small part of the multifarious activities which led to a public scandal when its chairman, Wilfred Harvey, was alleged to have paid himself more expenses than the company could afford. B.P.C. were involved with Pergamon (see below) in the sale of certain encyclopaedias which enjoyed a large loss, as did the fortnightly part-works which were promoted in a great flurry by Richard Holme, who had come from Penguin and went on to further merchandising in America in 1970. The particular imprints which B.P.C. absorbed included some which had quietly published saleable books under expert direction before the publicity arc lights were directed on to them. Chief of them was Macdonald's. For some twenty years E. R. H. Harvey, John Foster White and James Taylor-Whitehead had run the editorial side, and Walter Parrish had been production director. In 1967 James MacGibbon became managing director and stayed for nearly three years, during which time the imprint appeared to gain a new lease of life. Alongside the general books which were MacGibbon's particular concern a very broadbased juvenile list was promoted with deserved success. But, as in the Granada group, the heads of executives fell swiftly in the B.P.C. organization, and the *Times* gossip writer had many a paragraph recording the departure of this or that senior employee. The group took over John Lehmann Ltd early in our period and Max Parrish a few years later, in neither case retaining the services of the man whose name was given to the imprint. Similarly with the military list of Gale & Polden; E. R. Polden resigning the managing directorship in 1965 owing to 'fundamental differences of opinion between him and Mr Wilfred Harvey'. Sampson Low, Old-bourne and T. V. Boardman Ltd were later absorbed, and in 1968 the Bancroft children's list was added. In 1971 the book publishing departments of B.P.C. were reorganized, and in April 1973 Ronald Whiting became managing director of Macdonald and Janes, with responsibility for all general books.

The Lock and Shipton families had continued to own and manage Ward Lock, living mostly off the backlist, bringing out new editions of the famous Red Guides and of Mrs Beeton's various cookery books. In 1971 they were bought by the First National Finance Company which already owned the religious house of Marshall, Morgan & Scott. Anthony Shipton, who had become managing director in 1969, was succeeded by Frank Herrmann.

Pergamon was 38 per cent American owned in 1970, following a highly publicized takeover bid by Leasco Data Processing Corporation in 1969, after which dealing in shares was suspended and a Board of

Trade inquiry instituted. Robert Maxwell, who until then had had the majority holding, was ousted from the board, but was invited back in 1971 in a consultative capacity, by which time it appeared that Leasco wished to sell their shares. Following the collapse of Simpkin's, Maxwell had concentrated on building up Pergamon which published textbooks, encyclopaedias and scientific journals. Its ramifications were wide and Maxwell was a true son of his time in buying all he could lay hands on, including the Exeter printers and booksellers Wheaton & Co., the Religious Education Press and a number of bookshops. He failed to buy Butterworth's, as we have seen, and some of his other projected deals, including a bid for the *News of the World*, did not come off. In 1964 he became Labour M.P. for Buckingham, but lost his seat in 1970. Arthur Minshull moved over to Pergamon from Simpkin's and stayed until 1960, when over a hundred publishers subscribed to a donation which enabled him to fulfil a wish to visit Canada.

It is difficult to know where to fit in W. H. Allen because that old-established imprint was sold by Mark Goulden to Doubleday in 1961, bought back by him in 1968, re-sold to the Walter Reade Organization of America in 1970, and then returned to British ownership (Howard & Wyndham) a few months later. During all these changes Goulden retained control of the list, and Jeffrey Simmons and Donald Morrison, two senior colleagues of long standing, remained loyal to him and he to them. They published much American fiction during this time and introduced at least one important young English novelist, Alan Sillitoe, whose *Saturday Night and Sunday Morning* was an outstanding success of the mid-'fifties. Through American tie-ups there were agencies for the Yoseloff list, and in non-fiction there was a tendency to specialize in books of Jewish lore and humour, and in biographies of film stars. They also had the Sasek books on various cities of the world, *This is London* becoming thickly buttered bread for booksellers in the capital.

Lastly, Kaye & Ward, a small group formed in 1955 and owned by Straker's, the printers. It was born of Nicholas Kaye Ltd and Nicholas Vane Ltd, both of which began in 1947, and Edmund Ward Ltd. Ward had published his first book in Leicester in 1942, and became well known for the Thomas the Tank Engine series of books for young children written by the Reverend Awdry (sales of three million by 1970) and the equally successful Ant and Bee series of readers. They produced many books on sport and athletics as well as other series for the juvenile market.

The Book Centre, on London's North Circular Road, in unprepossessing Neasden, was the instrument through which an increasing number of publishers mentioned both above and later distributed and invoiced.

In 1945 its annual turnover was £500,000; in 1970, including the Publishers' Computer Service used by those who distributed for themselves, was £21,500,000. The Orders Clearing service, started in 1956, handled 1,390,000 orders in 1960 and over 4 million in 1970, by which date some London booksellers had stopped using it and were collating their order through B.O.D. (Booksellers Order Distribution) on the initiative of B.A. London Branch members.

G. A. Davies was general manager and company secretary of Book Centre until 1953, when J. Neilson Lapraik became the first managing director. He was succeeded by Frank Sanders in 1958 and it was under Sanders' leadership that the Publishers' Computer Service was started, as well as Parcels Clearing for all publishers. The number of parcels cleared weekly in 1960 was 8,000, and in 1970, by the time the Publishers' and Booksellers' Delivery Service (P.B.D.S.) had commenced, 84,000.

Frank Sanders was succeeded in 1969 by B. C. (Ben) Winter-Goodwin, an executive from outside the book trade who instantly applied his perceptive brain to the new problems before him. He made many friends, among them his predecessor, who remained on the board, and also some enemies, since he was not shy of hitting back at those who complained about his organization. In 1970 the Book Centre serviced 1,250,000 orders for those of its members whose distribution and warehousing it also managed, and another 1,300,000 for those who used only its computer for invoicing and collection of accounts.

By 1970 there was also a warehouse at Southport, Lancashire, which was to play its part in an important change in policy ushered in two years later when the number of publishers allowed to use the full Book Centre service was sharply decreased.

6

Foreign-Owned Groups

North-American controlled groups: Thomson—Crowell, Collier-Macmillan—Praeger; U.S. publishers represented in the U.K.: Harper & Row—Heath—R. R. Bowker—McGraw-Hill—Prentice-Hall—Leonard Hill Group; T.A.B.S.; American Book Supply Ltd; Angus & Robertson.

The Thomson Group of Publishers came into being when the Canadian newspaper magnate bought Illustrated Newspapers, to which Michael Joseph had sold a majority of his shares in the 'fifties. Roy (later Lord) Thomson caused a crisis in the affairs of Joseph in 1962, because following his acquisition of the firm there were mass resignations: the joint managing directors Charles Pick and Peter Hebdon, the editorial director, Roland Gant, who had come from Heinemann in 1956, and the chief London representative, Ian Kiek announced that they would be joining Jonathan Cape, Allen Lane having agreed to buy a substantial part of the equity in that house (see p. 459). The deal fell through; Pick moved to Heinemann; Gant to Secker, Kiek to Hutchinson, and Peter Hebdon returned to Joseph's, which, in the meantime, had formed an association with Cassell's, two of whose directors joined the board to steer it through a difficult period.

Michael Joseph's enjoyed great success during the ten years following the war, particularly with the fiction of H. E. Bates, Paul Gallico, John Masters, Monica Dickens, C. S. Forester, John Wyndham and Joyce Cary. It was a list on which aspiring and established novelists were happy to appear because it had the justified reputation of being sold by a lively sales force who, on Michael Joseph's instructions, never oversold, and who read other publishers' books.

Michael Joseph, whose second wife, Anthea, was a member of the board, sold out to Illustrated Newspapers because he needed fresh capital to finance his expanding list. Robert Lusty, who had managed the business during the war, went back to Hutchinson's, and Charles Pick and Peter Hebdon, who had grown up with the firm, took command when Joseph died in 1958.

After his return to Joseph's, Peter Hebdon became increasingly involved in the higher management of the Thomson empire as other imprints were acquired. The extra responsibilities and taxing overseas travel which this necessitated undoubtedly led to his death in 1970, at the age of fifty-three. Whilst keeping up a front of utter ruthlessness, Peter Hebdon could never, for long, hide a deep affection and concern for those he worked with and published. He was not made for the large organization because he had learned his craft from a great individual publisher, but he was supremely confident and energetic in managing the growth of Joseph's after the Thomson takeover. He built up the subsidiary imprint, Pelham Books, which William Luscombe came from Stanley Paul's to manage and further expand.

During the 'sixties the Joseph list, although retaining many of the novelists of its early days, branched out into non-fiction and especially, through Pelham, into sporting books. It was traditional practice for books by leading sportsmen to be ghosted by professional writers. Pelham carried the operation a stage further when they published ghosted novels by famous sportsmen.

Amongst Joseph's major successes in the 1960s was a beautifully illustrated volume, *The Concise British Flora in Colour*, compiled by an elderly clergyman, H. Keble Martin, who had devoted his spare time for many years to collecting specimens from all over the British Isles. Published at a time when what was thought of as pornography was flooding the bookshops, this became a refreshing book to sell, and sell it did, in huge quantities. Other non-porn items were the Shell Guides to Britain, England, Scotland, etc. Walter Allen, whose own novels were published by Joseph, but whose critical works came from Phoenix House, was chief reader to Joseph's for much of this period; Edmund Fisher, son of the naturalist James Fisher, became managing director when Peter Hebdon died. Raleigh Trevelyan succeeded Roland Gant in 1962.

Thomson, having become a book publisher by accident, went on to develop his new empire. Thomas Nelson was purchased in 1962, for a reported price of 'little short of £2 million', and Jocelyn Baines was appointed as managing director of the 164-year-old imprint. The rather staid list of classics, juveniles, philosophy and schoolbooks, was embellished with coffee-table items such as Robert Carrier's *Great Dishes of the World* and some handsome volumes on English houses and palaces. Neil McFarlane remained as sales director until the end of 1969, and then on his retirement joined Michael Joseph part time, thus, after all, handling the sales of *The Concise British Flora* which Nelson had rejected. Frank Hermann came briefly from Methuen as managing director.

Hamish Hamilton's is a list which it would be easy to underestimate in a history being written so close to its achievements. Hamilton sold out to Thomson, whose publishing group had an overall managing director in Gordon Brunton, on the understanding that he would retain complete editorial independence during his lifetime. It was Thomson's policy to allow his newspaper editors similar freedom, provided their publications were run profitably.

Hamilton was responsible in the late 'forties for an outstanding series of reprints — the Novel Library. They had varying patterned designs on the dust jackets and binding which blended when placed together on a shelf, and they were impeccably printed. The size (foolscap 8vo) made them a joy for the traveller or armchair reader, and it was a matter for great regret that the series was allowed to die. Hamish, known as 'Jamie', Hamilton never seemed to care much for establishing a back-list which would last over several decades, although in fact many of the books he published did enjoy success for a long time. He had the knack of producing the unexpected bestseller, and his authors included Alan Morehead, J. K. Galbraith, Albert Camus, Jean-Paul Sartre, Georges Simenon, Nancy Mitford, L. P. Hartley and J. D. Salinger, whose *The Catcher in the Rye*, first published in the U.K. in 1951 with mild success but critical acclaim, became perhaps *the* seminal novel of the era. Salinger bridged two generations, and when the Penguin edition eventually appeared teenagers were affronted to be told that my generation had already discovered and been excited by it. Hamilton also had a strong line in political and musical memoirs and the children's list, built up by Richard Hough, a prolific author on many subjects including naval history, grew in stature and was eventually managed expertly by Julia MacRae (ex-Collins), one of several women who made this important field of publishing peculiarly their own.

Hamish Hamilton relinquished the managing directorship in 1971 in favour of a newcomer, Gillon Aitken, but remained as chairman. Aitken had had eight years publishing experience, mainly with Chapman & Hall, followed by four years as partner in a literary agency, and had also become known as a translator of Pushkin and Solzhenitsyn.

George Rainbird, the last member of the group, was in a special category. Rainbird created books at the request of fellow publishers, and also suggested to others what they should publish in a particular format. George Rainbird had been concerned with the making of books for a long while before 1951 when he produced, for Collins, a large format, colour-plate edition of Thornton's *Temple of Flora*. This was Rainbird's introduction to publishing, and the venture began in Billy Collins's office where he saw and admired a Thornton print. Rainbird and his partner, Ruari McLean, went on to produce other splendid volumes for Collins, including the *Album de Redouté*, during the next five years. They then turned their attention to creating fine books from original material, and formed a small company to produce six volumes on *Old Garden Roses*, some drawings by Augustus John and Henry Moore's *Heads, Figures and Ideas*. The books were published in limited editions at between fifteen and one hundred guineas, which invariably sold out, and in standard editions at between seven and ten guineas, which did not. The operation proved uneconomic, and *Old Garden*

Roses was abandoned with only two volumes published. Meanwhile sponsored books for large companies such as Shell and Ilford were proving very profitable, and in 1965 the Rainbird-designed *The Concise British Flora* (see above) was the bestseller of the year. At the end of '66 Rainbird sold to Thomson, and by 1968 he had John Hadfield and Edward Young with him, and was regularly publishing 12 in. × 10½in. volumes which were recognizable as Rainbird books. Amongst their huge successes were Nancy Mitford's study of Louis XIV, *The Sun King* (Hamish Hamilton); Angus Wilson's *The World of Charles Dickens* (Secker); Hammond Innes's *The Conquistadors* (Collins) and J. B. Priestley's *The Edwardians* (Heinemann). The authors did not get as high a royalty as they received from their other books because the illustrations were realistically regarded as being as important in sales appeal as the text, but they enjoyed an international sale, the American and German markets being especially important. Rainbird's did not have their own sales organization, except for foreign rights, and distributed through the publishers whose books they produced. Each year they took on trainees whose year's apprenticeship included working with a printer for a few weeks and in a book shop for two or three months.

The ties between Macmillan, New York, for long a separate company, and its London parent grew weaker after the war and, eventually, nonexistent. The American company opened a London office and the British Macmillan started the St Martin's Press in New York in 1952. In the 'sixties there were various takeovers by the American company involving new names, and by the time the company had become markedly acquisitive in the U.K. it was known as Crowell, Collier-Macmillan Ltd. Under its own imprint it brought out mainly technical and academic books, but also introduced one popular cartoon animal to the British public in Max, a hamster whose creator was Giovanetti. In 1968 Crowell, Collier bought Studio Vista and Geoffrey Chapman, and in 1969 Cassell's, all of which companies had already absorbed a number of others.

To understand the evolution of Studio Vista it is necessary to keep a cool head. The Studio, which had been the family business of the Holmes since 1893, was sold to Edward Hulton in 1957; two years later he sold it to Odham's Press, which was taken over by I.P.C. in 1963. I.P.C. sold what was then known as Studio Vista to the Rev. Timothy Beaumont, who five years later disposed of it to Crowell, Collier.

Edward Hulton was a magazine publisher who started *Picture Post* in 1938. In 1949 he branched out into books, and even after the sale to Odham's he retained one imprint for his own independent use. Timothy Beaumont, a Church of England clergyman who inherited a fortune, was not able to indulge his political ambitions because his calling precluded him from sitting in the House of Commons. However he became active in the Liberal Party, was made its chairman and was rewarded with a life peerage which enabled him to sit in the Lords with his bishops. During the years of his proprietorship of Studio Vista he maintained a close interest in its affairs. His friend Peter Whiteley, a farmer, was brought in as managing director, and from 1966 David Herbert, with a career in teaching, bookselling, paperback publishing and the theatre behind him, became editorial director. Studio Vista's expansion was conducted with a certain missionary fervour in those years, and it was deliberate policy to produce books for creative leisure. The little Studio imprint almost sank without trace, but many of the elaborate and pocket-sized volumes which issued from Blue Star House, Highgate Hill, had their origins in it. An attractively designed paper series of pocket poets were taken over from Hulton and extended, and so were the excellent Vista Guides, partly historical, partly topographical, and French in origin. In the Beaumont era there were new series of paperbacks and an absolutely unexpurgated coffee-table edition of *The Drawings of Aubrey Beardsley*, for publishing which, the reverend gentleman declared, he took complete personal responsibility in the event of prosecution for obscene libel. In fact, no action was taken. David Herbert (who joined George Rainbird in 1972) remained in command editorially after the Crowell, Collier takeover, when those who had formerly been travellers for one company found themselves carrying the books of the entire group.

Cassell's fortunes after the war were very much built on Winston Churchill. First there were the six volumes of war memoirs, then four of the *History of the English-Speaking Peoples* and, after that, a sumptuous one-volume heavily illustrated version of the latter called *The Island Race*. Churchill's sales were phenomenal, and it was entirely fitting that he should have been invited to lay the foundation stone of Cassell's new building in Red Lion Square, Holborn, which was opened in 1957. There were other books on the list, however, and in fiction they had a big bestseller in Nicholas Monsarrat's war novel *The Cruel Sea* (1951), which sold one million copies in its original hardback edition in six years, and another in Alec Waugh's *Island in the Sun*. They also continued to publish many of their pre-war authors; the longstanding loyalty between Cassell's and their writers is exemplified by Ernest Raymond, who in 1973 had been with them for fifty-one years, and whose wife Diana had joined the list in the 'fifties. Robert Graves headed the poetry list; Margaret and Desmond Flower compiled an excellent anthology of English poems; the music list remained strong, with David Ascoli, sales director for many years, taking an active interest in it; and there was popular success with teenage pony fiction written by the show-jumper Pat Smythe. David Ascoli made the rare transfer from sales to editorial in 1967, by which time Desmond Flower had become chairman and the company had opened an Australian branch, bought George Blunt's, library suppliers in north-west London, and formed Baillière, Tindall & Cassell, out of Baillière, Tindall & Cox. Bryen Gentry, who had followed his father into Cassell after completing his war service, became managing director in 1968, but resigned some months after the American takeover, and announced a new imprint using his own name. Aubrey Gentry died in 1961. (Both Flower and Ascoli had resigned by the end of 1972.)

Geoffrey Chapman, an Australian lawyer, started publishing from his home in Wimbledon in 1957. When Pope John died he flew to Rome to bid successfully for his memoirs; these he published as *Journal of a Soul*, and thereafter his success was rapid. He took over Duckett's bookshop in the Strand and in 1969 bought from the printers Morrison & Gibb their publishing interests in Johnston & Bacon, the map specialists, (Johnston was Geographer Royal to Queen Victoria and the firm dated back to 1826; Bacon's bought it in 1944.) Chapman had by then sold to Crowell, Collier for cash, but remained in charge of what was a wholly owned subsidiary of the American group, which added further to its empire when the Woolston Book Company of Nottingham and Claude Gill's bookshop in Oxford Street, London, were also purchased.

Another American company which bought its way into British publishing was Frederick A. Praeger, Inc. (Praeger's were themselves acquired by the Encyclopaedia Britannica Company in 1966.) They bought the Pall Mall Press, a small imprint of recent origin specializing in books on international affairs, and then bought the Phaidon Press in 1967, on Dr Bela Horovitz's death. The Phaidon list, which had been kept carefully pruned by Horovitz, who brought out a few finely produced new titles each year, was encouraged to branch out. Paperback editions, in clumsily large format, of the more popular titles such as Gombrich's *Story of Art* were successfully marketed. Harvey Miller, Dr Horovitz's son-in-law, who had stayed as managing director under Praeger's left after three years, thus confirming the pattern. Life was apparently tough for most of those British publishers who tried to work for their new American masters.

Harper's, which in 1962 became Harper & Row, kept on their London office (which Piers Raymond managed for a short while between leaving A.B.P. and going to Dent), but many of the books on their list seemed to be unobtainable at any one time. (This was not untypical of American publishers' activities in the U.K., at least in the experience of one bookseller.) The Heath company of Boston, whom Harrap had represented for the whole of the century, set up a British office at Farnborough in 1970, and the R. R. Bowker Company, proprietors of the *Publishers Weekly*, installed Gerry Davies as managing director of a London subsidiary when he left the B.A.

American publishers were seldom satisfied with the promotion of their books in the U.K., and constantly changed their agents, but when they arrived to do the job themselves they often fell down as badly. The great exception was McGraw-Hill. In 1963, when they had already been represented in the U.K. for many years, they appointed W. Gordon Graham as managing director. Graham, a Scot, had lived and worked in the States and the Far East, where he first made contact with McGraw by writing for their publication *World News*. In due course, as British-based international sales manager, he became responsible for sales throughout Europe and the communist countries, a 'territory' extended in 1971 to include West Africa and the Middle East. Only the Pope had a larger diocese.

There were also Prentice-Hall, Inc., with many expensive technical tomes and a paperback lit. crit. series, all sold at poor terms which did not endear them to booksellers, and the Leonard Hill Group, which was aquired by Grampian Holdings in 1961 for approximately £225,000. Leonard Hill was another technical imprint with a leaning towards agricultural books established during the Second World War. Abelard Schuman, which came under the same umbrella, opened in London in 1955 and was managed for much of the 'sixties and after by a German ex-bookseller, Klaus Fluegge, who presided over an increasingly inter-esting general and juvenile list.

Obtaining books from American publishers who were not repre-sented in the U.K. was an exasperating business often involving weeks or even months of waiting, and, unless exchange rates and bank charges were calculated accurately, resulting in a net loss. A number of companies were represented by T.A.B.S. (Transatlantic Book Services Ltd) and the American Book Supply Co., but a host of others were not, and their books had to be ordered direct from the States. By 1970 some booksellers were soft-pedalling on such orders, and advising customers to get their books sent to them by a friend on the other side of the Atlantic.

Angus & Robertson's activities in London changed during this period. Previously they had bought British books for their Australian shops and sold their publications and those of other Australian imprints in Britain. By 1971 the London office was solely concerned with publishing, and was managed by John Ferguson whose father George, a most active and distinguished president of the Australian Booksellers' Association, had been in charge of it pre-war.

From 1963, by which date Walter Butcher had succeeded Stanley Amor as London manager, Angus & Robertson had the services of Barbara Ker Wilson, another leading children's editor. She had had experience with Collins and other houses before emigrating to Adelaide, where it became her task to alter the image of children's publishing in Australia. She had to persuade Australian authors to write for Aussie publishers so that the children 'down-under' were no longer constantly baffled by the essentially English background to many of the books they read. Miss Wilson wrote many books herself.

Hachette of Paris did not do any publishing from London but were the main wholesalers for French books for most of this time; Barmerlea Books Sales Ltd, run by the highly efficient Miss Faith, supplied books from Germany, Italy and elsewhere on the Continent.

7

Paperbacks

Penguin; Pan; Panther; Mayflower; New English Library; Corgi.

'Penguin' came to mean 'paperback' during the postwar era, which was as much a compliment to the men and women at Harmondsworth as it was an irritant to those struggling to establish their own imprints. Of the three Lane brothers only John, who was killed in action in 1942, did not survive to see the amazing expansion which gathered momentum in these years. The pre-war birds were joined by new species; some of the newcomers did not make the grade, and a few of the old ones were honourably retired, but for most of the flock the flight was exhilarating.

The first Penguin Classic, *The Odyssey* of Homer, appeared in January 1946, translated into modern English by Dr E. V. Rieu, who had undertaken that labour as an antidote to boredom whilst fire-watching during the blitz. Dr Rieu became editor of this new series and translated many other classics for it, among them *The Four Gospels*, work on which contributed to his conversion to Christianity. His principal colleague until 1960 was Alan Glover, who was also responsible for Pelicans.

Other wartime or postwar ventures included Penguin Prints, which never, alas, really got under way; Penguin Modern Painters, edited by Sir Kenneth Clark; Penguin Music Scores; and the Buildings of England. Modern Painters eventually foundered, but enjoyed considerable success when they first appeared at 3s. 6d. (17½p) each, which was marvellous value for thirty-two plates, half of them in full colour. The Music Scores were started when Allen Lane became bored at an editorial meeting, and Jack Morpurgo, recognizing the danger signs, thought it expedient that someone should come up with an idea; the next day he was instructed to get the series going. The fact that Morpurgo was an historian and not a musician was irrelevant to Lane who, if he liked a suggestion, wished to see it followed through at once. It was his genius not to question or cost a project which had the true Penguin flavour of daring and originality, but to expect those whom he employed to make it economically possible. If, after much trial, it could not pay its way then it had to be discontinued or subsidized, as were the Buildings of England volumes. That incomparable series was born in Allen Lane's rose garden one afternoon soon after the war, when he asked his guest, Professor Nikolaus Pevsner, what he would most like Penguin to publish. Pevsner replied unhesitatingly, and rapidly out-lined a series on all the buildings of England from Stonehenge onwards in about fifty volumes. For good measure he also suggested another series on the history of world art. Lane undertook at once to publish both. The Pelican History of Art and Architecture started as hardbacks, but reappeared in paper versions in 1970. The Buildings of England began in paper at 6s. (30p) in 1951, but new titles and reprints were all in stiff bindings by 1970, when the price of some of them was as much as 50s. (£2·50). Even so they were good value, and represented years of painstaking work by Pevsner and those who assisted in the authorship of later volumes. No reference books were ever more pithily and wittily written.

It was appropriate that Penguin 1,000, in 1954, should have been *One of Our Submarines*; Edward Young, its author, was one of the original staff down in the crypt of Holy Trinity Church. Allen Lane delighted in such acts of sentiment, which helped to keep the firm human. The thousandth Pelican did not come until 1968, by which time there were 2,662 books in print from the entire list, and the new warehouse at Harmondsworth housed 24 million books and could hold 40 million. By 1960 twelve titles had sold a million copies each, among them E. V. Rieu's translation of *The Odyssey*, E. M. Forster's *A Passage to India* and *Howards End*, H. D. F. Kitto's *The Greeks*, H. G. Wells's *Short History of the World*; and George Orwell's *Animal Farm* and *1984*. Clearly, quantity went hand in hand with quality.

In 1956, after twenty-one years, Penguin's was still a private limited company, with Allen and Richard Lane owning all the shares. In 1961 they went public, and put 750,000 ordinary shares on the stock market. These were oversubscribed, and rose from 12s. (60p) to 17s. (85p) on the first day. At this time Allen Lane increased his holding to 51 per cent, and three years later made a personal gift of £100,000 to create a staff pension fund in memory of his kinsman, John Lane. He safe-guarded the future of Penguin's by forming a trust, one of the four trustees being Sir Edward (later Lord) Boyle, minister of education in the Macmillan government, and one of those left-of-centre Tories who found it unrealistic to look for higher preferment in his party. He joined Penguin as an educational adviser and member of the board, but ceased to be active when he became vice-chancellor of Leeds University.

The early 'sixties were also important in the history of the company in that they brought Tony Godwin to Harmondsworth for seven years as chief editor. Under him the egghead Peregrines were introduced, and the confusingly named Modern Classics. He brought his own par-ticular vigour to the job, and perhaps a clash of personalities was inevitable because both he and Allen Lane were very much accustomed to having their own way, and both could be prickly. The final row revolved around the question of selling to other than book trade outlets. Godwin had to write to the press refuting the idea that he had advocated 'popping Penguins into garages and grocers', and pointed out that as a former bookseller of twenty-one years' experience, he had veered towards the expansion of Penguin shops and departments. Nevertheless, he went, but a number of his editorial team wrote a letter to *The Bookseller* stating that Godwin had 'extended the range of the list with vision and imagination, and we who were his editorial colleagues felt at every point his intense concern for quality and purpose'.

Amongst the signatories to this letter were Dieter Pevsner (son of Nikolaus); Oliver Caldecott; Giles Gordon and Charles Clark, all of whom had also resigned or signalled their departure by mid-1972. One who signed and stayed was Kaye Webb, who took over the editorship of Puffins when Eleanor Grahame retired. Under her direction the reputations of such excellent contemporary writers for children as Joan Aiken, Leon Garfield, Clive King and Alan Garner were much enhanced. She began the Puffin Club which, four times a year, sent its young members a magazine lightly written, wittily illustrated and brimful of competitions and news of club outings and plays. Directly in the Allen Lane tradition Kaye Webb introduced original Puffins, Clive King's *Stig of the Dump* being her particular favourite; it was subsequently published in hardback by Hamish Hamilton. By 1970 there were some twenty originals, plus about one-third of the Young Puffin list, an extension of the series which she started. A journalist before joining Penguin, she was married for many years to the cartoonist Ronald Searle, with whom she collaborated on a number of books published under the Perpetua imprint distributed by Michael Joseph. During the five years from 1963 to 1968 Puffin sales trebled (three and a quarter million sold in 1968), and in 1970 they had the greatest growth of all the birds.

The turnover of top executives at Penguin was sometimes nearer to the American than the British rate, but there were those who stayed the course. Amongst them were Harold Paroissien, who ran the Baltimore office for many years and then returned to Harmondsworth as managing director until his retirement at the beginning of 1970, and Hans Schmoller, a distinguished typographer who joined the board in the 'fifties; many of his books were featured in the Annual Book Design Exhibition sponsored by the N.B.L. Schmoller became vice-chairman of Allen Lane, The Penguin Press, in 1970, which was appropriate because during its short life that imprint had already made an impact through the excellence of its production. It also published one remarkable bestseller in Ronald Blythe's *Akenfield*, a work of genuine sociology (no charts, no graphs) and literature, anatomizing a Suffolk village.

Other editors in the crucial early years were Eunice Frost, who joined at twenty-one as Lane's secretary, and stayed to become a director who influenced both the Penguin and Puffin lists and Sir William Emrys Williams, who combined the job of chief editor with being secretary-general of the Arts Council. In a memoir published by The Bodley Head in 1973 Williams notes how the editorial meetings during the first twenty years were usually started, most informally, in his West End office and then continued all afternoon over a prolonged lunch in a small Spanish restaurant.

After the departure of Bruce Hepburn in 1962, Ronald Blass gradually assumed overall direction of sales. Blass had an extraordinary history with the company, rising from odd-job man in the early 'forties to deputy managing director and one of Allen Lane's trustees in 1970. He packed, drove a van and made himself generally useful in the early part of the war before he was called up. After demobilization he returned to Harmondsworth to find out his prospects, and was told by the company secretary that he could re-start at £4. 15s. (£4.75) per week. The offer was refused, but on his way out he met Allen and Richard Lane cycling in. He was greeted enthusiastically, and the King Penguin seemed distressed to hear that the young man was not rejoining them. He promised to speak to the company secretary and write later that day. Next morning Blass received an offer of £5 per week and so admired the effrontery of it that he accepted. He was soon being used for special missions, travelling abroad a lot to organize warehousing at overseas bases and even, on one occasion, being packed off to Florida for a holiday. As sales director he stage-managed the introduction of the computer and the vast extension to the warehouse, and had the simple but brilliant notion of selling Penguin's own delivery vans and renting those belonging to W. H. Smith, having perceived that the latter's vehicles were used during the night but idle in the day, and that there were, anyhow, more of them. He also furthered the establishment of Penguin bookshops in separate premises or within existing shops. There were over a hundred of them at the end of 1969. Penguin's made a generous contribution to fitting them, arranging for other paperback publishers to join in the subsidy but undertaking the design themselves.

The man who actually succeeded Allen Lane as managing director was Christopher Dolley. He had made a great success of the American house after Harry Paroissien returned to the U.K., and had also edited a volume of Penguin short stories. He was Unilever-trained, and played a key role in the negotiations with Longmans over the merger of 1970. Under his influence a great many new sub-series of Pelicans and Penguins, many concerned with the social sciences, were inaugurated and, for a while, green covers ceased to adorn crime novels — destroying at a stroke an image carefully nurtured over thirty years. (Fortunately, commonsense prevailed and the decision was revoked.) Already installed as managing director of the new Penguin Education division when Dolley came back from the States was Charles Clark, who had been deputy chief editor for the whole series from 1961 to 1966. Clark, who had been legal editor with Sweet & Maxwell, and had also been called to the bar, before moving to Harmondsworth, quickly succeeded with his new imprint, which challenged traditional methods of education and illuminated the whole scholastic scene. But he moved on to succeed Sir Robert Lusty at Hutchinson, whilst Dieter Pevsner and Oliver Caldecott started yet another new imprint, Wildwood House. Peter Calvocoressi, who had been writing books on world affairs and lecturing at Sussex University since resigning from Chatto, became chief editor in 1971 and succeeded Dolley as publisher in 1973. Calvocoressi, in a newspaper interview, said he supposed he was not an ideal editor because he thought that authors should write their own books, but his appointment with widespread approval in the trade.

And the man who began it all was, deservedly, the one who gained probably the greatest pleasure from it, and certainly the greatest wealth. Lane had a villa in Spain, a farm in the Home Counties, a house near Harmondsworth and a flat in Whitehall Court, Westminster, where he frequently threw parties from which, when boredom overtook him, he was not unknown to flee ahead of most of his guests. He also presided over numerous Penguin parties, especially during 1961, the twenty-fifth birthday year, but he rarely made speeches on these occasions and never orated at length. Nor did he play much part in P.A. affairs, having no aspirations to the presidency and not being a committee man. Nonetheless, official honours came his way—he was knighted in 1952, became a Companion of Honour in 1969 and in that year also received the Gold Albert Medal of the Royal Society 'for his contribution to publishing and education'. Unofficially he was honoured wherever Penguin books were read.

The records of other paperback companies pale by comparison, but there were some important competitors to Penguin, the first of which was Pan. It was started in 1944 as an independent subsidiary of the Book Society, with Aubrey Forshaw as managing director, a position he held until Ralph Vernon-Hunt succeeded him in 1970. Forshaw said of Pan, 'We are in middle-of-the-road entertainment,' and this remained true for most of the time, although they published a number of higher-brow titles in their Pan Piper non-fiction series.

In the early days after the war, Pan did their printing near Paris and the books were shipped down the Seine and across the Channel in a vessel called *Laloun*, which flew the Pan house flag. This colourful practice was discontinued in the next decade.

Ralph Vernon-Hunt, who had been a bookseller's assistant at Hudson's in Birmingham after being demobbed, became sales director of Pan in the 1950s. He became well known for his habit of telling booksellers that their shops were forbidding to would-be readers. This he did without giving offence because his forthrightness and humour won him respect, and he was certainly one of those who helped, through the paperback revolution, to make bookshops less intimidating.

Pan concentrated on expanding their sales without making too large a backlist. They had sold 25 million copies of the James Bond titles bought from Cape by the beginning of 1969, but in 1968 the total number of all books sold, 15 million, was a considerable drop on the previous year, but one which resulted in higher profits. In 1955 they sold over 8 million books per year against Penguin's 10, but they had 150 titles in print and Penguin's had 1,000. In 1969 Heinemann bought a one-third share in Pan, Macmillan and Collins owning the other two.

By the end of this period Pan had undertaken publication of the titles produced by Friends of the Earth, one of the many organizations formed as people became increasingly aware of the environmental crisis.

The early Panther books would not have won a prize from anyone for production, but in 1962, under the joint managing editorship of William Miller and John Boothe, they took on an appearance of quality as well as turning to books of greater literary merit. Nabokov, Mary McCarthy, Jean Genet and Doris Lessing added lustre to the list, which also sprouted individual bestsellers such as *The Naked and the Dead* and the *Kama Sutra*. In the late 'sixties the Paladin series of Pelican-type titles was planned by Tony Richardson, an ex-Harmondsworth man who tragically did not live to see their publication.

By then Mayflower, as well as Panther, was part of the Granada group. Mayflower had achieved some notoriety when under the ownership of Feiffer and Simons, and directed by Gareth Powell (a truck driver who became a reporter on Smith's Trade News before taking to publishing), by bringing out the unexpurgated *Fanny Hill*, the 'memoirs' of an eighteenth-century prostitute whose exploits had been a good line on the secondhand porn market throughout the century. Mayflower were prosecuted, and Powell later moved on to the New English Library, Christopher Shaw succeeding him. Feffer and Simons sold eventually to another American company, Dell, who subsequently sold to Bernstein.

The New English Library was owned by the New American Library, run by Victor Weybright. It absorbed Four Square Books, a paperback list started by a tobacco company which had already taken over Ace Books, for many years edited by Frank Rudman. Through N.E.L., the Signet and Mentor American paperbacks, many of them quite unnecessarily duplicating classic works of English literature which were already in several other series, were distributed in Britain.

Another paperback imprint which made its mark was Corgi (Transworld Publishers Ltd), who often paid larger advances than their competitors and obtained such plums as *Catch-22* and novels by James Baldwin and Michener. As they grew older, and under the influence of Pat Newman and Alan Earney, they learned to produce their books more elegantly. Almost from the outset Michael Legat was chief editor, joining from The Bodley Head in 1950, and assuming editorial responsibility two years later, apparently because no one else was about to take on the task. The fact that the cap fitted was proved in the years that followed and was given permanent record in an instructive and amusing compilation of imaginary letters which Legat published with Pelham Books in 1972, under the title *Dear Author*.

There was also the Thomson-owned Sphere, one of those which survived in 1970, by which time the feast was over. Some paperback firms estimated that they received back 40 per cent of what they sold, which was obviously quite uneconomic for both publisher and bookseller. The days of being able to sell anything because it was in paperback had ended.

8

Specialist Publishers

*Technical publishers: Ginn; Edward Arnold; Crosby Lockwood & Son;
Technical Press; Macdonald & Evans; George Philip & Son; John Bartholo-
mew & Son; Architectural Press; Lund Humphries; Samuel French; Ian
Allan; Folio Society; religious publishers: S.P.C.K.; S.C.M. Press; Epworth
Press; Carey Kingsgate Press; Lutterworth Press; Burns, Oates; Mercier Press;
official publishers: H.M.S.O.; B.B.C.: Greater London Council.*

In educational publishing many old-established firms held their own
against the newcomers—George Bell, the University Tutorial Press,
Edward Arnold, E. J. Arnold, James Nisbet and Ginn & Co., for instance. The latter was sold more than once, passing in and out of the
Odham's and I.P.C. networks. The postwar London directors of this
American-based firm, A. P. Davis and A. C. Wilson, bought the British
company in 1954 with the help of a finance corporation. Two years
previously they had introduced Ronald Ridout's English Workbooks,
which were something of an innovation in teaching textbooks and
achieved great popularity. A colleague of Davis and Wilson during this
time was Ken Hills, who survived subsequent ownerships and was still
with the company in 1972 by which time the Xerox Corporation of
America owned both it and the original parent company.

At Edward Arnold's, B. W. Fagan continued in charge for many
years. Like Arnold, Fagan believed that a publisher should be convers-
ant with every aspect of his business and should not publish more books
than he could midwife himself. He died in 1971, having outlived his
senior colleague, Thomas H. Clare, by six years. Clare, whose father
was foreman packer to Arnold, and whose mother was resident care-
taker of the Maddox Street premises, spent all of his working life with
the firm and rose to be chairman. Their tradition was carried on by
J. A. T. Morgan as chairman and Anthony Hamilton as managing
director.

A. W. Ready, one of the most respected of educational publishers,
died in office as managing director of George Bell in 1967. Always
primarily concerned with school textbooks, Bell's nevertheless had a
healthy small general list, overseen by S. L. Dennis, and began publication in 1970 of a definitive multi-volumed edition of Samuel Pepys's
diaries.

516

Technical publishing thrived, and in this division the publishers often saw the merit of giving better discounts than their educational colleagues, so that their books were actually stocked by booksellers. Crosby Lockwood gained a new lease of life in 1944 when John W. Wilson bought the company, whose premises had been destroyed in the blitz, from Hatchard's. The Technical Press, which grew out of Crosby Lockwood's troubles in the 'thirties, was also bombed and burnt out in 1940. After the war the Press was bought by C. F. G. Henshaw and Oliver Stobart, who had begun their negotiations in Italy during the battle on the River Garigliano and concluded the deal in the swamps of Salonika. In 1957 they started the Common Core series which had sold over a million copies by 1969. At Crosby Lockwood, Humphrey Wilson succeeded his father, and sold to Granada in 1972.

Macdonald & Evans put their handbooks into paperback; many firms such as Pitman's and Temple Press produced car manuals and other technical literature to do with vehicles two or more wheeled, and at Griffin's, the seventh generation in the person of James R. Griffin succeeded C. F. Rae Griffin as managing director at the end of 1970.

As foreign travel increased during the years after the war, so did the demand for maps and guides. George Philip continued to have a large stake in this field, but in 1970 they lost the agency for ordnance survey maps which were, thereafter, handled by the government department which produced them. Many of the most popular maps in use in the U.K. were printed in Europe for Michelin, Hallwag and Kummerley and Frey. The first-named were supplied through the Dickens Press, a surviving unit of the *News Chronicle* newspaper which suddenly ceased publication in the early 'sixties.

Bartholomew's of Edinburgh continued successfully in map publishing, and the firm founded in 1826 was still family owned in 1970, with John, Robert and Peter of the sixth generation in active management. Their half-inch sheets, covering the whole kingdom, and first produced between 1875 and 1903, were distributed by Frederick Warne's for many years.

The specialist policies of the Architectural Press were continued, but they also produced, at irregular intervals, volumes of general interest to lay observers of architecture and those concerned with bettering the environment. They had one popular bestseller in *London Night and Day*, illustrated by Osbert Lancaster, and another in Nan Fairbrother's *New Lives, New Landscapes*, one of the best-written and best-argued studies of the enviroment, a subject which spawned hundreds of books as well as new imprints (see p. 514).

Lund Humphries, old-established fine art publishers, produced a high proportion of coeditions with American firms, although they were printed and manufactured in this country. The Penrose Annual, an international review of the graphic arts, appeared for the sixty-fourth time in 1971. Dr Bruno Schindler, their publishing manager for nearly twenty-five years, retired in 1962; during his time Alec Tiranti, another fine art publisher, and a bookseller, became Lund Humphries's London trade counter.

Samuel French, the play-publishing house which was built up to serve the amateur theatre spread its wings to serve 'the profession' as well. When Cyril Hogg, whose father had succeeded French, died in 1964 his two sons were left in command, with Noel Woolf as their editorial director. The continued success of Ian Allan Ltd must also be recorded. The ex-railway clerk, who had got into trouble with the Southern Railway over his first wartime publication, went from strength to strength and removed in the 'sixties into new premises by the side of Shepperton station. There the board of directors met in a first-class Pullman carriage, Malaga, housed on a strip of rail. In addition to publishing, Ian Allan started train-spotting clubs and a travel agency which organized cheap flights to the Frankfurt Book Fair. An eccentricity of his was to have the flag outside his premises raised and lowered daily.

A specialist firm of a different nature was The Folio Society, a quality book club founded in 1947 'to produce editions of the world's greatest literature in a format worthy of the contents, at a price within the reach of everyman'. The first directors were Alan Bott, Christopher Sandford and Charles Ede, and they started in offices shared with the Golden Cockerel Press on a top floor in Poland Street, Soho. Finances were distinctly shaky in these early years when distribution was through normal trade channels, with Cassell's travellers and sales department handling orders. In 1949 it was decided to approach the public direct, and from then on membership grew steadily and Folio was often on the move to larger premises, from Poland Street to Ryder Street, where it had its first showroom; to Brook Street, where, because there was a lovely garden, the Folio Club was started, and then into Stratford Place, off Oxford Street.

In its first twenty-one years, 243 titles were published. About one-fifth of these were either original publications or became the only editions in print. Brian Rawson became editorial director in 1956, and it was under him that the number of non-fiction titles increased, the initial policy of choosing only safe classics having long been abandoned. Trade distribution was eventually discontinued. Charles Ede sold a controlling interest to Halfdan Lynner and John Letts in 1971.

The S.P.C.K. continued its missionary work at home and abroad. On the publishing side they were producing forty to fifty new titles each year by 1969 for the home market, and more, in other languages, for Asia and Africa. There were no fireworks attached to their activities, they went quietly about their business and upset neither the faithful nor the heathen. The same could not be said of the Student Christian Movement Press, which amazed the book trade by pulling a bestseller out of the bag in 1963. *Honest to God*, by the Bishop of Woolwich, sold more than a million copies in thirteen languages and caused controversy inside and outside the Church. The Church of England was going through a rather prolonged thin phase, and not surprisingly someone in its hierarchy felt the need for a basic re-examination — not that there had ever been a lack of unorthodox clergy, even on the supposedly orthodox side. The S.C.M. Press was non-sectarian, having had Baptist, Church of Scotland and Anglican editors, and modestly enjoyed the immense publicity which it attracted through publishing *Honest to God*. The Epworth, Carey Kingsgate and Lutterworth Presses were never the centre of such a storm. The latter also entered the general market, scoring successes with animal books by David Attenborough and with many juveniles. Carey Kingsgate ceased to publish when their bookshop in Southampton Row closed in the 'sixties.

The Roman Catholic publishers had a less prosperous time after the Second Vatican Council. Burns, Oates had already suffered years of upheaval, having been bought back, with its subsidiary Hollis & Carter, by members of the family from the Eyre Trust in 1948. Until 1965 Tom Burns, ably assisted by David James, was chairman of a reorganized company; then D. C. Hennessy succeeded him, and in 1967 Herder & Herder of Dublin (with a parent company in Freiburg, West Germany) bought the company.

Mercier Press, of Cork, were more fortunate. Realizing that the bottom was falling out of the Catholic theological market, John Feehan built up a list of books about Ireland and the Irish. André Deutsch took over his U.K. distribution in 1970.

Her Majesty's Stationery Office continued to be the largest of British publishers, printing twenty million books and pamphlets each year, and having a backlist of 40,000 titles. It published the *London Gazette*, the oldest newspaper in the country, some 250 guides to ancient monuments, national monuments, forests and parks, and about 100 booklets on careers for young people, in addition to the weekly output of white and blue papers necessary to government. Occasionally it produced a title that people actually wanted to read as distinct from consult. Such a one was Sir Ernest Gowers' *Complete Plain Words*, which sought to instruct the bureaucrat in good English. This even became a Pelican.

George Thompson was the man on the book side of H.M.S.O. who was known to the trade, and who proved to his purely commercial counterparts that human beings stood behind the formidable reports which it was his job to publish. H.M.S.O. distributed through the trade and had their own shops in London, Edinburgh, Cardiff, Belfast, Manchester, Birmingham and Bristol, as well as forty bookseller agents.

The Stationery Office's activities sometimes concerned the P.A., although no commercial publisher was anxious to obtain the rights in White Papers, but B.B.C. Publications needed to be watched because they had call on broadcasters and telecasters who were also authors contracted to traditional houses. For a long while the B.B.C. contented itself with publishing its year book and smallish pamphlets to do with particular languages, to tie-up with actual programmes. Gradually, however, they began to branch out and when Kenneth Clark's *Civilisation* was screened in 1969 the B.B.C. shared publication with John Murray in hard and paperback. Many titles developed from their children's programmes, including the popular *Blue Peter Annual*. By 1970 they had issued nearly six hundred publications, and the annual Reith Lectures on scientific and philosophical subjects began to be published by B.B.C. Publications, whereas previously they had come from various imprints. Many publications were distributed direct to schools to tie in with broadcasts, and booksellers were clumsily categorized for the scaling out of new titles. Had there been six hundred categories instead of six it might have been more successful, but B.B.C. Publications remained curiously inflexible in the face of criticism and seemed to forget that although, quite properly, they had a constitution free from political interference, they were owned by the public, which included those booksellers and publishers who sometimes had cause to resent official arrogance from this quarter.

The Greater London Council also showed a tendency to enter publishing, which, considering the haphazard way they went about it, might have been better delegated to someone else. There was nothing wrong with the actual publications; only with the inadequate organization for selling them to the trade.

British Books in Print listed 4,629 publishers for 1970. Of these, 314 were full members, and 38 associate members, of the Publishers' Association as at January 21st, 1971.

9

Bookselling: Universities

Three principal groups: University Bookshops Oxford, Bowes & Bowes, Dillon's University Bookshop; universities which ran their own bookshops: Leicester, Sussex; group of shops opened by Robert Maxwell in Oxford, Glasgow and on campus of University of Lancaster; Birmingham; Hull; Leeds; Sheffield; Manchester; Liverpool; Nottingham; Reading; Exeter; Cardiff; Swansea; Glasgow; Edinburgh; Dundee; Dublin.

Nepotism can break a family firm as easily as it can make for its continued progress. Basil Blackwell was fortunate in the two sons who followed him into his Oxford business and contributed energetically to its expansion, and wise in that he also made room for others, not of his blood, to augment their talents.

From being the wealthy and established leading booksellers to one of the two main university cities in the U.K., and publishers of note, Blackwell's rapidly developed into important exporters and became the home base for a large chain of university bookshops in England, Scotland and Wales. The bookshop in Broad Street, Oxford, which had started in an area of twelve square feet, grew to absorb the premises on either side of it and to be extended underground into the spacious Norrington Room; and it also took over other Oxford shops and opened offices elsewhere in the city to cope with its mail order business. By the late 'sixties it employed 625 people and served 96,000 customers in all parts of the world, whilst remaining, in its native setting, an inviting and peaceful shop in which town and gown could browse uninterruptedly. At Blackwell's there were notices informing customers that they would not be approached by salesmen unless they signalled for attention. Despite this courteous policy the company was managed in a thoroughly businesslike manner. Blackwell's, with their large buying power, were the first to demand better trading terms for other booksellers as well as themselves, and individual executives of the company were always prominent in trade affairs.

Basil Blackwell's elder son, Richard, developed the export business; his younger, Julian (known as Toby), was responsible for the transformation of a vast area lying beneath Trinity College into the Norrington Room. Here a great cavern of books, entered down a ramp from the original bookshop, was intriguingly designed to allow vistas of an

521

acreage of books below, above and beside one. The room was named
after the president of Trinity, and its mausoleum-like tendencies were
nicely tempered by such homely architectural touches as retaining an
iron spiral staircase which had performed some function in the original
cellar, and letting in actual daylight through a window high up on one
side. It was a striking achievement of modern design and engineering,
and it provided a splendid foil to the nineteenth-century aspect of the
Broad Street shop front, where some of the doors almost evoked a
knock before entering.

In 1946 Blackwell's and the Alden Press acquired the school bookshop
at Eton College, and ten years later Alden sold out to the Oxford booksellers. In another five, Parker's, on the opposite side of Broad Street, in
which Blackwell's had a deliberately non-controlling interest, opened a
paperback shop. But the largest home development came in 1964, when,
with the Oxford University Press, University Bookshops Oxford, Ltd
(U.B.O.), was formed to extend the services of university bookselling to
other cities and towns. An equal, majority or total holding was purchased in an existing business. Willshaw's of Manchester joined in 1964,
and John Prime, who had been assistant general manager of Collet's
Bookshops in London, was appointed managing director; a year later
Parry's of Liverpool came in, under Alan Wilson; in 1966 Eric Bailey of
Lear's, Cardiff, entered the group, followed in 1967 by William Smith
of Reading, in 1968 by Thomas Godfrey (York), W. Hartley Seed
(Sheffield) and Thorne's Student Bookshops, Newcastle-upon-Tyne and
in 1969 by Bisset's of Aberdeen. It was a formidable line-up geared
to meeting the heavily increased market in academic books created by
the new universities and the expansion of some of the old. George's of
Bristol, which had long been under Blackwell's ownership, and Blakey's
of Exeter were outside U.B.O. J. F. Blakey had been a bookseller in
Exeter for many years, and left Wheaton's after Maxwell had taken
over that company. When he started the shop bearing his name
George's took a controlling interest.

Chief amongst the non-family members of the board of Blackwell's
was H. L. Schollick, known as 'Uncle Henry', of whom mention has
already been made in connection with Book Tokens and other extra-
mural activities. Another was Per Saugman, a Dane who joined the
board soon after the second war, remaining an executive also of Munks-
gaard in his native country. Other Blackwell employees who joined the
chiefs from the Indians were the brothers Sam and Harry Knights, who
started as apprentices but became directors. On the family side, Miles,
son of Richard, represented the fourth generation, and failed each
morning (in company with his father and uncle) to arrive ahead of the
Gaffer, as Sir Basil was known to all the trade. The patriarch reckoned
to be on duty twenty minutes before any other executive to view his

juggernaut getting into motion, and to contribute his sage advice as to its direction. His seventieth birthday in 1959 was celebrated with a lunch at Quaglino's and, years later, he was still an active speaker on mainly social occasions.

In Cambridge the Heffers prospered, following a similar, if less extensive, course to the Blackwells; the Boweses, however, died out and gave way to another group bearing their name but owned by W. H. Smith. George Brimley Bowes retired in 1946, having been a bookseller for fifty years, and died a few months later. The business passed to Denis Payne, who developed the publishing side with a series of critiques of European writers, and then sold the bookselling side to W. H. Smith in 1953, later establishing himself on the Continent as a representative for many publishers. Smith's appointed Esmond Warner manager in 1957, and it was under him that the Bowes & Bowes group of university shops, of which he became chairman, was formed. Warner, son of the distinguished cricketer Sir Pelham Warner, had run a distribution centre in Cairo during the war and afterwards made a notable success of managing the W. H. Smith shop in Brussels. At Trinity Street he gutted the shop and rebuilt it internally from basement to roof. He installed new fittings and lighting, but left the exterior untouched; it was, after all, the oldest bookshop in the country. In 1963 he opened a Science Bookshop further along the street, and, a few years later, a Modern Languages Branch was added next door to it. By 1970, with Heffer's three shops in the same winding, narrow thoroughfare, Trinity Street had as great a density of bookshops as Charing Cross Road. The simple shelving which Warner designed consisted basically of a wall unit with a deep browsing ledge formed by a bunk unit at table height, and canopy lighting above. There were also island fittings using the same standard units.

Warner had tremendous drive, and a flair for selecting the right staff. In 1961 empire-building commenced when Sherratt & Hughes of Manchester was transferred from W. H. Smith, who had bought it on the retirement of the owners in 1946. Ben Mendelssohn, who had worked at Trinity Street, went to Manchester as manager, and Joe Cheetham, Junior, remained in the business until 1967 when he reached W. H. Smith's compulsory retirement age of sixty-five. He had then been bookselling for over fifty years, apart from a short spell as a pupil farmer to which task his bookselling father had put him because 'there was nothing to be made out of books'.

In 1963 came *their* first campus shops, at Southampton (the University Bookshop), Norwich (where the premises were in a Nissen hut behind the barbed-wire fence protecting public and students from each other) and, in the following year, a shop was opened in the main buildings of the University of Essex in Wivenhoe Park, a few miles outside Colchester.

This last shop was roughly U-shaped, which provided the management with a permanent shop-lifting problem, that bane of every bookseller's life being as much in evidence amongst the bleak grey tower-blocks of Wivenhoe as elsewhere.

In Bath, the W. H. Smith shop in fashionable Milsom Street was transferred to Bowes in 1965, and Bryce's of Museum Street, Bloomsbury, became part of the group in the same year. Three years later Alan Ward sold both of his Sheffield shops and with them his own services for a limited period. It was the policy of Bowes & Bowes to take over the previous owners as well as their shops, but Smith's retirement rule was rigid, and Ivan Chambers, to the great regret of his colleagues in the trade and of his customers, departed from the business he had made so very much his own after the death of William Jackson Bryce. He was followed almost immediately, early in 1971, by Esmond Warner himself, who handed over day-to-day management to his deputy, M. A. C. (Tony) Reavell, Simon Hornby becoming chairman. He left behind, though not for long, his colleague F. Reeve, archivist of the company, and author of *Victorian and Edwardian Cambridge* for Batsford. By 1971 Truslove & Hanson's in Sloane Street (the Clifford Street and Oxford Street branches had closed in 1958 and 1963) had been added to Bowes, and additional premises were taken elsewhere in the same thoroughfare. They were managed for a time by Richard Davies, whom the Thomson organization had placed in control of The Times Book Club during its last years (a story which comes later). A name associated with Truslove's of Sloane Street for much longer was that of Miss Mary Hawker, buyer for many years, and daughter of another long-serving employee of the company.

Heffer's moved out of their rambling Petty Cury premises in 1970 and into a new shop in Trinity Street which rivalled Blackwell's Norrington Room in ingenuity of design, use of space and splendour of fittings. It occupied a smaller area than Blackwell's, but a split-level layout utilized every square inch effectively and made for excellent vistas in most parts of the shop. Ernest Heffer died in 1948. He was succeeded by his son Reuben, who brought his sons Nicholas and William (who defected into antiques in 1971) into the business and adopted the current trend of going beyond the family in search of senior colleagues. John Welch, who had been with Kaye & Ward and in the London office of Hawthorn Books (an American connection of Prentice-Hall), returned to the city from which he had graduated, to become general manager in 1964. Four years later he was appointed managing director and organized the move to Trinity Street, where the children's bookshop was the first to open, opposite the site which became the new main premises. It also faced the paperback shop which had been started soon after Welch's arrival, on part of the ground floor of the old Deighton, Bell shop. The children's book shop was another triumph of design in a very small area at pavement and basement levels. The architect of both new shops was Peter Lord (Blackwell's was in the hands of the old established Canterbury firm of Wiltshier's). Heffer's also had, from 1957, a Penguin bookshop opposite Cambridge University Press.

Bowes & Bowes and Heffer's dominated Cambridge bookselling, but others continued to exist. Gustave David's son, Hubert, kept his stall in the market and his two shops in St Edward's Passage; the sons of the first Porter of Galloway & Porter also took over from their father; and the Student's Bookshop, which moved from Trumpington Street to Silver Street in 1965, also established main branches in the University of Keele and in Hanley. Deighton, Bell's became entirely antiquarian in 1963, four years after the share capital had been bought by William Dawson's, the London wholesalers and exporters.

U.B.O. and Bowes & Bowes did not have it all their own way, although the latter had formidable footholds in inner London. A third group emerged, based on Dillon's University Bookshop in Bloomsbury, and there were also an increasing number of large and small independent shops catering for the academic market.

Una Dillon moved shop across Store Street during the war when a bomb damaged her first premises. Hers was, at that time, a small general bookshop with an academic slant, although the wartime evacuation of the University of London put a temporary halt to developing the latter side. When the university returned to Bloomsbury, however, she soon realized that she needed larger premises. With the particular aid of Mrs Veronica Whatley she laid the foundation of a department specializing in books on education and on Africa, the latter prompted by the attendance at the shop of so many students from the Commonwealth. She was unable, however, to find either bigger premises or the capital with which to lease or purchase them. The solution came from the university authorities themselves, who bought a row of empty shops at the corner of Malet Street and Torrington Place, a few minutes walk from the Senate House, and invited Miss Dillon and another bookseller to run it in partnership. When this plan came to nothing she was asked to run it alone and given a minority shareholding in a new company which was started on £11,000 capital. This was in 1956, when Peter Stockham joined her from the campus bookshop at Keele and organized the move from Store Street to Malet Street. Ten years later Dillon's University Bookshop was turning over £600,000 a year and held a stock valued at just on £115,000. The gross profit was 24·1 per cent which reflected the poor terms given on academic books by most publishers. (When the High Hill Bookshop, in Hampstead, opened a university department in 1970 the gross profit fell from 28·4 per cent to 26·1 per cent in a single year, although the turnover increased by £20,000.) Peter Stockham led the battle for improved terms for those who stocked academic books but not enough publishers followed the example of Associated Book Publishers and Faber's in granting them.

Stockham succeeded Miss Dillon, who retired from active management of the ever-expanding shop in 1967. By then the business occupied four houses and five floors on each, some of which space was given over to office accommodation to deal with the large mail order department which had grown up. There was a staff of 109 and the ratio of sales to each was £6,132, compared with £6,963 the previous year, which reflected the growing number of personnel necessary behind the scenes. It was a long shot from the Store Street days when Una Dillon or 'Nique' Whatley did the collecting on an old bicycle whilst the other minded the shop. A branch was opened in Queen Mary College in the Mile End Road in 1966, and another, in 1968, at the small town of Wye, in Kent, noted for its farming college. Then, when Alec Rae, a Canterbury bookseller, withdrew from running the bookshop for the new university of the county, Dillon's took that over and, a few months later, also obtained the concession, previously held by Sisson & Parker, from Nottingham University to run their shop. Cyril Mercer, who had been with Dillon's for some years, administered the organization of these additional shops, and he and Michael Seviour, who had had experience at Bumpus and Better Books and was brought into Malet Street to manage the ground-floor shop, were Peter Stockham's principal *aides*. Miss Dillon remained on the board and took an active part in trade and British Council affairs. Rayner Unwin became a director in the late 'sixties.

Some universities chose to run their own bookshops, the first of these being at Leicester, where the authorities claimed that local booksellers had declined the offer to instal a campus shop. (The decision was taken during a summer holiday period when it was not possible for the B.A. to arrange to send delegations to protest, as they did on other occasions elsewhere.) So the head of the history department, Professor Jack Simmons, suggested a do-it-yourself operation, and the first manager was H. Hunter who had had many years experience with Foyle's Educational Ltd. When the faculty at Sussex took a similar decision, for similar reasons, Hunter went to manage their shop, and was succeeded at Leicester by G. F. Cousins, who had formerly managed the Student's Bookshop at Keele. Turnover at Leicester grew from £8,785 in 1958-9 to over £100,000 in 1967-8. Students were not allowed to open credit accounts, which did not deter them from using the shop, the space allotted to which grew by some 300 square feet during the first five years. At Sussex Hunter was followed by R. J. Marshall, who had managed the University of Lagos bookshop in West Africa. There were more rumbles of official book trade disapproval when Sussex, and then Warwick, decided to run their own shops. Both trade associations tried to dissuade them, but without the success that attended their similar appeals to the university authorities in Birmingham and Swansea. The result, at Leicester, anyway, was not perhaps harmful in the long run and it is worth quoting L. C. Sykes, who was on the faculty there, who wrote in an article in the *Journal of Documentation* (vol. 22, no. 1) that because the students had frequented the university bookshop and made the buying of books a habit, Leicester's graduates were likely to buy more books than their parents had from those booksellers who looked askance at its foundation. And perhaps there were more booksellers than anyone had ever counted who were justifiably cautious of entering a market fraught with the twin problems of less than economic discounts and increased likelihood of pilfering.

The publisher Robert Maxwell also formed a group of shops, opening on Magdalen Bridge, Oxford (the main premises of which were later closed), in Glasgow and on the campus of the University of Lancaster. In Birmingham, Hudson's remained the principal booksellers,* opening a shop at the University of Edgbaston in 1962, and the College House Bookshop, opposite the University of Aston, two years later. The main shop in New Street was enlarged, and covered 13,000 square feet by 1968, when there were 170 employees at the three branches. The New Street premises also housed the public library supply department, a canteen and staff training-room. A non-contributory pension scheme was started in 1964, and a personnel manager and training officer were appointed in 1968. E. F. Hudson died in 1951, and his wife Elsie, who had worked in the business before their marriage, outlived him by nearly twenty years. Their daughter Pat became chairman and managing director in 1970. She and her brothers John and G. W. (Barry) were all active in the expansion of the family business during this time, and rather more nepotism was evident on their board than Blackwell's or Heffer's. But there was much delegation of duties, with the result that by 1967 none of the Hudsons did any of the buying personally, and the proportion of stock to turnover was rising. This was a problem met by many booksellers large and small; with rare exceptions, buyers who were not owners tended to buy more than they would if they had been using their own money.

Combridge of Birmingham became a public company in 1954 and joined the Lonsdale and Bartholomew Group, which also included Universal Stationers, of Watford and elsewhere, in 1969. They were not exclusively concerned with books by any means, having a large trade in office equipment and commercial stationery, wholesale and retail.

* Until 1972, when they sold out to Marshall, Morgan & Scott for half a million.

Cornish's, under Walter Finch, moved from New Street out to Sutton Coldfield in 1963, but the Midland Educational continued to direct its operations from Corporation Street where G. R. Wasley, who joined the company in 1949, became a director in 1957. There were many branches by 1969, when Wolverhampton was opened; the old-established business of Mark & Co. of Northampton was also acquired.

Brown's of Hull opened a college shop at the invitation of the university soon after the war. Frank Bacon retired in 1964 and died four years later; he was a bookseller for seventy-five years, and his son Arthur followed him both in the shop and, from 1946, on the board.

Brum bristled with branches of Hudson's; Leeds was liberally endowed with Austick's shops, which catered not only for the student population but for industry and the general public as well. A university bookshop was opened in Woodhouse Lane in 1950, and moved to Blenheim Terrace in 1965; the original premises were then transformed into Student Stationers, dealing also in magazines and newspapers. A medical bookshop was opened in 1952, the Polytechnic Bookshop in Cookridge Street remained the headquarters, and the Headrow Bookshop came in 1967. The Austicks, David and Paul F., who succeeded the founder, also opened bookrooms in the Huddersfield College of Technology, and Trinity and All Saints College, Horsforth. The general policy of Austick's was to keep a comprehensive stock, employ above-average staff and to take a personal interest in both them and customers; few cities were as well served with bookshops as was Leeds, and few bookselling businesses had formulated their policy and guiding principles, writing them down for all to see, as clearly as had Austick's. In Leeds there was also Walker's, which was still in Albion Street when Henry Walker retired in 1950. The Jackson brothers, L. N. B. and B. H., then became partners, the former attending to general administration and the institutional accounts, the latter managing the shop. In 1966 they decided to separate, the shop was moved to the new Arndale Centre at Headingley, and a new company, Walker's Educational Supplies Ltd, was formed and housed at Ripley Lodge, Wortley. Mowbray's closed down their Leeds branch in 1969, after thirty years; other chains were, however, still represented, and the railway bookstall on the central station was notorious at one time for the enormous numbers of copies of sensational paperbacks which it sold.

Sheffield, like Manchester, came to have both U.B.O. and Bowes & Bowes shops, after the principal booksellers had sold out. Mr and Mrs Duffield together ran W. Hartley Seed from 1943 until Mr Duffield's death in 1957, after which Mrs Duffield carried on with a small turnover of senior staff and a large turnover of junior, reflecting a pattern which was nation-wide and contributed to inefficiency. In the 'sixties Hartley Seed took new premises in West Street with a shop front sixty feet long

—in contrast to the tiny box-window of the original. Alan Ward's shop was moved three times, but always remained in narrow, winding Chapel Walk. Close by is the Methodist Bookshop, whose eccentric shape was determined by being built on to the side of a Nonconformist chapel whose architect had not favoured straight lines; it boasted a large children's section in its basement. Miss Hilary Pattison left Ward's Leavygreave, in 1968 to take John Prime's place at Willshaw's, in Manchester, swapping groups in the process. Another senior colleague of Alan Ward's was Victoria Ohrenstein, a Jewish refugee from Austria who obtained a work permit in 1941 and stayed in Chapel Walk until her retirement in 1969, in which year the Sheffield City Council attempted to deal the local booksellers a body blow by announcing that, in future, it proposed to deal direct with publishers for its educational books in order to obtain higher discounts. This caused great bitterness because in the previous year, at the request of the Chief Educational Officer, Ward's, Hartley Seed, the Methodist Bookshop and others had opened a showroom for local teachers. They closed it in 1970 because it wasn't being used. By then most publishers, strongly urged by the B.A., had refused to supply the local authority direct. Had it been only a question of allowing the City Council to buy its textbooks from educational publishers, and nothing more, the Sheffield booksellers would probably have made no more than a token fuss, and been secretly glad to be rid of such uneconomic business. But they were fearful that they would lose the valuable school library business in net books, and it was this factor alone which determined the attitude of many booksellers in all parts of the country to supplying schools.

In Manchester Oxbridge had a lot of competition. Haigh & Hochland opened near the university in 1959 to serve those interested in academic and scientific study and research, and claimed to be the first specialized university bookshop to start in the provinces. Ernest Hochland quickly took to operating a mailing service on index cards, and by 1969 two-thirds of their turnover came from mail order. (Blackwell's started a similar operation at the same time without knowing what Haigh & Hochland were doing.) He had three shops by the end of the 'sixties, one specializing in technological books and another in paperbacks, with a total staff of forty-one including three working directors. There was also a minute shop in Portland Street, which was much more competitive than it looked, because Miss Jardine and Miss Davison who ran it built up many connections during their long years of trading in the city. Miss Jardine, whose name the shop bore, retired first; Kathleen Davison was an active member of the N.W. Branch of the B.A. and a member of the first Charter Booksellers' Committee. She sold the business to Paul Underhill, a publisher's rep., who opened a branch in Knutsford, Cheshire, soon after.

Frank Gabbutt moved his recently acquired Willshaw's to larger premises in John Dalton Street in 1956. According to his successor, John Prime, Gabbutt, who had survived in Blackburn during the lean years, never closed his mind to new ideas and anticipated the demands of late-twentieth-century bookselling, zestfully promoting the expansion of his Manchester shop at an age when most would have been thinking of retirement.

Many Manchester shops closed during the period following the war, including the once-famous Cornish; but in the city at the other end of the ship canal most of the closures had taken place between 1919 and 1939 when, as we have seen, only the strong survived. After 1945 the Liverpool trio of Philip, Son & Nephew, Charles Wilson, and Henry Young still remained the principal booksellers, but there were many others. Philip, Son & Nephew opted out of school contracting in 1969, having already grown retail branches in West Kirby, Formby and Southport, thus concentrating on the most profitable side of bookselling, which is to sell net books from stock for cash. Alan Wilson bought Parry's from the Yateses in 1948, and was sole proprietor until he sold to U.B.O. in 1965. It was not until 1946 that Parry's began to sell new books to cater for science and medical students at the university. A new shop was opened in September 1968 opposite the students' union, the largest until then built specifically to serve the needs of a provincial university.

At Nottingham, Sisson & Parker opened a University Bookshop in Portland Buildings and there, and at their main shop in Wheeler Gate, they claimed in 1963 to have a range of books unequalled outside London and Oxbridge (although they still found the Bible to be their bestseller). Walter Gisborne, a nephew of Walter Sisson, who died in 1947, became managing director. Woolston's, the Nottingham library suppliers, opened a showroom in London in 1959 at which time their capital was increased to £120,000. (In 1945 it had been raised to £40,000.) Tom Woolston and Bob Crosby were elected to the board in 1952, the year F. Crosby died, and Miss Corden became managing director. Crowell, Collier-Macmillan bought all the shares in the company in 1969, and Tom Woolston was appointed managing director.

Kenneth W. H. Adlam bought William Smith's of Reading from H. W. Brown in 1960, opened a branch in the new library building of the university four years later, and joined U.B.O. in 1967. Reading had several other well-stocked bookshops. These included the old-established James Golder, which became a company in 1945, J. H. Simpson subsequently being appointed managing director; branches of W. H. Smith, one of which, in 1969, still appeared to be more of a bookshop than anything else, which was unusual; and the headquarters of Paperback Parade Ltd, a small chain which was started by Leslie

Hannon in 1962. Branches of the latter followed at Southampton, Luton, Guildford and Salisbury.

F. J. Morrish became a partner in Pitts of Exeter in 1946, and continued as a director after becoming part of Varsity Bookshops Ltd (another small group with shops in Bristol and Cardiff) in 1969. By then Pitts had a branch in Torquay, providing that culturally deprived seaside resort with a proper bookshop at last. Pitts had also opened a paperback shop in the Cathedral Yard at Exeter, where the S.P.C.K. catered for the students of Exeter University in a first-floor room hidden away in a passage beside the canteen, which seemed to reflect official and architectural contempt for books. Similarly inadequate and badly sited accommodation was arranged at York, which was surprising because the faculty there was more liberal and progressive than many. That, however, was the situation as I saw it in 1968. The energetic Polish-born manager, J. S. Janiurek, may have improved it since.

H. E. Bailey, of whom we have already heard, joined Lear's of Cardiff in 1946; he was a stepson of the Lear who was then owner. A year later W. C. Davenport, who had started as a station bookstall manager for Wyman's, became a director. He retired in 1962, having been largely responsible for transforming Lear's from a small theological bookshop into a large general shop. The university shop, nearby but not on the campus, was opened in 1961 in a basement. Later the ground floor was acquired. Competition came from the University Bookshop (Beti Rhys) and, later, from Brunel, an imposing three-storey modern bookshop opposite the castle, which was part of Varsity Bookshops Ltd, already mentioned. A. F. Way, the old-established Swansea bookseller, foundered in the 'sixties, and the multiples held sway in that city of 170,000 people, although Leslie J. Thomas ran the independent Uplands Bookshop in Gwydr Square and had the university concession. At Newport (population 106,000) the situation was much worse; bookselling was represented only by branches of Smith's and Boot's, whilst in the great mining towns it was almost as difficult to buy a Book Token as a book.

The two great cities of Scotland did not need outside help in coping with their student population. John Smith's had been meeting the demands of Glasgow University for many decades. They had suffered lean years in the 'thirties when they closed their Technical Bookshop, but their steady if unspectacular expansion as John Knox, head of the firm until 1969, described it, took account of all developments in local bookselling, and when he handed over to his ward, Robert Clow, he gave up the reins of one of the finest businesses in the U.K. Clow had been occupied for some years with the shops in Gibson Street, near the university, and had used his architectural training and knowledge to turn a relatively small shop into one which appeared much larger.

Paradoxically, he achieved this result by actually making it smaller, building an inner wall on three sides and creating the effect of a stage set with clever use of perspective. There were intriguing items of decor at the main shop in St Vincent Street, also; an enormous metal mezzanine floor, resembling the deck of a warship, hung over the pavement-level shop, and to make a ramble round the premises that much simpler (although the layout was too complicated for it ever to be quite straightforward), several feet of solid Glasgow stone, once the sturdy party wall of two separate shops, had been hewn away. John Smith's had an impressive stock in highly sympathetic and bookish surroundings, not only in its own main premises but also in Sauchiehall Street, at John B. Wylie's.

Smith's bought Wylie's, then in Gordon Street, in 1947, and Ross Higgins went there as manager, and later became managing director. He had been an assistant to Knox, and had come to bookselling from advertising. Higgins built up a personal business, partly dependent on mail order but always on the force of his personality, and created a haven of peace in an area of Glasgow for years heavily under the developer's bulldozer. On the ground floor, customers entered something resembling the hall and library of a country house, where stood a large round table on which books were carefully but apparently informally arranged. There was even an open fireplace, although it was not much used. At the back, on a dais, was a stationery department, and up the pleasant wooden staircase was the children's department and Higgins's office, not unlike an actor's dressing-room with its signed photographs of authors and its homely lived-in atmosphere. Not that the bookseller was one to stray too often from the floor of his shop, which he even opened during the evenings at busy seasons for the benefit of those who could not easily do their shopping during the day. When Sauchiehall Street became somewhat depressed owing to all the rebuilding, which gutted the centre of Glasgow, Higgins moved over to St Vincent Street to join Robert Clow in generally directing the main business.

In 1970 Smith's opened a university shop at Stirling, where Maxwell, for a brief period, had opened in the front room of a small terrace house. John Knox could not have handed over to two more devoted booksellers, the youth of the one tempered by the longer experience of the other. Knox was a bachelor, and had cared for Clow when his missionary parents were lost, and for long thought to be dead, in China.

Of the other Glasgow booksellers, W. & R. Holmes became a company in 1947 and later merged with George Outram, publishers of the *Glasgow Herald*. They closed their shop in Dunlop Street and moved first to the *Herald* building in Buchanan Street, and later into Wylie & Lochhead's. Here, although it seemed to the public that the book department was part of the store, it was in fact independent. By then Holmes had absorbed McDougall's of Edinburgh; Blacklock Ferries of Dumfries, founded in 1910 as a one-man business by William Blacklock; the Standard Bookshop at Kilmarnock; and Jackson, Son & Co. of Glasgow, whose Italian-gothic-styled shop closed down in January 1968, Alan Jackson staying on with Holmes for a short while. Jackson, who had run the Western Book Club and gave up the presidency of the B.A. when he joined the forces in 1940, was perhaps the most colourful Scottish bookseller of his time, and much loved by his colleagues.

The Grant Educational Company occupied a rabbit warren of premises, with a basement reached by the curving marble stairway down which intending train travellers had once stepped. R. Charlton Paton joined them in 1944 and became head of the firm; his son was amongst his colleagues there. Grant Educational was sold to Howard & Wyndham in 1973.

In Edinburgh the Thins and the Bauermeisters presided over the bulk of the university trade, with both shops almost on the campus in South Bridge and George IV Bridge. Thin's occupied the older premises, rambling across several buildings with the same abandon as John Smith's in Glasgow. James Thin IV joined the family partnership in 1950, started the mail order side and in 1966 brought in a computer (the first to be owned and operated by a bookseller) to handle its affairs; his cousin, Ainslie, joined him at the end of the 'fifties. The Thins tended to dislike their computer and to express regret at having gone into the mail order business, but they appeared to thrive in their lovely city which, as always, supported numerous bookselling businesses, new and second-hand.

Bauermeister's moved in 1966 from the Mound to George IV Bridge into a modern shop built on to the old premises of W. F. Henderson, theological bookseller. It had a spacious air compared with Thin's, and increased its business ten times in the years from 1959 to 1969. During the war Bauermeister's was sold out of the family, although a daughter of the founder remained as managing director. When William, her brother, returned from the services, he was able to re-purchase all the shares from the Mound Bookshop Company which then owned them, and to have his wife and son join him in partnership. He opened a university branch in Dundee in 1964, but sold it two years later to Frank Russell. William Bauermeister should be mentioned as a shop-floor bookseller. I think it is worth recording that when I was in Glasgow and Edinburgh in August 1968 I frequently encountered the principals of businesses behind their counters or serving customers; this was not nearly so often the case in England.

In Dublin the chief booksellers were still those mentioned in earlier sections. The A.P.C.K., under the management of Arthur Gray (a popular figure at B.A. conferences and much missed after his death in 1971), had a foot in both Eire and Ulster. So did Eason's, the chairman of which from 1941 to 1958 was J. C. M. Eason, son of Charles, the second of that name. Browne & Nolan, another distinguished bookseller and publisher, formed an associated company with Longmans in 1967 to publish for the educational market. All Irish booksellers (and publishers) were constantly beset by the censorship problem, which was aggravated by the fact that laymen as well as priests could and did demand the banning of books for dogmatic reasons. The Irish booksellers were ever on good terms with their British colleagues, but the comparative poverty of their Emerald Isle, and the absurd rigours of their censorship, made it a difficult business to sell books there. Victor Gollancz is said to have remarked that he sold more books to Harrod's in one week than he did in Ireland in a whole year.

NOTE (see p. 522): Sam Knights died suddenly in September 1972. Much loved and respected by his colleagues on both sides of the trade, he was, according to Sir Basil Blackwell, 'essentially a front shop assistant who not only assimilated the spirit of Blackwell's but did much to mould it as his career developed'. His former chief, Ewart Hine, said he was the best bookseller he had ever known; his place as the director in charge of the actual shop in Broad Street was difficult to fill even with Blackwell's resources. He had, wrote Sir Basil of one whom he described as a 'precious colleague', a marvellous memory for titles, authors and publishers and for the history of particular books. No bookseller could wish for a better epitaph.

IO

Bookselling: the Chains

W. H. Smith & Sons; Menzies; S.P.C.K.; Bookland; Boot's; Countryside Libraries.

The place of W. H. Smith & Sons Ltd as booksellers during this period was unique and complicated. The company operated more bookshops than any other firm, in many places offering the only retail outlet available to the public, but often its shops were not primarily bookshops at all, but newsagents, stationers and selling points for numerous other goods ranging from gramophone records to toys. The branches which had previously stocked predominantly books, or had at least given the impression of being bookshops, were deliberately changed into stores offering a multiplicity of assorted merchandise including books. The closure of their commercial library system led to Smith's allocating more space within their shops for goods other than books, and the space that was left for the printed word was, in the opinion of some, most ineffectively used. Paperbacks, particularly, and sometimes hardbacks as well, were shelved in a manner that made it extremely difficult for customers to pull them out for inspection. It seemed to be a company ruling that books should be stacked horizontally, so that titles printed along the spine, instead of across, could be read without bending the neck. In reality it was much simpler for a customer to bend his neck, which is designed for that very act, than to extract the bottom book of a pile without making the others cascade on to his feet. What was of even more concern to publishers was the high level policy promulgated in 1970 to concentrate buying on fewer new titles from fewer publishers, and to cut out most lines which might not be expected to sell in bulk quantities. Because of this, Smith's, which had already ceased to be a general wholesale outlet, stopped being a retail outlet for some smaller publishers. To be fair to W.H.S. it has to be understood that by the 'sixties they were a large public company, dealing in many commodities, and that their first commercial priority was to make profits for the shareholders. In many trades and industries a more ruthless policy would have been implemented. It was greatly to the credit of those who directed W.H.S. that they permitted Bowes & Bowes to evolve without wishing upon such pedigree bookshops dump bins of plastic toys and ballpoint pens. Smith's also introduced an annual literary award in the

1960s which went to such distinguished writers as Leonard Woolf and
E. H. Gombrich—whose books one would not have automatically
expected to find in the average W.H.S. shop.

The company was sneered at in the trade by those who felt that
bookshops should be purely and simply emporiums in which literature
was sold to an elite who would purchase their more mundane requirements elsewhere. This rather grand attitude did not allow for the fact
that in, say, a small market town such as Buckingham no one had been
willing to open a pedigree bookshop, and that at least the local W.H.S.
was willing to stock books and to order some if not all of what a customer might require; but the cost of each special order, already a
worry to private booksellers by the late 'sixties, was even more of a
worry to such a huge organization. In 1967 the wholesale service of
Smith's which, after the demise of Simpkin Marshall, was the principal
one remaining, and which had been moved with a minimum of fuss
from Strand House, off Kingsway, to Bridge House in Lambeth, was
transferred to Swindon in Wiltshire where a computer was installed.
Service to independent booksellers soon ceased, and there was no
evidence, by 1970, of any intention to re-start it. That the decision was
wise in commercial terms was proved by increased profits in 1970.
That it became more and more difficult to obtain particular books
which were not in stock did not concern the shareholder, unless, perhaps, he was the person who wanted the book, but by then he had
become accustomed to the extreme problems attached to getting anything quickly from an expensive motor-car to a catch for a gas-oven door.

In 1959 Smith's had 371 branches, and 1969, 318. It was estimated
that these would be further reduced to some 295 by 1973. Of the many
titles in stock at the Swindon warehouse in 1969 a considerable percentage were thought to produce only £50 per annum turnover each.
So that the policy of reducing the number of new books to eliminate
those which gave a small return was really no different from that
favoured by any bookseller who wished to stay in business and make a
reasonable living. The open question was, could books really be
marketed in such a way as to ensure a proper distribution of what was
available (i.e. in print) to the public which wanted them. W.H.S.'s
answer had to be that their policy was the viable one for them but that
others, including the shops in the Bowes & Bowes group, could carry a
larger range.

The modernization of their branches cost the company huge sums of
money, and despite the effect it had on individual shops of reducing
the range of titles available at many outlets, Smith's remained very
important customers for nearly all publishers. None, for instance, was
indifferent to the potential sales at the Waterloo Station bookstall, if he
had a popular new novel or biography; few who dealt in mass market

juveniles, gardening and cookery books or do-it-yourself titles would be uninterested in having them displayed and sold in the vast Ealing branch, in west London, where the store resembled the entrance and waiting-room to a main-line rail terminal, and where the books were placed on great floor stands with so much room left for customer circulation that an agoraphobiac dared not enter. And in fact in some towns, such as Winchester, the local W. H. Smith held a stock of titles which enabled it to compete with the neighbouring privately owned bookshops. So there must have been more elasticity to the new buying policy than was announced.

Smith's, with its fifty-two main wholesale houses and sixty-nine sub-depots, was still a powerful organization for the dissemination of books, not only in Britain but also overseas, and whatever shortcomings its smaller branches undoubtedly had as bookshops, it was still the channel through which millions of books were sold each year.

From 1943 the head of the book buying department was Kenyon Foat, who took over from David Roy. He was succeeded in 1952 by Reggie Last, who had been a manager at Sevenoaks, Oxford, Ealing and in Sloane Street (Truslove & Hanson). Last was under constant pressure from publishers large and small to buy in big quantities for W. H. Smith, but he contrived to do his best for the company and remain on friendly terms with the trade, both publishers and booksellers. He handed over to Tom Hodges in 1965 and joined the board of Bowes & Bowes. The life of a chief buyer for such an organization demanded an iron nerve and persuasive charm to enable him to hold at arm's length those who attempted to oversell. Both Reggie Last and Tom Hodges kept their integrity and their friends.

Smith's also ran a magazine, *Trade News*, and a bibliographical service headed by F. Seymour Smith (not one of the family), who joined in 1950 after working as a public librarian for a quarter of a century. Frank Seymour Smith was one of the most distinguished bibliographers of his time and he compiled *An English Library*, described by Edmund Blunden as 'a masterly list of standard reading'. The W. H. Smith advertising company had as its managing director Sydney Hyde, author of a book on selling, who was much concerned, through Book Tokens, on whose board he sat, to publicize books for the benefit of the entire trade.

Another development within the Smith empire was the formation of Book Club Associates with Doubleday of New York, the purpose of which was to issue cheaper book club editions of new books simultaneously with the original publication. This was started in 1966 with a cookery-book club which gained 60,000 members in two years, and in 1968 the Literary Guild began offering 25 per cent off new publications, which did not offend against the Net Book Agreement.

Book Club Associates bought, for £280,000, the Reprint Society (World Books) in 1966. It then had a membership of around 50,000, having dropped from the quarter million figure of the late 'forties, and having lost 100,000 over the previous two years. A six-figure membership was reached again within eighteen months. The Hon. David Smith became governing director of W. H. Smith when his elder brother died in 1948, and was later appointed chairman. Amongst the directors in the late 1960s were his son J. D. Smith, and a third generation Hornby, Simon. The deputy chairman was Charles Troughton, who was also retail managing director; his brother-in-law Peter Barnett was another managing director, in charge of corporate planning and finance.

The Menzies chain expanded vigorously from 1945, in which year it had only five retail shops, to 1965, when there were 150. The latter figure included all those shops previously known as Wyman's and Stoneham's. Stoneham's shops, mostly in the City of London, had belonged to Simpkin Marshall who sold them during the Second World War to Hatchard's. In 1952, 23 shops were sold to Wyman's and when the great wholesalers crashed in 1955, the export division of Simpkin's also went that way. Some of the Stoneham shops were so tiny as to become economically unviable—the premises, for instance, in Cullum Street, a medieval-shaped lane off Lime Street; others were sizeable and could hold a representative stock—for example the branches in Old Broad Street and Cheapside, where Chris Pemberton displayed large photographs of authors to indicate that although he was part of a chain dealing in all manner of goods, his was first and foremost a bookshop. All of these shops were renamed Wyman's, only Stoneham's Public Library Service Ltd retaining a name which was very famous in its time. It had been a separate entity run for a time by Phil Piratin, Communist M.P. for Stepney, and latterly owned by Zwemmer's. The name of Wyman disappeared too from the retail shops, but was kept alive by the printing firm of Cox & Wyman, which was formed as an independent company (later sold to Heinemann) when Menzies bought up Wyman's in 1959. It was also perpetuated by Wyman-Marshall, the company incorporated in 1963 to deal with wholesale activities. The 'Marshall' referred not to Simpkin's but to Horace of that ilk, a nineteenth-century firm purchased in 1962. Norman Wilson was appointed managing director of Wyman-Marshall.

As Menzies gradually altered all the fascia boards yet again, so that only their name remained, the shop fronts and interiors came to have a great similarity with those of W. H. Smith, rather as different makes of cars began to resemble each other. Menzies, based still on Edinburgh, also bought a number of private businesses such as Douglas & Foulis, in the Scottish capital, the Helensburgh Bookshop, David Robertson's of Perth, Dunn & Wilson's of Falkirk and numerous others. There were actual Menzies still in the company during all this time, and John Maxwell Menzies succeeded his grandmother as chairman in 1951. The group book manager during the latter part of this period was Willie Kay. Menzies, of course, were much concerned with newspapers, periodicals and stationery, but their total book purchases made them a powerful buying unit.

By 1969 the S.P.C.K. had fifty shops in the U.K. and twenty-four overseas. In Salisbury, Wiltshire, their attractive premises in an old building on three floors in the cathedral precincts held the best stock of new books in the city; at Lincoln the panting visitor climbing Steep Hill to the cathedral could pause to browse in their branch there, whilst in Brighton, Winchester, Bristol and elsewhere small but well-kept book rooms were maintained. In London the central shop at Great Peter Street was enlarged and modernized in 1968 and officially reopened by the Bishop of London. Their Durham shop was appointed bookseller to the university in 1957, and from 1966 to 1969 eleven shops were opened at teacher-training and municipal colleges. Wilson's, of Kirkgate, Bradford, an old-established business, was acquired in 1968 and eventually merged with the existing S.P.C.K. shop in the town.

John Elsley joined his parents in Bookland & Co., based on Chester, in 1945, after serving a year's apprenticeship with Charles Wilson of Liverpool. By 1969, when his father was still active in the business, though his mother had died in 1960, he had established himself as a leading provincial bookseller, and was optimistic about the future, writing to me that he believed prospects to be bright, with the trade increasing and attracting more capable people to work in it. He then controlled a staff of over a hundred, in two shops and a wholesale house in Chester, three in Bangor (which were formed into a separate company) and one each in Stafford, Newcastle-under-Lyme, Wolverhampton and Wallasey. Individual managers were allowed considerable freedom to run their shops as they wished, but accounting and research were centralized as far as this was compatible with local efficiency. Bookland did much important pioneer work in establishing good bookshops in towns where there had been none. In Wolverhampton, for instance, a city of over 200,000 inhabitants, Bookland's only serious competition until the arrival of the Midland Educational came from Beattie's department store. In Chester their old-established rivals Philipson & Golder closed down in 1970. Bookland would have opened many more branches, and John Elsley was often offered them in towns which needed bookshops, and where he believed a reasonable turnover could have been achieved in two or three years, but he was usually deterred by the exorbitantly high rents pertaining. In Bangor, which had for long had a university college, Miss Hodgson retired from

Galloway & Hodgson in 1945 and J. G. Galloway, son of the founder, sold to Bookland twenty years later.

As an outlet for books, Boot's Pure Drug Stores declined sharply during this period, although for a time in the late 'fifties, under Philip ('Books Can be Sold Like Soap') Jarvis, the book departments were administered with great zest. Boot's, however, never had been primarily concerned with books, and with the decline of the circulating libraries their importance to the book trade decreased, although a stock of books continued to be maintained in many of their branches. Jarvis left to join Hamlyn, where he exercised his soap theories with much success; Allen Binney succeeded him at Boot's, but it was Tim Law who had the doleful task of overseeing the closure of the famous library, the last branch of which ceased to issue books in 1966, three days after the death of E. S. Moore, who was head librarian from 1941 to 1963. The shutting down of this chain, and of Smith's, plus the disappearance of most of the libraries in independent bookshops, had a serious effect especially on the sale of fiction and led to the closure of another small chain, Countryside Libraries Ltd, which Audrey and Basil Donne-Smith had run so successfully, mainly in East Anglia, for thirty years. The twenty-five branches dwindled to one in Hitchin, which was closed in 1966. The Donne-Smiths moved to semi-retirement in Somerset, at Crewkerne Abbey, where visitors noticed a discreet plate on the old stonework indicating that Countryside Libraries still went on. From the ancient crypt, 'Donne' issued small lists of remainders from time to time. He was one of the most prominent trade politicians of the period and wrote and spoke much about the economic plight of booksellers, despite which he and his wife were well liked.

II

Bookselling: Provincial Independents

Newcastle-upon-Tyne; Gateshead; Hexham; Lichfield; Durham; Sunderland; Middlesbrough; Bolton; Preston; Blackpool; Oldham; Southport; Huddersfield; Altrincham; Chesterfield; Coventry; Hanley; Stoke-on-Trent; Keele; Shrewsbury; Burton-on-Trent; Dudley; Rugby; Grimsby; Buxton; Stratford; Ipswich; Norwich; King's Lynn; Peterborough; Exeter; Bristol; Dartmouth; Bath; Marlborough; Lymington; Penzance; Truro; Bournemouth; Dorchester; Sherborne; Blandford Forum; Shaftesbury; Southampton; Winchester; Havant; Emsworth; Aylesbury; High Wycombe; Slough; Woking; Guildford; Caterham; Virginia Water; Walton-on-Thames; Farnham; Reigate; Redhill; Richmond; Surbiton; Esher; Kingston-on-Thames; Hastings and St Leonards; Eastbourne; Brighton; Hove; Worthing; Crowborough; Uckfield; Tunbridge Wells; Maidstone; Bexley; Chatham; Rochester; Gillingham; Canterbury; Whitstable; Thanet; Deal; Folkestone; Dover; Tenterden; Bromley; Westerham; St Albans; Hertford; Stevenage; Welwyn Garden City; Henley-on-Thames; Marlow; Maidenhead.

Take a population map of the British Isles and mark on it those places which had well-stocked and efficiently run bookshops in 1970, and no very clear pattern emerges. Many of the largest cities were reasonably well served (by British standards), but many others were not; some comparatively small places supported one or more bookshops. In many of the sprawling suburbs of large cities the absence of a bookshop was explained because book-buying was done at lunchtime by workers in the city centre; but there were exceptions to this, as well, which did not always reflect the affluence of the particular suburb. Banstead (population 41,870)* had a small but good shop; nearby Sutton (79,500) did not; Altrincham (41,130), a mainly residential town in Cheshire, at one time had two, so plainly the inhabitants were not buying their books in nearby Manchester or Warrington.

The answer lay, probably, in the quality of the bookseller, and proved correct Miss Santoro's theory (see p. 389) that a stockholding bookshop creates its own trade. So if this is taken into account the businesses mentioned in this next section will, I hope, seem a less unbalanced selection than would appear to be the case if they were compared with the areas of dense population on the map.

In Newcastle-upon-Tyne (253,780) the Morgans of Mawson, Swan

---

* The population figures in this chapter are taken from the 1961 census.

& Morgan continued to be represented, Esmond Thomas being joined by his son Stewart Lindsay in 1947. The latter together with his brother-in-law Douglas Miller became the executive heads of the company operating the store with a prominent book department in 1952, when Esmond Thomas died. There were numerous other bookshops in the great ship-building city, including W. Robinson's and Dring's, who sold their site for development in 1962 and with the proceeds opened up in Savile Row and also in Carlisle—at the other end, roughly, of Hadrian's wall. In 1969 T. Robson Dring finally retreated from Newcastle whilst half the city was being rebuilt. Probably Newcastle drew off the cream of the trade in the area. Certainly in Gateshead (101,200), a mainly working-class town on the southern bank of the Tyne, there were not even representatives of any of the stores; only, curiously, one J. Lehmann, who specialized in Hebrew religious books and had the largest stock of them in the whole of Europe; one wonders what market there was for his line in Gateshead. (This Lehmann was no relation of the publisher of that name.) At Hexham the picture was even more discouraging; in this busy market town (population 9,710, but serving a wide area) with some excellent shops books were little in evidence. The local store of William Robb had been taken over by W. H. Smith and the small book department was in a cul-de-sac on a raised part of the ground floor with a large notice stating NO EXIT, thus discouraging entrance. T. & G. Allan, a small North-Eastern chain, had a branch there but, again, the book department consisted in 1969 of a very few books indifferently displayed at the back of the shop. Going much further south, in Lichfield, Staffordshire (21,130), the birthplace of Dr Johnson and David Garrick, even the W. H. Smith branch had closed in the summer of 1969 (and displayed no evidence on its empty premises that it was moving elsewhere), whilst the only other member of the B.A. had one map in his window and little sign of books in the interior. Yet there was an excellent and large second-hand shop just off the market square where Johnson's father's house and bookshop was being redecorated as a museum. (It was officially re-opened by Sir Basil Blackwell in 1971.)

To return to the North-East, at Durham (24,210), the House of Andrews was bought in 1963 by E. A. Moulding and John Bartle from Jack Smart, who went to Weston-super-Mare to continue his career. At Sunderland (187,650), Hill's survived, and were the only chartered booksellers in the city in 1969. At Middlesbrough (150,000), G. N. Boddy took over the family business on the death of his father in 1952; there were also branches of W.H.S. and Boot's, but none of the book-shops who had failed during the depression had been replaced, and the other large industrial towns of the district catered little for the would-be book buyer.

Industrial Lancashire provided paradoxes, with some of the best shops in the whole country, and yet with some vast, smoky towns— Bolton (157,200) for instance—with only branches of the chains and the Send the Light Trust. In Preston (107,400), Harold Sweeten, whose father had died ten years earlier, bought Robinson's Bookshop in 1955. There, in drab Fishergate, near the centre of a city of no great beauty, he and his two sons created a light, modern shop on a different site from where Robinson had operated, with fitted carpet and two entrances from adjacent streets. Sweeten's was a veritable oasis of learning and apparently well-supported by the local population, although the proprietors resolutely insisted that new publications would not sell in Preston, where the stock consisted of backlist items and a big technical and educational section where the short-terms books were double-priced (5s. 6d. — 27½p—for one to five copies, say; 4s. 6d. — 22½p—for six or more). The Sweetens prided themselves on their professionalism and businesslike approach, and it was good for Blackpool (151,300) that, having closed their shop there in 1965, they decided to re-open in other premises five years later. Blackpool was not well served by bookshops, and the original Sweeten shop there was nothing like as finely stocked as the Preston one. David and Christopher Sweeten were the third generation in the family business, and it was their father's opinion that they would be better booksellers and businessmen than he had been; and it could be said that he had done notably well.

Bardsley's continued in Oldham (110,000) as the Oldham Bookshop, and in Blackburn (101,790) Seed & Gabbutt's two shops formed half of the local membership of the B.A.; Southport (79,940) and other Lancashire towns still had the big library suppliers, Askew's, Holt-Jackson and Jackson's Library Service, and it was a quirk of the system that so many books went north from London to these ever-expanding businesses only to be returned to points south later. (It was perhaps more of a rationalization than was at first evident for the Book Centre to plan to move close to them.) F. T. Bell became manager of Holt-Jackson in 1946, the year in which the founder sold out to Marlborough, the London wholesaler, and remained so until 1969. He was much respected and liked by publishers because his was a creative library supply business. He bought speculatively, as did some of the others in his line, and sold positively, sending his travellers round to librarians and establishing personal contact with his institutional customers. The staff at Holt-Jackson increased from 8 in 1945, housed in three rooms, to 175 in 1968, occupying premises of 20,000 square feet, and accounting for over a million pounds worth of business annually. Like other suppliers, Holt-Jackson processed books (3,500 a day in their case), fitting them with plastic jackets and generally performed a great many of the tasks which older librarians had been trained to do themselves, and which some considered they still should do. The charge for processing provided an area for competition amongst library suppliers, many of whom performed the service at cost, and it was a subject of some bitterness amongst booksellers who would have liked a larger stake in the whole business but, being small, could not afford to engage the staff to do this work.

In Yorkshire there was a stronghold of library supply in Woodfield & Stanley, started in 1946 and specializing in children's books from its headquarters in Huddersfield (132,260), a town more renowned for its devotion to the sung than to the written word. There were black spots in the Ridings, a number of its most heavily populated areas having nothing that could seriously be taken for a bookshop. This was also true of many cities in the Midlands. Happily, there were exceptions. At Altrincham, in Cheshire (41,130), Norman E. Lucas opened on a poor site, as he himself described it, in 1946, and because books were in short supply he had to display his stock face outwards, thus accidentally learning an important lesson in how to increase turnover. It is unfortunate that this method cannot be more often employed in all bookshops but it is unlikely to become generally possible whilst the over-production of new titles continues. Lucas stayed for sixteen years on his 'poor site', during which time he built up his business with libraries and schools, in the process doing more credit than cash business. To offset this he moved to a better shopping area, which instantly increased his cash trade. A further improvement was effected by one of his rivals moving out of the centre of the town. Another competitor was Harold Rawlinson, who had started in 1947 and ran literary luncheons to attract fresh custom. He was a sociable and trade-minded man who spent much time not only on B.A. affairs but with the Stationers' Association, the Fine Arts Guild, and others; he was assisted in his business by his wife. They sold to Johnstone's of Wilmslow in 1968.

At Chesterfield (70,170) the Ford family business suffered the loss of Geoffrey Ford, son of the founder, in 1969, but his wife and children continued as active directors of the firm. At Coventry (331,950) G. J. T. Collier, whose shop was destroyed in the war, reopened in Trinity Street. Collier was a member of the Reconstruction Committee for Coventry Cathedral, and the rebuilding of the central shopping area was part of the general scheme. It was a pity that he did not persuade a bookseller to take premises in the new two-level pedestrian precinct which was a much admired feature of the developed city, but perhaps neither he nor anyone else could afford the rent. In Hanley, one of Arnold Bennett's five towns, Student's Bookshops catered for a population of 276,300, and it was as well they did because little other provision was made in the Potteries; Stoke-on-Trent itself boasted only one B.A. member, a W. H. Smith branch. Student's Bookshops moved into

Hanley at the suggestion of the local Workers' Educational Association. That was in 1948; two years later they had the first campus bookshop in the country at Keele, and became the main booksellers in the area, serving both the general public and the students. Shrewsbury (52,450) had Wilding's and at Burton-on-Trent (50,140) one Dr Paul opened Byrkley Books. At Dudley (64,050) in Worcestershire G. W. M. Blewett started in 1949 and operated from various premises, surviving the experience despite conditions which he described in a letter to the *Bookseller* in 1967 as never having been worse; the general public, he complained, would not buy books even at sale prices, and he blamed publishers for not supporting small booksellers. Illogically, he said they could not afford to lose such outlets!

Over's at Rugby (57,190) apparently prospered, despite moving the bookshop on to the first floor to allow expansion of the stationery department. This was done in order to retain the character of the book department, and customers were not upset by it. In the 'sixties Over's developed a Technical Book Service. The managing director, in 1968, was A. E. H. Gilbert, C. E. Pearce, one of the original members of George Over's staff, having retired in 1957. The family firm of Gait's in Grimsby (96,030) continued to do 60 per cent of its business in goods other than books, but in 1970 they moved to premises three times the size of those they had previously occupied, and they were amongst those who battled on, determined to keep an outlet for books in a difficult area. For a while they ran a branch in Scunthorpe (70,980), but that closed in 1967. Another bookseller tried his luck in Grimsby after the war, but closed in 1952, as did so many others in various parts of the U.K. who started hopefully in the brave new world of 1946-7.

Of the non-industrial towns which might have been thought likely to support pedigree bookshops there were at least two notable exceptions in the spa of Buxton in Derbyshire and Stratford-upon-Avon. Buxton (20,100) had good shops, large hotels and an air of prosperity, but it did not have even one moderately well-stocked bookseller in 1969. Stratford (18,840), busy market town as well as main tourist centre, had branches of W. H. Smith and Midland Educational, selling as many souvenirs as books by the look of the stock, but their sales may well have been affected by the fact that Shakespeariana was also on sale in the local shrines, such as Anne Hathaway's cottage, which had an effectively stocked bookstall and opened on Sundays.

East Anglia was ever a problem area for trading, and had never supported bookshops much outside Ipswich (121,280) and Norwich (118,100). The Ancient House at Ipswich was sold by the Harrison family and later bought by Collins, but remained in its attractive, although inconveniently structured, building. Publisher's travellers always referred to East Anglia as 'the graveyard', and there was some rejoicing, therefore, when in 1968 John Prime, then of Willshaw's, announced his intention of opening in the market town and port of King's Lynn. An attractive shop, wide and deep, in a narrow street was found and fitted afresh, and Sir Allen Lane officially opened it at a party attended by many booksellers and publishers. From the first day the public came to buy, and Prime had the entire goodwill and good wishes of the trade in his venture. Although the population of King's Lynn was only 28,000, it served a wide area. At Peterborough (65,760) Collet's had opened a shop on two floors in 1967, so there were definite signs of a revival of bookselling in this region. But there was no guarantee of automatic success. Essex, like East Anglia, was a depressed area, but there again there were signs of revival by 1970.

In the south-west there was little to get excited about outside Exeter (93,010) and Bristol (427,786). An exception was the Harbour Bookshop, started by Christopher Milne and his wife in 1951 at Dartmouth. The small Devonshire port had a population of only 7,000, but the Milnes served a large hinterland and took particular interest in building up sales to schools by holding exhibitions, at which they sold, in the classrooms of the county. They drove their mobile showroom within a radius of sixty miles and were really dedicated booksellers.

Gladys Searight bought an old-established mostly antiquarian business in Bath (85,870) in 1947, when the area devoted to new books had dwindled to occupy but one room out of ten. As the paperback boom took hold, two rooms of the shop, which was on five floors, were allocated to Penguins and other ranges, and the emphasis on new books became marked. Gordon Nicholas, who had been an assistant when Miss Searight took over, became managing director in the mid-1960s and the business was sold to Douglas O'Shea, a publishers' freelance rep., in March 1972.

The White Horse Bookshop at Marlborough (6,040), in the famous wide market high street, was opened in the late 'forties and taken over by a Mr Evans twenty years later. It depended much on school and county library business, but in 1969 this spruce shop held, for its size, a large stock which presumably turned over satisfactorily.

King's of Lymington Ltd (32,120) prospered and expanded and also remained in the family. A new shop-front was put in in 1961 and additional offices were built two years later. In 1968 current trends were reflected by the provision of a staff-room (still unknown in the majority of bookshops), and a basement was converted from a box-room into a large paperback department.

In the extreme south-west tip of the country, Bridger's of Penzance (18,960), bought by George Linfoot in 1937 and the only purely book-selling business to have survived in Cornwall since the turn of the century, unhappily closed its doors in 1970, leaving the Truro Bookshop as the main stockholding shop in the county.

But in Hampshire the picture was brighter. At Bournemouth (151,460), J. F. Hyams ran the book department at Beale's store until he joined W. H. Smith in London in 1970, and Miss E. A. Turll opened Modern Books in 1944 and devoted all of its 1,400 square feet to bookselling. (Hyams was author of a Batsford book on the neighbouring, mostly agricultural county of Dorset, which had only two population centres of over 40,000, despite which Dorchester [13,360], the county town in the heart of the Hardy country, Sherborne [8,020], Blandford Forum [3,650] and Shaftesbury [3,410] all had purposefully managed and stocked small shops.) Along the coast at Southampton (209,370) H. M. Gilbert's thrived after their wartime bombing ordeal, and B. L. Gilbert, son of Owen (who died in 1952), re-acquired the Winchester branch from another member of the family in 1963. In both towns Gilbert's were booksellers pure and simple, not trading in other lines. Winchester (30,970) had excellent shops, in fact more and better for its size than any town in the U.K. In addition to those mentioned earlier, Michael Harrington was in Parchment Street, on two floors; the Gallery Book Shop was in the Square; across the cathedral grounds, in College Street, P. & G. Wells were still serving the school, but catering more than before for the town as well, from their pleasant, tranquil premises. This business, too, remained in the family; John Wells, who had been in banking, came in in 1945, his elder brother having died during the war. His daughter and son-in-law came to England from Czechoslovakia three years later, and when John Wells died in 1961 whilst in office as president of the B.A., Mrs Monique Fuchs, his daughter, became the head of the firm and watched over the growth of the children's department. A branch was opened at Farnham in 1947. Warren's of Winchester, which was one of the largest bookshops in the town, closed its book department in 1955, and thereafter concentrated on printing and stationery.

There were two formidable women booksellers in Hampshire: Irene Babbidge at Havant (86,040), and Molly Way at Emsworth (5,320). Miss Babbidge, after selling the Ibis at Banstead, set up as a librarian and bookseller in 1941, moving in 1953 to larger premises. From 1965 she sold only books in an urban district serving some 100,000 population; before the war it had served 12,000. She was one of the principal witnesses at the defence of the Net Book Agreement, and on her retirement in 1971 amongst those who paid tribute to her as a bookseller was Rayner Unwin, then president of the P.A. Miss Babbidge was in the great tradition of personal booksellers, and wrote a small book on her craft which André Deutsch published.

In the Home Counties it was often better for a bookseller to be farther away from London than in the sprawling suburbs, because there was less likelihood of the local population going up to town for a shopping spree, and the working population which commuted to the capital on five days a week might well prove to be customers on Saturdays. At Aylesbury (35,990), Frank Weatherhead, whose son Nicholas joined him in 1956, maintained a sizeable shop in the centre of the town some thirty-five miles from London. The business tended to develop more on the antiquarian than the new side, which reflected the interests of both father and son. An associated shop was the Wycombe Bookshop, opened in Castle Street, High Wycombe (55,170), in 1958, and run almost entirely on new books by John Aspland, who had formerly been with Better Books. Slough (92,070), nearer to London, was no less successful, although it was an improbable place in which to run a bookshop. Slough might be described as 'industrial Windsor', and John Betjeman had even invoked his muse against it ('Come friendly bombs and fall on Slough'), but nevertheless it provided the setting for a haven of comparative peace amongst the glitter and chrome of jazzy department stores, just as Sweeten's did in Preston. Leslie and Louie Wheeler started up in 1945 in partnership with Herbert Carter, who withdrew two years later, after which all the shares were owned by the Wheelers. Their shop was completely re-fitted in 1966-7, and additional premises were taken next door in 1969 to house a Penguin bookshop. When the Wheelers ceased to live in the flat above their shop and moved to a more peaceful domestic setting, their former living-quarters were turned into much needed offices.

At Woking (77,220), in the small Nancy Leigh Bookshop, Tom Dally, who bought it in 1962 from the lady after which it was named, maintained a watchful eye on the local inhabitants who made their purchases in London. He was one of those who resisted placing a surcharge on special orders and short-terms items for fear of losing native trade. He became a partner in the Fleet Bookshop in 1969 and also dabbled in literary dinners for authors to publicize his presence in a well-to-do suburb on the main line to Waterloo. The nearby town of Guildford (55,520) was not well served until the University of Surrey opened. Then, in the late 'sixties, Hatchard's opened a branch in Plummer's store, and Paperback Parade Ltd started its fourth shop, in Bridge Street.

One Surrey bookseller, Christopher Barclay, saw the potential of paperbacks when the boom was only just getting under way, in 1959. (He then owned South County Libraries, started in 1948.) Bookwise, his new company, a wholesale service to outlets inside and outside the book trade on a sale or return basis, became important to paperback publishers in expanding their market for them. By 1970 there was a sales force of approximately forty servicing some five thousand accounts south of Newcastle-upon-Tyne. Barclay, brother of the bookseller at Waterlooville (see p. 549) also started Books for Students Ltd as an offshoot of Bookwise. This provided exhibitions in schools and colleges over a large area of southern England. A colleague of Barclay's for many years was Charles Pizzey, who bought Pelican's Caterham (36,930) branch in 1955 and continued it under his own name, selling books and only books, a fact of which he was rightly proud.

At Virginia Water (6,633) Mrs Peggy Pegler, daughter of Charles Evans of Heinemann, opened a bookshop which was later sold to the actor and film director Bryan Forbes, who contrived to devote part of his busy life to it. In the same county, in Walton-on-Thames (50,220), M. W. Dashwood and his wife started the Fountain Bookshop in 1954. At first they went out after every sort of business, but later their attitude to supplying institutions hardened. They flatly refused to service books for public librarians and would not offer schools more than 5 per cent discount on non-net items. On the positive side, they took a separate shop for their children's books and were rewarded by greatly increased sales. They were a microcosm of small-town book-selling.

At Farnham (30,060) where, as we have seen, Wells's of Winchester had already opened a branch, Charles Hammick, a newcomer to the trade, opened in November 1968 with resounding success. He turned over £30,000 in his first year, and estimated in December 1969 that his takings would be 40 per cent up in the second year. He won the Ronald Politzer Award, given by the Publishers' Publicity Circle, for 'an admirable and enterprising business which deserves the support of all publishers'. Not all booksellers, to put it mildly, met with such un-qualified praise from their suppliers, and Hammick's advent into the book trade seems to warrant mention from this fact alone. The Ancient House Bookshop at Reigate (55,270), part of whose building dated back to Elizabethan times, opened in 1931 and was bought by Tom Langdon in 1945. It had no connection with the Ipswich shop, and unlike its namesake sold only books, becoming the sole bookshop in the town when Payne's, in the High Street, closed in 1966. By then Bruce Barclay had also sold his shop in the linked town of Redhill (20,238) and gone off to pursue his career at Waterlooville, Hampshire at the Bay Tree Bookshop.

At Richmond (181,130), much nearer to London, another husband-and-wife team, the Houbens, ran a pleasant shop in Church Court, a paved way off the main shopping street. The Christian Bookshop, in Eton Street, was equally bright and attractive, although very much down a side-turning. By contrast, in 1969 the W. H. Smith branch on George Street had a glaring display of Kleenex, cards, stationery, gramophone records and so on, with the bound books placed right at the rear of the shop.

Michael Lancet, who had been with the American publishers,

Abelard-Schuman, opened three shops in the 'sixties, one in 1962 at Surbiton (63,760), another in a rickety ancient building at the south end of the High Street in Esher (63,120) in 1964, and the third at Kingston (146,470) in 1966. He also went in for literary luncheons and for local publishing, a history of Esher appearing under his auspices in 1966. One of the wealthiest of the south London suburbs, with huge estates reached down private shrub-lined driveways, Esher was an obvious place in which to run a bookshop, and it was surprising that no one had thought of it before. In fact the father of Martyn Goff, who bought the Ibis, Banstead, from Miss Babbidge and Evelyn Folds-Taylor in 1950, had thought of it, but his son could not, or would not, take premises there. At Banstead (42,100), instead, he built up a personal business and became well known, even notorious, in the trade for his argumentative and sometimes amusing letters and articles in *The Bookseller,* where he was most vociferous in putting forward the case of the small retailer. Goff also wrote novels, published by Putnam and André Deutsch, and various other books on gramophone-record collecting and teenagers. In 1970 he left the day-to-day management of the business to his assistant of many years, Mrs Emily Taylor, when he became director of the National Book League. His shop was small but, especially after its refitting by Wiltshier's of Canterbury, extremely attractive, and carefully stocked. He was himself a super salesman, and at his first shop, in St Leonards-on-Sea, Sussex, he caused something of a sensation by clearly labelling one section of books SEX, an unheard-of innovation in a provincial bookshop in a respectable south-coast resort in 1948. His main competition there came from Kenneth Saville, brother of the writer Malcolm Saville, who had an old-fashioned and old-established, slightly fly-blown, shop in Robertson Street, Hastings. (The population of Hastings and St Leonards was 66,850.) Saville neglected his business to be president of the B.A., and although he subsequently moved to smaller premises he eventually sold those, also, and left Hastings without a central bookshop. St Leonards, likewise suffered, because Goff found the pace rather slow for him on the sleepy coast and removed himself to Banstead.

Along the coast at Eastbourne (68,200), another town badly hit during the war by evacuation and bombing, Johnson's Bookshop survived, changed hands a couple of times, and in the late 'sixties was completely re-fitted with an open window to replace the old-style pre-war frontage.

At Brighton (164,680), never to be associated with the sleepy south coast, although on it, Bredon & Heginbotham became K. J. Bredon's Bookshop after Margot Heginbotham left to be married. They had bought the business from Frank Ward at the end of the war, and Kenneth Bredon proceeded to expand steadily, taking over premises in

Prince Albert Street for an antiquarian department, and forming a Penguin Bookshop within the main premises at East Street. It was a pleasantly designed shop and one of the least over-stocked in the whole country, Bredon being the wisest of buyers, an attribute not always appreciated by representatives. Up the road from his shop was Beal's Store (nothing to do with the one at Bournemouth, which sported an additional 'e') with a good book department amongst the fancy goods and toys, and around the corner, near the Lanes, were the S.P.C.K. and Robinson's. Leslie John Robinson, who had started with Stoneham's in 1922 and became a manager of Q Bookshops in Brighton, started on his own in 1959, dealing in general and technical books. He was a firm believer in training assistants on the floor of the shop, as distinct from sending them on courses, which was, perhaps, ironic considering that he took over the Brighton College of Education Shop in 1967, two years before his death. His son-in-law, T. P. Brown, continued the business.

At adjoining Hove (72,600), the Combridge business was sold in 1960 to a company which operated in conjunction with a Brighton wholesale stationer. At Worthing (81,100), Mason sold his share to Hodges and his wife in 1962; elsewhere in Sussex, either on the coast or inland, shops opened and closed, changed ownership, went steadily on or declined, perhaps doing better than the outsider supposed, perhaps worse; only Miss Santoro's at Crowborough (8,169) seems to attract the historian, although he may well be wrong. In 1968 Miss Santoro moved her shop into new premises which were more commodious and, very important, close to a large car park. She closed her library service in 1966 and sold her Uckfield (4,412) branch to its manager in 1956, when her partner, Miss Frampton, was unable, through illness, to continue. In 1969 The Book Club, Crowborough, served twenty-six schools and had a wide overseas market for personal shoppers. Few, if any, small towns in the whole of Britain had a bookshop with as comprehensive a stock as Miss Santoro's, or were owned by anyone as compulsively dedicated to her task.

T. H. Rayward continued at Tunbridge Wells's (43,930) Goulden & Curry's until 1956, when the onset of blindness led to his retirement from the splendid book department which he had created. In 1969 when J. H. Fall, who had joined as a £3 a week apprentice in 1948, was manager of the department, two-thirds of the book business was still with private customers and one-third with libraries and schools.

Maidstone (66,650) was more fortunate than many market towns because Gordon Larkins, who had been with Ivan Chambers at Bryce's, secured premises in the High Street in 1966 when he opened his County Town Bookshop, which was attractively laid out in keeping with its surroundings but without being either aggressively modern or historically fusty. For the traveller in Kent, to come upon the lively County Town Bookshop, knowledgeably and sympathetically run, was a tonic after the desperate desert of Bexley (90,160) with one B.A. member; Chatham (51,220) and Rochester (54,200) with six between them, and Gillingham (82,830) where there was a W. H. Smith and G. & E. Nicholls, founded in 1922, which had only 252 square feet to devote to books.

Canterbury (32,790), as might be expected, had good shops—the S.P.C.K. inside one of the cathedral gateways, and the Pilgrim's Bookshop in Margaret Street. The Pilgrim's Bookshop was started by A. Egerton-Jones, formerly a teacher at King's School, but it was sold eight years later in 1955 to Alec Rae, who had retired early from the colonial civil service, the colonies being a non-growth industry at that time. Rae's wife, Jill, became a partner in 1963 and they built up a personal business, also dealing in foreign books which took them to the Frankfurt Book Fair most years in search of new lines.

The Kent coast was less well served than the Sussex, indeed, much less so. Apart from Whitstable (23,120), on the Thames Estuary, where Marjorie N. White ran the Book House, bookselling activities by the seaside were not exciting in Deal (27,190), Folkestone (44,070) and— even Dover (35,970), although there Denis Weaver had found himself a good site in the Market Square in the late 'sixties.*

Surprisingly, at Tenterden, an inland town (5,490), there was more interesting activity with the Tenterden Bookshop, started in 1962, literally linked to a chemist shop and buying all its stock from a wholesaler. H. V. Roberts bought the pharmacy, and his wife, disliking the stationery which was then in the adjoining shop, opted for books instead; in 1969 she had a bright and clean-looking stock. The following year there was news of another bookshop being opened in the same town.

In the northern part of the county Martin Hook opened a much needed shop in Bromley (301,680), the first independent bookselling business there since 1932. He had already opened in Westerham (4,228), near Sevenoaks. But Bromley being part of Greater London, his second venture belongs more properly to the next chapter.

Hertfordshire boasted two small but well-run and well-stocked shops: in St Albans (52,650), Paton Books, opened in 1962 by Miss Catherine Paton, an ex-assistant at Ward's in Chelsea's Kings Road; and in the county town (18,560), The Book Worm, owned by Mrs Shackleton. The new towns of Hertfordshire were not adequately endowed with bookshops except at Stevenage (60,370), which had an S.P.C.K. branch. At Welwyn Garden City (41,150), the department-store book department suffered the death of B. N. Langdon-Davies in 1952, a year after

* The Albion group of shops, based on Thanet, emerged in the 'sixties.

he had published his *Practice of Bookselling*, a useful textbook for the time.

Although I have tried not to be unfair, the selection in this chapter must appear invidious, and perhaps overlooks some who were struggling to provide good retail outlets in urban and country districts. In the Thames Valley, especially, several new businesses opened towards the end of this period, and one hopes they will make good. Mrs Bunty McNeil started at Henley-on-Thames (10,600) in 1966, providing a much-needed bookshop in that town. Circumstances required her to resign three years later and open another shop in nearby Marlow (10,750). In Maidenhead (44,980) a new shop appeared in 1970 supported by the obvious goodwill of publishers. Mrs McNeil and others were the brave new booksellers of the latter part of this history, and I dearly hope that the next edition will record their success.

Meanwhile it has to be noted that between fifty and a hundred population centres of over 40,000 inhabitants had no bookshop worth the name, and that it was usual, rather than the reverse, for a community rich in dry cleaners, supermarkets, laundrettes, boutiques and instant fried chicken bars not to be served by a stockholding bookshop. Whether or not this was owing to the public's total indifference to books, to the excellence of the 'free' (i.e. paid for out of the rates) public library service, or to an insufficiency of good booksellers who could create a market for books, must remain open to argument.

Apart from those bookshops mentioned above, and others perhaps overlooked because information was not made available to me, there were certain specialist retailers in many parts of the country. One, in unlikely Gateshead, I have already mentioned ; another was Landsman's in Bromyard, Herefordshire, a part of the country not noted for thriving bookselling. Landsman's was started in 1945 as a postal lending library for books on country subjects. It later sprouted a mobile bookshop which was taken round to agricultural and flower shows, selling as well as lending. In 1955 the library was dropped, and pure farming and gardening books superseded the 'country' books. However, David Spreckley, who had begun this enterprise, became more interested in selling and constructing caravans, and sold the book side to two farmers, Mr and Mrs John Young, who took this part of the business to Llangollen where they then lived. When John Young died in 1961 his widow was joined by her cousin, whose husband, an ex-R.A.F. test pilot, came in too. They worked from the base at Bromyard, after other temporary homes had been tried out, and reckoned to cover the whole country, exhibiting at all major shows concerned with their subject. Landsman's was a unique manifestation of bookselling, relatively unknown to the trade

as a whole, but emphasizing the importance of selling specialist literature without the backing of a permanently sited bookshop. It was an
extension of the mail order principle used by other booksellers, the
major part of whose business was done through the post but who had a
fixed address always open to the public. Most firms of the latter category
were based on London—Hersant, with a small shop in Highgate
specializing in aircraft books, for instance—but some large provincial
bookshops also had sidelines in specialist subjects. Many other booksellers, throughout the land, also attempted to build mailing lists in
general books, but it was often the case that unless the actual literature
was inclined to what was supposed to be pornographic the exercise was
not commercially successful.

Provincial bookselling was always more difficult than retailing in
London, where postal and carriage charges were not usually imposed,
and where many trade counters remained open so that urgent items
could be collected. The provincial bookseller who made a go of his
business was probably forced to be more astute than his London colleague, although he often did not have to face such high overheads.

Bookselling: London

Hatchard's; J. & E. Bumpus; W. & G. Foyle; Better Books; A. Zwemmer; Collet's; Economist's Bookshop; Denny's Booksellers; Barker & Howard; Jones & Evans; Alfred Wilson; A. R. Mowbray; G. Heywood Hill; Books and Careers; Claude Gill Books; Harrod's; Army & Navy Stores; Selfridge's; William Dawson; Gordon & Gotch; William Jackson (Books) Ltd; O. M. Watts; Fabian Society; Labour Party; Housman's; Horseman's Bookshop; Ecology Bookshop; H. K. Lewis; St John Thomas; Luzac; Probsthain; Kegan Paul; S.P.C.K.; Burns, Oates; Duckett's; Epworth Press; Carey Kingsgate Press; Hachette; Grant & Cutler; Woodfield & Stanley; Children's Book Centre; Mary Glasgow & Baker—Scholastic Productions; H.M.S.O.; Berger & Tims; F. J. Ward; Chelsea Bookshop; John Sandoe; H. Karnac; High Hill Bookshop; Belsize Bookshop; Mandarin Bookshops; Highgate Bookshop; Burgess' Bookshop; Caxton Bookshop; Langston's Bookshop; Hill Bookshop; Fielder; Greenwich Bookshop; Woolland's; Don Gresswell.

Sir Thomas Moore gave up control of Hatchard's in 1954, and for two years after that it was owned by Theodore Cole, who sold it to Collins, thus ensuring its continuance as one of London's leading quality bookshops. When he retired from the Army & Navy Stores in 1965, Thomas Joy was appointed managing director, and it was he who developed Hatchard's other activities, opening branches in stores, in Guildford, for example, and at Debenham and Freebody's, in London's Wigmore Street, which was left without a general bookshop when The Times closed down. (This last remark with due respect to the Scripture Union Bookshop, which had an attractive frontage but which was primarily a specialist business, as its title suggests.) Tommy Joy also bought Better Books in Charing Cross Road from Tony Godwin, but this was later disposed of to another publisher, John Calder. Before Joy's reign, in 1962, Prince's Bookshop, started in Piccadilly by Frank Francis some thirty years before, had been purchased along with the services of its owner. Peter Giddy joined Hatchard's as shop manager after Bumpus left Baker Street, and other refugees from that once-great retailing business who found themselves working alongside him were John Wilson (son of J.G.) and Dickie Bland, who arrived via The Times Bookshop; A. Donati, popular buyer at the Piccadilly shop for many years, survived the various changes. Another innovation of the Joy regime was the annual Authors of the Year party held on the fourteenth floor of New Zealand House, a great modern glass box which was erected in the Haymarket. Hatchard's, which had been in the doldrums more than once in its long history enjoyed a new phase of prosperity after Collins bought it (see also p. 455).

The story of Bumpus for most of this period was one of fading glory and near extinction. In the 'thirties J. G. Wilson had raised the money to buy the business, but after the war he failed to realize the value of the Oxford Street lease, and when it came up for renewal he was faced with having to pay a totally uneconomic rent. Once the war boom was over Bumpus had lean years, and 'J.G.' had to seek support from publishers, a consortium of whom took out debentures and approached Tony Godwin in 1958 to become managing director. By then the end of the lease in Oxford Street was approaching and new premises had already been taken in Baker Street. At this time the company was losing £1,800 per month, had a staff of nearly fifty, many of whom were over seventy, and had made no provisions for pensions. Numerous accounts, including those of some very celebrated personages indeed, had not been settled for years, and the shelves were heavily overstocked. It was necessary for Godwin to be ruthless, to reduce the staff to about a dozen and to refuse long-term credit, thus ridding himself of customers who were of no use to Bumpus. Every bookseller in London felt the repercussions, and some learned to be equally ruthless in refusing Bumpus's fleeing customers the terms to which they had become accustomed. The foreign department was sold to Dillon's, and the Book Society was bought for £12,000. The latter with its 10,000 members was undoubtedly a good buy and it helped to restore the fortunes of the bookshop, but in 1960 Allen Lane, one of the publishers who backed Bumpus, offered Godwin the chief editorship at Penguin. Godwin accepted, and Gordon Grimley was appointed in his place at Baker Street. Soon after, the company was sold to Bendor Drummond, who had not previously been connected with the trade, despite bids by W. H. Smith and Claude Gill. Drummond moved to Mount Street to premises which for a long time had been Day's Library, but were not for long to be Bumpus. Drummond sold out to Robert Maxwell in 1966 and Bumpus was merged with the Library supply business of Haldane's which Maxwell had bought from Foyle's in the same year.

Charing Cross Road remained the principal book street in London, although much of it was under the threat of demolition from the 'fifties onwards. Foyle's vast premises were extended in 1966 when the Goldbeaters' House Building was opened at a cost of £250,000. The firm at that time received 3,000 letters a day from all over the world and had thirty-two departments. The Literary Luncheons continued to attract the public and the press, which also gave considerable space to a strike of shop staff in the 1960s. The strike lasted some two weeks, during which time the shop remained open but picketed. Some publishers supported the strikers and refused deliveries, perhaps in order not to damage their own industrial relations, perhaps because they had some sympathy with the assistants, who were certainly lowly paid. The wage structure was capricious, and the wonder is that union interference did not occur earlier. The strike did not markedly improve conditions for bookshop assistants generally, and after it was settled Foyle's tended to employ temporary foreign labour.

William Foyle died in 1963, having spent some of his fortune on purchasing an abbey at Beeleigh in Essex. His son Richard predeceased him, and the effective control of the shop was in the hands of Christina Foyle and her husband Ronald Batty, who had come to Foyle's as an antiquarian bookseller. Foyle's Educational was run as a separate company under Gilbert, who founded an educational trust in 1944 to provide grants to university students. Eric and John, his sons, succeeded him, whilst Richard's son, Christopher, joined his aunt's side of the company. Foyle's had a tremendous turnover of staff, but amongst those who stayed was Ben Perrick, the advertising manager, who was a well-known figure in the trade. Here, as in all bookselling businesses, shop-lifting was a considerable problem, undefeated by the employment of store detectives and constant prosecutions.

Something has already been said of Better Books and its acquisition by Tony Godwin. His manager for many years was Ken Fyffe, who had been at the shop before the war but had left to become a publishers' rep. Better Books had a corner site but also acquired the adjoining premises in Charing Cross Road which were used for various purposes over the years, finally becoming a showroom and sales point for Oxford University Press books only. When Collins's took over they naturally did not wish to have a whole shop full of another publisher's books, so the Oxford showroom was accommodated in one of Zwemmer's premises further down the road. Zwemmer's continued primarily to be an art book shop, and became a company in 1949 with Desmond and John, sons of the founder, and E. Beeson as directors. They continued as agents for Skira books and, on the publishing side, built up a good remainder business. Their near neighbours were Collet's who took a lease of 64 Charing Cross Road, near to the old 'Bomb Shop', and under the influence of what had happened at Better Books they created a splendid light modern shop. Besides opening many other shops in other parts of London, Collet's opened a Penguin bookshop at 52 Charing Cross Road in 1962. Tom Russell, who had been manager of the London Philharmonic Orchestra, was general manager until 1969, and the other chief executives during this period of tremendous expansion were Olive Parsons, Joan Birch, John Prime and William Norris. Miss Reckitt remained active in the business which she had started, and celebrated her eightieth birthday in 1970. The head office was moved to Wellingborough (Northants) in the late 'sixties, and by then the policy was to concentrate on fewer outlets. Most of the gramophone record shops they had opened had already been sold off, as had some of the small general bookshops, but the Russian Bookshop in Museum Street remained. To return to Better Books, John Calder bought it with the intention of making it an outlet for his own and other publishers' avantgarde literature, threatening to set up stalls outside the shops of those booksellers who did not stock his books. He planned to open other shops, the first of which started in Edinburgh in 1970.

Bryce's and Dillon's have already been referred to in the section on university bookselling; another academic shop, the Economists', has not. This was started in 1947, close to the London School of Economics as a joint venture of *The Economist* journal and the L.S.E. The first manager was Mrs Gerti Kvergic, another remarkable woman bookseller, and she completed twenty-one years before handing over to Gerald Bartlett, who had been assistant manager for many years. Mrs Kvergic, a refugee from Hitler, worked on Sir Basil Blackwell's dictum that a good bookshop must be able to function behind closed doors and mail order business was sought from the beginning. Her first shop in St Clement's Passage had an old-fashioned bay window supported by a few spindly iron rods; the steps up to the door were heavily worn. In her first year she turned over £12,000, but by 1968 this had risen to £250,000 and the shop occupied new premises in Clare Market, as well as having a mail order department in the Hampstead Road. Half the turnover came through the post, much of it from overseas, which was of great benefit because L.S.E. suffered more than most during the student riots which were universal during the latter part of this period. Gerald Bartlett was a bookseller in the Blackwell-Schollick tradition, actively managing his own business whilst finding time to take a very positive part in trade politics. He was a persistent worker for better wages for bookshop staff and a great supporter of training schemes. His senior colleague at the Economists' for most of this time was Anthony Comerford, one of the many booksellers who was also an author. Bartlett, too, made claims in that direction by editing a series of books on Better Bookselling which were published by Hutchinson.

Edgar Gladwin, of Denny's, died in 1945 after nearly fifty years in the trade. Five years later Charles Bathurst and Miss Dorothy Denny became directors, the shop in the Strand was closed, and the business was concentrated on the premises in Ludgate Hill where, in the basement, there was much activity in library supply. The business transferred to Carthusian Street in 1967. Of the other city booksellers, Barker & Howard extended their activities by taking a new shop in the Barbican development around St Paul's Cathedral, but retained the old premises in Fenchurch Street; Jones & Evans, under George Downie, functioned in small premises in Queen Victoria Street where Mr Downie continued to exercise his prejudices against Book Tokens and paperbacks and yet remain a good personal bookseller; and Alfred Wilson Ltd followed Simpkin Marshall's into the receivers' hands. The former business was turning over £100,000 per annum in books in its three shops and export department in 1955, and publishers struggled to save it. Hubert Wilson bought back the export books and magazine subscriptions departments from the receiver; the shop in Ship Tavern Passage was sold to Tony Godwin; that in Victoria Street was closed down and the lease was disposed of; and the Hampstead High Street branch was sold to a very large private bookseller who remained anonymous. When Godwin, in his turn, sold what became known as the City Bookshop, his manager, Elwyn Fisher, started the New City Bookshop in 1964, in Byward Street. It occupied a brand new site covering 1,600 square feet and specialized in books on business and travel.

Mowbray's turned from theological to general bookselling, and became an unquoted public company. They opened and closed various branches in various provincial cities, but in London settled into redesigned premises in Margaret Street, near Oxford Circus, where Alfred G. R. Harrison was manager from 1952–64. F. G. Bryant, chairman and managing director for many years, retired in 1957 on his seventieth birthday.

At Heywood Hill's in Curzon Street, Handasyde Buchanan, who had been concerned in another nearby shop before the war, joined and presided over an emporium which had an air of carefully organized muddle without a speck of dust. He also wrote and edited books for Eyre & Spottiswoode and others.

Cyril Edgeley, who had been manager at Hatchard's during the Hatry regime, became manager of The Times Book Club in 1949, succeeding the Hon. Andrew Shirley. He remained there until 1968, by which time the library had been closed and the remaining subscribers transferred to Harrods. A branch opened in the Times building in the new Printing House Square in 1963 lasted only four years. In the year of Edgeley's retirement the shop was sold to W. H. Smith who closed it and transferred the goodwill to Truslove & Hanson in Sloane Street where, as we have seen, it became part of Bowes & Bowes. As with Bumpus, a sad story of decline.

Of the new businesses, Books and Careers, which became Claude Gill Ltd, was the most formidable. At one stage Books and Careers had branches in Moorgate, in the City, in Victoria Street, South Audley Street and, outside London, in Southampton. These were all gradually closed (Victoria Street lost nearly half a dozen bookshops in the 'fifties) and the business was concentrated in large premises in Oxford Street where Jim Hume succeeded Claude Gill as manager. Gill, after whom the business was re-named, retired in 1967 when R. P. Wellsman became managing director. Crowell, Collier-Macmillan acquired it soon after. They also opened in 1968 a Management and Training Centre, at 481 Oxford Street, to display a comprehensive range of books on those subjects, in addition to audio-visual aids and training equipment.

Bookselling was active in the stores, throughout this period, particularly at Harrods, where the subscription library was maintained despite closures almost everywhere else in the country. Cadness Page retired in 1965 and joined Pergamon Press for a while as managing director; he was succeeded by J. M. Whiting, and Geoffrey Van Danzig remained buyer for the book department. David Leck, who bought for the library for many years, moved to the Army & Navy Stores in 1960 when George Depotex, who had succeeded Thomas Joy as book buyer, left to become sales manager of André Deutsch. Joy started the subscription library when he came from Harrods at the end of the war to take on the task of rehabilitating the rather stricken book department in the Victoria Street store. At Selfridge's, Jock Elliot was succeeded by Gordon Cool, and at the Civil Service Stores, Audrey Graham-Jones was manageress until she bought her own bookshop in Rottingdean, Sussex. The book department of this store was reached through a separate entrance until it was moved up to the third floor in 1969. It was a haven, during Miss Graham-Jones' reign, for reps who had had a bad time with other buyers; she always provided the words of comfort they needed.

Wholesale exporting declined from 1939 to 1970, but did not disappear altogether. William Dawson's, of Macklin Street, whilst continuing their retailing operations elsewhere, closed down their wholesale book service in October 1970 and handed over orders received after that date to Gordon & Gotch (already merged with Alfred Royle & Willan) who had bought the export agency of W. H. Smith a few months before. William Jackson (Books) Ltd moved from Took's Court to Southampton Row, where a retail shop was added to the export side. It was an eccentric and typically Frederick Joiner arrangement that customers were not allowed to handle the books or to use the front door on to the street. Instead they had to enter by the side passage to the export department, present themselves at a counter which barred access to the stock, and ask for what they wanted. Joiner went blind in 1954 and died some ten years later. The bookshop is no longer.

There were many specialist book businesses in London. Captain O. M. Watts in Albemarle Street dealt entirely in maritime literature. He obtained his Master's Ticket in the Merchant Navy as a young man but took up retail business in the 'twenties, adding books to his other lines in 1927. The Fabian Society had its own retail outlet in Dartmouth Street, near Parliament Square, and the Conservative Party operated a bookshop, also dealing in general literature, in Victoria Street for many years. The Labour Party had a kind of shop on an upper floor of Transport House in Smith Square, but it was not open to the public. Also politically orientated was Housman's, run by the Peace Pledge Union. J. A. Allen ran the Horseman's Bookshop in Buckingham Palace Road; there was an Ecology Bookshop in Lower Belgrave Street; H. K. Lewis's of Gower Street remained the leading medical booksellers; and St John Thomas, of David & Charles, opened a shop in Woburn Place in 1969 specializing in social and economic history, industrial history and archaeology, thus reflecting the main preoccupations of the D. & C. list. In Great Russell Street, facing the British Museum, were a number of small shops concerned with orientalia: Luzac, still in the hands of the Knight-Smith family; Probsthain; and Kegan Paul, a subsidiary of Routledge's since 1911.

Besides Mowbray's and S.P.C.K., other theological shops were Burns, Oates (Roman Catholic), whose Victoria Street shop was sold to the Daughters of St Paul, and then closed; Duckett's, now Gill's, in the Strand (R.C. but with a general stock as well); the Epworth Press (Methodist); and the Carey Kingsgate Press (Baptist).

Hachette moved into new premises in Regent Place, off Regent Street, in 1964, when W. G. Corp was manager. Another shop much favoured by those who wished to buy foreign books was Grant & Cutler in Buckingham Street, close to Charing Cross Station. They dealt in all foreign books, and had a reputation for being able to obtain items which other booksellers could not.

There was a children's bookshop owned by the Huddersfield library suppliers, Woodfield & Stanley, in Great Russell Street for many years, but this closed in the late 'fifties. It's successor, in Kensington Church Street, was the Children's Book Centre, founded by Eric Baker in 1966. It was the only Central London bookshop specializing in juveniles, although a number opened in the suburbs and provinces, and it arranged displays in schools and colleges as well as organizing informal gatherings of children to meet authors and artists. It grew out of Mary Glasgow & Baker, which had started at the same address a few years previously. In 1966 Mary Glasgow decided to concentrate on publishing, so Baker formed a separate company to attend to the bookselling.

The arrival of a children's bookshop in Kensington Church Street was also linked with the establishment of a paperback readers' club aimed at selling books, through schools, to children from non-bookish homes. In its first year, encouraged by an ex-teacher turned author, Edward Blishen, and by one of the most active of children's publishers, Mrs Grace Hogarth, it sold 100,000 books in 1,000 secondary schools. Mary

Glasgow & Baker created the organization in conjunction with Scholastic Magazines Inc. of America, and from 1964, when Simon Boosey became managing director, it was known as Scholastic Productions Ltd, and was run by a staff of idealistic but highly professional men and women working under him. It is impossible to estimate the benefit it has been to publishers and booksellers in bringing books before children who were previously unaware of them because of parental indifference.

The particular importance of catering for young people was emphasized outside London as well, and the Domino Children's Bookshop (1964) in Beckenham (in Kent but within the confines of Greater London) should be noted. It excited the attention of at least one sales director of a large publishing company as being 'a most attractive shop' which suggested to him a smaller version of Eric Baker's Children's Book Centre. And part of his excitement — even allowing for idealism, which is not entirely foreign to all sales personnel — must have been due to actual sales made.

The government ran other specialist shops under the aegis of H.M.S.O. One of these, in Oxford Street, was closed down in 1968 for the rather curious reason that it was doing too much business; apparently the shop could no longer accommodate the vast Stationery Office output and funds would not stretch to additional premises.

As one outlet closed, so another opened, and there was a revival of bookselling in Victoria Street when Berger & Tims, library suppliers, who had formerly occupied a basement near the Alfred Wilson shop, started a retail department in the new Watney-Mann development near Victoria.

S.W.1, S.W.3 and N.W.3 were good areas for bookselling. In the King's Road Frank Ward opened a shop when he returned from the war, and was joined by his former assistant, Edward Sheppard, who took over when Ward died. Ted Sheppard was for many years also the London manager of the Ward Gallery, an associated company which published greeting cards. He attended to his duties at both so conscientiously that he worried more than was necessary; this probably contributed to his untimely death in 1971. Further down King's Road Elizabeth Weiler had the Chelsea Bookshop, and round the corner in Blacklands Terrace John Sandoe started an attractive small shop on three floors in 1957. In Gloucester Road, Harry Karnac, who had been a bookseller in Edgware, opened in 1950, specializing in psychology. He was the one who survived! Several others in the neighbourhood closed as the character of Kensington and Knightsbridge changed. In 1950 Karnac said Kensington was still in the hands of the Galsworthian middle classes who thought paperbacks were vulgar, so that revolution reached S.W.7 a little later than elsewhere but not in time to prevent a number of shops from going out of business.

When the tax loss of Alfred Wilson was sold, it was necessary for the new owners to keep open a branch of the business, so the Hampstead High Street shop remained with myself as manager. In 1957 the name was changed to the High Hill Bookshop, and in 1964, by which time the freehold property it had occupied had been sold and the shop moved a few doors down the street, it was sold to Alan Steele and me. Later the business moved in and out of other premises in that part of the High Street, but by 1971 it had settled into three linked shop-units occupying some 3,000 square feet. The turnover in books in 1956 was approximately £8,000 ; in 1970 it was £110,000 of which some 60 per cent was in direct retailing over the counter. In 1961 Collet's branch at Belsize Park, N.W.3, was sold to High Hill, who kept it for ten years before selling it to the manager, Donald Woodford. At High Hill for many years, and for a short while as manager at Belsize, was Ralph Abercrombie. This brilliant man, who never realized his own abilities, was a bookseller *par excellence*; when he was not fighting sickness he had a near-photographic memory, and was widely read, with the talent to 'read-in' books, as he put it, a process by which he seemed to extract all that was essential without reading every word. High Hill also benefited from the nonsense of the Library Association, who would not recognize the qualifications of New Zealand library assistants; they were thus able to keep Monica Carolan, who became a director of the company in 1969, when John Ford joined from Seager's, of East India Dock Road. This John Ford should not be confused with another of that name, who was a Central London rep. for Collins for many years and a pillar of the B.P.R.A., for whom he helped organize numerous functions.

Also in the Hampstead area, at Swiss Cottage, was Harry Saunderson, who had also opened a shop in Notting Hill Gate a year or two before. Both shops were called Mandarin Bookshop. In Highgate Antony Wilson, ex-publicity department at The Bodley Head and ex-manager of the Belsize Bookshop, opened his own shop in 1966.

Elsewhere in North London for many years there was no shop with a sizeable stock between High Hill in Hampstead and Miss Paton's in St Albans, twenty miles away. As I write there have been a number of recent openings, and it must be hoped that the situation will improve.

In the outer suburbs shops were sparse indeed. At Brentwood in Essex Alec Bunch moved from the High Street into the Ongar Road into a pleasant two-storied new shop. At Romford an ex-policeman, A. C. Andrews, had a shop in three-hundred-year old premises in the Market Place until he moved, in 1968, into new large premises in a shopping development. At Twickenham, Langton's bookshop carried a large stock in rambling premises consisting of two seventeenth-century houses knocked together. It was owned in 1970 by Mr and Mrs Holtom. South London Stationers had a number of shops, including the

Hill Bookshop at Wimbledon, which was managed for some years by an ex-actor, Freddy Walker, who later became sales manager of Studio Vista. After his departure Noel Frieslich became manager. Nearer to Wimbledon Station was Fielder, who had been long established in a district which, like Hampstead and Chelsea, was peopled by those who could tell books from magazines, and were prepared to buy them. Blackheath, another such district, was not equally blessed, although down the hill by Greenwich Pier Nigel Hamilton opened a shop in 1966 from which he subsequently published a handsome book on the community, with a foreword by Arthur Bryant. Distinguished authors also proved willing to contribute to the books published from High Hill — Ernest Raymond, Ivor Brown and Eleanor Farjeon amongst them. A number of booksellers turned to publishing, particularly for books about their own locality, because the fact that so many copies could be sold over their own counters at full price allowed a lower costing to be placed on a small run.

Harrow had several bookshops, including Woollonds (now closed) and a branch of Universal Stationers, and at Enfield Don Gresswell expanded his business so prodigiously that in 1965 he built himself a new three-storey factory, nicely surrounded by newly planted trees, and gave up retailing. Instead of a bookshop he had a first-floor showroom with perhaps the best stock of books for children (as distinct from children's books) anywhere in Britain. This was manned by a receptionist, and the public were welcomed, but as it was not in a main shopping area visitors were usually teachers and parties of school children. Gresswell's sons, Patrick and Philip, joined him in the business, which supplied all forms of school equipment, as well as books, to libraries and schools all over the world. Brian Alderson, who managed the retail shop for many years, remained an adviser to the firm after he had left to pursue a distinguished career as a lecturer in librarianship and a writer on children's literature; he established himself as an authority on the latter subject.

Don Gresswell trained as a mechanical engineer; Leslie Wheeler was a sanitary inspector before he became a bookseller; Alec Rae, a colonial civil servant; Ross Higgins, an advertising agent; Una Dillon, a social worker. I do not know of anyone who combined bookselling with undertaking, as did the Egyptian mentioned on the first page of this history, but the trade continued to attract those who began their working lives in quite different occupations. It is worth noting that scarcely any of the most successful booksellers of this period had any official training in their craft; this was much in the tradition of Robert Dodsley, who began life as a footman and lived to be publisher of Johnson's *Dictionary*. Personally I hope bookselling will always be a free-entry trade; some occupations, and this is one of them, need common sense and a willingness to work hard more than paper qualifications.

Postscript

As the comedian discussing the weather remarked, the only predictable thing about the future is that it will be unpredictable. Nonetheless, this edition has been so long in the making that a few guesses may be hazarded, based on trends already observable, about what the next edition may record.

A significant number of publishers have left the conglomerates to go it alone preferring, as one of them stated, to begin his real publishing at 9.30 in the morning instead of in the late afternoon after all the office conferences. Some of those who have bravely started their own houses will be recorded in the 1984 edition as having merged, been taken over or ceased business; it will be difficult for any of them (as for their predecessors) to survive without becoming part of a conglomerate.

The effect of Britain entering the European Economic Community in 1973 may well lead to unions with continental publishers, and the larger bookselling businesses may also establish branches in France and elsewhere, as W. H. Smith did long ago. Whether or not there will be more or less American ownership of British-born firms depends much on the state of the international money market. The enlargement of the E.E.C. may make for tighter world economic units and greater American concentration on infiltrating other countries which were once Britain's traditional overseas selling points. In the nations which formed the now disintegrated British Empire there will be more indigenous publishing, and our publishers will continue to protect their own interests by operating separate companies within those territories.

At home, in an ever more complex society relying increasingly on the new technology, methods of printing, publishing and distribution will become more automated, and, with any luck, more humanized, than they have been in the initial stages of computerization and mass production. The pace of change will continue to accelerate, unless those few voices which warn us now of the dangers of going too far too fast are heard — and it would be a starry-eyed optimist indeed who forecast confidently that they will.

There will be wider use of cassettes, tapes, photo-copying and audio-visual equipment, but it is unlikely that the book will become obsolete as an instrument of instruction. It has not been killed by the invention of moving pictures, radio or television, and I daresay there will always be those who find the book a convenient storage place for knowledge, and the index a useful retrieval system.

In the early 'seventies many new bookshops opened, mostly small in size (1,000 square feet or less—often much less), in communities which had formerly lacked this amenity. Whether or not they can survive in the face of inflationary rents and other overheads must be very questionable, but it is not unlikely that they will have to face whatever future they have without relying overmuch on institutional trade. Local government is being reorganized into larger units with greater buying power, and it would be ostrich-like to suppose that the inevitable demands for centralized book-buying direct from publishers will not be seriously heard. Healthy bookselling will depend more and more on retail sales over the counter or through the mail (assuming that there is one) and the cost of servicing institutional orders will continue to rise so that this business, if it does not go direct to the publisher, may well become even more concentrated than it is now in the hands of a few large library and educational contractors.

The various trade institutions will prosper or decline, adapt to new conditions or dissolve into new formations. Prediction can, finally, be no more than a stimulating parlour game; but what is as certain as a defective copy in every edition is that publishers will go on over-producing and believing that the majority of booksellers do not try to sell positively; that booksellers will insist that they could sell more effectively if distribution improved and if they were allowed better terms; and that authors will remain eternally convinced that their books are insufficiently advertised and displayed. And from the ranks of all three there will arise new colourful personalities who will earn their places in future histories, even if these have to be inscribed on stone because we have squandered all our other natural resources.

Appendixes

APPENDIX A

These tables, reprinted by permission of J. Whitaker & Sons, Ltd, show the books recorded in *The Bookseller*

CLASSIFICATION	1937 (Pre-war record year)				1943 (Lowest war year total)				1955 (Record year)			
	Total	Reprints and new edns.	Trans.	Edns. de luxe	Total	Reprints and new edns.	Trans.	Edns. de luxe	Total	Reprints and new edns.	Trans.	Edns. de luxe
Aeronautics	50	9	—	—	148	19	1	1	107	37	1	—
Annuals and Serials	123	101	—	—	47	33	—	2	52	50	—	—
Anthropology	46	5	2	—	23	1	—	—	38	2	1	—
Archaeology	60	6	3	—	17	—	—	1	58	9	4	—
Art and Architecture	230	46	6	9	67	12	1	1	591	89	33	22
Astronomy	43	3	1	—	21	2	—	—	78	21	1	—
Banking and Finance	42	13	—	—	40	14	—	—	220	82	—	—
Bibliography	98	44	3	3	55	4	—	—	304	47	9	9
Biography	789	188	43	4	281	40	5	1	496	89	34	3
Botany and Agriculture	178	39	1	1	58	6	1	2	285	78	5	4
Calendars	67	31	1	—	7	1	—	—	15	14	—	—
Chemistry and Physics	133	27	4	—	52	16	1	—	335	71	8	—
Children's Books	1597	552	6	1	671	110	4	8	1756	482	14	—
Classics and Translations	87	57	40	3	26	15	8	4	64	27	22	—
Dictionaries	62	15	—	—	22	5	—	—	116	22	—	—
Directories	166	92	—	—	16	9	—	—	411	258	2	—
Domestic Economy	79	12	—	—	45	11	—	—	221	42	—	—
Educational	1337	223	20	—	312	41	1	—	1844	383	10	—
Engineering	155	53	3	—	101	26	—	—	413	165	3	—
Essays	462	96	16	1	124	26	1	2	118	25	12	3
Facetiae	61	9	—	—	54	11	1	—	66	10	5	—
Fiction	5097	2944	81	6	1408	347	30	1	3702	1453	255	6
Geology	56	10	—	—	18	2	—	—	157	67	12	—
History	458	87	22	1	192	20	4	2	235	40	15	1
Illustrated Gift Books	234	31	2	21	39	1	—	4	32	9	—	—
Law and Parliamentary	248	97	2	—	103	29	1	—	437	164	3	—
Maps and Atlases	30	4	1	—	15	1	—	—	81	22	—	—
Mathematics	38	4	1	—	46	14	—	—	87	22	3	—
Medical and Surgical	543	155	9	1	212	72	2	—	785	239	13	—
Music	83	13	3	—	43	12	2	—	121	25	7	—
Natural History	186	34	1	1	48	7	—	—	295	57	6	2
Nautical	99	18	—	1	14	3	—	—	133	57	4	—
Naval and Military	62	6	—	—	229	21	5	—	305	86	18	—
Occultism	58	13	2	—	28	5	1	—	48	17	2	—
Oriental	169	25	11	2	34	5	4	—	15	4	7	—
Philately	13	6	—	—	11	2	—	—	23	12	—	1
Philosophy and Science	164	36	18	—	62	5	3	—	187	41	31	1
Poetry and Drama	569	211	20	9	329	56	15	4	658	104	29	14
Politics	633	66	23	2	596	44	23	—	651	122	15	—
Psychology	59	1	—	—	25	5	1	—	119	26	13	—
Religion	927	135	60	3	425	41	6	1	1058	202	81	3
Sociology	264	26	2	—	165	10	1	—	405	96	10	1
Sport and Pastimes	260	34	5	2	57	9	—	—	433	129	10	6
Technical Handbooks	322	80	2	—	104	44	1	—	881	320	4	2
Topography	139	18	—	—	59	6	—	—	399	59	12	4
Trade	81	22	—	—	47	9	—	—	626	246	3	—
Travel and Adventure	411	107	19	—	102	18	5	1	199	31	31	—
Veterinary and Stockkeeping	38	11	1	—	73	6	—	1	204	84	—	—
Wireless	19	5	—	—	34	5	—	—	98	33	2	—
Totals	17137	5810	434	17	6705	1201	129	28	19962	5770	750	81

CLASSIFICATION	Total	1960		
		Reprints and new editions	Trans.	Ltd editions
Aeronautics	148	43	1	—
Annuals and Serials	33	33	—	—
Anthropology and Ethnology	50	4	3	—
Archaeology	85	16	7	—
Art and Architecture	614	87	86	7
Astronomy and Meteorology	140	34	7	—
Banking and Finance	206	79	—	—
Bibliography and Literary History	452	88	13	—
Biography and Memoirs	566	85	39	5
Botany, Horticulture and Agriculture	252	50	13	1
Calendars, Booklets and Albums	23	—	—	—
Chemistry and Physics	574	88	27	—
Children's Books	2295	304	63	—
Classics and Translations	79	40	37	—
Dictionaries and Encyclopaedias	84	21	2	—
Directories and Guide Books	512	313	5	—
Domestic Economy	193	33	5	—
Educational	2075	390	17	1
Engineering, Electricity and Mechanics	601	187	16	—
Essays and Belles-Lettres	129	20	6	3
Facetiae	133	18	3	2
Fiction	4209	1820	353	1
Geology, Mineralogy and Mining	174	50	6	—
History	412	89	17	2
Illustrated Gift Books	25	2	2	—
Law and Parliamentary	554	154	4	—
Maps and Atlases	169	44	—	—
Mathematics	222	49	15	1
Medical and Surgical	1116	293	28	—
Music	157	27	20	—
Natural History, Biology and Zoology	372	51	20	—
Nautical	155	50	1	—
Naval and Military	331	83	11	1
Occultism	70	7	1	—
Oriental	24	4	3	—
Philately	39	10	—	1
Philosophy and Science	253	61	28	1
Poetry and Drama	721	86	59	19
Politics, Political Economy and Questions of the Day	923	109	16	—
Psychology	132	30	11	—
Religion and Theology	1247	220	134	2
Sociology	431	77	12	—
Sports, Games and Pastimes	387	102	4	—
Technical Handbooks	922	274	9	1
Topography, Local History and Folklore	396	58	19	3
Trade, Commerce and Industry	526	144	1	—
Travel and Adventure	170	31	18	—
Veterinary Science, Farming and Stockkeeping	255	80	1	—
Wireless and Television	147	51	5	—
Totals	23783	5989	1148	51

CLASSIFICATION	1965				1970			
	Total	Reprints and new editions	Trans.	Ltd editions	Total	Reprints and new editions	Trans.	Ltd editions
Aeronautics	149	31	1	—	151	34	2	—
Agriculture & Forestry	313	42	6	—	235	66	3	—
Architecture	209	26	8	—	340	78	17	2
Art	649	100	69	6	967	217	49	9
Astronomy	88	11	5	1	91	22	22	—
Bibliography and Library Economy	238	51	1	3	464	94	1	1
Biography	707	125	44	2	940	265	61	11
Chemistry and Physics	828	139	46	—	803	125	23	—
Children's Books	2484	343	105	—	2406	575	77	—
Commerce	507	83	3	—	759	199	5	1
Customs, Costume, Folklore	61	7	4	—	116	46	7	1
Domestic Science	264	41	9	—	354	142	3	1
Education	562	63	2	—	973	206	8	—
Engineering	756	166	42	—	1015	252	20	—
Entertainment	161	25	10	1	295	57	21	1
Fiction	3877	1633	307	—	4449	2129	213	11
General	41	8	2	—	102	45	2	—
Geography and Archaeology	229	36	8	—	371	122	13	3
Geology and Meteorology	165	30	6	—	187	34	9	—
History	1073	233	65	1	1556	568	56	2
Humour	104	23	1	—	148	61	—	—
Industry	561	130	23	—	481	126	9	—
Language	292	45	3	—	337	104	7	—
Law and Public Administration	526	109	3	1	960	367	10	1
Literature	745	121	63	1	1320	375	107	7
Mathematics	466	87	47	—	530	99	13	—
Medical Science	1227	262	31	—	1285	313	12	—
Military Science	94	12	7	1	141	29	5	5
Music	178	32	11	1	272	96	9	3
Natural Sciences	690	146	23	—	928	216	33	—
Occultism	70	14	2	—	165	40	12	1
Philosophy	230	39	18	—	405	120	59	4
Photography	86	18	4	—	51	17	2	—
Plays	220	47	19	—	287	112	45	1
Poetry	361	34	20	13	840	133	50	100
Political Science and Economy	1559	221	40	—	2575	815	70	1
Psychology	268	38	6	—	399	103	0	—
Religion and Theology	1227	179	88	—	1245	375	101	2
School Textbooks	1869	175	31	—	1875	293	24	—
Science, General	113	11	3	—	115	37	9	—
Sociology	525	70	8	—	699	168	16	1
Sports and Outdoor Games	353	59	5	1	534	159	7	—
Stockbreeding	170	29	3	—	167	51	4	—
Trade	313	47	—	1	350	144	2	—
Travel and Guidebooks	545	129	27	—	637	316	16	1
Wireless and Television	205	43	8	—	169	32	2	—
Totals	26358	5313	1237	33	33489	9977	1229	170

Appendix B

OFFICERS OF THE PUBLISHERS' ASSOCIATION

Date	President	Vice-President	Treasurer
1896–98	C. J. Longman	John Murray	Frederick Macmillan
1898–1900	John Murray	C. J. Longman	Frederick Macmillan
1900–2	Frederick Macmillan	John Murray	C. J. Longman
1902–4	C. J. Longman	Frederick Macmillan	John Murray
1904–6	Reginald J. Smith	William Heinemann	C. J. Longman
1906–9	Edward Bell	C. J. Longman	William Heinemann
1909–11	William Heinemann	Edward Bell	Arthur Waugh
1911–13	Frederick Macmillan	William Heinemann	James H. Blackwood
1913–15	James H. Blackwood	Frederick Macmillan	John Murray
1915–17	Reginald J. Smith	James H. Blackwood	W. M. Meredith
1917–19	W. M. Meredith	Humphrey Milford	G. S. Williams
1919–21	Humphrey Milford	W. M. Meredith	C. F. Clay
1921–3	G. S. Williams	Humphrey Milford	C. F. Clay
1923–4	C. F. Clay	{ G. S. Williams / Humphrey Milford }	H. Scheurmier
1924–5	C. F. Clay	G. S. Williams	H. Scheurmier
1925–7	H. Scheurmier	G. S. Williams	G. C. Rivington
1927–9	{ W. M. Meredith / Edward Arnold }	H. Scheurmier	G. C. Rivington
1929–31	W. Longman	G. C. Rivington	Bertram Christian
1931–3	Bertram Christian	W. Longman	Stanley Unwin
1933–5	Stanley Unwin	Bertram Christian	W. G. Taylor
1935–7	W. G. Taylor	Stanley Unwin	G. Wren Howard
1937–9	G. Wren Howard	W. G. Taylor	Geoffrey C. Faber
1939–41	Geoffrey C. Faber	G. Wren Howard	Walter G. Harrap
1941–3	Walter G. Harrap	Geoffrey C. Faber	R. J. L. Kingsford
1943–5	R. J. L. Kingsford	Walter G. Harrap	B. W. Fagan
1945–7	B. W. Fagan	R. J. L. Kingsford	R. H. C. Holland
1947–9	R. H. C. Holland	B. W. Fagan	J. D. Newth
1949–51	J. D. Newth	R. H. C. Holland	Kenneth B. Potter
1951–3	Kenneth B. Potter	J. D. Newth	Ralph Hodder-Williams
1953–5	Ralph Hodder-Williams	Kenneth B. Potter	J. Alan White
1955–7	J. Alan White	Ralph Hodder-Williams	Ian Parsons
1957–9	Ian Parsons	J. Alan White	R. W. David
1959–61	R. W. David	Ian Parsons	John Boon

Date	President	Vice-President	Treasurer
1961–3	John Boon	R. W. David	John Brown
1963–5	John Brown	John Boon	John Attenborough
1965–7	John Attenborough	John Brown	Peter du Sautoy
1967–9	Peter du Sautoy	John Attenborough	Mark Longman
1969–71	Mark Longman	Peter du Sautoy	Rayner Unwin
1971–3	Rayner Unwin	Mark Longman	Colin Eccleshare
1973–5	Colin Eccleshare	Rayner Unwin	Peter Allsop

Appendix C

THE BOOKSELLERS' ASSOCIATION OF GREAT BRITAIN AND IRELAND

Date	Chairman	Hon. Secretary	Hon. Treasurer
1895–9	H. W. Keay, J.P.	E. Pearce	
1900–2		E. Pearce	F. Calder Turner
	President		
1903–11	H. W. Keay, J.P.	E. Pearce	F. Calder Turner
1912–20	H. W. Keay, J.P.	E. Pearce	F. Hanson
		Secretary	
1921	H. W. Keay, J.P.	W. J. Magenis	F. Hanson
1922	H. W. Keay, J.P.	W. J. Magenis	H. Shaylor
1923	F. A. Denny	W. J. Magenis	H. Shaylor
1924	F. A. Denny	W. J. Magenis	H. Shaylor
1925	G. A. Bowes	W. J. Magenis	H. Shaylor
1926	G. A. Bowes	W. J. Magenis	H. Shaylor
1927	C. Young	W. J. Magenis	W. J. Prior
1928	C. Young	W. J. Magenis	W. J. Prior
1929	H. E. Alden	W. J. Magenis	H. L. Jackson
1930	H. E. Alden	Miss H. M. Light	H. L. Jackson
1931	T. N. Philip	Miss H. M. Light	H. L. Jackson
1932	F. Bacon	Miss H. M. Light	H. L. Jackson
1933	F. Bacon	Miss H. M. Light	H. L. Jackson
1934	Basil Blackwell, M.A., J.P.	Miss H. M. Light	H. L. Jackson
1935	Basil Blackwell, M.A., J.P.	Miss H. M. Light	H. L. Jackson
1936	David Roy	Miss H. M. Light	H. L. Jackson
1937	David Roy	Miss H. M. Light	H. L. Jackson
1938	C. H. Barber	Miss H. M. Light	H. L. Jackson
1939	{ A. S. Jackson J. H. Ruddock }	Miss H. M. Light	H. L. Jackson
1940	J. H. Ruddock	Miss H. M. Light	H. L. Jackson
1941	J. H. Ruddock	Miss H. M. Light	H. L. Jackson
1942	H. L. Jackson	Miss H. M. Light	F. G. Bryant
1943	H. L. Jackson	Miss H. M. Light	F. G. Bryant
1944	A. F. Mason	Miss H. M. Light	F. G. Bryant
1945	F. J. Aldwinckle	Miss H. M. Light	F. G. Bryant
1946	F. J. Aldwinckle	Gordon M. Smith	F. G. Bryant
1947	H. M. Wilson	Gordon M. Smith	F. G. Bryant
1948	H. M. Wilson	P. B. Hepburn	F. G. Bryant

Date	President	Secretary	Hon. Treasurer
1949	K. V. Saville	P. B. Hepburn	F. G. Bryant
1950	K. V. Saville	P. B. Hepburn	F. G. Bryant
1951	F. G. Bryant	P. B. Hepburn	T. A. Joy
1952	F. G. Bryant	P. B. Hepburn	T. A. Joy
1953	Cadness Page	P. B. Hepburn	T. A. Joy
1954	Cadness Page	P. B. Hepburn	T. A. Joy
1955	Basil Donne-Smith	G. R. Davies	H. H. Sweeten
1956	Basil Donne-Smith	G. R. Davies	H. H. Sweeten
1957	T. A. Joy	G. R. Davies	H. H. Sweeten
1958	A. B. Ward	G. R. Davies	H. H. Sweeten
1959	A. B. Ward	G. R. Davies	H. H. Sweeten
1960	J. Wells	G. R. Davies	H. H. Sweeten
1961	H. S. Hitchen	G. R. Davies	H. H. Sweeten
1962	H. S. Hitchen	G. R. Davies	H. H. Sweeten
1963	C. R. Edgeley	G. R. Davies	R. Blackwell
		Director	
1964	H. H. Sweeten	G. R. Davies	R. Blackwell
1965	H. H. Sweeten	G. R. Davies	H. E. Bailey
1966	R. Blackwell	G. Lane	H. E. Bailey
1967	R. Blackwell	J. Newton	H. E. Bailey
1968	Ross Higgins	J. Newton	G. R. Bartlett
1969	Ross Higgins	J. Newton	G. R. Bartlett
1970	H. E. Bailey	G. R. Davies	D. Ainslie Thin
1971	H. E. Bailey	G. R. Davies	D. Ainslie Thin
1972	T. Hodges	G. R. Davies	D. Ainslie Thin
1973	T. Hodges	G. R. Davies	D. Ainslie Thin

Appendix D

THE JOINT COMMITTEE, 1927-9

Publishers: G. H. Bickers (George Bell); Jonathan Cape; C. W. Chamberlain (Methuen); G. Duckworth; C. S. Evans (Heinemann); William Longman; Harold Raymond (Chatto & Windus); G. C. Rivington; W. Symons (Blackie); Stanley Unwin; G. S. Williams (Martin Hopkinson); G. Wilson (A. & C. Black, vice-chairman)
Booksellers: H. E. Alden (Simpkin Marshall); G. B. Bowes (chairman); F. Brown (Educational Supply Association); F. A. Denny; Gilbert Foyle; F. J. Hanks (Blackwell); D. Roy (W. H. Smith); A. Stevens (The Times Book Club); E. Story (York); *later*: J. Norman Read (Bolton); J. Ainslie Thin; T. C. Ward (Midland Educational); W. S. Sisson (Nottingham); C. Young (London)
Secretary: Maurice Marston

THE 1948 BOOK TRADE COMMITTEE

Chairman: Hubert M. Wilson
Vice-Chairman: J. D. Newth (A. & C. Black)
Publishers: J. E. Allen (Chambers); John Baker (Phoenix House); F. J. Martin (Dent); B. W. Fagan (Edward Arnold); Walter G. Harrap; Ralph Hodder-Williams; B. Howard Mudditt (The Paternoster Press); Kenneth B. Potter (Longmans); Harold Raymond (Chatto & Windus); A. W. Ready (Bell); R. F. West (Baillière, Tindall & Cox)
Booksellers: F. J. Aldwinckle (Midland Educational); A. Coleridge; F. E. K. Foat (W. H. Smith); F. B. Gabbutt (Seed & Gabbutt); Don Gresswell; R. G. Heffer; W. E. Hill; T. A. Joy (Army & Navy Stores); B. N. Langdon-Davies (Welwyn Department Store); Cadness Page (Harrod's); T. H. Rayward (Goulden & Curry); K. V. Saville (Brooker & Saville, resigned 1949); H. L. Schollick (Blackwell's, resigned 1949)
Secretary: F. D. Sanders

BOOK TRADE WORKING PARTY, 1970-72

Publishers: Charles Allen (Collins); Anthony Blond; Charles Clark (Penguin); A. T. G. Pocock (O.U.P., joint-chairman); Michael Turner (Eyre-Methuen)

Booksellers: Julian Blackwell (joint-chairman); T. W. Dally (Woking);
Ian Norrie (High Hill Bookshop, resigned April 1972); David Sweeten
(Preston); John Welch (Heffer)
Secretary: John Chesshyre

Appendix E

U.K. BOOK SALES

Year	Total	Home	Export	Percentage Export
	£	£	£	
1939	10,321,658	7,167,059	3,154,599	30·0
1949	34,297,252	24,498,414	9,798,838	28·6
1959	66,945,183	41,551,223	25,393,960	37·9
1965	104,876,998	58,753,808	46,123,190	43·9
1966	119,578,145	68,160,359	51,417,786	43·0
1967	125,782,262	71,943,844	53,838,418	42·8
1968	137,981,324	75,869,164	62,112,160	45·0
1969	145,693,000	77,170,000	68,523,000	47·0
1970	153,677,000	85,835,000	67,842,000	44·1

Main Sources for Part Two

Only printed publications are acknowledged here but, as explained in the Preface, much information, especially about bookselling, came to me in private letters and notes and from conversations and observation. Where a book or article is included in the Bibliography it is referred to here in abbreviated form (e.g. James Hepburn, *The Author's Empty Purse and the Rise of the Literary Agent*, O.U.P., 1968, is shown as 'Hepburn, *Author's Empty Purse*'); where there is no corresponding entry in the Bibliography, a full reference is given.

SECTION I: 1870–1901

INTRODUCTION

Ensor, Sir Robert, *England, 1870–1914* (O.U.P., 1936). Volume in The Oxford History of England
Nowell-Smith, *Letters to Macmillan*
John Smith, *Short Note on a Long History*
The Story of Bowes & Bowes (privately circulated)
The House of Menzies (privately published)
James Thin, 1848–1948
Centenary *Bookseller*, 1958
Butler & Tanner *Newsletter*, no. 108, p. 11

1. TRADE AFFAIRS

Morgan, *House of Macmillan*
Nowell-Smith, *Letters to Macmillan*
Centenary *Bookseller*, 1958
Corp, *Fifty Years*
Barnes, *Free Trade in Books*
Kingsford, *Publishers' Association*
Hepburn, *Author's Empty Purse*
Two London Telephone Directories, (David & Charles, 1970)
Nowell-Smith, *International Copyright*
Unwin, *Truth about a Publisher*
Centenary *Bookseller*, 1958

2. OXFORD UNIVERSITY PRESS; CAMBRIDGE UNIVERSITY PRESS; S.P.C.K.

Hudson, *Oxford Publishing*
Roberts, *Evolution of Cambridge Publishing*
Bookseller, 24.7.71, p. 189

3. THE ESTABLISHED PUBLISHERS: FATHERS AND SONS

Blagden, *Fire More than Water*

Gibbings, John, 'John Murray's' (two articles in *The Bookseller*, 26.10.68 and 2.11.68)

Centenary *Bookseller*, 1958

Keir, *House of Collins*

Blackie, *Blackie and Son*

'J.D.N.', *A. & C. Black*

Whitaker's *Reference Catalogue of Current Literature*, *1940*

Turnbull, *William and Robert Chambers*

Junor, John, *Footprints in the Sands of Time*

Cumbers, *Book Room*

King, *House of Warne*

Nowell-Smith, *Letters to Macmillan*

Morgan, *House of Macmillan*

Liveing, *Adventure in Publishing*

Nowell-Smith, *House of Cassell*

The Dictionary of National Biography, (O.U.P.)

Warner, ed., *Century of Writers*

Doran, *Chronicles of Barabbas*

Swinnerton, *Bookman's London*

4. THE NEW IMPRINTS

Mumby, *From Swan Sonnenschein*

Bolitho, *Batsford Century*

Unwin, *Publishing Unwins*

Centenary *Bookseller*, 1958

Whitaker's *Reference Catalogue of Current Literature*, *1961*

Darwin, *Fifty Years of Country Life*

H.M.S.O. As Publisher (brochure)

Dent, *Memoirs*

Swinnerton, *Bookman's London*

The Dictionary of National Biography, (O.U.P.)

Whyte, *William Heinemann*

Ryder, *Bodley Head*

Richards, *Author Hunting*

Whitaker's *Reference Catalogue of Current Literature*, *1940*

Hepburn, James, ed., *Letters of Arnold Bennett*: vol. i., *Letters to J. B. Pinker*, (O.U.P., 1966)

Phelps, *The Literary Life*

5. BOOKSELLING: LONDON

Note: In all the chapters on bookselling either the source of the information or the clue to it often lay in the columns of *The Bookseller* or of *Bookselling News.*

Laver, *Hatchard's*
Centenary *Bookseller*, 1958
The Menzies Group
Bookseller, 11.1.69, p. 88
Publishers' Circular, 29.2.51, pp. 172–3

6. BOOKSELLING: SCOTLAND

John Smith, *Short Note on Long History*
The Grant Educational Company, 1897–1947
James Thin, 1848–1948
House of Menzies

7. BOOKSELLING: PROVINCIAL, WELSH, IRISH

Story of Bowes & Bowes
Industrial Nottingham, October 1963, p. 10 (Nottingham Chamber of Commerce)
Birmingham Evening Mail, April 1968
Centenary *Bookseller*, 1958
Our Story, 1860–1960 (A. Brown, Hull, 1961)
Gore's Liverpool Directory, 1870
White's Directory for Norfolk, 1890
Manchester Directory, 1873
Lancashire Directory, 1890

SECTION II: 1901–39

1. TRADE AFFAIRS

Unwin, *Truth about a Publisher*
Kingsford, *Publishers' Association*
Centenary *Bookseller*, 1958
Hepburn, *Author's Empty Purse*
Corp, *Fifty Years*
Thrush, *Representative Majority*
Swinnerton, *Bookman's London*
Baker, *Low Cost of Book Loving*

2. THE DYNASTIES

Blagden, *Fire More than Water*
Nowell-Smith, *Letters to Macmillan*

Morgan, *House of Macmillan*
Keir, *House of Collins*
Dent, *Memoirs*
Kingsford, *Publishers' Association*
'J.D.N.', *A. & C. Black*
Blackie, *Blackie & Co.*
King, *House of Warne*
Bolitho, *Batsford Century*
Whitaker's *Reference Catalogue of Current Literature, 1940*
Bookseller, 2.11.68, p. 1536
Dick, *Ivy and Stevie*: Bibliography (Duckworth, 1971)
Bookseller, 8.2.69, p. 448
Bookseller, 22.2.69, p. 1444
The House of Hodder, (brochure)
Liveing, *Adventure in Publishing*
Swinnerton, *Bookman's London*

3. THE UNIVERSITY PRESSES

Hudson, *Oxford Publishing*
Roberts, *Evolution of Cambridge Publishing*
Crutchley, *Two Men*
Whitaker's *Reference Catalogue of Current Literature, 1961*

4. OTHER NINETEENTH-CENTURY PUBLISHERS

Whyte, *William Heinemann*
Hepburn, James, *Letters of Arnold Bennett*: vol. 1, *Letters to J. B. Pinker*
    (O.U.P., 1966)
Centenary *Bookseller*, 1958
Warburg, *Occupation for a Gentleman*
Mumby, *From Swan Sonnenschein*
Unwin, *Truth about a Publisher*
Unwin, *Publishing Unwins*
Nowell-Smith, *House of Cassell*
Warner, *Century of Writers*
Richards, *Author Hunting*
Duckworth, *Fifty Years*
Arnold, *Orange Street and Brickhole Lane*

5. THE NEW PUBLISHERS

Warburg, *Occupation for a Gentleman*
Whitaker's *Reference Catalogue of Current Literature, 1940*
Centenary *Bookseller*, 1958
Darwin, *Fifty Years of Country Life*
Woolf, *Beginning Again*

Woolf, *Downhill All the Way*
Howard, *Jonathan Cape, Publisher*
The Dictionary of National Biography, (O.U.P.)
Gollancz, *My Dear Timothy*
Unwin, *Truth about a Publisher*
Dickson, *House of Words*
The Penguin Story
The Times, 22.4.69, article on Sir Allen Lane

6. BOOKSELLING: LONDON

The Menzies Group
Centenary *Bookseller*, 1958
Publishers' Circular, 24.2.51
Hampden, *The Book World*
Unwin, *Truth about a Publisher*
Foyle's Fifty Years
Whitaker's *Reference Catalogue of Current Literature*, *1940*
Grant, *Harold Monro*
Guttmann, *Seven Years' Harvest*
Bookseller, 6.2.71, pp. 340–42
Joy, *Mostly Joy*
London Post Office Directory, 1914, 1919, 1929, 1939

7. BOOKSELLING: PROVINCIAL, WELSH, SCOTTISH

Hampden, *The Book World*
Kelly's Birmingham Directories for 1913 and 1929
White's Directory for Stafford, 1851
Bookselling News, September 1969
The Bookseller, 3.1.53, p. 4
The Bookseller, 15.4.69, p. 1919
The Bookseller, 10.1.69, p. 85
Kelly's Kent Directory, 1913
Kelly's Lancashire Directory, 1913
House of Menzies
James Thin, 1848–1948
Bristol Directory, 1913
Kelly's Birmingham Directory, 1913, 1939
White's Directory for Stafford, 1851
Kelly's Directory for Stafford, 1928

SECTION III: 1939–50 — WAR AND PEACE

Centenary *Bookseller*, 1958
P. A. Official Reports 1939–40, 1942–3, 1945–6, 1947–8, 1950–51
Bolitho, *Batsford Century*

Morgan, *House of Macmillan*
Dickson, *House of Words*
Keir, *House of Collins*
Howard, *Jonathan Cape, Publisher*
Ian Allan 25 Years (privately circulated)
Lidderdale, *Dear Miss Weaver*
Publishers' Association, *1948 Committee Report*
Williams, *The Penguin Story*

SECTION IV: 1950–70

I. TRADE AFFAIRS

Centenary *Bookseller*, 1958
P.A. Official Reports: 1953–4, 1954–5, 1955–6, 1958–9, 1962–3, 1966–7
Bookseller, 9.4.55, pp. 1188–9
Bookseller, 31.12.55, pp. 1962–4
Shorter Oxford English Dictionary (O.U.P.)
Books in Schools: A Factual Statement (Educational Publishers' Council, 1970)
Bookseller, 3.1.70, p. 22
Bookseller, 16.9.67 (article on Dillon's)
Bookseller, 7.1.50, p. 13
H.M.S.O., R.B.C.41, Wages Council Notice
Kingsford, *Publishers' Association*
Bookseller, 25.12.54, p. 1947
Unwin, *Publishing Unwins*
Bookseller, 21.9.68, pp. 956–61
Bookseller, 3.4.71 (obit. Edmund Segrave)

2. THE UNIVERSITY PRESSES

Hudson, *Oxford Publishing*
Bookseller, 9.5.70, pp. 2292–7
Bookseller, 4.1.69, p. 42
Authors and O.U.P. (brochure)

3. THE OLDER INDEPENDENT PUBLISHERS

Whitaker's *Reference Catalogue of Current Literature, 1961*
Bookseller, 2.11.68 (article by John Gibbings on Murray's)
Bookseller, 20.6.70, p. 2662
Booksellers, 27.12.69 and 4.1.70, 'The Book Trade in 1969'
Booksellers, 2.1.71 and 9.1.71 'The Book Trade in 1970'
Nowell-Smith, *Letters to Macmillan*
Keir, *House of Collins*

Bookseller, 18.10.69, pp. 2215, 2218
Howard, *Jonathan Cape, Publisher*
King, *House of Warne*
Unwin, *Truth about a Publisher*
Unwin, *Publishing Unwins*
Centenary *Bookseller*, 1958

4. THE NEW PUBLISHERS

Van Thal— *Tops of the Mulberry Trees*
Whitaker's *Reference Catalogue of Current Literature, 1961*
Blond, *Publishing Game*
Bookseller, 25.11.67, pp. 2500–2504

5. BRITISH-OWNED GROUPS

Blagden, *Fire More than Water*
Bookseller, 29.5.71, p. 2328
          Footprints in the Sands of Time
Bookseller, 31.12.49, p. 1568
Bookseller, 30.12.61, p. 2485
Bookseller, 5.1.52, p. 8
Bookseller, 30.12.61, p. 2486
Bookseller, 6.5.50, p. 1004
Bookseller, 13.5.50

6. FOREIGN-OWNED GROUPS

Howard, *Jonathan Cape, Publisher*
Whitaker's *Reference Catalogue of Current Literature, 1961*
Bookseller, 28.12.57, p. 2148
Bookseller, 20.5.67, p. 2290
Bookseller, 19.4.69, p. 2140
Times, 29.12.71 (article on Barbara Ker Wilson)

7. PAPERBACKS

Penguin Story
Penguin's Progress
Times obituary of E. V. Rieu (May 1972)
Bookseller, 28.1.67, pp. 240–42 (article by Nikolaus Pevsner)
Booksellers, 13.5.67 and 20.5.67 (concerning Tony Godwin's resignation
     from Penguin)
Observer, 27.4.69 (article on Penguin)
Legat, *Dear Author*
Trade News, 25.1.69 (article on Pan)

8. SPECIALIST PUBLISHERS

Letters and notes, various
Folio Society: 25 Years
Whitaker's *Reference Catalogue of Current Literature, 1970*
H.M.S.O. as Publisher (brochure)

9. BOOKSELLING: UNIVERSITIES

Centenary *Bookseller*, 1958
Bookseller, 16.9.67 (article on Dillon's)
Journal of Documentation. v. 22 No. 1 (Leicester University Bookshop)
Sheffield Morning Telegraph, 12.12.67 (Hartley Seed)
Industrial Nottingham, October 1963, p. 10
Bookseller, 12.7.69, pp. 87–8

10. BOOKSELLING: THE CHAINS

Bookseller, 8.4.72 (obituary of Seymour Smith)
The Menzies Group
The House of Menzies

12. BOOKSELLING: LONDON

The Foyle Story

Bibliography of
Publishing and Bookselling

By *William Peet*

[*Reprinted, with additions by F. A. Mumby, Monica Carolan and others, from*
NOTES AND QUERIES *by kind permission of the Editor*]

'The largest collection of books devoted to the subjects of book-producing and bookselling in all its many branches', wrote William Peet in introducing his bibliography, 'will be found in the library of the *Börsenverein der Deutschen Buchhändler* at Leipzig. The catalogue of this library is in two vols (Vol. I, 1885; Vol. II, 1902), and contains several thousands of titles of works in all languages. I am considerably indebted to this catalogue, although I had nearly finished my list before I had the opportunity of consulting it. Works on printing and the production of books are noted only when they contain matter bearing incidentally on publishing or bookselling, while copyright, book-collecting and the sport of book-hunting are beyond my scope. Works dealing with the freedom of the Press, actions for libel, or prosecutions for publishing blasphemous or seditious books are not systematically included. They form, however, a very large section in the Leipzig catalogue.' When William Peet died at the close of 1916 he left material for a revision and extension of his bibliography. This was incorporated, and the work brought up to date by F. A. Mumby, for his first edition of this book in 1930. Further lists were added for subsequent editions, and for this fifth edition Monica Carolan has added nearly as many entries as were in the original. All four lists have now been combined to make one alphabetical bibliography.

ABBOTT, J. — The Harper Establishment, or How the Story Books are Made. Harper, 1855.

ADAMS, S. — The O.P. Market; A Subject Directory Bowker: Whitaker, 1945.

ALCUIN PRESS, Chipping Campden, Glos. — An Introduction to the Work and Aims of Chipping Campden, 1932.

ALDIS, H. G. — The Book-Trade, 1557–1625. (Reprinted from 'The Cambridge History of English Literature', vol. iv, pp. 378–420.) 8vo, reprinted for private circulation, London, 1909. *Pp. 415–20 are devoted to a bibliography of the subject during the period specified.*

A List of Books printed in Scotland before 1700, including those printed furth of the Realm for Scottish Booksellers. With Brief Notes on the Printers and Stationers. Edinburgh Bibliographical Society, 1905.

Book Production and Distribution, 1625–1800. (Reprinted from 'The Cambridge History of English Literature', vol. xi, chap. 14.) London, 1914. *See also under McKerrow, R. B.*

ALDIS, W. G.—The Printed Book. Revised by J. Carter and B. Critchley. C.U.P., 1950.

ALLAN, IAN, LTD—25 Years, 1942–67. Ian Allan, 1967.

ALLEN, A.—The Story of the Book. Faber, 1952.

ALLEN, C. E.—Publishers' Accounts, including a Consideration of Copyright. 8vo, London, 1897.

ALLEN, GEORGE—Copyright and Copy-wrong: The Authentic and Unauthentic Ruskin. Allen & Unwin, 1908.

ALLEN, GEORGE, & UNWIN LTD—George Allen and Unwin Ltd. Allen & Unwin, 1933.

ALMON, JOHN, 1737–1805—Memoirs of John Almon, Bookseller, of Piccadilly. 8vo, London, 1790. *Famous as John Wilkes's publisher, and as having been prosecuted for selling Junius' Letters.*

AMERICAN LIBRARY ASSOCIATION—Blueprint for British Book Week. A.L.A., 1943.

AMES, JOSEPH, 1689–1758—Typographical Antiquities, being an Historical Account of Printing in England, Memoirs of the Ancient Printers, and a Register of Books printed by them from 1471 to 1600. 4to, London, 1749. *For various editions, see Lowndes.*

Index to Dibdin's Edition of the 'Typographical Antiquities', first compiled by Joseph Ames, with some references to the intermediate edition by William Herbert. Bibliographical Society, 8vo, 1899.

AMORY, THOMAS, 1691?–1788—Life of John Buncle, Esq., 1756–66, and subsequent reprints. *Amory was a bookseller in London and Dublin. 'John Buncle' contains fragments of autobiography, a character of Edmund Curll, etc.*

ANDREWS, W. L.—The Old Booksellers of New York. P.p., 1895.

ANNUALS—*See 'The Annuals of Former Days' in the 'Bookseller', 29 November and 24 December 1858.*

See also 'Publishers' Circular', 27 June 1891.

ANTIQUARIAN BOOKSELLERS' ASSOCIATION—A.B.A. Annual, 1952: incorporating the first annual lecture by Michael Sadleir. William Dawson, 1952.

APPLETON, HOUSE OF—*See under Overton, Grant.*

ARBER, EDWARD—List of London Publishers, 1553–1640. 8vo, London, 1889. *This was only a trial proof of 32 pp. in vol. v. of Professor Arber's 'Transcript of the Registers of the Stationers' Company'.*

See also 'Catalogues'; 'Stationers' Company'.

Contemporary Lists of Books, printed in England (Bibliographia, vol. iii, pp. 173–91).

ARCHAEOLOGIA, vol. xxix, p. 101—Copies of Original Papers illustrative of the Reign of Queen Elizabeth. Communicated by (Sir) Henry Ellis. 4to, London, 1834.

ARMITAGE, G.—Banned in England: An Examination of the Law Relating to Obscene Publications. Wishart, 1932.

ARMSTRONG, A. C.—Bouverie Street to Bowling Green Lane: Fifty-five Years of Specialised Publishing. Hodder & Stoughton (Temple Press), 1946.

ARMSTRONG, ELIZABETH—Robert Estienne, Royal Printer: An Historical Study of the Elder Stephanus. C.U.P., 1954.

ARNOLD, E. J., LTD—A Service to Education. E. J. Arnold, n.d.

ARNOLD, RALPH—Orange Street and Brickhole Lane. Hart-Davis, 1963.

ASSOCIATED BOOKSELLERS OF GREAT BRITAIN AND IRELAND—The Code of Practice for Booksellers, 1931.

Training for the Retail Book Trade. A.B., 1950.

Code of Practice for Booksellers. A.B., 1931.

The Net Book System. A.B., 1931.

Summary of Publishers' Terms (confidential). A.B., 1931.

See also under Book Trade Organization; and Book Clubs.

ASTBURY, R. (ed.)—Libraries and the Book Trade. Bingley, 1968.

ATKINSON, SIR E. T.—Obscene Literature in Law and Practice. Christopher's, 1937.

ATKINSON, J.—100 Years of Steady Progress, 1837–1937. Illus. Atkinson. Ulverston.

AUTHORS' AND BOOKSELLERS' CO-OPERATIVE PUBLISHING ALLIANCE—A New Departure in Publishing. 8vo, London, 1901.

AUTHOR'S HAND-BOOK, THE—A Guide to the Art and System of Publishing on Commission. 8vo, London, 1844.

AUTHOR'S HANDBOOK, 1940, THE—Edited by D. Kilham Roberts. 8vo, London, 1940.

AUTHOR'S PRINTING AND PUBLISHING ASSISTANT, THE—A Guide to the Printing, Correcting, and Publishing of New Works. Crown 8vo, London, 1845.

AUTHORS' PUBLICATION SOCIETY—Reasons for Establishing one, by which Literary labour would receive a more adequate Reward, and the Price of all New Books be much reduced. 8vo, London, 1843.

AUTHOR AS PUBLISHER, THE, OR WHY DO NOT AUTHORS PUBLISH THEIR OWN BOOKS—By O. L. G., London, 1912.

See also under Swinnerton, Frank.

AUTHORS' SOCIETY—Grievances between Authors and Publishers. Crown 8vo, London, 1887. *See also the volumes of the 'Author', 1890, etc.; and Author's Handbook, 1940.*

AUTHOR'S WALLET: Narrative of Messrs James Lackington, 1745–1815, and John Chapman, 1822–94, concerning the price fixing of books. Macy, N.Y., 1934.

AVIS, F. C.—Bookmen's Concise Dictionary. Avis, 1956.

BABBIDGE, IRENE—Beginning in Bookselling. Deutsch, 1965.

BAGSTER, HOUSE OF—A Century of Publishing: a Chat with Mr Robert Bagster. With Illustrations and three Portraits—*St. James' Budget*, 27 April 1894.

Centenary of the Bagster Publishing House, established 19 April 1794. Crown 8vo, London, 1894.

BAGSTER, ROBERT—Centenary of the First Pocket Reference Bible issued by Samuel Bagster, 1812. (An account of the publishing house of Bagster.) Bagster, 1912.

BAILEY, H. E.—Economics of Bookselling. Hutchinson, 1965.

BAILEY, HERBERT SMITH, JNR—The Art and Science of Book Publishing. Harper & Row, 1970.

BAIN, JAMES STODDART—A Bookseller Looks Back. The Story of the Bains. London, 1940.

BAIN, L.—John Sharpe, Publisher and Bookseller, Piccadilly, 1800–40. Lavercock Press, privately circulated, 1960.

BAKER, A.—Life of Sir Isaac Pitman. Pitman, 1908.

BAKER, JOHN—The Low Cost of Bookloving. An account of the first 21 years of Readers' Union. R.U., 1958.

BALLANTYNE, HOUSE OF—*See Lockhart's 'Scott', passim; also*
A Refutation of the Misstatements and Calumnies contained in Mr Lockhart's Life of Sir Walter Scott respecting the Messrs (James and John) Ballantyne. By the Trustees and Son of the late James Ballantyne. 8vo, London, 1838.

The Ballantyne Humbug Handled. By John Gibson Lockhart. 8vo, Edinburgh, 1839.

Reply to Mr Lockhart's Pamphlet, entitled 'The Ballantyne Humbug Handled'. By the Authors of 'A Refutation of the Misstatements and Calumnies', etc. 8vo, London, 1839.

History of the Ballantyne Press. 4to, Edinburgh, 1871.

The Ballantyne Press and its Founders, 1796–1908. By W. T. Dobson and W. L. Carrie. Post 4to, Edinburgh, 1909.

Life of John Gibson Lockhart, by Andrew Lang. 2 vols, 1897. Vol. ii, chap. xvii; xx, p. 169.

See also Carswell, Donald.

BALSTON, THOMAS—William Balston—Paper-maker. Methuen, 1954.

BARKER, R. E.—The Book Trade in Czechoslovakia. P.A., n.d.
Canada: The Expanding Book Market. P.A., 1963.
Ghana: A Short Survey of the Book Market. P.A., 1965.
Copyright at the Crossroads. P.A., 1969.
International Copyright: A Search for a Formula in the '70s. P.A., 1969.
International Copyright: A Formula Emerges. P.A., 1970.
Nigeria: A Short Survey of the Book Market. P.A., 1964.
The Revised Berne Convention. The Stockholm Act, 1967, with an article-by-article summary of its provisions. P.A., 1967.
The United States of America: A Short Survey of Methods. P.A., 1963.

BARKER, R. E., AND DAVIES, G. R.—Books are Different: An Account of the Defence of the Net Book Agreement. Macmillan, 1966.

BARNES, JAMES J.—Free Trade in Books. O.U.P., 1964.

BARTLETT, G. R. (ed.)—Better Bookselling. Hutchinson, 1969.
Bookselling by Mail. Hutchinson, 1966.
Stock Control in Bookselling. Hutchinson, 1965.

BASKERVILLE, JOHN, 1706–1775—A Memoir. By R. Straus (with R. K. Dent). 4to, London, 1907.

BASON, FRED—Fred Bason's Diary: edited and introduced by Nicolas Bentley. Wingate, 1950. Fred Bason's 3rd Diary: edited and introduced by Michael Sadleir. Deutsch, 1955.

BATSFORD, THE HOUSE OF—An illustrated brochure commemorating the removal of Messrs B. T. Batsford, Ltd., to Mayfair, giving an account of architectural publishing in Holborn since 1611, as well as a history of the firm for nearly a century. London, 1931.

A Batsford Century: The Record of a Hundred Years of Publishing and Bookselling. Edited by Hector Bolitho. London, 1943.

BATTLE OF THE BOOKS, 1940—*See under National Book Council.*

BATTY, R. F.—How to Run a Twopenny Library. Gifford, 1938.

BAYLISS, F. C.—The Master Salesman. W. H. Smith, 1916.

BEACH, SYLVIA—Shakespeare and Co. Illus. Faber, 1960.

BEALE, C. H. (ed.)—Catherine Hutton and Her Friends. P.p., Birmingham, 1895.

BEAUMONT, CYRIL W.—The first Score: An Account of the Foundation and Development of the Beaumont Press and its First Twenty Publications. January, 1927.

BEEMAN, NEVILLE—Bookselling: A Decaying Industry. *New Century Review*, January 1898.

BEEVERS, S.—Publishers' Accounts. Gee, 1929.

BELL, EDWARD, 1844–1926—Contributed a 'Narrative of the Dispute between *The Times* Book Club and the Publishers' Association' to Sir Frederick Macmillan's account of the 'Net Book Agreement, 1899, and the Book War, 1906–1908'. Privately printed, 1924.

BELL, F. T. AND SMITH, F. SEYMOUR—Library Bookselling. Grafton Books, 1966.

Further reference will be found to F. T. Bell in the text. Following his retirement from active work, he wrote many articles, especially on library supplying, for The Bookseller, *during the early 1970s.*

BELL, GEORGE, 1814–90—George Bell, Publisher: A Brief Memoir. By Edward Bell. Printed for Private Circulation at the Chiswick Press, 1924.

BELL, H.W.—The Bookseller is Sent Forth to the Elect Every Little While. P.p., 1901.

BELL, JOHN, 1745–1832—See under Morison, Stanley.

BEMROSE, H.H.—The House of Bemrose, 1826–1926. Bemrose Press, 1926.

BENN, SIR ERNEST—Confessions of a Capitalist. Benn, 1948.

BENN, J.—Publishing as a Craft. Benn, 1948.

BENNET, H. S.—English Books and Readers, 1485–1557. C.U.P., 1952.

English Books and Readers, 1558–1603. A Study of the Book Trade in the Reign of Queen Elizabeth. C.U.P., 1965.

English Books and Readers, 1603–1640. Being a Study in the History of the Book Trade in the reigns of James I and Charles I. C.U.P., 1970.

BENNET, T., AND CLEMENTS, H.—Notebook (1686) with some Aspects of Book Trade Practice. Edited by Hodgson and Blagden. O.U.P., 1956.

BENTLEY, HOUSE OF—Some Leaves from the Past. Swept together by Richard Bentley. With eleven Portraits and other Illustrations. 8vo, privately printed, 1896.

Richard Bentley and Son. By Ernest Chesneau. Reprinted from *Le Livre* of October 1885. With some additional Notes. With 3 Illustrations. Royal 8vo, privately printed, 1886.

Richard Bentley, 1794–1871 – *The Bookseller* (p. 811), 1871.

BERESFORD, JAMES (1764–1840) – Bibliosophia, 8vo, 1810. *A work provoked by Dibdin's 'Bibliomania'.*

BERJEAU, JEAN PHILIBERT – The Book-worm: a Literary and Bibliographical Review. 5 vols, London, 1866–71.

BESANT, SIR WALTER – The Pen and the Book. 8vo, London, 1899.

Literary Handmaid of the Church (the S.P.C.K.). Crown 8vo, London, 1890.

See also the volumes of the 'Author', 1890, etc.

BESTERMAN, T. (ed.) – Publishing Firm of Cadell and Davies, Select Correspondence and Accounts, 1793–1836. O.U.P., 1938.

BIBLIOGRAPHER, THE – A Journal of Book-lore. Edited by Henry B. Wheatley. 5 vols, London, 1882–4.

See Indexes throughout.

BIBLIOGRAPHICA – 3 vols, 4to, London, 1895–7.

An Elizabethan Bookseller (Edward Blount, 1564?). By Sir Sidney Lee. Vol. i, p. 474.

Two References to the English Book-trade, *circa* 1525. Vol. i, p. 252.

The Booksellers at the Sign of the Trinity. By E. Gordon Duff. Vol. i, pp. 93 and 175.

English Book-sales, 1676–1680. By A. W. Pollard. Vol. i, p. 373.

The Long Shop in the Poultry. By H. R. Plomer. Vol. ii, p. 61.

The Early Italian Book-trade. By R. Garnett. Vol. iii, p. 29.

BIBLIOPHILE'S MISCELLANY, 1931. London, 1930. *The offspring of the 'Bibliophile's Almanack', edited in 1921 and 1928 by Oliver Simon and Harold Child.*

BIBLIOPHOBIA – Remarks on the Present Languid and Depressed State of Literature and the Book-trade. In a letter addressed to the author of the 'Bibliomania'. By Mercurius Rusticus (T. F. Dibdin). With Notes by Cato Parvus. London, 1832.

(BIGG, JAMES) – The Bookselling System: a letter to Lord Campbell respecting the late inquiry into the regulations of the Booksellers' Association in reference to the causes which led to its dissolution ... and the consequences to authors likely to result from unrestricted competition in the sale of new works. By a Retired Bookseller. Westminster, 1852.

BIGMORE AND WYMAN'S BIBLIOGRAPHY OF PRINTING, 3 vols, 1880–86. *See for connection of the early printers with the booksellers and publishers.*

BINGLEY, CLIVE – Book Publishing Practice. New Librarianship Series. Crosby Lockwood, 1966.

BINGLEY, WILLIAM, 1738–99 – A Sketch of W. Bingley, Bookseller. With Portrait and a Prospectus of his Proposed Reprint of Nos. 1–46 of the *North Briton*. London, 1793.

The New Plain Dealer; or, Will Freeman's Budget, 1791–4. *Contains autobiographical details.*

BIRKETT, SIR NORMAN, and others – Books are Essential. Deutsch, 1951.

BIRRELL, AUGUSTINE—Essays on 'Book-Buying', in *Obiter Dicta*, Second Series, 1887; 'Books Old and New', and 'Book-Binding', in *Men, Women and Books*, 1894; and 'Bookworms', 'First Editions', and 'Old Booksellers' in *In the Name of the Bodleian*, 1905.

Seven Lectures on the Law and History of Copyright in Books. Cassell, 1899.

BLACK, ADAM & CHARLES, 1807–1957. Some Chapters in a History of a Publishing House, initialled 'J.D.N.' Illus. Black, 1957.

BLACK, ADAM, 1784–1874—Memoirs of Adam Black. Edited by Alexander Nicolson, LL.D. With Portrait. Second Edition. Crown 8vo, Edinburgh, 1885.

BLACKIE, AGNES—Blackie & Son, 1809–1959. Blackie, 1959.

BLACKIE, HOUSE OF—Origin and Progress of the Firm of Blackie and Son, 1809–74. 8vo, London, 1897.

BLACKIE, J. S.—Letters of John Stuart Blackie to His Wife with a few earlier ones to his Parents. Blackie, 1909.

BLACKIE, W. W.—A Scottish Student in Leipzig: Being Letters to W. G. Blackie, his Father and his Brothers in the years 1839–40. 1932.

John Blackie, Senior (1782–1874): Some Notes collected by his grandson, Walter W. Blackie. Printed for private circulation, London, 1933.

BLACKWELL, BASIL—The Idea of a British Book Trade Association. An Address. Society of Bookmen, 1937.

The Nemesis of the New Book Agreement (An address delivered to the Society of Bookmen on 5 January 1933). Society of Bookmen, 1933.

A New Order in the Book Trade? Society of Bookmen, 1943.

School Books: Why Not Net? An Address. P.p., 1934.

See also under Dent Memorial Lectures; and Hampden, John.

BLACKWELL, B. H.—A Note on the New Buildings of B. H. Blackwell Ltd. Illus. Blackwell, 1938.

BLACKWOOD, HOUSE OF—Annals of a Publishing House: William Blackwood and his Sons, their Magazine and Friends. By Mrs Oliphant. With 4 Portraits. Vols i and ii. 8vo, Edinburgh, 1897.

Vol. iii, John Blackwood. By his Daughter, Mrs Gerald Porter. With 2 Portraits. 8vo, Edinburgh, 1898.

The Early House of Blackwood. By I. C. B. Post 4to. Printed for private circulation, Edinburgh, 1900. *This was intended to supply a deficiency in Mrs Oliphant's history of the firm.*

Blackwood's Magazine—A Letter to Mr John Murray, occasioned by his having undertaken the publication in London of *Blackwood's Magazine*, 1818.

The Bookseller, 26 June, 27 August, 26 September, 1860.

The Critic, 7 July 1860, and five successive weeks—a series of articles by F. Espinasse.

The Bookman, special article, with portraits, etc. November, 1901.

A Selection from the Obituary Notices of the late John Blackwood, Editor of *Blackwood's Magazine*. Privately printed. Small 4to, Edinburgh, 1880.

BLACKWOOD, W., & SONS—A Catalogue of Blackwood Exhibitions. National Library of Scotland, 1954.

BLADES, W.—The Enemies of Books. Illus. Elliot, Stock, 1888.

BLAGDEN, CYPRIEN—Fire More than Water. Longmans, Green, 1949.

BLAKEY, DOROTHY—The Minerva Press. Bibliographical Society, 1939.

BLOCK, A.—A Short History of the Principal London Antiquarian Book-sellers and Book Auctioneers. Archer, 1933.

BLOND, ANTHONY—The Publishing Game. Cape, 1971.

BLOUNT, EDWARD—Sir Sidney Lee.

BLUMENTHAL, W. H.—Bookmen's Browse. Toucan Press, 1967.

BLUNDEN, EDMUND—Keats's Publisher: A Memoir of John Taylor (1781–1864). London, 1936.

BLUNT, SIR ANTHONY, and others—Anton Zwemmer. P.p., 1962.

BOHN, HENRY GEORGE, 1796–1884— *The Times*, 25 August 1884; *Athenaeum*, 30 August 1884; *The Bookseller*, September 1884; *Bibliographer*, October 1884; *Book Monthly* (with portrait), April 1904.
See also Hazlitt, W. C., and Lowndes, W. T.

BOOK AUCTIONEERS—*See The Bookseller*, 8 April 1902; and Lawler's *Book Auctions*, forward.
See also under Sotheby's; Hodgson and Company; Karslake, F., and Book-Prices Current.

BOOK AUCTIONS IN ENGLAND—*See Notes and Queries*, 2 S. xi, 463; 5 S. xii, 95, 211, 411; 6 S. ii, 297, 417; 9 S. vi, 86, 156; 10 S. viii, 246, 266.
Longman's Magazine, April 1893—Article by A. W. Pollard, 'The First English Book-Sale'.
List of catalogues of English Book-Sales, 1676–1900, now in the British Museum. 8vo. Issued by the British Museum, 1915.
Harrison, Canon F.—A Book about Books. London, 1943.

BOOK CLUBS—The Third Report of the Joint Committee on Book Clubs appointed by the Publishers' Association and the Associated Booksellers, dated 10 May 1939. Published in *The Bookseller*, 1 June 1939.

BOOK CLUBS AND PRINTING SOCIETIES OF GREAT BRITAIN AND IRELAND—Harold Williams. First Edition Club, 1929.

BOOK CRISIS, THE—Contains the speeches made by Sir Hugh Walpole, J. B. Priestley, Geoffrey Faber, Dr J. J. Mallon, Kenneth Lindsay, M.P., and Henry Strauss, M.P., in opposing the proposed tax on books. With an introduction by the editor, Gilbert McAllister. London, 1940.

BOOK OF ENGLISH TRADES, THE—The Bookbinder, the Bookseller, the Printer, etc. New Edition, with 500 Questions for Students. 12mo, London, 1824.

BOOK TOKENS: A Statement. Pamphlet, 1943.
See also under British Book Trade Organization.

BOOK TOKENS COMMITTEE. Book Tokens Today: A Report. Book Tokens, 1934.

BOOK TRADE HANDBOOK, 1937—Edited by William G. Corp. London, 1937. Includes chapters on 'Publishing To-day', by Harold Raymond; 'Some Problems of New Bookselling', by Kenneth V. Saville; 'The Press and the Book Trade', by Geoffrey Grigson; and 'The Net Book Agreement', by W. G. Corp.
Book Trade Handbook. National Newsagent, 1953.

BOOKKEEPING, A MANUAL OF—For Booksellers, Publishers, and Stationers on the principle of Single, converted periodically into Double Entry. By a Bookseller. 8vo, London, 1850.

BOOK-LORE—A Magazine devoted to Old-Time Literature. 4 vols, London, 1884–6. See Indexes throughout.

'BOOKMAN', THE—Directory of Booksellers, Publishers, and Authors. 4to, London, 1893.

BOOKMAN'S GLOSSARY, THE—A Compendium of Information relating to the Production and Distribution of Books. By John A. Holden, New York, 1925.

BOOKMEN, SOCIETY OF—Report of the Book Trade Delegation to Holland and Germany, 19–28 June 1926. London, 1926.

BOOK-PRICES CURRENT—Edited by J. H. Slater. Being a Record of the Prices at which Books have been sold at Auction, the Titles and Descriptions in Full, the Names of the Purchasers, etc. Vols i to xvii. 8vo, London, 1887–1903, and periodically.

Index to the First Ten Volumes of Book-Prices Current (1887–96). Constituting a Reference List of Subjects and, incidentally, a Key to Anonymous and Pseudonymous Literature. 8vo, London, 1897, and periodically.

See also under Karslake, F., and Livingston, L. S.

BOOK PUBLISHING IN SOVIET RUSSIA. U.S.A. Public Affairs Press, 1948.

BOOKSELLER, THE—founded 1858. Jubilee Number, 24 January 1908: 'Fifty Years of *The Bookseller* and Bookselling. London, 1908'.

Centenary Number, 3 May 1958. 'The Bookseller, One Hundred Years'. *Contains extracts from the trade journal for each year of issue, and biographical notes on its editors.*

BOOKMAN'S GLOSSARY—Bowker: Whitaker, Third edition, 1951.

BOOKSELLER, THE SUCCESSFUL—A Complete Guide to Success to all engaged in a Retail Bookselling ... Business. 4to, London, 1905.

BOOKSELLERS, PROVINCIAL. English, Scotch, Irish, and American. See *Notes and Queries, 11 S. i, 303, 363, 423; 10 S. v, 141, 183, 242, 297, 351, 415, 492; vii, 26, 75; viii, 201; x, 141; and indexes throughout.*

Durham and Northumberland, 10 *S. vi*, 443. Cirencester, 11 *S. xi*, 141.

Hampshire. See 10 *S. v*, 481; vi, 31.

St Neots. See 10 *S. xii*, 164.

'BOOKSELLERS AND NEWSPAPERS IN THE ISLE OF MAN'—(In *The Bookseller*, 1882.)

BOOKSELLERS' ASSOCIATION, 1852—See *Publishers' Circular*, 15 April and 1 June 1852.

Sales Promotion for Books; a Report on the Nottingham Book Festivals. B.A., 1955.

And see s.n. J. W. Parker and John Chapman.

Directory of British Publishers. B.A., 1960 and usually annually.

List of Members. B.A., 1958 and annually.

List of Overseas Publishers' Representatives in Great Britain. B.A., n.d.

Opening a Bookshop. B.A., 1964.

Publishers' Terms. B.A., 1951.

Trade Reference Book. B.A., 1969.

BOOKSELLERS' ASSOCIATION AND PUBLISHERS' ASSOCIATION—Report of the 1948 Book Trade Committee. P.A., 1954.

BOOKSELLERS' ASSOCIATIONS.
See Bowes.

BOOKSELLERS EAST OF ST PAUL'S— *The Bookseller*, 2 September 1873.

BOOKSELLERS' HANDBOOK, 1947. National Newsagent, Bookseller, Stationer, 1947.

BOOKSELLING—The Government Bookselling Question. Memorial to the Chancellor of the Exchequer on ... with Correspondence and Remarks. 8vo, London, 1853.

BOOKSELLING QUESTION, THE [*i.e.* Underselling]: Additional Letters. 8vo, London, 1852.

BOON, JOHN—The Book Trade in the U.S.S.R. P.A., 1965.

BOOSEY, Y.—Assumed Copyright in Foreign Authors: Judgment in the Case of Boosey *v.* Purday. F. Elsworth, 1848.

BOOTH, W. S.—A Practical Guide for Authors in their Relations with Publishers and Printers. Houghton, Mifflin, 1907.

BOOT'S LIBRARY—*See under Milne, James.*

BOSWELL, E.—*See under Stationers' Company.*

BOSWORTH, T.—On 'Rattening' in the Book Trade. Bosworth, 1968.

BOTT, ALAN—The Book Trade: A Plan for Expansion. Society of Bookmen, 1943.

BOUCHOT, HENRY—The Book: its Printers, Illustrators, and Binders, from Gutenberg to the Present Time. With a Treatise on the Art of collecting and describing Early Printed Books, and a Latin–English and English–Latin Topographical Index of the Earliest Printing Presses. Containing 172 Facsimiles of Early Typography, Book Illustrations, Printers' Marks, Bindings, numerous Borders, Initials, Head and Tail Pieces, and a Frontispiece. Royal 8vo, London, 1890.

BOUTELL, H. S.—First Editions of Today and How to Tell Them. 8vo, London, 1930.

BOWES, G. B.—Education and the Book Trade. A.B., 1920.

Some Cambridge Booksellers. Dent, 1933.

BOWES, ROBERT—Biographical Notes on the Printers ... in Cambridge. A Reprint from the Cambridge Antiquarian Society's Communications, vol. v, no. 4. Privately printed, Cambridge, 1886.

Catalogue of Books printed at Cambridge 1521–1893. 2 parts.

Booksellers' Associations, Past and Present. Printed for Private Circulation for the Associated Booksellers of Great Britain and Ireland. 4to, Taunton, 1905.

And see E. Marston's Sketches of Some Booksellers of the Time of Dr Johnson (fcap. 8vo, 1902), chap. vii, for an account by Mr Bowes of a Booksellers' Club, 1805–11, 'The Friends of Literature'. See also under McKerrow, R. B.

BOWES AND BOWES—*See under Gray, George J.*

BOWKER, B.—Lectures on Book Publishing, 1st and 2nd series. The Typophilo, New York, 1943–5.

BOWKER, R. R.—Copyright, Its Law and Literature. *Publishers' Weekly*, 1886.

BOYNTON, H. W.—Annals of American Bookselling, 1683–1850. Wiley, 1932.

BRADBURY, S.—*See under Dobell, Bertram.*

BRADSHAW, HENRY (1831–86). Librarian of Cambridge University— Collected Papers, edited by F. J. H. Jenkinson. 8vo, Cambridge University Press, 1889. *Includes his 'Notes on the Day Book of John Horne'; list of founts and woodcut devices of fifteenth-century Dutch printers; and other bibliographical and typographical papers.*

BRADSHER, EARL L.—*See under Carey, Matthew.*

BRIGGS, W.—The Law of International Copyright. Stevens & Haynes, 1906.

BRITISH BOOK TRADE ORGANIZATION—A Report on the Work of the Joint Committee. Edited by F. D. Sanders, with an introduction by Stanley Unwin. 1939.

BRITISH COUNCIL, THE—Programme of a Course on Book Production and Publicity. B.C., 1951.

BRITISH MUSEUM, THE—List of Catalogues of English Book Sales 1676–1900. B.M., 1915.

BRITISH STANDARDS INSTITUTION—Book Sizes and the Dating of Books (B.S. 1413). B.S.I., 1947.
  Specification for Page Sizes for Books, second revised edition (Metric Units). B.S.I., 1970.

BRITTON, JOHN, 1771–1857—The Rights of Literature; or, an Enquiry into the Policy and Justice of the Claims of certain Public Libraries on all the Publishers and Authors of the United Kingdom, for Eleven Copies, on the Best Paper, of every New Production. 8vo, London, 1814. *The eleven copies were claimed by the following libraries: British Museum; Zion College; The Universities of Oxford, Cambridge, Edinburgh, Aberdeen, Glasgow, Perth; The Advocates' Library, Edinburgh; Trinity College, Dublin; King's Inn, Dublin. See 'Quarterly Review', No. 41, May 1819, on the subject of the compulsory eleven copies, with list of pamphlets, etc.*

BROPHY, JOHN—Britain Needs Books (A survey of book production in wartime). National Book Council. London, 1942.

BROTHERHEAD, W.—Forty Years Among the Booksellers of Philadelphia. 1891.

BROWN, A., & CO.—Brown's Bookstall. 3 vols. Illus. Brown and Co., Aberdeen, 1892–4.

BROWN, HORATIO R. F., 1854–1903—The Venetian Printing Press: an Historical Study. 4to, London, 1891. *Contains several chapters on the book-trade of Venice, the laws of copyright, etc., during the sixteenth and seventeenth centuries.*

BRYDGES, SIR EGERTON, 1762–1837—A Summary Statement of the great Grievances imposed on Authors and Publishers, and the injury done to Literature, by the late Copyright Act (and other pamphlets by the same author). London, 1817–18. *This refers to the compulsory eleven free copies. See note under Fisher, Thomas.*

BUCHANAN, ROBERT—Is Barabbas a Necessity? A Discourse on Publishers and Publishing. 8vo, 32 pp. London, 1896.

BUCHLER, W.—Publishing for Pleasure and Profit. Useful Publications, 1946.

BUHLER, C. F.—The Fifteenth Century Book. Illus. The Rosenbach Fellowship in Bibliography Series. Pennsylvania U.P./O.U.P., 1961.

BULMER PAPERS—Vol. 1, no. 1. Allenholme Press, 1960. Irregular. (William Blackwood, 1757–1830.)

BUMPUS, J. & E., LTD—Bumpus (Booksellers). Bumpus, 1930.

BURDEKIN, R.—Memoirs of Mr Spence of York, Bookseller, 1927.

BURGER, KONRAD—The Printers and Publishers of the Fifteenth Century, with Lists of their Works. Index to the Supplement to Hain's Repertorium Bibliographicum. 8vo, London, 1902.
And see s.n. Hain.

BURKE, P.—Law of International Copyright Between England and France: In English & French. Sampson Low, 1852.

BURKE, T., etc.—The Bookworm's Turn: Introduction to the Book Guild. Book Guild, 1948.

BURLINGAME, R.—Endless Frontiers: The Story of McGraw-Hill. McGraw Hill, 1960.
Of Making Many Books: 100 Years of Reading, Writing and Publishing. Scribners, 1946.

BURNS AND OATES—Early Chapters in the History of Burns and Oates. Privately circulated, 1949.

BURNS AND OATES—Early Chapters in the History of Burns and Oates. London, 1908.

BURTON, J. H.—Authors' Records and Accounts ... Including the Problem of Taxation. Gee, 1946.

BUSHNELL, G. H.—From Papyrus to Print. Grafton, 1947.

BUTTON, W. A.—Libel and Slander. Second edition. Sweet & Maxwell, 1946.

CALDER-MARSHALL, A.—The Book Front. John Lane, 1947.

CAMBRIDGE BOOKSELLERS, SOME—*The Bookmark*, Autumn, 1933.

CAMBRIDGE UNIVERSITY PRESS—Historical Sketches. Cambridge, 1910.
Cambridge Books and Printing: Catalogue of Exhibition held at Bumpus's Bookshop, 1931. Cambridge, 1931.
Cambridge University Press. A Brief History. C.U.P., 1955.
A List of Some Books Printed in Cambridge at the University Press, 1521–1800. Illus. C.U.P., 1935.
Notes on Its History and Development. C.U.P., 1934.
A Short Note on the Cambridge University Press. Illus. C.U.P., 1911.
See also under Roberts, S. C., and Catchpole, P. A.

CAMPBELL, G. A.—Making of a Book. O.U.P., 1955.

CAMPBELL, T. C.—Battle of the Press as Told in the History of the Life of Richard Carlile. 1899.

CANFIELD, C.—The Publishing Experience. Rosenbach Fellowship in Bibliography. Pennsylvania U.P./O.U.P., 1969.

CANNONS, H. G. Y. (Borough Librarian, Finsbury)—Bibliography of
Library Economy. A Classified Index to Library Economy, Printing,
Methods of Publishing, Copyright, etc. London, 1910.

CANT, R. M.—The Application of Salesmanship to Bookselling. Whitaker,
n.d.

CAREY, A.—The History of the Book. Cassell, 1890.

CAREY, MATTHEW. Editor, Author, and Publisher—A Study in American
Literary Development. By Earl L. Bradsher. New York and London,
1912.

*From 1785 to 1824 Matthew Carey was at the head of the greatest publishing and
distributing firm in the United States, and was its sole owner during the greater part of
that period.*

CARLILE, RICHARD, 1790–1843—The Life and Character of Richard
Carlile. By George Jacob Holyoake. London, 1848.

The Battle of the Press, as told in the Story of the Life of Richard Carlile.
By his Daughter, Theophila Carlile Campbell. London, 1899.

CARNIE, R. H.—Publishing in Perth Before 1807. Abertay History Society,
1960.

CARRICK, J. C.—William Creech, Robert Burns' Best Friend. 1903.

CARSWELL, DONALD—SIR WALTER: A Four-Part Study in Biography.
8vo, London, 1930. *Includes the first clear picture of Scott's business affairs and
his relations with Constable and the Ballantynes.*

CARTER, J.—Binding Variants in English Publishing, 1820–1900. Illus.
Constable, 1932.

CARTER, JOHN—ABC for Book-Collectors. Hart-Davis, 1952.

CARTER, JOHN, AND POLLARD, GRAHAM—The Firm of Charles
Ottley, London, and Co.: footnote to an enquiry. Hart-Davis, 1948.

CARTER, JOHN, AND SADLEIR, MICHAEL—Victorian Fiction: An
Exhibition of Original Editions. 8vo, London, 1947.

CARTER, ROBERT, HIS LIFE AND WORK, 1891.

CARTER, WALTER, AUTOBIOGRAPHY AND REMINISCENCE (1807–89),
1901.

CASSELL, JOHN, 1817–65—The Life of John Cassell. By G. Holden Pike.
Crown 8vo, London, 1894.

The Bookseller, April and May 1865.

Publishers' Circular, 13 January 1894.

*See also 'A Few Personal Recollections. By an Old Printer' (John Farlow Wilson).
Printed for private circulation, 1868. Also under Vizetelly, Henry.*

CASSELL AND COMPANY—The House that Cassell Built. 12mo, London,
1906.

See also Flower, Sir Newman.

CASSELL'S DIRECTORY of Publishing in Great Britain the Commonwealth and Ireland, 1964–5. Cassell, 1964, and later editions.

CATALOGUES—The First Part of the Catalogue of English Printed Books,
which concerneth such matters of divinitie as have bin either written in
our owne tongue, or translated out of anie other language; and have bin
published to the glory of God, and edification of the Church of Christ in
England. Gathered into alphabet, and such method as it is, by Andrew

Maunsell, Bookseller. London, printed, by John Windet for Andrew Maunsell, dwelling in Lothburie, 1595.

A Catalogue of the most vendible Books in England, orderly and alphabetically Digested; under the Heads of Divinity, History, Physick, and Chyrurgery, Law, Arithmetick, Geometry, Astrologie, Dialling ... etc. With Hebrew, Greek, and Latin Books, for Schools and Scholars. The like Work never yet performed by any. (By William London.) London, 1658. *The first systematic catalogue issued in England.*

Catalogus Librorum ex variis Europae partibus advectorum, apud Robertum Scott, Bibliopolam Regium. 4to, Londini, 1687.

The systematic enumeration of catalogues is rendered superfluous by the publication of Mr Growoll's 'Three Centuries of English Book-trade Bibliography', 1903. See forward; also an article by E. Marston in the 'Publishers' Circular', 16 March 1907.

The Term Catalogues, 1668–1709. With a Number for Easter Term, 1711. A Contemporary Bibliography of English Literature in the Reigns of Charles II, James II, William and Mary, and Anne. Edited from the very rare Quarterly Lists of New Books and Reprints of Divinity, History, Science, Law, Medicine, Music, Trade, etc., issued by the Booksellers, etc., of London. By Edward Arber, F.S.A. 3 vols, 4to. Vol. i, 1668–82; vol. ii, 1683–96; vol. iii, 1697–1709 and 1711. Privately printed, London, 1903. *The original compiler of some of these Term Catalogues was probably R. Clavell.*

A collection of Trade Catalogues referring to sales of books and copyrights, ranging from 1704 to 1768, giving details of prices and purchasers, is in the possession of Longmans. An account of these by W. H. Peet will be found in *Notes and Queries*, 7 S. ix, 301.

Catalogue of a collection of works on Publishing and Bookselling in the British Library of Political and Economic Science. London School of Economics and Political Science (University of London), 1936.

Catalogue of the Library of the National Book Council. N.B.C., London, 1944.

See also under Book Auctions in England.

CATCHPOLE, P. A.—Fifty Years with the Cambridge University Press. Cambridge, 1932.

CATNACH, JAMES, 1792–1841—The Life and Times of James Catnach (late of Seven Dials), Ballad Monger. By Charles Hindley. With 230 Woodcuts, of which 42 are by Bewick. 8vo, London, 1878.

The History of the Catnach Press, at Berwick-upon-Tweed, Alnwick and Newcastle-on-Tyne, in Northumberland, and Seven Dials, London. By Charles Hindley. With many Illustrations. 4to, London, 1886.

CAVE, EDWARD, 1691–1754—The Life of Edward Cave. By Samuel Johnson. *Gentleman's Magazine*, February 1754, and reprinted with Johnson's 'Works'.

The Rise and Progress of the *Gentleman's Magazine*. With anecdotes of the Projector and his early associates. By John Nichols. With 2 Portraits. 8vo, London, 1821.

Cave's Life will be found in Johnson's 'Lives of the English Poets and Sundry

Eminent Persons', *Tilt's edition, crown 8vo, London, 1831. See also Nichols's 'Literary Anecdotes', vol. v.*

CAVE, RODERICK—The Private Press. Illus. Faber & Faber, 1970.

CAVE, RODERICK, AND ROE, THOMAS—Private Press Books. Private Library Assoc., 1960.

CAXTON, WILLIAM, 1422–91—The Old Printer and the Modern Press. By Charles Knight. Crown 8vo, London, 1854.

Life and Typography of William Caxton. By William Blades. London, 1861–3.

CHAMBERS, WILLIAM, 1800–83; ROBERT, 1802–71—Memoir of Robert Chambers, with Autobiographic Reminiscences of William Chambers. Crown 8vo, 1872. 12th Edition, with Supplementary Chapter, 1884.

No mention is made in this book of the fact that Robert Chambers was the author of 'The Vestiges of the Natural History of Creation' (1844), and William Chambers wished the secret to die with him. An account of the authorship and publication will, however, be found in Alexander Ireland's Introduction to the twelfth edition of 'The Vestiges', 1884.

See James Payn's 'Some Literary Recollections', 1886, for a chapter on the two brothers. Payn never concealed his dislike of William Chambers, and it is understood that the Sir Peter Fibbert of 'For Cash Only' is to some extent a portrait of him.

The Story of a Long and Busy Life. By William Chambers. Crown 8vo, Edinburgh, 1884.

Lives of Illustrious and Distinguished Scotsmen, from the Earliest Period to the Present Time. By Robert Chambers. With Portraits. 4 vols, 8vo, Glasgow, 1833–5.

Supplement [and continuation to 1855]. By the Rev. Thomas Thomson. 8vo, Glasgow, 1855.

Memories of the Chambers Brothers. Edited by D. Maggs. Illus. Limited edition. Galahad Press, 1967.

CHAMBERS'S ENCYCLOPAEDIA—*See articles 'Book-trade', etc.*

CHANDLER, JOHN E.—*See under Longman, House of.*

CHAPMAN, JOHN, 1822–94—*See Herbert Spencer's autobiography; 'Life of George Eliot', vol. i, p. 225; also Kegan Paul's 'Biographical Sketches', 1883.*

Chapman was a somewhat remarkable man, and made a reputation as the publisher of books by the 'Philosophical Radicals'. He edited the 'Westminster Review' for many years after he had retired from publishing and was practising as a physician.

Cheap Books and how to get them: being a reprint from the *Westminster Review*, April 1852, of the article 'The Commerce of Literature', together with a brief account of the origin and progress of the recent agitation for free trade in books. 8vo, London, 1852.

The Bookselling System. 8vo, London, 1852.

A Report of the Proceedings of a Meeting (consisting chiefly of Authors) held 4 May 1852, at the House of Mr John Chapman, for the Purpose of hastening the Removal of the Trade Restrictions on the Commerce of Literature. 8vo, London, 1852.

Selections from Chapman's Diary were printed in the *Nottingham Guardian*. 4 May, 25 June 1915. The Diary was found in a Nottingham bookstall.

CHAPMAN & HALL—*See under Waugh, Arthur.*

CHARMIER, D.—Law Relating to Literary Copyright and the authorship and Publication of Books. Effingham Wilson, 1895.

CHAYTOR, H. J.—From Script to Script: An Introduction to Medieval Literature. Cambridge, 1945.

CHENEY, O. H.—Economic Survey of the Book Industry, 1930–31. Bowker, 1949.

CHESNAU, E.—Richard Bentley and Son. Illus. P.p., 1886.

CHILCOTT, TIM—A Publisher and His Circle: Life and Work of John Taylor, Keats's Publisher. Routledge & Kegan Paul, 1972.

CHURCH, A. J.—Authors and Publishers, in *Nineteenth Century*, May 1907.

CHURTON, E.—The Author's Handbook: A Complete Guide to the Art and System of Publishing on Commission. Third edition, with additions. 8vo, London, 1835.

CITY BIOGRAPHY, containing Anecdotes and Memoirs of the Rise, Progress, Situation, and Character of the Aldermen ... of the Corporation and City of London. 8vo, London, 1800. *Contains Lives of Boydell, Newman, Cadell and other London booksellers and printers.*

CLAPPERTON, R. H.—*See under Dent Memorial Lectures.*

CLARK, T. AND T.—The Publishing House of T. and T. Clark, Edinburgh. 12mo, Edinburgh, 1882.

CLARKE, ADAM, 1760–1832—A Bibliographical Dictionary, containing a chronological account, alphabetically arranged, of the most curious, scarce, useful, and important Books, which have been published in Latin, Greek, Coptic, Hebrew, etc., from the Infancy of Printing to the Beginning of the Nineteenth Century. With Biographical Anecdotes of Authors, Printers, and Publishers. 6 vols, and supplement 2 vols. 8vo, London, 1802–6.

CLARKE, ARCHIBALD—The Reputed First Circulating Library in London (*c.* 1740). *See* article in the *Library*, June 1900.

CLARKE, W. K. L.—A Short History of S.P.C.K. S.P.C.K., 1919.

CLASSIFIED CATALOGUE of a Collection of Works on Publishing and Bookselling in the British Library of Political and Economic Science. L.S.E.P.S., 1962.

CLEGG, JAMES (ed.)—The International Directory of Booksellers, and Bibliophile's Manual. Including Lists of the Public Libraries of the World, Publishers, Book Collectors, Learned Societies, and Institutes; also Bibliographies of Book and Library Catalogues, Concordances, Book-plates, etc. Crown 8vo, 1909 (published periodically).

CLEGG'S INTERNATIONAL DIRECTORY of the World's Book Trade. James Clarke, 1950.

CLOUTMAN, B. MACKAY, V.C., AND LUCK, FRANCIS W.—Law for Printers and Publishers. Demy 8vo, London, 1929. Second revised edition, Staples, 1949.

Law Relating to Authors and Publishers. Bale, 1926.

CLOWES, A. A.—Charles Knight. Illus. Richard Bentley, 1892.

CLOWES, W. B.—Family Business, 1803–1953. Illus. Clowes, 1953.

CLYDE, W. M.—The Struggle for the Freedom of the Press from Caxton to Cromwell. O.U.P., 1934.

COBBETT, WILLIAM, 1762–1835 — The Life of William Cobbett. By his Son. London, 1837.
Cobbett was in business as a bookseller in Philadelphia; in Pall Mall at the sign oj 'The Crown, the Bible, and the Mitre' at 11 Bolt Court, Fleet Street, and at 183 Fleet Street.
The Life and Letters of William Cobbett. By Lewis Melville. 2 vols, London, 1913.

COLE, JOHN — Bookselling Spiritualised, Books and Articles of Stationery rendered Monitors of Religion (only 40 copies printed). Scarborough, 1826.

COLLET, COLLET DOBSON — History of the Taxes on Knowledge. 2 vols, London, 1899.

COLLIER, J. PAYNE (1789–1883) — Bibliographical and Critical Account of the Rarest Books in the English Language. 2 vols, 8vo, 1865.
See also under Stationers' Company.

COLLINS, A. S. — Authorship in the days of Johnson: The Relations between Author, Patron, Publisher, and Public, 1726–80. London, 1927. New edition, 1928.
The Profession of Letters: A study of the Relations of Author to Patron, Publisher, and Public, 1780–1832. London, 1928.

COLLINS, WILLIAM, SONS, AND CO. — The Story of a Great Business, 1820–1909. London and Glasgow, 1909.
See also Keir, David.

COLMAN, GEORGE, THE YOUNGER, 1762–1836 — Eccentricities for Edinburgh (containing a poem entitled 'Lamentation to Scotch Booksellers'). 8vo, 1816.

COMMITTEE OF WELSH LANGUAGE PUBLISHING. Report 1952. Home Office.

CONKLIN, G. — How to Run a Rental Library. Revised edition, Bowker: Whitaker, 1947.

CONSTABLE, ARCHIBALD, AND HIS LITERARY CORRESPONDENTS. By his Son Thomas Constable. 3 vols, 8vo, Edinburgh, 1873. *See appendix to vol. i for 'what may be called a* catalogue raisonné *by my father of the chief booksellers in Edinburgh at the end of the last [eighteenth] century'.*
See also under Scott, Ballantyne and Carswell.

COPINGER, W. A. — On the Law of Copyright. Ninth revised edition. James, F. E. S. Sweet & Maxwell, 1958.

CORNHILL MAGAZINE — Publishing before the Age of Printing. January 1864.
Bookselling in the Thirteenth Century. April 1864.
And see s.n. George Smith.

CORP, W. G. — Fifty Years: A Brief Account of the Associated Booksellers of Great Britain and Ireland, 1895–1945. Blackwell, 1945.
See also under Book Trade Handbook, 1937.

COST OF PRODUCTION, THE (Society of Authors). Crown 8vo, London, 1891.

COTTLE, JOSEPH, 1770–1853 — Reminiscences of Coleridge, Southey, etc. Post 8vo, London, 1847.

COUPER, W. J.—The Millers of Haddington, Dunbar and Dunfermline: A Record of Scottish Bookselling. T. Fisher Unwin, 1914.

COURT OF THE QUEEN'S BENCH. The Hichlin Case, and Judgment Pronounced in 1868 Governing the Law Relating to the Publication of Obscene Libels. Dent, 1937.

COURTNEY, W. P.—*See under Dodsley, Robert, and Payne, Thomas.*

COWAN, SAMUEL (of Perth), 1914—Humorous Episodes in the Life of a Provincial Publisher extending over Fifty years. Birmingham, 1912.

COX, GREGORY STEVENS (ed.)—Bibliography of Private Publishing. Illus. Brewhouse, 1970.

COX, HAROLD—*See under Longman, House of.*

CRAIG, A.—Above all Liberties. Allen & Unwin, 1942.
The Banned Books of England. Allen & Unwin, 1931.

CRAWFORD AND BALCARRES, EARL OF—Authors, Publishers and Critics. *Nineteenth Century*, April 1931. *Discussing the influence of book clubs, log-rolling, limited editions, and other aspects of modern publishing.*

CREECH, WILLIAM, 1745–1815—Edinburgh Fugitive Pieces. New Edition, with Memoir. Edinburgh, 1815.
A famous Edinburgh Bookseller. Published for Burns, Blair, Dugald Stewart, and Beattie. Lord Provost, 1811–13.
Creech, William, Robert Burns' Best Friend. By the Rev. J. C. Carrick, B.D., Minister of Newbattle. F'cap. 8vo, Dalkeith, 1903.

CRITIC, THE (weekly newspaper).—F. Espinasse contributed a series of articles on various publishing houses as follows (see his 'Literary Reminiscences', chap. xx, 1893):
Charles Knight. May (two articles) 1860.
Longman, House of. 24 March, 7, 21 April 1860.
John Murray, House of. 7, 14, 21, 28 January 1860.
Blackwood, House of. 7, 14, 21, 28 July, 4, 11 August 1860.

CROPPER, P. J.—The Nottinghamshire printed chap-books, with notices of their printers and vendors. 4to, Nottingham, 1892.

CROSS, G.—Paper and Books. Things We Use Series. Illus. Longmans, 1953.

CROWELL, C. R.—Book Shop Accounts and Records. Nat. Assoc. Book Publishers, New York, 1928.

CRUDEN, ALEXANDER, 1701–70—Life, by Alexander Chalmers. *This is prefixed to many of the editions of the Bible Concordance. Cruden opened a book-seller's shop under the Royal Exchange in 1732, and it was there that he composed his great work.*

CRUSE, AMY—The Englishman and his Books in the Early Nineteenth Century. London, 1930.
The Victorians and their Books. London, 1935.

CRUTCHLEY, BROOKE—Two Men: Walter Lewis and Stanley Morison at Cambridge. Printed for his friends by the University Printer, 1968.

CUMBERS, F. H.—The Book Room: The Story of the Methodist Publishing House and Epworth Press. Illus. Epworth, 1956.

CUNARD, NANCY—These Were the Hours: Memories of My Hours Press, Réanville and Paris, 1928–31. Illus. Illinois U.P., 1969.

CURIO, THE (an illustrated monthly magazine)—'The Great Booksellers of the World', by Max Murray. Bernard Quaritch of London; Ludwig Rosenthal of Munich; Damascene Morgand of Paris; Henry Sotheran of London; E. Bonaventure of New York. With 2 Portraits. 4to, New York, 1887–8.

'Eminent Publishing Houses', by G. Hedeler.

CURLE, R.—James Stevens Cox. Learmouth, 1962.

CURLL, EDMUND, 1675–1747—The Curll Papers. By W. J. Thoms. *See 'Notes and Queries', 2 S. ii, iii, iv, ix, x, and privately reprinted, 1879.*

Pope's Literary Correspondence, 1704–34. (Curll's Edition.) 4 vols, 12mo, 1735–6.

The Unspeakable Curll. Some Account of Edmund Curll, Bookseller; to which is added a full list of his Books. By Ralph Straus. London, 1927.

CURWEN, HENRY, 1845–92—A History of Booksellers, the Old and the New. With Portraits. Crown 8vo, London, 1873. *Curwen was editor of the 'Times of India'. See 'Notes and Queries', 9 S. vi, 288, 388, 376, 454.*

DAKERS, ANDREWS—Publishing. Hale, Target Books, 1961.

DALE, T. C.—Descendants of Robert Richardson of Great Woodhouse. P.p., 1924.

DANIELS, W. M.—Censorship of Books. W. & R. Holmes, 1954.

DANISH BOOK TRADE—*See under Unwin, Sir Stanley.*

DARLEY, L. S.—Bookbinding: Then and Now: James Burn and Co. Faber, 1959.

DARLING, SIR WILL Y.—The Bankrupt Bookseller. Robert Grant, Edinburgh, 1947. *Originally published anonymously in 1931 by Oliver and Boyd, as 'The Private Papers of a Bankrupt Bookseller', and reprinted by Jonathan Cape, in the Travellers' Library, in 1936.*

The Bankrupt Bookseller Speaks Again. Oliver and Boyd, 1938. *This volume was also issued anonymously.*

Darling was Lord Provost of Edinburgh from 1941–4, and subsequently Member of Parliament for South Edinburgh. His memoirs were imaginary; he was in fact a draper, but his firm was next door to a bookseller's.

DARTON, F. J. H.—'Children's Books', reprinted from 'The Cambridge History of English Literature', vol. xi, 1914.

Children's Books in England. Second revised edition. C.U.P., 1958.

See also under Sawyer, C. J.

DARWIN, BERNARD—Fifty Years of *Country Life*. Country Life, 1947.

DAVENPORT, C.—The Book: its History and Development. Illus. Constable, 1907.

DAVID OF CAMBRIDGE; Some Appreciations. Illus. C.U.P., 1937.

DAVIES, D. H. M.—The Copyright Act, 1956. Sweet & Maxwell, 1957.

DAVIES, DAVID W.—The World of Elseviers, 1580–1712. Batsford: Elsevier, 1954.

DAVIS, WILLIAM (bookseller and bibliographical writer)—An Olio of Bibliographical and Literary Anecdotes and Memoranda. 12mo, London, 1814.

A Journey round the Library of a Bibliomaniac; or Cento of Notes and

Reminiscences concerning Rare, Curious, and Valuable Books. 8vo, London, 1821.

A Second Journey round the Library of a Bibliomaniac. 8vo, 1825.

DAWSON, T.—The Law of the Press. 2nd ed. Staples, 1947.

DAY, G. P.—The Function and Organisation of University Presses. Yale U.P.: O.U.P., 1945.

DEALERS IN BOOKS. Sheppard Press, 1955–6, and later.

DELL, HENRY, fl. 1756—The Booksellers, a Poem, 1766.

DE MORGAN, AUGUSTUS, 1806–71—On the Difficulty of Correct Descriptions of Books. With Introduction by Henry Guppy. Reprinted from the *Library Association Record*, June 1902.

DE RICCI, SEYMOUR—English Collectors of Books and Manuscripts (1530–1930), and Their Marks of Ownership. The Sandars Lectures, 1930. Cambridge, 1930.

DENHARD, C. H.—The Autobiography of a Book. *New York Times*: National Book Fair.

THE HOUSE OF DENT

DENT, J. M., & SONS LTD—Dent: Aldine House, 1926.
The Memoirs of J. M. Dent, 1849–1926. London, 1928
New edition commemorating the jubilee of the firm, with additional chapters by Hugh R. Dent, 1938.

DENT, J. M., MEMORIAL LECTURES—Annual public lectures published by Dent's in uniform volumes:
The World of Books: A Panoramic Survey. By Basil Blackwell, 1931; Authors and Publishers: A Study in Mutual Esteem. By Michael Sadleir, 1932; The Printer: His Customers and His Men. By John Johnson, 1933; Paper and its Relationship to Books: By R. H. Clapperton, 1934; Modern Bookbinding. By Douglas Leighton, 1935; A Publisher on Book Production. By Richard de la Mare, 1936; Book Illustration: A Review of the Art as it is To-day. By R. P. Gossop, 1937; Publishing and Bookselling: A Survey of Post-War Developments and Present-Day Problems. By Harold Raymond, 1938; The Reviewing and Criticism of Books. By Frank Swinnerton, 1939.

DERBY, J. C.—Fifty Years Amongst Authors, Books and Publishers, 1833–83. 1884.

DIBDIN, THOMAS F., 1770–1847—Bibliomania, or Book-Madness, 1811.
The Bibliographical Decameron, 1817.
Bibliophobia, 1832.
For other works see Lowndes, W. T., and Ames, Joseph.

DICKSON, LOVAT—The House of Words. Macmillan, 1963.
The author, in a second volume of autobiography, describes the setting up of his own publishing house; its subsequent demise; and his years as a director of Macmillan's.

DILNOT, G.—The Romance of the Amalgamated Press. Illus. Amalgamated Press, 1925.

D'ISRAELI, ISAAC, 1766–1848—The Calamities and Quarrels of Authors: with some Inquiries respecting their Moral and Literary Characters, and Memoirs for our Literary History, 1812–14. New Edition. Edited by his son, Benjamin Disraeli. In one volume. Crown 8vo, London, 1859.

Contains extracts from Bernard Lintot's account-book showing his dealings with Pope, Gay, Theobald, etc.

Curiosities of Literature. New Edition. Edited, with Memoir and Notes, by the Earl of Beaconsfield. 3 vols, Crown 8vo, London, n.d.

DIX, E. R. M. and C.—*See under McKerrow, R. B.*

DOBELL, BERTRAM, BOOKSELLER AND MAN OF LETTERS. By S. Bradbury. 8vo, London, 1909.

DOBSON, AUSTIN—Eighteenth-Century Vignettes (Fine Paper Edition), Series I contains, 'An Old London Bookseller' (Francis Newbery); Series II, 'At Tully's Head' (Robert Dodsley), 'Richardson at Home', 'The Two Paynes'; Series III, 'Thos. Gent, Printer'. F'cap, 8vo, London, 1906–7.

DODSLEY, ROBERT, 1703–64—*See* W. P. Courtney's articles, *Notes and Queries*, 10 S. vi, 361, 402; vii, 3, 82, 284, 404, 442; viii, 124, 183, 384, 442; ix, 3, 184, 323, 463; x, 103, 243, 305, 403; xi, 62, 143, 323; xii, 63. See also *Northern Notes and Queries*, vol. i, nos 7 and 8, pp. 200, 234. Newcastle-upon-Tyne.

The Economy of Human Life. With a Memoir and Portrait of Dodsley. 12mo, London, 1809.

New Notes about Robert Dodsley and the Dodsley Family. By A. Stapleton (of Nottingham). 1909.

Poet, Publisher, and Playwright. By Ralph Straus. With Portrait and 12 other Illustrations. 8vo, London, 1910.

DORAN, G. H.—Chronicles of Barabbas, 1884–1934. Methuen, 1935. Further Chronicles and Comment, 1952. Rinehart, 1952.

DORNE, JOHN (Oxford bookseller, sixteenth century)—Diary of John Dorne. Edited by F. Madan. Oxford Historical Society. 8vo, Oxford, 1885.

See also 'Half Century of Notes on the Day Book of John Dorne', by Henry Bradshaw, in his 'Collected Papers', Cambridge Press, 1889.

DORSTEN, J. A. VAN—Thomas Basson, 1555–1613, English Printer at Leiden. Illus. O.U.P., 1961.

DOUGHTY, D. W.—The Tullis Press, Cupar, 1803–49. Abertay Hist. Soc., 1967.

DOWDING, GEOFFREY—An Introduction to the History of Printing Types. Wace, 1962.

DOWNEY (EDMUND)—Twenty Years Ago: a Book of Anecdote Illustrating Literary Life in London (1875–83). 8vo, London, 1905. *Largely deals with the author's connection with William Tinsley, the publisher.*

DREDGE, JOHN INGLE—Devon Booksellers and Printers of the Seventeenth and Eighteenth Centuries. Reprinted from the *Western Antiquary*. 8vo, privately printed, Plymouth, 1885.

DUBLIN BOOKSELLERS—*Notes and Queries, 9 S. iii, 428.*
Has an Index of London booksellers' signs before 1558.

Early Chancery Proceedings concerning Members of the Book-Trade—Article in the *Library*, October 1907.

The English Provincial Printers, Stationers, and Bookbinders to 1557. Crown 8vo, 153 pp. C.U.P.

The Stationers at the Sign of the Trinity in St Paul's Churchyard. Bibliographica, 1895.

The Printers, Stationers, and Bookbinders of York up to 1600. Transactions of Bibliographical Society, vol. v, 1899.

See also under McKerrow, R. B.

DUCKWORTH—Fifty Years, 1898–1948. Duckworth, 1948.

DUFF, E. GORDON—The Printers, Stationers, and Bookbinders of Westminster and London from 1476 to 1535. The Sandars Lectures at
Cambridge, 1899 and 1904. Crown 8vo, Cambridge, 1906.

A Century of the English Book-Trade. Short Notices of all Printers,
Stationers, Booksellers, and Others connected with it from the Issue of
the First Dated Book in 1457 to the Incorporation of the Company of
Stationers in 1557. Bibliographical Society, 1906.

DUFF, E. GORDON, PLOMER, H. R., AND PROCTOR, R.—Hand-lists
of English Printers, 1501–56, viz., Wynkyn de Worde, Julian Notary, R.
and W. Faques, John Skot, R. Pynson, R. Copland, J. Rastell, P.
Treveris, R. Bankes, L. Andrewe, W. Rastell, T. Godfray, J. Byddell.
2 vols, small 4to, with facsimiles. Bibliographical Society, 1895–6.

DUFFUS, R. L.—Books: their Place in a Democracy. 8vo, 1930. *An up-to-
date account of the American book trade.*

DUNCAN, R.—Editor, Notices and Documents illustrative of the Literary
History of Glasgow during the last century (principally on the Foulis
Press). 4to, Glasgow, 1831. Reprint, 1886.

DUNTON, JOHN, 1659–1733—The Life and Errors of John Dunton, Citizen
of London (and Bookseller). New Edition. With Memoir by J. B. Nichols.
2 vols, 8vo, Westminster, 1818.

*Many of Dunton's letters and agreements are in the Bodleian Library, Rawlinson
MSS. (See Nichols's edition of 'Life and Errors', Appendix.)*

Religio Bibliopolae; or, the Religion of a Bookseller. By John Dunton and
Benjamin Bridgewater.

The Dublin Scuffle: being a Challenge sent by John Dunton to Patrick
Campbel, Bookseller in Dublin. Together with the Small Skirmishes of
Bills and Advertisements. 8vo, London, 1699.

*See 'Notes of Biographies', by Ed. Harley (second), Earl of Oxford, Brit. M. Harl.
MS. 7, 544.*

EASON & SON LTD—1886–1936. Illus.

ECONOMIC DEVELOPMENT COMMITTEE FOR PRINTING AND PUB-
LISHING. Printing in a Competitive World: Report of the P. &
P.E.D.C.'s Joint Mission to Printing Firms in Five Countries. H.M.S.O.,
1970.

EDDY, J. P.—The Law of Copyright. Butterworth, 1958.

EDE, C. (ed.)—The Art of the Book: Some Record of Work Carried Out in
Europe and the U.S.A., 1939–50. Studio, 1951.

EDITOR AND PUBLISHER'S INTERNATIONAL YEARBOOK. Pub. &
Dist., 1950.

ELLIOT, ANDREW GEORGE—Who's Who and What's What in Publishing,
including announcements by a number of British Publishers. Right Way
Books, 1960.

ELLIS, SIR HY—Printers and Stationers: Paper illustrative of the Management of their Trade in the Reign of Elizabeth. Archaeologia, 1832.

ELLIS AND ELVEY—The Hundredth Catalogue of Rare, Curious, and Interesting Books . . . . To which is prefixed a Short Account of the Bookselling Business carried on continuously at this Shop (29 New Bond Street, London, W.) since its establishment in 1728. F'cap, 8vo, London, 1903.

The Oldest London Bookshop: a History of Two Hundred Years. By George Smith and Frank Benger. To which is appended a Family Correspondence of the eighteenth century. London, 1928.

The Letters of Dante Gabriel Rossetti to his Publisher, F. S. Ellis, edited by Oswald Doughty, London, 1928.

ENCYCLOPAEDIA BRITANNICA. Tenth edition, Supplement, vol. iv. Art., 'Bookselling'. Supplement, vol. viii. Art., 'Publishing'. By Joseph Shaylor. Fourteenth edition, 1929. Articles on Books, Book-Collecting, Bookselling, and Publishing. By various english and American writers. *And subsequent editions.*

ERNST, M. L. AND LINDEY, A.—Hold Your Tongue: Adventures in Libel and Slander. Methuen, 1936.

ESCARPIT, R.—The Book Revolution. Trans. from French. UNESCO, 1966.

ESDAILE, ARUNDELL—A Student's Manual of Bibliography. 8vo, London, 1931. The British Museum Library. 8vo, London, 1946.

ESPINASSE, F.—*See under 'Critic', The.*

EVANS, B. A.—If I Had My Way with Publishers. Illus. ASLIB, 1955.

EWART, K.—Copyright, C.U.P., 1952.

EXMAN, E.—The House of Harper. Harper & Row, 1968.

EYRE, FRANK—British Children's Books in the 20th Century. New edition. Illus. Longmans, 1971.

FABER, GEOFFREY—A Publisher Looks at Booksellers. Extracts from a Paper read before the Society of Bookmen. *Publisher and Bookseller*, 3 April 1931.

An Address delivered at Harrogate. A Paper read at the Annual Conference of the Associated Booksellers of Great Britain and Ireland. Printed in the *Publisher and Bookseller*, 5 and 12 June 1931.

A Publisher Speaking. London, 1934.

See also under National Book Council ('Battle of the Books').

FABES, GILBERT H.—Modern First Editions: Points and Values. 8vo, London, 1929.

The Autobiography of a Book. Elsevier, 1926.

See also under Foyle W. and G., Ltd.

FEARMAN, W.—A Letter in Reply to the Ridiculous Threats of Mr John Ballantine, Bookseller for Scotland. 1819.

FIELDS, ANNIE—Authors and Friends, 1896.

FIELDS, JAMES T. (Ticknor and Fields, Boston, U.S.), 1817–81—Biographical Notes and Personal Sketches, with Unpublished Fragments and Tributes from Men and Women of Letters. 8vo, Boston, U.S., 1881.

Harper's Magazine, vol. lxii, p. 391.

Yesterdays with Authors. Crown 8vo, Boston, U.S., 1871.

FISHER, THOMAS—The Present Circumstances of Literary Property in England Considered. London, 1813.

Mr Fisher protested against the Act of Parliament which required eleven copies of all new books to be presented to Public Libraries. This was reduced to five copies by the Copyright Act of 1842. And see s.n. Britton, Brydges.

FITZGERALD, J.—The Recollections of a Book (Trade) Collector, 1848–58. By J. Fitzgerald. F'cap. 8vo, Liverpool, 1903.

FLEMING, C. McCLUNG—R. R. Bowker: Militant Liberal. University of Oklahoma Press, 1953.

FLETCHER, W. Y.—English Book Collectors, 1902.

FLOWER, D.—Century of Bestsellers, 1830–1930. National Book Council, 1934.

The Paperback: Its Past, Present and Future. Arborfield, 1959.

FLOWER, SIR NEWMAN—Just as it Happened. Cassell, 1950.

FOLIO SOCIETY—Folio 21: A Bibliography of the Folio Society, 1947–67, with an Appraisal by Sir Francis Meynell. Folio Society, 1968.

FONTAINE, L.—Creative Bookshop Staffing. Hutchinson, 1968.

FORSYTH, ISAAC (Bookseller at Elgin), 1768–1839—A Memoir of Isaac Forsyth. By his Grandson, Major-General J. Forsyth McAndrew. With Portrait. 8vo, London, 1889.

FOULIS, T. N.—Descriptive Catalogue of the Books Issued by T. N. Foulis (with History of the Firm). Illus. Foulis, 1912.

FOYLE, W. AND G. LTD—The Romance of a Bookshop, 1904–29, by Gilbert H. Fabes. Privately printed, London, 1929. *The story of the brothers William and Gilbert Foyle and their bookshop in Charing Cross Road, commemorating its twenty-fifth birthday.*

Foyles' Fifty Years, 1904–54. Foyle, 1954.

FRANCIS, JOHN, 1811–82—John Francis and the *Athenaeum*. With 2 Portraits. 2 vols, Crown 8vo, London, 1888.

FRANCIS, JOHN COLLINS—Notes by the Way. Post 4to, London, 1909. *Chap. xiii contains notes on various publishing houses, Trade Dinners, etc.*

FRANKLIN, BENJAMIN, 1706–90—The Autobiography of Benjamin Franklin. Edited (with a continuation) by Jared Sparks. Crown 8vo, London, 1850–54.

Many other editions.

FRASER, JAMES, ?–1841—*Literary Gazette*, 9 October 1841; *Fraser's Magazine*, January 1837.

James Fraser was the proprietor and publisher of 'Fraser's Magazine', but it was projected by a namesake, Hugh Fraser. See 'The Maclise Portrait Gallery', edited by William Bates. New edition, p. 521. Crown 8vo, London, 1898; and also Froude's 'Carlyle's Early Life', for an account of Fraser's first offer for and final acceptance of 'Sartor Resartus', 1833.

FRASER'S MAGAZINE—Publishers and Authors. October 1848.

The Makers, Sellers, and Buyers of Books. (Reprinted from *Fraser's Magazine*.) 8vo, London, 1852.

FRENCH BOOK, THE ART OF THE, from early manuscripts to the present time. Introduction by Philip James. London, 1947.

FRIEDBERG, M.—Russian Classics in Soviet Jackets. Columbia U.P., 1962.

FRIEDRICHS, H.—Life of Sir George Newnes. Illus. Hodder, 1911.

FUCHS, MONIQUE—Accounting for Booksellers. Hutchinson, 1965.

FRY, JOHN, 1792–1822—Bibliographical Memoranda in Illustration of Early English Literature. 4to, privately printed, Bristol, 1816. *Contains articles on Osborne's Catalogues.*

GALE, NORMAN—A Famous Bookshop. Illus. George Over, 1914.

GARDINER, WILLIAM NELSON (Bookseller, Pall Mall, *d.* 1814)—'A Brief Memoir of Himself', *Gentleman's Magazine*, vol. lxxxiv, pp. 622–3.

He was an eccentric man, with a considerable knowledge of books, and a spirited engraver. He committed suicide, leaving behind him a letter to a friend ending: 'I die in the principles I have published—a sound Whig.' With the letter was enclosed the 'Memoir of Himself', printed in the 'Gentleman's Magazine', June 1814.

GARNETT, DAVID—Never Be a Bookseller. Knopf, 1929.

GARNETT, R.—*See under Bibliographica.*

GASKELL, P.—The Foulis Press. Soho Bibliographies. Hart-Davis, 1964.

GATTEY, J. C. C.—Libel and Slander. Edited by R. O'Sullivan and Brown, R. G. Fourth revised edition. Sweet & Maxwell, 1953.

GEDUDD, HARRY MAURICE—Prince of Publishers: A Study of the Work and Career of Jacob Tonson. Indiana U.P., 1969.

GENT, THOMAS, 1691–1778—The Life of Mr. Thomas Gent, Printer of York. Written by Himself. With Portrait. 8vo, London, 1832.

Gent was author, printer, publisher, bookseller. For some further details see 'Longman's Magazine', April 1896: 'Thos. Gent, Printer', by Austin Dobson.

Annales Regioduni Hullini: a Facsimile of the Original Edition of 1735. With Life. By the Rev. George Ohlson. 8vo, Hull, 1869.

GENTLEMAN'S MAGAZINE, THE—General Index, 1731–1818. 4 vols, 8vo, London, 1789–1821.

Index to the Biographical and Obituary Notices, 1731–80. 8vo, London, 1891.

Gentleman's Magazine Library: Being a Classified Collection of the Chief Contents of the *Gentleman's Magazine* from 1731 to 1868. Edited by G. L. Gomme. 30 vols, 8vo, London, 1883–1905.

GERRING, C.—Notes on Printers and Booksellers. 8vo, London, 1900.

GETTMAN, R. A.—Victorian Publisher: A Study of the Bentley Papers. Illus. C.U.P., 1960.

GEYER, A.—Reference Directory of Booksellers and Stationers in U.S. and Canada. 1894.

GIBSON, S.—Abstracts from the Wills of Binders, Printers, and Stationers of Oxford, 1493–1638. 4to, printed for the Bibliographical Society, 1906.

Early Oxford Bindings. Bibliographical Society, 4to, 1903.

See also under McKerrow, R. B., and Johnson, John.

GIBSON, S. AND JOHNSON, J. (eds)—The First Minute Book of the Delegates of the Oxford University Press. New impression. O.U.P., 1966.

GILL, ARTHUR ERIC ROWTON—An Essay on Typography. Reset edition. Illus. Dent, 1960.

GILL, R. S.—The Author Publisher Printer Complex. Third revised edition. Illus. Williams & Wilkins, 1958.

GINSBERG, RALPH—An Unhurried View of Erotica. Secker & Warburg, 1959.

GLAISTER, G. (ed.)—Glossary of the Book. Illus. Allen & Unwin, 1960.

GLASGOW—Some Notes on the Early Printers, Publishers, and Booksellers of Glasgow. *See* 'Book-Auction Records', edited by Frank Karslake, vol. v, part 3, April–June 1908.

GODWIN, WILLIAM, 1756–1836—William Godwin: his Friends and Contemporaries. By C. Kegan Paul. 2 vols, 8vo, London, 1876.

William Godwin: a Biographical Study. By George Woodcock. London, 1946.

GOLDEN COCKEREL PRESS—Catalogue 1932.

Cockalorum ... a Bibliography of the Golden Cockerel Press, 1943–8. Golden Cockerel Press, 1950.

GOLDSACK, S. J.—Salesmanship. Collins, 1936.

GOLDSCHMIDT, E. P.—The First Cambridge Press in its European Setting. C.U.P., 1955.

GOMME, G. L.—Book-Making and Book-Selling. Edited by G. L. and G. *Gentleman's Magazine* Library. London, 1888.
See also under Gentleman's Magazine Library.

GORDON, GILES—Books 2000: Some Likely Trends in Publishing. Occasional Papers. Association of Assistant Librarians, 1969.

GOVERNMENT BOOKSELLING QUESTIONS. 1853.

GRAF, T.—The Fifty Years Clause of the Copyright Bill Will Destroy the Poor Man's Bookshelf. Grafton, 1910.

GRAHAM, B.—Bookman's Manual. Revised Hoffman. Seventh revised edition. Bowker: Whitaker, 1954.

GRANNIS, C. B. (ed.)—What Happens in Book Publishing. O.U.P., 1957.

GRANT, JOY—Harold Monro and the Poetry Bookshop. Routledge, 1967. *A history of the Poetry Bookshop and an assessment of Monro as a poet.*

GRANT EDUCATIONAL LTD—Jubilee of the Grant Educational Co. Ltd, 1897–1947. Grant Ed., n.d.

GRAY, G. J.—William Pickering, the Earliest Bookseller on London Bridge, 1556–1751. Transactions of Bibliographical Society, vol. iv, 1898, pp. 57–102.

The Booksellers of London Bridge and their Dwellings. *Notes and Queries*, 6 *S. vii*, 461 (16 June 1883).

Index to W. C. Hazlitt's Bibliographical Collections and Notes, 1893.

The Earlier Stationers and Bookbinders and the First Printer of Cambridge. Bibliographical Society Monographs, no. xii, 1904.

'Cambridge Bookselling and the oldest Bookshop in the United Kingdom', Cambridge, 1925. *An address reprinted from the 'Cambridge Chronicle' of 9 December 1924, tracing the history of the bookshop occupied by Messrs Bowes and Bowes at No. 1 Trinity Street: a record extending over 340 years.*
See also under McKerrow, R. B.

GRAY, G. J. AND PALMER, W. M.—Abstracts from the Wills and Testamentary Documents of Printers, Binders and Stationers of Cambridge, 1504–1699. Bibliographical Society, 1915.

GREAT BRITAIN—Statutes. Printers Imprints Act, 1961. 9 and 10 Elizabeth
    II. H.M.S.O., 1961.
  Statutes. Defamation Act, 1952. H.M.S.O., 1952.
  Home Office. Report of the Committee on Welsh Language Publishing.
    H.M.S.O., 1952.
GREEN, S. G.—Story of the Religious Tract Society for 100 Years. 1899.
GREENSLET, F.—Under the Bridge. Autobiography. Collins, 1944.
GREG, SIR WALTER WILSON—Some Aspects and Problems of London
    Publishing. 1550–1650. O.U.P., 1956.
  Licensers for the Press, etc., to 1640: A Biographical Index. Oxford
    Bibliographical Society, 1962.
  What is Bibliography? Transactions of Bibliographical Society, vol. xii,
    1914.
  See also under Stationers' Company.
GRIEST, GUINEVERE L.—Mudie's Circulating Library and the Victorian
    Novel. David & Charles, 1970.
GRIFFEN & COMPANY—The Centenary Volume of Charles. With Fore-
    word by Lord Moulton, 1920.
GRIFFITH, F. G.—The Swedenborg Society, 1810–1960. Illus. Swedenborg
    Society, 1960.
GRIFFITHS, RALPH, 1720–1803—The *European Magazine*, January 1804.
    *The 'memoir' by Dr Griffiths' son, mentioned in the article as being in preparation,
    I cannot trace, and it was probably never published.*
GRIGSON, GEOFFREY—*See under Book Trade Handbook, 1937.*
GROSS, G.—Publishers on Publishing. Secker & Warburg, 1962.
GROSS, JOHN—The Rise and Fall of the Man of Letters. Weidenfeld &
    Nicolson, 1969.
GROWOLL, A.—A Bookseller's Library and How to Use It. *Publishers'
    Weekly*, 1891.
  The Profession of Bookselling. 2 vols, Sampson Low, 1893–5.
GROWOLL A., AND EAMES, WILBERFORCE—Three Centuries of
    English Book-trade Bibliography: an Essay on the Beginning of Book-
    trade Bibliography since the introduction of Printing, and in England
    since 1595. By A. Growoll. Also a List of the Catalogues, etc., published
    for the English Book-trade from 1595–1902, by Wilberforce Eames, of
    the Lenox Library, New York. New York, published for the Dibdin
    Club by M. L. Greenhalgh, and London, 1903. *This book treats of the
    bibliography of catalogues, and only incidentally gives a few biographical details.*
GUTMAN, SIDNEY (compiler)—Seven Years' Harvest. An Anthology of
    the Bermondsey Book. 1923–30. Heinemann, 1934.
GUY, THOMAS, 1644–1724—A True Copy of the Last Will and Testament
    of Thomas Guy, Esq., late of Lombard Street, Bookseller. Third edition.
    London, 1725.
  An Essay on Death-bed Charity, exemplified in Mr. Thomas Guy, Book-
    seller. By John Dunton, 1728.
  A Biographical History of Guy's Hospital (Life of Thomas Guy, pp. 1–73).
    By Samuel Wilks, M.D., and G. T. Bettany, M.A., B.Sc. With Portrait
    of Thomas Guy. 8vo, London, 1892.

HÄBLER, K.—Early Printers of Spain and Portugal. 4to, Bibliographical Society, 1897.

HACKETT, A. P.—Fifty Years of Bestsellers, 1895–1945. Bowker, 1945.
Seventy Years of Bestsellers. Bowker, 1968.
Sixty Years of Bestsellers, 1895–1955. Bowker, 1955.

HAIGHT, ANNE LYON—Banned Books. Second edition. Bowker, 1955.

HAIN, L.—Repertorium Bibliographicum. 2 vols, 8vo, Stuttgart, 1826–38.
Repertorium Bibliographicum. Indices opera C. Burger. 8vo, Lipsiae, 1891.
Supplement to Hain's Repertorium Bibliographicum. By W. A. Copinger.
3 vols, 8vo, London, 1895–1902.
Appendices ad Hainii-Copingeri Repertorium Bibliographicum. Edidit D. Reichling. 8vo, Monachii, 1905, etc.

HAMILTON, GAVIN—Short Memoir of Gavin Hamilton, Bookseller in Edinburgh in the Eighteenth Century. Privately printed, 1840.

HAMILTON, HAMISH (ed.)—Majority; 1931–52: An Anthology of 21 Years of Publishing. Hamish Hamilton, 1952.

HAMPDEN, JOHN—The Book World. London, 1935. *A Symposium by authors closely associated with the book trade, edited by John Hampden. Introduction by Sir Stanley Unwin. Chapters on 'Authorship', by Frank Swinnerton; 'The Literary Agent', by D. Kilham Roberts; 'Publishing' by W. G. Taylor; 'Book Production', by G. Wren Howard; 'Reviewing', by Gerald Gould; 'Bookselling in London', by J. G. Wilson; 'Provincial Bookselling', by Basil Blackwell; 'Second-hand Bookselling', by J. Ainslie Thin; 'English Books Abroad', by Sir Stanley Unwin; 'The Public Library', by Charles Nowell; 'The Circulating Library', by F. R. Richardson; 'A List of Books', by John Hampden.*
(Ed.) The Book World Today: A New Survey of the Making and Distribution of Books in Britain. Allen & Unwin, 1957. *Twenty-two essays by well-known authors, booksellers, librarians, publishers etc., with an introduction by Sir Stanley Unwin.*

HAMPSHIRE BOOKSELLERS AND PUBLISHERS—By F. A. Edwards. *Notes and Queries*, 10 S. v, 481–3.

HAMPSTEAD ANNUAL, THE, 1904–5—Edited by Greville E. Matheson and Sydney C. Mayle. Containing an article on publishers in Hampstead, George Bell, George M. Smith, Charles Knight. With portraits. Hampstead, 1895.

HANDOVER, PHYLLIS MARGARET—Printing in London from 1476 to Modern Times. Illus. Allen & Unwin, 1960.

HANFF, HELENE—84 Charing Cross Road. Deutsch, 1971. *Letters exchanged between a bookseller at Marks & Co. and an American customer who hated buying newly published books.*

HARLEY, E. S. AND HAMPDEN, J.—Books: From Papyrus to Paperback. Outline Series. Illus. Methuen, 1964.

HARMAN, E. (ed.)—The University as Publisher. Toronto University Press, 1962.

HARPER, J. H.—The House of Harper. Illus. Harper, 1912.
Harper Centennial, 1817–1917. Harper, 1917.

HARRAP, GEORGE G.—Some Memories—A Publisher's Contribution to the History of Publishing. London, 1935.

HARRAP, GEORGE, & CO.—Partners in Progress. P.p., Harrap, 1961.

HARRISON, FREDERICK—A Book about Books. London, 1943.

HARRISON, T.—The Bookbinding Craft and Industry: An outline of its history, development and technique. London, 1926.

HARRISON, THE HOUSE OF—Being an account of the family and firm of Harrison & Sons, Printers to the King. London, 1914.

HART, HORACE—Charles, Earl Stanhope and the Oxford University Press. Illus. Printing History Soc., n.d.

Notes on a Century of Typography at the University Press, 1693–1794. Oxford, 1900.

HATCHARD'S—Memorials of the House of Hatchard. (Piccadilly Bookmen.) By Arthur L. Humphreys. London, 1893.

Publishers' Circular, 21 November 1903, Mr Edwin Shepherd, with portrait.

HAUPT, H. L.—Life of the Book. Illus. Abelard-Schumann, 1962.

One Hundred Books about Book Making. O.U.P., 1949.

The Book in America. Second edition. Bowker, 1951.

HAVERCROFT, R. H.—A Book Is Made for You. Illus. Harrap, 1961–70.

HAWKER, G.—A Biographical Sketch of Francis James Blight. F.R.S.E., Publisher. Illus. Elliot Stock, 1931.

HAZELL, R. C.—Walter Hazell, 1843–1919. 8vo, London, 1919.

HAZLITT, WILLIAM CAREW, 1834—Collections and Notes (towards English Bibliography). With Index. 6 vols, 8vo, London, 1876–92.

The Confessions of a Collector. Crown 8vo., London, 1897. *This has notes and reminiscences of H. G. Bohn, B. Quaritch, F. S. Ellis, Joseph Lilly, etc.*

HEINEMANN, W.—Bookselling: the System adopted in Germany for the Prevention of Underselling and for Promoting the Sale of Books. (A Paper read before a meeting of the Associated Booksellers of Great Britain and Ireland, April 1895.) 8vo, Taunton, 1895.

The Hardships of Publishing. Privately printed, London, 1893.

William Heinemann—A Memoir. By Frederic Whyte. London, 1928.

HENDRICK, B. J.—*See under Page, Walter H.*

HEPBURN, JAMES—The Author's Empty Purse and the Rise of the Literary Agent. O.U.P., 1968.

HERBERT, SIR ALAN (A. P.)—Public Lending Right: Authors, Publishers and Libraries. Wilding & Son, privately circulated, 1960.

HERBERT, WILLIAM—*See under Ames, Joseph.*

HERTZBERGER, M. (ed.)—Dictionary for the Antiquarian Book Trade. Sawyer, 1956.

HEWITT, G.—Let the People Read: A Short History of the United Society for Christian Literature. Illus. Lutterworth, 1949.

HEYWOOD, G. B.—Abel Heywood and Son Ltd, 1832–1932. Illus. A. Heywood, 1932.

HICKSON, O. S., AND CARTER-RUCK, P. F.—The Law of Libel and Slander. Faber, 1953.

HIGH HOUSE PRESS, THE—A Short History and Appreciation. By S. Mathewman. Shaftesbury, Dorset, 1930.

HIGHLEY, S.—Record of the Life-work from 1844–85 of Samuel Highley, Publisher, etc. 1886.

HILL, JOSEPH—The Book-Makers of Old Birmingham: Authors, Printers and Booksellers. Illus. Birmingham, 1908.

HILL, L. W.—Making Known: The Partnership of Author, Publisher and Bookseller in the Advancement of Science and Technology. Stratford Press, 1954.

HINDLEY, CHARLES—The Life and Times of James Catnach (late of Seven Dials), Ballad-Monger. Illus. Facs. First edition 1878. Seven Dials Press, 1970.

HISCOCK, ERIC—Last Boat to Folly Bridge. Cassell, 1970.

HOBSON, G. D.—Notes on the History of Sotheby's. Privately printed, 1917. Maioli, Canevari, etc. Ernest Benn, 1926.

HODGSON AND CO.—A Century of Book-Auctions, being a Brief Record of the firm of Hodgson and Co. London, 1907.

HOLBROW, R. N.—Bookseller's Handbook. National Newsagent, 1947.

HOLDEN, JOHN A.—*See under Bookman's Glossary.*

HOLLAND, JOSIAH GILBERT—Life of, by H. M. Plunkett. 1894.

HOLMES, C. J.—Self and Partners, Mostly Self. Illus. Constable, 1936.

HOLT, H.—Sixty Years as a Publisher. Allen & Unwin, 1923.

HONE, WILLIAM, 1780–1842—Early Life and Conversion. Written by Himself. London, 1841.

William Hone—His Life and Times. By F. W. Hackwood. A popularly written biography, consisting largely of Letters and Autobiographical and other contemporary matter. London, 1912.

HOPKINS, G. (ed.)—Battle of the Books. Wingate, 1947.

HOPKINSON, C.—Dictionary of Parisian Music Publishers, 1700–1950. Illus. Hopkinson, 1951.

HOPPÉ, A. J.—A Talk on *Everyman's Library*. Printed as a *brochure* by Dent's, 1938.

HORAE BEATAE MARIAE VIRGINIS; or, Primers of Sarum and York Use. With an Introduction by Edgar Hoskins, M.A. 8vo, London, 1901. *This contains 'A List of Printers and Booksellers, with a List of Places', from the fifteenth to the eighteenth century.*

HORROCKS, SIDNEY—The State as Publisher. Library Association, 1952.

HOTCHKISS, J. T.—Bookstore Advertising, Publicity and Window Display. 1926.

HOTTEN, JOHN CAMDEN—1832–73. A List of Books edited by him. *See Notes and Queries. 8 May 1915, pp. 357–8.*

Literary Copyright. Hotten, 1871.

HOUGHTON, HENRY OSCAR—*See 'Publishers' Weekly', with portrait, vol. xlviii, no. 10 (New York, 1895); vol. li, no. 21 (New York, 1897).*

HOW TO PRINT AND PUBLISH A BOOK. 8vo, Winchester, 1890.

HOWARD, G. WREN—*See under Hampden John.*

HOWARD, MICHAEL S.—Jonathan Cape, Publisher. Cape, 1971.

HOWE, GERALD—Of the Making of CXXV Books: a Publisher's Bibliography. London, 1934.

HOWE, P. P.—Malthus and the Publishing Trade. London, 1913.

HUDSON, DEREK—Oxford Publishing since 1478. O.U.P., 1966.

Writing Between the Lines. High Hill Books, 1965. *An autobiography which includes chapters relating to the author's work as an editor at O.U.P.*

HUGHES, T.—On Chester Literature, Its Authors and Publishers during the Sixteenth and Seventeenth Centuries. Chester, 1858.

HULTON READERSHIP SURVEY. Hulton, 1947.

HUME, ABRAHAM—Learned Societies and Printing Clubs of the United Kingdom, 1853.

HUMPHRIES, C.—Life of Charles Humphries. Wickliffe Press, n.d.

HUMPHRIES, CHARLES, AND SMITH, WILLIAM C.—Music Publishing in the British Isles from the Earliest Times to the Middle of the Nineteenth Century: A Dictionary. Cassell, 1954.

HUNT, CECIL—Ink in my Veins. 8vo, London, 1948.
How to Write a Book. Jenkins, 1952.

HUNTINGDON BOOKSELLERS—*Notes and Queries*, 10 S. viii, 201; xii, 164; 11 S. vi, 207.

HUTTON, WILLIAM, 1723–1815—The Life of William Hutton, F.A.S.S., including a Particular Account of the Riots at Birmingham in 1791. To which is subjoined the History of his Family, written by himself, and published by his Daughter, Catherine Hutton. With Portrait. 8vo, London and Birmingham, 1816.
Catherine Hutton and her Friends. Edited by Mrs C. H. Beale. Small 4to, cloth. Birmingham, 1895. *This is a record of the only daughter of the celebrated William Hutton, historian of Birmingham, and a bookseller there.*

HUXLEY, GERVAS—Market Promotion and the Book Trade. (Talk to the Society of Bookmen.) Privately printed for the Society by Chatto, 1951.

HUXLEY, LEONARD—*See under Smith, Elder, The House of.*

HYDE, SYDNEY—Sales on a Shoestring: How to Advertise Books. Deutsch, 1956.

IFLIN, M.—Black on White: The Story of Books. Routledge & Kegan Paul, 1932.

INDIAN BOOK TRADE AND LIBRARY DIRECTORY, Pub. & Dist., 1953.

INSTITUTE OF ECONOMIC AFFAIRS—Libraries: Free for All? Illus. I.E.A., 1962.

ISBISTER & CO.—*The Bookman*, February 1893.

JACKSON, HOLBROOK—*The Anatomy of Bibliomania*. 2 vols, London, 1930–31. *Treats of every branch of book-collecting and book-lore, with chapters on the care of books, libraries, bindings, and the like.*
The Fear of Books. London, 1932.
William Caxton. London, 1933.
The Printing of Books. London, 1938.
Bookman's Holiday. London, 1945.
See also under Morison, Stanley.

JACOBI, CHARLES T.—On the Making and Issuing of Books. 4to, London, 1891.
Some Notes on Books and Printing (and Publishing). 8vo, London, 1902.

JAGGARD, WILLIAM—Shakespeare's Publishers: Notes on the Tudor–Stuart Period of the Jaggard Press. Liverpool, 1907.
Lists of omissions from D.N.B., containing a considerable number of book-

sellers. *Notes and Queries. See* 10 *S. ix*, 21, 83; *x*, 183, 282; *xii*, 24, 124, 262; 11 *S. ii*, 11.

JAMES, G. P. R., 1801–60 – Some Observations on the Book-trade, as connected with Literature in England. *Journal of the Statistical Society of London*, vol. vi, Part I. London, February 1843.

JAMES, PHILIP – English Book Illustration. 8vo, London, 1947.

JARROLD'S, 1823–1923, The House of – A History of One Hundred Years. Privately printed, 1924.

JEFFREY, J. B. (ed.) – Growing Up with Books: An Annotated List. National Book League, 1966.

JENKINSON, FRANCIS J. H. – List of Incunabula collected by G. Dunn, to illustrate the history of Printing. Transactions of Bibliographical Society. 8vo, London, 1923.

JENNET, SEAN – The Making of Books. Faber, 1951.

JERDAN, WILLIAM, 1782–1869 – Illustrations of the Plan of a National Association for the Encouragement and Protection of Authors. 8vo, London, 1838.

JERROLD, S. – Handbook of English and Foreign Copyright. Chatto & Windus, 1881.

JESSOP, AUGUSTUS, 1824–1913 – A Plea for the Publisher. Contemporary Review, March 1890.

JEWITT, L. – Life of William Hutton and History of the Hutton Family. Warne, 1872.

JOHNSON, JOHN, AND GIBSON, STRICKLAND – Print and Privilege at Oxford in the year 1700. Oxford University Press, 1947.
See also under Dent Memorial Lectures.

JOHNSON, JOSEPH – By-gone Manchester Booksellers: I. William Willis, 1807–61, and others. II. Samuel Johnson, 1783–1868, and other members of his family. *These notices appeared in W. T. Johnson's Manchester Catalogue (28 Corporation Street), December 1883 and February 1884, and were all that were published.*
Liverpool Booksellers. *See 'Bookseller', September 1861, January 1862.*
Manchester Bookseller. *See 'Bookseller', February 1861.*

JOHNSON, SAMUEL, 1709–84 – The Life of. By James Boswell.

JOHNSTON, W. AND A. K. – 100 Years of Mapmaking. Illus. Johnston, 1930.

JONES, THOMAS – The Gregynog Press. O.U.P., 1954.

JONES, W. – Religious Tract Society: Jubilee Memorial, 1799–1849.

JOSEPH, MICHAEL – Adventure of Publishing. Wingate, 1949.
Commercial Side of Literature. Hutchinson, 1925.
The Sword in the Scabbard. London, 1942.

JOVANOVICH, W. – Now, Barabbas. Longmans, 1965.

JOY, THOMAS – Bookselling. Pitman, 1952.
Mostly Joy: A Bookman's Story. M. Joseph, 1971.
The Right Way to Run a Library Business. A. G. Elliot, 1949.
The Truth About Bookselling. Pitman, 1964.

JUDGE, C. B. – Elizabethan Book Pirates. Harvard, 1934.

JUNOR, JOHN – Footprints on the Sands of Time, 1863–1963: The Story of the House of Livingstone. E. and S. Livingstone, 1963.

JUSTICE OF THE PEACE AND LOCAL GOVERNMENT REVIEW—Obscene Publications. Justice of the Peace, 1955.

KAHANE, J.—Memoirs of a Book-legger. Michael Joseph, 1939.

KARSLAKE, F.—Book-Auction Records. A Record of London Book-Auctions. London, issued quarterly.

KEIR, DAVID—The House of Collins. Collins, 1952.

KEITH, ALEXANDER—Aberdeen University Press, 1840–1963. Ab.U.P., 1963.

KELLY, THOMAS, 1722–1855—Passages from the Private and Official Life of the late Alderman Kelly (Lord Mayor), 1836–7. By the Rev. R. C. Fell. With Portrait. F'cap. 8vo, London, 1856.

KELLY'S DIRECTORY of Stationers, Printers, Booksellers, Publishers, and Paper Makers in Great Britain. Royal 8vo, London, 1900 and periodically.

KELMSCOTT PRESS—*See under Sparling, H. Halliday.*

KENNEDY, RICHARD—A Boy at the Hogarth Press. Illus. Limited edition, Whittington Press, 1971; Heinemann, 1972. *Contains witty drawings of the Woolfs at work.*

KEYS, C.—The Truth about Certain Publishing. British Commonwealth Agencies.

KEYNES, SIR GEOFFREY—William Pickering, publisher, a memoir and check list of his publications. Illus. Facs. Galahad Press, 1969.

KILGOUR, R. L.—Estes and Lauriat: A History 1872–98: with a Brief Account of Dana Estes & Co., 1898–1914. Illus. O.U.P., 1957.

Messrs Roberts Brothers, Publishers. Illus. Michigan U.P., 1952.

KING, ARTHUR, AND STUART, A. F.—The House of Warne. Illus. 1965.

KING, PHILIP STEPHEN, 1819–1908—Reminiscences of an Octogenarian. Privately printed, 1905.

Mr King was the founder of the well-known firm of Parliamentary publishers and booksellers. These reminiscences, however, only relate to Mr King's life up to the time of his commencing business for himself in 1853.

KINGSFORD, R. J. L.—Books in the Immediate Post-War Period. British Federation of Master Printers, 1944.

The Publishers' Association, 1896–1946 (with an epilogue). C.U.P., 1970.

KIRKMAN, FRANCIS, publisher and dramatic writer, 1632–(?)—Memoirs of his own life. *This is mentioned by Dunton, but I cannot find any other reference to it or proof of its publication.*

KITCHEN, F. H.—Moberley Bell and His Times. Illus. P. Allen, 1925.

KNIGHT, CHARLES, 1791–1873—The Pursuit of Knowledge under Difficulties (see chaps x–xi, 'Literary Pursuits of Booksellers and Printers'). 12mo, London, 1830.

The Struggle of a Book against Excessive Taxation. 8vo, London, 1850.

The old Printer and the Modern Press. Crown 8vo, London, 1854. *Part II deals with eighteenth- and nineteenth-century methods of publishing and bookselling.*

Two articles on Charles Knight by F. Espinasse appeared in the *Critic* during May 1860.

Passages of a Working Life. 3 vols, Crown 8vo, London, 1864.

Shadows of the Old Booksellers. Crown 8vo, London, 1865. A New Edition published by Peter Davies with a preface by Stanley Unwin. London, 1927.

A Sketch. By his Granddaughter, Alice A. Clowes. With a Portrait. 8vo, London, 1892. *Contains a list of works written, edited, or conducted by Charles Knight.*

Charles Knight, Publisher. By Alexander Strahan. *Good Words*, September 1867.

KOGAN, H. — The Great E.B.: The Story of the Encyclopaedia Britannica. Chicago U.P./C.U.P., 1958.

KÜNSMÜLLER, F. A. S. — T. J. Cobden-Sanderson as Bookbinder. Trans. from German, by I. Grafe. Illus. Tabard Press, 1967.

LABOUR AND NATIONAL SERVICE, MINISTRY OF — Journalism and Publishing. Revised edition. H.M.S.O., 1954.

Careers for Men and Women Series.

LACKINGTON, JAMES, 1746–1815 — Memoirs of the First Forty-five Years of James Lackington, the present Bookseller in Chiswell Street, Moorfields, London. Written by Himself in Forty-six Letters to a Friend. With Portrait. 8vo, London, 1791. *For other editions see Lowndes.*

The Confessions of J. Lackington, late Bookseller at the Temple of the Muses, in a Series of Letters to a Friend. Second Edition. Crown 8vo, London, 1804.

LACKINGTON'S CONFESSIONS, rendered into narrative, to which are added observations on the Bad Consequences of Educating Daughters at Boarding Schools. By Allan Macleod, Esq. F'cap. London, 1804. *Written in ridicule of Lackington's book, partly in verse. A futile performance.*

LAING, DAVID (bookseller, antiquary, *d.* 1878). *Scottish Historical Review*, July 1914, and separately 1915.

LANE, JOHN — *See under May, J. Lewis.*

LANGDON-DAVIES, B. N. — The Practice of Bookselling. Phoenix House, 1951.

LATHAM, H. S. — My Life in Publishing. Sidgwick & Jackson, 1966.

LAVER, JAMES — Hatchard's of Piccadilly. Hatchard's, 1947.

LAWLER, JOHN — Book Auctions in England in the Seventeenth Century (1676–1700). With a Chronological List of the Book Auctions of the Period. Crown 8vo, London, 1898.

LAWLER, JOHN — The H. W. Wilson Company: Half a Century of Bibliographic Publishing. University of Minnesota Press/O.U.P., 1950.

LAWRENCE, D. H. — Pornography and Obscenity. Faber, 1929.

LEAPER, W. J. — Copyright and Performing Rights. Stevens, 1957.

LEAVIS, Q. D. — Fiction and the Reading Public. Chatto & Windus, 1932; new edition, 1970.

LEE, SIR SIDNEY — An Elizabethan Bookseller (Edward Blount). *Bibliographer*, vol. i, 1895.

See also under Smith, George M.

LEGAT, MICHAEL — Dear Author: Letters from a Working Publisher to Authors, Practised and Prospective. Pelham Books, 1972.

LEHMANN, JOHN—I am My Brother. Autobiography, vol. ii. Longmans 1960.

The Whispering Gallery, Autobiography, vol. i. Longman, 1958.

LEIGHTON, DOUGLAS—*See under Dent Memorial Lectures.*

LEMOINE, HENRY, 1755–1812—*See 'T. P.'s Magazine', February 1911; Art. by John o' London, 'Up and Down Old Broad Street'.*

LETTER TO THE SOCIETY OF BOOKSELLERS, on the Method of forming a True judgment of the Manuscripts of Authors: and on the leaving them in their hands, or those of others, for the determination of their merit: also, of the knowledge of new books, and of the method of distributing them for sale ... 8vo, London, 1738.

LEVY, H.—Retail Trade Associations (Report to Fabian Society). Routledge & Kegan Paul, 1942.

LEWIS, A. W.—Books. Third edition. E.S.A., 1956.

LEWIS, H. K.—Lewis' 1844–1944. A Brief Account of a Century's Work. H. K. Lewis, 1945.

LEWIS, H. K., & CO. LTD.—Respice-Prospice: 1844–1931. H. K. Lewis, 1931.

LEWIS, JOHN—The Left Book Club: An Historical Record. Foreword by Margaret Cole. Gollancz, 1970.

LEWIS, WILMARTH—Collector's Progress. Constable, 1952.

LIBRARY, THE. New Series. Vol. i, 1900, and in progress. *See Indexes throughout for many interesting and valuable articles.*

LIBRARY, THE CIRCULATING—*See under Hampden, John; Milne, James; and Book Trade Organization.*

LIBRARIES AND THE BOOK TRADE IN THE SEVENTIES: One-Day Conference at Holborn Central Library, 8 April 1970. North-West Polytechnic School of Librarianship, 1970. (Distributed by Duckworth.)

LIDDERDALE, JANE, AND NICHOLSON, MARY—Dear Miss Weaver: Harriet Shaw Weaver, 1876–1961. Illus. Faber, 1970.

LINDSAY, T. M.—An Oxford Bookseller in 1520. Stirling and Glasgow Public Libraries, 1907.

LITTLE, BROWN, AND CO., BOSTON—An Article reprinted from the *Publishers' Weekly*. New York, 1898.

LIVEING, EDWARD—Adventure in Publishing: The House of Ward, Lock, 1854–1954. Ward, Lock, 1954.

LIVERPOOL BOOKSELLERS—*See s.n. Joseph, Johnson.*

LIVINGSTON, L. S.—America Book Prices Current. From 1895. Auction Prices of Books. 4 vols, 1905.

LIVINGSTONE, E. AND S., LTD—80 Years of Publishing, 1864–1944. Livingstone, 1944.

LLOYD, B., AND GILBERT, G.—The Censorship and Public Morality: An Australian Conspectus. Angus & Robertson, 1930.

LONDON, WILLIAM—*See under Catalogues.*

LONDON BOOKSELLERS' SIGNS—*See the 'Bibliographer', vol. ii, 112, 143, 174; iii, 45, 67, 94; iv, 76; vi, 22. London, 1882–4.*

See 'Publishers' Circular', 12, 19 March, 2, 16 April, 28 May, and 20 August 1892; 'Notes and Queries', 6 S. vi, 283, 302 (1590–1713); 6 S. v, 4 (1612–40); 6

S. iii, 404, 464; iv, 242 (1623–1714); *6 S. ii, 141 (1737–43). St. Paul's Church-yard, 5 S. ix, 9–10 (1515–87); xi, 94 (1548–1738); xiii, 489 (1593–1723); viii, 461 (1593–1763); ix, 97 (1611–52).*

See also under Spielmann, M. H.

LONDON BRIDGE BOOKSELLERS—*See s.n. Thomson, R., and Gray, G. J.*

See also the articles, 'Notes and Queries', 6 S. v, 221, 222; vi, 444, 465, 531; vii, 103, 461; x, 163, 237, 317; xi, 293; 7 S. iv, 164.

LONGMAN, HOUSE OF—A series of articles appeared in the *Critic*, 24 March, 7, 21 April 1860, by F. Espinasse.

The House of Longman, with a Record of their Bicentenary Celebrations, 1724–1924. By Harold Cox and John E. Chandler. Printed for private circulation, London, 1925.

Longman, Sir Rees T., and Britton, John. Reminiscences of Literary London, 1779–1893, pp. 42–61.

Longman's Notes on Books, Extra Number, 8 December 1908. *This contained the succession of partners and imprints of the firm from 1724, and was reprinted in 'Notes and Queries', 10 S. xi, 2.*

The Bookseller, August 1859 and 30 June 1865.

British and Colonial Printer and Stationer, 24 December 1884.

Publishers' Circular, 13 August 1892.

Sketch, 30 May 1894.

Bookman, special article, with portraits, etc., March 1901.

Public Opinion, 26 February 1904.

LONGMANS & CO. AND MURRAY, J.—On the Publication of School Books by the Government at the Public Expense. Longman and Murray, 1851.

LONGMAN, THOMAS, 1804–79—*Athenaeum*, 6 September 1879; *Standard*, 2 September 1879; *Daily Telegraph*, 1 September 1879; *Publishers' Circular*, 16 September 1879.

LONGMAN, WILLIAM, 1813–77—An article by Henry Reeve in *Fraser's Magazine*, October 1877; *Athenaeum*, 18 August 1877; *Publishers' Circular*, 1 September 1877; *The Bookseller*, 4 September 1877.

LONGMAN, WILLIAM (President of the Publishers' Association, 1930–31)— Tokens of the Eighteenth Century connected with Booksellers and Bookmakers (Authors, Printers, Publishers, Engravers and Papermakers). Illus., 90 pp. 8vo, London, 1916.

LOW, D. M., and others—A Century of Writers, 1855–1955, with Introduction by Oliver Warner. Chatto, 1855. *Contains a short history of Chatto & Windus in the Introduction.*

LOWNDES, THOMAS, 1719–84—A bookseller in Fleet Street. 'He is supposed to have been delineated by Miss Burney, in her celebrated novel *Cecilia*, under the name of "Briggs"' (Timperley's 'Dictionary of Printers').

LOWNDES, WILLIAM THOMAS (1798–1843)—The Bibliographer's Manual. Four vols, 8vo, 1834. New Edition in ten parts, ed. H. G. Bohn, 1857–64. *The first systematic work of its kind.*

The British Librarian, 8vo, 1839–42.

* 'This list (1623–1714) is an alphabetical list of London publishers carried down to 1834, but 1714 is the last dated sign mentioned, apparently.' Mr W. McMurray ('*Notes and Queries*', 11 S. i, 402).

LUCAS, E. V.—Charles Lamb and the Lloyds. With Portrait. Crown 8vo, London, 1898.

Robert Lloyd (1778–1811) was a bookseller in Birmingham, being a partner in the firm of Knott and Lloyd. See imprint of W. Hutton's 'Roman Wall', 1802.

A Bookseller's Rubaiyat. Being verses written by E. V. Lucas and read by him at Methuen and Co.'s Dinner, at which a number of members of the Bookselling Trade were present on 15 November 1912. For private circulation only.

Lines Written for the Dinner of the B.P.R.A. P.p. 1929.

Travellers' Joy, or the Keeper of the Stall. W. H. Smith, 1919.

MCALLISTER, G. (ed.)—Book Crisis. Faber, 1940.

MACAULAY, LORD, 1800–59—The Life and Letters of Lord Macaulay. By Sir G. O. Trevelyan, Bart. 2 vols, 8vo, 1876, and other editions. *See throughout for Macaulay's connection and transactions with Longmans.*

MCCLURE, S. S.—The Autobiography of. London, 1914.

The adventurous American publisher, founder of McClure's Magazine, who was the prototype of Pinkerton in R. L. Stevenson's 'The Wrecker'.

MACGIBBON, JAMES, AND BATSFORD, BRIAN—Book Publishing in the British Zone of Germany. Typescript, 1947.

MACGILLIVRAY, E. J.—Copyright. 1926. Royal Inst. Chem., 1926.

Copyright Cases, 1924–5. P.A., 1926.

MCKENZIE, D. F.—The Cambridge University Press, 1696–1712. Vol. 1. Illus. 2 vols. C.U.P., 1966.

MCKERROW, R. B. (General Editor)—A Dictionary of Printers and Book-sellers in England, Scotland, and Ireland, and of Foreign Printers of English Books, 1557–1640. By H. G. Aldis, Robert Bowes, E. R. M. and C. Dix, E. Gordon Duff, Strickland Gibson, G. J. Gray, R. B. McKerrow, Falconer Madan, and H. R. Plomer. London. Bibliographical Society, 1910.

Printers' and Publishers' Devices in England and Scotland, 1485–1640. London. Bibliographical Society, 1913.

An Introduction to Bibliography for Literary Students. 8vo, London, 1927.

MACKINNON, M., AND BELL, A.—Libel for Laymen. Hurst, 1933.

MACLEHOSE, J.—Books Published by James MacLehose from 1838 to 1881, and by J. MacLehose and Sons, to 1905. Presented to the Library of the University of Glasgow. With Portrait. 8vo, Glasgow, 1905.

MACLEHOSE, J.—The Glasgow University Press, 1638–1931. Illus. Glasgow U.P., 1931.

MACLEHOSE, R.—Report to the Society of Authors on the Discount Question: A Criticism. MacLehose, 1897.

MCLEAN, RUARI—Modern Book Design. Longmans Green for British Council, 1951.

MCLEISH, A. A.—A Free Man's Books. Peter Pauper, N.Y., 1942.

MACLEOD, R. D.—The Scottish Publishing Houses. W. and R. Holmes, 1953.

MACMILLAN, DANIEL, 1813–57; MACMILLAN, ALEXANDER, 1818–96 —Memoir of Daniel Macmillan. By Thomas Hughes. With Portrait. Crown 8vo, London, 1882.

The Life and Letters of Alexander Macmillan. By C. L. Graves. 8vo, 1910.

MACMILLAN, SIR FREDERICK—*See under Net Book Agreement.*

MACMILLAN, THE HOUSE OF (1843–1943)—By Charles Morgan. London, 1943.

A Bibliographical Catalogue of Macmillan and Co.'s Publications from 1843 to 1889. With portrait of Daniel Macmillan from an oil painting by Lowes Dickinson, and of Alexander Macmillan from an oil painting by Hubert Herkomer, R.A. 8vo, London, 1891.

MACMILLAN, LETTERS TO. *See under Nowell-Smith.*

MACMILLAN, M. K.—Selected Letters. Illus. P.p., 1893.

McMURTIE, D. C.—The Book: The Story of Printing and Book Making. Illus. O.U.P., 1943.

MADAN, F.—Books in Manuscript. Kegan Paul, 1893.

The Early Oxford Press: a Bibliography of Printing and Publishing at Oxford, 1468–1640. With Notes, Appendices, and Illustrations. 8vo, Oxford, 1900.

A Chart of Oxford Printing, 1468–1900. With Notes and Illustrations. 4to, Oxford, 1903. *Deals mainly with the Oxford University Press. Contains a list of Oxford printers and publishers, 1481–1900.*

A Brief Account of the University Press at Oxford. With Illustrations. Oxford, 1908.

Oxford Books. A Bibliography of Printed Works relating to the University and City of Oxford, or printed and published there. Vols 1 and 2, 1895–1912.

See also under Dorne, John; and McKerrow, R. B.

MAGGS BROTHERS LTD—The House of Maggs. Illustrated Pamphlet. London, 1939.

MANCHESTER GUARDIAN—Publishers of Distinction: Supplement to *Manchester Guardian Weekly,* 1932. *Manchester Guardian.*

MANCHESTER PUBLIC LIBRARIES. Reference Library Catalogue: Private Press Books. Manchester Public Library, 1960.

MARE, RICHARD DE LA—Publisher on Book Production. Dent, 1936.

MARE, WALTER DE LA—An Introduction to 'Everyman'. Dent, 1938.

MARSTON, EDWARD, 1824–1914—Copyright, National and International, from the point of View of the Publisher. Sampson, Low, 1879.

Copyright, National and International, with some remarks of position of Authors and Publishers. Sampson, Low, 1877.

Sketches of Booksellers of other days. With 9 Illustrations. F'cap. 8vo, London, 1901.

Sketches of some Booksellers of the Time of Dr Samuel Johnson. With 9 Illustrations. F'cap. 8vo, London, 1902. *In chap. vii will be found an interesting account, by Robert Bowes, of Cambridge, of a Booksellers' Club, 1805–11, 'The Friends of Literature', taken from the minute-book and a collection of letters and receipted accounts bought at the sale of the Phillips MSS.*

After Work: Fragments from the Workshop of an Old Publisher. By Edward Marston. With Portraits. London, 1904. *In an appendix, Mr Marston gives a list of the London publishers and booksellers 'whom I remember over fifty years ago'.*

MARTIN, J., 1791–1855—Bibliographical Catalogue of Privately Printed Books, 8vo, London, 1834; Second Edition, 1854. *Includes the productions of the Bannatyne, Maitland and Roxburghe Clubs, and the chief private presses of the day.*
Martin was a London bookseller, but retired from business in 1826 and ten years later became librarian to the Duke of Bedford.

MASON, A. F.—Address of Annual Conference of Associate Booksellers. B.A., 1945.

MASON, J. H.—A Selection from the Notebook of a Scholar Printer, made by his son, John Mason. Illus. Twelve by Eight, Leicester, 1961.

MASON, K.—Publishers' Directory, 1963. K. Mason.
Mason's Publishers: An Annotated Directory of the Publishing Trade. Third revised edition. P. Milward ed. K. Mason, 1969.

MASSEY, H. G.—During Six Reigns, 1776–1926. H. & M. Massey, 1826.

MATHESON, CYRIL—Catalogue of the Publications of Scottish Historical and Kindred Clubs and Societies, 1908–1927. Aberdeen, 1928. *A Supplement to Professor Sandford Terry's Catalogue.*

MATHIAS, THOMAS JAMES, 1754?–1835 (reputed author)—The Pursuits of Literature, a Satirical Poem in Four Dialogues, with Notes. To which are added an Appendix; the citations translated; and a Complete Index. Sixteenth Edition. 8vo, London, 1812.

MAUNSELL, ANDREW—*See under Catalogues.*

MAY, J. LEWIS—John Lane and the Nineties. London, 1936.

MELCHER, F. G.—So you Want to Get into Book Publishing. Bowker: Whitaker, 1956.

MELCHER, F. G., and others—Successful Bookshop. Revised edition. Bowker, 1951.

MELVILLE, L.—Life and Letters of William Cobbett. 2 vols, John Lane, 1913.

MEN OF THE REIGN. Edited by Thomas Humphry Ward. Crown 8vo, London, 1885.

MENZIES, JOHN & CO. LTD—The House of Menzies. P.p., 1958.
The Menzies Group. John Menzies, 1965.

MERRYWEATHER, F. SOMNER—Bibliomania in the Middle Ages, etc. 1849.

METHUEN, SIR ALGERNON, 1856–1926—Sir Algernon Methuen, Baronet: A Memoir. Privately printed, London, 1925.

MEYNELL, SIR FRANCIS—The Nonesuch Centenary: A History, with bibliography by Desmond Flower and 'appraisement' by A. J. A. Symons. London, 1935.
English Printed Books. London, 1947.
My Lives. Illus. Bodley Head, 1971.

MILLER, B. M.—Illustrators of Children's Books, 1946–56. Illus. Horn Books Inc.; Stevens and Brown, 1959.

MILLER, GEORGE, 1770–1835—Latter Struggles in the Journey of Life; or, the Afternoon of my Days: ... Illustrating ... the real life of a country Bookseller, who exercised that Profession in his little Provincial Locality (Dunbar, East Lothian) ... 8vo, Edinburgh, 1833.

MILLER, GEORGE, Bookseller of Dunbar, 1770–1835, and JOHN MILLER, Printer and Publisher, 1778–1852, Bibliography of. *See articles by T. F. U(nwin)*, '*Notes and Queries*', *10 S. xii, 1, 42, 374.*

MILLERS, THE, OF HADDINGTON, DUNBAR, AND DUNFERMLINE— By W. J. Couper. 8vo, London, 1914.

MILLER, THOMAS, 1808–74—*See Notes and Queries, 8 S. v, 124, 251, 314, 372; Thomas Cooper's 'Autobiography', 1872; and Amcoats' Gainsborough Annual, 1892, article by C. Bonnell.*
   The 'Basket-Maker Poet' was a bookseller in Newgate Street and afterwards on Ludgate Hill.

MILLER, WILLIAM—The Book Industry. Columbia U.P., 1949.

MILNE, J.—A London Book Window. John Lane, 1924.
   Printer's Devil, or How Books Happen. Epworth, 1948.

MILNE, JAMES—A Library of To-day (Boots). Reprinted from the *Cornhill* for private circulation, n.d.

MILTON, JOHN, 1608–74—Areopagitica: or, A Speech for the Liberty of Unlicenc'd Printing. 1644.

MINERVA PRESS—*See Blakey, Dorothy.*

MORAN, J.—Wynkyn de Worde: Father of Fleet Street. W. de W. Society, 1960.

MORGAN, CHARLES—*See under Macmillan.*

MORGAN, F. C.—Hereford Bookseller's Catalogue of 1695. F. C. Morgan, 1943.

MORGAN, PAUL—Warwickshire Printed Notices, 1799–1866. Illus. Dugdale Society, 1970.

MORGAN, R. C., HIS LIFE AND TIMES—By his son, George E. Morgan. 8vo, London, 1909.
   Founder of the firm of Morgan and Chase, afterwards Morgan and Scott.

MORGAN AND SCOTT—The House of Morgan and Scott Ltd. Illus. Marshall, Morgan & Scott, 1915.

MORISON, STANLEY—The Art of the Printer. London, 1925.
   John Bell, 1745–1832—Bookseller, Printer, Publisher, Typefounder, Journalist, etc. Cambridge University Press, 1930.
   John Fell: The University Press and the 'Fell' Types. O.U.P., 1967.
   Four Centuries of Fine Printing. Illus. Benn, 1960.

MORISON, STANLEY, AND JACKSON, HOLBROOK—A Brief Survey of Printing History and Practice. London, 1923.

MORISONS, THE, OF PERTH: A NOTABLE PUBLISHING HOUSE (*c.* 1770–1874). By John Minto. *See the 'Library', June 1900.*

MUDIE'S LIBRARY—*See Preston, W. C.*

MUIR, P. H.—Book Collecting. Cassell, 1949.
   Minding My Own Business: An Autobiography. Illus. Chatto & Windus, 1956.

MUMBY, F. A.—The Romance of Bookselling. With a Bibliography of Publishing and Bookselling, by W. H. Peet. With Illustrations. 8vo, London, 1910.
   Re-written and brought up-to-date in *Publishing and Bookselling*: A History from the Earliest Times to the Twentieth Century. 8vo, London,

1930. Re-issued in Academy Books, 1934; new and revised edition, 1956.

The House of Routledge, 1834–1934. With a History of Kegan Paul, Trench, Trübner and other Associated Firms. London, 1934.

MUMBY, F. A., AND STALLYBRASS, FRANCES H. S.—From Swan Sonnenschein to George Allen & Unwin. Allen & Unwin, 1955.

MURRAY, JOHN (HOUSE OF)—A Publisher and his Friends: Memoir and Correspondence of the late John Murray (II) (1778–1843), with an account of the Origin and Progress of the House, 1768–1843. By Samuel Smiles. With portraits. 2 vols, 8vo, London, 1891.

See vol. i of 'Portraits of Public Characters', by Author of 'Random Recollections of the Lords and Commons' (James Grant) 2 vols, Crown 8vo, London, 1841.

A series of articles by F. Espinasse appeared in the *Critic*, 7, 14, 21, 28 January 1860. Also an article by the same writer, with portraits and other illustrations, in *Harper's Magazine*, September 1885.

Bookman, special article with portraits and other illustrations, February 1901.

Public Opinion, 5 February 1904; *Temple Bar*, art. by W. Fraser Rae, vol. xcii, pp. 343–61; *M.A.P.*, 23 November 1901; *Sketch*, 4 July 1894, 29 November 1899.

John Murray (III) (1808–1892), *The Times, Daily Telegraph, Daily News*, 14 April 1892. 'A Brief Memoir', by John Murray (IV), 8vo, London, 1920.

The Origin and History of 'Murray's Handbooks'. By John Murray (III) *Murray's Magazine*, November 1889.

From the Archives of Albemarle Street. By George Paston. *A series of articles covering the reign of John Murray III. Published serially in the 'Cornhill' beginning August 1930. Reprinted by John Murray in 1932 under the title 'At John Murray's': Records of a Literary Circle, 1834–92.*

MURRAY, JOHN, LTD—Catalogue Illustrative of the History of the House of Murray. Murray, 1931.

John Murray and A. H. Hallam Versus Walter and others. Murray, 1908.

John Murray (IV), 1851–1928. *The Times, Daily Telegraph*, 1 December 1928. 'In Memoriam', a Tribute, by C. E. L. (C. E. Lawrence) in the *Quarterly Review*, January 1929.

John Murray, 50 Albemarle Street, 1768–1930. An illustrated *brochure*, commemorating changes in the historic publishing office. Privately printed, 1930.

MYERS, ROBIN (ed.)—Handlist of Books and Periodicals. Articles on British Book Design Since the War. Galley Club: Collins, 1967.

NAIRN, A.—Jacob's Ladder: A Sermon. Associated Booksellers, 1927.

NASH, EVELEIGH—I Liked the Life I Lived. 1941.

NATESAN, B.—In the Service of the Nation. Illus. Natesan, Madras, 1947.

NATION AND ATHENAEUM—Books and the Public. Hogarth, 1927.

NATIONAL BOOK COUNCIL—Booksellers' Reference Library. N.B.C., 1929.

The Cheapest Amusement. N.B.C., 1935.

Memorandum on Co-operative Advertising for the Book Trade. N.B.C., 1930.

National Book Council to National Book League. A Plan for Development. N.B.C., 1944.

Report on Plan for Increasing National Interest in Books. N.B.C., 1934.

Script for the Visual and Sound Sequences of the Documentary Film *Cover to Cover*. Shenval Press, 1938.

A Survey of Fourteen Years' Work, N.B.C., 1940.

The Battle of the Books. Recording the successful campaign against the Purchase Tax in 1940. N.B.C., 1940.

See also under Catalogues.

NATIONAL BOOK COUNCIL AND A.B.G.B.I. SALES PROMOTION COMMITTEE—Proposal for a Classified Index of New Books. N.B.C., 1927.

NATIONAL BOOK LEAGUE—An Appeal to Bookmen. Illus. N.B.L., 1950.

Books and Readers. N.B.L., 1945.

Books about Books: Catalogue of the Library. C.U.P. for N.B.L., 1955.

Books for the Teachers and the Child. N.B.L., 1961.

British Book Production. N.B.L., 1971.

British Children's Books. N.B.L., 1964.

Next Stage. N.B.L., 1949.

Number 7. N.B.L., 1961.

Planning a Book Exhibition, illus. n.d.

Science for All. N.B.L., 1964.

Seven Albemarle Street: An Appeal to Bookmen. 1945.

Touring Exhibitions and Book Lists. 1971–2. N.B.L.

NATIONAL VIGILANCE ASSOCIATION—Pernicious Literature: Debate in the House of Commons: Trial and Conviction for the Sale of Zola's Novels. 1889.

NELSON AND SONS LTD—How Books are Made. Nelson, 1947.

NELSON, WILLIAM, 1816–87—A Memoir. By Sir Daniel Wilson, LL.D., F.R.S.E. With Portrait. Printed for private circulation. 8vo, 1889. *Contains also a sketch of Thomas Nelson, 1780–1861, the founder of the firm.*

NET BOOK AGREEMENT, 1899, AND THE BOOK WAR, 1906–8: Two Chapters in the History of the Book Trade, including a Narrative of the Dispute between The Times Book Club and the Publishers' Association. By Edward Bell, M.A., President of the Association, 1906–8. By Sir Frederick Macmillan. Privately printed, 1924.

NEWBERY, JOHN, 1713–67—A Bookseller of the Last Century: being Some Account of the Life of John Newbery, and of the Books he Published, with a Notice of the later Newberys. By Charles Welsh. 8vo. London, 1885.

Records of the House of Newbery from 1274–1910. By A. Le B. Newbery. 1911.

See Austin Dobson's 'Eighteenth-Century Vignettes', First Series (art. 'An Old London Bookseller'). London, 1906.

NEWTH, J. D.—*See under Adam and Charles Black.*

NICHOLS, JOHN, 1745–1826 (Printer, Antiquary, and for nearly fifty years Editor of the *Gentleman's Magazine*)—Memoir of. By Alexander Chalmers. *Gentleman's Magazine*, December 1826.

Biographical and Literary Anecdotes of William Bowyer. 8vo, London, 1782.

Literary Anecdotes of the Eighteenth Century. 9 vols, 8vo, London, 1812–15. *For alphabetical list of Booksellers, etc., with biographical details, see vol. iii, pp. 714–42.*

Illustrations of the Literary History of the Eighteenth Century, continued by John Bowyer Nichols. 8 vols, 8vo, London, 1817–58.

For alphabetical list of Booksellers, etc., with biographical details, see vol. viii, pp. 463–529.

Memoir of John Nichols, Esq., F.S.A. With tributes of respect to his memory. With portraits. 8vo, privately printed, 1858.

Minor Lives: A Collection of Biographies, annotated and with an introduction on John Nichols and the Antiquarian and Anecdotal Movement of the Late Eighteenth Century, by Edward L. Hart, etc. Harvard: O.U.P., 1971.

Hart has collected 28 of Nichols' biographies of antique booksellers, illustrators and designers., etc.

Memoir of John Bowyer Nichols, 1779–1863. By John Gough Nichols. *Gentleman's Magazine*, December 1863.

Memoir of the late John Gough Nichols, F.S.A. By Robert Cradock Nichols, F.S.A. With portraits. 4to, privately printed, 1874.

Historical Notices of the Worshipful Company of Stationers of London. By John Gough Nichols, Jun. 4to, London, 1861.

NICHOLSON, M.—Manual of Copyright Practice for Writers, Publishers and Agents. Second edition. O.U.P., 1956.

NICOLL, HENRY J.—Great Movements and those who Achieved Them, 1881. 'Cheap Literature: Constable, Chambers, Knight, Cassell', pp. 151–88. 'The Repeal of the Fiscal Restrictions on Literature: T. Milner Gibson, Cassell, Chambers, John Francis', pp. 265–339.

NICOLSON, A.—Memoirs of Adam Black. Second edition. Black, 1885.

NISBET, JAMES, 1785–1854—Lessons from the Life of the late James Nisbet, Publisher, London: a Study for Young Men. By the Rev. J. A. Wallace. Crown 8vo, London, 1867.

NORTH, ROGER, 1650–1733—Life of the Right Hon. Francis North, Sir Dudley North, and the Hon. and Rev. Dr. John North, vol. iii, p. 293. 8vo, London, 1826. *A reference to the Little Britain Booksellers.*

NORRIE, IAN (ed.)—The Book of Westminster. Illus. High Hill Books, 1964. *Contains essay 'A Bookman's Westminster' and essays on other subjects by G. R. Davies, Martyn Goff and J. E. Morpurgo, all contemporary bookmen.*

NORWAY AND SWEDEN: BOOK TRADE ORGANIZATION IN—*See under Unwin, Sir Stanley.*

NOWELL-SMITH, SIMON—The House of Cassell, 1848–1958. Illus. Cassell, 1958.

International Copyright Law and the Publisher in the Reign of Queen Victoria. Illus. O.U.P., 1965.

(ed.)—Letters to Macmillan. Macmillan, 1967.

'O & Y.'—The Author as Publisher, or Why Don't Authors Publish Their Own Books? Grant & Words, 1912.

O'BRIEN, M. B. — A Manual for Authors, Printers, and Publishers. London, 1890.

OLDYS, WILLIAM, 1696–1761 — A Literary Antiquary: Memoir of William Oldys, Esq., Norroy King-at-Arms. Together with his Diary, Choice Notes from his Adversaria, and an Account of the London Libraries (with Anecdotes of Collectors of Books, Remarks on Booksellers, and of the first publishers of Catalogues). [By James Yeowell.] Reprinted from *Notes and Queries*. 12mo, London, 1862.

OLIVIER, E. — Eccentric Life of Alexander Cruden. Faber, 1934.

ORCUTT, W. DANA — In Quest of the Perfect Book: Reminiscences and Reflections of a Bookman. London, 1926.

Kingdom of Books. Murray, 1927.

Master Makers of the Book. London, 1929. *The story of fine printing from the earliest days to the twentieth century.*

OVER, G., LTD — Over's Bookshop, 1928. Illus. Over, 1928.

OVERTON, GRANT — Portrait of a Publisher [William Worthen Appleton] and the first Hundred Years of the House of Appleton, 1825–1925. New York and London, 1925.

OXFORD, UNIVERSITY OF — Report of Committee of University Press. Illus. O.U.P., 1970.

OXFORD BOOKSELLERS, SOME — The *Bookmark*, Summer, 1933.

OXFORD UNIVERSITY PRESS, 1468–1926 — Some Account of the. 4to, Oxford, 1926. An official, illustrated record.

See also under Madan, F.; Hart, Horace; Hudson, Derek; and Johnson, John.

PAGE, WALTER H., of Doubleday, Page and Co., New York, 1913–18 — A Publisher's Confessions. Crown 8vo, New York, 1905. New Edition, with an Introduction by F. N. Doubleday. London and New York, 1924.

The Life and Letters of Walter H. Page, by B. J. Hendrick. London, 1922. Third vol. 1925. *Ten chapters on 'The Ruinous Policy of Large Royalties', 'Has Publishing become Commercialised?' 'The Advertising of Books', etc.*

PALIN, JOHANN PHILIP, 1760–1806 — Bookseller of Nuremberg. Shot on Napoleon's orders for publishing a pamphlet reflecting on the French. See Timperley's Dictionary, p. 824; *Notes and Queries, 11 S. x, 10, 55, 76, 131, 196.*

PARK, R. B. — Book Shops: How to Run Them. Doubleday, 1929.

PARKER, C. J. — Parker's of Oxford. Parker, 1914.

PARKER, J. W., 1792–1870 — The Opinions of certain Authors on the Bookselling Question (*i.e.*, Underselling). 8vo, London, 1852.

This is the circular letter (dated 4 May 1852) announcing Mr Peter's retirement from the Booksellers' Association, and asking for an expression of opinion from authors as to the action of the Association in refusing to supply books to undersellers.

Copies of this circular letter, together with many original replies from authors, among whom were Carlyle, Dickens, Leigh Hunt, J. S. Mill, and Herbert Spencer, are now in the possession of the Publishers' Association.

PARRY, SIR E. A. — Report of the Facts of the Copyright Action Brought by E. A. Parry against Alexander Moring and Israel Gollancz. Sherratt, 1903.

PARTINGTON, WILFRED—Thomas J. Wise in the Original Cloth: The Life and Record of the Forger of the Nineteenth-century Pamphlets. R. Hale, 1946.

PARTON, J.—Biographical Sketch of G. W. Childs. 1870.

PARTRIDGE, ERIC—The First Three Years: An Account of the Scholartis Press, with a Discursive Bibliography. London, 1930.

PARTRIDGE, R. C. B.—History of the Legal Deposit of Books Throughout the British Empire. Library Association, 1938.

'PASTON, GEORGE' (Miss E. M. Symonds)—*See under Murray, John.*

PAUL, C. KEGAN, 1828–1902—Biographical Sketches (including George Eliot and John Chapman). Crown 8vo, 1883.

Faith and Unfaith, and other Essays. (Including an article on the Production and the Life of Books) Crown 8vo, London, 1891.

Memories. Crown 8vo, London, 1899.

Publishers' Circular, 26 July 1902, Obituary Notice, with portrait.

See also under Godwin, William.

PAUL AND CO., KEGAN—*See Mumby, F. A.*

Memories of C. Kegan Paul. 1st edition reprinted with foreword by Colin Franklin. Routledge & Kegan Paul, 1971.

William Godwin, His Friends and Contemporaries. 2 vols. 1876.

PAYNE, THOMAS—At the Mews-Gate—*See Notes and Queries, 10 S. vii, 409, 492; Mathias's 'Pursuits of Literature'; Gentleman's Magazine, vol. lxix, pp. 171–2; D.N.B., art. by W. P. Courtney; and Austin Dobson's 'Eighteenth-Century Vignettes', Second Series, art. 'The Two Paynes' (Thomas Payne II, 1752–1830).*

PEACHAM, R. G.—Library and Educational Supply in Bookselling. Hutchinson, 1966.

PEDDIE, R. A.—Notes on Provincial Printers and Booksellers. Essex. Library World, September 1904.

PENDRED, J.—The Earliest Dictionary of the Book Trade. 1785. Edited by Pollard. Bibliographical Society, 1955.

PENGUIN BOOKS—Penguin's Progress, 1935–60. Penguin, 1969.

PERILS OF AUTHORSHIP . . . containing copious instruction for publishing books at the slightest possible risk. By an Old and Popular Author. 18mo, London, n.d. (?1835).

The Author's Advocate and Young Publisher's Friend: a Sequel to 'The Perils of Authorship', By an Old and Popular Author. London, n.d.

PERKINS, M. E.—Editor to Author: The Letters of Maxwell E. Perkins. Edited by J. H. Wheelock. Scribner's, 1950.

[PETHERAM, JOHN.] Reasons for establishing an Authors' Publication Society, by which Literary Labour would receive a more adequate Reward, and the Price of all New Books be much Reduced. 8vo, London, 1843.

PERTHES, FRIEDRICH CHRISTOPHER (OF GOTHA), 1772–1843— Memoirs of, 1789–1843. 2 vols. 8vo, London. 1856.

The Life of, By his Son, Clemens Theodor. Translated into English. New Edition. Crown 8vo, London, 1878.

PHELPS, ROBERT AND DEANE, PETER—The Literary Life. Illus. Chatto & Windus, 1969.

PHILIP, G.—Story of the Last Hundred Years: A Geographical Record, 1834–1934. Illus. Philip, 1934.

PHILIP, I. G.—William Blackstone and the Reform of the Oxford University Press in the 18th Century. Illus. Oxford Bib. Soc., 1957.

PHILLIPS, SIR RICHARD, 1768–1840—Memoirs of the Public and Private Life of Sir Richard Phillips. By a Citizen of London and Assistants. (? By Ralph Fell and — — Pinkerton, and by Phillips himself.) See Shorter's 'George Borrow and his Circle'. 1913, p. 88. F'cap. 8vo, London, 1808.

An Old Leicestershire Bookseller (Sir Richard Phillips). By F. S. Herne. *Journal of the Leicester Literary and Philosophical Society*, January 1893.

Walks and Talks about London. By John Timbs. 1864. Art. 'Recollections of Sir Richard Phillips'.

A Memoir appeared in the *Gentleman's Magazine*, August 1840.

PICKERING, WILLIAM, PUBLISHER, 1796–1854—A Memoir and a Hand-list of his Editions. By G. L. Keynes. London, 1924.

PIKE, G. H.—John Cassell. Illus. Cassell, 1894.

PINTRESS, V. G.—Publishing: Crisis or Chaos? A. J. Philip, 1938.

PITMAN, A.—Half a Century of Commercial Education and Publishing. Illus. P.p., 1932.

PITMAN, SIR ISAAC, & SONS LTD—The House of Pitman, 1930. Illus. Pitman, 1930.

PITMAN, SIR ISAAC, THE LIFE OF (1813–97)—By Alfred Baker. With 50 illustrations. 8vo, London, 1908.

PLANT, A.—Economic Aspects of Copyright in Books. London School of Economics, 1934.

The New Commerce in Ideas and Intellectual Property. Athlone Press, 1953.

Supply of Foreign Books in U.K. Library Association, 1949.

PLANT, MARJORIE—The English Book Trade: An Economic History. London, 1939.

PLANTIN FAMILY (Antwerp), 1514–1876—Christophe Plantin, Imprimeur Anversois. Par Max Rooses. Illustrée de plusieurs centaines gravures, portraits, vues, lettrines, titres de livres, frontispieces. Royal 8vo, Antwerp, 1897.

Annales de l'Imprimerie Plantinienne. Par—Backer et Ruelens. Brussels, 1865.

Correspondance de Plantin. Editée par Max Rooses. 2 vols. Ghent, 1884–6.

La Maison Plantin. Par Degeorge. Troisième édition. Paris, 1886.

The Plantin Museum—*Harper's Magazine*, August 1890; *Macmillan's Magazine* (art. by W. Blades), August 1878.

Catalogue du Musée Plantin–Moretus. Par Max Rooses, Conservateur du Musée. Antwerp, 1893.

PLOMER, H. R.—New Documents on English Printers and Booksellers in the Sixteenth Century. Transactions of Bibliographical Society, vol. iv. 4to, London, 1898.

St. Paul's Cathedral and its Bookselling Tenants. Art. in the *Library*, July 1902.

Abstracts from the Wills of English Printers and Stationers, 1492–1630. Printed for the Bibliographical Society. 4to, London, 1903.

Robert Wyer (fl. 1529–56), Printer and Bookseller. With Facsimiles of Types and Marks. Small 4to. Bibliographical Society, 1897.

A Dictionary of the Booksellers and Printers who were at Work in England from 1641 to 1667. Bibliographical Society, 1907; supplementary volume bringing the Record from 1668 to 1725, issued by the same society in 1922.—See art. on 'British Provincial Book-Trade, 1641–6', *Notes and Queries*, 10 S. x, 141.

Notices of English Stationers in the Archives of the City of London. Transactions of Bibliographical Society, vol. vi, 1901.

The Booksellers of London Bridge. (The *Library*, New Series, vol. iv, 1903.) *See also under Bibliographica; Duff, E. Gordon; McKerrow, R. B.; and Wyer, Robert.*

PLUNKETT, H. M.—Life of Josiah Gilbert Holland. Scribner, 1894.

POCOCK, A. T. G.—A Survey of Distribution Times. P.A., 1963.

POETRY BOOKSHOP, THE—See article by Ernest Rhys, *Everyman*, 21 March 1932. Also under Grant, Joy.

POLITICAL AND ECONOMIC PLANNING—Economics of Book Publishing. P.E.P., 1951.

Publishing and Bookselling. P.E.P., 1956.

POLLARD, A. W.—Commercial Circulating Libraries and the Price of Books. Bibliographical Society, 1929.

Last Words on the Title-Page. London, 1891.

Westminster Hall and its Booksellers.—Art. in the *Library*, October 1905.

'Book-collecting' and 'Bibliography' articles in *Encyclopaedia Britannica*. Eleventh Edition, 1910–11.

POLLARD, A. W., AND REDGRAVE, G. R.—A Short-Title Catalogue of Books printed in England, Scotland and Ireland . . . 1475–1640 . . . Bibliographical Society, London, 1926.

See also under Bibliographica; and Book Auctions in England.

POLLARD, H. GRAHAM—English Market for Printed Books. Sanders Lecture in Bibliography. H. R. Creswick: Univ. Library, Cambridge, 1960.

POPE, ALEXANDER, 1688–1744—The Dunciad, 1728–9. *Mentions Edmund Curll, John Dunton, Bernard Lintot, Thomas Osborne, Jacob Tonson, etc.*

PORTRAITS OF PUBLIC CHARACTERS—By the Author of 'Random Recollections of the Lords and Commons' (James Grant, 1802–72, editor of the *Morning Advertiser*). 2 vols. Crown 8vo, London, 1841. *See vol. ii for John Murray and Thomas Tegg.*

POWELL, L. C.—. . . And Brown. P.p., Stevens and Brown, 1959.

POWER, JOHN—A Handy Book about Books for Book-Lovers, Book-Buyers, and Book-Sellers. London, 1870.

PRATT, J. B.—Century of Book Publishing, 1838–1938. Illus. Barnes & Noble, 1938.

PRATT, R. D.—A Thousand Books on Books. R. D. Pratt, Weston-Super-Mare, 1967.

PRESTON, W. C.—Mudie's Library. Reprinted from *Good Words*. October 1894.

PRINCE, J. H., Bookseller—His Life, Adventures, Pedestrian Excursions, and Singular Opinions. 12mo, 1806.

PRINTERS—*For information as to the connection of the early printers with publishers and booksellers, see Bigmore and Wyman's 'Bibliography of Printing', 3 vols, 1880–86.*

The Revival of Printing: A Bibliographical Catalogue of Works issued by the chief modern English Presses. With an Introduction by R. Steele. The Medici Society, London, 1912.

Modern Book Production: *Studio* Monograph. London, 1928.

The Times Literary Supplement Printing Number, 13 October 1927. Including Chapters on Bindings, Illustrations, and other aspects of Modern Book Production. Reprinted by *The Times*. London, 1927.

Printing in the Twentieth Century: A Survey. Reprinted from the Special Number of *The Times*, 29 October 1929. London, 1830. Including Chapters on fine Editions, the Size of Books, Private Printing Presses, and other Allied Topics, as well as the History of Printing at Home and Abroad.

The Times Commemoration of the 500th Anniversary of the Invention of Printing. Special Supplement. 15 February 1940.

Select Bibliography of the Principal Modern Presses, Public and Private, in Great Britain. G. S. Tomkinson, First Edition Club. London, 1928.

Private Presses and their Books. By Will Ransome, New York, 1927.

For the whole subject of printing, see Catalogue of the William Blades Library, 1899, and Catalogue of the Passmore Edwards Library, 1897. These are both compiled by John Southward. The two collections of books are in the library of the St Bride Foundation Institute, Bride Lane, London, E.C.

For 'Title-Page' see Pollard (A.W.). See also under Morison, Stanley; and Jackson, Holbrook.

PRINTERS' AND BOOKSELLERS' 'PRIVILEGES' AND LICENCES OF THE OLDEN TIMES: I. General: II. England; III–IV. Scotland. *British and Colonial Printer and Stationer*, 17 January, 7 March, 23 May, 25 July 1907.

PRIVATE BOOK COLLECTORS IN THE U.S. AND CANADA. Bowker, 1953.

PUBLIC OPINION—Fifteen Articles on 'The Leading Publishers', 5 February to 13 May 1904.

PUBLISHERS' ADVERTISING: Being the Reactions of a Practising Publisher–Advertiser to the Exhortations of non-Publisher Theorists. Based on articles first published in 'Constable's Monthly List'. 8vo, London, 1930.

The Reactions of a Practising Publisher–Advertiser to the Exhortations of Non-publisher Theorists. 56 pp. 8vo, London, 1930. *A detailed account of the problem, with its social and moral, as well as its economic implications. See also under Sadleir, Michael.*

PUBLISHERS ASSOCIATION (THE LONDON), founded 1896—List of Members and Rules, published annually.

Book Distribution: A Handbook for Booksellers and Publishers. P.A., 1961.

Book Production War Economy Agreement. P.A., 1942.

Book Publishing as a Career for University Graduates. P.A., 1950.

Book Tokens: A Statement. Pamphlet, 1943.

Canada, the Market for British Books. Third edition. P.A., 1952.

Getting into Publishing. P.A.

Guide to Royalty Agreements. Third edition. P.A., 1952.

How to Obtain British Books. P.A., 1955.

Joint Committee Reports, 1928–9.

Purchase Tax and Books. P.A., 1940.

Report on the Book Trade in U.S. and Canada. P.A., 1943.

Report on Granting of Trade Terms (Home). P.A., 1928.

Regulations for the Book Clubs. P.A., 1939.

Report and Recommendations on the Operations of Book Clubs. P.A., 1938.

Supply of Books to Schools. P.A.

The Times and the Publishers. P.A., 1906.

Trade Follows the Book. P.A., 1945.

See also Book Trade Organization; Book Tokens; and Book Clubs.

PUBLISHERS ASSOCIATION AND NATIONAL BOOK COUNCIL. Book Trade Statistics. Interim Report. 1939.

PUBLISHERS ASSOCIATION AND SOCIETY OF AUTHORS—Photocopying and the Law. P.A.

PUBLISHERS AND THEIR ADDRESSES. Issued annually. Whitaker.

PUBLISHERS' CIRCULAR, THE, 1837.

PUBLISHERS' MARKS (Books and Book-plates). Vol. iv. 1903–4.

PUBLISHERS AND PUBLISHING A HUNDRED YEARS AGO. From Materials collected by Aleck Abrahams. With some Notes by E. Marston. *Publishers' Circular*, 6, 13 January 1906.

PUBLISHERS' WEEKLY, New York. *See throughout for obituary notices, etc.*

PUTNAM, GEORGE HAVEN—Memories of My Youth, 1844–65. New York and London, 1914.

Memories of a Publisher, 1865–95. New York and London, 1915.

Authors and Publishers. Containing a Description of Publishing Methods and Arrangements, etc. First edition, post 8vo, New York and London, 1883; seventh edition, post 8vo, New York and London, 1900.

Authors and their Public in Ancient Times: a Sketch of Literary Conditions and of the Relations with the Public of Literary Producers, from the Earliest Times to the Fall of the Roman Empire. 12mo, first edition, New York and London, 1893; 12mo, third edition, revised, New York and London, 1896.

Books and their Makers during the Middle Ages: a Study of the Conditions of the Production and Distribution of Literature from the Fall of the Roman Empire to the Close of the Seventeenth Century. 2 vols. 8vo, New York and London, 1897.

International Copyright. Putnam, 1879.

Question of Copyright. Third edition. Putnam, 1904.

PUTNAM, GEORGE PALMER, 1814–72—A Memorial of George Palmer Putnam, together with a Record of the Publishing House founded by him. Privately printed, New York, 1903. New edition, New York and London, 1912.

PUTNAM, G. P.—Wide Margins: A Publisher's Autobiography. Harcourt, Brace, 1942.

QUARITCH, BERNARD, 1819–99—U(lm), A(dolph). Bernard Quaritch in London. Separat-Abdruck aus Petzholdt's *Neuern Anzeiger für Bibliographie und Bibliothek-wissenschaft*, Heft 11. 8vo, Dresden, 1880.

(Wyman, C.) B. Q., a Bibliographical Fragment. (24 copies printed.) 16mo, London, 1880.

Bernard Quaritch's Annual Trade Sale, 1885. Karl W. Hiersemann. Sonder-Abdruck aus dem *Börsenblatt für den Deutschen Buchhändel*, No. 265. 8vo, Leipzig, 1885.

Mr Bernard Quaritch, the eminent Bibliographer. By F. M. Holmes. With portrait. *Great Thoughts*, Third Series, vol. ix, No. 226. London, 1897.

Bernard Quaritch's Semi-Centennial. With portrait. *Publishers' Weekly*, vol. lii, No. 19. New York, 1897.

A Catalogue of Books and Manuscripts Issued to Commemorate the One Hundredth Anniversary of the Firm of Bernard Quaritch, 1847–1947.

With a Portrait Study of the Founder by his Daughter, Charlotte Quaritch Wrentmore. Quaritch, 1947.

QUARITCH LTD—One Hundredth Anniversary. 1847–1947. Quaritch, 1947.

QUARTERLY REVIEW—The History of Bookselling in England. January 1892.

RAE, T. AND HANDLEY-TAYLOR, GEOFFREY—The Book of the Private Presses. Signet Press, n.d.

RALPH, JAMES, 1705 (?)–62—The Case of Authors by Profession or Trade Stated; in Regard to Booksellers, the Stage, and the Public. 8vo, London, 1758.

RAMSAY, ALLAN, 1688–1758—Poems, with a Memoir by George Chalmers. 2 vols, 8vo, London, 1800.

Life. By Oliphant Smeaton. Crown 8vo, Edinburgh, 1892.

Celebrated as the author of 'The Gentle Shepherd', Allan Ramsay deserted his first business as a wigmaker for that of bookseller and publisher.

RANSOME, W.—Private Presses and their Books. Bowker: Whitaker, 1929.

RAWLINGS, G. B.—The Story of Books. Hodder, 1901.

RAYMOND, HAROLD—Publishing and Bookselling. Dent, 1938.

Trade or Profession. Society of Bookmen, 1933.

See also under Book Trade Handbook, 1937; and Dent Memorial Lectures.

REDGRAVE, G. R.—*See under Pollard, A. W.*

REED, A. H. AND A. W.—The House of Reed. A. H. Reed: Bailey Brothers, 1957.

Books are my Business. Illus. Educational Explorers, 1966.

T. A.—Biography of Isaac Pitman, Inventor of Phonography. Illus. Griffith, Farron, Okeden and Welsh, 1890.

REES, THOMAS, 1777–1864, and BRITTON, JOHN, 1771–1857—Reminiscences of Literary London from 1779 to 1853. With Interesting Anecdotes of Publishers, Authors, and Book Auctioneers of that Period. Privately printed, 1853. New edition, 'Edited by a Book-Lover', London, 1896.

RELIGIOUS TRACT SOCIETY—The Jubilee Memorial of the Religious Tract Society, containing a Record of its Origin, Proceedings, and Results, A.D. 1799 to A.D. 1849. By William Jones, Corresponding Secretary. Large 8vo, London, 1850.

The Story of the Religious Tract Society for One Hundred Years. By Samuel G. Green, D.D. 8vo, London, 1899.

RÉPERTOIRE INTERNATIONAL DE LA LIBRAIRIE. International Directory of the Book Trade, 1912. Berne. Congrès International des Editeurs.

RESULTS OF BOOKSELLING, 1948–52, a Report of an Investigation made by Messrs Chalmers, Wade. B.A., 1953.

RHYS, ERNEST—Everyman Remembers. Illus. Dent, 1931.

RICHARDS, GRANT—Memories of a Misspent Youth (1872–96). Introduction by Max Beerbohm. London, 1932.

Author Hunting by an Old Sportsman: Memories of Years mainly spent in Publishing (1887–1925). Hamish Hamilton, 1934. New edition, Unicorn Press, 1960.

RICHARDSON, SAMUEL, 1689–1761—The Correspondence of Samuel Richardson. With Memoir by Mrs A. L. Barbauld. 6 vols, Crown 8vo, London, 1804.

The Collected Works of Samuel Richardson. With a Sketch of his Life by the Rev. E. Mangin. 19 vols. Crown 8vo, London, 1811.

Samuel Richardson: a Biographical and Critical Study. By Clara Linklater Thomson. With portrait. Crown 8vo, London, 1900.

Miss Thomson's book has a full Bibliography of Richardsoniana.

RIDDELL, J. R.—A Few Historical Notes on the Worshipful Company of Stationers. St Bride Foundation Printing School, 1921.

RIDGE, L.—A Scheme for Promoting the Interests of the Country Booksellers and Publishers. 4to, Grantham, 1868.

RIVINGTON, C. R.—*See under Stationers' Company.*

RIVINGTON, HOUSE OF—The House of Rivington. By Septimus Rivington. 8vo, London, 1894. Second enlarged edition, 1919.

Publishers' Circular, 15 January 1885; 2 June 1890. *The Bookseller,* January 1885; 6 June 1890.

RIVINGTON, R. T.—*See under Stationers' Company.*

RIVINGTON, S.—Publishing Family of Rivington. Illus. Rivingtons, 1919.

ROBERTS, D. KILHAM—*See under Author's Handbook; and Hampden, John.*

ROBERTS, S. C.—A History of the Cambridge University Press, 1521–1921. Cambridge, 1921.

The Evolution of Cambridge Publishing. C.U.P., 1956.

ROBERTS, WILLIAM—The Earlier History of English Bookselling. Crown 8vo, London, 1889; new and cheaper edition, London, 1892.

Printers' Marks, 8vo, 1893.

'The Book-hunter in London'. 8vo, 1895.

Book-Verse: Anthology of Poems of Books, etc. 8vo, 1896.

Catalogues of English Book-Sales. Reproduced from *Notes and Queries*. 8vo, 1900.

Bookselling in the Poultry. *City Press*, 16 August 1890.

ROBERTSON, G. S.—Law of Copyright. O.U.P., 1912.

RODD, THOMAS, Bookseller of Great Newport Street. (Thomas Rodd I, 1763–1802 (?); Thomas Rodd II, 1796–1849.)—*See 'Gentleman's Magazine', June 1849; 'Morning Post', 24 April 1849; 'Morning Herald', 18 July 1851; 'Evening Standard', 30 April 1849; 'Athenaeum', 28 April 1849; 'Literary Gazette', 28 April 1849.*

ROLFE, FREDERICK (WILLIAM), BARON CORVO—Letters to Leonard Moore. Edited with introduction by Cecil Woolf and Rabbi Bertram W. Korn. Limited edition. Vane, 1960.

ROLPH, C. H.—The Trial of Lady Chatterley. Penguin, 1961.

ROME—The Book Trade of Ancient Rome. See *Book-Lore* vol. iv, p. 121, London, 1886.

ROSENBACH, A. S. W.—Books and Bidders: The Adventures of a Bidder, 1928.

ROSNER, CHARLES—The Growth of the Book Jacket. Sylvan Press, 1954.

ROSSETTI, D. G.—Letters to his Publisher, F. S. Ellis. Edited by Doughty. Limited edition. Scholartis Press, 1928.

RUBINSTEIN, MICHAEL—Wicked, Wicked Libels. Routledge & Kegan Paul, 1972.

RUDDIMAN, THOMAS, 1674–1757 (Book auctioneer, printer, Latin grammarian)—The Life of Thomas Ruddiman, Keeper for almost Fifty Years of the Library belonging to the Faculty of Advocates at Edinburgh. By George Chalmers. 8vo, London, 1794.

RUSKIN, JOHN, 1819–1900—Fors Clavigera, 1871–84. (The References are to the numbers of the letters.)

The Author's Battle with Booksellers, a Losing Game at First, but now nearly won, 62; and those they hire, 89.

Bookselling Trade, Author's principles as managed by Mr Allen, 6, 11, 16, 62, 89 (and see Notes and Correspondence, 10, 14, and 15).

Publishing and Bookselling Trade, abuses of, 53, 57.

Ruskin and his Books. An Interview with his Publisher. (*Strand Magazine*, December 1902.)

RYDER, JOHN—The Bodley Head, 1887–1957. Privately circulated, 1971.

RYLANDS, W. H.—Booksellers in Warrington, 1639, 1657. Proceedings of Liverpool Historic Society, vol. xxxvii. 8vo, Liverpool, 1888.

SADLEIR, MICHAEL—Authors and Publishers: A Study in Mutual Esteem. Dent, 1932.

Bentley's Standard Novel Series: Its History and Achievement. Reprinted from *The Colophon*, 1932.

The Evolution of Publishers' Binding Styles. London, 1930. No. 1 of

'Bibliographia', a series, edited by Michael Sadleir, devoted to 'Studies in Book History and Book Structure, 1750–1900'.

Minerva Press Publicity. Bibliographical Society, 1940.

Nineteenth-Century Fiction: A Bibliographical Record Based on his own Collection. 2 vols. Constable: California University Press, 1951.

Publishers' Advertising. A detailed account, with its social and moral, as well as its economic implications. London, 1930.

See also under Carter, John; and Dent Memorial Lectures.

SANDERS, F. D.—*See British Book Trade Organization.*

SAWYER, C. J. AND DARTON, F. J. H.—English Books, 1475–1900: Signposts for Collectors. 2 vols, Westminster, 1927.

SAYLE, R. T. D.—Notes on the South East Corner of Chancery Lane. 1119–1929. Illus. Sweet & Maxwell. 1929.

SCHLEMMINGER, J.—German–English–French Dictionary for Book Trade and Library Use. Second revised edition. Bailey Bros.

SCHOLES, J. C.—Bolton Bibliography and Jottings of Book-Lore. With Notes on Local Authors and Printers. 12mo, Manchester, 1886.

SCINTILLA, or a Light Broken into Darke Warehouses. With Observations upon the Monopolists of Seaven Severall Patents and Two Charters. Practised and Performed by a mysterie of some Printers, Sleeping Stationers and Combining Booksellers. 4to, London, 1641.

SCOTT, SIR WALTER, 1771–1832—The Life of Sir Walter Scott. By John Gibson Lockhart.

And see Ballantyne, House of. Also under Constable, Archibald, and Carswell, Donald.

SCRIBNERS, CHARLES, AND SONS LTD. Illus. Scribners, 1931.

SEELEY, J. J.—The Profitable Lending Library: How It Should Be Run. Seeley, Service, 1936.

SEELEY, THE HOUSE OF—The *Bookman*, with portraits, April 1904.

SHAYLOR, JOSEPH—On the Selling of Books. *Nineteenth Century*, December 1896.

Booksellers and Bookselling. *Nineteenth Century*, May 1899.

On the Life and Death of Books. *Chambers's Journal*, 1 July 1899.

Bookselling and the Distribution of Books. *Literature*, 9 February 1901.

Sixty Years of Bookselling. *Publishers' Circular*, 5 June 1897.

A Few Words upon Book Titles. *Publishers' Circular*, 27 November 1897.

Bookselling and some of its Humours. *Publishers' Circular*, 5 March 1898.

Fiction: Its Classification and Fashion. *Publishers' Circular*, 14 May 1898.

The Revolution in Educational Literature. *Publishers' Circular*, 13 August 1899.

Some Old Libraries. *Publishers' Circular*, 14 January 1899.

More Bookish Humour. *Publishers' Circular*, 12 May 1899.

On the Manufacture of Books. *Publishers' Circular*, 17 November 1900.

On the Decline in Religious Books. *Sunday Magazine*, June 1898.

Hymns, Hymn-Writers, and Hymn-Books. *Young Man*, June 1899.

The Problem of Titles. *Book Monthly*, November 1903.

Booksellers' Trade Dinner Sales. *Fortnightly Review*, December 1907.

The Fascination of Books. *Odd Volume*, 1908.

Reprints and their Readers. *Cornhill Magazine*, April 1905.

The Christmas Book. *Cornhill Magazine*, December 1905.

The Issue of Fiction. *Publishers' Circular*, 15 October 1910.

Two articles on 'Bookselling' and 'Publishing', with notices of British and American publishing houses. *Encyclopaedia Britannica*, tenth edition. Supplementary volumes, vols. iv and viii.

Some Thoughts on Bookselling: Its Past and its Future. *Publishers' Circular* (written in the Spring of 1915). 4 March 1916.

Most of the above were collected by the author in 'The Fascination of Books', 1912; 'The Pleasures of Bookland', 1912; and 'Sixty Years a Bookman', 1923.

SHEAVYN, PH.—Writers and the Publishing Trade, *c.* 1600. *See the 'Library', October 1906.*

SHEEHAN, D. H.—This was Publishing. Indiana U.P., 1952.

SHEFFIELD PUBLIC LIBRARIES. Book Printed by John Garnet, Sheffield's First Known Printer. City Libraries, 1969.

SHEPARD, ERNEST HOWARD—Drawn From Life. Illus. Methuen, 1961.

SIMPKIN MARSHALL LTD—The Lending Library: How to Run it for Profit. Second edition, Simpkin Marshall, 1930.

Simpkin's: Origin and Progress. Illus. Simpkin Marshall, 1924.

SIMPSON, W.—Old Inverness Booksellers. Carruthers, Inverness, 1931.

SISSON AND PARKER LTD—A Short Account 1854–1924. Illus. Sisson & Parker, 1924.

SMEATON, O.—Life of Allan Ramsay. 1892.

SMELLIE, WILLIAM, 1740–95—Memoirs of the Life, Writings, and Correspondence of William Smellie, F.R.S., late Printer in Edinburgh, etc. By Robert Kerr, F.R.S. With portrait. 2 vols, 8vo, Edinburgh, 1811.

Partner with W. Creech (q.v.) and friend of Robert Burns. Smellie was the first editor of the 'Encyclopaedia Britannica'.

SMILES, SAMUEL, 1816–1904—Authors and Publishers. *Murray's Magazine*, January–February 1890.

See also under Murray, House of.

SMITH, ELDER AND CO.—The *Sketch*, with portraits and illustrations, 3 July 1895. The *Bookman*, with illustrations, October 1901. The *King*, with portrait of Mr Reginald Smith, 18 January 1902. *Public Opinion*, 12 February 1904.

The House of Smith, Elder. By Dr. Leonard Huxley. London, 1923. *A privately printed history of the firm throughout the hundred years of its existence from 1816 to 1916. Leonard Huxley, as literary adviser and editor of the 'Cornhill', was associated with the late Reginald Smith, K.C., in the business of this firm for many years.*

SMITH, MRS E.—John White: A Memoir. Illus. Hodder, 1896.

SMITH, F. SEYMOUR—Bibliography in the Bookshop. Deutsch, 1964.

SMITH, GEORGE MURRAY, 1824–1901—Memoir of George Smith. By Sidney Lee. Prefixed to vol. i of the Supplement to the 'Dictionary of National Biography'. With portrait. Royal 8vo, London, 1901.

In Memoriam, George M. Smith. By Sir Leslie Stephen. *Cornhill Magazine*, May 1901.

SMITH, G., AND BENGER, F.—The Oldest London Bookshop. Illus. Ellis, 1928.

SMITH, JOHN, AND SON (GLASGOW) LTD—A Short Note on a Long History, 1751–1921. Illus. P.p., John Smith, n.d.

SMITH, JOSEPH, 1819–96—Quaker, Bookseller and Bibliographer. The Journal of the Friends' Historical Society. January 1914.

SMITH, WILLIAM HENRY, 1825–91—The Life and Times of the Right Hon. William Henry Smith, M.P. By Sir Herbert E. Maxwell, Bt. With Portrait. 2 vols. 8vo, London, 1893.

SMITH, W.—Spilt Ink. Illus. Ernest Benn, 1932.

SMITH, W. H., AND SON—The *World's Work*, October 1903.

The Story of W. H. Smith and Son. By G. R. Pocklington, 1921.

The Art of Bookselling. A Collection of Eight Essays and Divers useful Hints to those who would become Good Booksellers. Printed for private circulation amongst the Managers and Assistants at W. H. Smith and Son's Bookstalls and Bookshops, 1907.

Guide for the Use of Managers of W. H. Smith's and Sons Bookshops. Illus. W.H.S., 1908.

A National Service. Illus. W.H.S., n.d.

Special Displays. Illus. W.H.S., 1914.

Viscount Hambleden, 1868–1928. Illus. P.p., n.d.

Viscount Hambleden, 25 July 1903–31, March 1948. P.p., 1950.

W. H. Smith and Son: Romance of a Great Business. W.H.S., 1931.

SMYTH, RICHARD, 1590–1675—The Obituary of Richard Smyth, Secondary of the Poultry Compter, London: being a Catalogue of all such Persons as he knew in their life: extending from A.D. 1627 to A.D. 1674. Edited by Sir Henry Ellis, K.H. Small 4to, printed for the Camden Society, 1849. Reprinted in *Willis' Current Notes*, February 1853.

'This gentleman was one of the most ardent of the book-loving maniacs of whom we have any notice during the period stated. He mentions the names of most of the early booksellers of Little Britain, Paternoster Row, and other bookshops he almost daily visited.'—Extract from Catalogue of W. Ridler, 53 High Street, Bloomsbury, W.C., 1903.

SNOW, PHEBE—How a Book is Made. Illus. Routledge & Kegan Paul, 1960.

SOCIETY OF AUTHORS—Cost of Production. S. of A., 1891.

Forms of Agreement issued by the Publishers' Association. Second edition. S. of A.

The Grievance between Authors and Publishers: the Report of the Conference, held March 1887. 8vo, London, 1887.

See also under Author's Handbook, 1940.

SOCIETY OF BOOKMEN—Co-operative Advertising of Books. S. of B., 1924.

Report of the Commercial Circulating Libraries Sub-Committee. S. of B., 1928.

The Society of Bookmen: A Short History. 1920–36. Third edition. S. of B., 1936.

SONNENSCHEIN AND CO., SWAN—The *Bookman*, February 1893.

See also under Mumby, F. A.—'The House of Routledge'.

SOTHEBY'S—*See under Hobson, G. D.*

SOTHERAN, H., LTD—Piccadilly Notes, 1933–4. Sotheran, 1934.

SOUTHAM, A. D.—From MS to Bookstall. Southam, 1894.

SOWLE, TATE—The publisher of Quaker Books in the early part of the eighteenth century. He was a very dilatory man apparently. See 'A Quaker Post Bag'. Edited by Mrs G. Locker Lampson, 8vo, 139 pp. 1910.

SPARLING, H. HALLIDAY—The Kelmscott Press and Wm Morris: Master Craftsman. London, 1924. *An intimate record based upon some ten years of close association with Morris in his numerous activities.*

SPEDDING, JAMES, 1810–1881—Publishers and Authors. Printed for the author. Crown 8vo, London, 1867. *Two papers which were intended to appear in a magazine or review, but which, from the nature of the assertions made as to certain publishing methods, were refused insertion. It is interesting to note that Mr Spedding suggests that the system of paying authors by means of a 'percentage upon the retail price of the volume sold' should be more generally adopted. This system of 'royalties' was a novelty in England when Mr Spedding wrote. He says that it was introduced to his notice by Mr H. O. Houghton, of Messrs Hurd and Houghton, of New York.*

SPENCE, JOSEPH, 1698–1768—Anecdotes, Observations, and Characters of Books and Men. 8vo, London, 1820.

SPENCER, D. H.—The Hill of Content: Books, Art, Music, People. Angus & Robertson, 1960.

SPENCER, HERBERT, 1820–1903—The Bookselling Question (1852)— Views concerning Copyright—Book-Distribution—The 'Net-Price' System of Bookselling—Publishing on Commission—American Publishers. See 'Various Fragments', enlarged edition, 8vo, London, 1900.

An Autobiography. 2 vols, 8vo, 1904.

See Index as follows: John Chapman, Williams and Norgate, Longmans and Company, Experiences of Publishing, Booksellers' Dispute with Authors in 1852.

SPENCER, W. T.—Forty Years in My Bookshop, 1923.

SPIELMANN, M. H.—Booksellers' Signs, *The Times Literary Supplement*. A series of six articles, 11 and 18 October 1917; 3 January, 7 February, 28 February, and 28 March 1918.

SPON, ERNEST—How to Publish a Book. London, 1872.

SPOTTISWOOD AND COMPANY, LTD—The Story of a Printing House: Being a short account of the Strahans and Spottiswoods. Privately printed, London, 1911. Second edition, 1912.

SPRIGGE, S. S.—Methods of Publishing. London, 1890.

SPRING, S.—Risks and Rights in Publishing, T.V., etc. Allen & Unwin, 1951.

STANDING, J.—The Private Press Today. Brewhouse, 1967.

STANFORD, EDWARD, 1827–1904—EDWARD STANFORD. With a Note on the History of the Firm, from 1852–1901. With Illustrations. 4to. Privately printed, London, 1902.

A memoir of Edward Stanford, by John Bolton, appeared in the 'Geographical Journal', December 1904.

STATIONERS' COMPANY—Extracts from the Registers of Works entered
    for Publication between 1557 and 1570. With Notes and Illustrations
    by J. Payne Collier. 2 vols, 8vo, printed for the Shakespeare Society,
    1848.
A Transcript of the Registers of the Company of Stationers of London,
    1554–1646. Edited by Edward Arber. Vols i–iv (text), royal 4to, 1875–7;
    vol. v (index), royal 4to, 1894. Privately printed, London, 1903.
Historical Notices of the Worshipful Company of Stationers of London.
    By John Gough Nichols, Jun. 4to, London, 1861.
A Short Account of the Worshipful Company of Stationers. By Charles
    Robert Rivington, Clerk to the Company. Imperial 4to. Privately
    printed, London, 1903.
The Worshipful Company of Stationers: A Short Account of its Charter,
    Hall, Plate, Registers and other matters connected with its History. By
    Reginald T. Rivington, Clerk to the Company. Privately printed, 1928.
A Short Account of the Worshipful Company of Stationers. Anonymous.
    Privately printed, 1930.
Records of the Court of the Stationers' Company, 1576–1602, from Register
    B. Edited by W. W. Greg and E. Boswell. Bibliographical Society,
    London, 1930.
Transcript of the Registers of the Company, A.D. 1554–1640, edited by
    Edward Arber. Reprinted, 5 vols. P. Smith, 1949–50.
See also Transactions of the London and Middlesex Archaeological Society, vols ii
and vi.
STAVELEY, R.—The Reader, The Writer and Copyright Law. London
    University School of Librarianship, 1957.
STEELE, R.—See under Printers.
STEINBERG, SIEGFRIED HEINRICH—Five Hundred Years of Printing.
    Illus. Faber, 1959; Penguin, 1961.
STEUART, BASIL, 1794–1886—Manager at John Murray's and publisher.
    See 'Chambers' Journal', September 1903.
STEVENS, A. A.—Recollections of a Bookman. Witherby, 1933.
STEVENS, BENJAMIN FRANKLIN, 1833–1902—Memoir of. By G. Manville
    Fenn. With 4 Portraits and 3 other Illustrations. Crown 8vo. Printed for
    private circulation, London, 1903.
STEVENS, GEORGE, AND UNWIN, STANLEY—Best Sellers: are they
    Born or Made? Concludes with Frank Swinnerton's essay on 'Authors
    and Advertising'. London, 1932.
ST JOHN-STEVAS, NORMAN—Obscenity and the Law. Secker & Warburg,
    1956.
STOCK, ELLIOT, 1837–1911—See The Times, 3 March 1911.
STOCKHAM, PETER—University Bookselling. Hutchinson, 1965.
STOKES, H. P.—Cambridge Stationers, Printers, Bookbinders, etc. 1919.
STOTT, DAVID—The Decay of Bookselling. Nineteenth Century, December
    1894.
STRAHAN, ALEXANDER—Twenty Years of a Publisher's Life. Appeared
    serially in the 'Day of Rest', 1881 (Strahan and Co.). Announced in volume form
    by Chatto & Windus, 1882, but not published.

STRAUS, RALPH—A Whip for the Women: The Present State of the Novel Market. Chapman & Hall, 1931.
See also under Baskerville, John; Dodsley, Robert; and Curll, Edmund.

STRONG, C. A. G.—The Writer's Table. Methuen, 1953.

SUCCESSFUL BOOKSELLER, THE—A Complete Guide to Success to all engaged in a retail Bookselling, Stationery, and Fancy Goods Business. 4to, London, 1906.

SUPER, R. H.—The Publication of Landor's Works. Bibliographical Society, 1954.

SUTTABY, THE FIRM OF, 1801–90—*See The Bookseller,* 5 July 1890.

SWINNERTON, FRANK—Authors and the Book Trade. London, 1932. Reprint, with new preface, 1933.
See also under Dent Memorial Lectures; Hampden, John; Stevens, George, and Book Trade Handbook, 1937.
Authors and Advertising. Constable, n.d.
The Bookman's London. Wingate, 1952; re-issued John Baker, 1970.

TAUBERT, SIGFRED—Bibliopola: Pictures and Text about the Book Trade. 2 vols. Illus. Allen Lane, Penguin Press, 1966.
The Book Trade of the World. Vol. i. Deutsch, 1972.

TAUCHNITZ, THE FIRM OF—The Tauchnitz Edition: the Story of a Popular Publisher. By Tighe Hopkins. With Illustrations. *Pall Mall Magazine,* October 1901.

TAYLOR, JOHN, Keats's Publisher—*See under Blunden, Edmund.*

TAYLOR, W. G.—The Book Market: Expansion or Deadlock. Society of Bookmen, 1937.

TAYLOR, W. G.—*See under Hampden, John.*

TEGG, THOMAS, 1776–1846—Memoir of the late Thomas Tegg. Abridged from his Autobiography by permission of his son, William Tegg. By Aleph (*i.e.* Dr Harvey of Lonsdale Square). From the *City Press* of 6 August 1870. Printed for private circulation.
See vol. ii of 'Portraits of Public Characters', by the Author (James Grant) of 'Random Recollections of the Lords and Commons'. 2 vols, Crown 8vo, London, 1841.
Thomas Tegg was generally supposed to have been the original of 'Twigg' in Hood's novel 'Tilney Hall'.

TEMPLE PRESS—*See Armstrong, A. C.*

TERRY, PROFESSOR SANDFORD—Catalogue of the Publications of Scottish Historical and Kindred Clubs and Societies, 1780–1908. Glasgow, 1909.

THAYER, J. A.—Astir: A Publisher's Life-Story. 8vo, Boston, Mass, 1910. Another edition: 'Getting On: The Confessions of a Publisher'. 8vo, London, 1911.

THIEME, H. C. A.—The Society of Authors and the Publishers. Thieme, 1893.

THIN, JAMES, 1824–1915—James Thin, 1848–1948. P.p., n.d.
Reminiscences of Booksellers and Bookselling in Edinburgh in the Time of William IV. An Address delivered to a Meeting of Booksellers' Assistants ... Edinburgh, October 1904. With a Portrait of James Thin. Post 4to. Privately printed, Edinburgh, 1905.

THOMASON, GEORGE, Bookseller, The Rose and Crown, St Paul's Church-
yard, *c.* 1602–66—Catalogue of the Pamphlets, Books, Newspapers, and
MSS, relating to the Civil War, the Commonwealth and Restoration,
1640–1661, now in the British Museum, and known as the 'Thomason
Tracts', 2 vols, Royal 8vo, London, 1908. *A life of George Thomason, by
G. K. Fortescue, is prefixed to the Catalogue.*

THOMPSON, G. C.—Remarks on the Law of Literary Property in Different
Countries. National Press Agency, 1883.

THOMS, WILLIAM JOHN, 1803–85—Curll Papers. (Notes on Edmund
Curll.) *See under Curll, Edmund.*

THOMSON, C. CAMPBELL—I Am a Literary Agent. Sampson, Low,
1951.

THOMSON, RICHARD, 1794–1865—Chronicles of London Bridge. By an
Antiquary. 8vo, London, 1827.
See ante, for 'London Bridge Booksellers'.

THORNTON, J.—A Tour of the Temple Press. Dent, 1935.

THREE ADDRESSES: An Essay in Publishing Ecology by Indiaman,
1936–47. Illus. Longmans, 1947.

THREE PROFILES—John Calder (Stuart Middleton and Christopher
Dawson); Norah Smallwood (Josephine Leahy and Angela Holland;
Anthony Blond (John Rhodes and Kathleen Kellogg). Illus. Oxford
College of Technology, 1969.

THRING, G. H.—Addenda to the Methods of Publishing. Society of
Authors, 1902.
The Marketing of Literary Property, Book and Serial Rights. Constable,
1933.

THRUSH, ARTHUR—Representative Majority: 21 Years of the Book
Publishers' Representatives Association. B.P.R.A., 1945.

'TIMES, THE'—Booksellers, the Public and the Publishers: Being a History
of *The Times* on the Warpath. Glaisher, 1906.
History of the Book War; Fair Book Prices versus Publishers' Trust Prices.
The Times, 1907.
See also under Printers.

'TIMES, THE', BOOK CLUB, AND PUBLISHERS' ASSOCIATION AND
THE ASSOCIATED BOOKSELLERS—See *The Times*, and other daily
and weekly papers, 1906–8; *Publisher and Bookseller*, 1906–8; *Bookseller*,
1906–8; *Publishers' Circular*, 1906–8; 'Murray, John and A. H. Hallam, *v.*
Walter and others'. Crown 8vo, (privately printed, 1908); and Edward
Bell's 'Narrative of the Dispute between The Times Book Club and the
Publishers' Association', contributed to Sir Frederick Macmillan's
volume on 'The Net Book Agreement and the Book War, 1906–1908,
(privately printed, 1924).

TIMPERLEY, CHARLES H., 1794–1846—A Dictionary of Printers and
Printing, with the Progress of Literature, Ancient and Modern; Bibliographical Illustrations, etc. Royal 8vo, London, 1839. *This volume is
especially useful as containing biographical notices of English printers, publishers,
and booksellers, from the earliest times to 1838.*
Encyclopaedia of Literary and Typographical Anecdote. Royal 8vo,

London, 1842. *This is a second edition of the 'Dictionary of Printers', and has a continuation of the biographical matter (chiefly of booksellers), 1839–42.*

TINSLEY, WILLIAM, 1831–1902 — Tinsley, Edward, 1835–66. Random Recollections of an Old Publisher. By William Tinsley. 2 vols, 8vo, London, 1900

See also E. Downey's 'Seventy Years Ago'. 8vo, 1905.

TOMKINSON, G. S. — *See under Printers.*

TOWERS, M. — Some Notes on Publishers Advertising. Towers, Richmond, n.d.

TREDREY, F. D. — The House of Blackwood. Blackwood, 1954.

TRELOAR, SIR WILLIAM PURDIE, 1843–1923 — Ludgate Hill, Past and Present. With Illustrations. Second edition, London, 1892.

TRÜBNER, NICHOLAS, 1817–84 — In Memoriam Nicholas Trübner. By William E. A. Axon. The *Library Chronicle*, vol. i, No. 2, London, April 1884.

In Memoriam Nicholas Trübner. By A. H. Sayce. *Trubner's American, European, and Oriental Literary Record*, Nos 197–8. London, April 1884.

TRÜBNER & CO. — *See under Mumby, F. A.*

TURNBULL, A. — William and Robert Chambers, 1800–1883. Chambers, n.d.

ULLSTEIN, H. — Rise and Fall of the House of Ullstein. Nicholson & Watson, n.d.

UNESCO — Copyright Laws and Treaties of the World. U.N.: H.M.S.O., 1956.

Educational Publishers. U.N.: H.M.S.O., 1962.

Records of the Inter-Governmental Copyright Conference. UNESCO, 1955.

Universal Copyright Convention. H.M.S.O., 1953.

UNETT, JOHN — Management for Small Traders. Iliffe, 1956.

UNWIN, PHILIP — Publishing from Manuscript to Bookshop. C.U.P. for the N.B.L., 1955.

Book Publishing as a Career. Hamish Hamilton, 1965.

The Publishing Unwins. Heinemann, 1972.

UNWIN, SIR STANLEY — The Truth about Publishing, London, 1926. Fifth edition, 1947; sixth edition, 1950; seventh edition, 1960. *Deals in detail with every aspect of the subject, from the receipt of the MS. to the sale of the book.*

The Price of Books. A pamphlet reprinted from the *Nation* and *Publishers' Circular*, 1925. Afterwards included as a chapter in 'The Truth about Publishing'.

English Books Abroad, A Broadcast. Printed in the *Publisher and Bookseller*, 2 January 1931.

Book Trade Organization in Norway and Sweden, 1932.

Danish Book Trade Organization, 1937.

Book Distribution in Germany: an address to the Society of Bookmen, subsequently reprinted in the *Publishers' Circular*, and expanded in a new chapter in 'The Truth about Publishing'. Third edition, 1929.

Publishing in Peace and War. Based on the author's 'Discourse' at the

Royal Institution. With some notes on 'The Future of English Books on the Continent after the War', and 'The Status of Books'. Allen & Unwin, 1944.

How Governments Treat Books. Allen & Unwin, 1950; new edition, John Baker, 1969.

The Book in the Making. Allen & Unwin, 1937.

On Translation: With Some Notes on 'Our Universal Language'. Allen & Unwin, 1946.

The Status of Books. Allen & Unwin, 1941.

The Truth About a Publisher. Allen & Unwin, 1960. *Unwin's autobiography.*

Unwin, Sir Stanley; Tributes from some of his Friends. Allen & Unwin, 1954.

See also under Hampden, John; British Book Trade Organization; Stevens, George; and Knight, Charles.

UNWIN, T. FISHER—The *Bookman*, May 1893.
See also under Miller, George.

UPHAM, JOHN (of Bath), and GARRETT, WILLIAM (of Newcastle)—Printing and Literature: a Collection of Notices of the Origin of Printing, Anecdotes of Celebrated Booksellers, etc. *This was in MS. only, and is taken from the Catalogue of W. H. Gee, Bookseller, Oxford, 1880.*

VAN THAL, HERBERT—The Tops of the Mulberry Trees. Allen & Unwin, 1971. *Autobiography of a publisher and literary agent.*

VAUGHAN, ALEXANDER—Modern Book Binding. New edition. Skilton, 1960.

VINCENT, W.—Seen from the Railway Platform: 50 Years Reminiscences. Illus. T. Fisher Unwin, 1919.

VIZETELLY, HENRY, 1820–94—Glances back through Seventy Years. 2 vols, 8vo, London, 1893.

WAGNER, L.—How to Publish a Book or Article. 8vo, London, 1898.

WALFORD, C.—Early Laws and Regulations concerning Books and Printers. Transactions of the Library Association, vol. vi, 1886.

WALFORD, E.—Editor versus Publisher. Third edition. Walford, Hampstead, 1881.

WALL, THOMAS—The Sign of Doctor Hay's Head: Being Some Account of the Hazards and Fortunes of Catholic Printers and Publishers in Dublin from Later Penal Times to the Present Day. Illus. M. H. Gill, 1958.

WALLACE, J. A.—Lessons Form the Life of the Late James Nisbet, Publisher. London, 1967.

WARBURG, FREDRIC—An Occupation for Gentlemen. Hutchinson, 1959.

WARDE, B. L.—The Same Book. P.p. 1940.

WATERS, A. W.—A List of the Eighteenth-Century Tokens issued by Publishers, Printers, and Booksellers. With Illustrations. *Publishers' Circular*, 11 and 18 May 1901.

WATSON, E. H. LACON—'Barker's', a Novel. Crown 8vo, London, 1910. *In this novel the author deals with many details of authorship and publishing.*

WAUGH, ARTHUR—A Century of Publishing: Being a History of the House of Chapman and Hall, from 1830 to 1930. London, 1930.

One Man's Road: Being a Picture of Life in a Passing Generation. London, 1930.

WELCH, C.—St Paul's Cathedral and its early Literary Associations (Containing a List of London Printers and Booksellers, 1556). 8vo, London, 1891.

WELSH, CHARLES—Publishing a Book: Being a few Practical Hints to Authors as to the Preparation of Manuscript, the Correction of Proofs, and the Arrangement with the Publishers. Boston, U.S.

A Bookseller of the Last Century: John Newbery. Griffith, Farran, Okeden & Welsh, 1885.

And see s.n. Newbery.

WEMMS, M. (ed.)—Libraries and the Book Trade. Conference Papers. Herts. County Library, 1969.

WEST, WILLIAM, 1770–1854—Fifty Years' Recollections of an Old Bookseller; consisting of Anecdotes, Characteristic Sketches, and Original Traits and Eccentricities of Authors, Artists, Actors, Books, Booksellers, and of the Periodical Press of the last Half Century. With Portrait. 8vo, Cork, 1837.

An important series of articles on Booksellers and Publishers, by William West, also appeared in the *Aldine Magazine*, 8vo, London, 1838–9.

WESTON, R.—A Visit to the United States and Canada in 1833 (the author was a Bookseller). 8vo, Edinburgh, 1836.

WHEATLEY, H. B.—Prices of Books: an Inquiry into the Changes in the Price of Books which have occurred in England at Different Periods. Crown 8vo, London, 1898. *See also under Bibliographer, The.*

Dryden's Publisher. *See the* 'Cambridge History of English Literature', vol. viii.

WHELAN, F.—The Bookshops (Ltd). Proof, Private and Confidential. Illus. 1902.

WHITE, F.—A Bachelor's London: Memoirs of the Day Before Yesterday. 1889–1914. Illus. Grant, Richards (Fronto Ltd), 1931.

WHITE, T. A. B.—Copyright. Stevens & Son, 1949.

WHITEHOUSE, J. HOWARD—The Craftsmanship of Books. London, 1929.

WHYTE, FREDERIC—*See under Heinemann, William.*

WILBERFORCE, WILFRID—*See under Burns and Oates.*

WILES, R. M.—Serial Publication in England Before 1750. C.U.P., 1957.

WILEY, J., & SONS, INC.—The First 150 Years, 1807–1957. Illus. Chapman & Hall, 1957.

A Guide for Wiley Authors: Publishing Procedures from MS. to Bound Book.

WILKS, S., AND BETTANY, G. T.—Biographical History of Guy's Hospital. Illus. 1892.

WILLIAMS, B. J. S., etc.—Micro Publishing for Learned Societies. National Reprographic Centre for Documents, 1968.

WILLIAMS, G. S.—A Lecture on Publishing. London School of Printing, 1925.

WILLIAMS, HAROLD—Book Clubs and Printing Societies of Great Britain and Ireland. First Editions Club, 1929.

WILLIAMS, IOLA A.—Elements of Book-collecting. 8vo, 1927.

WILLIAMS, SIR WILLIAM EMRYS—The Penguin Story, 1935–56. Illus. Penguin, 1956.

WILLIAMSON, H.—Methods of Book Design. Illus. O.U.P., 1956.

WILLIAMSON, R. N.—Bits from an Old Book Shop. By R. M. Williamson of the Waverley Book Store, Leith Walk, Edinburgh, London, 1903.

WILSON, SIR D.—William Nelsom. Illus. P.p., 1889.

WILSON, EFFINGHAM, 1783–1868—A Biographical Sketch, reprinted from the *City Press*, 18 July 1868, etc. With Portrait. Printed for private circulation, 1868.

WILSON, HUBERT—An Old City Bookshop in a New Home. Illus. P.p. n.d.

WILSON, J. F.—A Few Personal Recollections. By an Old Printer (John Farlow Wilson, *d.* 6 February 1916, aged 87). Printed for private circulation, London, 1896. *Contains an account of the career of John Cassell.*

WILSON, JOHN G.—Modern Limited Editions. *Publisher and Bookseller*, 11 April 1930.

The Business of Bookselling: Three Lectures given at the London Day Training College under the auspices of the London County Council. 8vo, London, 1930; second edition, A.B.G.B.I., 1945.

Aspects of Modern Bookselling. Stationers Craft Lecture, 1924.

WILSON (JOHN), HOGG (JAMES), LOCKHART (JOHN GIBSON)—Translation from an Ancient Chaldee Manuscript. *Blackwood's Magazine*, October 1817. Reprinted in vol. iv of the collected edition of Professor Wilson's Works, with Notes by Professor Ferrier, 1855–8. *In this squib, among the persons satirized, or otherwise described, are Blackwood, Constable and John Ballantyne.*

WILSON, R. N. D.—Books and their History shown to the Children. London, 1930.

WILSON, R. B.—Old and Curious: The History of James Wilson's Bookshop. J. Wilson, Birmingham, 1960.

WINTER, JOHN STRANGE—Confessions of a Publisher, London, 1888. *A melodramatic story of an imaginary and despicable publisher by the author of 'Bootles' Baby' (Mrs Stannard).*

WINTERICH, J. T.—Books and the Man. New York and London, 1930. *A series of articles on famous books and their history, with bibliographical details, collected from the 'Publishers' Weekly'.*

WOLTERS, W. P.—The Oldest Bookselling Firm in Europe. (E. J. Brill, of Leyden)—*Trübner's American, European, etc., Record*, Nos 191–2. 8vo, London, 1883.

The succession is as follows: Elzevier (1580–1617), Luchtmans, Brill.

WOOD, F. T.—Notes on London Booksellers and Publishers, 1700–1750, *Notes and Queries*, 18 July and 22 August 1931.

WOOD, WILLIAM, AND COMPANY, New York—One Hundred Years of Publishing (1804–1904). A Brief Historical Account of the House of

William Wood and Company. With Portraits and other Illustrations. Crown 8vo, New York, 1904.

WOODCOCK, GEORGE—*See under Godwin, William.*

WOODHOUSE, JAMES, 1735–1820—The Life and Poetical Works of James Woodhouse. 2 vols, 4to, London, 1896. *Though Woodhouse was better known as 'the poetical shoemaker', he was in business for some years from 1803 at 211 Oxford Street, as a bookseller. See 'Blackwood's Magazine', November 1829, art. 'Sorting my Letters and Papers'.*

WOOLF, LEONARD—Beginning Again. Hogarth Press, 1964.
Downhill All the Way. Hogarth Press, 1967.
The Journey not the Arrival Matters. Hogarth Press, 1969.
Volumes iii, iv and v of Woolf's autobiography, containing much about the organization and finances of the Hogarth Press.

WOON, BASIL—The Current Publishing Scene. Exposition Press, N.Y., 1952.

WORMAN, ERNEST JAMES—Alien Members of the Book-Trade during the Tudor Period: Being an index to those whose names occur in the Returns of Aliens, Letters of Denization, and other Documents published by the Huguenot Society. With Notes. Small 4to, Bibliographical Society, 1906.

WRIGHT, JOHN, & SONS LTD—125 Years of Printing and Publishing. 1825–1950. Bristol: Stonebridge Press. Wright, 1952.

WYER, ROBERT, fl. 1529–56—Robert Wyer, Printer and Bookseller. By H. R. Plomer. With facsimiles of types and marks. Small 4to, Bibliographical Society, 1897.

WYLIE, DAVID, afterwards DAVID WYLIE AND SON—A Century of Bookselling, 1814–1914. Reprinted from the *Aberdeen Book-lover*, November 1914.

WYMAN AND CO.—Authorship and Publication: a Concise Guide for Authors in matters relating to Printing and Publishing. Third edition, London, 1883.

YARD, R. STERLING—The Publisher, 1913. *An American book, but with a good deal of matter of interest to British readers.*

YATES, EDMUND, 1831–94—Recollections and Experiences. 2 vols, 8vo, London, 1884. *References made to Smith, Elder and Co. and the 'Cornhill Magazine', David Bogue, John Maxwell, Edward Tinsley, George Bentley, George Routledge, and others.*

YOUNG, CHARLES—A Bookseller looks at Publishers. Paper read before the Society of Bookmen. Extracts published in the *Publisher and Bookseller*, 24 April 1931.
The Craft of Bookselling. Lecture delivered under the auspices of the Stationers' Company and Printing Industry Technical Board. Printed in the *Publisher and Bookseller*, 1 May 1931.

YOUNG, JOHN L.—'Books: From the MS. to the Bookseller'. London, 1929. A manual in Pitman's 'Common Commodities and Industries' series. Revised edition, 1947.

Index